THE C

Latin love elegy is one (ie Augustan era, also known as the ... lume brings together leading scholars from Australia, Europe and ... ca to present and explore the Greek and Roman backdrop for Latin love elegy, the individual Latin love elegists (both the canonical and the non-canonical), their poems and influence on writers in later times. The book is designed as an accessible introduction for the general reader interested in Latin love elegy and the history of love and lament in Western literature, as well as a collection of critically stimulating essays for students and scholars of Latin poetry and of the classical tradition.

A complete list of books in the series is at the back of the book.

THE CAMBRIDGE
COMPANION TO

LATIN LOVE ELEGY

THE CAMBRIDGE COMPANION TO

LATIN LOVE ELEGY

EDITED BY

THEA S. THORSEN

Norwegian University of Science and Technology, Trondheim

CAMBRIDGE
UNIVERSITY PRESS

CAMBRIDGE
UNIVERSITY PRESS

University Printing House, Cambridge CB2 8BS, United Kingdom

Published in the United States of America by Cambridge University Press, New York

Cambridge University Press is part of the University of Cambridge.

It furthers the University's mission by disseminating knowledge in the pursuit of education, learning and research at the highest international levels of excellence.

www.cambridge.org
Information on this title: www.cambridge.org/9780521129374

First published 2013

Printed in the United Kingdom by TJ International Ltd. Padstow Cornwall

A catalogue record for this publication is available from the British Library

Library of Congress Cataloguing in Publication data
The Cambridge companion to Latin love elegy / [edited by] Dr. Thea S. Thorsen.
pages cm – (Cambridge companions to literature)
Includes bibliographical references and index.
ISBN 978-0-521-76536-7 (hardback)
1. Elegiac poetry, Latin – History and criticism. 2. Love poetry, Latin – History and criticism. 3. Influence (Literary, artistic, etc.) I. Thorsen, Thea Selliaas, editor. II. Title: Latin love elegy.
PA6059.E6C36 2013
874'.01093543 – dc23 2013016981

ISBN 978-0-521-76536-7 Hardback
ISBN 978-0-521-12937-4 Paperback

CONTENTS

NOTES ON CONTRIBUTORS

FEDERICA BESSONE is Associate Professor of Latin language and literature at the University of Turin. She has produced the critical edition and commentary *P. Ovidii Nasonis Heroidum Epistula XII. Medea Iasoni* (1997), and *La Tebaide di Stazio. Epica e potere* (2011), as well as numerous articles on Augustan elegy, the 'poetry book' of Ovid's *Heroides*, Flavian epic and the Roman novel.

MEGAN O. DRINKWATER is Associate Professor of Classics at Agnes Scott College. She has published articles on Ovid's *Heroides* (2007) and on Tibullus' Marathus cycle (2012), in which she explores her interest in elegy, ancient sexuality and gender in early Augustan Rome. She has revised Amy Barbour's *Selections from Herodotus* (2011).

LAUREL FULKERSON is Professor of Classics at Florida State University. She is the author of *The Ovidian Heroine as Author: Reading, Writing and Community in the Heroides* (2005), *No Regrets: Remorse in Classical Antiquity* (2013) and numerous articles on Greek and Latin poetry and prose. She is the editor of the *Classical Journal.*

ROY GIBSON is Professor of Latin at the University of Manchester, and the author of a commentary on *Ovid: Ars Amatoria 3* (2003), and of *Excess and Restraint: Propertius, Horace, and Ovid's Ars Amatoria* (2007), as well as co-editor with A. Sharrock and S. Green of *The Art of Love: Bimillennial Essays on Ovid's Ars Amatoria*. Recently he has begun to work on both Plinys, and is co-author with R. Morello of *Reading the Letters of Pliny the Younger: an Introduction* (2012), and co-editor with R. Morello of *Re-Imagining Pliny the Younger* (2003) and *Pliny the Elder: Themes and Contexts* (2011).

ROGER P. H. GREEN was Professor of Humanity (Latin) in the University of Glasgow from 1995 to 2008, and is now Honorary Professorial Research Fellow there. He has written extensively on Latin writers of Late Antiquity, and his books include *The Works of Ausonius* (1991), a translation of Augustine's treatise

On Christian Teaching (1995, 1997) and *Latin Epics of the New Testament* (2006). His interest in Latin writers of early modern Scotland has led him to edit George Buchanan, *Poetic Paraphrase of the Psalms of David* (2011) and to co-edit *George Buchanan, Poet and Dramatist* (2009).

STEPHEN HARRISON is Professor of Latin Literature at the University of Oxford and Fellow and Tutor in Classics at Corpus Christi College. He has published extensively on Augustan poetry, the ancient novel and the reception of Roman literature. He is the author of *A Commentary on Virgil, Aeneid 10* (1991), *Apuleius: A Latin Sophist* (2000) as well as *Generic Enrichment in Virgil and Horace* (2007), and editor of numerous volumes, including *A Companion to Latin Literature* (2005), *The Cambridge Companion to Horace* (2007) and *Living Classics: Greece and Rome in Contemporary Poetry in English* (2009).

LUKE B.T. HOUGHTON is Lecturer in Classics at the University of Glasgow. He is the author of publications on Latin love elegy and its reception in neo-Latin poetry, and co-editor with M. Wyke of *Perceptions of Horace* (2009). He is currently working on a history of Virgil's fourth *Eclogue* in later art and literature, and editing (with G. Manuwald) a collection of essays on neo-Latin poetry in the British Isles.

RICHARD HUNTER is Regius Professor of Greek at the University of Cambridge and Fellow of Trinity College. His publications on Hellenistic poetry include *The Argonautica of Apollonius: Literary Studies* (1993), *Theocritus and the Archaeology of Greek Poetry* (1996) and (with M. Fantuzzi) *Tradition and Innovation in Hellenistic Poetry* (2004). His interests in ancient literary criticism and the reception of Greek poetry at Rome are explored in works such as *The Shadow of Callimachus* (2006), *Critical Moments in Classical Literature* (2009) and (with D. Russell), *Plutarch: How to study poetry* (2011). His collected papers were published in 2008 as *On Coming After: Studies in Post-Classical Greek Literature and its Reception.*

ANDREW KAHN is Professor in Russian at the University of Oxford and Fellow at St. Edmund Hall, Oxford. His scholarly research draws on Greek, Latin and French literature, in addition to Russian. He is the author of many studies of Russian poetry and Enlightenment thought, including Pushkin's *The Bronze Horseman* (1998), *Pushkin's Lyric Intelligence* (2008), and editor of *The Cambridge Companion to Pushkin* (2007). He has published translations of Karamzin's *Letters of a Russian Traveler* (2003) as well as poems by Pushkin and Osip Mandelstam.

ALISON KEITH is Professor of Classics at the University of Toronto, where she also holds cross appointments in the Centre for Medieval Studies, the Centre for

Comparative Literature and the Women and Gender Studies Institute. She is the author of *The Play of Fictions: Ovid's Metamorphoses Book 2* (1992), *Engendering Rome: Women in Latin Epic* (2000) and *Propertius, Poet of Love and Leisure* (2008). She is the co-editor of *Metamorphosis: the Changing Face of Ovid's Metamorphoses in Medieval and Early Modern Europe* (2007) and *Roman Dress and the Fabric of Roman Society* (2008).

MAREK THUE KRETSCHMER is Professor of Medieval Latin literature at the Norwegian University of Science and Technology. He has published several articles on Medieval Latin literature, especially on historiography and poetry. He is author of *Rewriting Roman History in the Middle Ages* (2007) and contributes to the forthcoming *Cambridge Companion to Roman Comedy*. He is also a member of the research group *Interfaces* at the Centre for Medieval Literature (Centre of Excellence at the Universities of Southern Denmark and York), where he currently is co-authoring a chapter about medieval poetry on the subject of Troy with Professor Francine Mora.

PARSHIA LEE-STECUM is Senior Lecturer in Classics at the University of Melbourne. He is the author of *Powerplay in Tibullus: Reading Elegies Book One* (1998) and numerous articles on Augustan literature, magic in the ancient world, Roman ethnicity and mythology.

JOHN F. MILLER is Professor of Classics at the University of Virginia. He is the author of *Ovid's Elegiac Festivals: Studies in the Fasti* and *Apollo, Augustus, and the Poets*. His many articles include studies of the Latin elegists and other Augustan poets, and of the reception of Ovid in literature and art. He edited the periodical *Classical Journal* for seven years and has co-edited three collaborative volumes on Greek and Latin topics.

PAUL ALLEN MILLER is Professor of Classics and Comparative Literature at the University of South Carolina, Columbia. He is the author of *Lyric Texts and Lyric Consciousness: The Birth of a Genre from Archaic Greece to Augustan Rome* (1994), *Subjecting Verses: Latin Love Elegy and the Emergence of the Real* (2004) and *Postmodern Spiritual Practices: The Reception of Plato and the Construction of the Subject in Lacan, Derrida and Foucault* (2007) as well as numerous articles. Among his edited volumes are *Latin Erotic Elegy: An Anthology and Critical Reader* (2002) and *Desire of the Analysts: Psychoanalysis and Cultural Criticism* (2008).

VICTORIA MOUL is Lecturer in Latin Language and Literature at King's College London. She works on a range of topics in classical poetry and its reception, translation and imitation, with a special interest in Horace, Virgil and Pindar. Her interest in the early modern classical tradition encompasses English translations and imitations as well as neo-Latin poetry. She is the author of *Jonson, Horace and the Classical Tradition* (2010) as well as a number of articles.

LISA PIAZZI is Research Fellow at the Scuola Normale Superiore di Pisa. She is the author of *Lucrezio e i presocratici: un commento a De rerum natura 1:635–920* (2005), the critical edition and commentary on Ovid's *Heroidum Epistula VII: Dido Aeneae* (2007) and *Lucrezio: Il De rerum natura e la cultura occidentale* (2009). She was G. B. Conte's research assistant as he prepared the critical edition of Virgil's *Aeneid* for the Bibliotheca Teubneriana (2009).

EMMANUELLE RAYMOND is Maître de Conférence at University of Angers. Her research interests include the forms and aspects of memory in epic literature and especially in Virgil's *Aeneid*. She is the editor of the anthology *Vox Poetae: Manifestations auctoriales dans l'épopée gréco-latine* (2011).

ALISON SHARROCK is Professor of Classics at the University of Manchester. She is the author of *Seduction and Repetition in Ovid's Ars Amatoria 2* (1994) and *Reading Roman Comedy: Poetics and Playfulness in Plautus and Terence* (2009), based on her 1999 W.B. Stanford Memorial Lectures, as well as numerous book-chapters and articles. She is the author (with R. Ash) of *Fifty Key Classical Authors* (2002), (with H. Morales) *Intratextuality: Greek and Roman Textual Relations* (2000) and co-editor (with R. Gibson and S. Green) of *The Art of Love: Bimillennial Essays on Ovid's Ars Amatoria and Remedia Amoris* (2006).

MATHILDE SKOIE is currently Head of the Department of Philosophy, Classics, History of Art and Ideas at the University of Oslo. She is the author of *Reading Sulpicia* (2002) and the co-editor of *Pastoral and the Humanities. Arcadia Re-Inscribed* (2006) and *Romans and Romantics* (2012). She has written articles on elegy and pastoral and contributed to several introductory manuals on the topic of Classics and their reception.

THEA SELLIAAS THORSEN is Associate Professor in Latin at the Norwegian University of Science and Technology. She is the author of *Ovid's Early Poetry* (forthcoming) and *Do Not Enter without Desire* (in Norwegian, 2011), a collection of essays on literature from ancient Mesopotamia to contemporary Norwegian poetry. She is the editor of *Greek and Roman Games in the Computer Age* (2012) and, with Stephen Harrison, co-editor of *Sappho at Rome: Receptions from Lucretius to Martial* (in preparation). She is co-founder and co-editor of *Trondheim Studies in Greek and Latin*. Her metrical translations of Ovid's entire erotic-elegiac output are the first ever into Norwegian (2001–2009).

THEODORE ZIOLKOWSKI is Class of 1900 Professor Emeritus of German and Comparative Literature at Princeton University. In addition to many books on

German Romanticism, literature and religion, and literature and law, he has written widely on the reception of classical antiquity in the twentieth century. Besides articles on Catullus, Horace, Juvenal and Seneca, he has published *Virgil and the Moderns* (1993), *Ovid and the Moderns* (2005), *Minos and the Moderns* (2008) and *Mythologisierte Gegenwart: Deutsches Erleben in antikem Gewand* (2008). His most recent work is *Gilgamesh Among Us: Modern Encounters with the Ancient Epic* (2011).

PREFACE

Long disregarded as frivolous poetry, Latin love elegy currently enjoys widespread recognition as a powerful vehicle for dazzling aesthetics, political poignancy, social provocation and challenging gender-representations. This *Companion* explores Latin love elegy as a form of expression that is both playfully light and gravely serious within the context of earlier Greek and Roman poetry, as well as that of later literature. Designed as a comprehensive introduction to the main characteristics of the literary genre, it also includes cutting-edge research and fresh scholarly approaches, in the hope of inspiring future endeavours in the increasingly blooming field of erotic-elegiac scholarship.

The contributors to this volume merit my heartfelt thanks. It has been a pleasure, and an immensely enlightening one, to work with scholars capable of producing works that are as informative as they are stimulating. I also wish to thank Professor Alessandro Barchiesi and Dr. Martin Dinter for their inspiration and moral support, which provided the *sine qua non* for the future of this volume at early stages. My greatest thanks are however due to Professor Stephen Harrison, whose exceedingly generous and learned help has been indispensable throughout the entire process. My thanks to him are also due to the fact that he kindly acted in an editorial capacity for my own contributions to the volume. Similarly, I owe thanks to the various anonymous readers who have been involved at different stages in the process. The staff at the Bodleian Library and – not least – the staff at the University of Science and Technology Humanities Library both merit my humble thanks: their patience has been impressive. Thanks are also due to Terje Breigutu Moseng for consolidating the bibliography and to Professor Lasse Hodne and Svein Henrik Pedersen for helping me find the right jacket picture. Finally, at the Cambridge University Press I owe heartfelt thanks to senior editor Michael Sharp for his expertise, support and patience during some four years and to editor Elizabeth Hanlon for rewarding collaboration, especially during the final lap. Thanks are also due to production editors Elizabeth Davey and Rachel Cox for their assistance and to Andrew Dyck for copy-editing the volume.

ABBREVIATIONS

AE	*L'Année Épigraphique*
A&P	Aris and Phillips Classical Texts
AP	*Anthologia Palatina*
BT	Bibliotheca Teubneriana
CEG	*Carmina Epigraphica Graeca*
CIL	*Corpus Inscriptiarum Latinarum*
FLP	*The Fragmentary Latin Poets*, ed. Courtney
K-A	*Poetae Comici Graeci*, R. Kassel and C. Austin
LIMC	*Lexicon iconographicum mythologiae classicae*
LTUR	*Lexicon topographicum urbis Romae*, ed. Steinby
OCD	*Oxford Classical Dictionary*, 3rd edn, ed. Hornblower and Spawforth
OCT	Oxford Classical Texts
OLD	*Oxford Latin Dictionary*
PIR	*Prosopographia Imperii Romani*
PC	The Penguin Classics
PL	*Patrologiae Cursus*, series Latina, ed. Migne
RE	*Real-Enzyklopädie der klassischen Altertumswissenschaft*
LCL	Loeb Classical Library
WC	The World's Classics

THEA S. THORSEN

Introduction

Latin love elegy

'If only Christ had read the Latin love elegists!'
– Joseph Brodsky[1]

Ever since antiquity the art form of elegy has proved astonishingly vital. Elegy provided inspiration for artistic achievements throughout the Middle Ages, the Renaissance, the Enlightenment and even today.[2] Nevertheless, compared with its rich reception history, the period during which Latin love elegy flourished is surprisingly brief. The poetic body of Latin love elegy was fashioned by a relatively small group of poets who were active some fifty years in ancient Rome, during the transition between the Roman Republic and the monarchy of Augustus.

The Latin love elegists revived and refined an existing art form, that is poetry in a certain metrical pattern known as elegy, attested in ancient Greece from around 700 BC. During the centuries when elegies were composed in Greek, this literary form was to accommodate an astonishingly wide range of themes.[3] However, at the time when the Latin love elegists were active,

I am grateful to Stephen Harrison and the anonymous reader at the Press for precious feedback on this introduction.

1 According to the Polish poet Adam Zagajewski, as confided to me in oral communication.

2 For examples of such artistic achievements throughout these and other periods, see 'Part V: Receptions' in this volume. Two recent, particularly noteworthy examples are Ezra Pound's *Hommage to Sextus Propertius* (1919) and Nobel laureate Derek Walcott's 'A Propertius Quartet' from his *Arkansas Testament* (1987). Walcott's 'A Propertius Quartet' is partly addressed to and partly written about the Latin love elegist Sextus Propertius and his beloved Cynthia (for further details about the couple, see below) and the fatal love between 'she whose first syllable was Sin, as yours was Sex' (1987: 97). I am grateful to Lars Morten Gram and Steffen Hope for drawing my attention to these poems.

3 It remains hard to reconcile the modern understanding of elegy as 'lament' with pre-Alexandrian Greek elegy, despite several insightful attempts made by outstanding scholars (cf. e.g. Francke (1816), Page (1936) and Nagy (2010); see also Harvey (1955) 168–72). Existing specimens of Greek literature marked by an 'elegiac mode' before the age of Alexander the Great belong to a great extent to well-defined genres that are not elegy, such as epic and tragedy, while examples of poems in the metre of elegy (i.e. the elegiac couplet; see below) rarely seem 'elegiac' in the modern sense of the word, despite dealing with many types of subject matter (see West (1974) 1–21), Aloni (2009) and

elegy was principally associated with a tradition of loss and lament.[4] The great achievement of the Latin love elegists was that they merged the mode of lament with a concept of totalitarian love.

Love

The ideal of love in Latin love elegy represents a turning point in the literary history of the West. This is not to say that love is an unimportant theme in classical literature outside Latin love elegy, but rather that love within this literary genre is of a different kind. Love for love's sake: that is the rule in the world of Latin love elegy. Latin elegiac love has no explanation; it appears as its own cause and effect and seems self-sufficient.

In other ancient literature,[5] love may regularly be explained by factors that are external to the experience of love itself.[6] Thus, love may be represented as madness due to divine will, as is often the case in the literary genres of

Hunter in this volume). In this context the 'elegy' of Andromache in Euripides' eponymous tragedy (ll. 103–16), where a lament occurs in the elegiac metre within the framework of tragedy, remains unique.

4 The explanation of the origin of elegy as lament is attested in Horace, who writes *uersibus impariter iunctis querimonia primum,/ post etiam inclusa est uoti sententia compos;/ quis tamen exiguos elegos emiserit auctor,/ grammatici certant et adhuc sub iudice lis est* (*Ars P.* 75–8, [elegy was] first a lament composed with unequally joined verses, thereafter a thought with the power of a granted prayer was included; but grammarians fight over which author first produced little elegies, and the debate is still awaiting its final judgement). See also *miserabilis... elegos* (Hor. *Carm.* 1.33.2–3, 'sad elegies') in an erotic context. Similarly, Ovid explicitly stresses the plaintive quality of elegy throughout his poetic career: *elegi quoque flebile carmen* (*Her.* 15.7, 'elegy is also a tearful form of poetry'); *flebilis... Elegia* (*Am.* 3.9.3, 'tearful Elegy'); *flebilis ut noster status est, ita flebile carmen* (*Tr.* 5.1.5, 'as tearful as my life now is, is my song'). Later authors refer to a tradition that precedes these testimonies of elegy as lament, such as the dedicatory inscription by Echembrotus (*fl.* during the latter half of the sixth century BC), quoted by Pausanias 10.7.6 (see West (1971), 4 and Nobili (2011): 34–6). Among attempts at establishing a connection between elegy and lament by means of (false) etymologies, Horace's contemporary Didymus, based in Alexandria, launched the suggestion that the term stems from εὖ λέγειν ('to speak well', quoted in Orion *Etymologicum* 58.7 Sturz). Later sources repeat this explanation, along with the suggestion that the term 'elegy' derives from ἒ ἒ λέγειν ('to say "woe", "woe"', cf. e.g. Marius Plotius Sacerdos, *Gramm. lat.* 4.509.31 Keil, Porph. *ad Hor.* Carm. 1.33.2 and *Suda* E 774). For more recent attempts at unlocking the origin of elegy by means of etymology, see West (1971) 8.

5 For love in ancient literature, see esp. Calame (1999). Nilsson (2009) is also helpful.

6 The subsequent survey focuses on the *function* of love in ancient literature, rather than on love as *problem*, which is how philosophical writings in prose and poetry alike tend to conceive the emotional state in question. For an exposition of the similarities and differences between the concept of love in philosophy compared to that of Latin love elegy, see Allen (1950) 259–64, Caston (2012) 21–47 and Piazzi (Chapter 14) in this volume.

epic and tragedy. Love may also be linked to simple sexual satisfaction, as in Attic comedy. A pretext for marriage is a further function of love in classical literature, as exemplified by the theatrical genre of New Comedy. Here, the love of a young man for his girl has the precise purpose of unfolding a plot, which is destined to close with the marital union between the two.

There are reminiscences of almost all these kinds of love in Latin love elegy. To be sure, the elegiac concept of love may occasionally resemble a divine curse. Especially the child-god Amor (Love), also called Cupid (Lust), is prone to inflict pain and misery on the Latin elegiac lover. However, because of the inconstancy with which the elegiac child-god is depicted, this divinity never seems to acquire the rationale of a wronged god in search of vengeance, as in epic and tragedy. Furthermore, the concept of Latin elegiac love does include sexual pleasure. Yet such pleasure rarely provides lasting satisfaction for the Latin elegiac lover, who longs for his beloved's affection as much as her body.[7] Finally, a number of features of New Comedy reverberate through Latin love elegy.[8] However, marriage as a consequence of love remains a concept starkly alien to this poetic genre. The ambition of Latin elegiac love is decidedly neither marriage nor offspring.

Latin elegiac love has no objective but to worship the beloved, even in the face of danger, rejection and humiliation. As such, Latin elegiac love resembles most closely the kind of love which in other ancient literature is most vigorously explored in the homoerotic tradition. In Greek archaic lyric, the woman poet Sappho (latter half of the seventh century BC) is one of the most prominent exponents of this tradition, which is later extended by the body of pederastic love-poetry for beautiful boys. In the homoerotic tradition of same-sex longing and despair, love can have no cause other than the beauty and person of the beloved and no aim other than the bliss that the lover may experience if the beloved should grant him – or her – access. This is also the case in Latin love elegy.

In contrast to the tradition of homoerotic and pederastic poetry, Latin elegiac love is employed in predominantly heterosexual relationships.[9] The

[7] A body to which the elegist rarely gains access, cf. Connolly 2000.

[8] Cf. James (1998, 2003, 2006 and 2012), Konstan (1986) and Piazzi (Chapter 14) in this volume.

[9] In fact, homoeroticism appears to be an evanescent feature in the Latin erotic-elegiac corpus when considered as a whole. In Tibullus there are the Marathus poems (Tib. 1.4, 1.8 and 1.9), which are outright homoerotic, while Propertius models his very first poem (Prop. 1.1) on a homoerotic epigram by Meleager (*Anth. Pal.* 12.101) and later compares homoeroticism and heterosexual love (e.g. Prop. 1.20). Finally, Ovid considers – just the once, as a preliminary option – the possibility of loving a boy in the first poem of his *Amores*, where the future poet-lover pleads that in order to become an elegist, he must find someone to love: *aut puer aut... puella* (*Am.* 1.1.20, 'either [with] a boy or a girl').

heterosexual relationships of Latin love elegy regularly consist in a male character featured as the elegist himself and a female character featured as his beloved. Latin love elegy is in fact the classical genre that most systematically combines heterosexual relationships with a concept of love presented not as divine retribution, carnal hedonism or social function serving the establishment by producing heirs, but as love for love's sake. The fact that the couple consists of a man and a woman, normally the prerequisite for upholding family and tradition by producing heirs, enhances the elegiac experience of impossible, yet inescapable and therefore irrational love.

From the point of view of our present day the concept of such 'impossible' love between a man and woman may seem trivial. However, the seeming triviality is a sign of success: after Latin love elegy, love for love's sake in heterosexual relationships is the rule in Western literature and indeed in Western culture.

Genre

Latin love elegy is a perfect case for studying a literary genre. A distinct unity makes this genre easily identifiable among ancient literary forms;[10] this unity concerns the genre's era (50–1 BC), location (Rome), theme (love) and form (the elegiac couplet). An elegiac couplet consists of a dactylic hexameter, followed by a dactylic pentameter (see Chapter 23), and the Latin love elegists adapted it from Greek elegy to the prosody of the Latin language. When considering the genre of Latin love elegy from a metrical perspective, it is useful to recall that the elegiac couplet also occurs in a different yet similar poetic genre known as epigram. This Greek term means 'inscription' and originally denoted inscribed verses in various metres, often on tombs in commemoration of deceased persons. From the third century BC, Greek epigram was cultivated as a literary genre, accommodating a wide range of topics. At the time of the Latin love elegists, there was a considerable body of epigrammatic poetry in elegiac couplets on such topics as grief and love (cf. Keith 2011). Consequently, there are overlaps in form as well as content between the genres of epigram and elegy. However, epigrams are normally short, often no more than two couplets (= four lines) long; in Latin love elegy a poem usually runs for more than four couplets (= eight lines). The genre's appearance in one place at one time is thus matched not only by one theme, but also one form, namely a certain number of elegiac couplets.

[10] Thus, of all the ancient genres available, Latin love elegy is the case in point of Farrell's exposition of 'classical genre in theory and practice', since '"Latin love elegy" is . . . easy to define': Farrell (2003) 397. I am grateful to the author for a copy of the article.

Furthermore, Latin love elegy is profoundly *literary* in a way that facilitates meta-generic reflection. In the universe of this genre, there is a mostly insurmountable gap between what the elegiac lover desires and what he experiences. The contrast between what the Latin elegiac lover longs for (joy, mutual fidelity and love until death) and what he gets (disillusionment) creates the very *raison d'être* of Latin love elegy – as poetry. When the Latin elegiac lover does not get what he wants, he writes about it instead. The continuous experience of non-fulfilment urges the elegiac lover to vent his frustration in verse, along with repeated attempts at seduction, sometimes accompanied by memories of occasional bliss, which explains the erotic-persuasive (cf. *blanda . . . Elegia*, Ov. *Rem. am.* 379, 'charming Elegy') and, more frequently, erotic-pathetic (cf. *flebilis . . . Elegia*, Ov. *Am.* 3.9.3, 'tearful elegy') modes of Latin love elegy. In the Latin elegiac world, life can in fact consist in one of only two activities: love-making, if the beloved is present and accessible, and writing about past joys, future hopes and imminent anguish, if the lover is denied access to his beloved (not infrequently by the beloved herself). Making love and making poetry are thus the only two modes of existence in the world of Latin love elegy. The fiction of Latin love elegy is consequently that there is no fiction. The artistic accomplishment of such non-fictional fiction is enhanced by the use of the elegists' own names and, allegedly, pseudonyms for the names of the 'real' girls they love (cf. Ov. *Am.* 2.17.29–30, *Ars* 3.538 and Apul. *Apol.* 10) in their elegiac outputs.

Canon

To the characteristics one time, one place, one theme and one form that mark Latin love elegy, 'one canon' can be added. In Chapter 1 Richard Hunter points out a number of features that must have proved fruitful to the Roman elegists in the wide diversity of Greek elegy.[11] The rich chapter includes a

[11] From the viewpoint of ancient Rome, there seems to have been a Greek canon of erotic elegists as well. The names that may be included in such a canon are Mimnermus of Smyrna, later claimed for Colophon, see fr. 9 West (latter half of the seventh century BC); Antimachus (*fl.* c.400 BC), Hermesianax (early third century BC), both from Colophon, and Hermesianax's friend Philitas from Cos; and the contemporary of the latter two, Callimachus of Cyrene. Hermesianax clearly regards Mimnermus, whom he calls the 'inventor of the pentameter' and inflamed lover of the woman Nanno, a canonical representative of the elegiac genre, along with Antimachus, whom Hermesianax portrays as a sad mourner of his beloved Lyde (fr. 3.35–46 Lightfoot). In the same fragment, but outside Hermesianax's literary canon *sub specie amoris*, where elegy features among the genres of epic, lyric and tragedy, the elegist Philitas, reportedly in love with the woman Bittis, is paired with a contemporary philosopher (3.75–8 Lightfoot). As many as four Greek elegists are thus evoked through Hermesianax's fragment, if the very work to which this fragment belongs, the elegiac

large number of poets from different places and spans several centuries. By contrast, ancient sources (Ov. *Tr.* 4.10.53–4, cf. *Ars* 3.536–8 and Quint. *Inst. Or.* 10.1.93) provide us with a neat canon of four Latin love elegists, who all flourished in Rome during the last half of the first century BC:

- Cornelius Gallus (70/69–27/26 BC), who is said to have composed four lost books of elegies entitled *Amores* (Servius *ad Buc.* 10.1, 'Loves'), centred on the female figure of Lycoris
- Tibullus (between 55 and 48 to 19 BC), the author of two poetry books (centred on the female figures of Delia and Nemesis, respectively), both of which are transmitted together with a third book of compositions by other poets, also known as the *Appendix Tibulliana* (cf. Tränkle 1990)
- Propertius (born between 54 and 47, died after 16 BC), who produced four books of elegies where Cynthia is the leading lady
- Ovid (43 BC–AD 17), who composed a number of erotic-elegiac works, among which the three books of elegies entitled *Amores*, centred on the female figure of Corinna, are the most conventional.

Appearance in one place, then, during the course of one half-century, of one kind of theme, one metrical form and one canon of poets, these are the hallmarks of the genre of Latin love elegy. But despite these well-defined features, problems in defining Latin love elegy remain.

The dispute continues over whether Catullus (*c.*84–54 BC) should be counted among Latin love elegists (cf. Wray 2012). The ambiguity of Catullus' elegiac status is reflected in this *Companion*, where the poet is represented as an elegiac predecessor by Federica Bessone in Chapter 2 and as an elegist proper by Paul Allen Miller in Chapter 10. Catullus uses the elegiac couplet in longer elegies as well as in epigrams. However, the love for his

Leontion, presumably named after Hermesianax's beloved, is taken into account. In addition to Hermesianax, Callimachus also seems to regard Mimnermus as an erotic-elegiac ideal (cf. *Aet.* 1.11 Pfeiffer), as does Propertius (cf. Prop. 1.9.11). Antimachus may also be mentioned as an elegist in Callimachus (fr. 398 Pfeiffer), but in Rome he is recorded as an epic poet (Prop. 2.34.45 and Quint. *Inst.* 10.1.53), while Philitas, who is probably also invoked by Callimachus (cf. *Aet.* 1.9–10), is mentioned by both Propertius and Ovid (cf. Prop. 2.34.29–32; 3.1.1–2, see also Prop. 3.3.51–2, 3.9.43–6 and 4.6.1–4 and Ov. *Ars* 3.329 and *Rem. am.* 760). Of Hermesianax and Callimachus, the former is never named by the Roman elegists, whereas the latter is acknowledged as extremely influential (see Hunter in this volume, with references). Nevertheless, Hermesianax's catalogue of poets may indeed anticipate conceptions of canons of Greek and Latin erotic elegy at Rome (see below), as Farrell (2012) argues. It should however be kept in mind that Philitas, Sappho and Anacreon (also included in Hermesianax's *Leontion*, cf. fr. 3.48–52 Lightfoot) are repeatedly mentioned in the Greek sections of Ovid's literary catalogues (*Ars* 3.329–33, *Rem. am.* 759–62), which are therefore perhaps better understood as histories of *love* literature than as canons of elegy.

puella ('girl') Lesbia, which is as obsessive and tormented as the love of any of the canonical elegists, does not know the metrical boundaries of Latin love elegy. The lyrical versatility of Catullus, who masters many metres, marks his distance from canonical erotic elegy. Nevertheless, Catullus' portrayal of Lesbia and the feelings he claims that she provokes in him aligns him with the other Latin elegists.

Even within the canon of Latin love elegists, there are problems concerning chronology. Ovid, who must be responsible for the self-serving concept of *four* canonical elegists, repeatedly mentions Tibullus before Propertius among them (cf. Ov. *Rem. am.* 763–4, *Tr.* 2.445–68 and *Tr.* 4.10.51–4). In Chapter 2, Bessone draws a suggestive picture of the intense literary activity that marked the end of the Roman Republic, whose fragmentary poetic remains are still being recovered. In Chapter 3 Emmanuelle Raymond challenges the notion that Gallus was the 'first inventor' of the genre and suggests that the fragmentary state of the generation of poets to which Gallus belongs allows for well-founded doubts as to whether he single-handedly introduced the genre, or rather refined an existing trend.

In Chapter 6 on Propertius, Alison Keith corroborates the general view that Propertius' first book of elegies, the *Monobiblos* ('one book'), preceded the first book of Tibullus' elegies (for a different view, see Knox 2005). On this assumption, Propertius' elegiac debut is the earliest complete work we possess of Latin love elegy. But the four poetry books of the Propertian corpus certainly did not precede Tibullus' two collections of elegies in their entirety. Rather, the chronology of the oeuvres of the two poets intertwined, with Tibullus' first book seemingly appearing before the second book of Propertius, which in turn preceded the second book of Tibullus (cf. Lyne 1998a = 2007: 251–82).

The Ovidian order of canonical elegists is reflected in this *Companion* in the sense that the chapter on Tibullus comes before Propertius. This organization is not meant to challenge the ruling opinion that Propertius' *Monobiblos* is the first extant elegy book in Latin so much as to reflect the principal place of Tibullus in a different kind of order, based on *auctoritas* ('authority'), that certain ancient literary critics recognized in his elegiac works, and that forms the intriguing point of departure for Parshia Lee-Stecum's Chapter 4. From another point of view – of retrospect, with Ovid – Tibullus' work certainly terminated earlier than Propertius', and fame 'beyond the reach of carping criticism' conventionally began with the poet's death and its elegiac lamentation (Ov. *Am.* 1.15.39–40); for the funeral of Tibullus and Tibullan elegy, see Ov. *Am.* 3.9.[12]

[12] I owe this formulation to the anonymous reader for Cambridge University Press.

Lee-Stecum's chapter also treats the non-canonical poet Lygdamus, whose elegies are transmitted as a part of the Tibullan corpus along with a number of other poets in the *Appendix Tibulliana*. The much discussed date of Lygdamus, whose identity has remained a puzzle throughout the centuries, may be as late as the Flavian period (cf. Antolín 1996; see however *OCD*: 899). The fact that Lee-Stecum's chapter gives ample space to Tibullus, the poet who may be regarded as the principal erotic elegist in terms of ancient conceptions of authority, *but also* includes Lygdamus, who was possibly the latest of the classical (but non-canonical) elegists, should serve as a reminder of the uncertainty besetting established chronologies of ancient literature.

Ends

The self-contained universe of Latin love elegy reveals an obsession with its own well-defined borders. In fact, the genre's unity – i.e. one time, one place, one theme, one form, one canon – proves an excellent point of departure for exploring the 'other' by means of both contrasts and similarities. The genesis and immediate development of the genre that is so easy to pinpoint allows us to observe Latin love elegy as a literary laboratory, where poetic experiments are carried out. During these experiments, not only the drawing but also the violation of the genre's limits occurs, two processes that both – however paradoxically – contribute to the ultimate assertion of the generic identity of Latin love elegy. This dynamic is most obvious in the case of Ovid, whose erotic output in elegiac couplets sports a wide range of diverse realizations of the genre, as I try to demonstrate in Chapter 7.

Nonetheless, even the classic examples of Latin love elegy, Ovid's arch-elegiac *Amores* included, encompass features that herald the genre's end. Most shocking, perhaps, is that none of the extant canonical elegists remains true to the 'one' love they profess, as Roy Gibson shows in Chapter 13, directly challenging orthodox erotic-elegiac scholarship. Similarly, in Chapter 14, Lisa Piazzi demonstrates how erotic-elegiac promiscuity extends through the field of literary genres as she points out how Latin love elegy frequently engages in 'adulterous' liaisons with other forms of poetry. However, Piazzi concludes her chapter by suggesting that the elegists' zealous interest in other genres expresses nostalgia for a literary past, rather than anticipation of its own closure. Perhaps the marked genesis, *floruit* and end of the erotic-elegiac genre enhanced a particular elegiac consciousness, as it were, of the literary landscape it 'left behind'? Perhaps this would be equally true of what lay ahead for the genre? In Chapter 15 John F. Miller demonstrates how the power of the erotic-elegiac genre prevails even as the last two canonical love elegists, Propertius and Ovid, explicitly distance themselves from the genre by turning to aetiological projects.

Gender

felix Eois lex funeris illa maritis
quos Aurora suis rubra colorat aquis.
namque ubi mortifero iacta est fax ultima lecto,
uxorum fusis stat pia turba comis,
et certamen habent leti, quae uiua sequatur
coniugium: pudor est non licuisse mori.
(Prop. 3.13.15–20)

Happy is that funeral custom [= suttee] for the husbands of the East, whom reddening Aurora colours with her waters. For when the last torch is thrown onto the corpse-bearing pyre, the righteous crowd of wives stand with dishevelled hair, and there is a competition between them to be the one who follows her husband alive: it brings shame not to be allowed to die.

A complex representation of gender is a hallmark of Latin love elegy. This passage from Propertius 3.13 is as an example of how Latin love elegy may serve as a vehicle for male chauvinist ideals. Here, the elegiac lover's envy of Indian men for the practice of suttee, according to which it is morally unacceptable for a woman to live after her husband's death, discloses a destructive wish to control women. The ideal in this passage is that a woman should exist only for her man; when he is dead, her reason for living ceases. The fact that the passage contains a reference to an historical practice (which persisted in India until the nineteenth century) should serve as a reminder of the intimate way in which Latin love elegy is interwoven with a world of historically real men and women, where sexism is the rule.

However, it is precisely against this socio-historical backdrop of sexism and male chauvinism that Latin love elegy frequently represents both genders in irregular, counter-cultural and even subversive ways. There is dispute over the extent to which Latin love elegy is in fact counter-cultural or rather a symptom of the general promiscuity and increased liberty for women that evidently marked the end of the Roman Republic. At any event, the all-consuming nature of Latin elegiac love alienates the lover from *traditional* Roman society and ideals of masculinity. In Chapter 9 Alison Sharrock brilliantly captures the dynamics of this alienation in the concept of *nequitia* ('badness'), which renders the life of the poet-lover pointless, yet naughty and therefore ultimately potent as a socially subversive form of existence from the traditionalist's point of view.

In Latin love elegy, the poet-lover is regularly portrayed as being just as weak as the beloved woman is strong. The poet-lover excels in *mollitia* ('softness'), a quality associated with the feminine and effeminate. As Sharrock points out in Chapter 9, Propertius even casts himself – outrageously – in the position of an *uniuira* ('woman who has had only one husband', cf. Prop. 2.1.47–8). By contrast, the beloved is normally portrayed not only as *dura* (hard), but also as *domina* (owner/mistress). The unequal relationship between the elegiac man and woman is consequently represented as the elegiac lover's *seruitium amoris* ('slavery of love'), which is the topic of Chapter 11 by Laurel Fulkerson. The concept of the poet-lover's slavery entails not only the subversion of traditional roles of men and women, but also of social class, again to the ultimate empowerment of the elegiac poet-lover. Fulkerson points out how this seemingly paradoxical process has literary consequences in that there seems to be a closer relationship between the elegiac lover and the *seruus callidus* ('clever slave') of comedy than has previously been recognized in erotic-elegiac scholarship.

Scholarly awareness of the complexities and importance of gender in Latin love elegy has transformed our conception of that genre during the last few decades. Feminist approaches and studies of erotics have not only contributed to profounder insights into the genre proper, but have challenged and changed our understanding of Latin literature and literary culture in general.[13] As with the genre of Latin love elegy itself, issues concerning gender now permeate studies on the topic (see below). A similar approach is applied in this *Companion*: no single chapter is allotted to gender, and the issue is instead addressed throughout the various chapters. Furthermore, one entire chapter is dedicated to Sulpicia, who is usually assumed to be the daughter of the Servius Sulpicius Rufus, who died in 43 BC (cf. *Serui filia Sulpicia* [Tib.] 3.16.4, 'Sulpicia, daughter of Servius', see Lyne (2007), 341–67 and Skoie (Chapter 5) in this volume). Sulpicia is the only woman among Augustan poets, and she is a composer of elegiac couplets, whether her poems are considered epigrams (her longest poem runs to ten lines) or *elegidia* ('little elegies').

Sulpicia is of great significance to Latin love elegy, although she does not make the elegiac canon, and her corpus, which is transmitted in the *Appendix Tibulliana*, is even smaller than that of Lygdamus (see above). For centuries even the possibility of her existence was in doubt. Sulpicia is nevertheless important because she embodies the subversion of established gender models that is so fundamental to the dynamics of Latin love elegy. While the beloved

13 I owe much of this formulation to the anonymous reader of the *Companion* for Cambridge University Press.

woman of the male erotic elegists regularly sports traditionally masculine qualities by appearing as strong, hard and dominating, it is important to bear in mind that she emerges as such by being mediated through the matrix of the poet-lover's text; she rarely speaks, and she remains elusive as a subject in her own right. Nevertheless, the poet-lover constantly hints at the reality of the woman he worships, and scholarly debate continues over the degree to which the elegiac *puella* is purely *scripta* ('written', cf. Prop. 2.10.8) and the fictitious object of the poet's creation. Even the female voice recorded in Ovid's *Heroides* 1–15 ('Heroines'), a work that consists of love (and hate) letters purportedly penned by women from legend and literature, remains a work written by Ovid (as he underscored e.g. in *Am.* 2.18). Most, but not all, scholars now agree that Sulpicia is not a *puella scripta*; instead, she represents the genuine subject position of a woman who wrote about her love for the male character Cerinthus in Latin elegiac couplets.[14] In Chapter 5 Mathilde Skoie updates both Sulpician and erotic-elegiac scholarship by gauging the extent to which this poet adheres to the genre of Latin love elegy.

Politics

Latin love elegy remains ambiguous in the context of ruling Augustan ideology. The establishment of the Augustan regime coincides in time and place with the floruit of the genre. In Chapter 8 Stephen Harrison outlines the profound ways in which this poetic genre reflects and refashions the contemporary setting of the elegists during the latter half of the first century BC in Rome against the backdrop of the emergent Augustan regime. In this contemporary setting, the anti-social posture of the elegiac poet-lover, captured in the concept of *nequitia* as explored by Sharrock in Chapter 9, has plenty of political poignancy.

The ambition of Augustan ideology is totalitarian. All aspects of life, official roles as well as intimate relationships, were to be regulated according to the regime's fictive hierarchy of values and moral codes. As already pointed out, Latin elegiac love is also totalitarian and competes as such with the ruling ideology of the contemporary world of the elegists. The clash of

[14] Pointing out the most severe problem concerning Sulpicia, namely that what is presumed to be her own composition ([Tib.] 3.13–18, a total of 40 lines) is preceded by five poems that represent a series of exchanges between herself and her beloved Cerinthus ([Tib.] 3.8–12, a total of 114 lines), the anonymous reader asks: 'So we are meant to think Cerinthus and Sulpicia sat down together to write their answering sequence? *That* is the problem for those who believe Sulpicia wrote "Sulpicia's poems".'

these two regimes, that of love and that of politics, is a part of the fiction of Latin love elegy and produces numerous dilemmas for the poet-lover, so that he ultimately has no choice but to submit himself to love, however outrageous this may seem from a conventional point of view. The trope of *militia amoris* ('soldiering of love'), freshly explored by Megan O. Drinkwater in Chapter 12, is illustrative: while pleading that he is completely useless in the army of Rome, the poet-lover feels obliged to enrol in the army of love.

The end of Latin love elegy in its classical form coincides with the consolidation of the Augustan regime. The postures of the Latin love elegists are politically provocative. For how long could such postures be sustained against the consolidation of Augustan power? Harrison, who poses this question in his chapter, suggests that the 'social and political loosening which marked the end of the Roman Republic was an apt moment of genesis for an essentially countercultural genre, while moral legislation and an increasingly authoritarian monarchy clearly contributed to its passing'. In Chapter 6, Keith's presentation of the poetic career of Propertius corroborates this view. While totalitarian love rules the first book of Propertius, erotic absolutism gradually breaks down in the next two books, while the final collection of elegies, which is dedicated to *Roma* rather than *Amor*, focuses on legendary origins of Roman monuments and customs in the aetiological tradition. The development of Propertius' poetic career may thus be understood as gradually complying with emergent Augustan ideology, as already touched upon. In Chapter 15, John F. Miller shows, however, how arch-elegiac issues related to gender subversion not only prevail, but arguably become more acute in Propertius' professedly non-erotic final book of elegies.

Literary history

Latin love elegy is highly significant in Western literary history. Broadly speaking, the legacy of the genre in question is twofold: as already noted, Latin love elegy embodies a turning point in the West's rich tradition of literary conceptions of *love*; furthermore, the genre in question represents a formative phase in its tradition of *lament*. Love elegy is thus seminal for understanding these two often entangled themes in Western literary history. In a narrower sense, too, posterity's constant engagement with this classical genre attests not only Latin love elegy's enduring inspiration, but also the individual characteristics of each period that found fresh approaches to the genre – approaches that reflect back on the genre itself and highlight crucial aspects of the ancient model.

In recognition of the significance of Latin love elegy within the context of literary history, a substantial section of this *Companion* is dedicated to receptions of the genre. The reception history featured here pertains to different languages and literary forms. Several of the chapters focus on literary works in the Latin language at times when responses to ancient erotic elegy were also found in the vernacular. This organization reflects not a lack of interest in responses to Latin love elegy in the vernacular, but rather a wish to grasp the opportunity – inasmuch as this is a companion to *Latin* love elegy – to focus on the rich, but neglected tradition of erotic-elegiac compositions in the Latin language after antiquity. From the eighteenth century onwards, however, the focus is on literary responses to the genre in other languages. The elegiac metre, which is the formal criterion by which the genre is technically identified, plays a varying role throughout the reception of Latin love elegy. In the history of the reception of this genre the couplet, also called distich, remains a recurrent feature, but feet, rhythm and syllables may vary. Nevertheless, wit, naughty sexiness, pre-romantic romanticism, artistic originality and the aesthetics of exquisite refinement associated with the tradition after Callimachus of Cyrene (first half of the third century BC) are all aspects of the ancient genre that are variously underscored at different stages of its reception in Western literary history, whatever the language and whatever the form.

During the Christian eras of Late Antiquity and the Middle Ages, learned men (and the occasional woman) who were inspired by the erotic-elegiac tradition celebrate – seemingly paradoxically – the humour and sexiness of Latin love elegy. The main focus of Roger Green's Chapter 16 is on the often hilarious regrets of the lover in the elegiac corpus attributed to Maximianus, who probably lived in the sixth century AD, but who until the nineteenth century was mistaken for Cornelius Gallus, thanks to the successful manipulation of Pomponio Gaurico (1482–1530) in his edition of the poet in 1501. In Chapter 17 Marek T. Kretschmer shows how the medieval response to Latin love elegy both concentrates on Ovid and results in the creation of a surprisingly rich variety of further literary forms, including elegiac comedy and biography. In his chapter, Kretschmer evokes Ludwig Traube's term *aetas Ouidiana* ('Ovidian age') in order to describe the impact of the elegist during the tenth and eleventh centuries. By extension, at least when the focus is on the reception of ancient erotic elegy, the Renaissance and early modern era could be called an *aetas Propertiana* (Propertian age), as Chapter 18 by Luke B. Houghton and Chapter 19 by Victoria Moul clearly demonstrate, while the long eighteenth century is an *aetas Tibulliana* (Tibullan age), as shown in Chapter 20 by Stéphanie Loubère and Chapter 21 by Andrew Kahn.

The aesthetic ideals of poetic refinement, oblique allusions and artistic innovation that are associated with the Callimachean tradition were of paramount importance to the Augustan poets, including the love elegists. In Houghton's chapter on Renaissance responses to the classical genre, a similar Callimacheanism is also a key feature. The chapter demonstrates how the ancient vocabulary related to Callimachean aesthetics, not least represented by the Propertian corpus, nourishes the reception of Latin love elegy first and foremost in Italian, but also in Dutch, French and German Renaissance poetry. Latin love elegies composed in England during the sixteenth and seventeenth centuries are the topic of Moul's chapter, which reveals a near-Augustan quest for artistic originality and that updates the genre to include 'the inhabitants of Thames right side', a Cupid who 'sports a musket' and the female voice of ancient elegy transposed to the kingdom of plants in the botanical garden of the University of Oxford, no less.

Furthermore, the reception of Latin love elegy plays a vital, yet neglected role in the transition between the ages of Enlightenment and Romanticism. Both Loubère's chapter on the French eighteenth century and Kahn's chapter, which covers Russian responses to the tradition of Latin love elegy throughout the so-called long eighteenth century, contribute to a profounder understanding of the transitional dynamics of Enlightenment and Romanticism. Both Loubère and Kahn stress how important the ancient elegists were for leading French and Russian writers of those eras, such as Évariste de Parny (1753–1814), André Chénier (1762–1794), François-René Chateaubriand (1768–1748) and Alexander Pushkin (1799–1837).

Similarly, the reception of Latin love elegy in German-speaking areas of Europe eventually paved the way for the invention of 'German elegy'. In Chapter 22, Theodore Ziolkowski outlines the development of this particular German poetic form, which reached its sublime summit in the compositions of Johann Wolfgang von Goethe (1749–1832), Friedrich Schiller (1759–1805) and Friedrich Hölderlin (1770–1843) and which winds up being parodied by Bertolt Brecht (1898–1956) in Hollywood, thus signalling the genre's dissemination into popular culture.

Scholarship

It remains a striking coincidence that the sixties BC saw the first sprouts of Latin love elegy, which first found profound scholarly appreciation from the sixties onwards of the twentieth century. Latin love elegy, whose motto could have been 'make-love-your-war', thus seems to have resonated particularly sympathetically with the spirit of the generation famous for the motto 'make-love-not-war'.[15]

Along with other significant publications on Hellenistic poetry, Augustan literature and the individual elegists, three books appeared every new decade from the sixties onwards that contributed to the rich and sophisticated appreciation of the erotic-elegiac genre among classicists today. Luck's *The Latin Love Elegy* (1959) marks the beginning of this era in classical scholarship. Luck's erotic-elegiac monograph, especially its revised edition of 1969, still contains valuable observations on the characteristics of the Roman genre against its Hellenistic background. Luck's revised edition was soon accompanied by Stroh's important monograph *Die römische Liebeselegie als werbende Dichtung* (1971), which stressed the erotic-persuasive quality of Latin love elegy. Finally, almost ten years later, Lyne's comprehensive study *The Latin Love Poets* (1980) appeared, featuring the Latin love elegists along with Catullus and Horace and focusing on their various representations of love against the background of the social changes that marked the end of the Roman Republic.

From the 1980s onwards there was an increase in the frequency with which erotic-elegiac studies were produced. Veyne's *L'élégie érotique romaine: l'amour, la poésie et l'occident* (French original 1983, English translation 1988) is one of the first and also most provocative of these studies. The greatest merit of Veyne's book is that it destabilizes the theoretical grounds on which our understanding of Latin love elegy is built. As already pointed out, the fundamental fiction of Latin love elegy is that there is no fiction. Consequently, the genre abounds with allusions to the extra-textual world of the elegists' contemporary Rome, such as the elegists' own names, which in the phrase of the French literary critic Roland Barthes (1915–1980) create what may be called *l'effet de réel*: 'the reality effect'.[16] Much erotic-elegiac scholarship has been, and still is, centred on the nature of the relationship between reality and representation in this genre. The risks linked to the 'biographical fallacy', that is the fallacy of reading a poet's word as an historical document of his own, flesh-and-blood existence, are

[15] Before the 1960s, an important part of erotic-elegiac scholarship centred on the question of objective versus subjective elegy. Scholars recognized how the combination of a personal voice and mythical exempla and excursuses distinguished Latin love elegy from other kinds of literature. The dispute was over the degree to which this combination was an original invention on the part of the genre in question, or rather the continuation of a (mostly) lost Hellenistic tradition. The debate, excellently outlined by Bessone (Chapter 2) in this volume, was largely settled by the synthesizing approach of Cairns in his book on Tibullus (1979a).

[16] Barthes (1968).

always immanent in attempts to identify extra-textual facts or more fleeting features such as social attitudes and ideology through the matrix of poetry. Nevertheless, because of numerous reminders of the world outside the text in Latin love poetry from Catullus onwards, such scholarly quests for the historically real remain to some extent responses to invitations embedded in this kind of poetry itself. The biographical fallacy is, as it were, a consequence of the reality effect of erotic-elegiac fiction at the receiving end.

The complexity and sophistication of *l'effet de réel* of Latin love elegy evokes equally complex and sophisticated scholarly approaches to the genre. One of the greatest merits of Veyne's monograph is that it remains an influential contribution to such theoretical refinement of erotic-elegiac scholarship. Inspired by the 'epistemic' conception of history deployed by his friend Michel Foucault (1926–1984), in which continuity and communication through time is envisaged as little more than wishful thinking, Veyne systematically attacks reductionist understandings of Latin love elegy as a genre that chronicles real experiences of real love by real subjects in the real Rome. By thus pointing out what Latin love elegy is *not*, Veyne successfully paves the way for fresh approaches to the genre.

Conversely, Veyne's presentation of what Latin love elegy *is* remains less satisfactory, if not outright shocking. By drawing attention to the genre's semiotics, that is system of signs, Veyne sees the genre as playfully witty, even brilliant. However, this brilliance remains dead in his eyes: its aesthetics and artifice were as pointless at the time of its creation, Veyne contends, as they are to us today. The gap between Latin love elegy and us is consequently bridged by boredom. 'For my part,' Veyne confesses, 'I think I can understand what these poets meant to do, but I admit that reading them can be boring' (1988: 33). While Veyne's book has been duly regarded as being representative of various intellectual approaches now labelled as 'French theory', less attention has been paid to how Veyne's confessed boredom links him to a longer intellectual tradition in France. Since the eighteenth century, French intellectuals have vented complaints about being bored with elegists, ancient as well as modern,[17] as Loubère points out in her chapter, which thus contributes to the contextualization of Veyne's stark attitude towards the genre.

Veyne's monograph reveals an ambition to situate the Latin love elegists within the greater framework of Western literary history. Contrary to his confessed boredom while reading the Latin love elegists, this ambition remains constructive. But the ambition is only vaguely communicated

[17] 'The fact is that, despite the great number of elegies that are produced, there are few of them that can be read without boredom': Leblanc: (1731) 3, translated by J. Lloyd.

through the study, and it even seems to run counter to the epistemic approach inspired by Foucault. Nevertheless, the context of Western literary history remains formative for the conception of Veyne's book, a fact that is heralded by its original subtitle of *l'amour, la poésie et l'occident* ('love, poetry and the West'). This subtitle alludes to *L'Amour et l'Occident* ('Love and the Western World'), a classic within the disciplines of comparative literature and history of ideas, written by Denis de Rougemont (1906–1985).[18] Any reader familiar with the Latin love elegists would expect ample exposition of their corpus in a book with a title such as de Rougemont's; however, although de Rougemont treats many themes related to love that are first developed in a uniquely systematic manner by the Latin love elegists, these poets are nowhere mentioned in his book. Though Veyne modestly claims that he does not intend to 'rewrite Love in the Western World in [his] own terms', (1988: 140–1), he concludes his brief and critical account of the work by de Rougemont (whose name he omits) with a remark that in fact is a most serious charge against *L'Amour et l'Occident*: 'elegiac poetry,' Veyne asserts, 'will remain for twenty centuries the model for all amorous poetry' (1988: 140–1). By including a substantial section on the reception of Latin love elegy, this *Companion* subscribes to Veyne's ambition of contextualizing the Latin love elegists within the literary history of the West.

Veyne's conceptualization of Latin love elegy has been met with much criticism in classical scholarship. One of the earliest critics of Veyne, and certainly one of the most influential contributors to Latin studies today, is Gian Biagio Conte. In his seminal paper 'Love without Elegy: The *Remedia amoris* and the Logic of a Genre' (1989, Italian original 1986),[19] Conte dedicates a lengthy footnote to the criticism of Veyne (1989: 451–2). Conte's sophisticated and influential exposition of the genre of Latin love elegy provided by the *uia negatiua* of Ovid's *Remedia amoris* ('Cures for Love') nicely balances Veyne's conception of the genre, where Veyne's pointless playfulness (and attitudinizing with aesthetic *ennui*)[20] is replaced by Conte's rules of the game that disclose the meaning of it, if understood properly.

Conte's brilliant analysis of the genre appeared at the beginning of a new golden age for the appreciation of Augustan poetry, including Latin love elegy. The following works are select highlights from this golden age, presented in their approximate order of appearance. Holzberg's *Die römische*

[18] *Love in the Western World* (and not 'Love and the Western World') is the title of the English translation of the work, published in 1983. The work was first published in French in 1939, and was continuously revised by the author until its final version in 1972.

[19] 'Love without Elegy' was republished in *Genres and Readers* (1994b) 35–65.

[20] I owe this observation to the anonymous reader for Cambridge University Press.

Liebeselegie: eine Einführung (1990) is the first work that merits attention as it aims to introduce the genre in an all-embracing manner. However valuable the first edition of this work is, the substantially revised version of 2001, which draws on, debates and assesses the scholarly endeavours of the 1990s, is even more rewarding. Just one year after Holzberg's revised introduction to Latin love elegy appeared, Pinotti published her *L'elegia latina: storia di una forma poetica* (2002), another stimulating introduction to the genre, which provides an overview that extends both further back and further ahead of the ancient timeline covered by Holzberg and which thus necessarily touches upon non-erotic as well as erotic elegy in Latin.

Between the appearance of these two thorough and thought-provoking introductions to the genre, the following works proved especially influential in enhancing scholarly understanding of Latin love elegy: Kennedy's refined *The Arts of Love: Five Studies in the Discourse of Roman Love Elegy* (1993), which marries the sophistication of literary theory with the genre of Latin love elegy; Greene's *The Erotics of Domination: Male Desire and the Mistress in Latin Poetry* (1998), where the key of gender-related perspectives unlocks the essential dynamics of the genre; and Wyke's *The Roman Mistress: Ancient and Modern Representations* (2002), whose first part collects the author's groundbreaking works on the literariness of gender representations in Latin love elegy since 1987.

James' *Learned Girls and Male Persuasion: Gender and Reading in Roman Love Elegy* (2003) pursued the fruitful approach already opened up by works such as Wyke's and Greene's (see also Ancona and Greene 2005) by exploring gender-related issues further. At the same time, James stressed the erotic-persuasive quality of Latin love elegy, and thus updated Stroh's important concept of the genre as *werbende Dichtung* ('courtship poetry'). In terms of theoretical refinement in scholarly approaches to the genre, P.A. Miller's *Subjecting Verses: Latin Love Elegy and the Emergence of the Real* (2004) is perhaps the most ambitious attempt to date to capture the genre's intricate, literary and psychodynamic game of realities and representations.

Fundamental to the appreciation of Latin love elegy today is the rigorous, yet vital strain of textual criticism and close analysis in erotic-elegiac scholarship. Few book-length works embody this tradition as broadly as Lyne's *Collected Papers on Latin Poetry* and Cairns' *Papers on Roman Elegy: 1969–2003*, two volumes that both appeared in 2007. As many as eleven of the nineteen essays included in Lyne's volume treat erotic-elegiac topics, while all of Cairns' volume is dedicated to the genre in question. Both collections take us through a number of tough and thought-provoking trials concerning textual challenges in Latin love elegy, as well as more than thirty years of valuable scholarship.

Today, textual criticism, awareness of gendered dynamics and theoretical refinement blend into erotic-elegiac scholarship to the benefit of a profounder understanding of the art form that is Latin love elegy. Fine examples are the anthology *Elegy and Narratology: Fragments of Story* (2008), edited by Liveley and Salzman-Mitchell and the book *Gendering Time in Augustan Love Elegy* (2013) by Gardner, which provide fresh approaches to the genre by focusing on the particular ways in which narratives are employed in erotic-elegiac poetry. Valuable are also the cognate, yet highly different monographs Dolor *und* Ingenium: *Untersuchungen zur römischen Liebeselegie* by Baar (2006) and *The Elegiac Passion: Jealousy in Roman Love Elegy* (2012) by Caston, which both investigate how representations of emotions (pain and jealousy) contribute to the formative framework of the genre of Latin love elegy at Rome. Finally, *The Oxford Handbook to the Elegy*, edited by Weisman (2010), and *A Companion to Roman Love Elegy* (2012), edited by Gold, offer recent reference tools in the increasingly blooming field of elegiac scholarship. Weisman provides the broader scope both in terms of culture (including the Judaic tradition), timeline and different media (e.g. film and photography) in which forms of elegy are located. However, the all-inclusive approach tends to dilute the concept heralded in the title, which perhaps should have been 'lament' rather than 'elegy'. One consequence is that an otherwise fine chapter on Latin love elegy underplays the importance of the genre in the elegiac tradition as 'the peculiar story of elegy in Rome' (cf. P.A. Miller 2010), asking 'What's love got to do with it?' as if the erotic aspect of elegy represents an anomaly. In contrast, Gold's companion solidly concentrates on the genre in question and – to some extent – the influence it has exercised throughout two millennia. The volume does indeed provide a 'rich trove of material' (Gold 2012: 6), outlining a number of themes and chronologies that cross each other throughout the thirty-three chapters of the eight sections into which the volume is divided.

Companion

Needless to say, this *Companion* benefits from a favourable situation. In the hope of producing clarity of exposition, the twenty-two helpful, important and thought-provoking chapters of this volume are organized in five sections. In the first part, 'History and Context', Latin love elegy emerges as a 'Roman *reductio*' against the variegated background of Greek elegy (Hunter) and a generic 'son-of-nobody' that nonetheless claims to be heir to a rich tradition, a claim that appears as much an invention as an actual 'birthright' (Bessone), thus explaining the profound difference between Greek and Roman elegy. The second part, 'The Latin Love Elegists', gives ample space to the major poets: Gallus (Raymond), Tibullus (Lee-Stecum), Propertius (Keith) and Ovid (Thorsen), including Lygdamus (together with Tibullus, cf. Lee-Stecum) and Sulpicia (Skoie), who are the known elegiac poets of the *Appendix Tibulliana*. The third part, 'The Elegiac World', outlines the historical setting of the genre (Harrison), the major protagonists of the poet-lover (Sharrock) and his *puella* (P.A. Miller), as well as the major erotic-elegiac tropes of *seruitium amoris* (Fulkerson) and *militia amoris* (Drinkwater). The fourth part, 'The Ends of Latin Love Elegy', explores the confines of the genre in terms of multiple loves (Gibson), other genres (Piazzi) and violation of self-imposed rules (J. Miller). Finally, the fifth part, 'Receptions', traces the influence of the genre throughout Late Antiquity (Green), the Middle Ages (Kretschmer), the Renaissance (Houghton), early modern times (Moul and Ziolkowski), the eighteenth century (Loubère, Kahn and Ziolkowski) and the nineteenth and the twentieth centuries (Ziolkowski). At the very end, there is a chapter dedicated to technical as well as semantically significant aspects of the Latin elegiac couplet (Thorsen). All chapters include a section of recommendations for further reading, often identifying areas within erotic-elegiac scholarship that need more coverage. The chapters on the individual elegists also contain information about texts, commentaries and translations into English.

Whether the reader decides to go through these parts consecutively or pick and choose chapters as he or she sees fit – both approaches have their merits – it is my hope that the scholar and student alike will find an informative, stimulating and cutting-edge *Companion* to the classical genre of Latin love elegy, which is of such great importance to literary history.

PART I

History and context

1

RICHARD HUNTER

Greek elegy

Archaic Greek elegy

We possess passages of Greek poetry in elegiac couplets by Callinus, Archilochus and Tyrtaeus from probably the middle of the seventh century BC, i.e. within a few decades of the most commonly accepted date for Hesiod and Homer. The elegiac couplet itself belongs to a recognizable group of 'strophic' metres and is presumably considerably older than our earliest evidence for it; it is composed of a dactylic hexameter followed by two 'hemiepes' always separated by word division (–⏑⏑–⏑⏑ || –⏑⏑–⏑⏑–), the so-called 'pentameter'. It seems clear that, from the earliest period, poets thought and composed in couplets or groups of couplets, rather than 'verse by verse';[1] features such as the relative frequency of enjambment, by comparison with that in stichic hexameter verse, and the fact that replacement of two short syllables by a long syllable does not occur in the second hemiepes of the pentameter, which thus always presents the same rhythm, point to a fundamental distinction between hexameter and elegiac verse. Nevertheless, from the earliest period there is a closeness between the basically Ionic *Kunstsprache* of Homeric poetry and that of elegiac verse, even where that verse treats 'non-Homeric' subjects and where local, epichoric features of dialect are also clearly in evidence; panhellenic epic infused the texture of elegy, whose metrical pattern provided of course a ready home for many of the linguistic structures of epic.[2] This similarity and virtual symbiosis, which for those concerned, as Roman poets were to be, with the history of literary forms naturally accentuates the importance of (sometimes small) differences of style, subject and treatment, was to determine to an important degree the reception of Greek elegy at Rome.[3]

[1] On elegiac metrics cf., e.g., West (1982) 44–6, Adkins (1985), Raalte (1988), Barnes (1995), Garner (2011); on composition by 'stanza' Faraone (2008).

[2] Cf., e.g., Page (1964) and Garner (2011). On 'local' dialect features in early elegy cf. D'Alessio in Budelmann (2009) 120–3.

[3] The subject of this chapter makes some overlap with Hunter (2006), (2012) and (2013) inevitable.

Unfortunately, time has not been kind to Greek elegy of the archaic period.[4] For elegiac compositions down to the middle of the fifth century we have the following sources of evidence:

1. Papyri, notably of Archilochus and Simonides (see below) and Tyrtaeus.
2. An anthology, preserved in manuscript tradition,[5] of nearly 1400 verses ascribed to Theognis of Megara, but certainly containing the work of several poets, including Mimnermus, Solon and Tyrtaeus, ranging in date from the seventh to the early fifth century at least; the collection is introduced by four invocations: to Apollo (two), Artemis and the Muses and Graces. The last part of the anthology (1231–1389, 'Book 2') gathers together largely pederastic verse. The origin and date of the anthology remain unclear and disputed,[6] but some parts at least may go back to the fourth century.
3. Quotations of elegiac verse in later authors (Plutarch, Athenaeus, Stobaeus etc.) and lexica; worthy of special note is a quotation of an extended passage of one of Solon's political elegies by Demosthenes (19.254 = Solon fr. 4 W).
4. Information in later writers and lexica about poets and the performance of elegy.
5. Epigrams ascribed in the *Palatine Anthology* and other written sources to early poets such as Anacreon; issues of authorship always arise in such cases. Of particular importance is the body of epigrams ascribed to Simonides, many on matters concerned with the Persian Wars.[7]
6. Inscribed epitaphs and dedications.[8] The earliest inscribed poetry is not in elegiacs, but elegiacs become regular from about the end of the sixth century.

It is a reasonable guess that elegiac compositions varied very greatly in length, though there is no sign of monumental composition on a 'Homeric scale'; Plutarch tells us that Solon's poem on Salamis was one hundred verses long (we have a poem (fr. 13 W) of seventy-six verses), and the evidence suggests that some of Simonides' celebratory elegiac poems (cf. below) will have been rather longer than that. Poems of several hundred verses on subjects of local legend and history are not hard to imagine.[9] It

4 There is an introductory survey by Gerber (1997) and cf. also Aloni (2009) and Lulli (2011). Gerber (1991) offers a helpful and detailed bibliographical survey.

5 For a brief summary of the transmission cf. West (1971/1992) xi–xiii.

6 Cf. West (1974) 40–61, Bowie (1997), Selle (2008) esp. 381–93.

7 Cf. Petrovic (2007). 8 Cf. Hansen (1983) (= *CEG*).

9 The contributions of Bowie (e.g. 1986, 2001) are fundamental in this area. It is difficult to know how to evaluate the report that Panyassis' *Ionika* was seven thousand verses in length.

is likely that the great majority of elegiac poetry (except of course inscribed verses) was 'sung' to the accompaniment of the *aulos* (a reed instrument not unlike our oboe, though 'flute' is the conventional translation); the fact that a poet or singer could therefore not accompany himself must have made the later shift to unaccompanied, purely 'written' verses relatively uncomplicated. Moreover, despite the musical nature of early elegy, and the fact that it shares many themes and attitudes with more properly 'lyric' or 'melic' poetry from which some elegy is distinguishable only by metre,[10] ancient scholars always treated elegy, together with hexameter poetry and *iambos*, as on the spoken side of the sung/spoken divide. This too will have encouraged Roman poets to see elegy and epic as, from one perspective, the opposed members of a single group and to have explored and enlarged those differences.

How much archaic Greek elegy was available to Roman poets or familiar at Rome is a difficult question, but it would be dangerous to be over-optimistic; the archaic elegist most important to Roman love elegists, namely Mimnermus, had been identified in the Hellenistic period as the 'inventor' of the elegiac couplet (Hermesianax fr. 7.35–8 Powell) and immortalized by Callimachus (fr. 1.11), and he may have been little more than a famous name.[11] On the other hand, a good case can be made for believing that contemporary Greek writers had at their disposal considerably more than we do of, say, Mimnermus and Solon during the first two Christian centuries.[12] Quintilian, however, for whose purposes Greek elegy has little to offer, exceptionally names two, as we would say, Hellenistic poets, Callimachus and Philitas, as occupying first and second place in this genre (*Inst.* 10.1.58), and we should consider the possibility that this reflects not merely a qualitative judgement, but also the fact that texts of archaic elegy were simply not very accessible, perhaps in part because of a relative neglect by Alexandrian scholarship.

Much of what survives of early elegy either assumes or would be perfectly at home in the setting of a symposium. In a famous passage (vv. 237–54), Theognis envisages how his poetry, addressed to the *erômenos* Kyrnos, will be sung at future symposia to the accompaniment of 'clear-sounding pipes'. The delights of *erōs* and reflection on themes such as the brevity of youth find a natural place in the poetry of the symposium, and it was to prove important for Roman poets that Hellenistic epigram inherited and

10 For these terms and for the difficulties of classification see the Introduction to Budelmann (2009), citing earlier bibliography.

11 Cf. Hunter (2006b), (2013).

12 There is a helpful survey in Bowie (1997) 58–60.

developed many of these themes of archaic elegy,[13] which were then transmitted to Rome in the late second to early first century, in a process far from fully understood, though one in which Meleager's 'Garland' will have played an important role.[14] Among these themes was the conduct of the symposium itself; a preserved twenty-four verse passage of Xenophanes (late sixth century) describes and prescribes the appropriate setting and behaviour for the symposium, and the importance of 'purity' of word and deed which runs through that poem foreshadows Callimachean themes which were to become dear to Roman poets.[15] This theme of the proper conduct of the symposium may be traced back at least as far as the *Odyssey*, notably to Odysseus' famous 'golden verses' which introduce his tales to the Phaeacians (*Odyssey* 9.2–11) and which may, for all we know, themselves echo elegiac poetry.[16]

Sympotic space was of course very capacious in the poetic themes it could accommodate. Exhortation to young men to be brave and steadfast in battle is the subject of some of our best known pieces of early elegy (Callinus fr.1, Tyrtaeus *passim*), and this too would not be out of place at a symposium, though of course the verses could well have subsequently been re-performed in other contexts, including on the battlefield itself, as indeed is reported for Tyrtaeus.[17] So too, the political verse of Solon and aristocratic complaints about the power of money and the stupidity of the citizens which run through the *Theognidea* would fit perfectly into what we know of the symposium. Early Greek elegy was certainly not politically unengaged.

While it is clear that narrative of various kinds must have played a part in the more expansive elegies devoted to legendary and/or historical subjects, the extent of elegiac narrative in the early period remains unclear. In 2005 Obbink published a new elegiac passage of Archilochus (*POxy.* 4708) in which the story of the defeat by Telephus in Mysia of the Greek army destined for Troy seems to have been told as an exemplum, perhaps as a consolation for a retreat which the poet and his comrades had been forced to make. Very much remains uncertain,[18] but we now have a rather better sense of how early elegy could be expansive, as well perhaps as a better understanding of 'Longinus'' apparent contrast between Archilochus and Eratosthenes in the field of elegy (*Subl.* 33.5).[19] Narrative is also at the heart

13 Cf. e.g. Giangrande (1968), Bowie (2007).

14 Bibliography in Fantuzzi-Hunter (2004) 463.

15 Cf. Hunter (2006a) 36–7.

16 On this tradition of *symposiodidaxis* cf. Bielohlawek (1940), Hunter (1983) 186.

17 On the poetry of martial exhortation cf. Irwin (2005) 19–62; for Tyrtaeus' unusual 'communal' voice cf. D'Alessio (2009) 150–6.

18 The bibliography is already of course large; see further Obbink (2006), Aloni-Iannucci (2007) 205–37.

19 Cf. further Hunter (2010).

of much debate as to how to interpret the significant fragments of (almost certainly) more than one elegy by Simonides published by Peter Parsons in 1992 (*POxy.* 3965, overlapping with 2327 = frr. 2–22 West).[20] The most significant fragment (fr. 11) is concerned with the Spartan victory at Plataea in 479 BC. The departure from Sparta of the army under Pausanias is described, but the fragment begins with a description of the death of Achilles, complete with an 'epic' simile; this leads to (? the return of) the Greek army itself and praise of Homer who is responsible for the *kleos* (Gr. 'fame') of the Greeks; the poet then bids farewell to Achilles and invokes the Muse to help him with his song of the Spartans. This complex structure, replete with hymnic features, presumably formed part of a poem (of at least a hundred verses and probably rather more) which, not improbably, was commissioned by Spartans for public performance and commemoration. In the context of this chapter its primary significance is that it provides yet another illustration of the extraordinary range and variety of early Greek elegy; accustomed as we are to the restricted thematic range of Latin elegy, produced by poets all living within a very restricted time frame, it is easy to forget just how rich the elegiac tradition was (though there is as yet no evidence for archaic elegy in the area of natural philosophy). It is, of course, this Roman *reductio*, as much as anything else, which requires explanation. Here too, however, the 'new Simonides' may perhaps be suggestive. The new fragments include not just the martial 'Plataea' verses, but also reflections, some already known from later quotations, on the evanescence of youth, on desire and the certainty of death (frr. 19–22 West); there was, within the elegiac tradition, a recurrent set of preoccupations waiting to be distilled into an 'elegiac' sensibility.

Greek elegy in the Classical and Hellenistic periods

Apart from inscribed epigram, we have in fact little evidence for elegiac verse in the late fifth and fourth century. Clearly some poetry of traditional type continued to be composed (the fragments of Ion of Chios deserve notice), and there are some fragments from Athens (Dionysius Chalcus, Critias etc.) which attest to a continuing tradition of sympotic verse, but these are no more than scraps. More significant from the perspective of later poetry was the *Lyde* of another poet who straddles the fifth and fourth centuries, Antimachus from Colophon, who also wrote epic poetry (which – as far as our pitifully little evidence allows us to judge – does not, in

[20] Amidst the vast bibliography may be mentioned Boedeker-Sider (2001) and Kowerski (2005).

fact, seem to have been stylistically much differentiated from his elegy); Antimachus was also, like several important Hellenistic poets, a scholar of Homer. Sources tell us that when the poet's wife or mistress Lyde ('the Lydian lady') died Antimachus wrote a consolatory elegy for himself 'full of unhappy heroic stories, thus lessening his own grief through others' sorrows' (T 12 Matthews); 'he filled books with lamentations' (Hermesianax fr. 7/45 Powell = T 11 Matthews), a description which certainly seems to foreshadow the Roman conception of *flebilis Elegia* (Ov. *Am.* 3.9.3, 'tearful Elegy'). The poem was in at least two books, and although our fragments are exiguous, it is clear that some stories, such as that of the Argonauts (from which Apollonius of Rhodes was later to borrow), were told at some length and detail.[21] It is likely, though not absolutely certain, that the poet wrote himself into the poem, perhaps through a first-person prologue; if so, we would have an interesting resonance between the poet's own erotic experience and that of some of his mythological characters, to whose 'lamentations' Hermesianax presumably refers,[22] which would look forward (*inter alia*) to some of the uses of mythology in Roman poetry. Although for us the *Lyde* is a mere shadow, it was a poem with a very rich *Nachleben* in the Hellenistic period, when attitudes to it seem to have become something of a touchstone of poetic taste.[23] It may also have been in this poem that Antimachus laid emphasis upon Mimnermus as a poetic predecessor, thus fashioning that poet's 'Nanno' (perhaps a poetic title which Mimnermus himself never used) into the first in what was to become a long line of elegiac poems celebrating beloved women.[24]

In the third century, the range of the elegiac couplet extends into virtually every area of poetic endeavour, with the probable exception of large-scale martial epic; elegiac didactic poetry is another apparent absentee, though if two elegiac fragments (31–2 Gow-Scholfield) ascribed to Nicander and recounting popular beliefs about snakes and other dangerous creatures belong to the *Ophiaka*, then that poem at least was 'didactic' in some sense.[25] The capacious subject-range of elegiac epigrams incorporated and

[21] On the *Lyde* cf. Cameron (1995) Index s.v. Antimachus of Colophon, Matthews (1996) 26–39, citing earlier bibliography.

[22] It seems very probable that some at least of Antimachus' characters' κακά were erotic in nature.

[23] To Cameron (1995) and Matthews (1996) add Krevans (1993).

[24] Cf. West (1974) 74–6.

[25] For didactic elegiacs in the imperial period cf. Obbink (1999) 67–109. There is a helpful survey of Hellenistic elegiac poetry in Lightfoot (1999) 24–31; Lightfoot emphasizes the very great difference between the third century, on one side, and the second and first on the other. For surveys of the range of Hellenistic elegiacs cf. Lightfoot (1999) 17–31, Lulli (2009), Murray (2010).

thus transmitted lyric, as well as traditionally elegiac, themes; Nossis of Locri, who saw herself as Sappho's heir, and Anyte of Tegea, whose themes include foreshadowings of pastoral poetry, are striking proof that women, as well as men, were masters of the form. Elegiac mythological narrative may be exemplified, on the one hand, by some of the poetry of Philitas of Cos, who straddles the fourth and third centuries, and, on the other, by the *Erigone* of Eratosthenes. Philitas' *Demeter* (of uncertain length) seems to have told the story of the goddess' visit to Cos during her wanderings in search of her daughter and will have been replete with allusions to Coan myth and sacred geography; it is all but certain that echoes of the *Demeter* are to be found in Callimachus' *Hymn to Demeter* and in Theocritus' seventh *Idyll*, the 'Thalysia' set on Cos. In view of the links, at least from the Roman perspective, between elegy and lamentation, the necessarily unhappy subject of this famous poem is worth noting, and three fragments ascribed to it by Stobaeus, plus one other which modern scholars add to them with great probability, are indeed expressions of grief or consolation (frr. 5–8 Sbardella = 9–10, 12–13 Spanoudakis). Eratosthenes' *Erigone* too, which 'Longinus' disdainfully calls a 'flawless little poem', tells a sad story of wanderings, this time the Attic story of Erigone, whose father Ikarios was killed by peasants who thought he was trying to poison them with Dionysus' new gift of wine, and who subsequently hung herself; at the end of the poem father, daughter and faithful dog were all catasterized.[26] Had we more of this poem, we would very probably see its influence in Ovid's *Metamorphoses*.

Mythological narrative also had a central place in Callimachus' *Aetia* (see below), and the story of Teiresias' blinding for having inadvertently seen Athena naked is central to Callimachus' elegiac *Hymn to Athena*. A wider tradition of elegiac hymnography is perhaps suggested by the two elegiac hymns of Isidorus inscribed on a temple in the Egyptian Fayum in the first century.[27] Be that as it may, one set of partly mythological poems which seem to have been important for Roman poets took the form of poetic catalogues.[28] Hermesianax's *Leontion* recounted love stories from all over the Greek world, including the (largely fictitious) loves of (*inter alios*) poets and philosophers: in the current context its greatest significance probably lies in what it tells us of the erotic poetry of Antimachus and Philitas (fr. 7 Powell). Phanocles' *Loves* or *Beautiful Boys* did something similar for pederastic love, and the one surviving fragment of any length tells the story of Orpheus' death at the hands of Thracian women for having introduced pederastic practices. There is some sense in seeing such poems as a

[26] Cf. Rosokoki (1995). [27] Cf. Fantuzzi-Hunter (2004) 350–71.
[28] Cf. Magnelli (1999) 15–26, Hunter (2005) 259–65, Asquith (2005).

kind of blend of the perceived 'essential core' of the Hesiodic *Catalogue of Women* with the tradition of Antimachus' *Lyde*. Although martial narrative remained essentially the domain of the hexameter,[29] it is clear that elegy was also used for ruler encomium (cf. *SH* 958, 969)[30] and to celebrate the traditions of local cities and worthies. A particularly interesting example of the latter is the sixty verse 'Pride of Halicarnassus' (*SGO* 01/12/02) of the late second or first century, found inscribed on the site of Salmakis on the harbour of Halicarnassus (Bodrum), which seems to show clear traces of the influence of Callimachus.[31] Such poems may be seen as distant descendants of archaic elegies in praise of cities and local traditions. Elegy also found its way into pastoral (Theocritus 8 and 9) and 'curse poetry' (the 'tattoo elegy'),[32] the 'genre' which Ovid imitated in the *Ibis*. There are, moreover, a few anonymous fragments preserved on papyrus which offer tantalizing hints of elegy which used examples of mythical lovers to reflect upon the poet's own situation; if so, this would of course be of the greatest interest for Roman elegy, but unfortunately the date and interpretation of these poems remains very debated.[33] Further surprises in the future about Hellenistic 'erotic elegy' would not in fact be a great surprise.

Parthenius of Bithynia came to Rome as a prisoner-of-war (probably) in the latter part of the first century BC and seems to have played an important role in introducing Alexandrian poetry and poetics to Rome, though not perhaps with the revolutionary influence with which he has sometimes been credited.[34] His very scanty fragments show clear signs of Callimachean influence, and an epigram of imperial date groups him together with that master (Pollianus, *AP* 11.130 = Parthenius T 5 Lightfoot). Among his elegiac productions was a three-book *epicedion* ('lament') for his wife Arete, which may have stood in the tradition of Antimachus' *Lyde* and which may have been more influential upon Catullus and subsequent elegy than we can now tell; it has often been guessed that this poem was reflected in Calvus' elegy for Quintilia (frs. 15–16 Courtney, cf. Catullus 96). That Parthenius wrote a *Metamorphoses* is obviously of some interest, though it is not certain that

29 There has been much debate about the existence or otherwise of hexameter 'epic' poetry in the Hellenistic period, but Alan Cameron's argument that most of our evidence points not to large-scale 'epic' but to shorter, often encomiastic, poems is now broadly accepted in its outlines. It is worth bearing in mind that Propertius ends his 'history' of Greek martial epic with the *Persika* of Choerilus (Prop. 2.1.22).

30 Cf. Barbantani (2001), with excellent bibliography and survey of the tradition. *SH* 961 (an epithalamium for a royal marriage?) probably also belongs here.

31 Recent discussion and bibliography in Gagné (2006) and Romano (2009).

32 Cf. Huys (1991), *SSH* 969.

33 Cf. Butrica (1996a), Lightfoot (1999) 26–8, *SSH* 1187.

34 Lightfoot (1999) is the fundamental study where further details and bibliography should be sought.

this was verse rather than prose; it has been suggested that some fragmentary elegiacs (*POxy.* 4711) which tell briefly the stories of Adonis, Asteria and Narcissus may belong here, but the matter is far from certain.[35] Parthenius' other importance rests on his collection of erotic and novelistic narratives taken (largely) from Greek poetry, the *Sufferings in Love* (ἐρωτικὰ παθήματα), which he dedicated and sent to Cornelius Gallus to be used in his 'hexameters and elegiacs', though the stories lacked 'stylistic polish'. It was, however, the classics of Hellenistic poetry themselves which would show Gallus and his successors how to achieve the stylistic 'something special' (τὸ περιττόν) in both hexameters and elegies.

Callimachus' *Aetia* and Roman love elegy

The best known, and certainly most influential, elegiac product of the high Alexandrian period is the *Aetia* of Callimachus;[36] it was this poem which, for the subsequent tradition, gave Callimachus his place at the very top of the list of elegists. In four books (perhaps some five thousand verses in all) Callimachus recounted the 'causes' or 'origins' of city foundations, local myths and cultic practices from all over the Greek world; Propertius book 4 and Ovid's *Fasti* represent two Romanizations of the idea of the *Aetia*.[37] Callimachus' work was introduced by a polemical and programmatic prologue, the famous 'Reply to the Telchines' (fr. 1 Pf.), in which the poet allusively set out some poetic principles and proclaimed them as endorsed by Apollo; perhaps no passage of Greek poetry was echoed in Roman poetry more frequently than the 'Reply'.

Whether or not the *Aetia* went through two editions with books 3 and 4 added many years after books 1 and 2 (a much disputed subject), there is a clear difference in arrangement between the two halves of the poem. In the first pair, the poet recalls a dream conversation he had with the Muses on Mt Helicon in which he asked them questions and listened to their answers, as well as displaying his own knowledge; the structure is one of a number of ways in which the *Aetia* is marked as a 'Hesiodic' and indeed 'post-Hesiodic' work. If Hesiod's *Theogony*, in which the poet is given his poetic mission by the Muses, explained the creation and organization of the Olympian world, then the *Aetia* provides (*inter alia*) an account of how humans react to that world through myth and religious practice. The material of

35 For bibliography and sceptical discussion cf. Bernsdorff (2007).

36 The bibliography is vast. For the principal arguments about structure and arrangement cf., e.g., Cameron (1995) and Fantuzzi-Hunter (2004) 42–88; and Harder (2012) 2–12.

37 Miller (1982) provides a helpful overview of Callimachean aetiology in Roman elegy.

Books 3–4 seems to have been more varied (and some of the individual *Aetia* may have circulated as discrete poems), but of particular importance for Roman poets was the fact that this pair of books was framed by elegiac encomia of Callimachus' royal patrons. Book 3 was introduced by the 'Victoria Berenices', a grand epinician elegy in honour of the Cyrenean princess who married Ptolemy III Euergetes,[38] which told the story of Heracles' founding of the Nemean games, but gave pride of place within that story to Heracles' entertainment by the peasant Molorchus who eked out a humble living in land devastated by the Nemean lion; the description of Molorchus' battle with mice takes poetic precedence over Heracles' battle with the lion. This poem finds many echoes in Roman poetry, and features as a principal model at the opening of the third book of Virgil's *Georgics*.[39] The final place at the end of Book 4 was given to the 'Coma Berenices', the witty celebration of the catasterism of a lock of Queen Berenice's hair; through Catullus' translation of this poem (Poem 66), it too found an honoured place in the Roman tradition. One other episode from book 3 which deserves mention is the story of the founding of the Cean dynasty of the Akontiadai through the marriage of Acontius of Ceos to Cydippe of Naxos; this famous episode, of which a substantial fragment from the end survives (fr. 75 Pf.), was central to the Roman elegists' reception of Callimachus (cf. especially Ov. *Her.* 20–21) and may have been principally responsible for the ease with which Callimachus could be represented as a 'love poet'.[40]

Three aspects of the *Aetia* which deserve special mention in the context of reception at Rome are the attention which Callimachus obviously gave to juxtaposition and arrangement within the overall structure, the style of the poem, and the use of poetic voice. As to the first, the key aim appears to have been *poikilia* 'variety', an aim which means that episodes (or 'poems') on similar subjects are sometimes juxtaposed (e.g. the 'Lindian sacrifice' (frr. 22–23) and 'Theiodamas and Heracles' (frr. 24–25)) and sometimes it is difference which is highlighted; the Callimachean way of dealing with the problems of arrangement within a 'catalogue poem' was to prove influential both in the arrangement of books of Roman elegy and for Ovid's *Metamorphoses*. Secondly, it is important that stylistic difference between the *Aetia* and Callimachus' hexameter narrative, the *Hecale*, is observable:[41] the latter, perhaps unsurprisingly, is closer to 'epic norms' of both language and technique (similes etc.), and this of course is an area which was to prove very important to Roman elegists; several modern scholars have argued that it

38 Cf. esp. Fuhrer (1992). 39 Cf. Thomas (1983).

40 Cf. further below. For the reception of 'Acontius and Cydippe' in Roman poetry cf., e.g., Kenney (1983), Barchiesi (1993) 353–63.

41 Cf. Cameron (1995) 437–47, Fantuzzi-Hunter (2004) 197–8.

was precisely for not differentiating stylistically between his elegiac *Lyde* and his hexameter *Thebais* that Callimachus took Antimachus to task. Finally, no aspect of the *Aetia* is more prominent than the ever present voice of the poet, which intrudes itself into our reading not just through insistent first-person asides and parentheses (again a feature lacking from the *Hecale*), but also through word-order, diction, the use of proverbial wisdom and sometimes extraordinary perspective and percipience.[42] It was the *Aetia* which showed how the poet could be a character in his own poem; Callimachus' familiarity with the iambic tradition of Hipponax may well have been very influential on this aspect of his elegiacs.

Allusion to and evocation of the *Aetia* are pervasive in Roman elegy, though nowhere more so, perhaps, than in Propertius' 'programmatic' poems:

> quaeritis unde mihi totiens scribantur amores,
> unde meus ueniat mollis in ora liber.
> non haec Calliope, non haec mihi cantat Apollo:
> ingenium nobis ipsa puella facit.
> siue illam Cois fulgentem incedere cerno,
> totum de Coa ueste uolumen erit;
> seu uidi ad frontem sparsos errare capillos,
> gaudet laudatis ire superba comis;
> siue lyrae carmen digitis percussit eburnis,
> miramur faciles ut premat arte manus;
> seu cum poscentes somnum declinat ocellos,
> inuenio causas mille poeta nouas;
> seu nuda erepto mecum luctatur amictu,
> tum uero longas condimus Iliadas;
> seu quicquid fecit, siue est quodcumque locuta,
> maxima de nihilo nascitur historia.
>
> Prop. 2.1.1–16[43]

You (pl.) ask from where it comes that I write love poems so often, from where comes to the lips my soft book. Calliope does not sing this to me, nor Apollo: my girl herself inspires me. If I see her process, gleaming in Coan silks, a whole book will be made of Coan stuff; or if I have seen her locks scattered and straying across her brow, proudly she rejoices in an encomium of her hair; or if with her ivory fingers she strikes a song on the lyre, we are amazed at how skilfully she works her supple hands; or when she lowers her eyes which demand sleep,

[42] Perhaps there is no more potent example than the opening of fr. 75 from 'Acontius and Cydippe', cf. Fantuzzi-Hunter (2004) 61–3.

[43] Heyworth's text; the textual uncertainties in the verses do not affect the points being made.

> I find a thousand new causes for my poetry; or when, her dress torn off, she struggles naked with me, then indeed I compose long Iliads; whatever she has done, whatever she has said, a very great history is born from nothing.

These verses at the head of Propertius' second book are replete with signposts back to Greek elegy, and particularly Callimachus' *Aetia*;[44] some we see on second reading, others leap to the eye at once. *quaeritis unde... unde* evokes the aetiological focus of Callimachus' major poem; his questions to the Muses may be framed by κῶς 'why, how comes it that...?' (frr. 3, 7.19 Pf. = 5, 9.19 M) – 'he enquires for what *aitia* X happens', as the ancient scholiasts put it – and elsewhere his insistent questions to a human interlocutor are introduced in successive verses (cf. *unde... unde*) by κῶς... τεῦ δ' ἕνεκεν 'how comes it that... for what reason' (fr. 178.24–5 Pf. = 89.24–5 M). *totiens* very likely evokes (and goes beyond) πολλάκι (Gr. 'many times', 'often'), all but certainly the opening word of the *Aetia*;[45] *amores* evokes not just the title of Gallus' Latin poetry, but also Ἔρωτες as a Greek title (cf. Phanocles, above); *mollis* recalls μαλακός, the epithet which Hermesianax had given to Mimnermus' new creation, elegiac poetry (fr. 7.36); *miramur* picks up the 'wonder' (Gr. θάμβος) which prompts Callimachean poetry (fr. 43.85 Pf. = 50.85 M).[46] The allusions to Callimachus' 'Causes' in *causas* (v. 12) – here, paradoxically, 'new' – and to his acknowledged forerunner, Philitas of Cos, in vv. 5–6 (cf. Prop. 3.1.1–2) have long been noticed; just, however, as the inspiration of the poetry differs from that of Callimachus (vv. 3–4, cf. below), so Propertius' *copia*, his *ubertas* (*totiens*, *mille*, *longas*, *maxima*), stand in tension with Callimachus' stress upon the smallness of his poetry and the large scale of that which he rejects. The 'stuff' of Propertius' poetry, its 'Coan fabric', is here marked by the reference to the rhetorical concept of *inuentio* (v. 12),[47] another forceful reminder that traditional notions of divine inspiration are not relevant here. Moreover, this is not going to be the usual fictional material of poetry; this is poetry drawn from real life, from the appearance and actions of the beloved. It resembles in fact history, *historia*, in being the record, not of 'what Alcibiades did or suffered' (Aristotle, *Poet.* 1451b11), but of whatever Propertius' beloved 'did or said' (v. 15), a girl who, we are to understand, is no less real than is Maecenas who, had Propertius been going to write Roman epic instead, would have

44 Bibliography in Fedeli (2005) 39; there is of course much else going on in these verses, but I limit myself to their relation to Greek elegy, and I have also not thought it worthwhile to record who first made which 'Callimachean' observation.

45 I wonder whether Propertius has moved from πολλάκι to the rhythmically identical τοσσάκι (Gr. 'so many times', 'so often').

46 Cf. Fantuzzi-Hunter (2004) 59.

47 Cf. Hunter (2006a) 81–2.

been 'woven into' (v. 35) the poetry, just as certainly as the girl is woven into the elegies.

In the second couplet, the pair of Apollo and Calliope evoke the sources of inspiration for at least Books 1 and 2 of the *Aetia*;[48] Apollo gives the poet his instructions in the 'Reply to the Telchines', and Calliope – in any case, the leading Muse – answers some of the poet's questions (cf. fr. 7.22 Pf. = fr. 9.22 M). There is perhaps another significance in the choice of Calliope here. At the very end of the *aition* of 'Acontius and Cydippe' Callimachus explains 'from where' (ἔνθεν, cf. *unde*) he got the story of Acontius' 'fierce love', namely from the annalistic writings of Xenomedes of Ceos; it was from him that 'the child's story ran down to my Calliope' (fr. 75. 76–7 Pf.). The poem moves from the παῖς and Κυδίππη to the παῖς and Καλλιόπη (fr. 67.2 ~ fr. 75.76–7);[49] the distorted ring composition, with Καλλιόπην not just as the final word but also standing emphatically in a place in the elegiac verse where Κυδίππην, otherwise so similar, could not stand, foregrounds Callimachus' poetic story-telling: Callimachus needs a Calliope, because Cydippe is not his girl, his inspiration, but rather Acontius'. Propertius' couplet retraces the same arc, but he has no need of a Muse: love for Cydippe made Acontius a poet, and Propertius is in pretty much the same situation – *ingenium nobis ipsa puella facit*.[50] This *puella* is to Propertius what Cydippe was to Acontius, what Galateia was to the Cyclops.

Another Callimachean lady may also resonate here. It is clear that the catalogue of vv. 5–16 evokes the style of hymns, and v. 5 in particular suggests the radiant and stately divinity of the beloved (*fulgentem incedere*), as befits someone taking the place of a Muse. In the *Aetia* it is possible, no more, that Callimachus added Arsinoe, the sister-wife of Ptolemy II Philadelphus, as a tenth Muse in the dream sequence which followed the 'Reply'.[51] If so, then the Roman poet's beloved girl/Muse evokes Callimachus' royal patronesses who, in their own way, were also responsible for the poet's *ingenium*; this would certainly sit well with the hint of poetic encomium in

48 *Ingenium* (v. 3) perhaps alludes to the same argument about Callimachus as does Ovid's claim that *Battiades* ... *quamuis ingenio non ualet, arte ualet* (*Am.* 1.15.13–14), although the descendant of Battus (in Cyrene = Callimachus) is great not because of poetic talent, but because of art).

49 Cf. Fantuzzi-Hunter (2004) 65–6.

50 It was almost proverbial Greek wisdom that 'love teaches the poet' (cf. the material assembled by Kannicht under Euripides fr. 663), and this is perhaps what the opening of the poem (fr. 67.1–3) leads us to expect; note the postponement of τέχνην (Gr. 'trick/art'). As it turns out, Love teaches Acontius both a trick and the art of poetry.

51 Cf. Cameron (1995) 141–2. Observe the very similar sequence at 2.3.9–24 where the catalogue of the beloved's accomplishments is followed by a prediction of her apotheosis.

vv. 7–14 and, in particular, with the glance at the Callimachean/Catullan 'Coma Berenices' in v. 8.

However that may be, it is clear that 'Acontius and Cydippe' was central to the image of Callimachus which Propertius and Ovid, particularly, fashioned. It is possible, again no more, that Callimachus' poem, or perhaps just Acontius' lament within it (cf. fr. 73 Pf.), was (or could be) known to the Romans as the 'Cydippe' (cf. Ov. *Rem. am.* 382); if so, this will be one way in which that poem was seen not only as an ancestor of Propertius' own 'Cynthia' (Book 1, the *Monobiblos*), but also as belonging in the tradition of Antimachus' *Lyde*, Hermesianax's *Leontion* and Philitas' *Bittis*, whether or not these poems, perhaps quite imaginary in the last instance, were actually known in any detail to the Romans.[52] No doubt the name of Cydippe filled Acontius' song, as Corydon's song in Virgil, *Eclogue* 2 is framed by 'Alexis'. Of particular interest in this regard is the description of the bereaved Orpheus in the fourth book of the *Georgics*:

> ipse caua solans aegrum testudine amorem
> te, dulcis coniunx, te solo in litore secum,
> te, ueniente die, te decedente canebat.
>
> Virgil, *Georgics* 4.464–6

> As he consoles his sickened love on the hollow lyre, it is you, sweet wife, by himself on the lonely shore, you whom he sang as the day came and the day went away.

As is generally understood,[53] much in the presentation of Orpheus is either 'elegiac' or suggestive of the elegiac poet. In song he finds consolation, as Antimachus is said to have done (T 12 Matthews); his song is insistently sad and complaining (vv. 512, 514, 515, 520), and he himself is like the quintessentially elegiac nightingale (vv. 511–13).[54] If we ask 'What song did Orpheus sing?', the most obvious answer is that he sang a song called (either by him or the subsequent tradition) *Eurydice* and that it was in elegiacs.[55]

'Acontius and Cydippe' was, of course, not the only episode of the *Aetia* which foregrounded love; also in the third book Callimachus told the story of Phrygius and Pieria, a version of the familiar 'Romeo and Juliet' motif of lovers from opposed camps. Above all, in poems 65 and 66 Catullus had drawn attention to the 'Coma Berenices', the complaint of a lock of the

[52] Ovid's linking of Antimachus' *Lyde* and Philitas' *Bittis* at *Tristia* 1.6.1–2 does not really help in this matter.

[53] Cf. esp. Conte (1986b) 135–7.

[54] Cf. Hunter (2006a) 30.

[55] So too, I think that we are to imagine Phanocles' Orpheus singing an elegiac *Kalais*, cf. fr. 1.1–6 Powell, where 'singing his *pothos*' is nicely ambiguous.

queen's hair cut off and now catasterized, separated from the beloved mistress as the queen had been separated from her beloved husband.[56] Whatever else Virgil's famous allusion to this poem at *Aeneid* 6.458–60 might mean, it marks how the story of Dido and Aeneas had in part been fashioned to the aesthetic of a Roman Callimacheanism. Beyond subject matter, however, there was style. A few memorable passages of Callimachus – the 'Reply to the Telchines', the end of the *Hymn to Apollo*, Epigram 28 Pf ('I hate the circling poem . . . ') – had created a set of critical terms (sweet, loud-thundering etc.), images and dichotomies (small ~ large, familiar ~ untrodden, pure ~ unclear etc.) whose lack of fixed definition and reference both provoked and offered opportunities for exploitation, self-definition and the marking of poetic space. In particular, although Alan Cameron's argument that the concerns of the 'Reply to the Telchines' are with style rather than 'genre' and, principally, with stylistic difference within elegy rather than between elegy and hexameter epic is now broadly accepted in modern criticism,[57] Callimachean aesthetic language seemed indeed to offer a way for Roman elegists to mark their space against the traditional style and ideology of Roman epic.[58] If doing so meant the creative 'misrepresentation' of both the Roman poetic heritage and of Callimachus, then this mattered little; the literary history of poetry is always designed to serve more than historical ends. If the Callimachean Muse was 'graceful' and 'sweet', then it was hardly a very great leap to associate it with the poetry of love and desire.

Propertius book 4 and Ovid's *Fasti*, in particular, warn us against exaggerating the narrowness of the Roman reception of the *Aetia*, or – perhaps rather – remind us that there was evolution over time in that reception. It is perhaps a cheering irony that Roman poets eventually came to see (or at least publicly to acknowledge) that Callimachus' great poem was not a call-to-arms against the past and its poetry, but rather a creative engagement with the past, an act of preservation, though not a simple antiquarian recording; in this, Propertius and Ovid have proved forerunners of the history of modern approaches to the *Aetia* and to Hellenistic poetry more generally.

[56] For a survey of Callimachean echoes in Catullus cf. Fantuzzi-Hunter (2004) 464. Observe that Catullus may have 'introduced' the 'Coma' with an allusion to 'Acontius and Cydippe' (Hunter (2006a) 88–9, 101–2, citing earlier bibliography). Puelma (1982) remains an important study of the Callimachean background to Roman love elegy.

[57] The bibliography is too vast to allow the necessary nuancing here; some guidance can be found through the entry for Callimachus fr. 1 in Hunter (2006a) 'Index of passages discussed'.

[58] Wimmel (1960) remains the fundamental study; for further reflections on this subject cf. Hunter (2006a) 1–6.

Further reading

The standard collection of texts of pre-Hellenistic 'literary' elegy is West (1971/1992), but Gerber (1999) also offers a reliable text and translation; for an introduction to many of the issues raised by this material cf. Gerber (1997), Aloni (2009), Nagy (2010). Faraone (2008) is an innovative study of stanzaic structures in early elegy. Gutzwiller (1998) is an excellent introduction to the books of Hellenistic epigrams which were very influential on the Latin elegists, and for the transition from Greek to Latin literature in general see Hunter (2006a). On Callimachus' *Aetia* see Fantuzzi-Hunter (2004) chap. 2 and the introduction to Harder (2012). Cameron (1995) and Murray (2010) touch on many major issues about elegiac poetry in the Hellenistic period.

2

FEDERICA BESSONE

Latin precursors

'The origins': ancient and modern constructions

'The origins of Latin elegy', a crux of classical studies for more than a century, can serve as a paradigm of the difficulties and the theoretical traps of all genetic criticism. In his *Ars poetica*, Horace was ironical about the confusion of the ancients regarding the πρῶτος εὑρετής (Gr. first inventor) of the elegiac distich (*Ars P.* 77–8), a confusion that continues in modern attempts to trace the genealogy of Augustan elegy. A minor genre thus appears branded by the stigma of its obscure origins – even if, in Rome, that son-of-nobody could display a respectable and rather crowded family tree.

The twentieth-century approach to the question begins with confrontation of Leo's and Jacoby's theories, the former supporting a derivation of Latin elegy from lost Hellenistic elegy – an intermediate that could explain the similarities with comedy[1] – and the latter claiming among other things a more autonomous expansion of Hellenistic erotic epigram by Roman elegists.[2] The two theories were largely founded on hypothesis: Leo postulated the existence of subjective erotic elegy in the Hellenistic world; Jacoby was sure this would never be found. That controversy opposed two different critical constructions of Latin literature, one still conditioned by the notion of 'subordination' and by a positivistic conception of literary genetics, the other ready to recognize that the Roman poets elaborated a ready-made poetic form to a higher complexity, expanding the first-person expression of erotic experience in epigram.[3]

Translated by Arietta Papaconstantinou.

1 See also Piazzi (Chapter 14) in this volume.

2 Leo (1895) 126–7; (1900); (1912) 143–4 (reply to Jacoby); Jacoby (1905 = 1961); (1909–1910 = 1961). Jacoby's thesis was developed by Day (1938), Rostagni (1956), Stroh (1971) 197–226; (1983) (after the 'new Gallus'); on its merits and limits cf. Fedeli (1974). The importance of Hellenistic elegy was assumed behind the complexity of Catull. 68 by Heinze (1919) 127–9, cf. § 10.

3 On Jacoby's precursors (among whom Wilamowitz) and on his method, close to Heinze's and attentive to the *Arbeitsweise* of Roman poets, cf. Galasso (2006) and Conte (2006).

The presupposition that oriented the discussion for decades was a dichotomy between Latin 'subjective' elegy and Hellenistic 'objective' elegy,[4] which rigidly applied modern categories and was based on the only Hellenistic elegy known at the time: narrative elegy, mythological and catalogue-like, as well as aetiological as represented (besides Callimachus' *Aetia*) by the fragments of Hermesianax, Phanocles and Alexander Aetolus.[5]

After the edition of the 'new Gallus' papyrus (1979), the publication in 1987 of a second-century papyrus containing fragments of a Greek erotic elegy (*POxy.* LIV 3723) opened a new perspective: in the last verse, the narration of homoerotic myths seems interrupted by the monologic incursion of the poetic 'I', in a manner that is close to that of Latin elegy.[6] Despite the uncertain date of this and other texts preserved by the papyri attributed to the Hellenistic or the imperial period,[7] these finds document the existence of a Hellenistic elegy with subjective elements, of which these texts are either direct witnesses or later re-elaborations.

The new discovery drove scholars to reconsider several already published papyri (*POxy.* XXXIX 2885, fr. 1 [=*SH* 964], ll. 1–20; ll. 22–45; *POxy.* XXXIX 2884, fr. 2 [=*SH* 962]), in addition to the fragments of the indirect tradition and to ancient *testimonia*. It was now possible to give greater value to connections between myth and personal 'reality' introduced by Hellenistic elegists; one could identify a range of functions for exempla – pragmatic, didactic, cautionary or self-consolatory – deployed in relation to the subjective situation, which is presented by the authorial voice as 'real'. The connection between narration and erotic experience became evident: the 'autobiographical' construction of the poetic persona could emerge as the frame, or connecting tissue, of the catalogue-style series of allusions to stories told in other texts.

One could thus appreciate that an antecedent of Hellenistic elegy such as Antimachus' *Lyde*, described by Plutarch as a self-consolation, must have framed the mythical account with the expression of pain and love for the deceased wife; that the catalogue of unhappy loves in Hermesianax' *Leontion* was interrupted by asides to the beloved, however evanescent; that the

4 For reactions cf. Cairns (2006a) 70–1 (= 1979a) 215–16; Binder-Hamm (1998) 14 n. 4.

5 See also Hunter in this volume.

6 Cf. Morelli (1994); Butrica (1996a); Cairns (2006a) 69–70 and 87–95 (additions to 1979a: ch. 9, where the importance of personal frames in Hellenistic elegy was already supposed).

7 Imperial age: Bremer-Parsons (1987); Parsons (1988); Morelli (1994); Hellenistic age: Butrica (1996a); the thesis of Hose (1994), that these texts may be influenced by Latin elegy itself, is perplexing.

personal element would have been prominent in Parthenius' *Arete*, a lament and encomium for his deceased wife written by a key figure in negotiations between Hellenistic and Roman poetry; meanwhile e.g. Philitas' *Bittis* remained an unknown quantity, except for its very title.[8] On the other hand, when the polemical-programmatic personal elements of Callimachus' *Aetia* came to light in the prologue published in 1927 (followed in 1935 by the *scholia* on it), this at a stroke transformed our grasp of how a Hellenistic poet could speak of himself in an elegiac work that was narrative and 'objective'.

Leo's hypothesis that there existed a subjective Hellenistic elegy has been in part confirmed by new finds, but Jacoby's position still retains some value, supported by the increasingly well-established debt of Latin elegy to Hellenistic epigrams and of Roman elegy books to collections of epigrams such as Meleager's *Garland*.

Study of Latin love elegy has long since moved on. In 1938, Day carried out a survey of the literary forms that were rethought by the Roman elegists, from elegy to epigram, to rhetoric, bucolics and comedy, with a glance at late epistolography. Since then, scholarship has explored the dynamics of such relations, but developments in theory, abandoning *Quellenforschung*, have opened up new approaches to our question, in terms of genre, modelling and literary memory.

At the beginning of the new century, we can say that all the work of comparison with previous poetic experiences has rendered more evident the decisive transformation achieved by Latin elegists. A gap still continues to separate Latin elegy from Hellenistic elegy as we know it today. Few compositions of Propertius, Tibullus and Ovid reveal a pattern similar to those restored to us by the papyri, while their production maintains an unmistakeable profile: the meaning of common elements such as *seruitium amoris* changes in the new context; the hierarchy between myth and 'autobiography' is turned upside down; above all, erotic experience has become the declared centre of poetry and of life.

The critical need for a subjective Hellenistic elegy was to be partly satisfied only in the 1980s; yet already from the middle of the century the progress made in the knowledge of Callimachus and in the study of Roman Callimacheanism, marked by Pfeiffer's edition (1949–53) and by Wimmel's book (1960), and the sharper attention paid to neotericism and to the elegiac

[8] For an outline of Hellenistic elegy, and for Parthenius, cf. Lightfoot (1999) 23–39; on Philitas, Knox (1993); on Antimachus, Krevans (1993). See also Hunter (Chapter 1) in this volume.

verses of Catullus, had drawn the line from Callimachus to Catullus as the basis of Augustan elegy.[9]

The masterpiece of elegy's *princeps* (cf. Quint. *Inst.* 10.1.58, 'leader'), the *Aetia*, together with the rest of the Callimachean production, now appears more than ever as the foundational model for the establishment of this new poetry, even before the treatment of the love theme: it is a lesson in poetics, in style, in verse technique and in the architecture of the book. Callimachus is the author without whom Latin elegy would not have existed; but Augustan elegy would not have been what it was without the rethinking of Callimachus by Catullus. Even more than its Greek models, Augustan elegy presupposes its Latin precursors.

Method should be considered here. We know how potentially misleading the dichotomy between 'subjective' and 'objective' can be: that is demonstrated by the very debt of the Roman elegists to Callimachus' *Aetia*. Beyond the lesson in form and technique afforded by Hellenistic narrative elegy, its exploration of erotic psychology and of the expressive modes of mythical characters can be just as important for the development of a personal discourse in Latin elegy as any passage of 'subjective' poetry in the first person: Acontius' monologue in Callimachus is one of the most influential models for the Roman construction of the elegiac persona.[10]

And yet, the apparently simple gesture with which an Augustan elegist transformed himself, the poet-lover, into an Acontius, is a revolution, and owes to the neoteric revolution the audacity of a crucial passage: that from the subjectivization of the narrative, and from the projection of oneself into myth, to the 'autobiographical' construction of the myth of oneself. Even more than Hellenistic epigram, behind this new poetic appreciation of the experience of love there is the experience of Catullus; and there is the model of a multiform poetry book in which the love story of the poet who says 'I' can be felt as a unifying centre. At the zenith of the neoteric season, Callimachean aesthetics combined in Rome with a choice of life: the tormented choice of existential and poetic *otium* (Lat. 'leisure'), which is a totalizing conception of *erōs*. Catullus declares this through an appropriation of Sappho's lyric that borders on identification: and conciliating Callimachus and

[9] The importance of the *Aetia* as a model for Latin elegy was claimed by Puelma (1982). On Callimachus in Rome, after Wimmel, cf. Cameron (1995); Hunter (2006a). For the different phases of Roman Callimacheanism, Labate (1990). On Callimachus and Catullus, cf. Clausen (1970); Hunter (2006a) 88–108 and the critical survey by Knox (2007).

[10] On Acontius as a model for Latin elegy: Cairns (1969); Rosen-Farrell (1986); Barchiesi (1993); Heinze (1919), with psychologizing approach; on the double-sided subjectivity of the *Aetia* cf. Puelma (1982) esp. 229.

Sappho is what is suggested in the Catullan *Liber* by the correspondence between the two translations, poems 51 and 66. The Callimachean poetic programme thus aspires to become a programme of life and poetry, in which love for a single woman, represented as devastating and of tragic seriousness, occupies a central place.

The poet of Lesbia, the pioneer of elegiac form, the interpreter of Callimachean poetics: this, and much more, is what Catullus meant to the Augustan elegists. Above all, the same poet who in poem 64 'lyricized' the Hellenistic forms of the *epyllion*, narrating mythical love in the language of his own love lyric, is also the elegiac experimenter who, in poem 68B, merged autobiography and myth into new forms, in a union that is deeper and more complex than in the Hellenistic examples.

If we turn towards 'immanent' literary history, the assertions of Augustan elegists (instrumental, but important) make clear what their main points of reference were, however many new fragments of Hellenistic elegy might still be recovered in Egypt. In addition to the Greeks Callimachus and Philitas, as well as Mimnermus,[11] Propertius and Ovid mention Catullus and Calvus as their precursors. The two recognized Hellenistic masters of 'slender' verse, and an archaic elegist celebrated – by Callimachus himself – for his 'sweet' love poetry and for his 'soft' pentameter, would not have sufficed to give birth to Roman elegy without the revolution of the *neoteroi*. It is in the elegiac genre that continuity between Augustan and neoteric poetry appears most evidently: in the combination of a rigorous Callimacheanism, alien to grand genres, with the poetic-existential choice of Catullus.

Propertius closes his second book with a list of Latin poets who had written about love before him, and he begins with the *neoteroi*. Propertius 2.34, a programmatic elegy addressed to the rival-friend and epic-tragic poet Lynceus includes the announcement of the *Aeneid* in a survey of Virgil's works that gives prominence to the slender erotic poetry of the *Eclogues* and recognises the relative proximity of the bucolic Virgil to the neoteric and elegiac world.[12] In this confrontation between epic and 'minor' poetry with amorous themes we meet the series of four poets, each associated with the name of the woman he sang – poets among whom Propertius aspires to be included (Prop. 2.34.85–94):[13]

[11] Declarations of loyalty to Callimachus and Philitas, underestimated in the past as conventional (Rostagni (1956)), are valued today as revealing, even in so far as they are tendentious: Hunter (2006a) 128–9; for the judgment on Philitas and Mimnermus in the *Aetia* prologue cf. also Cameron (1995) 307–9; Hunter (2006b) 120–1.

[12] On this proximity cf. Kenney (1983). [13] Cf. Fedeli (2005).

haec quoque perfecto ludebat Iasone Varro,
    Varro Leucadiae maxima flamma suae;
haec quoque lasciui cantarunt scripta Catulli,
    Lesbia quis ipsa notior est Helena;
haec etiam docti confessa est pagina Calui,
    cum caneret miserae funera Quintiliae.
et modo formosa quam multa Lycoride Gallus
    mortuus inferna uulnera lauit aqua!
Cynthia quin uiuet uersu laudata Properti,
    hos inter si me ponere Fama uolet.

Such themes also did Varro sport with, his tale of Jason ended, Varro, the brightest flame of his Leucadia; such themes also the verse of wanton Catullus sang, which made Lesbia better known than Helen herself; such passion also the pages of learned Calvus confessed, when he sang of the death of hapless Quintilia. And in these recent days how many wounds has Gallus, dead for love of fair Lycoris, laved in the waters of the world below! Yea, Cynthia glorified in the verse of Propertius shall live, if Fame consent to rank me with bards like these. [Transl. adapted from G. P. Goold]

The approach to the elegiac genre is progressive. The series begins with Varro Atacinus who, in inverse order to Virgil, wrote love poetry (elegiac?) after the Argonautic epos. It continues with the *neoteroi*: Catullus, who gave to Lesbia, in varying forms and verses, greater fame than Homer gave to Helen, and Calvus ('learned' author of epyllia, epithalamia, epigrams in various metres), who mourned in elegiac distichs the death of his beloved Quintilia. The list ends with the image of Gallus who washes in the infernal waters the love wounds received from Lycoris, held responsible for his death: here is the elegiac universe in a single distich.[14]

The power of erotic poetry to immortalize the beloved woman lends nobility to a minor literary form, which can become the unique commitment of a literary career and the *raison d'être* of an entire life. This is the programme of the elegiac genre, which Propertius here delineates on a poetic-'existential' level, thus supplementing Philitas' and Callimachus' proclamation as stylistic models at Prop. 2.34.31–2. In the family album put together by the Augustan elegists, Catullus and Calvus appear as precursors of Gallus, who is recognized as directly preceding Propertius; Catullus, Calvus and Gallus, according to Ovid, welcome Tibullus in Elysium (*Am.* 3.9.61–4); while it is the line of succession Gallus-Tibullus-Propertius-Ovid that constitutes the canon of the elegists, set out by Ovid in *Trist.* 4.10.51–4 (cf. *Ars* 3.536–8 and Quint. *Inst. Or.* 10.1.93).

14 On Varro Atacinus, Calvus, Gallus cf. Courtney (1993); Hollis (2007).

Latin love elegy does not only trace its own genealogy, but also paints a self-portrait. What had been in archaic Greece an open, flexible genre (an aspect that would always remain productive),[15] heads in Augustan Rome towards a selection of features. Indeed, for a season, it takes on such an individualized physiognomy that it becomes an individual. In *Amores* III, Ovid makes this visible through two personifications: Elegy is identified with its presumed etymology and origin, as a figure of bereavement, when she has to mourn the death of Tibullus (*Am.* 3.9.3–4), thus fulfilling the theory current in antiquity (Hor. *Ars P.* 75–6);[16] on the other hand, modern Elegy is embodied by a sexy *puella* with seductive uneven feet, in a *tenuissima uestis* (*Am.* 3.1.9–12). Lament and love, attitude of bereavement and Alexandrian elegance: it is in the tension between these poles that Latin erotic elegy shapes itself.

In the typically Augustan confrontation of poetic genres, multiple exterior gazes see in mourning the dominant trait of contemporary elegy and contribute to a definition of the genre as an incessant love lament and expression of bereavement: it is so in the exploration of the boundaries between bucolic and elegy in Virgil's tenth *Eclogue*, the consolation-reproach of Pan to Gallus, who weeps incessantly for love (Virg. *Ecl.* 10.28–30), or in the finale of the *Georgics*, in opposition to the didascalic model of Aristaeus, the representation of Orpheus as an inconsolable elegiac poet-lover (*G.* 4.463–466, 507–515).[17] In Horace's lyrical works, with invitations to put an end to the incessant weeping addressed to Valgius, as an elegiac poet, and, probably, to Tibullus (Hor. *Carm.* 2.9, *non semper . . . tu semper . . . nec . . . semper*; cf. *Carm.*1.33.1–4); thus also in *Epode* 14, where the *flere amorem* of the Anacreontics, assimilated to elegy and a paradigm for the *mollis inertia* prevents Horace from finishing the book of the *Iambs* (Hor. *Epod.* 14.10–12).[18] 'To mourn love' is the definition of elegy in the epigram on the death of Tibullus (Dom. Mars. fr. 7.3 Courtney, . . . *elegis molles qui fleret amores*).

It is again Catullus who anticipates this distinctive trait of Latin elegy, in his poems 65, 68A and 68B, giving it symbolic representation in the image of the nightingale, as well as a formulation, in the key of fraternal love, that *a posteriori* sounds programmatic: *semper amabo* [*sc. te*], / *semper maesta tua carmina morte canam* (Catull. 65.11–12, 'I will always love you, because of your death I will always sing sad songs'), where the phrase *semper canam*

15 Aloni and Iannucci (2007) 91, 107–8; cf. La Penna (1977) 29.

16 Cf. Brink (1971) on *Ars P.* 75–8; Hinds (1987b) 103–4; Aloni and Iannucci (2007) 13–19 and 81–2 (on Simonides' Plataea elegy).

17 Cf. Conte (1984 = 1986b) and (2002 = 2007).

18 On Horace and elegy: Labate (1994); Barchiesi (1997a), with bibliography; Syndikus (1998); on *Epode* 14, elegy and Catullus: Labate (1994) 71–5; Watson (2003) 438–40.

puns on the Greek ἀηδών, 'nightingale', from ἀεὶ ἀείδω (Gr. I always sing).[19] The Augustans develop this programme of 'bereavement' poetry.

Catullus' discovery of the 'poetry of the affections' (Traina (1998)) opens the way to Latin elegy – the affections being identified with life. The Augustans carry out a *reductio ad unum*. In Catullus' *libellus*, love for Lesbia and love for his brother, and even friendship, sung with the same absoluteness, could exchange their traits; the elegists condense the space of the affections to the unique and totalizing erotic passion. If, in Catullus, elegy was born as a lament for his dead brother, into which was woven in a unity of tone the poetry for Lesbia, in the Augustans love lament becomes funereal, a lament for suffering experienced as bereavement.

At the end of his experiments with distichs, the major poet of the second Augustan generation could reflect on the position acquired by elegy in the system of genres of the Latin classics. In his elegiac career Ovid, who presented himself as the climax of the canon of love elegy, challenged erotic-elegiac conventions in a series of provocative works, then experimented with aetiology along the lines of Callimachus and Propertius 4 and finally, in his exile poetry, excluded himself from the canon, marking an evident rupture – and a semi-hidden continuity – with his own erotic elegy (*Trist.* 5.1.15–20).

The author of the *Tristia* and the *Epistulae ex Ponto* opened a new avenue to the genre, but this was in fact an old avenue, since it not only recovered, in the poetics specific to the sad elegy, the presumed original function of elegy as *thrēnos* (Gr. 'lament'), already re-purposed by Catullus in poems 65 and 68 (A and B), but it also re-appropriated, in yet a different form after the *Fasti*, the encomiastic function that elegy performed as court poetry in Callimachus and in the Hellenistic world.[20]

Ovid, the Augustan poet who more than any other constructed, and deconstructed, the features of elegy thus delivered to subsequent poetry a genre which had been renewed several times, but which was still intimately aware of its long Greek and Latin history.

Hellenistic genres in Rome from the preneoterics to Catullus

Love poetry in distichs began in Rome as epigram, between the second and the first century BC, in the context of the socio-cultural transformations of

[19] This erudite, Homeric-tragic simile of the nightingale becomes an emblem of elegy as *thrēnos*, programmatically repeated in *Georgics* 4.511–15 and in the *Epistula Sapphus* (Ov. *Her.* 15.155); Rosati (1996a); Bessone (2003); Monella (2002) and (2005) 221–51. The authenticity of the *Epistula Sapphus*, which conventionally holds the closing place of Ovid's single *Heroides*, is disputed; see Thorsen (forthcoming) and Chapter 7 in this volume.

[20] On the new directions of elegy beginning with the later Ovid cf. Rosati (2005).

the late Republic and of a new poetic tendency, which anticipated the neoteric movement.[21] Valerius Aedituus, Porcius Licinus and Lutatius Catulus experimented with a new form which after Ennius had been developed in Lucilius and became the first observable laboratory for the erotic theme in Latin. Gellius preserved for us the epigrams of these 'preneoterics', recited by the rhetor Antonius Iulianus to his Greek guests, as the closest approximation to the poetry of 'Anacreon' (or rather of the *Anacreontea*) and Sappho. The two epigrams by Aedituus, centred on the Sapphic symptomatology of passion (fr. 1 Courtney) and on the comparison between the torch of the torchbearer and the inextinguishable flame of love (fr. 2 C.), are followed by Porcius Licinus' bucolic variation on the conceit of the fire of love (fr. 7 C.) and by the re-elaboration of a pederastic epigram of Callimachus signed by Lutatius Catulus.

The best-known personality of the triad, Catulus, who has given his name to a presumed 'circle', sums up the novelties of that trend: the mannered exercise in style in a minor Hellenistic genre, light and disengaged poetry as an entertainment for *otium*, now a favourite pastime of a senator and consul who gives first-person expression to the erotic theme, in this case pederastic. This all happened within a direct comparison with the Alexandrian models – without forgetting the great archaic Greek lyric –, with a rhetorical exploration of the theme of love that is pushed to conceit, and an exploitation of the resources of the Latin language and its poetic tradition.

Having come into contact with Greek poets such as Antipater of Sidon and then Archias, Roman aristocrats not only promoted, but in their free time also practised, a refined and not austere literary activity, a poetic and amateur *lusus* (Lat. 'game') considered by that time elite and prestigious: this is the phenomenon of rupture with the archaic Roman tradition attested by Pliny (*Ep.* 5.3). Beyond offering their Roman protectors celebratory poetry with a Hellenistic stamp, Greek professional poets, often by means of improvisation, spread the occasional use of minor poetry, which came to be part of the social life of the upper classes, and prepared the ground for the experiments of the *neoteroi*. From the same period, Laevius' *Erotopaegnia*, primarily in lyrical metres, represent a precious experiment in mythologico-sentimental poetry (e.g. *Protesilaodamia*), traces of which can be glimpsed in Ovid's *Heroides*.[22]

The contact with Callimachus sought by Lutatius Catulus is interesting.[23] The epigram on the flight of the *animus* to 'Theotimus' (fr. 1 C., cf. Callim.

[21] Cf. Morelli (2000), also on the relation with Greek epigram and Meleager's *Garland* and on the problems of relative chronology, with bibliography (177–85 and 225–6).

[22] Tandoi (1992) I 112–27. [23] Cf. Perutelli (2002 = 1990).

Epigr. 41 Pf. = 4 GP) shows a proximity to the language of comedy (Terence, rather than Plautus), to its world of characters, evoked by the metaphor of the *fugitiuus*, and to the structure of the comic monologue: an affinity detected in Catullus, for example, in poems 8 and 85. Comparison with the Catullan revival of an epigram of Callimachus (Catull. 70, cf. Callim. *Epigr.* 25 Pf. = *Anth. Pal.* 5.6) reveals a different way of proceeding: the neoteric poet breaks up the syntax of his model into a syncopated rhythm, with dramatisation and pathetic effect; Catullus adheres more narrowly to the stylistic values of Callimachus.[24] The neoterics asserted a new phase of Roman Callimacheanism, more demanding after the indiscriminate one of the archaic poets; but some of the conditions were in place a generation earlier. The epigram of Catulus on Roscius (Cic. *Nat. D.* 1.79 = fr. 2 C.) exalts the beauty of the famous actor as superior to that of a god, and alludes polemically to an epigram by Ennius on Scipio: from every point of view, a challenge to Roman tradition.

The distich epigram is one of the first expressions of *eros* in the first person in Rome, a sparkling form that could reduce the lyric of Sappho to the epigrammatic effect or vary Callimachus' intellectualizing reflection on the division of the I. It is almost in the same years that Meleager's *Garland* was published: Roman poets were in pace with the avant-garde trends of Greek epigrammatic production. The making of that poetry did not avoid virtuoso artifice – far from the 'sophisticated spontaneity' of Catullus – nor did it suggest a profound valuation of erotic experience, but its historical importance is evident.

The relation between epigram and elegy in Rome involves the debated question of the relationship between the two genres.[25] Elegy and epigram in distichs have histories that are distinct, but partly intertwined, ever since, in archaic Greece, epigram separated from the epigraphic medium and entered the world of sympotic recitation, becoming a form of short elegy with its own characteristics, which recall its original destination and use. The passage from performance to book further reduced the distance. In the Hellenistic period the literary epigram became part of collections or anthologies in which there was not always a clear distinction between forms that shared the elegiac metre – as well as between παίγνια (Gr. 'games'/'jokes') in different metres – but in which proper epigrams could appear next to compositions

[24] Knox (2007) 159–60.

[25] Cf. Gentili (1968) esp. 43–68; Morelli (1994) 415 n. 1; Puelma (1996); Gutzwiller (1998) 4–5; Aloni and Ianucci (2007) 60–6. The missing codification and distinction of forms in distichs in ancient theory, which led Crusius (1905), Reitzenstein (1907) and Wilamowitz (1924) to deny the difference between elegy and epigram, rather reveals a gap between poetic theory and praxis: a balanced judgement in La Penna (1977) 26.

that one would be in doubt whether to define as long epigrams or short elegies: this is the situation documented by two third-century AD papyri, *PVindob.* G 40611 and *PPetrie* II 49a (*PLond. Lit.* 60 = *SH* 961).[26] Meleager's *Garland* itself included compositions that were longer and programmatic in the initial and final positions.[27]

The enigma of the 'new Gallus', with divisions in the papyrus after verses 1, 5 and 9, has led scholars to think, among other things, that it was another series of 'epigrams', perhaps placed at the end of the book, even though different hypotheses remain possible, such as a selection of passages from longer elegies.[28] The first book of Propertius closes with two short, quasi-epigrammatic compositions: a variation on the sepulchral epigram and an autobiographical *sphragis* (Fedeli 1980). The making of a book of elegies here plays suggestively on the contiguity of the two forms in distichs, setting an erotic epigram of Meleager (*Anth. Pal.* 12.101) as an incipit and exhibiting an epigrammatic sequence as an ending; between them, as in Tibullus and Ovid, various elegies inscribe within themselves a monodistich epigram (Ramsby 2007), reproducing in the text the model of *epi-graphē* and showing the compatibility between different elegiac 'tissues'.

Osmosis between the two forms in distichs is obvious when they share the identical theme of love: elegy and erotic epigram exploit a common repertoire, as the register of contacts between Augustan elegy and Hellenistic epigrams testifies; conversely, Hellenistic erotic epigram seems to claim its difference from elegy by avoiding, more than other sub-genres, the hybrid form of the 'long epigram' (Morelli 2008a: 18–20; 2008b: 83). It is however the novelty of the epigrammatic collections, among which Meleager's *Garland* is the leading example, which proves crucial for the genesis of Latin elegy: the cycles of erotic epigrams for recurring characters, which follow the evolution of a relation, sketching 'an exemplary amorous autobiography',

[26] On Hellenistic epigram books, and on papyrus testimonies of elegiac-epigrammatic books, cf. Gutzwiller (1998) 20–36; (2005) 6–7 and n. 14. *PVindob* G 40611, an index of incipits transcribed or selected from a collection of *epigrammata* in at least four books, has stichometric indications, from which elegies of 20, 40 and 52 verses seem to be attested; signalled by Harrauer (1981), it is still unpublished: cf. Parsons (1988) 74; Cameron (1993) 9–10, 385; Puelma (1996) 128–9; Gutzwiller (1998) 23–4; Argentieri (1998) 12–13; Krevans (2007) 133. On *PPetrie* II. 49 a, part of an epigrammatic collection which began with an elegy of at least 24 verses on the wedding of Arsinoe I or II (Posid. 114 Austin-Bastianini), cf. Morelli (1994) 415–7; Gutzwiller (1998) 25; Argentieri (1998) 9; Cairns (2006a) 95.

[27] Gutzwiller (1997) 170; (1998) 279–81; Barchiesi (2005) 322. On distich poems with varying geometry in the initial and final position of a book, Morelli (2008a) 44–5.

[28] Gall. fr. 2–5 Bl. = 2 C. = 145 H.; cf. Courtney (1993) 263–8, esp. 264; Hollis (2007) 241–52, esp. 250–2; for the hypothesis of epigrams at the end of an elegiac book: Nisbet in Anderson-Parsons-Nisbet (1979) 149–51; Petersmann (1983); Holzberg (2001) 33–4.

create a model for the development of the love story in the Augustan books of elegies.[29]

Thus, if ancient theory does not make distinctions between ἐλεγεῖα (Gr. pl. 'elegiac couplets'),[30] ancient practice shows awareness of difference, but also interest in experimentation at the border between the two forms of longer elegies and shorter epigrams. Callimachus himself, who distinguished clearly between elegiac narration and epigrams (perhaps never published by the author), had borrowed from epigrammatic technique the expedient of the speaking object introduced in *Aetia* III-IV: a novelty that Catullus reproduced in his translation of the *Lock of Berenice* (Catull. 66), and repeated in a humble version in the contiguous elegy to the door (Catull. 67).[31]

In Rome, elegies and epigrams in distichs are side by side in poems 65 to 116 of Catullus' *Liber*, which according to some was a separate collection with authorial design; in any case, an example of the attention paid to the architecture of the book by editors, compilers, copyists and readers alike, in conformity with the more indeterminate model suggested by Hellenistic books of epigrams such as the 'new Posidippus'.[32]

While the elegiac poems from 65 to 68B can be linked to the *carmina longiora* or *docta* (61–64), poems 69 to 116 are 'epigrams', including erotic ones (Hartz 2007, Fain 2008). Among them we can observe a metamorphosis from epigram to elegy, or rather the exploration of an intermediate zone where compactness and epigrammatic closure fade into more articulated structures. A 'long epigram', or proto-elegy, like poem 76 (26 verses) exemplifies not simply a widening of the epigrammatic form, but a re-elaboration of different literary cues, which forces the distinctions into a search for a new form:[33] the development of the monologue surpasses the internal dynamics of the Meleagrean epigram (Gutzwiller (2007)), touches upon wisdom attitudes of the brief Theognidean elegy (Laurens (1989) 191–4) and foregoes Sappho's invocation of reciprocity in love, appealing to virtue as its own reward and ultimately to divine succour as liberation from passion (Traina (1954)), while the epigrammatic fragmentation of the I intensifies in the

29 Morelli (1994) 405 and 414, with bibliography; (2000) 326–37, esp. 327; (2007) 537–8; Holzberg (2001) 9–10; Ypsilanti (2005); Gutzwiller (2007) 331–2.

30 Cf. West (1971) 2–4.

31 Cf. Puelma (1982) 228–32; Hutchinson (2003).

32 On the debated question of the arrangement and edition of the Catullan *Liber*, well-informed critical discussion in Skinner (2007); cf. Bellandi (2003) 65–96. On Catull. 65–116 as a third *uolumen* edited by the author, after Quinn (1972) 264–5, cf. e.g. Morelli (2000) 317; Holzberg (2002a) 151–211; Skinner (2003) XXII–XXVIII, 1–28; on the opportunity of imagining a 'fuzzier model', however, Barchiesi (2005) 333–42, esp. 338.

33 On Catull. 76 (and 99) as an experiment in 'long epigram' cf. Morelli (2008b).

observation of failure and mortal illness. Erotic discourse, constructed in the legal and political language of Roman *amicitia* (Lat. 'friendship') – with *foedus amoris* (Lat. 'bond of love') – leads into a prayer to the gods as guarantors of *fides* (Lat. 'fidelity') and *pietas* (Lat. 'dutiful respect'), and shows how the thrusts for the creation of Latin elegy could converge from several directions to make an original synthesis. The stylistic characters, which would rather seem to differentiate this poem from the 'learned' elegies, do not in themselves substantiate inclusion in this or that genre. The generally higher level of elegy in relation to epigram, and of 65–68B in relation to 69–116, does not impede the fluidity of the transitions between the two sections, in which the register of each composition is determined by its destination (Morelli 2008b: 101–5). With its 'irregularities', which make it less elegant than the more 'epigrammatic' poem 96 (the homage to Calvus), poem 76 is considered as a full-blown elegy.[34] The other long poem, Catullus 99 (16 verses), merges epigrammatic language and themes with the amplitude and regularity of metre and syntax of elegy, and constitutes a model for Martial's long epigrams.

Catullan experimentation, which can press the torn I into a monodistich (Catull. 85: Feeney 2009), surprises expectations even outside the erotic theme. Thus, after the elegiac sequence of 65–68A–68B, poem 101 develops the motif of the death of the brother, transfiguring the funerary epigram;[35] detaching himself from the modes of the epitaph, and from the model of Meleager, Catullus constructs a lyrico-dramatic monologue which harmonizes interior meditation and ritual action, and closes in an epigraphic funeral farewell a poem that opens with a reminiscence of the incipit of the *Odyssey*: by its complexity, a 'brief elegy'.

The neoterics also anticipated Augustan elegy with the epyllion[36] – a form that Propertius recreated in distichs in 1.20. Calvus' *Io* and Cinna's *Zmyrna*, hailed by Catullus in a homage that is his Callimachean manifesto (Catull. 95), developed Hellenistic taste for myths of unhappy love narrated in sentimental style: the *Sufferings in Love* (ἐρωτικὰ παθήματα), which Parthenius reduced to prose and gave to Gallus so that he could draw from it 'poems in epic and elegiac metre'. Catullus transformed that 'subjective' narration into lyricism, converting his personal poetry into myth. Ariadne's monologue in poem 64, which presupposes perhaps the Phyllis of the *Aetia* and Hellenistic elegiac models (Callim. fr. 556 Pf.; *SH* 962–63 = *POxy*. XXXIX

[34] Wilamowitz (1924) I 234. On the basis of metric-stylistic features, Catull. 76 is considered an elegy by Bishop (1972), an epigram by Ross (1969) 164, 167, 171–3, within the framework of an excessive differentiation between the more innovative polymetrics and elegies on one side, and the epigrams, of Roman tradition, on the other.

[35] Biondi (1976), Feldherr (2000), Bellandi (2003).

[36] Cf. Perutelli (1979).

2884), is assimilated to the laments for Lesbia's infidelity and becomes the prototype for the lament of the *relicta* (Lat. 'abandoned woman') in Roman 'female elegy', whether mythological or not, from Propertius 4 to Ovid's *Heroides*.[37]

Catullus' longer elegiac poems (65–68B)

Catullus' entire *Liber* was absorbed into Latin elegy: this is shown on a small scale by Propertius 1.3, which recapitulates poem 64 between incipit and conclusion – between the paradigm of the abandoned Ariadne and the lament of the jealous Cynthia – and repeats the scene of the apple as an erotic gift from Catullus 65, including a hemistich from Catullus 76 on ungrateful love.[38] Catullus' experience as a whole is a prelude to elegy: his most important legacy – the choice of a love that is irregular, transgressing Roman morality and transforms traditional values such as matrimonial *fides* to an alternative code of ethics –[39] permeates every form, from polymetres to epigrams.

However, the mid-section of the Catullan *Liber* closes with a series of long poems in elegiac couplets that seem to formally condition the subsequent development of the genre. While Catullus 68 is acknowledged as an archetype of love elegy, the entire sequence of poems 65–68B[40] is increasingly recognised as a complex elegiac experiment, opening directions that Augustan elegy was to follow in successive phases of its development: elegiac epistle, aitiological elegy, elegiac dialogue, elegiac encomium, mixed with funerary and love elegy, which blend myth and 'autobiography' – a great part of the past and the future of the genre is summarized here.

The influence of Callimachus is of great importance to Catullus' *carmina longiora* in elegiac couplets.[41] Poem 65[42] is an epistle that accompanies poem 66, a translation of the *Lock of Berenice*, which concludes the *Aetia*: Catullus 65 thus emerges as a Callimachean preface to a translation from Callimachus.[43] The single period (which spans twenty-four verses, a

37 Rosati (1992).

38 Ross (1975) 54–6; Fedeli (1980); Knox (2006) 130–1 (for the Catullan character of Prop. 1, as 'circle poetry', cf. Citroni (1995) 381–92).

39 Cf. Conte (1986a).

40 Ample commentary in Syndikus (1990).

41 For Catull. 65–68B and Callimachus, esp. regarding the use of simile, cf. Hunter (2006a) 88–108.

42 Van Sickle (1968); Hunter (1993) and (2006a) 88–9, 101–2; Barchiesi (1993) 363–5; Citroni (1995) 93–99; Tatum (1997); Fantuzzi-Hunter (2002 = 2004) 546–8; Formicola (2003); Fernandelli (2004–5); Sweet (2006).

43 For the hypothesis of Catull. 65 as a programmatic introduction to the distich poems, perhaps designed by Catullus, cf. Wiseman (1969) 17–18; (1979) 176–9, where he

concessive protasis interrupted at verse 5 by a long parenthesis and taken up again by the apodosis at verse 15) expresses fidelity to poetry despite bereavement (*Etsi*, 65.1, 'even if'). The 'constant pain' drives the poet away from the 'learned virgins' and impedes him from 'bringing to light the sweet fruit of the Muses' (*dulcis Musarum expromere fetus*, 65.3) – his brother is dead, but Catullus will always love him and always sing mournful poetry for his death, just as the nightingale of the myth sings to mourn the death of her son. Still, 'in such great mourning' (Catull 65.15), the poet sends his friend *haec expressa . . . carmina Battiadae*, 'this poetry translated from Callimachus', so that he will not think he has forgotten his words (*tua dicta*, 65.17), perhaps a request for poetry, to which the translation replies as a surrogate.

Poem 66[44] ensured great fortune for another erotic-elegiac theme of Callimachean origin: the 'lament of the *relicta*', which found an embodiment in the translation of the *Lock* that was as vital as the figure of the abandoned Ariadne in Catullus 64. Through the ironic prism of the talking object of the lock, Catullus inaugurated a favourite piece of the elegiac repertoire: the lament of the abandoned woman, separated from her lover because of war, in a melodramatic scenario, which includes tearful farewell and vows for safe return. With delicate irony, the motif is duplicated: just as Berenice mourns her separation from her spouse and 'brother', so the *coma* (feminine in Latin) poses as the lover who suffers from the separation of the beloved body and from the fraternal affection of the sister's hair, also because of the 'iron', whose inventor is cursed – as in the antimilitaristic Tibullus 1.10 or Propertius 4.3.

The courtly homage that closed Βερενίκης πλόκαμος (*The Lock of Berenice*, fr. 110 Pf., 94a), not translated in the conclusion of poem 66, seems to be dissonantly echoed in the opening of poem 67: by dislocating the distich, probably expunged when the *Lock* came to form the finale of the *Aetia*, Catullus exhibits learned awareness of the history of Callimachus' text; and he recreates between 66 and 67 the difference in style anticipated in the epilogue of the *Aetia* as Callimachus passes to the *Iambs*.[45] The door in Verona is endowed with speech and assumes the role of informant such as that of the Muses in *Aetia* I and II, answering the poet's question by revealing a provincial story of adultery and incest, in opposition to the chaste 'fraternal' marriage of the Ptolemaic court; the matrimonial *leitmotif*

accepts the thesis of Quinn (1972) 264–5, of Catull. 65–116 as a third book; Forsyth (1977) 353; Block (1984) 50–1; Hinds (1987b) 102 and n. 14; Barchiesi (1993) 363–5 and (2005) 333–6; Hubbard (2005) 269–75 (cf. also, on the Callimachean character of 65–116, King (1988)); *contra*, Bellandi (2007) 77–8.

44 Cf. Marinone (1997); Binder-Hamm (1998); Warden (2006); Höschele (2009).

45 Fantuzzi-Hunter (2002 = 2004) 549 and 562, n. 69.

is varied in comical style and in dialogue form, a model for the elegy of the door in Propertius 1.16.[46]

Catullus 68 remains the recognized incunabulum of Latin love elegy, despite the unresolved problems of the unity of its composition, the identity of its addressee, the repeated verses, lacunae, *cruces* and interpretive uncertainties.[47] The letter to Mallius (Allius? Manlius?), 68A, is Catullus' *recusatio*, excuse, for not being able to answer a request for love poetry (*munera . . . et Musarum . . . et Veneris*, cf. Anac. fr. 2 W. = 56 Gentili) as consolation for a lover's pain; fraternal bereavement wrenched away poetry and every other joy from Catullus, and the bitter-sweet past of love and poetry appears lost – in addition to that, isolated in Verona, the poet has with him a single box of books. *Ignosces igitur, si . . .* (Catull. 68A.31, 'You will therefore forgive me, if . . .') – writes Catullus – the expectation can no longer be satisfied. Repeating the Catullan hemistich, Propertius, in his quasi-epistolary poem 1.11, justifies the change of his poetry's hue from joyful to sad, fearing that Baiae is tearing away Cynthia from his poems: Cynthia who is 'everything' for him, joy and family, just as the brother is for Catullus.

To make poetry out of one's own incapacity to make poetry, because of pain: the *recusatio* of 65 and 68A resonates in that of Horace's *Epode* 14 to Maecenas, while the tension between 'bereavement' and art (which in Prop. 1.7 sees the choice of elegy as a service to *dolor*, pain, rather than to *ingenium*, poetic talent) was exacerbated by Ovid's invention of elegiac exile where, in the affectation of a sad elegy as a spontaneous product of *dolor*, exile was the equivalent of death.[48] Ovid's *Tristia* 5.1, an Augustan counter-programme which repudiates the Callimachean aesthetics of *dulce*/γλυκύ[49] and a past of *lusus*, of delicate love poetry – erotic elegy, which now appears by contrast as happy elegy – echoes the sad elegiac 'programme' of Catullus in 65 and 68A.[50] Ovid makes explicit the self-consolatory role, the resistance to 'wearing oneself out in constant worries' (*assiduis animum tabescere curis*, *Tr.* 5.1.77), contaminating the 'constant pain' and 'worry' for the fraternal bereavement of Catullus (65.1, *assiduo confectum cura dolore*) and the

[46] On Catull. 67 cf. MacLeod (1983); Levine (1985); Murgatroyd (1989).

[47] On Catull. 68 (A and B): Coppel (1973); Lyne (1980) 52–60; Sarkissian (1983); Citroni (1995) 79–93; Tuplin (1981); Feeney (1992); Hunter (2006a) 102–8; critical survey in Theodorakopoulos (2007); commentary, as a unitary poem, in Maggiali (2008). Jacoby (1905) 51 was criticized for denying the status of elegy to Catull. 68, which he considered an epistle and an encomium: cf. Galasso (2006) 136; on the poem as an archetype of elegy cf., e.g., Fedeli (1974) 40–1; Pasoli (1980); La Penna (1982) 125; Traina (1998) 49–50.

[48] On Ovid's exile poetics cf. Nagle (1980), Labate (1987), Williams (1994).

[49] Hunter (2006a) 35–6; (2006b).

[50] Bonvicini (2000); Bessone (2003).

'constant pining in tears' for the erotic passion (68B.55, *assiduo tabescere lumina fletu*).

The poetic *munus* (Lat. 'gift') of 68B, if an attempt to unify the name of the addressee may be accepted, can be considered a response to the request from the same friend in 68A. The frame is an encomium of Allius (or Manlius), who has made possible Catullus' love relationship by putting his house at his disposal for an encounter between the poet and his beloved woman. Within a vertiginous concentric structure complicated by a fugue of similes, commemoration of the first love encounter arouses the memory of the myth of Laodamia and Protesilaus and this in turn provokes a curse upon Troy, tomb of heroes and of the poet's brother, whose 'sweet love' Catullus identified with the joy of life (68B.95–6 = 68A.23–4), like Laodamia's love for her spouse (68B.105–7) and that of Catullus for his lady (68B.159–60). The original blend of autobiography and myth (around the key image of the house, *domus*) gives form to Catullan obsessions and contradictions, which are already in part those of the elegists: love and death; the woman who is *diua*, *domina* and *era* (Lat. 'goddess', 'mistress' and 'lady of the house'); loyalty and *furta* (Lat. stolen joys); adulterous or irregular relations and matrimonial nostalgia. Catullus sings Lesbia in many different forms, but when he does so in elegy (without naming her), he does it by blending life with myth and love with death, representing himself in incessant tears (68B.55–6) and alternating regret and hope, absolute aspirations and bitter irony, so as to soften the pathos (68B.135–40): Catullus here strengthens the complexity of elegiac love discourse, elegy as a poetry of weeping and as the poetic form of nostalgia.[51]

Latin love elegy begins here, where poem 68 ends, in an envoi that could easily come from Propertius: *lux mea, qua uiua uiuere dulce mihi est*, (Catull. 68B.160, my light, which as long as it lives makes my life sweet).

Further reading

General studies on Latin elegy inform about the broad debate on its origins, e.g. Luck (1959), Holzberg (2001), Pinotti (2002), Gibson (2005), cf. La Penna (1977) 23–31; specific contributions are: Alfonsi (1965); Pasoli (1980); Stroh (1983); Gärtner (2006); Lucarini (2008). On Hellenistic genres in the Republican age cf. La Penna (1982). On Latin elegy and Hellenistic epigram see now Keith (2011). For Catullus' Latin text, see Mynors (1958), Goold (1983) and Ancona, Maltby et al. (2004); for Catullus' Latin text and en-face translations into English, see Goold and Cornish (1988). For

[51] See also P.A. Miller (Chapter 10) in this volume.

English translations of Catullus, see Lee (1998) and Godwin (1995, 1999). For commentaries on Catullus, see Fordyce (1961), Quinn (1970) and Godwin (1995, 1999). On the various aspects of Catullus as a precursor of elegy, and on critical views thereon: Miller (2007); cf. Ross (1975): 1–17, Granarolo (1980).

PART II

The Latin love elegists

3

EMMANUELLE RAYMOND

Caius Cornelius Gallus

'The inventor of Latin love elegy'[1]

Caius Cornelius Gallus haunts almost every discussion of Latin Love Elegy. From Antiquity onwards, authors and critics have ascribed a prominent place to Gallus in the elegiac tradition but his prominence is counterbalanced by a striking scarcity both of information about the poet and of his extant poetry.

The discrepancy between Gallus' fame as the father of Roman elegy[2] and the poverty of reliable evidence for his life, career and poetry is something of a puzzle. Nevertheless, what we do know about Gallus gives an alluring picture of the poet. He lived in a context of transition between the dying Republic and the newborn Principate, had well-known friendships with the greatest statesmen and poets of Augustan Rome such as Asinius Pollio,[3] Virgil, his fellow student,[4] and Augustus, his friend.[5] Gallus ended his life by committing suicide,[6] after having fallen into disgrace (see below).[7]

Indirect references to Gallus[8] only allow critics a vague overview, and the loss of his poems makes it impossible to dispel the mystery of Gallus. From what may have amounted to four books of elegy, just one single line was known[9] before the sensational discovery at Qaṣr Ibrîm, which recovered some ten lines of Gallus, saw its *editio princeps* in 1979.[10] Despite the scarcity of Gallus' poetic remains, his fame is due precisely to his poetic

Special thanks to Thea S. Thorsen, Anton Powell, Zara Torlone.

1 Syme (1939) 252. On the title of *inuentor*/ εὑρετής, see Bardon (1956) 39.

2 Putnam (1970) 354.

3 Cf. Cic. *Fam.* 10.32 (= 415 SB) and, less certainly, *Fam.* 10.31 (= 368 SB); see Hollis (2007) 226.

4 *Condiscipulus* cf. Pseudo-Probus, *Ecl. Praef.* Thilo and Hagen (1961) 328.

5 Cf. Ovid *Am.* 3.9.64.

6 In the year 27 BC cf. Jer. *Chron.* (ed. Helm (1956) 164), see also Cass. Dio 53.24.

7 Cf. Ovid *Am.* 3.9.64–5.

8 Cf. Hollis (2007) 219–23.

9 C. Cornelius Gallus fr. 1 (*FLP*).

10 Anderson, Parsons and Nisbet (1979) 125–55.

achievements; and, as Virgil asked, *neget quis carmina Gallo?* (*Ecl.*10.3, 'who would deny Gallus poems?').[11]

Gallus' mysterious life

On Gallus' life we find only dubious testimony, which has driven scholars to a variety of hypotheses.[12] On his life and political career, a few words may suffice to illustrate his shadowy nature. Neither year nor places of birth and death are known; on these points modern authors profoundly disagree.[13] Guesses have also been made about Gallus' modest origins.[14] As he was already present in Pollio's circle during the 40s BC, he probably was a famous poet and a statesman before Virgil began his own work. We can neither precisely date the beginning of his political career nor define the exact nature of his military deeds before 29 BC. During these years, we hear from Servius (*ad Buc.* 10.1) that Gallus had a love affair with an actress named Cytheris – a freedwoman whose real name was Volumnia – who abandoned him to follow Mark Antony in Gaul. This courtesan may be the model of Lycoris, the *domina* (mistress) of Gallus' poetry, who allegedly put him through acute love pangs.[15] There are also reasons to believe that his four books of poetry, in which Lycoris featured, were called *Amores* (Servius *ad Buc.* 10.1, 'Loves').

After 29 BC, we possess an inscription probably commissioned by Gallus himself in which he listed his exploits as the first prefect of Roman Egypt rather immodestly and without the necessary regard for the authority of Augustus.[16] Subsequently, according to ancient authors, Octavian withdrew

11 The line is famously ambiguous, translating as both 'who would refuse to dedicate poems to Gallus' and 'who would forbid Gallus to write poems' (= who would censor Gallus?).

12 Most critics are extremely cautious concerning Gallus' biography; nevertheless see Boucher (1966), Nicastri (1984), Manzoni (1995).

13 Boucher (1966) 5–9; Torlone (1999) 24–5.

14 Suetonius, *Aug.* 66.1 (*ex infima fortuna*). For Strabo 17.819.53 and Cass. Dio 51.9 it was his military deeds which allowed Gallus to become prefect of Egypt. See also Jer. *Chron.* ibid.

15 Cf. Propertius 2.34.91–92, Ovid *Am.* 1.15.29–30 and *Ars* 3.537 and Martial 8.73.5–6.

16 *CIL* III (1414)7. The trilingual inscription of Philae, and that of the Vatican obelisk quoted above, testify, somewhat conflictingly, to Gallus as a self-promoting but nonetheless obedient prefect of Egypt: 'Caius Cornelius Gallus, son of Cnaeus, Roman knight, after the defeat by Caesar the son of divine Caesar, first prefect of Alexandria and Egypt, victor over the sedition in Thebais in less than fifteen days during which he twice crushed the enemy in pitched battle, conqueror of five cities, Boresis, Coptos, Ceramice, Diospolis Magna and Ophieus, after having arrested the sedition's captains, after having driven the army beyond the Nile's cataracts, where the Roman people, the Egyptian king had not driven their army, after having extracted Thebais from the fear of

his trust and friendship from Gallus and the Senate decreed that Gallus was to be exiled and his estate confiscated.[17] Suetonius (*Gram.* 16.1) reports that Gallus helped Q. Caecilius Epirota, who had offended a family member of Augustus, and thus outraged the *princeps*. Ovid (*Tr.* 2.1.445–6) attributed Gallus' downfall to his *licentia* when drunk. Gallus' subsequent suicide probably took place in 27 or 26 BC. The shortage of ancient testimony may suggest a *damnatio memoriae*,[18] which would also explain the striking loss of his poetry.[19] It is hard to say if Virgil's alleged withdrawal of 'the praises of Gallus' (*laudes Galli*) at the end of the fourth book of the Georgics (replacing the passage with the Aristaeus episode) is reliable evidence of Gallus' *damnatio* (Servius *ad Buc.* 10.1; *ad Geor.* 4.1). Although Servius is our only witness for Virgil's alterations, it seems plausible that it was hard or dangerous for contemporary poets to express sympathy or admiration for Gallus after his fall from grace.[20]

Gallus' poetic remains

As mentioned, until 1979 we possessed only a single line of Gallus and could not assess for ourselves the place ascribed to the poet by ancient authors. The quotation, which is a so-called golden line,[21] that Vibius Sequester had excerpted from Gallus is the following line about the river Hypanis,

kings, after having heard out the Ethiopian king's ambassadors near Philae and after having received this king under the Roman people's protection, after having placed a tyrant in Triakontaschoenundium of Ethiopia, he inscribed this dedication to local gods and to the helpful Nile.' See also Boucher (1966) 33–8, with a photograph, and Hoffmann, Minas-Nerpel and Pfeiffer (2009).

17 Suet. *Aug.* 66.2, Cass. Dio 53.23, Amm. Marc. 18.4.5.

18 Skutsch (1904) 122, 124–5. The silence of historians such as Livy and Velleius Paterculus on Gallus' condemnation seems to confirm the idea of a *damnatio memoriae* (cf. Boucher (1966) 28). The obelisk, now in Saint Peter's Square in the Vatican, reused by Caligula in his circus, shows an ancient inscription which mentioned Gallus: IVSSV IMP. CAESARIS DIVI F./ C. CORNELIVS CN. F. GALLVS/ PRAEF. FABR. CAESARIS DIV. F./ FORVM IVLIVM FECIT ('On the order of Caesar imperator, son of divine Caesar, Caius Cornelius Gallus, son of Cnaeus, *praefectus fabrum* of divine Caesar's son, built the *Forum Iulium*'). This inscription, which gives Gallus' title of *praefectus fabrum* and the dedication by him of a *Forum Iulium* in Alexandria, had probably been removed after Gallus' *damnatio*; Boucher (1966) 33–8, 56–7; Flower (2006) 127–9 fig. 19–21; Hollis (2007) 225.

19 See Flower (2006) 125–9; Hollis (2007) 230 justifies the loss of Gallus' poetry on the grounds of poetic technique inferior in comparison with younger rivals.

20 Haarhoff (1960) 101–2.

21 A golden line (or golden verse) is a Latin dactylic hexameter with an interlocking pattern of different grammatical forms. Gallus' line also combines two numbers (*uno/duas*) which produce an ABAB alternation of cases (ablative-accusative/ablative-accusative) and a chiasmus with a number-noun/noun-number arrangement.

separating Europe from Asia: *uno tellures diuidit amne duas* (divided two lands with one river).[22]

The discovery of the papyrus of Qaṣr Ibrîm revived discussion of Gallus' lost works. The fragment[23] is composed of one pentameter on the *nequitia* (misbehaviour, wickedness) of Lycoris, then two elegiac couplets of national inspiration about Caesar's victories, then two couplets about the poet's *carmina* and his *domina* and finally one isolated word:

    Tristia nequit[ia . . . .]a,[24] Lycori, tua
Fata mihi, Caesar, tum erunt[25] mea dulcia, quom tu
    maxima Romanae pars eri<s>[26] historiae
postque tuum reditum multorum templa deorum
    fixa legam spolieis deiuitiora tueis.
. . . . .] . . . .tandem fecerunt c[ar]mina Musae
    quae possem domina deicere digna mea.
. . . .]atur idem tibi, non ego, Visce
    . . . .] . . . . . .] Kato,[27] iudice te uereor.
    ] . . . [   ].
    ] . . . .[   ].Tyria.[28]
                    ].

. . . sad, Lycoris, by your misbehaviour. My fate will then be sweet to me, Caesar, when you are the most important part of Roman history, and when I read of many gods' temples the richer after your return for being hung with your trophies.

22 Hellenistic influence (Hollis (2007) 237–8), precisely that of Euphorion of Chalcis (*Ecl.* 10.50 *Chalcidico . . . uersu*, Serv. *Praef. ad Buc.* 10.1, Quint. 10.1.56; *contra* Courtney (1993) 261–2 and *Ecl.* 6.67–73, Serv. *ad Buc.* 6.72; see also Diomedes *GLK* 1.484, Hollis (2007) 203–4; 237–8) and the *Sufferings in Love* (ἐρωτικὰ παθήματα) by Parthenius – who had dedicated this work to Gallus (fr. 1, Lightfoot (2009) 550; cf. Boucher (1966) 74–7; Barchiesi (1981), Cairns (2006b) 238; 244; Hollis (2007) 238–40), as well as Callimachus (Cairns (2011)) has been assumed. Cairns (2011) explores further echoes of Gallus' pentameter in Propertius (1.12.3–4, 9–10) and Ovid (*Fast.* 6.495–6; *Her.* 18.125–6; *Her.* 19.142; *Pont.* 4.10.55–6). On the assumption that *Ecl.* 10 and Prop. 1.8 have a common source that either was Gallus or one he had made use of, it has been suggested that he introduced the *propemptikon* to Augustan poetry (McKeown (1998) 222), and that this line was a part of such a farewell poem to Lycoris (Boucher (1966) 83–4; Nicastri (1984) 20–1).

23 Anderson, Parsons and Nisbet (1979) 140 (text and translation), 140–8 (commentary). For a line-by-line commentary see also Van Sickle (1981); Verducci (1984) 132–6; Capasso (2003) 50–74; Hollis (2007) 242–52.

24 *fact*]*a Nisbet.* 25 *Tum, Caesar, erunt* Lyne.

26 *Erit* pap., corr. Nisbet and Parsons. 27 *pla*]*kato*, i.e. *placato* prop. Hutchinson.

28 *Syria* prop. Capasso.

> At last the . . . Muses have made poems for me to utter as worthy of my mistress. . . . . the same to you, I do not, Viscus, I do not, Cato, fear . . . ., even if you are the arbiter . . . Tyrian . . . [29]

Although these lines pertain to the only extant fragment displaying more or less plausible thematic connections,[30] it remains hard to say whether what we read are fragments of several short poems or parts of a single poem which might be an amoebaean contest,[31] a *recusatio*, since grave political thoughts follow a more frivolous couplet,[32] or an anthology of Gallus' poetry, whether some extracts of his *Amores* or a collection of his epigrams.[33] Without trying to solve this mystery,[34] let us comment on the lines separately.

Other Augustan poets[35] may allude to the first line, which points toward Gallan authorship, through the beloved's name. It can be seen as Gallus' programmatic introduction to his love poetry, here confirmed as subjective love-elegy.[36] The first line has sometimes been interpreted as part of an epigram or an elegy based on the theme of *seruitium amoris*[37] and addressed to the *saeua domina Lycoris*, whose debauchery inflicts pain on the *poeta amator*,[38] maybe unto death. Hollis (2007) 244–5 is convinced that *fata mea* refers to the death of the *amator* from the *nequitia* of the *domina* and understands *legam* (5) as meaning to scan, to survey. This puzzling

[29] Text and translation from *editio princeps* (1979). On line 1, Hollis (2007) 224 proposes '<made> sad Lycoris, by your wantonness', with caution. Lines 4–5 Hollis: 'when after your return, I survey the temples of many gods'. Line 6, Hollis proposes the addition: 'the Muses have made <these> poems <for me>'. Line 8, Hollis understands: '<And if she tells> you the same'. Line 9, Courtney (1993) 268 favours the restoration *quae canit ulla Kato*, i.e. *non uereor ulla (carmina) quae canit Kato* . . . Then 8 might have begun with something like *quodsi iam uideatur* (Nisbet): 'if you, Viscus, agree with my judgment of the quality now at last attained by my poetry, then I need not fear comparison with that of Cato.'

[30] Cf. Anderson, Parsons and Nisbet (1979) 149; Van Sickle (1981) 116–20. *Contra* Verducci (1984) 121–2 and Courtney (1993) 264.

[31] Fairweather (1984) 167.

[32] Verducci (1984) 125.

[33] Nicastri (1984) 17 thinks of several epigrams, followed by Hollis (2007) 250 with discussion.

[34] Discussion in Torlone (1999) 37–8.

[35] The *topos* of the *duritia* of Gallus' *puella* may have inspired Virgil, cf. *Ecl.* 10.10, and Propertius, cf. 2.1.78.

[36] For 'subjective elegy' as opposed to 'objective elegy', see Bessone (Chapter 2) in this volume.

[37] Cf. Capasso (2003) 51–2.

[38] Cf. Nicastri (1984) 15 n. 3; for the figure of the *poeta amator*, see Sharrock (Chapter 9) in this volume.

legam,[39] linked with the problematic identification of Caesar,[40] is key to the interpretation of the text: whereas Nisbet sees the line as meaning 'I will read about historiographic accounts of your conquests', Courtney construes *templa legere* i.e. 'I will read the inscriptions on temples'. Miller (2004) 76 insists that *legam* refers to the poet's presence at the dedication of Caesar's victorious trophies in certain temples. The next stanza (6–9) introduces the theme of inspiration through the figure of the Muses and the stylish quality of the verse, finally composed.[41] The satisfaction shown by the poet through *tandem* (6) underscores the arduous difficulty of writing poetry, as confirmed by the common representation of the Muses as co-*auctores* while the poet stands back.[42] As the Muses inspire his *digna scripta* (marked by a striking alliteration), the poet should be able to charm his perhaps over-critical *domina*.[43]

As the end of the passage lapses into unreadable fragments, it is hard to propose a convincing interpretation. Hollis (2007) 247 thinks of possible confrontation between Lycoris as *testis* facing Viscus as *iudex*. Less conjectured is the Virgilian echo (cf. *Ecl.* 2.26–7), which could imply allusion to Theocritus in Gallus. In that lines 8 and 9 raise the insoluble questions of the identity of Viscus and of Kato spelt with a *K*, interpretation is baffled. The last word *Tyria*, preferred in the *editio princeps* to *Syria*, may allude to the Latin colour common for clothes for women or of the triumphant victor's toga. Whether Gallus in subsequent lost verses returned to the figure of Lycoris or to Caesar's victories is impossible to determine.[44]

However scanty these poetic remains may be, a scattering of features of these lines, such as the linguistic sophistication, the morally difficult

39 For interpretations of *legam*, cf. Capasso (2003) 57.

40 Hutchinson (1981) 37–42 identifies Caesar as Octavian conquering Illyria in mid-30 BC or crushing Egypt after Actium. On the contrary, following Nisbet in Anderson, Parsons and Nisbet (1979) 152 and Courtney (1993) 265, Hollis (2007) 243 goes back to Julius Caesar and his plan to invade Parthia, which could be seen, unlike Octavian's conquest of Illyria or his siege of Alexandria, as one of the greatest parts of Roman history, pushing into the background Crassus' shameful defeat against the Parthians. As shown by Putnam (1980) 49–56, Propertius 3.4 can be seen as confirmation of Gallus' Caesar being Julius Caesar.

41 Nisbet in Anderson, Parsons and Nisbet (1979) 150, Courtney (1993) 266 and Hollis (2007) 250 argue that lines 6–9 could be the poetically self-conscious concluding lines of a preceding book or a kind of triumphant epilogue.

42 See in particular Euphorion fr. 118 Powell; *AP*. 9.63, 9.513; Lucr. 1.24; Horace *Epist.* 2.2.92 and Prop. 4.1.133.

43 Courtney (1993) 267 thinks that the word *idem* (8) alluded to a judgment expressed in the passage. Hollis (2007) 247 connects the idea of some critics with the *saeua domina* evoked before.

44 Capasso (2003) 73–4.

concept of *nequitia*,[45] the beloved's meaningful though elusive name, the figure of the mistress/*domina* related to that of the elegiac *puella*,[46] the ambivalent relationship between poetry and politics,[47] will become themes that the elegiac successors of Gallus imitate, develop and enhance in their compositions.[48]

'A moving force in the genesis of Augustan poetry'[49]

Although we possess so little of Gallus today, his impact on other poets was important and immediate. The best-known literary response to Gallus' poetic achievements is famously found in the first work of his contemporary colleague Virgil, whose allusions to Gallus' poetry are clearly attested by Servius (*ad Buc.* 10.46).[50]

In the sixth *Eclogue*, the bucolic framework is a poetic artifice destined to provide a continuation of the Callimachean refusal of epic poetry and to yield a catalogue of poets whose works Virgil appreciated, through the mouth of the herdsman Silenus, turning into a remarkable literary critic. Behind the Theocritean drape of pastoral poetry, the main theme is poetry as conceived by Callimachus and his successors, embodied by Gallus.[51] In Virgil's list of renowned poets, only Gallus is explicitly named (64) and Virgil's representation of him as Hesiod's heir (69–70) has led modern scholars to think of a Virgilian recomposition of Gallus' *persona* under the guise of a Callimachean vision.[52] According to Virgil's lines, Gallus leaves the valley of Permessus for the mountains of Helicon, which can be interpreted as a literary movement from love elegy to the higher level of Callimachean aetiology. Gallus' poetic initiation and the overall Hellenistic prism of the sixth *Eclogue* are aptly created to match Virgil's own generic programme.[53]

Modelled on Theocritus' *Idyll* 1, the tenth *Eclogue* is a tribute paid by Virgil to Gallus' love poems. The lines combine feelings of friendship (2; 72), and admiration for a poet who has succeeded in his poetical life as well as in his political life (71). Thus Gallus is the dedicatee of an entire eclogue, appended by Virgil to the collection upon publication. This particular

45 See further Sharrock (Chapter 9) in this volume.
46 See P.A. Miller (Chapter 10) in this volume.
47 See Harrison (Chapter 8) in this volume.
48 Miller (2004) 74. 49 Van Sickle (1977) 327.
50 The Virgilian framing of Gallus' poetic *persona* has clearly been taken into account by later elegiac poets such as Tibullus but above all by Propertius in 1.10. In Propertius, Gallus is addressed in 1.5, 1.10, 1.13, 1.20, and probably alluded to in 1.1, 1.8, 1.18, 1.21, 1.22. The second Book offers only one direct mention (2.34); after that Gallus vanishes from Propertius' lines. Is that also a consequence of his *damnatio memoriae*?
51 Clausen (1994) 177. 52 Torlone (1999) 58. 53 Torlone (1999) 60.

honour at the end of the work is bound to underline for the reader the influence of Gallus' poetry throughout Virgil's poetry book. The couple Gallus and Lycoris are brought together in the same line (2), and the word *amores* (6) arguably stands for Gallus' entire output. The Virgilian portrait thus seems complete, bringing together the poet Gallus, his mistress Lycoris as *domina* of his verses, and the poetic result of their inspirational relationship, the four books of *Amores*. Virgil's representation of Gallus as imitating the real Gallus uses several *topoi* from the repertoire of the disconsolate elegiac lover – which is thereafter reused by elegiac poets – such as prostration beneath a lonely crag (10.14),[54] the increasing madness of the lover (22; 44), the blind veneration of the beloved, the melancholic and self-satisfied pleasure to be seen and remembered as a dying lover whose lines will join the poetic heritage (31).[55]

The first canonized elegist

Contrary to prevailing opinion, Gallus was not the first Latin love elegist. There were poets composing elegies before him, similarly inspired by the love of a mistress.[56] Gallus remains, however, the first poet in the canon of Roman erotic elegists.[57] It is perhaps not accidental that Ovid, who presents himself as the last contributor to the canon of Latin love elegy, most insistently promotes the idea that Gallus comes first in this canon (*Tr.* 4.10.53). If Ovid indeed invented the inventor, it has proved to be a successful concept for teaching in schools since Quintilian (*Inst.* 10.1.93).[58] Quintilian famously also called Gallus the *durior* ('harder'/ 'harsher') of the elegists and if Ovid and Quintilian agree on the primordial place of Gallus in the Latin elegiac canon, Quintilian's verdict continues to be challenged by

54 For this topos, see Prop. 1.9.3, 1.16.23–24, 2.14.32, Tib. 2.4.22, 2.5.109–11 and Ov. *Am.* 2.10.15 and *Ars* 2.238.

55 Prop. 1.17.19–24, 1.19, 2.13.17–58 and Tib. 1.1.59–68, 3.53–66 show the same penchant for morbid description of their fictive death.

56 Catull. 75, 79, 83, 86, 87, 92 and 107 are in elegiac couplets and feature the name of Lesbia (cf. also Catull. 86 and P.A. Miller in Chapter 10). According to Porphyrio *ad* Hor. *Carm.* 1.22, the sixteenth book of Lucilius was dedicated to a Collyra, who was his *amica*, (girl friend). The only extant fragments in elegiac metre are however only from books 22–5 of Lucilius. Calvus' poem to Quintilia (cf. Catull. 86 and Prop. 2.34.88–9) was an elegy, but if Terentius Varro Atacinus' poem(s) about Leucadia were in elegiac distichs, then that would be the only known example of a non-hexameter composition among his works. See also Bessone (Chapter 2) in this volume.

57 Ross (1975) 1.

58 Even in modern scholarship Gallus outshines previous elegiac poets' works, and has been dubbed both εὑρετής and the uncaused cause (Miller (2004) 73) of Roman elegy.

Ovid's question: *Quis poterit lecto durus discedere Gallo?* (*Rem. am.* 765, 'Who can go on being harsh after having read Gallus?').

Further reading

Critical literature about Gallus divides into two periods, before and after the discovery of the papyrus at Qaṣr Ibrîm (Anderson, Parsons and Nisbet (1979)). Works written before that date are generally allusive and speculative (Syme (1939), Bardon (1956), Haarhoff (1960), Boucher (1966)). Recent contributions to Gallan scholarship of importance are Crowther (1983), Nicastri (1984), Manzoni (1995), Stickler (2002) and Capasso (2003). Indispensable are recent editions with commentary (Courtney (1993) and Hollis (2007), with English translation) to which shorter studies remain valuable additions (Hutchinson (1981), Van Sickle (1981), Fairweather (1984), Verducci (1984) and Cairns (2011) on the 'old' Gallus). On Gallus' trilingual inscription, see Hoffmann, Minas-Nerpel and Pfeiffer (2009). On Gallus' influence on Virgil's Eclogues, see Putnam (1970); Perkell (1996); Woodman (1997); Clausen (1994). On Gallus and Propertius see Putnam (1980); most recently Cairns (2006) and (2011a) and Heyworth (2007a and b). On Gallus and Ovid, see McKeown (1989), (1998) and Cairns (2011). Also relevant are monographs about Hellenistic influence on Gallus' style (Lightfoot (1999), (2009) and Hunter (2006a)) and general works about Augustan poetry (Miller (2004); Ross (1975)).

4

PARSHIA LEE-STECUM

Tibullus in first place

hic multorum iudicio principem inter elegiographos optinet locum.[1]

In the opinion of many he holds the first place among writers of elegy.

This line from the brief *Vita Tibulli* (Life of Tibullus) raises many questions about a poet who is little read today outside the circles of academic Latinists and whose profile even among classicists is still dwarfed by those of Propertius and Ovid. Who are the many whose opinion rated Tibullus in first place? Stylistic hints in the *Vita* suggest it is drawn in large part from the *De Poetis* section of Suetonius' *De Viris Illustribus* (On Famous Men).[2] If so, the statement is made after 125 years of reading Tibullus' work. For how much of this period the opinion was held is unclear. It may be an overview of general judgements over the full course of the period from around 26 BC (when the first Book of Tibullus was first circulated) until around AD 105–10, or it might represent an immediately contemporary assessment of reading tastes in the Trajanic period when Suetonius was writing.

Equally intriguing is the question of what 'first place' might entail. A simple meaning of 'first to write elegies' must be precluded. From the *Vita* and other sources we can deduce that Tibullus was probably born in the late 50s or early 40s BC, that he was of equestrian rank, that he served with distinction in at least one campaign under his patron, Marcus Valerius Messalla Corvinus, that he owned an estate in the *regio Pedana* (ten or so miles east of Rome), and that he died in 19 BC.[3] These bare details in themselves place Tibullus' brief floruit at a time and in a social context of intense poetic production and interaction. While difficulties with relative dating persist, patterns of poetic response and counter-response seem to place Tibullus book 1 subsequent to Propertius book 1, and the second book of Tibullus

[1] For discussion of this and other evidence for the high regard in which Tibullus' poetry was held in antiquity, see Cairns (1979a) 3–6.

[2] On the *De Viris Illustribus* and its possible structure, see Brugnoli (1968) 41–60. For the attribution of the *Vita Tibulli* to Suetonius, see Rostagni (1979) 133–8.

[3] A full list of *testimonia* for Tibullus is collected by Maltby (2002) 33–9.

subsequent to Propertius books 2 and 3.[4] Even if later Roman generations believed that Tibullus' first collection was published before Propertius', any claim to primacy that excluded Gallus would be unsustainable. A statement of chronological primacy would be more clearly indicated by *primus*, a term for an originator which Tibullus himself uses on several occasions. In contrast to *primus*, *princeps locus* evokes a traditional Republican language of influence, respect and authority.[5] *Princeps* was already becoming during Tibullus' lifetime a term redolent of the authority (*auctoritas*) and leadership of one man (Augustus), and was even more closely identified with the position of the Emperor in Roman society by the time of Suetonius. To give Tibullus the 'first place among writers of elegy' is thus to accord his work a degree of authority, influence and esteem in the elegiac field equivalent to that which the great *principes* of the Republic, or even the Emperor himself, possessed in the socio-political field.

While his work has been highly esteemed in different periods and places over the centuries since the judgement of the *Vita*, the difference between this opinion and Tibullus' present literary reputation is stark. What was it in the work of this poet, recently described as 'absurdly under-valued',[6] that led Suetonius' 'many' to see him as a literary leader in his field? In some respects it may represent a stylistic preference and echo Quintilian's more famous statement that 'for me the author, Tibullus, seems most refined and elegant (*tersus atque elegans*)' (*Inst.* 10.1.93).[7] But additionally, Tibullus' work engages critically with many of the most important themes that run through the elegies of Propertius and Ovid. These are the very themes that give Roman elegy its particular identity. Like the imperial *princeps* in the socio-political field, Tibullan elegy forms an *exemplum* to which others must respond.[8]

The *Corpus Tibullianum*

As well as two poetic collections that are certainly by Tibullus, a series of additional poems, now commonly numbered as a third book and recently

4 See Solmsen (1962) and especially Lyne (1998a). Knox (2005), however, tries to argue for an earlier date of Tibullus book 1.

5 On *princeps* see: Gruen (2005) 34; Wickert (1974) 10–25; Brunt (1988) 506–8; and Syme (1939) 311–12.

6 Wray (2003) 219.

7 For analysis of the critical vocabulary applied by Quintilian to Tibullus here, see Cairns (1979a) 3–5.

8 The most explicit response is Ovid's lament for Tibullus at *Amores* 3.9: see Huskey (2005) especially 367 n. 3, which lists earlier discussions of the response in 3.9 to Tibullus 1.3 and Tibullan poetry generally.

designated the *Appendix Tibulliana*, were attached to the poet's name sometime in antiquity.[9] The three books were henceforth circulated as a collected *Corpus Tibullianum*. In addition to a sequence of poems by or to Sulpicia,[10] the *Appendix* contains the *Laudes* (or *Panegyricus*) *Messallae* ('The Praises of Messalla'), and two brief elegies (of twenty-four and four lines respectively). In the first of these two elegies, the poet refers to himself as 'Tibullus', although it is far from certain whether these are really the work of Tibullus himself. The *Appendix* begins with a sequence of six longer elegies by a poet who refers to himself by the pseudonym Lygdamus (3.2.29). Traditionally understood as a collection of writings by poets surrounding Messalla Corvinus (the 'circle of Messalla'), closer examination has suggested that the make-up of the *Appendix* is more complex.[11]

The identity and date of Lygdamus has been particularly vexed. Perhaps he is a son or nephew of Messalla, a young Tibullus, a young Ovid or a post-Ovidian poet? It has also been claimed, not implausibly, that Lygdamus is a poet of the late-Flavian period (born AD 69).[12] Although a final answer to the *quaestio Lygdamea* remains elusive, a post-Tibullan date seems the most likely. Certainly the poems of Lygdamus are in some ways quite distinct in form and approach from those of Tibullus books 1 and 2. Not least, Lygdamus writes of his beloved, Neaera, as *coniunx* (wife), holds a dialogue with the Muses (3.1) that explicitly outlines his neoteric poetic principles, and echoes Ovidian elegy on a number of occasions.[13] Yet at the same time Lygdamus' construction of his elegies around the poetics of presence and the blending of discourses (erotic, poetic, religious, familial) in a framework that is 'dream-like'[14] positions his mini-collection in direct relation to the Tibullan example. This position the Lygdamus sequence shares with all post-Tibullan Roman elegy.

Just as the *quaestio Lygdamea* remains without a conclusive answer, so it is impossible to determine when the works of the *Appendix Tibulliana* were first collected together or added to the first two collections as a 'third book' of Tibullus. Material from the corpus is not explicitly referred to in the ancient *testimonia* for Tibullus and may not have been joined to

[9] The title *Appendix Tibulliana* was coined by Tränkle (1990) in his commentary on the poems of 'book 3'.

[10] See Skoie (Chapter 5) in this volume.

[11] On the transmission of the *corpus Tibullianum* see Fisher (1981), Reeve and Rouse (1983), and Antolín (1996) 25–40.

[12] For a complete survey of opinion on the question of Lygdamus' date and identity (the *quaestio Lygdamea*), see Antolín (1996) 3–20.

[13] For Ovidian echoes see Lee (1958–9).

[14] In fact, Lygdamus' fourth poem (usually numbered 3.4) explicitly discusses *somnia*, ('dreams') and describes a particular dream-vision (of the god, Apollo) in detail.

books 1 and 2 until late antiquity or even the early medieval period. But it is very likely that the works themselves, regardless of their own merits, owe their survival to association with Tibullus' name and thus the *princeps locus inter elegiographos*.

Tibullus' work comprises not simply a presentation of common or representative elegiac themes but an analysis and exposure of the mechanisms of these themes that integrates them with, rather than separates them from, the broad range of Roman experience. He is not (chronologically) the first to develop such an approach. Catullus, Gallus and Hellenistic poetry before them provide important models and intertexts for Tibullan elegy.[15] But his poetic achievement provides a touchstone, at least in the opinion of 'many', for elegy in its Roman form.

Presence

In simple terms, desire is the focus of Roman elegy, and Tibullus develops and exploits this focus to the fullest extent. This is not a matter only of longing for the fulfilment of sexual desire. Nor is it limited to a desire for the fidelity of the beloved. Desire for presence is the driving force of Tibullan poetry. Most obvious is the genre-defining desire for the presence of a beloved who is absent or separated from the poet/lover. This desire directs the words of the Tibullan poet in ways that are not always clear at first. Amatory motivations are gradually revealed, or suddenly exposed at work behind decisions, assertions and other forms of desire that might initially seem independent.

The opening poems of both Tibullan collections begin, and continue for some time, with seemingly non-amatory desires. Poem 1.1 expands on the poet's desire to avoid the anxieties of military service (*militia*) in favour of life as a farmer. Poem 2.1 expresses desire for the presence of rural deities in the style of a traditional prayer. In both cases it is suggested later that desire for the beloved's presence has determined the poet's choices. In 1.1 the poet is unable to go on campaign because he is immobilized by amatory desire expressed as his physical confinement outside the doors of his beloved, Delia (1.1.53–6). In contrast, others, such as the *alius* (someone else) of 1.1.1 or the patron, Messalla, with whom the poet's immobilization is directly compared at 1.1.53–4, may choose *militia*. Hints of the influence of *amor* are present in 2.1 (lines 67–80), but it is only in a later poem, 2.3, that the cause of the

[15] For Hellenistic models see Cairns (1979a); Luck (1969), ch. 5; Bulloch (1973). For Catullus, see Cairns (1979a) 224–8 (also discussing the influence of Gallus). For the influence of Gallus see Crowther (1983) 1641–5; Ross (1975).

poet's presence in the country and rustic concerns are explicitly stated as amatory (2.3.1–2).

The opening poems of the two collections are also revealing for the other competing desires expressed. While *amor* is exposed as the controlling desire, overwhelming all others and structured by the absence (behind a door, in the country) of the beloved, 1.1's initial desire for a rustic life encompasses both the secure presence of the beloved and freedom from the anxieties of male, elite expectations (*militia*). The invocation of rural gods in 2.1 expresses a wish for release from the controlling force of amatory desire, just as it craves a productive and protected rustic community. These desires remain unfulfilled as the power of amatory desire overwhelms all else. The variety of competing desires has also contributed to Tibullus' recent reputation as a 'dreamer'.[16] The multiplication of unfulfilled desires and the eventual domination of the master-desire (*amor*) are, indeed, characteristic of Tibullan elegy. In all cases, that which is desired remains unattained and absent.

The revelation of amatory desire behind the poet's valuation of *rura*, rejection of *militia*, interactions with his patron or choice of physical position and behaviour emphasizes the controlling and structuring command of *amor* over elegiac poetry. While Tibullus also makes more explicit statements of amatory slavery (*seruitium amoris*, such as 2.4.1), the poetics of revelation vividly dramatizes the invasive creep of desire as *amor* extends its power into areas of Roman elite behaviour (and discourse) where it might otherwise be expected to be absent. Although often represented in a more direct and explicit manner, such creep is a hallmark of Roman elegy, possibly since Gallus.[17]

It is not simply that the thwarted desire for the beloved's presence dominates all the elegist's choices. The poet's need for presence expands well beyond the amatory. The two books of Tibullan poetry are littered with appeals for presence and lamentations for its lack. The presence of the gods is invoked through the conventional language of ritual. In some cases, the underlying influence of *amor* is revealed at work here too (as, for example,

[16] The analogy of the dream has been proposed in Tibullan scholarship since the early twentieth century, not always as a negative assessment. It has recently been re-substantiated as a powerful critical tool by Miller's analysis of Tibullan elegy as 'dream-text': Miller (2004) 93–129, parts of which first made an appearance as Miller (1999).

[17] The exact relationship between *militia* and *amor* in Gallus' poetry remains obscure. But our surviving fragment may hint at a poet held back from participation in a military campaign by the power of *amor*. For this interpretation of lines 2–5 of the papyrus fragment of Gallus' elegies (*PQaṣr Ibrîm inu.* 78–3–11/1), see Courtney (1993) 264. For a similar conclusion on the basis of Virgil's depiction of Gallus in *Eclogue* 10, see Cairns (1979a) 226. But for the poet of the fragment as an active soldier longing for peace, see Merriam (1990) 448–9.

in the invocation of Isis to assist in the poet's safe return to his beloved at 1.3.27–32). But the need for divine presence to provide security, potency and prophetic/poetic inspiration is also apparent in the appeal to Natalis in poem 2.2, the role of agricultural deities in 2.1 or the power of Apollo in 2.5. Consistent with Roman religious discourse, divine presence is never taken for granted. It must be requested, fostered, celebrated in prospect, and its absence feared. In this it offers a close parallel to the desired presence of the beloved. Elegy's representation of its beloveds as godlike in other ways furthers this parallel: both the female beloveds of Tibullus (Delia and Nemesis) bear the names of gods or their cultic epithets.[18] In Tibullus, however, the parallel is more than another metaphor for the much-desired presence of the beloved. The inclusion of developed prayers in recognizably liturgical language, the representation and celebration of real religious events such as the Ambarualia (2.1) or the induction of Messallinus as one of the *quindecemuiri sacris faciundis* (2.5),[19] demonstrate that Roman religious discourse, and thus the Roman view of the powers that drive the universe, is already structured around the desire for presence. In the cases of both the elegiac *amor*-relationship and religious discourse, the desire issues from a subject position less powerful than the object of desire. The anomalous poet/lover, who seems in many ways to distinguish his desires and choices from the conventional paths of the Roman elite, appears representative of some very Roman and very conventional patterns of behaviour, expression and belief. *Amor*, which seems in many ways to be a force quite distinct or even oppositional to the dynamics and demands of conventional elite life, is exposed as operating according to some very recognizable rules. Tibullan elegy reveals that the anomaly is also the norm.

How amatory desire might reflect upon and expose the desires that drive Roman society more generally is suggested by another longed-for presence in Books 1 and 2: the presence of the poet's great friend (or 'patron') Marcus Valerius Messalla Corvinus. As with all other Roman poets, Tibullus never refers to Messalla as 'patron' or explicitly employs the language of *clientela* to describe their relationship.[20] The relationship is expressed through the poet's unfulfilled desire for the patron's presence. Poem 1.3 dramatizes this

[18] 'Nemesis' is the name of a goddess, while 'Delia' suggests Delos (site of Apollo's and Diana's birth) and the cult of Apollo Delius. Tibullus follows the practice of Gallus (Lycoris: Apollo Lycoreus) and Propertius (Cynthia: Apollo/Diana Cynthius/Cynthia). Lygdamus' Neaera is an exception, as is the male beloved of Tibullus book 1 (1.4, 1.8, 1.9), Marathus. On Marathus see Gibson (Chapter 13) in this volume.

[19] The *quindecemuiri sacris faciundis* were the group of priests primarily responsible for consultation and interpretation of the prophetic Sibylline books.

[20] See White (2005) 328–31 on Tibullus' relationship with Messalla, and White (1993) 27–34, on Augustan poets' avoidance of the language of patronage.

desire. The poet is immobilized due to illness as the patron sails off on campaign (1.3.1–4). Continued presence has almost been achieved – the poet has made the first stage of the journey, as far as Corfu – but it is finally elusive. The presence of the great man of aristocratic action is aligned with the norms of Roman elite behaviour. In 1.3 to be in the presence of Messalla is to be on *militia* and to participate in Roman dominance and governance of the empire. This alienation from the conventional patterns and expectations of elite male behaviour is signalled in the first Tibullan elegy by the statement which most clearly lays bare the poet/lover's underlying motivation for the rejection of *militia*:

O quantum est auri pereat potiusque smaragdi
    quam fleat ob nostras ulla puella uias!
te bellare decet terra, Messalla, marique
    ut domus hostiles praeferat exuuias:
me retinent uinctum formosae uincla puellae,
    et sedeo duras ianitor ante fores.

1.1.51–6

Oh may all gold and every emerald perish
    before any girl cry because of my departure!
It is right that you wage war on land and sea, Messalla,
    so your home may display spoils taken from the enemy:
The chains of a beautiful girl hold me bound,
    and I sit as doorman before her hard door.

In a manner typical of the *militia amoris* motif throughout Roman elegy, these lines emphasize both the difference and the similarity between Messalla and the beloved. Active pursuit of one precludes the pursuit of the other, however much the presence of both may be desired. Yet the poet is displayed outside the home of the beloved in the same way as Messalla, a *triumphator*, might display the trophies of his military triumphs. The poet is chained as the captives displayed in Messalla's triumph were chained. The apparent similarities of the two systems notwithstanding, the irony for the Tibullan poet is that whichever he chooses to pursue, presence is denied him. Even when he sets out on *militia*, in 1.3, Messalla finally sails away without him. As the second elegy's expansion on the *ante fores* of 1.1.56 demonstrates, the beloved's role is also to be absent, although perhaps enticingly close, just behind closed doors (1.2.5–6).

The linking of the beloved and the patron in this way finds clear expression in the poet's fantasy of Messalla's visit in which Delia is the dutiful, conventional wife on the poet's estate at 1.5.31–34. The reconciliation of the two potent but absent objects of desire can only find expression in an imagined future, just as elsewhere in the two Tibullan collections presence is retrojected into a more or less idealized past (the Age of Saturn, 1.3.35–48; early Rome, 2.5.19–66). The most famous Tibullan celebration of Messalla is itself a commemoration of past events.[21] Poem 1.7 asserts, in language that recalls the separation of poet and patron in 1.3 (line 1), the poet's presence with Messalla on past campaigns (1.7.9–12: *non sine me est tibi partus honos*, 'Not without me was your glory won'). In this complex poem, Messalla is also paralleled with divine presence through a 'hymn' and final invocation of the god Osiris (1.7.29–54). These lines focus at first on the past interaction between god and mortals, figured as the teaching of agricultural techniques. Rapidly, however, the teaching role is taken over by the fruits of agriculture, the liquor of wine. While the wine may offer some abiding divine presence in its metonymic incarnation of Bacchus (1.7.39, 41), Osiris remains a distant god. He is the god of potent and creative/generative gifts, but he is also the god of a distant land (Egypt). In the end, the presence of Osiris, as with other deities in the Tibullan collections, is desired and invoked (1.7.49–54). But as with the patron and the beloved, the presence of the deity lives only in desire or memory.

Amor and Rome

In an insightful article on 'what Tibullus does', David Wray draws attention to the distinction between 'making' and 'taking' (the poetic and the ctetic) in the poet/lover's ethical positions.[22] This distinction becomes active particularly in the most noted aspect of Tibullan poetry: the poet's adoption and promotion of a rural lifestyle, especially in the opening poems of each collection, and the opposition of that lifestyle to military service. The *rura*-versus-*militia* theme can be construed as a choice between the generative role of agriculture and the acquisitive drive of military conquest. The work of the farmer produces from the land (however small that produce may be), while the soldier takes from the defeated enemy (1.1.1–8).

As Wray states in comment on the opening lines of Tibullus 1.1, 'the speaker's hand possesses the quality of being *facilis* because it has turned

[21] Or at least it appears to be a commemoration of past events in most modern editions of the text. Knox, however, argues that, in 1.7, Messalla's triumph is still in the future (*portabit* should be read for *portabat* at 1.7.8): Knox (2005) 208–9. If this is correct, then the victory may be commemorated in the poem, but the triumph, like that of Messalinus in 2.5, can only be anticipated. The *Fasti Capitolini* record that Messalla's Aquitanian triumph was celebrated in September 27 BC (*CIL* I², p. 50): see Beard (2007) 297.

[22] Wray (2003) 231–2. Wray draws on the distinction between 'making' arts (ποιητική) and 'getting' arts (κτητική) made by Plato at *Soph.* 219a-c. 'What Tibullus Does' is the title of the first sub-section of Wray's article.

from 'getting' tawny (*fuluus*) gold through soldiery to the gentler art of 'making' golden (*flauus*) grain through farming'.[23] Agriculture as a 'making' art can be aligned with poetry itself.[24] The primary motivation behind Roman elegy, *amor*, can also be classed as a generative force, as Wray notes.[25] This, in fact, conforms well with the traditional Roman discourse of erotic desire, and even with the cultic persona of Venus Genetrix, mother of Amor, who combines agricultural fertility and sexual desire.[26]

The Tibullan poet would seem to make a clear choice: rejection of aggressive acquisition in favour of rural/poetic/amatory generation. While this position, expressed at the very opening of the two books, can be read as programmatic (a theme to be developed throughout the collections), it can also be read as a proposition to be tested in the poems that follow. There is the question of whether the poet will be able to follow the creative path he expresses as his ideal. Already in poem 1.1 there seems a potential clash between *rura* and *amor*: Delia's chains fix the poet in an urban setting in a manner which ironically echoes the spoils of war that he has rejected for himself (1.1.55–6). But, more significantly, there is the question of the nature of *amor* as generative force. Amor itself acts with aggressive acquisitiveness in its domination of lovers: it captures, possesses and immobilizes the free will of its captive (1.1.55–6; 1.2.91–2; 1.5.3–4; 2.3.81–4; 2.4.1–6). The poet attempts to present the god Amor as a farmer-deity, a product of the countryside, at 2.1.67–9 and 2.3.75–8. But even here the conquering drive of the god comes to the fore and is lamented from the poet/lover's point-of-view (2.1.70–74).

The similarities to imperial acquisition are clearest in the violence which *amor* generates. This goes beyond violence done upon the body and mind of the poet/lover himself. Tibullus magnifies the violence captured in the cliché of the cruel archer god, Amor/Cupid, by exploiting and extending the violence associated with lovers' battles in Hellenistic poetry and on the comic stage. In 1.10 such violence (*Veneris bella*, 1.10.53) erupts into the agricultural world (1.10.51–66). The disruptive force of *amor* is all the more emphatic as it is set within a long passage extolling and desiring *Pax* (peace). *Pax* in this case is represented as the catalyst of rural

[23] Wray (2003) 233.

[24] 'Farming is a "poetic" art, productive of the artifacts that are crops': Wray (2003) 233. See also Tzounakas (2006), who argues that *rura* in 1.1 asserts a particular *ars poetica*: 'Tibullus reveals his intention to lend "rural" characteristics to his own poetic composition': Tzounakas (2006) 115.

[25] Amor is an 'artisan': Wray (2003) 241–2.

[26] This is the divine persona of Venus expressed by Lucretius in the proem to *De rerum natura* (1.1–43). For the interplay of fertility/birth, the natural world, *uoluptas*, poetic inspiration and 'national goddess' in Lucretius' invocation, see Gale (1994) 208–23.

production and the suppressor of military violence and acquisition: *pace bidens uomerque nitent, at tristia duri / militis in tenebris occupat arma situs* (1.10.49–50, 'In peace the hoe and plough shine, while rust seizes / the hard soldier's grim weapons in the dark'). The poet finally steps back from the full force of amatory violence (64–6), but his desire for violent domination of the beloved is still vividly clear (1.10.59–66).

Such physical subjugation seems at odds with the concluding appeal to *Pax* as an ideal of generative potency (1.10.67–8). Amor does not simply act upon the lover as a violent, conquering soldier acts upon a slave; it promotes a desire in the lover to act in a similarly dominating manner upon the object of desire. The general impotence of the elegiac lover may prevent him from realizing the fantasy of violent control, but it remains clear in the closing passage of Book 1 that the effects of *amor* are more than purely generative.

Book 2 develops a more detailed picture of the aggressive and acquisitive mode of Amor. The collection also sketches a history of the apparently uneasy relationship between *amor* and *rura* with implications for Amor's blend of making and taking. Poem 2.1 describes Cupid as born *inter agros* but having changed the object of his hunt (2.1.71). The 'now and then' contrast of Amor's behaviour reflects the desire for a lost past expressed elsewhere in the poem and collection. More specifically, the actions of present-day Amor are described in terms of taking and enslaving: *hic iuueni detraxit opes, hic dicere iussit / limen ad iratae uerba pudenda senem* (2.1.73–4, 'He rips wealth from the young; he orders the old to speak shameful words at an angry woman's door'). This is consistent with the description of the poet himself as spoils before the door of Delia in 1.1.55–6. It also explicitly extends the conquests of Amor to language (*uerba*). The making of poetry, which *amor* generates, is also a taking of the lover, as surely as the soldier (*alius*) of 1.1.1–6 takes land and booty from the enemy.

The paradigm of the rich rival, which Tibullus also adapts from Hellenistic poetry, dramatizes the clash between taking and making (acquisition and generation) in the elegies. When a rival first appears at 1.2.65 he is called *ferreus* (made of iron) like the inventor of the sword (*ferrum*) which is the primary tool for violent acquisition at 1.10.1–4. The rival of 1.2, in a reversal of the poet's aspirations, chooses *militia* over *amor* and Delia. But it is clear that this soldier, whose career promises to bring him great wealth, might have had Delia for the taking (1.2.67). In what remains a cliché of the elegiac genre, the representative of violent acquisition holds the upper hand in the field of *amor*. In 1.5 the avarice of the beloved is encouraged and facilitated by a bawd (*lena*), another stock figure of elegy. The *lena callida* ('cunning bawd') is a *saga rapax* ('rapacious witch', 1.5.48 and 59). In contrast, the poet describes himself as able to offer only service: religious, menial and verbal (the *uota* of 1.5.10 and 16). His devotion is certainly productive. It generates the fantasies of presence (the dreams, such as at 1.5.19). It generates the elegies as a whole. But such generative potency gains no purchase in the realm of *amor*, as the poet complains: *heu, canimus frustra, nec uerbis uicta patescit / ianua, sed plena est percutienda manu* (1.5.67–8, 'Alas, I sing in vain! The door does not lie open, conquered / by my words, but must be knocked on by a hand full of cash'; see also 1.5.35–6).

Amor's integration of artistic generation and harsh, enslaving acquisition is captured in the poet's lament at 2.5.105–12. Cupid brings art (*ars*) and weaponry (*tela*) together, rendering art itself both good and bad (2.5.107–8). The lover's resulting pleasure in pain echoes Amor's combination of forces which might otherwise be thought opposites: *et faueo morbo, cum iuuat ipse dolor* (2.5.110, 'I cosset the sickness – the pain pleases me'). *Amor/eros* is traditionally fertile ground for the exploration of co-existing opposites.[27] Tibullus exploits these themes, but also aligns *amor*'s collapsing of the taking/making dichotomy with traditional Roman aristocratic roles and means to power.

Messalla, as he is presented in the collections, also integrates violent acquisition and production. In this case it is an integration representative of conventional elite Roman success. Messalla is the *triumphator* and successful warrior in 1.1, 1.3, 1.7, 2.1, just as it is prophesied his son, Messalinus, will one day be at 2.5. But the role of acquisitive warrior is combined with a productive cultural role. In 1.7 Messalla is first aligned with the divine culture hero, Osiris, before his achievement as a road builder is praised (1.7.55–62). It is an achievement that will, in turn, generate song from the world of agricultural production (*te canat agricola*, 61, 'May the farmer sing of you'), just as the patron will inspire the Tibullan poet's song at 2.1.35–6. But this act of making is not separate from the work of Messalla the conquering general. The *opes* from which the road is made (59) must come, in part at least, from the conquests detailed in the opening lines of 1.7. Messalla's actions stand within a Roman tradition of linked taking and making, conquest and building. In 2.5, Messalinus, Apollo and Messalla himself combine triumphal, religious and prophetic roles in the poet's celebration of a traditional aristocratic responsibility (*quindecemuir sacris faciundis*). The shared language of prophecy and poetic song (*cantet . . . canit . . . canat . . .*) emphasises the creative potency of Messalinus' role. Although Messalinus is represented as an interpreter of song rather than a creator himself,[28] Tibullus

[27] The most famous example is Catullus 85: *odi et amo*.

[28] For Messalinus as a 'reader' in 2.5, see Lee-Stecum (2000) 200–11.

closely integrates the creation of understanding with productive generation and acquisitive action through the examples of Sibylline prophecy he details from line 19. Aeneas must understand the Sibyl's prophetic song in order to take, through victory (45), the land and resources upon which Rome will be based. The nexus of song, interpretation, and violent acquisition upon which Rome is founded is repeated (or sustained) in the ritual role of Messalinus.

The choice of making instead of taking is represented as a desirable one for the poet. Creative and nurturing forces are associated with the choice in opposition to the acquisitive imperatives of Roman military conquest. But as with the apparent dichotomy of *pietas* and *furor* in the epic of Tibullus' contemporary, Virgil, the desired distinction collapses.[29] In Tibullus' elegies this collapse is first and foremost an effect of *amor*, inescapable and dominating. But production and acquisition are equally inextricable in the conventional Roman world the elegist seems to eschew. Just as the initial separation of rustic work from military service in 1.1 belies the traditional Roman ideological identification of the two, the dominant representative of elite Roman success in the collections, Marcus Valerius Messalla Corvinus, integrates production and violent, acquisitive conquest, not least through his support for and inspiration of Tibullus himself. It is not simply that the poet's desired pursuit of generative rustic and poetic endeavours exclusive of the violent, fearful forces of acquisitive imperialism is unrealistic, even in the context of his own elegiac collections. The collapse of desired difference also demonstrates the close alignment of elegiac *amor* and Roman male elite ideology and practice.

Conclusion

Tibullan *amor* is paradigmatic and all-encompassing. It dissolves distinctions into one another. It renders the poet's clean ethical choices unsustainable and distances him from his desires. The poet responds with a range of strategies that attempt to render the objects of his desire present: persuasive words, memory, appeals to divine power and prophecy. The success of these strategies is at best provisional and uncertain. In this sense, Tibullan poetry typifies Roman elegy's stance of profound alienation. Yet the revelation of the Tibullan collections is that this alienation is not a product of an anomalous state, but a result of conditions shared by the conventional world of elite Roman affairs. The poet has the opportunity, and the burden of expectation, to participate in conventional elite activities, but the alternative

[29] For a strong interpretation of this collapse as 'the triumph, if of *pietas*, of *pietas* redefined as *furor*', see Boyle (1986) 83–132 (quotation from 132).

path he seems to choose is revealed as no alternative at all, and not just because the poet must commence *militia* (in 1.3) or celebrate the *res gestae* of his patron (in 1.7 and 2.5). Rome, like *amor*, is paradigmatic and all-encompassing in the two books of Tibullan elegy.

It has often been emphasized that, unlike the works of Propertius and Ovid, Augustus is absent from Tibullus' text. The absence of the most dominant figure in the Roman world during the period of the collections' publication (roughly 26–19/18 BC) seems odd to modern readers familiar with Propertius, Ovid, Horace and Virgil.[30] Cultural elements closely associated with Augustus at the time (such as traditional festive religion, the *quindecemuiri* and prophecy, or even Aeneas in 2.5) are represented in connection with Messalla or Messalinus. This could be interpreted as a (re-)appropriation of the fields of Augustan *auctoritas*, but might more plausibly be understood as reflecting an Augustan allegiance.[31] Alternatively, Tibullus might simply represent the product of a different 'circle' of patronage, without direct connection to the Imperial family.[32] Books 1 and 2, and perhaps other elements of the *Corpus Tibullianum*, might be almost the lone survivors of a more voluminous poetic output which focused its concerns on different aristocratic patrons with very little, if any, direct reference to the *princeps*. However this might have been read by Augustus himself, the socio-political vision of Books 1 and 2, while addressing much that might seem consistent with Augustan ideology in the period, is broader than a single man or regime. The alienation, confusion of categories and lack of longed-for presence are consequences of forces, structures and demands that refuse to be identified with a single individual. Messalla operates successfully within this system (just as the poet/lover operates unsuccessfully), but neither of them are the system, any more than the (absent) Augustus is. By avoiding the iconic Augustan presence, Tibullus avoids the danger of this simplification.

Different fields of activity and different discourses (military, rural, religious, prophetic, erotic, poetic) bleed into each other and merge in a manner

30 For a concise and useful account of the complex relationship of Tibullan poetry and Augustus, see Maltby (2002) 53–5. Roman elegy's direct engagement with Caesar (possibly Julius rather than Octavian) seems to have begun with Gallus: *PQaṣr Ibrîm inu.* 78-3-11/1, line 2–3.

31 Maltby (2002) 53–4, who also draws attention to some themes that do not fit so comfortably with the apparent Augustan programme. As Maltby puts it, 'the question of political Augustanism in T.'s elegies is a complex one'.

32 Indifference rather than hostility has been the more common interpretation of the poet's attitude to Augustus: see Davies (1973), Little (1982), Cancelli (1986); and White (2005) 331.

that has been viewed as 'dream-like'. This is elegiac *amor* and it is Rome. The insight Tibullus takes from Catullus and Gallus and builds into a genre-defining dynamic is that discussion of *amor* can be a discussion of Rome and an examination of desire can be an examination of being Roman.[33] It is this dynamic that finally becomes blatantly explicit in the later work of Propertius (Book 4) and the elegies of Ovid (*Fasti*, *Tristia*, *Epistulae ex Ponto*) that followed it. Rather than an opposite, or even adversary, of the traditional demands of Roman aristocratic *uirtus*, elegiac *amor* mirrors those demands and their effects on the individual. Tibullus may not have been the first to see or to represent this, but after the publication of his work the genre could be no other way.

Further reading

The best and most accessible commentaries in English on Tibullus Books 1 and 2 are by Maltby (2002) and Murgatroyd (1980 and 1994). A dedicated commentary on Lygdamus, including a full survey of the range of opinions on the *quaestio Lygdamea*, is provided by Antolín, (1996). The best English translation remains that of Lee, (1990), which includes the entire *Appendix Tibulliana* with facing Latin text for all poems and a brief commentary; see also Juster's recent translation with notes by Maltby (2012), as well as that of Dennis and Putnam (2012), including poems from the *Appendix Tibulliana*. A thorough examination of the textual structure of Tibullus Books 1 and 2 is undertaken by Ball (1983).

For an elegant exposition of the 'dreamy' Tibullus see Elder (1962), 65–105. Cairns (1979a) remains an important starting point for study of Tibullus' poetry, and Bright (1978) is a readable, entertaining and still influential examination of Tibullan themes and persona. These two works, along with major works by Wimmel (1976 and 1983), were instrumental in stimulating a reassessment of Tibullan elegy in the 1980s and 1990s. Important

[33] Scholars have differed on how conscious Tibullus was of his work's engagement with the circumstances of Rome in his day and the demands of being (an elite, male) Roman at the time. Cairns' great work on Tibullus concludes: 'An implied reason why Tibullus is the greatest of Roman elegists may well be that he was in the fullest sense a man of his age, who understood and in his own literary persona portrayed its dilemma': Cairns (1979a) 230. Miller's sophisticated analysis of the Tibullan dream-text argues that the elegies 'manifest what Jameson would term the Augustan 'political unconscious', and concludes: 'Tibullus' poetry, thus, in its very plurivocity, in its insistent, repetitive articulation of a desire for the conjunction of the Imaginary and Symbolic registers of existence, stands as eloquent testimony of the early principate's status as a moment of ideological crisis': Miller (2004) 129.

contributions to this reassessment include Dettmer (1980), 68–82; Leach (1980); Gaisser (1983); Boyd (1984) Mutschler (1985) and Lee-Stecum (1998).

Those interested in more recent interpretations of Tibullan poetry can do no better than reading P.A. Miller (1999) and Wray (2003) in tandem. Miller (2004) incorporates a revision of his earlier article and situates Tibullus within an overall analysis of the elegiac genre.

5

MATHILDE SKOIE

'The woman'

... So, praise the gods, at last he's away!
And let me tend you this advice my dear:
Take any lover that you will, or may,
Except a poet. All of them are queer.

It's just the same – quarrel or a kiss
Is but a tune to play on his pipe.
He's always hymning that or wailing this;
Myself, I much prefer the business type.

That thing he wrote, the time the sparrow died -
(Oh, most unpleasant – gloomy, tedious words!)
I called it sweet, and made believe I cried;
The stupid fool! I've always hated birds...

Dorothy Parker (1893–1967)
'From a letter from Lesbia'

Though one can argue that Roman elegy is among so many other things playing with gender, the active players are almost exclusively male.[1] Cynthia, Delia and Corinna are objects of male desire and male poetry. Although these elegiac *puellae* can be both *dominae* and *doctae*, they are 'but a tune to play' on the poet's pipe. They are metaphors and muses, but mainly mute.[2]

I would like to thank Marianne Ophaug Wehus and Thea S. Thorsen for valuable input.

[1] Wyke (2002) 3 states: 'The gender play of Augustan elegy is now well established.' Yet, just how this gender play works – whether it is a kind of 'counter cultural feminism' as argued in Hallett (1973) or whether this is part of a rhetorical strategy for obtaining control within a lover's discourse as Kennedy (1993) and Greene (1998) would argue – is still much debated. Batstone (2000) argues that elegy is an 'obstinately male genre'. Wyke (2002) 155–191 gives a good overview of the debate so far as well as arguing for a performative function of elegiac gender play, i.e. elegy is itself a 'a technology of gender', a perspective which is in harmony with Spentzou's emphasis on the possibility of an interceptive reading of elegy at the point of reception: Spentzou (2003). For more recent views on gender and Latin love poetry, see Ancona and Greene (2005).

[2] When Cynthia finally speaks, she is either half-asleep (Prop. 1.3) or a ghost (Prop. 4.7), and the matron Cornelia is speaking from the grave (Prop. 4.11). Ovid can offer advice

There is an exception to this rule: the voice of Sulpicia. In this essay I shall look at how Sulpicia fits into what one might call the grammar of elegy. Is she an elegiac *ego* or elegiac *puella*, or does she make a 'room of her own'? Looked at from this perspective I shall argue that a reading of the poems written about and in the name of Sulpicia might shed important light on the world of elegy itself. The poems challenge our expectations as readers both in the way they conform to and differ from the elegiac rules. A closer reading of these poems may therefore end up expanding our views of elegy.

The corpus

The eleven poems concerning Sulpicia are located in book three of the *Corpus Tibullianum* (3.8–18) and were until the nineteenth century read as by Tibullus.[3] Of these, three are written in the third person about Sulpicia (3.8, 3.10 and 3.12) while eight are written from the first person perspective of Sulpicia herself (3.9, 3.11 and 3.13–18). While the first eight poems are between twenty and twenty-six verses, the latter six are much shorter – between six and ten verses each. This has given rise to different theories of authorship once Tibullan authorship of the entire corpus was ruled out.[4]

The most widely held hypothesis is that these poems make up two different groups. The short first-person poems, 3.13–18, are attributed to a real Augustan Sulpicia, *Serui filia* ('daughter of Servius'), as she presents herself in poem 3.16.4.[5] This Servius might be the son of Cicero's friend Servius Sulpicius, and Messalla, who is addressed in another poem (3.14), might be her maternal uncle and even guardian.[6] This places Sulpicia in one of the major literary circles of Augustan Rome and gives us a possible date for

to Perilla as a poet (*Tr.* 3.7), but we do not have her writing – thus even she remains a 'written' rather than a writing woman. On the other hand Ovid's letter-writing heroines, the *Heroides*, are all in one way or another mythical with the exception of the final heroine Sappho, whose Heroidean letter is disputed with regard to authenticity; see Thorsen forthcoming and in this volume (Chapter 7).

3 The *Corpus Tibullianum* is sometimes divided into three and sometimes four books. In this article I follow the three-book division which may be converted into the four-book division by subtracting six, e.g. 3.13 = 4.7.

4 Doubt was raised already in the eighteenth century, e.g. in Heyne (1755), but serious alternative theories originated with Gruppe (1838).

5 This is a slightly revised version of the theory raised by Gruppe (1838). It is elegantly made fun of in Parker (2006).

6 Lyne (2007) 344–5 gives a good overview of the prosopographic evidence. For Servius Sulpicius, see also Syme (1986) 206. Messalla might be her guardian if Sulpicia's mother never remarried; cf. the fact that Servius Sulpicius dies in 43 BC and the use of *propinque* (kinsman) in 3.14.6. In Hallett (2009b) Sulpicia is read within this fatherless context. Scaliger (1577) ad loc. suggests a different role for Messalla, namely that he was in love with Sulpicia himself; see Skoie (2002) 85–7.

the poems in the twenties BC.[7] The longer poems, 3.8–12, are within this paradigm regarded as by someone else. These poems are often called the 'garland of Sulpicia' or 'Sulpicia cycle' and ascribed to an *amicus Sulpiciae* or *auctor de Sulpicia*.[8] The idea is that these might be written by a poet who has taken Sulpicia's invitation in poem 3.13 – that someone might tell her joys (*mea gaudia narret*, 5) – seriously.[9] This fits nicely with a reading of the third book of the *corpus Tibullianum* as a kind of *Hauspoetenbuch*, a collection of poems written by different members of Messalla's literary circle who all knew each other and met in what one might call his literary salon.[10] This hypothesis is substantiated by the way several of the long poems elaborate on issues from the shorter ones as well as the idea of a poetic circle responding to Sulpicia.[11]

Though this twofold division of authorship between a real Sulpicia and another member of Messalla's circle is the basis of most editions of the text, there are other hypotheses. On the one hand some scholars have claimed that all the first-person poems or even all the poems are by Sulpicia,[12] while others on the contrary have argued that they are all by a male poet, either written as a kind of party-game or as a later fake.[13] A recent rediscovery of the elegiac epigraph of a Greek slave called Petale who identifies herself as perhaps 'Sulpicia the *lectrix*' ('woman who reads aloud') or 'Sulpicia's *lectrix*' ('the woman who reads aloud for Sulpicia') dated to the late twenties BC has given new, if inconclusive, impetus to the debate.[14]

Whether we are dealing with a real or imaginary woman's voice has influenced the interpretation and status of the poems throughout the history of their reception.[15] The poems have been treated either as windows onto the mind and love of a real Roman *puella* or poetic mimesis of the female

[7] For an analysis of the social context for the publication of Sulpicia's poetry, see Hemelrijk (1999).

[8] Some have also attributed them to a young Ovid: Radford (1923) attributes the entire third book of the *corpus Tibullianum* to him, while Breguet (1946) attributes only the *amicus*-poems to him. More recently, Bernays (2004) has supported the latter.

[9] Hinds (1987a) 46. [10] Norden (1954) 71.

[11] Most notably Sulpicia's illness, 3.17, is commented upon by the *amicus*-poet in 3.10. The third-person poet even answers Sulpicia's concern that Cerinthus (for this character, see below) might not care (1–2) by narrating how Cerinthus is praying for her recovery.

[12] Parker (1994) and Stevenson (2005) argue that all the first-person poems might be by Sulpicia, whereas Hallett (2002b) argues that all the poems are by Sulpicia.

[13] Holzberg (1999) argues that they are all post-Ovidian. Hubbard (2004/5) presents them as party pieces – perhaps a gift for the wedding of Sulpicia and Cerinthus – based e.g. on the many birthdays and the mentioning of a marriage in 2.2.

[14] *AE* (1928).73. Text and translation is given in Stevenson (2005). For discussion, see also Hallett (2009b).

[15] For an analysis of the impact of the gendering of the author on the interpretation of the poems, see Skoie (2002).

voice. In the first case they are important historical documents or examples of a feminine discourse without literary merit, in the second, they are poetic creations within the elegiac game. Despite the impact the idea of the author and her gender has on interpretation and the fact that the urge to have a real female voice is strong, I shall for the moment leave the issue of authorship and authenticity, and focus instead on the textual female voice, the *poetria amatrix* or *persona* Sulpicia. I will, however, return to the issue of authorship towards the end.

Kiss and tell

The most read of the first-person poems is poem 3.13, where Sulpicia rejoices over the love she is finally experiencing:

> Tandem uenit amor, qualem texisse pudore
>   Quam nudasse alicui sit mihi fama magis.
> Exorata meis illum Cytherea Camenis
>   Adtulit in nostrum deposuitque sinum.
> Exsoluit promissa Venus: mea gaudia narret,
>   Dicetur siquis non habuisse sua.
> Non ego signatis quicquam mandare tabellis,
>   Ne legat id nemo quam meus ante, uelim,
> Sed peccasse iuvat, uultus conponere famae
>   Taedet: cum digno digna fuisse ferar.

> At last a love has come of a sort that the rumour that I had hidden because of shame would be greater than the rumour of having revealed it to someone. Won over by my muses, Cytherea brought him and placed him in my embrace. Venus fulfilled her promises. Let my joys be told by all of those of whom it can be said that they do not have their own. I would not wish to trust anything to sealed tablets in order that no one might read them before my lover. On the contrary, it gives me pleasure to sin, I am sick of keeping up appearances; may I be said as a worthy woman to have been together with a worthy man.[16]

[16] The text used is that of Luck (1998). All translations are my own, but heavily informed by other translations, particularly that of the LCL (1995). The translations have no poetic pretensions. All the short poems are notoriously difficult to translate. Holzberg (1999) 174 describes the syntax of the poems as 'at times not immediately fathomable'. Lord Byron typically had a go at an imitation of 3.17, the easiest of them. Ezra Pound might be on to something when he observed that 'it would be worth ten years of a man's life to translate Catullus, Ovid or perhaps Sulpicia' in his article 'Horace' originally published in *The Criterion* 9 (1929–30); see Santirocco (1979) 231, Roessel (1990b) and Maxwell (2002). An interesting modern reworking of poem 3.13 is 'Sulpicia's Playlist' by Simon Armitage where the modern poet gives a popular song-title expressing the sense of almost every verse in the poem.

In this poem Sulpicia presents herself as the ardent lover and gives a framework for the reading of all the other poems, a sexual relationship with a man blessed by the goddess Venus. Though some commentators would like this to be no more than a kiss, *esse cum* is a common euphemism for sexual intercourse, cf. Varro *Ling.* 6.80. Furthermore *peccare* (to sin) has connotations of extramarital sex.[17] This worthy man is usually read as Cerinthus, who is the beloved of most of the other poems. The name is most likely a pseudonym in analogy with Cynthia, Delia and Corinna with equally rich connotations. *Cerinthum* (from the Greek κήρινθος) means bee-bread and thus has a connection both with honey and wax, love and literature.[18] Because of metrical equivalence and placement in the *Corpus Tibullianum*, many have read him as the Cornutus who is mentioned in Tibullus' poem 2.2.[19] In that case one might even argue that the couple got married – an attractive option for many a commentator.[20]

In the following short first-person poems as well as the longer first- and third-person poems we encounter different aspects of this love, including standard *topoi* such as the prospect of separation (3.9, 3.14 and 3.15), illness (3.9 and 3.17), birthdays (3.14, 3.11 and 3.12) and unfaithfulness (3.16). In poems 3.14 and 15 we also find that the poems themselves have a performative function. The first poem is a plea to Messalla for her birthday to be celebrated in town and not in the country where there is no Cerinthus, while the second is a happy message telling the reader that the trip is cancelled. As in Propertius 1.8A and B the poetry plays a part in the elegiac narrative. In these respects Sulpicia resembles the other elegiac poet-lovers. And as in the other elegiac *corpora*, the poems have lent themselves to further narrativization. Several scholars and translators have produced highly varied Romantic narratives in which the poems are regarded as fragments of a story.[21]

On the other hand, to return to poem 3.13, Sulpicia shows an unusual awareness of an aspect of poetry that does not seem to play any important

[17] *OLD* 3: 'To commit a moral offence, b. (of offences against the sexual code)'. Cf. e.g. Hor. *Sat.* 1.2.63. Interestingly *OLD* 1b: 'to make a slip in speaking' might also give this a programmatic touch in tune with the idea that this is a publication poem, see below.

[18] Roessel (1990a).

[19] Most recently Holzberg (1999) 184, Hubbard (2004/5) 183–4 and Stevenson (2005) 37, *contra* Roessell (1990a) 244 and Santirocco (1979) 236–7. The argument for Cornutus = Cerinthus is based on metrical equivalence as well as play on *cornus*/κέρας (despite the quantitative difference between the short e of κέρας and the long of κήρινθος). Furthermore, the sequence of consonants is the same: *crnts*.

[20] E.g. Smith (1913), Gruppe (1838), Dissen (1835).

[21] Closest to hand, perhaps, Smith (1913) and Creekmore (1966). The latter arranges the Sulpician poems into a sequence called 'No harm to lovers'. For an analysis of other sample narratives, see Skoie (2008).

part in the rest of the elegiac corpus, a concern with publishing.[22] In his commentary, Oliver Lyne goes so far as to call poem 3.13 a 'publication poem'.[23] In this poem Sulpicia is not only publishing her love, she is making a feature of the actual publication, or telling, of it.[24] Yet the actual publication is far from straightforward. While the statements might be called 'bravado', the way they are told is not quite as brave. The poem is notoriously difficult to translate precisely because she does not tell the story in a straightforward manner, but in a convoluted way using passive, subjunctive and hypotaxis.[25] Hence she does not say explicitly that she herself would rather tell it than hide it, but wraps this statement up in a passive construction (*sit mihi fama*, 2); likewise she does not say that she has been with a man worthy of her, rather she urges herself to 'be said' (*ferar*, 10) to have been with such a man. Thus there is a double process of telling and not telling. Likewise, she uses the metaphor of undressing (*nudasse*, 2) and what has been called a 'rhetoric of disclosure' while she at the same time verbally veils herself behind passive constructions.[26] A similar move is made in poem 3.18 where Sulpicia regrets having hidden her passion, but at the same time hides this same passion in what one scholar has called a 'bewildering web of multiple hypotaxis' at the very end of the poem.[27]

Just another Roman poet?[28]

The convoluted expressions and 'reluctant telling' are found mostly in the shorter poems (3.13–18). Together with the lack of any extensive mythological imagery this syntax has been used to argue that the shorter poems were written by an amateurish slip of a girl while the longer poems with their allusions, mythological imagery and more standard syntax were written by a professional male poet. Accordingly, for a long time the shorter poems received precious little by way of *literary* scrutiny. Rather they were regarded as social documents which happened to be written in verse.[29]

[22] Admittedly Propertius makes a feature of the publication of Cynthia, both when generally he plays on Cynthia as signifying both poetry collection and woman, and more specifically when he regrets having made Cynthia renowned in his verse (3.23). Yet there seems to be no concern about publishing his own feelings.

[23] Lyne (2006). [24] A similar move is seen in Emily Dickinson's 'The letter'.

[25] On Sulpicia's syntax, see Lowe (1988). [26] See Flaschenriem (1999).

[27] Lowe (1988) 198. He also gives a very succinct grammatical analysis of this web.

[28] This heading is modeled on the title of Merriam (2006): 'Sulpicia: Just Another Roman Poet'.

[29] The feminist scholar Pomeroy (1975) 173 is a neat example: 'she was not a brilliant artist; her work is of interest only because the author is female'. Tränkle (1990) 300 still takes as a premise for his reading that the poems were not meant for publication at all and that they have no poetic pretensions.

However, since Matthew Santirocco's significant reconsideration of their poetic qualities pointing out e.g. how the birthday poems 3.14 and 15 should not just be seen as occasional poetry or documents of an affair, but in the framework of *genethliaca* (the special birthday poem-genre), like Tib. 1.7 and 3.2.[30] Likewise the illness in 3.17 can be read within an elegiac context:

> Estne tibi, Cerinthe, tuae pia cura puellae,
> Quod mea nunc uexat corpora fessa calor?
> A ego non aliter tristes euincere morbos
> Optarim, quam te si quoque uelle putem.
> At mihi quid prosit morbos euincere, si tu
> Nostra potes lento pectore ferre mala?

> Have you, Cerinthus, any devoted concern for your girl, that now a fever torments my body? Ah, I would not wish to triumph over the gloomy illness unless I thought that you wanted it too. But what would it profit me to triumph over my illnesses, if you can bear my sufferings with an indifferent heart?

This is not simply a poem by which to diagnose Sulpicia[31] but a poem asking for proof of the beloved's feelings. In the *Ars* (2.315–36) Ovid recommends that the lover grab any opportunity to display his piety (*pietas*, 2.315); compare Sulpicia's *pia cura* ('true concern', 1).[32] Both Tibullus (1.5.9–18) and Propertius (2.9.25–8) describe similar situations. Further, as Santirocco points out, 'the sustained medical imagery on which the lines turn is standard in Latin love poetry, the calculated ambiguity between real fever and the heat of passion, between real disease and the illness that is love'.[33] Despite the fact that some of the terminology used is of a more technical nature, the reader is reminded of Catullus 76, where the disease is his love.[34] The use of *lentus* in verse 6 also links to amatory discourse, e.g. Prop. 1.6.12 where the lover exclaims that the man who can be indifferent (*lentus*) in love should perish.[35]

30 Santirocco (1979). Specifically on *genethliaca*, see 231–2 and Davies (1973) 33–5.

31 Creekmore (1966) 146 comments: 'The fever is apparently malarial.' This point was first made in Santirocco (1979) 233.

32 *Contra* Yardley (1990) thinks this is simply a poem about Sulpicia being ill and using the language of *amicitia*. In his reading the reference to *pietas* is linked primarily to this.

33 Santirocco (1979) 233.

34 E.g. *calor* and *euincere morbos*, see Lyne (2007) 363. *morbus* is, however, found in Catull. 66.25; see Hallett (2002a).

35 Also used in Prop. 3.23.12 in a similar context, that is, a context where the lover is asking for confirmation of the beloved's love and Ov. *Her.*1.1. On *lentus* and elegiac discourse, Knox (1995) *Her.*1.1: '*Lento*: not simply "slow" but "tarrying". The adjective forms a standard component in the elegists' arsenal of reproachful epithets for the less amorous partner in a love affair.'

Santirocco also pointed out various framing devices and read Sulpicia's syntax as part of a rhetorical strategy. This development led to a wave of more literary approaches to Sulpicia and her poetics. Poem 3.13 with its concern with publication might then be read not only as a poem about love and the publication of love, but as a metapoetic statement about the conditions for a female love poet. In many ways this may precisely be an attempt to answer the question, 'how would a female poet-lover speak?' within the elegiac world. The answer would then be, with difficulty, and within the space created between telling and not-telling. This would be a textual strategy rather than happening by accident or through lack of poetic training. Accordingly, Nick Lowe concludes that 'the syntactic mannerisms that have been blamed on amateurism and gender' are 'essential instruments of expression for an agile and distinctive poetic imagination'.[36] I would go still further and claim that these so-called mannerisms make up a particular poetics.

A reading of the poems as literature has opened up for exploration further intertextual possibilities, as well as expanding the context for reading Sulpicia's poems from the more restricted reality of Roman women to the world of literature. While scholars and commentators had found an abundance of poetic allusions in the longer poems,[37] scholars have only recently read Sulpicia in the light of Catullus,[38] Sappho,[39] Homer,[40] Horace,[41] Ovid,[42] Propertius[43] and Virgil.[44] Judith Hallett has used what she regards as a continuity of intertexts between the longer and shorter poems to argue for a single author.[45] Use of heroic material in an elegiac context might put the shorter Sulpician poems on a par with the other elegists and their use of epic. However, the particular relevant passage or context might not.[46] A case in point is the possible allusion to Virgil's Dido.

36 Lowe (1988) 205. 37 In particular to Ovid, see note 8 above.

38 Santirocco (1979), Lowe (1988), Hallett (2002a). Hallett also argues for family-connections between Catullus and Sulpicia as she suggests a relationship between the Valerii Catulli and the Valerii Messallae.

39 Merriam (2006) 12 argues for Sapphic influence regarding her use of Venus in 3.13.

40 Merriam (2006) 12–13, *Il.* 3.380–2 and 5.311–15 (Aphrodite rescuing Paris and Aeneas respectively).

41 In particular on the use of the name Cerinthus in *Sat.* 1.2.81, see Hallett (2009a) 148–9.

42 This has long been the case for the longer poems, see note above, but more recently also seen as relevant for the shorter ones, e.g. 3.16 and *Ars* 2.315 and *Am.* 2.16.47.

43 Especially Prop. 3.23, see Flaschenriem (1999) 41–2. It is, however, surprising that not more has been done in relation to Propertius given that the first word uttered by Cynthia in 1.3.35 is *tandem*, the first word in poem 3.13.

44 Keith (1997) especially *Aeneid* 4, see below.

45 Hallett (2009b). 46 Merriam (2006).

Along with concern with publication a striking feature of poem 3.13 is Sulpicia's concern about her *fama*, in the sense of slander or bad reputation. This term is used twice within the ten lines of poem 3.13 and thus works as a kind of frame.[47] When *fama* is used in relation to the poet-lover in the elegiac corpora of Propertius or Ovid, it is mostly in the context of programmatic statements about their own coming literary fame (positive).[48] *Fama* in the Sulpician sense is mostly used in relation to the elegiac *puellae* and invoked as a concern or threat that they might lose their reputations, e.g. Prop. 2.5.29 or 2.32.21. The latter makes it very explicit that it is the reputation of the *puella* and not the poet's: *sed de me minus est: famae iactura pudicae/ tanta tibi miserae, quanta meretur, erit* ('But this is less a question about me: for poor you, the reputation will be jeopardized to the extent that you deserve'). In this respect then the Sulpicia of 3.13 is different from the other poet-lovers and more like the elegiac *puellae*. However, another literary model may be at work. The most elaborate concern for one's *fama*, and that from an ardent female lover, is Dido in *Aeneid* 4.50.[49] Particularly pertinent perhaps since *fama* is not only a key concept in book 4, but also appears linked to another important term in 3.13.1, namely *pudor* ('chastity').[50] Accordingly Dido's concern about her *fama* in *Aeneid* 4 has been read as an important context for Sulpicia's moulding of her own sexual role.[51] In this way a literary reading of Sulpicia has not simply opened up for investigations of Sulpicia's poetics, but also, for her role as a lover, as we shall see below.

Elegiac *ego* or *puella*?

Sulpicia's position between telling and being told positions her somewhere between subject and object in the literary world. So too, Sulpicia's concern about her *fama* in poem 3.13 may place her amongst the elegiac *puellae* while the model of Dido offers her a place among the active lovers. However, Sulpicia does not only place herself in a literary world. In poem 3.16 she

47 Hallett (2006) 38.

48 A prime example might be Propertius 3.1.9. Hallett (2006) tries to read Sulpicia's *fama* into this male context as well, suggesting a literary reputation resulting in allusions in Ovid *Ars*. On this, see also Batstone (2000) and his discussion of poem 1.

49 This is explored by Keith (1997) and Hallett (2006). Merriam (2006) is more in doubt as to whether the chronology can actually work.

50 Cf. *Aen.* 4.321–23: . . . *te propter eundem/extinctus* pudor *et, qua sola sidera adibam,/*fama *prior* (my emphasis, 'on your account likewise my sense of Shame has been blotted out and my previous reputation, by which alone I approached the heavens'). Likewise, the use of *pietas* (*pia cura*) in poem 3.17 might make sense within this context. *Pudor* also plays a part when *fama* is used in Prop. 2.32.21; see quotation above.

51 Most extensively Keith (1997).

presents herself quite specifically in what is hard not to read as contemporary Rome – or at least a sociological Rome:

Gratum est, securus multum quod iam tibi de me
    Permittis, subito ne male inepta cadam.
Sit tibi cura togae potior pressumque quasillo
    Scortum quam Serui filia Sulpicia:
Solliciti sunt pro nobis, quibus illa dolori est,
    Ne cedam ignoto, maxima causa, toro.

> I am pleased that you, because you are so sure about me, now allow yourself so much so that I do not trip in some mad folly. Let love for a toga-dressed and a woolbasket-carrying whore be more worth for you than Servius' daughter Sulpicia. Some are worried about me, for whom it would be the biggest reason for pain if I surrendered to an ignoble bed.

In this highly ironic and difficult poem, Sulpicia, not only sets herself apart from her lowborn rival (the toga-dressed and woolbasket-carrying prostitute, 3–4), but also presents herself as very different from the elegiac *puellae*. First, she gives herself a proper Roman name which can be placed in Augustan society: she is a member of the *gens Sulpicia*, part of the aristocracy.[52] Second, while Paul Veyne famously called the elegiac *puellae* 'not such high society',[53] Sulpicia here places herself in 'high society deluxe'.[54] She is a noble woman, and class obviously matters in the powerplay with Cerinthus which seems to take place here. Unlike Cerinthus, who is so sure (*securus de me*), she is uncertain of his commitment. However, here Sulpicia uses the opposite tactics to 3.17 where she explicitly plays weak to prompt a response. Instead she uses the weapons she has at hand, her social status and those concerned about her (*solliciti*, 5) – presumably her peers.

The other elegists employ the metaphor of *seruitium amoris* ('the slavery of love') when describing the power structure involved in their love affairs. In this imagery the beloved woman is placed on top as *domina* in a gender-bending game. In poem 3.16 Sulpicia is admittedly presented as a *domina* in the social sense. It is more doubtful whether she also represents an elegiac or gender-bending *domina*. After all, she seems to have little power over her beloved. One might therefore ask what happens to gender-reversal when a

52 Literally part of Syme (1986): ch. XV.
53 This is a chapter heading in Veyne (1988).
54 However, Hinds (1987a) 44–5 also reads Sulpicia's poetic signature as a subtle allusion making her at the same time closer to the prostitute: in view of Roman history and one of the first kings, Servius Tullius, any Roman *puella* would be a daughter of Servius. Furthermore, *seruus* of course also means 'slave'. Have we here another *seruus amoris* or yet another similarity between the *scortum* and our *puella*?

woman plays the part of the weak lover?[55] Might not this simply reaffirm normal sexual roles in Augustan society?

Direct allusion to *seruitium amoris* appears only once in all these poems, in the opening couplets of poem 3.11, one of the long poems where Sulpicia is praying to the birthday spirit and Venus (1–4):

> Qui mihi te, Cerinthe, dies dedit, hic mihi sanctus
> Atque inter festos semper habendus erit:
> Te nascente nouum Parcae cecinere puellis
> Seruitium et dederunt regna superba tibi.

> The day which gave me you, Cerinthus, shall be holy for me and always counted among the festivals. When you were born the Parcae sang of a new slavery for girls and gave you proud realms of power.

What is this *nouum seruitium*, then? In the following lines Sulpicia prays for a mutual love (*mutuus adsit amor*, 7). Furthermore, the lovers should both be shackled in love's slavery:

> Nec tu sis iniusta, Venus: uel seruiat aeque
> Vinctus uterque tibi uel mea uincla leua;
> Sed potius ualida teneamur uterque catena,
> Nulla queat posthac quam soluisse dies.

> And be not unjust, Venus: either let each of us alike be your shackled slaves or remove my chains. But rather let us both be held by a powerful chain which no day after this may be able to loosen.

This emphasis on equality is also in tune with the punchline of 3.13 where the lovers are emphatically worthy of each other (*cum digno digna*, 10).[56]

Yet, are the two lovers in this *nouum seruitium* equal? What is the role of Cerinthus in this cycle? Cerinthus seems to a great extent to be cast in the same role as Cynthia, Delia and Corinna as a mute object of desire, a muteness explicitly commented upon:

> Optat idem iuuenis quod nos, sed tectius optat:
> Nam pudet haec illum dicere uerba palam.
> At tu, Natalis, quoniam deus omnia sentis,
> Adnue: quid refert, clamne palamne roget?

> The boy wishes the same as me, but he wishes it more covertly as he is ashamed to utter these words openly. But thou, Birth-spirit, since you as a god sense everything, nod favourably: What does it matter if he pleads in silence or aloud?

[55] I owe much of what follows to Hinds (1987a).
[56] Hallett (2002a) 49–50 reads the use of *dignus* in light of Catullus.

As Hinds has pointed out, 'the most interesting thing about these lines is that they are there at all'.[57] Given that none of the other elegiac *puellae* to whom he might be compared speaks much, this should not be a problem. His muteness is only a problem given an emphasis on mutuality. Within this perspective it also seems odd that none of the poems written from a third-person perspective are put in the voice of Cerinthus. In poem 3.10, which might be read as a response to poem 3.17 where Sulpicia is ill and asks for confirmation, the confirmation does not come from Cerinthus. An unknown third person prays to Phoebus that the illness go away and that Cerinthus no longer be tortured with fear for his mistress (11–12). What this goes to show, however, is that, just as Sulpicia is neither a straight poet-lover nor an elegiac *puella* in the poems looked at so far, so Cerinthus is not an unproblematic elegiac *puer*.[58]

Yet there is one poem where Sulpicia might be read as a straight elegiac *puella*, the very first poem about Sulpicia in the *Corpus Tibullianum*, poem 3.8. In this poem the third-person narrator dresses her up as an elegiac *puella*, this time to honour the god Mars on the festival of Matronalia. Like one of the *puellae* in Ovid's catalogue of women in *Am.* 2.4, Sulpicia is presented as a girl who is pleasing in whatever form she takes (7–14):

> Illam, quidquid agit, quoquo uestigia mouit,
>   Componit furtim subsequiturque Decor;
> Seu soluit crines, fusis decet esse capillis:
>   Seu composit, comptis est ueneranda comis.
> Vrit, seu Tyria uoluit procedere palla:
>   Vrit, seu niuea candida ueste uenit.
> Talis in aeterno felix Vertumnus Olympo
>   Mille habet ornatus, mille decenter habet.

> Her, whatever she does, wherever she sets her foot, Grace secretly composes and follows: if she loosens her hair it is becoming with flowing tresses, if she arranges it, she should be admired for adorned hair. She inflames if she wished to walk around in a Tyrian gown, she inflames if she comes in a snowy white dress. In the same way happy Vertumnus on eternal Olympus wears a thousand costumes, and wears a thousand attractively.

The comparison with Vertumnus draws attention to the way everything suits her, and how the narrator fantasizes about her in different attires in a process which Alison Sharrock dubbed 'womanufacture'.[59] Here this is

[57] Hinds (1987a) 40.

[58] Pearcy (2006) goes even further and argues that Cerinthus is almost erased – he has even lost his place as a privileged reader.

[59] Sharrock (1991).

made even more explicit in the term *componere*, which is used of both writing and more practical forms of arrangement, rendering Sulpicia what Maria Wyke called a 'written *puella*'.[60] However, bringing in Vertumnus, god of change, also emphasizes the possibility that she may play different roles.[61] Thus even here Sulpicia is no straight elegiac *puella*. As the first poem about Sulpicia in the collection this might be an important pointer to the reader. The different versions of dress and dressing/undressing in the corpus – including the toga-dressed whore of poem 3.16[62] – may likewise be read not only as metapoetic or rhetorical pointers, but also on a thematic level as a sign of the spectrum of roles available to a Roman writing *puella*.

Reading Sulpicia

So how are we to read the poems written about and in the voice of Sulpicia? They clearly pose a challenge to readers on several levels. For a reader of elegy they certainly seem to explore what might happen when a female voice enters the realm of elegy, yet the answer is far from clear-cut, as we have seen. Rather, the reading of these poems might inspire further and more nuanced readings of the gendering of elegy in general. Likewise our prejudices about the *poeta-amator* and elegiac *puella* might be somewhat challenged by the development of these roles in this little corpus. The use of different voices and different forms (short/long) can be read as an exploration of both gender and genre. Not least, the poems challenge our expectations of a female and male author respectively. The identity of the author or authors of this collection will probably never be resolved once and for all. We are locked in our own readings of the texts and contexts, our own horizons of expectation and our own notions of gender.

The poems are extremely concerned with their readers. Unlike the other elegists, where the intended readership within the fiction most often is the beloved, Sulpicia explicitly says that she does not want to seal her letters so that no one can read them before Cerinthus (3.13.7–8), and she asks people to tell her story (3.13.5). Another voice has done precisely this in poems 3.8, 10 and 12. Sulpicia also reminds us that others are concerned about her (3.16.5). Readers – whether poets or scholars – may not be so concerned about her as with her poems. In the reception of her poems, then,

60 Wyke (2002) *passim*, but 46–76 in particular.

61 So Wyke (2002) 84 reads Prop. 4.2 as a lesson on how to read the fourth book of Propertius.

62 Barchiesi (2006) 120 emphasizes dress code when discussing available female roles and links this to visibility and availability.

her *fama* might after all be closer to that of her male colleagues than the elegiac *puellae*.[63]

Further reading

On the gendering of elegy in general, see Wyke (2002): 155–91. For Sulpicia's Latin text with en face English translation, see Postgate, revised by Goold (1988, LCL). For commentaries on Sulpicia, see Tränkle, with Latin text (1990) and Lyne (2007). Though wonderfully romanticizing, Smith (1913) is still useful. Hallett (2009a): 142–4 gives a useful overview of the different theories on authorship. A superb parody of the debates on authorship is Parker (2006). An overview of Sulpician scholarship in general is Keith (2006). She, however, does not include the most recent scholarship, which includes the Petale-epigraph. For this, see Stevenson (2005). For a literary approach to the poems, see especially Santirocco (1979), Lowe (1988), Keith (1997), Merriam (2006) and Hallett (2006). For a gender-oriented reading of Sulpicia Wyke (2002) is perhaps still the most useful. On the reception of Sulpicia, see Skoie (2002).

[63] See also Hallett (2006).

6

ALISON KEITH

Propertius

Unlike the four other major Augustan poets whose works survived antiquity, Propertius seems not to have received a notice in Suetonius' *Lives of the Poets*, perhaps because he was not generally considered the pre-eminent Roman elegist.[1] That honour apparently belonged to his contemporary, Albius Tibullus, of whom Suetonius reports 'in the judgment of many, he took first place amongst the writers of elegy' (*Tib.*, see also Chapter 4). This notice is probably derived from the first-century AD educator Quintilian, who praises Tibullus as 'polished and refined' (*tersus atque elegans*), although he acknowledges that 'some prefer Propertius' (*sunt qui Propertium malint*, *Inst. Or.* 10.1.93).[2] By implication, Propertius was a minority taste. Whatever the explanation for Propertius' failure to receive a Suetonian Life, as a result our knowledge of the elegist's biography is even more than usually dependent on autobiographical statements in his own poetry and biographical comments about him in the works of other Roman authors. Even our knowledge of the poet's first name depends on a fortuitous reference in Suetonius, for although the elegist 'signs' eight poems with his *nomen* 'Propertius' (2.8.18, 14.27, 24.35, 34.93; 3.3.17, 10.15; 4.1.71, 7.49), it is the biographer who supplies his praenomen 'Sextus' when quoting a Propertian distich (2.34.65–6) as evidence for the pre-publication fame of the *Aeneid* (Suet. *Verg.* 30).

We know neither the year of Propertius' birth nor that of his death, although we may conjecture that he must have been born around 55 BC and know that he died after 16 BC.[3] Propertius himself offers scant

[1] Rostagni (1944) 136; cf. ibid. xxiii, 133–4.

[2] Quintilian probably derives his canon of four Latin elegists (Gallus, Tibullus, Propertius and Ovid) from Ovid's notices (*Ars* 3.333–4, 535–8; *Rem.* 763–6; *Tr.* 2.445–68, 4.10.51–4, 5.1.15–20). Velleius Paterculus' implicit 'canonization' of Virgil and Rabirius in epic, Livy in history and Tibullus and Ovid in elegy (2.36.3) reflects Propertius' early loss of establishment sympathy.

[3] Keyser (1992) has argued for a birthdate between 4 May and 24 June, 43 BC, on the basis of a presumed horoscope in 4.1.83–6, but this has not been widely accepted.

autobiographical information in his poetry. At the end of his first book of elegies he sets a *sphragis* or 'seal' to the collection that contains the information that his family was of Umbrian provenance (1.22) and specifies the location of his ancestral seat near Perusia (modern Perugia). The poet's emphasis on Etruscan Perusia (1.22.1–8) and its proximity to his own Umbrian homeland (1.22.9–10) probably encodes a compliment to his first patron Tullus, the scion of a distinguished Etruscan family from Perusia.[4] Propertius elaborates this brief autobiographical notice in elegy 4.1, where he proudly proclaims Umbria the fatherland of the 'Roman Callimachus', as he styles himself (4.1.64, *Vmbria Romani patria Callimachi*; cf. 3.1.1–6, 3.9.43–6),[5] and names his hometown Assisi (4.1.125). The details about his family and upbringing that emerge there include the early death of his father and the young Propertius' subsequent loss of his patrimony and removal to the protection of his maternal relatives, in whose household he dedicated his boyhood amulet and assumed adult dress (4.1.127–30). The loss of his patrimony is probably to be connected with the triumviral confiscations in the area of Perugia after Philippi and the foundation of a military colony at Spello (ancient Hispellum) near Assisi soon after. Elite Roman youths assumed the toga of adulthood between the ages of fourteen and seventeen, so if the poet was not yet of age in the late 40s BC, then his birth can be placed very approximately in the mid- to late-50s BC.

Propertius' early experience of civil war and the resulting diminution of his patrimony find suggestive parallels with those of his contemporaries Virgil, Horace and Tibullus, whose families' holdings were also purportedly diminished in the civil wars of their youth (or even earlier in Horace's case).[6] Like his contemporaries, however, Propertius in no way forfeited membership in the municipal elite or the census classification to which his aristocratic birth entitled him, despite the depredation of his paternal estates.[7] The epigraphic and textual records demonstrate that the Propertii retained their prominence in the poet's adulthood, when they produced not only the eminent elegist, who enjoyed the patronage of Augustus' intimate Maecenas (the dedicatee of 2.1 and 3.9) and even, perhaps, of Augustus himself (whose victory at

4 On the family see Bonamente (2004); Cairns (2006b).

5 Unless otherwise indicated, quotations of Propertius are from Fedeli (1984) and translations are my own. On the many difficulties of the manuscript tradition, see Butrica (1984); Tarrant (2006); Heyworth (2007c) vii–lxv, (2007b) *passim*.

6 Virgil: Suet. *Verg* 19.2, with Rostagni (1944) 84–5 ad loc. Horace: Suet. *Hor.* 1.1–2, with G. Williams (1995). Tibullus: Tib. 1.1.19–22 and 41–2 with Maltby (2002) 40. Cf. Ovid's proud boast in *Amores* 3.15 of his Paelignian provenance and the participation of the Paeligni on the side of the allies, against Rome, in the Social War of 91–87 BC.

7 For the wealth of Propertius' poetic contemporaries, cf. Suet. *Verg.* 13 and *Hor*; for Tibullus, cf. Hor. *Epist.* 1.4.7, with Maltby (2002) 40.

Actium is celebrated in 4.6), but also the first senator of the line in C. Propertius Postumus (*PIR*² P 1010). The recipient of both a Horatian ode (*Carm.* 2.14) and a Propertian elegy (3.12) in the late 20s BC, Postumus enjoyed considerable political favour, and his wife Aelia Galla,[8] named six times in Propertius' elegy (3.12.1, 4, 15, 19, 22, 38), no doubt enhanced his standing still further, for her name suggests that she was closely related to Augustus' second prefect of Egypt, L. Aelius Gallus (*pr. Aegypti*, 26–24 BC).[9] The name Galla may also link her directly to Propertius on his mother's side through his otherwise obscure kinsman 'Gallus', named in 1.21 and alluded to in 1.22 as an unburied victim of the Perusine war.[10] In the absence of hard evidence, the most that we can infer about Propertius' maternal family, whether or not they were Aelii Galli, is that our elegist came under their protection in the aftermath of the loss of his paternal estates and benefited from their wealth and connections in this period. Their resources must have been extensive, since they enabled him to obtain an expensive education in poetry (*carmine*, 4.1.133) and rhetoric (*uerba tonare Foro*, 4.1.134).

Propertius repeatedly acknowledges Umbria as his *patria*, but his elegies show him living, and writing, in Rome. His first book of elegies clearly made him famous, and the second book reveals him in the mid-20s BC as an established elegist in the clientele of a new patron, C. Maecenas. The opening poem of book 2 is addressed to this wealthy friend of Virgil and Horace, a prominent Augustan partisan who is named twice here (2.1.17, 73) and is also the addressee of 3.9. Propertius' Umbrian origins and Etruscan friends will no doubt have commended him to the Arretine Maecenas, celebrated by Horace as the descendant of Etruscan kings (Hor. *C.* 3.29.1; cf. Prop. 3.9.1).[11] Soon after the Battle of Actium, Maecenas began the construction of a palatial mansion and tower on magnificent grounds on the Esquiline, where Propertius represents himself as owning a house in the late 20s BC (3.23.23–4). He also notes the proximity of his house to Maecenas' famous gardens (4.8.1–2), whose location archaeological excavation has pinpointed quite precisely.[12] In this area the so-called Auditorium of Maecenas has also been excavated, on whose outer wall was inscribed a Greek epigram by

8 Propertius' modern editors unanimously correct the MSS' corrupt (because unmetrical) 'L(a)el(l)ia' to 'Aelia' in this line.

9 Nisbet and Hubbard (1978) 223–4; cf. Syme (1986) 308.

10 The suggestion was advanced by Fedeli (1983) 1915, and accepted by Bonamente (2004) 52 n. 119; *contra*, Cairns (2006b) 61–2, who suggests that the poet's mother came from the Volcacii/Volcasii and that the poet was related through her to his patron Tullus.

11 On Maecenas, see White (1991), (1993); Graverini (1997).

12 For the archaeological evidence, see Grüner (1993) and Coarelli (2004), both with further bibliography. For their location, see Richardson (1992) 200–1.

Callimachus (*Epigr.* 42), adapted by Propertius early in his first collection of elegies (1.3.13–14). Originally believed to be a recital hall, the building is now generally agreed to have been a grand dining room, but there can be little doubt that it once provided a congenial and appropriate context for poetic recitation, and it is tempting to imagine Propertius, Horace and others performing there, at Maecenas' invitation, after dinner.[13]

Propertius' domestic proximity to Maecenas' urban estate implies both his restoration of the family fortunes and his access to the poets of Maecenas' 'circle'.[14] These included most famously Virgil and Horace (both of whom also lived near Maecenas on the Esquiline),[15] as well as many other prominent contemporary poets and men of letters. As a result of moving to Rome and entering Maecenas' *clientela*, Propertius will also have enjoyed entrée into the most exalted political circles. The impact of acquaintance with Augustus can perhaps be discerned in Propertius' elegy 4.6, which commemorates the emperor's victory at Actium and has been taken as evidence that, at the end of the 20s BC, Propertius ultimately passed from Maecenas' patronage into that of the emperor Augustus himself.[16]

Several elegies in the second collection document the fame Propertius won with the publication of his first book in 29 or 28 BC.[17] Already in the opening couplet of elegy 2.1, for example, the poet represents his readers as inquiring into the inspiration for his amatory elegies (2.1.1–2), while a later elegy implies the wide popularity of his first book of poetry, which seems to have circulated under the title of 'Cynthia' (2.24.1–2): *tu loqueris, cum sis iam noto fabula libro | et tua sit toto Cynthia lecta foro?* ('How can you say this, when you've become the talk of the town because of your famous book, your Cynthia read in the whole forum?').[18] In the final poem of the

13 On Maecenas' 'auditorium', see *LTUR* III 74–5, dating the building's construction and decoration to the late republic/early principate. For the performance context (with particular reference to Horace), see Murray (1985).

14 On Maecenas' literary *clientela*, see Dalzell (1956); Williams (1990); White (1993) 326 index s.v. 'Maecenas, relations in Roman literary society'. For a stimulating, if necessarily speculative, reconstruction of Propertius' place in Maecenas' 'circle', see Cairns (2006b) 295–319.

15 See note above. Suetonius reports that Horace, after his death, was buried in Maecenas' gardens near his friend's tomb, *humatus et conditus est extremis Esquiliis iuxta Maecenatis tumulum* (*Hor.*).

16 Cairns (2006b) 320.

17 On the publication date of the first book, see Butler and Barber (1933); Fedeli (1980); Lyne (1998a); Cairns (2006b). The arguments of Knox (2005) have not won wide acceptance.

18 Prop. 2.24.1–2; cf. Mart. 14.189, a distich composed to accompany a presentation copy of Propertius' 'single book' (*Monobiblos Properti*): *Cynthia, facundi carmen iuuenale Properti, | accepit famam, nec minus ipsa dedit* ('Cynthia, the youthful work of eloquent Propertius, received fame, and herself conferred no less').

second book, Propertius represents himself as a well-known lover (2.34.55–60), a man of modest means devoted to the pleasures of the flesh and unfit by ancestry and temperament alike to the traditional Roman pursuits of politics and war. Leaving even the poetry of war to another, he hails Virgil's *Aeneid* as greater than the *Iliad* (2.34.65–6), and his summary of the epic suggests that he enjoyed pre-publication access through Maecenas' patronage. At the conclusion of the elegy, Propertius returns to his own literary reputation and includes himself as the last in the canon of Latin elegists (2.34.85–94). His reference here to the recent death of the elegist Gallus – by suicide in 27 or 26, after Augustus renounced his friendship – suggests a date of 28 to 25 BC for the composition of the second book of elegies.[19]

In his later poetry, Propertius occasionally represents himself as breaking with erotic verse, but he always capitulates to the elegiac imperative (3.3, 4.1). His recurrent self-definition as a prominent elegist reflects the renown that his collections of erotic verse garnered him, despite the silence of his contemporaries. Even Horace, who provides abundant evidence about the contemporary literary scene and exhaustively documents the shifting membership of Maecenas' literary *clientela*, never names Propertius, although his parodic representation of an unnamed elegist as a would-be Callimachus or Mimnermus in *Epistles* 2.2 (91–101), conventionally dated to *c.*19 BC, has been taken to be a portrait of our elegist since Propertius himself pays explicit homage to both Callimachus (2.1.40, 2.34.32, 3.1.1, 3.9.43, 4.1.64) and Mimnermus (1.9.11).[20] By contrast, Propertius figures importantly in Ovid's poetry.[21] Ovid includes several catalogues of amatory authors in his elegiac poetry (*Ars* 3.329–34, *Tr.* 2.427–68, *Tr.* 4.10.51–5), all apparently modelled on Propertius' *sphragis* at the end of 2.34 and according Propertius primacy. It was conventional not to name living poets in catalogues of famous poets, so Ovid's *Amores* 1.15 and 3.9, which contain catalogues of famous poets and elegists that do not include Propertius, are generally agreed to have been written before our elegist's death.[22] If our knowledge of the chronology of the composition of Ovid's works were secure, Propertius' absence from or inclusion in these notices could offer us more precise

[19] A publication date of 26–5 BC is widely accepted for book 2: see Butler and Barber (1933); Fedeli (2005) 21; and cf. Cairns (2006b) 257, 300, 321–42.

[20] Several passages in Horace's poetry (e.g., *Epistles* 1.19, 2.2.91–101) have been taken to refer, in uncomplimentary terms, to the elegist. On Horace's relations with Propertius, see Solmsen (1948); Flach (1967); Sullivan (1976); White (1993); Dimundo (2002) 295–303, with extensive bibliography.

[21] On Ovid's relations with Propertius, see Davis (1977); Morgan (1977); Boyd (1997); Dimundo (2002) 314–18, with extensive bibliography.

[22] See McKeown (1989) 395, on the catalogue of famous writers at Ov. *Am.* 1.15.9–30.

information concerning the date of his death. Ovid is our only contemporary witness to Propertius' fame in his own lifetime, and he locates his elder friend's pre-eminence in the late 20s and early teens BC, when he himself was just embarking on a poetic career (*Tr.* 2.45–6): *saepe suos solitus recitare Propertius ignes, | iure sodalicii, quo mihi iunctus erat* ('Propertius often used to declaim his passionate verse by right of the comradeship with which he was joined to me'). Propertius' own poetry makes no reference to events after 16 BC, and since our textual evidence for his life includes no further mention of him as active after that date, his death is conventionally placed *c.*15 BC.

Cynthia

Propertius' first poem opens with the name of a woman who, in company with the love god Amor, presides over the elegiac speaker's prostrate form (1.1.1–4): *Cynthia prima suis miserum me cepit ocellis, | contactum nullis ante Cupidinibus. | tum mihi constantis deiecit lumina fastus | et caput impositis pressit Amor pedibus* ('Cynthia first captured me, wretch that I am, with her eyes; before, I'd been touched by no Desires. Then Love cast down my glance of stubborn arrogance and trampled my head beneath his feet'). Cynthia does not reappear in 1.1, but she is the focus of the following elegy, in which the poet-lover praises her beauty extravagantly and specifies the details of her dress and appurtenances – a fancy hairstyle, expensive clothing and exotic perfumes, all of which he characterizes, in the last line of the elegy, as luxury items he wishes he could persuade her to forego (1.2.31–2). The luxury products of Cynthia's toilette, like her 'unchaste' life and Greek name, combine to characterize her as an expensive Greek courtesan[23] – or, perhaps, an independently wealthy woman of the Roman elite kitted out as an expensive Greek courtesan, her identity concealed by a Greek pseudonym.[24]

[23] On the courtesan status of the elegiac *puella*, see James (2003); cf. Sullivan (1976) 76–106; Griffin (1986) 112–41; Laigneau (1999) 197–202; Miller (2004) 62–3; and Fantham (2006) 187–9. For a historical analogue, cf. Gallus' reputed mistress the mime-actress Volumnia, freedwoman of P. Volumnius Eutrapelus, whose stage name Cytheris ('Aphrodite's girl') suggests her sexual availability. On the identity of Gallus' Lycoris, see Serv. *ad Buc.* 10.1.6.

[24] Cf. Caelius' description of Clodia Metelli as a 'fourpenny Clytemnestra, [dressed] Coan in the dining room, [but] Nolan in the bedroom' (*quadrantariam Clytemnestram, Coam in triclinio, Nolam in cubiculo*, Cael. *apud* Quint. *Inst. or.* 8.6.53). On the meaning of 'Nolam' (i.e. 'unwilling') in this riposte, see Hillard (1981). Boucher (1980) 447, 455–9, argues most strongly for Cynthia's status as Roman *matrona*; cf. G. Williams (1968) 529–30, 534.

Cynthia is also the focus of elegy 1.3, which opens with an extended comparison of the sleeping mistress to the heroines of Greek mythology (1.3.1–8) and casts the lover-poet in the role of the god Bacchus creeping up on the sleeping Ariadne (1.3.1–2).[25] The suggestion is enhanced by Propertius' allusion a few lines later to a famous epigram by Callimachus in which the speaker apologizes for a *kōmos* (drunken lover's vigil) at his beloved's house (Callim. *Epigr.* 42.3–4 Pf.): 'Wine (*Ákrētos*) and Love (*Érōs*) compelled me, of which the one (i.e. love) drew me on, and the other (i.e. drink) prevented me from laying aside my temerity'. The komastic context of Callimachus' epigram informs Propertius' scenario in 1.3 as we are invited to view the poet-lover, like his Callimachean model, returning late at night from drunken revels to his beloved's house. Despite the lover's caution, however, his mistress wakes when the moon's rays shine through the window on to her face (1.3.27–33) and she reproaches the poet-lover for his infidelity, documenting her chastity in a catalogue of her nocturnal activities – playing the lyre, singing and weaving (1.3.35–46).

The passion and immediacy of the Cynthia elegies have long provoked interest amongst Propertius' readers in the autobiographical origins of his elegiac poetry, and he himself plays on public curiosity about the intimate details of his love affair at the outset of the second collection (2.1.1–2): *Quaeritis unde mihi totiens scribantur amores, | unde meus ueniat mollis in ora liber* ('You [pl.] ask whence my love poems are so often written, whence my soft book comes to recital'). Few readers have been able to resist the invitation of these lines to biographical speculation, though the nineteenth century produced the most sustained efforts to reconstruct from Propertius' poems the course of his affair with Cynthia.[26] The challenge was taken up already in antiquity, as Apuleius shows (*Apology* 10): 'Propertius . . . says Cynthia to conceal Hostia'. A highly speculative case has been constructed in support of Apuleius' identification of Cynthia with a historically recoverable Hostia by biographically-minded critics, who have used Propertius' repeated emphasis on Cynthia's erudition to identify a literary ancestor for her in the republican poet Hostius, author of a lost epic *Bellum Histricum*.[27]

Social historians and literary critics alike, however, have called into question whether the identification of a supposed historical girlfriend concealed behind Propertius' pseudonymous Cynthia can provide meaningful access to the historical woman and the circumstances of her life, let alone explain

[25] Hunter (2006a) 69 n. 85.

[26] The biographical preoccupation already animating Lachmann (1816) is carried to its furthest extreme in Plessis (1884); in English Haight (1932) 81–124 is representative.

[27] See, most recently, Coarelli (2004) 110–15, with further bibliography.

her literary significance in Propertius' poetry.[28] Feminist critics have demonstrated that women enter classical literature as 'gendered' objects of (mostly) male writing practices and have explained how such 'written' women are further shaped by the literary genre in which their authors inscribe them.[29] Even if we accept the biographical speculations of historical and philological scholarship, therefore, we must explore Cynthia's symbolic import in Propertian elegy by considering the literary valence of the themes and images with which our elegist associates her throughout his verse.

Catullus sets the precedent for the naming practices of the Augustan elegists by concealing the identity of his beloved behind a pseudonym, 'Lesbia', that evokes the Greek poet Sappho. Propertius' debt to Catullus is evident not only in his explicit invocation of Catullan precedent (2.25.1–4, 32.45–6), but also in his representation of Cynthia as a poet herself (1.3.41–4, 2.3.19–22) who rivals comparison with the Greek poets Sappho and Corinna (2.3.19–22).[30] Even more significant is Propertius' debt to his admired model Gallus, who conceals the name of his mistress 'Cytheris' (itself a stage-name of the freedwoman and mime-actress, Volumnia) beneath the pseudonym 'Lycoris', a feminized form of the cult-title of Apollo at Delphi. Cynthia too is a feminized form of one of the god's cult-titles, appearing for the first time in Latin literature in a programmatically-charged passage at the opening of Virgil's sixth Eclogue that adapts into Latin the famous scene of Callimachus' Apolline commission in the prologue of the *Aetia* (fr. 1.21–4 Pf.).[31] Propertius thus endows his *inamorata* with a name that bears an intensely literary resonance, as we might expect of the 'Roman Callimachus' (4.1.64).[32]

The metapoetic interpretation of Cynthia is facilitated by the ancient practice of identifying literary works by their opening word or phrase. Propertius' first collection of elegies will thus have circulated under the title of *Cynthia* (1.1.1). Our poet plays with the double valence of Cynthia as both woman and text already in his first book, when he imagines writing her name on the bark of trees (1.18.21–2), self-consciously foregrounding his role as amatory elegist by inscribing 'Cynthia' on the original writing

28 Hillard (1989); Wyke (2002) 11–191; Kennedy (1993) 1–23.

29 Wyke (2002) 11–191; McNamee (1993); Keith (1994), (2000), (2008) 86–114; Oliensis (1997); Dixon (2001); James (2003). There is an extensive feminist critical literature on Propertian elegy. Wyke's early publications, collected in Wyke (2002), are seminal; see also Gold (1993) and Greene (1998).

30 On Corinna, see Snyder (1989) 41–54; Rayor (1993).

31 On Cynthia's name, see Randall (1979) 31–3. On the characterization of Cynthia, see also Boucher (1965) 441–74; Sullivan (1976) 76–106; Greene (1998); Sharrock (2000); Miller (2004) 60–73; Fantham (2006); O'Neill (2005); and the references above.

32 Wyke (2002) 46–114; McNamee (1993); Keith (2008) 86–114.

surface.[33] Cynthia's textualization is central as well to her characterization in book 2, where Propertius promises to write epic once his mistress has been 'written' (2.10.8); reflects on the fame the wide circulation of his *Cynthia* among contemporary Roman readers has brought him (2.24.1–2); and anticipates his readers' interest in his mistress/book at the very outset (2.1.1–16), implying that the unnamed *puella* who furnishes his inspiration in the new book is the Cynthia who gave her name to his first.[34]

Yet the very beauty and erudition that the poet-lover celebrates in the first book and opening elegies of the second incite his mistress to caprice and infidelity. Already in 1.15, the amatory speaker complains of her inconstancy, despite his elegiac service. He construes Cynthia's exemplary beauty, still manifestly an index of the stylistic perfection of his elegy (*leuitas, componere, uariare, formosa*), as evidence of potential infidelity, and his fears concerning her promiscuity cast a lengthening shadow over their relationship in the second and third books. Thus in elegy 2.4, the poet-lover complains of her 'many transgressions' (*multa delicta*, 2.4.1), while in 2.5 he contemplates a new liaison more worthy of his verse (2.5.5–6), and in elegy 2.6 he surveys her house, thronged like those of the storied courtesans of Greece (2.6.1–2). As Propertius' verse circulates, Cynthia's scandalous appeal increases, and rivals – both literary and amatory – proliferate (1.4, 5, 8; 2.8, 9, 16, 24, 25, 34; 3.19, 20, 24–5). The poet-lover's amatory service outdoes the inconstancy of rival lovers, even as his mistress's promiscuous circulation underlines his true devotion and confers on him the literary fame of which he boasts (e.g., 2.25, 34; 3.3).

The textualization of women such as Propertius' exquisite Cynthia, and their concomitant circulation among men, is a central gender dynamic of Roman lyric and love elegy. The literary renown that Cynthia's general circulation brings the poet-lover is thus an important factor to consider in his characterization of his promiscuous mistress/book. We have seen that the opening lines of elegy 1.1 describe the poet-lover's passionate love for her, but the poem itself plays a wider function in the collection since it is addressed to Propertius' patron Tullus. Cynthia, both the lover's mistress and the poet's book of elegies, is thereby subsumed into the gift presented to Tullus, who is the dedicatee of our poet's 'single book' and the addressee not only of elegy 1.1 but also of elegies 1.6, 14, and 22, as well as the later 3.22. Through his elegies, 'Cynthia' circulates between Propertius and his friends, patrons and rivals: Bassus (1.4), Gallus (1.5, 10, 13, 20), Ponticus (1.7, 9), Maecenas (2.1, 3.9), Demophoon (2.22), Lynceus (2.34) and Horos (4.1). Thus, when our elegist complains of his mistress's promiscuity (in e.g. 1.12,

[33] McNamee (1993) 228. [34] See also Hunter (Chapter 1) in this volume.

15; 2.5, 6, 8, 9, 16, 32 etc.), we should recall that his own elegies release Cynthia into public circulation, not only among Roman notables in general, but between the elegist and his friends in particular.

Propertius' poetry circulates among the Roman political elites within a culture of institutionalized social relations that consolidate male authority in and through women's bodies. The feminine clichés to which Propertius' portrait of Cynthia appeals not only strengthen male social bonds and elite authority (over female, foreigner, and slave) but also naturalize the hierarchy of the sexes on display in Latin literature and Roman culture. Propertian elegy thus makes explicit the poet's participation in the elite male homosocial network central to Latin political, rhetorical and literary culture.[35] By addressing members of the Roman social and political elites as patrons, friends and literary rivals, Propertius appeals to and consolidates the homosocial bonds of elite Roman male friendship and implicitly documents the social and political entitlements of his own class. Roman poetic composition and performance, like its rhetorical counterpart declamation, was an exercise in masculine co-operation and competition, as Propertius' genealogy of Latin love poetry illustrates (2.34.85–94). The distichs celebrating Roman elegiac poets and their poetry imply not only their practitioners' mutual interest in one another's verse but also each successive elegist's inspiration of the next.

Propertius' participation in the homosocial network of the Roman cultural and political elites is evident throughout his own elegiac corpus, especially in the first book, where a series of poems with named addressees signals the extent of his literary and social ambitions. In elegy 1.4, for example, he sets Cynthia into circulation between himself and the iambic poet Bassus in a complex negotiation of their mutual literary and amatory standing.[36] Throughout the elegy, the syntactic pairing of Propertius and Bassus establishes between them a symmetrical relationship, both amatory and literary, which distinguishes them sharply from Cynthia. The poem founds the structural congruence between the two poets on male homosocial desire and harnesses the sexual and textual exchange of women for the consolidation of literary and affective bonds between men. A similar rhetorical strategy undergirds the paired elegies 1.7 and 1.9, addressed to the epic poet Ponticus, whom Propertius represents as a rival in epic composition to Homer. He

[35] The adjective homosocial describes social bonds between members of the same sex in such arenas as 'friendship, mentorship, entitlement, rivalry, and . . . sexuality' (Sedgwick (1992) 1). On homosociality in general, see Sedgwick (1992), building on Girard (1976) and Irigaray (1985); and in the context of Augustan poetry, see Oliensis (1997), Miller (2004).

[36] Suits (1976) 89.

cautions Ponticus that, should he fall in love, he will find the Greek elegist Mimnermus – by implication Propertius' own generic model – more valuable than Homer (1.9.11): *plus in amore ualet Mimnermi uersus Homero.* Ponticus' epic themes of Cadmean Thebes, civil war, and fratricide find their structural antonym in Propertius' elegiac attention to 'love' (*nostros agitamus amores*, 1.7.5) and a 'harsh mistress' (*duram dominam*, 6), as living Roman poets supersede Greek masters. Yet the ostensible rivalry between successive pairs of poets – Ponticus ~ Homer, Homer ~ Mimnermus, Ponticus ~ Propertius – obscures the greater homology of the poetic pursuit of renown common to both epicist and elegist, Greek and Roman. Both elegies exemplify elite male homosocial competition in their appeal to clichés of masculine rivalry even as they enact elite male solidarity.

From first to last, Propertius remains an exponent of 'soft' and 'seductive' elegiac verse, but the horizon of his elegy expands from an exclusive focus on his beloved 'Cynthia' in book 1, to encompass contemporary political themes under Maecenas' patronage, fitfully in book 2, more frequently in book 3, and consistently in book 4. The poet's careful arrangement of the poems in the first collection has been well documented.[37] The three poems that conclude the book illustrate the frayed relations between lover and mistress by foregoing any mention of Cynthia, offering instead advice to Gallus about his homoerotic love affair (1.20) and two sepulchral epigrams (1.21–22). The themes of death and recent civil war in the epigrams illustrate particularly starkly their closural function in the book.

Book 2: the long love

I subscribe to the view that book 2 is a single collection, badly mauled in transmission, and I accept Richard Tarrant's attractive suggestion that the 'exceptional length [of the book] should probably be seen as a provocative feature... a witty literalization of 2.1's opening words (... *totiens amores*) and of the following references to superabundant composition (12, 14)'.[38] Although exceptionally long, the book exhibits the standard structural components of programmatic opening and closing poems (2.1, 34) and an internal sequence of programmatic poems (2.10–13) that functions as an off-centre 'proem in the middle'.[39] The opening poem of the second

[37] On the design of book 1, see Skutsch (1963); Otis (1965); Courtney (1968); King (1975/76); Davis (1977); Petersmann (1980); Fedeli (1983); Manuwald (2006).

[38] Tarrant (2006) 57.

[39] Classic discussion in Conte (1992). On the problems posed by book 2, see Skutsch (1975); Menés (1983); Camps (1967); Heyworth (1995); Butrica (1996b); Lyne

collection returns us to the *mise-en-scène* of the first in its celebration of the elegiac mistress's beauty and erudition (2.1.1–16), and recalls the early elegies of the first volume (1.2–3). Like the first collection, the second exhibits a narrative progression from the poet-lover's literary and amatory success to his increasing disillusionment with the elegiac mistress/book, 'Cynthia'. Thus in elegies 2.2 and 2.3, the amatory speaker accounts for his composition of elegy as the result of his love for an exceptional woman, rehearsing the attributes that attract him so powerfully, while the following elegies (2.4–9) rehearse the lover's disillusionment with his mistress's increasing caprice and infidelity, the poet's with her genre. Cynthia's caprice makes her unmarriageable but never to be parted from the poet-lover in 2.7, the object of a rival lover's pursuit in 2.8 (*eripitur nobis iam pridem cara puella*, 1), and apparently his rival's conquest in 2.9 (*iste quod est, ego saepe fui*, 1). The brief separation and immediate reconciliation recorded in elegies 2.10–13 then invite interpretation as the poet's re-commitment to the genre, for they initiate a new sequence of amatory success (2.14, 15), infidelity, and rupture, in which both Cynthia (2.16, 17, 19, 21) and the poet-lover (2.18, 20, 22) explore the attractions of other partners.

Of particular interest is Propertius' proud boast to his friend Demophoon in 2.22, that he finds many girls desirable (1): *scis here mi multas pariter placuisse puellas* ('you know that yesterday many girls proved equally attractive to me'). The very name of his addressee, meaning 'voice of the people', suggests the poet-lover's ready capitulation to the gossip that circulates about him (in e.g. 2.1, 3) and his mistress (in e.g. 2.5, 11, 18.37–8). But his new erotic interest in a multitude of potential girlfriends reverses an earlier profession of love for Cynthia alone (2.6.19): *tu mihi sola places: placeam tibi, Cynthia, solus* ('you alone please me: let me alone please you, Cynthia'). In forswearing the exclusivity of his relations with Cynthia, the lover reveals his readiness for erotic adventure, the poet his desire for literary experimentation (2.22.3–6).[40] The elegiac speaker then disavows his commitment to a singular mistress in 2.23, as the poet-lover evinces a new interest in the comic *meretrix* and lyric freedwoman. Propertius associates his resulting amatory and literary degradation with Cynthia herself in the following poem, which opens with an interlocutor's comment on her wide circulation (2.24.1–2, quoted above). The promiscuity of the elegiac book figures that of the elegiac mistress, and as Propertius' literary fame increases their notoriety redounds to his moral discredit, setting in play an unresolved,

(1998b), (1998c); Syndikus (2006). On the design of book 2 as we have it, see Camps (1967); Syndikus (2006); Tarrant (2006).

40 See also Gibson (Chapter 14) in this volume.

and perhaps unresolvable, tension between the mistress's erotic and literary circulation. The elegies that conclude the second book can be interpreted, through their employment of a series of closural themes, as illustrating the poet's increasing disengagement from his genre, the lover's from his mistress.

Book 3: the end of the elegiac *affaire*?

The plot of amatory disillusionment and literary disengagement intensifies in the third book, which opens with the substitution of literary for amatory programme in the 'Roman Elegies' (3.1–5),[41] and concludes with the poet-lover's final disavowal of his mistress (and amatory elegy) because of her promiscuity (3.19–25).[42] Within the book, Propertius includes fewer poems about Cynthia than in the earlier books, and he names and/or addresses her only in the closing sequence of elegies (3.21, 24–5). The elegies in which she appears, moreover, illustrate their recurrent dissension and frequent separation: elegy 3.6 reports the unfaithful poet-lover's hope for rapprochement with his mistress, despite her reproaches; 3.8 celebrates the lovers' quarrel that the elegiac speaker believes attests to his beloved's continuing love for him; 3.10 is a birthday gift for his mistress proposing a night of pleasures; 3.15 commemorates the first mistress of the elegiac *amator*, Lycinna; and 3.16 records the poet-lover's summons from Rome to his girlfriend's villa at Tibur, whereby he imagines his murder by brigands on the journey.

The sequence of five elegies that opens the third collection corresponds particularly closely to the thematically related sequence of six odes that opens Horace's third book of lyric poems, the so-called 'Roman Odes'. Throughout his sequence, Propertius explores his 'status as a poet of love'[43] and develops with special intensity the Horatian themes 'of his lack of interest in material acquisitions; of the equalizing function of death, which knows no distinction between rich and poor, noble and humble; of the general futility of human efforts'.[44] But Propertius' appropriation of the diction and themes of Horace's *Odes* tendentiously adapts Horatian lyric to the (im)moral project of his own elegiac verse, for he ostentatiously rejects the ethical valence of Horace's denunciation of wealth even as he appropriates it to his own elegiac poetic programme. The recuperation of public Horatian lyric for private elegiac ends also animates the narrative

[41] Nethercut (1970).

[42] On the design of book 3, see Courtney (1970); Putnam (1980); Comber (1998); Newman (2006).

[43] Nethercut (1970) 385, quoting Solmsen (1948) 105.

[44] Solmsen (1948) 106; cf. Flach (1967), Nethercut (1970), and Miller (1983).

trajectory of these elegies, in which Propertius retrofits Horace's celebration of Augustan *pax* to an erotic setting.[45]

Propertius' extensive renovation of the programmatic language, imagery, and themes of Horace's *Odes* in elegies 3.1–5 introduces contemporary Latin lyric into the third book as a significant new source of generic engagement and experimentation. In addition to his renovation of the 'Roman Odes' in his 'Roman Elegies', Propertius' *epicedion* for Paetus lost at sea (3.7) shares with Horace's Archytas ode, *Carm.* 1.28, a speech delivered by a shipwrecked man; elegy 3.9, addressed to Maecenas, the patron they share, is a *recusatio*, or refusal to write on grand themes, of the kind that Horace makes in *Carm.* 1.6; poem 3.11 can be appreciated as a 'Cleopatra elegy' inspired by Horace's 'Cleopatra ode', *Carm.* 1.37; elegy 3.12 addresses Postumus, the recipient of Horace's famous *Eheu fugaces*, *Carm.* 2.14; and elegy 3.13 handles the theme of Roman moral decadence that Horace treats extensively in the *Odes*. The criticism of avarice in particular is a prominent theme of Horatian lyric that recurs throughout the third book of Propertius' elegies (e.g., 3.7.1–8, 3.12.1–6, 3.13)[46] but in the distinctive form of the elegist's repeated expression of a singular commitment to love and concomitant indifference to wealth. Elegy 3.17, a dithyramb or hymn to Bacchus, illustrates Propertius' newly explicit engagement with lyric. Perhaps inspired by Horace's odes to the wine god (C. 2.19, 3.25) and his wine jar (C. 3.21),[47] the elegy announces itself as a Pindaric ode (3.17.39–40). If the final couplet humorously deflates lofty lyric sentiment (41–2), the poem as a whole offers sustained and successful expression of a distinctly non-elegiac programme. Like Fedeli and other recent critics, therefore, I view this poem's experimental departure from amatory elegy as marking a stage in Propertius' disengagement from the genre in book 3.[48]

The closing sequence of the third book constitutes an extended meditation not only on how the poet-lover can renounce elegy and the elegiac mistress, but also why he must. In elegy 3.19, the elegiac speaker takes his girlfriend's promiscuity as the starting point for an exploration of female wantonness (3.19.1–2), while in the following elegy, a rival lover's departure confirms his mistress's infidelity (3.20.1–6). Elegy 3.21 therefore proposes a sea voyage to cure the poet-lover of his infatuation. The lover's removal to Athens and the poet's immersion there in philosophy, rhetoric and even comedy (3.21.25–8) hold out the prospect of a cure for love, *remedium amoris*, such as the

45 On allusion to Gallus, fr. 145 Hollis, in Propertius' elegy 3.4, see Putnam (1980); Cairns (2006b) 406–12; and Hollis (2007) 243–4.

46 On Propertius' debt to Horace for this theme, see Flach (1967) 19–40.

47 So, e.g., Fedeli (1985) 512–16; Hunter (2006a) 68–72.

48 Cf. Neumeister (1983) 96–101; Fedeli (1985) 516; Lefèvre (1991); Miller (1991b).

elegist rejects in 1.1.25–38. Elegy 3.21 thus constitutes a valedictory address to the central themes – Rome, friends, and girlfriend – of Propertian elegy (3.21.15–16). The loss of his writing tablets in elegy 3.23 wittily instantiates the poet's renunciation of love elegy, and the closing elegy (or elegies)[49] commemorates the lover's final break with Cynthia. The lover renounces Cynthia in the very words with which the poet celebrated her in the opening collection, where her *forma* and *figura* furnished the subject of elegy 1.2 and her eyes inspired his love for her in elegy 1.1 (cf. 2.15.12), reducing him from arrogance (1.1.3) to submission (1.1.4, 32–8).[50] His mention in elegy 3.24 of friends (*amici*, 9) and a witch (*saga*, 10) also looks back to the opening poem of the first book (witches, 1.1.19–24; *amici*, 1.1.25–6), as do the themes of a sea-voyage (3.24.12, 15–16; 1.1.29), surgical remedies (3.24.11; 1.1.27) and slavery to Venus (3.24.14; 1.1.33). The closural function of such lexical and thematic recapitulation is abundantly clear and invites interpretation as Propertius' valedictory meditation on the circulation of 'Cynthia' among the Roman reading public. His mistress/book has made the poet famous, but the lover a laughing stock, and so he represents himself as tired of both love and love poetry. The sequence articulates Propertius' desire to bring the life of love to an end along with the composition of amatory elegy.

Book 4: aetiological elegy

The culmination of Propertius' homage to Callimachus comes in the final book of elegies where, as we have seen, he announces himself the Roman Callimachus and undertakes to commemorate in his elegiac verse specifically aetiological subjects (4.1.69–70). He is ostensibly deflected, however, from his proposed change of course by the soothsayer Horos, who bids him return to the amatory themes that have always distinguished his elegiac verse (4.1.135–46). The poems in the final book enact this competing programme of 'Callimachean' aetiological and 'Propertian' erotic elegy through the juxtaposition of aetiological and amatory subjects: poems 4.2, 4, 6, 9 and 10 treat the legends of Vertumnus' statue in the Vicus Tuscus, the Rock of Tarpeia, Actian Apollo, Hercules' foundation of the *Ara Pacis* and the *spolia opima* on display in the temple of Jupiter Feretrius, while poems 4.3, 5, 7, 8 and 11 explore amatory relationships from a variety of perspectives. In the complex imbrication of erotic and aetiological themes in the final collection we can trace Propertius' debt not only to Callimachean elegy per

[49] On the textual issues, see Fedeli (1985) 672–4. For 3.24–5 as a *renuntiatio amoris*, see Cairns (1972) 79–82.

[50] Fedeli (1985) 675–7; Fear (2005) 26–30.

se but also to the larger question of poetic book design which Callimachus and his contemporaries explored with extraordinary sophistication.[51]

The central elegy 4.6 functions as a 'proem in the middle' and provides a forum for reflection on the politics and poetics of Propertius' final collection. In its religious setting and explicit acknowledgment of Philitas and Callimachus as the source of his aesthetic inspiration, elegy 4.6 closely reworks the opening of elegy 3.1. In its accommodation of political panegyric to elegiac programme, the poem draws especially closely on the example of Callimachus' *Aetia*, in which statements of poetic principle (*Aetia* Prologue frr. 1–7 M, *Aetia* Epilogue fr. 112 Pf) frame praise of the Ptolemaic dynasty (*Victoria Berenices* (*SH* 254–69), *Coma Berenices* (*Aetia* 4 fr. 110 Pf)).[52] Where once Cynthia had furnished our elegist's inspiration and themes (2.1.1–16), now Apollo and Calliope, the sources of Callimachus' poetic inspiration in the *Aetia*, incite him to sing of Augustus' victory at Actium (4.6.11–12). The elegy celebrates Augustus Caesar's military victories over Egypt (13–68), the German Sygambri (77), Ethiopian Meroe (78) and the Parthians (79–84), and takes the form of panegyric (13–14): *Caesaris in nomen ducuntur carmina: Caesar | dum canitur, quaeso, Iuppiter ipse uaces* ('songs are being made for Caesar's glory: while Caesar is hymned, I beg you, Jupiter, to go without being sung'). Propertius showcases his own panegyrical elegy on the theme of Augustus' victory at Actium, which occupies pride of place (15–68), but he also includes notice of his fellow poets' panegyrics on related themes at a banquet after the victory celebration and he even seems to quote a snatch of a rival's song (4.6.77–84).

In elegy 4.6, the supreme patron has become the subject of poems exchanged between professional poets in a specially constituted context, displacing Cynthia to the following elegies (4.7, 8) as Propertius abandons amatory themes for imperial panegyric in public performance (cf. 4.10, 11). The elegist has finally come of age, leaving youth and its age-appropriate pursuits of love and love elegy behind (cf. 3.9.57), 'to devote his energies to the network of relations between men that constitutes the fabric of Roman society'.[53] His absorption into the purely homosocial society of poets in the central elegy of the final collection marks the social elevation his elegiac poetry has earned him in the public world of Roman culture.

[51] On the design of book 4, see Sullivan (1984); Janan (2001); DeBrohun (2003); Welch (2005); Günther (2006b); Hutchinson (2006).

[52] On Callimachus' two elegies for Berenice, and their structural and political importance in the *Aetia*, see Fantuzzi and Hunter (2004) 83–8. On the *Victoria Berenices*, see the *editio princeps* of Parsons and Kassel (1977) and the full discussion, with extensive bibliography, of Fuhrer (1992); on the impact of the poem on Latin poetry, see esp. Thomas (1983).

[53] Oliensis (1997) 152; see further Fear (2005).

Further reading

Propertius has enjoyed a protracted period of critical esteem in the last half-century or so, given impetus in the English-speaking world by the publication of Camps' sequence of commentaries on individual books of Propertian elegies (1961, 1965, 1966, 1967), followed by the seminal studies of Commager and Hubbard (both 1974), and in the Italian milieu by the *seriatim* publication of Paolo Fedeli's commentaries on individual books (1965, 1980, 1985, 2005). For translations of Propertius into English, see Lee (WC, 1994) Goold (LCL, 1990) and Katz (2004). Since the appearance of the two English monographs, Propertian elegy has been the focus of concerted scholarly attention, with the completion of two doctoral theses on the manuscript tradition (Butrica 1984, Heyworth 1986); the publication of several critical editions of the elegies (Fedeli 1984, Goold 1990 and Heyworth 2007c); the appearance of a number of scholarly commentaries on individual books of Propertius' elegies (Baker 1990; Booth forthcoming; Hutchinson 2006); and the publication of several important monographs on Propertius' literary style (Benediktson 1989; Keith 2008; Miller 2004; Newman 1997; Papanghelis 1987; Pinotti 2004), politics (Cairns 2006b; Stahl 1985) gender politics (Greene 1998; Wyke 2002) and aetiological elegy (DeBrohun 2003; Janan 2001; Warden 1980; Welch 2005).

7

THEA S. THORSEN

Ovid the love elegist

'I hate it when a page is shining all over and empty' (*Am.* 1.11.20, *odi cum late splendida cera uacat*) says Ovid, the last of the great Augustan poets and the most prolific of them all. Ovid (Publius Ovidius Naso) was born on March 20th 43 BC (*Tr.* 4.10.13–19) as the second son of a fairly well-off family of ancient equestrian rank (*Am.* 1.3.8, *Tr.* 4.10.7–8) in the city of Sulmo (*Am.* 2.1.1; 3.15.3, 8–14; *Tr.* 4.10.3).[1] In his autobiographical poem *Tristia* 4.10, written late in life, Ovid states that when he and his brother, who was exactly one year older, were still children, they made the roughly 150-kilometre journey to Rome, where their father financed their upper-class education in rhetoric and law (*Tr.* 4.10.15–16, Sen. *Controv.* 2.2.8–12, cf. 9.5.17). Ovid further tells us how he always felt the urge to compose poetry and that, although his father warned him that not even Homer died rich, all his attempts to write prose resulted only in the outpouring of verse (*Tr.* 4.10.21–25). Ovid embarked nevertheless on a career as a public official, but when he in due course was expected to take up a seat in the Senate, he decided to abandon any such career and dedicated himself entirely to poetry (*Tr.* 4.10.33–8).

Ovid was probably in his twenties when he made this decision. He had, however, pursued his poetic interests well before that. Perhaps he had even already made the acquaintance of Valerius Messalla Corvinus (cf. *Pont.* 1.7.27–8), the great aristocrat who famously sponsored poets, among whom Tibullus was the most prominent. Ovid claims that he at least caught a glimpse of Virgil, who died in 19 BC (cf. *Vit. Don.* 35); that Tibullus, who also reportedly passed away in 19 BC (Dom. Mars. fr. 7.3 Courtney), would have made a great friend; and that he enjoyed friendship with Propertius, who inspired him by reciting his own elegies (*Tr.* 4.10.45, 51–2). And while

I am grateful to Stephen Harrison for generous feedback on this chapter.

[1] The city is today's Sulmona in the Italian Abruzzi.

Ovid was still torn between his father's expectations and his poetic vocation, he did of course compose poetry, too:

> carmina cum primum populo iuuenalia legi,
> barba resecta mihi bisue semelue fuit.
> mouerat ingenium totam cantata per urbem
> nomine non uero dicta Corinna mihi.
> (*Tr.* 4.10.57–60)

When I first recited the poems of my youth in public, my beard had been shaven once or twice. Corinna, called thus by a name which was not true, inspired my talent, [and was] sung all over the city [of Rome].[2]

To judge from this passage, Ovid was only a teenager when he first performed in public at Rome, reciting from the work that was later to be known as the collection of elegies entitled *Amores* ('Loves'), centred precisely on Corinna as not the only, but the most important *puella* ('girl'). Ovid loved to write, and Ovid wrote of love: *tenerorum lusor amorum* (the playful poet of tender loves) is the title he chose for himself both in his imaginary epitaph (*Tr.* 3.3.73) and in his autobiography (*Tr.* 4.10.1).[3] And the love Ovid most frequently wrote of was of the elegiac kind, that is, sexy, elegant and light-hearted, but also unhappy, plaintive and even tragic. To be an elegist was a fundamental part of Ovid's poetic identity; he repeatedly claimed to be the successor of the canonical Roman elegists Gallus, Tibullus and Propertius (*Tr.* 2.467, 4.10.53), and he boasted that his elegiac achievement was only comparable to the epic accomplishment of Virgil:

> tantum se nobis elegi debere fatentur
> quantum Virgilio nobile debet epos.
> (*Rem. am.* 395–6)

Elegies admit they owe me as much as noble epic owes Virgil.

Love elegy of epic dimensions

Most of Ovid's elegies about love were produced during the first half of his poetic career, from the moment he made his public debut until he was about forty-five years old: the single *Heroides* ('Heroines'), the three books of the *Amores*, the three books of the *Ars amatoria* ('Art of Love') and *Remedia amoris* ('Cures for Love').[4] The chronological order of these works

[2] All translations are my own. [3] Cf. *Am.* 3.15.1.

[4] For the title of the *Heroides*, cf. Priscian (*Gramm. Lat.* 2.544.4 Keil); alternative titles are *Epistula(e)*, (*Ars* 3.345) and *Epistulae Heroidum* ('Letters of Heroines'). For the title of the *Amores*, cf. *Ars* 3.343. For the title of the *Ars amatoria*, see Seneca (*Controv.* 3.7.2); the metrical version is *Ars amandi* (*Ars* 1.1).

is notoriously difficult to establish. As we have seen, the *Amores* is the first work Ovid claims to have recited publicly, and this must indeed have been one of his very first poetic undertakings (see above, *Tr.* 4.10.59–60). But Ovid simultaneously confesses that in his youth he 'wrote a lot, but that which [he] found imperfect, [he] let the flames improve' (*Tr.* 4.10.61–2), and this claim seems to be substantiated by the introductory epigram of the *Amores* (*ipsius epigramma*), where the poet claims to have reduced the original five-book work to one of only three. Furthermore, the second book of the *Amores* refers to his now lost tragedy *Medea* and the single *Heroides* (*Am.* 2.18.13–14, 19–34), which makes it plausible that the extant *Amores* is a second edition, that might well have been begun before but finished after Ovid wrote *Medea* and the single *Heroides*. As a consequence, the single *Heroides* antedates the extant version of the *Amores*.

Curiously, there seems to be a reference to the *Ars amatoria* as well in the second book of the *Amores* (*Am.* 2.18.19–20). The implication that the *Ars amatoria* was produced before the *Amores* is hard to assess, since the *Ars amatoria* establishes a chronology of fiction by means of numerous allusions to 'previous' events that take place in the *Amores*.[5] To complicate matters still more, the last date that it seems possible to establish for the *Ars amatoria* (*c.*AD 2, cf. 1.177–212) coincides with that of the *Remedia amoris* (155–8), which certainly reads as a sequel to the *Ars amatoria*.[6] These complications do indeed hamper attempts to establish a clear-cut chronological order for Ovid's love elegies. At the same time the same complications also attractively suggest that not only did Ovid compose – or at least modify – all of these works more or less simultaneously, he may also at some point (around AD 2) have published them in a joint edition.[7]

In the *Ars amatoria* (3.205–8) there is furthermore a reference to Ovid's *Medicamina faciei femineae* ('Make-Up for Female Beauty'). This didactic work can rightly be categorized among Ovid's love elegies, but the extant fragment is arguably more concerned with *cultus* ('cultivation'/'culture') than the theme of love, although the two are cognate (cf. *Rem. am.* 45 and 50, and *Ars* 3.101 and *passim*).[8] The final work that belongs with Ovid's love elegies is the double epistles (16–21), often entitled *Heroides* despite (naturally) featuring as many heroes as heroines.[9] Persuasive arguments

[5] Cf. e.g. *Ars* 1.135–62 and *Am.* 3.2; *Ars* 1.417–36 and *Am.* 1.8; *Ars* 2.547–52 and *Am.* 2.5; *Ars* 2.169–72 and *Am.* 1.7.

[6] For the date of the *Amores*, see McKeown (1987) 74, n. 1. For the relationship between the *Amores*, the *Ars amatoria* and the *Remedia amoris*, see Syme (1978) 13–20, Murgia, (1986a) 80, 86, *passim*, (1986b) 203, Hollis (1977) xiii, Cameron (1995) 116 and Gibson (2003) 39–43.

[7] Syme (1978) 20, Harrison (2002) 84.

[8] Cf. Myerowitz (1985).

[9] Cf. Kenney (1996) 1, n. 1.

suggest that the double epistles were produced in Ovid's exilic period, which would imply that Ovid engaged in love elegy from the very beginning of his poetic career to its very end.[10] More important, perhaps, is that the single *Heroides* (*c.*2, 400 lines), the *Amores* (*c.*2, 400 lines), the three books of the *Ars amatoria* (*c.*2, 400 lines), the *Remedia amoris* (*c.*800 lines) and the double *Heroides* (*c.*1, 600 lines) represent almost ten thousand verses in total, an epic *quantum* (cf. again *Rem. am.* 395–6) matching that of Virgil's *Aeneid*. In the following we shall explore the world of Latin love elegy that these works constitute.

The single *Heroides*: Latin love elegy is *puella* poetry

At first glance, Ovid's single *Heroides* bear little resemblance to the love elegies composed by his elegiac precursors. Ovid makes no secret of this, choosing rather to vaunt the originality of his *opus*, in a passage where he imagines that a future admirer will recommend his *Heroides* thus (*Ars* 3.345–6):

'... uel tibi composita cantetur EPISTVLA uoce;
ignotum hoc aliis ille nouauit opus.'
(*Ars* 3.345–6)

'... or you could have a LETTER of well-composed words sung to you; he made that an original work, previously unknown to all others.'

The *Heroides* are indeed a novel creation that consist of versified letters, purportedly written by legendary heroines who address absent husbands and lovers and who are all referred to in Greek and Roman literature: Penelope, famous from Homer's *Odyssey*, writes to Odysseus (*Her.* 1); Phyllis, probably alluded to in Callimachus (fr. 556 Pf.), writes to Demophoon, (*Her.* 2); Briseis, famous from Homer's *Iliad*, writes to Achilles (*Her.* 3); Phaedra writes to Hippolytus, both famous from Euripides' eponymous tragedy

[10] In particular two features of the double *Heroides* suggest that they were written late in Ovid's career: the usage of *nec* in the sense of *et ne* in the introduction of direct speech, which Ovid applies only here and in the *Metamorphoses* and *Fasti*; and three instances of polysyllabic pentameter endings (*Her.* 16.290, 17.16 and 19.202), found only at *Fast.* 5.582 and 6.660 and in the exile poetry, cf. Courtney (1965) 63–4, Kenney (1996) 21–22 and Platnauer (1951) 16–17. Furthermore, Platnauer (1951) 9–10 observes the frequency of weak caesurae in the third foot of the hexameter in the double *Heroides* (*c.* 3.6%) and the exile poetry, including *Ibis* (*c.* 4%), while the works of Ovid's early poetry has a higher frequency of the same caesura (between 7.5 and 9%). There are also interpretative reasons to view this work in connection with Ovid's exile elegies, cf. e.g. Ingleheart (2010b) 21 and Barchiesi and Hardie (2010) 63.

(*Her.* 4); Oenone, attested in Hellenistic sources,[11] writes to Paris (*Her.* 5); Hypsipyle, famous from Apollonius Rhodius' *Argonautica* and maybe the lost Latin translation of this epic by Terentius Varro Atacinus, writes to Jason (*Her.* 6); Dido, famous from Virgil's *Aeneid*, writes to Aeneas (*Her.* 7); Hermione, attested in Sophocles' lost, eponymous tragedy and Euripides' *Andromache*, writes to Orestes (*Her.* 8); Deianira, famous from Sophocles' *Trachiniae*, writes to Hercules (*Her.* 9); Ariadne, famous from Catullus' *carmen* 64, writes to Theseus (Her. 10); Canace, attested in Euripides' lost tragedy *Aeolus*, writes to Macareus (*Her.* 11); Medea, famous from Euripides' eponymous tragedy, Apollonius Rhodius' *Argonautica*, perhaps Terentius Varro Atacinus' lost Latin version and Ovid's own lost tragedy, writes to Jason (*Her.* 12); Laodamia, featuring in Catullus' *carmen* 68, (probably) Euripides' lost *Protesilaus* and Laevius' fragmentary iambic dimeter poem *Protesilaodamia*, writes to Protesilaus (*Her.* 13); Hypermestra, known from several of Aeschylus' tragedies and Horace's *carmen* 3.11, writes to Lynceus (*Her.* 14); and finally, Sappho, famous in her own right as a lyric poet and attested in Attic and Latin comedy, writes to Phaon (*Her.* 15).[12]

From this brief outline it is evident that the single *Heroides* are heavily indebted to non-elegiac genres, primarily epic, tragedy and neoteric lyric. By focussing on the theme of love and the mode of lament within works that belong to the 'great' (and some 'minor') genres mentioned above, Ovid seems to locate generic loopholes through which he can translate the heroines into the world of elegy.[13] The main vehicle of this translation is the epistolary form of the heroines' poems, which famously has a pendant in Propertius' elegiac letter 4.3, in which Arethusa writes to her absent husband Lycotas.[14] Both in Propertius 4.3 and the single *Heroides* the act of writing letters fits into what might be called erotic-elegiac fundamentalism, where life consists of only one of two activities, depending on the beloved's presence or absence: making love or writing about love. The occasional improbability of the writing situation (e.g. *Her.* 10.135–40), as well as self-designations like

11 Parthenius tells the story in *Amat. narr.* 4; cf. Lightfoot (2009) 558–61. Ps.-Lycophron mentions Oenone in *Alexandra* 57–68. Quintus of Smyrna later wrote of Paris and Oenone in his *Posthomerica* (10).

12 Comic fragments and titles of relevance are Alexis (135; 136; 137 K-A), Amipsias (15 K-A), Amphis (32 K-A), Antiphanes (139; 140; 194 K-A), Diphilus (52 K-A; 70), Ephippus (20 K-A), Menander (fr. 258 Körte), Timocles (32 K-A), and Turpilius (2.113–18 Ribbeck; 29–37 Rychlewska). The ascription of *Heroides* 15 to Ovid is disputed, cf. Thorsen (forthcoming).

13 The verb *queri* (to lament) is far more frequent in the single *Heroides* than in any other work by Ovid; cf. Anderson (1973) 82, n. 11.

14 Prop. 4.3 is normally regarded as a model for Ovid's *Heroides*, but considering the chronological order of Ovid's work and Propertius' fourth book, the possibility remains that the latter is a response to the former. I owe this observation to Stephen Harrison.

scribentis imago (*Her.* 7.183 and *Her.* 11.5, 'the writer's image') subtly disclose the fiction of these letters, which of course are poems. Fittingly, a real woman poet, or rather, the woman poet, Sappho, purportedly writes the final elegiac epistle. Sappho also allows for the insertion of meta-elegiac reflections – a hallmark of Ovidian love elegy – into the single *Heroides*, as she ponders on the relationship between life and poetry (*Her.* 15.1–8; 79–84), defining elegy as *flebile carmen* (*Her.* 15.7, 'tearful composition').

Transformed and transported into Ovid's *Heroides*, the outlook, behaviour and experiences of the heroines resemble those of the *poeta-amator*, or the *poetria-amatrix,* as Holzberg (2002b: 71) has dubbed the concept (cf. *Her.* 15.183). Each letter represents a kind of *paraklausithyron* ('lament by the closed door'), except that in the single *Heroides* the door which conventionally bars the lover from the beloved is most frequently replaced by the sea over which the hero has sailed away, leaving the heroine in the situation of an *exclusa amans* ('rejected lover'). There are examples of the elegiac topos of *seruitium amoris* ('slavery of love', especially Briseis, cf. *Her.* 3.75–80, 101–102) and among the numerous instances that recall the topos of *militia amoris* ('soldiery of love') the two most arresting are perhaps those of Hypsipyle and Canace. The queen Hypsipyle is experienced in real warfare; she has led the army of women who killed all the men on her island of Lemnos and readily transfers military jargon to the field of love when she calls Jason's new wife Medea her *hostis* (*Her.* 6.82, 'enemy'). Canace is in an entirely different situation; she has no experience of war, as far as we can tell, and yet when she gives birth to the child she has conceived with her brother Macareus, she describes herself as a *rudis . . . et noua miles* (*Her.* 11.48, 'raw military recruit').

Remarkably, Hypsipyle's *hostis* and Canace's *miles* (soldier) are the only instances in the Latin language where these nouns are attested in the feminine. Rosati's astute observation that the *Heroides* is *L'elegia al femminile* ('women's version of elegy') is thus rendered true even on a lexical level (Rosati 1992). The implications of Ovid's elegiac 'feminization' have at least as much to do with genre as with gender. One of the most striking features of the new kind of poetry that emerges concurrently with Catullus, and is distilled into the genre of Latin love elegy by Propertius, Tibullus, Sulpicia and Lygdamus, is the figure of the *puella*. There are attestations of Greek-style predilection for pederasty even in Roman elegy, but the Latin *puer* remains totally eclipsed by the *puella*.[15] The term not only denotes a

[15] E.g. Tib. 1.4, 1.8; Valgius in Hor. *Carm.* 2.9; Ov. *Am.* 1.1.20 and *Ars* 2.864; also relevant are Catullus' Juventius poems. See Luck (1969) 83–99; relevant is also Miller (2004) 60–94.

morally and psychologically complex female figure, which vacillates between being the distinct other and similar for the elegist, but also occurs with such frequency in this poetry that it arguably assumes the function of a generic marker. Ovid's *ignotum opus*, with its astonishing range of heroines, who incessantly use the term *puella* about themselves and other women, thus highlights a crucial characteristic of Latin love elegy, namely that it is *puella* poetry.

The extant *Amores*: love elegy by the book and beyond

If the single *Heroides* tend to be unexpectedly elegiac (cf. Spoth 1992), the extant *Amores* have 'love elegy' written all over them. The title itself seems to be a tribute to the canonical proto-elegist Gallus, who probably also called his elegies *Amores* (Servius *ad Buc.* 10.1). Furthermore, Ovid's *Amores* are set in the contemporary world of Rome – with plenty of political poignancy – and the protagonist lover (*amator*) throughout the work is *Naso poeta* (*Am.* 2.1.2, Ovid the poet). He conventionally defends his own *nequitia* (*Am.* 2.1.2, 'morally reproachable incapacity and laziness') in the face of traditional masculine ideals (*Am.* 1.15.3, *mos patrum*) and produces *recusationes* ('excuses') not only for being a poet instead of something useful like a soldier or lawyer, but also, as a poet, for not writing of serious matters. But the poet claims that he must love and write about his love for (predominantly) Corinna, his *puella*, who has a meaningful name – notably that of the most famous female poet after Sappho,[16] which simultaneously is Greek for 'little girl'[17] – and appealing body language, but otherwise is virtually silent.[18] Nevertheless, she behaves like a wilful *domina* and only rarely accepts the advances of the poet, who suffers *seruitium amoris* (*Am.* 2.17), but also actively engages in *militia amoris* (*Am.* 1.9), exposing himself to the hardships befalling an *exclusus amator* (*Am.* 1.6) and complaining at the closed door of his beloved (*paraklausithyron*).

By including all these features, Ovid's *Amores* abide by the rules of Latin love elegy, which apply to all the works of the canonical Roman erotic elegists. But only in Ovid does Elegia appear in person:[19] the embodiment of the genre emerges as a luscious, slightly limping female figure (*Am.* 3.1.7–10) in a competition with another personification of a genre, the more serious Tragoedia. The two divinities contend for Ovid's poetic favours, and as

16 See Keith (1994) 32. Regarding Sappho and Corinna it is interesting to note that there were in fact statues of the two poets in ancient Rome; see Thorsen 2012.

17 Cf. Hardie (2002b) 2.

18 Cf. Prop. 2.3.19–21, McKeown (1987) 19–24, Hardie (2002b) 2.

19 Cf. Perkins (2011).

might be expected, Elegia triumphs (if only for the moment). The arguments she uses to win Ovid over are perhaps more surprising. First, she stresses that both she and the god of love are *leuis* (*Am.* 3.1.41) and that her gentle touch (that of a procuress) has refined even Venus. Furthermore, she reminds Ovid of how she has taught Corinna to dupe her husband and draws attention to the distress and degradation she, Elegia, continues to suffer – often in the shape of roughly treated letters – for the sake of love (*Am.* 3.1.41–58).

Ovid's Elegia is sexy (like the *Amores*), didactic (like the *Ars amatoria*) and not afraid of getting her hands dirty, even if that means assuming the shape of a common letter (like the *Heroides*).[20] This *leuis Elegia* seems alien to the definition of elegy as *flebile carmen* (*Her.* 15.7), but is later in the *Amores* juxtaposed with a second portrayal (*Am.* 3.9), where Ovid bids her to loosen her hair in grief at the bier of Tibullus:

> flebilis indignos, Elegia, solue capillos:
> a, nimis ex uero nunc tibi nomen erit!
> (*Am.* 3.9.3–4)

> Tearful Elegia, loosen the hair that you should not have had to loosen: ah, too much of a truth will your name now become.

The distribution of poems that contain meta-elegiac reflections and dramatizations constitutes one of the more important structures of the *Amores*. Metapoetic reflections are indeed embedded in the portrayal of Elegia, too, but also – and more explicitly – in the framing poems of each of the three books of the *Amores*. When the first book opens, Cupid has laughingly attacked Ovid and his fine intentions, reducing his hexameter on Virgilian *arma* (*Am.*1.1, 'wars') to a pentameter characterizing the present elegy.[21] Ovid reproaches the god of love for stepping out of line and asks *an, quod ubique, tuum est?* (*Am.* 1.1.15, 'or is everything everywhere yours?') The question seems rhetorical, but considering the imperialist strategy towards other, traditionally greater genres on behalf of love elegy in the *Heroides*, the question can also be genuine. The all-embracing ambition of the god of love, who finally shoots his dart into Ovid's heart, has a pendant in the finale of the first book, where Ovid asserts his place in the all-embracing history of Graeco-Roman literature (*Am.* 1.15.9–42).

The humorous drama of *Am.* 1.1 also stages a *recusatio* for not writing literature of a higher order, most prominently represented by epic and tragedy.

20 For Ovid's *Elegia* in the context of Propertius and Augustan politics, see Wyke (2002) 115–54.

21 For an attractive disclosure of the ambiguous vocabulary of *Am.* 1.1, see Kennedy (1993) 58–63.

And at *Am.* 2.1 it is precisely another attempt at epic, more precisely that of a *Gigantomachia* ('Clash of the Titans'), that must cede to elegy in a poem that also stages a topos of Latin love elegy, namely the *paraklausithyron*. Towards the end of the book we find the next poem with meta-elegiac qualities, *Amores* 2.18, in which Ovid, now an incurable love poet, challenges his epic-composing friend Macer to convert to elegy. Finally, two poems, *Am.* 3.1 and *Am.* 3.15, frame the third book, where the choice between tragedy and elegy is dramatized.

Between the framing poems of the *Amores* – which first invoke all genres versus elegy in book one, then epic versus elegy in book two, and finally tragedy versus elegy in book three – a love story evolves, not so much chronologically, perhaps, as thematically (Holzberg (2002b) 46–53).[22] McKeown (1987: 92–4) has however pointed out a strikingly coherent line of development that entails both love and lament, but not quite in the traditional elegiac manner. In *Am.* 1.3 Ovid declares that he will always be faithful to his beloved *puella* and not play 'love's acrobat' (*desultor amoris*),[23] and in *Am.* 1.5, the first poem in which Corinna is named, the two of them are in bed. In book two, however, Ovid confesses that he does have an eye for most women (*Am.* 2.4) and soon thereafter he reports to 'love' two girls at the same time (*Am.* 2.10). Each is more beautiful than the other, both are more pleasing; what can Ovid do with such abundance – for which he assures us he is man enough – but to wish to die of sex? And die in the embrace of a woman he will, but not in the way he imagines: at *Am.* 3.7 he finds himself in bed with a most able and attractive *puella*, but despite (as he brags) having recently satisfied Chlide twice, Pitho thrice and Corinna no less than nine times – a Catullan hyperbole (Catull. 32.8) – in one short night (*Am.* 3.7.23–6), still his member is lying *praemortua* (*Am.* 3.7.65, 'dead before time') and *turpiter languidiora hesterna rosa* (*Am.* 3.7.66, 'shamefully more drooping than the rose of yesterday').[24] Whatever the intentions, there is a lesson to learn from that!

The *Ars amatoria*: Latin love elegy is the art of love

In the *Ars amatoria* Ovid wants to help readers to be wise lovers who avoid failure, are loved in return and enjoy the pleasures of sex. With successful sex as the ultimate goal, Ovid sets out, entitling himself both *praeceptor amoris*

[22] For a splendid analysis of the traditionally most 'offensive' poems (e.g. about female baldness *Am.* 1.14 and abortion 2.13 and 2.14) included in this 'love-story', see James (2003) 155–211.
[23] See however Gibson (Chapter 13) in this volume. [24] Cf. Sharrock (1995).

(*Ars* 1.17, 'professor of love') and *Naso magister* (*Ars* 2.744, 3.812, 'Ovid the teacher'), to coach men (books one and two) and women (book three) through the stages of finding, seducing and enjoying a lover. By choosing the theme of love, Ovid aligns the *Ars amatoria* with the tradition of trivial sex manuals allegedly written by women (cf. Gibson 2003: 14–19). At the same time – by choosing a poetic form (the elegiac distich, cf. *Ars* 1.264), by rivalling the prototypically didactic poet Hesiod (*Ars* 1.25–8) and by inserting – almost as a slip of the tongue – a cosmogony (*Ars* 2.467–80), a hallmark of the didactic genre (cf. e.g. Hes. *Theog.* 115–20, Lucr. 5.416–508) – Ovid makes it clear that this time he has set out to conquer this 'great' genre for Latin love elegy.

Closer examination reveals that Ovid in his *Ars amatoria* continues to appropriate other non-elegiac genres *sub specie Amoris*. The all-pervasive erotic perspective seems to be vouched for by Venus, whom Ovid invokes in the first (*Ars* 1.30) and second book (*Ars* 2.15) and who finally appears to him when he writes the third book (*Ars* 3.43–56). Venus' epiphany is the last of three instances where a god addresses Ovid as poet. In the first book (*Ars* 1.525) Bacchus requires Ovid's attention, and the poet responds by telling how the god, accompanied by bacchantes, Silenus and satyrs, fell in love with Ariadne on the island where Theseus had abandoned her (cf. *Her.* 10). The narrative serves numerous purposes: erotically it provides a divine example of male desire and rape (cf. Catull. 64, *Fast.* 3.459–517, cf. Conte, 1986b: 59–63); metonymically it illustrates the usefulness of (moderate quantities of) wine in the process of seduction (*Ars* 1.565–9); and metapoetically it underscores that Bacchus presides as a vatic deity not only over tragedy, but also over its sexualized relative, the satyr play, in which Silenus is a stock figure.

The second book of the *Ars amatoria* opens with Ovid's appraisal of the god Apollo, who then, almost halfway through, actually appears to the poet (*Ars* 2.493–510). Both Bacchus and Apollo are patron gods of poetry in general (cf. *Her.* 15.23–4, *Am.* 1.3.11), but whereas drama is predominantly Bacchus' genre, Apollo is mainly the 'protector of epic singers and lyre-players' (Hes. *Theog.* 94), plus oracular verse and philosophy. Apollo has a habit of manifesting himself to poets (e.g. Callim. *Aet.* 1.1.21–4; Virg. *Ecl.* 6.3–5; Prop. 3.3.13–16; Hor. *Carm.* 4.15.1–4), urging them to pursue his different interests. In Ovid's *Ars amatoria* the god, conspicuously vatic – lyre in hand, laureate and *uates uidendus* (*Ars* 2.497, 'looking like a bard') – is both oracular and philosophical: he instructs the poet to 'know himself' and wants him to break off his cosmological excursion (which has been dangerously close to a natural history of beastly desires) so that he can pursue his teachings.[25] Fittingly, philosophical reflections on decay and mortality permeate the whole of this book, where Ovid, not denying the power of appearances in the game of love, asserts that inner qualities (enhanced, we will be pleased to know, by the knowledge of Greek and Latin, cf. *Ars* 2.121–2) are far more important: *ut ameris, amabilis esto* (*Ars* 2.107, 'in order to be loved, you must be loveable').[26]

Finally, Ovid chronicles his encounter with Venus. The goddess has ordered him to teach women as well as men and thus follow the example of the lyric poet Stesichorus; he was famously blinded by the Muses when he wrote poetry chastizing Menelaus' unfaithful wife Helen, but regained his vision when he subsequently composed palinodes in her praise. Ovid, who has already acquitted Helen of all blame (*Helenen ego crimine soluo*, *Ars* 2.371), rises enthusiastically to the occasion, not only to teach women to love the right men, but also to teach them about Augustan Rome – replete with political tensions – and himself as a poet. Towards the end of the poem (*Ars* 3.769–70) Ovid again reports the words of Venus as he hesitates with embarrassment before the task, assigned to him by the goddess herself, of describing different sexual positions, an undertaking he eventually embarks on – with bravado (*Ars* 3.771–88).

The idea that love can be taught is (still today) profoundly unromantic and seems to undermine the love elegist's very *raison d'être*. But by exploring the complex of love as systematically as the Roman erotic elegists do, they necessarily acquire a rare expertise in the field (cf. *Tr.* 2.447–66). Ovid insists that it is precisely his personal experience that enables him to appropriate even the didactic genre for love elegy (*Ars* 1.129–30): he has made his mistakes, and learned from them. An inevitable consequence of this profoundly elegiac insight is that the carefully crafted *effet de réel* of the genre is simultaneously disclosed as an act of art.

The *Remedia amoris*: suicidal tendencies

The *Remedia amoris* opens with a dramatic scene: Amor, god of love, has just read the title and furiously accuses Ovid of waging war against him (*Rem. am.* 1–2). In Ovid's ensuing defence he reassures the god that his *Remedia amoris* are only meant for the extreme cases of lovesickness that result in suicide (*Rem. am.* 15–22) and that he will not interfere with anyone who loves happily (*Rem. am.* 13–14). Love is fine, Ovid argues, but it has

[25] For the Augustan aspect of Apollo in *Ars* 2, see Miller (2009); for the Callimachean aspects of Apollo in *Ars* 2, see Sharrock (1994).

[26] Cf. Labate (1984).

nothing to do with death, since Amor is a peace-loving and playful deity, distant from all bloody atrocities (20, 23–4, 27–8), not unlike Elegia as she was portrayed in the *Amores* (3.1) and as she will reappear almost halfway through the *Remedia* (*Rem. am.* 379–80).

Ovid makes the connection between Amor and the genre of elegy, too, when he bids the god to continue to employ *iuuenes* (young men) and *puellae* (girls) in classical topoi of Latin love elegy, exemplified by the *paraklausithyron* and *furtiuus amor* ('stolen love'). Finally Ovid bids Amor: *modo blanditias rigido, modo iurgia, posti/ dicat et exclusus flebile cantet amans* (*Rem. am.* 35–6, 'let the shut-out lover both coax and swear at the unresponsive door and sing a tearful song').[27] But how is it possible to love happily at the same time as you are rejected and cry? There are at least two answers to this question: either Ovid, who often delights in the fine line between faking and aching, wants Amor to bid young people to act like elegiac lovers (as he does at e.g. *Ars* 1.611–12), or there is a genuine conflict at the heart of the poetic project of the *Remedia amoris*. In the following I will maintain the latter view.

One of the central lessons in the *Remedia amoris* is to unlearn to love women, but although Ovid keeps a sharp focus on saving lives by preventing heartache, he has such a hard time lecturing on how to be disgusted with girls that he literally begins to contradict himself: *'quam mala' dicebam 'nostrae sunt crura puellae'/ (nec tamen, ut uere confiteamur, erant)* (*Rem. am.* 317–18, cf. 319–20, 'I used to say "how ugly the legs of my girl are!" (And yet they were not, should I confess the truth)'). Ovid's denigration of the girl gains momentum only when he recalls her avarice, which enables him to reverse the arguments at *Ars* 2.657–62, proving yet again that a flaw can be an advantage – and vice versa – depending on the perspective.

What Ovid finds even more distressing than to teach men how to dislike girls is to instruct his readers not to read love poetry: *eloquar inuitus: teneros ne tange poetas; summoueo dotes impius ipse meas* (*Rem. am.* 757–8, 'I will speak against my will: do not touch the tender poets; I am sacrilegious and withdraw my own treasures (from you)'). Ovid then (re)produces a list (cf. *Ars* 3.329–34) of the erotic poets Callimachus, Philitas, Sappho, Anacreon and the Latin love elegists, before including himself thus: *et mea nescioquid carmina tale sonant* (*Rem. am.* 766, 'and my poems sound somewhat like these'). At this point, towards the end of the *Remedia amoris*, it is important to remember how the beginning of the work evokes all of Ovid's preceding elegiac compositions. The opening conflict with Amor recalls that of *Amores* 1.1, Ovid refers openly to the *Ars amatoria* (*Rem. am.* 43) and includes four

[27] Cf. *Her.* 15.7 and *Am.* 3.9.3.

of his *Heroides* in an exemplary catalogue of unhealthy love (*Rem. am.* 55–64, see also 591–608). The reader who is about to finish the *Remedia amoris* should now in hindsight grasp the severity of the conflict at the heart of the work, which is that Ovid's attempt to separate love from death is his own attempt at suicide as a poet.

A couple in the end of love or: a couple in love in the end?

As we know, Ovid survived. But what about Latin love elegy? Firstly, Ovid did not regard himself as the last love elegist in the history of Latin literature (cf. *Tr.* 2.467–8, *Pont.* 4.16). Secondly, if Ovid wrote his double *Heroides* while in exile, the *Remedia amoris* was not a final farewell to the genre even within the framework of his own literary career. The double *Heroides* include Paris' letter to Helen (*Her.* 16) and Helen's reply (*Her.* 17); both characters are famous in general, but especially from Homer's *Iliad*; Leander's letter to Hero (*Her.* 18) and Hero's reply (*Her.* 19), a couple which features in Virgil's *Georgics*; and Acontius' letter to Cydippe (*Her.* 20) followed by Cydippe's reply (*Her.* 21), whose relationship is described in Callimachus' elegiac *Aetia*.[28]

The three couples embody very different kinds of loves: Paris and Helen commit adultery, Leander and Hero share true love (i.e. mutual and exclusive, innocent and forbidden) and Acontius and Cydippe will be united in (forced) marriage. This diversity of erotic relations is furthermore furnished with a variety of elegiac features. Alessandro Barchiesi (1993) has brilliantly shown how the letters of Acontius and Cydippe re-enact the Callimachean origins of Latin love elegy, in which reading and writing are key components, by entering on a sophisticated game of creative genealogies and original repetitions, all features essential to Augustan poetry. While Acontius and Cydippe thus reiterate the poetic starting point of the genre in question, Paris writes as if he has been an eager reader of both Ovid's *Amores* and *Ars amatoria* (cf. *Her.* 16.215–18) and Helen sympathizes with her rival Oenone, as well as Hypsipyle, Ariadne and Medea (*Her.* 17.193–6, 231–4), all abandoned heroines from the single *Heroides*.

The Heroidean version of the elegiac topos of the *paraklausithyron* is furthermore activated in the case of Leander and Hero, as they desperately long for each other on opposite sides of the Hellespont. The young lovers would normally enjoy the elegiac *furtiuus amor* each time Leander swam across the strait, guided by the light in Hero's tower. But on the night he writes his epistle, a week-long storm prevents him from swimming. A sailor

[28] Cf. Hunter in this volume (Chapter 1).

dares to tempt the waters and Leander sends his letter off with him, assuring Hero that he would have jumped into the boat himself, were it not that his parents (who apparently would disapprove of their liaison) were watching the departure. Hero then receives Leander's letter, and replies.

Among the many meta-elegiac features of the letters of Leander and Hero is their shared obsession with death. True, romantic love knows no limits, not even those imposed by the end of life; this is fundamentally why (romantic) love and (plaintive) elegy are inseparable. Leander relishes his fantasies about his future death (*Her.* 18.169–79, 189–200) because it would prove his love for Hero. Her terrified fascination with the same deadly scenario – mediated through an ominous dream – reveals that she has got the message (*Her.* 19.191–204).

It was at dawn when the lamp in her tower was dying down that Hero had her dream vision. Although she does not attribute much importance to the detail as she writes her letter, it is of course fatal: at the same time as the flame flickers, Leander is swimming towards her, but as his guiding light vanishes, he gets lost and drowns. His body will soon be washed ashore on Hero's side of the strait, where she will find him and commit suicide by throwing herself from her tower.

The timing of Leander and Hero's letters is thus crucial to their tragedy, which is a tragedy that holds insights into the genre of love elegy. As in the case of the re-enacting closure of the letters of Acontius and Cydippe, reading and writing are key elements here too. Hero reads Leander's letter as he throws himself into the waves for the very last time, while she writes her reply virtually as he dies, and when her letter is written, she will soon be dead as well. The epistolary elegies of Leander and Hero thus frame a moment of death, but this death is at the same time overruled, as the lives that are lost during the time it takes to read and write the texts in question are simultaneously preserved in the eternal now of literature.

Further reading

The bibliography on Ovid's love elegies is enormous and the following titles are some highlights. First, Latin texts: for the *Heroides*, the only complete edition (1–21) and commentary remains Palmer and Purser (1898, reprinted with introduction by D. Kennedy 2005). Dörrie (1971 and 1975) is a somewhat more bewildering critical edition of *Her.* 1–21, with plenty of useful material for the patient reader. Splendid is Knox (1995), covering *Her.* 1, 2, 5, 7, 10, 11 and 15, as is Kenney (1996), covering *Her.* 16–21. In Italian there is a most commendable series published by Felice le Monnier and most recently de Gruyter of editions and commentaries on select *Heroides*: 1–3

(Barchiesi, 1992), 7 (Piazzi 2007), 8 (Pestelli 2007), 9 (Casali 1995), 10 (Battistella 2010), 12 (Bessone 1997), 13 (Reggia 2011) and 18–19 (Rosati 1996b). Kenney (1995) has brilliantly edited all of Ovid's amatory works (OCT), as has Ramírez de Verger (2003, BT). For *Amores* only, McKeown's Latin text and commentaries on book 1 and 2 are indispensable (1987–98), while Booth (1991) has produced a fine commentary to book 2 and Ingleheart and Radice have composed a fresh commentary to select poems of *Amores* book 3 (2011). Hollis (1977), Janka (1997), in German, and Gibson (2003) each provide highly valuable commentaries on the three books of the *Ars amatoria*.

Both the single and double *Heroides* are available along with the *Amores* in Latin with en face translation by Showerman (1977), revised by Goold (LCL), as are the *Ars amatoria and Remedia amoris* translated by Mozley (1929) (LCL). Furthermore, there are English translations of the *Amores* by Lee (1968), of the *Heroides* by Isbell (PC, 1990), the *Ars amatoria* and *Remedia amoris* by Melville (WC, 1998) and of the *Amores*, the *Heroides* and the *Remedia amoris* by Slavitt (2011).

Among overview works that present Ovid's entire output I recommend Hardie (2002b), Holzberg (2002b) and Volk (2010), which include stimulating outlines of Ovid's erotic-elegiac phase within the framework of his career. Conversely, Harrison (2002) is an original and compelling interpretation of Ovid's career, including the *Metamorphoses*, from an elegiac point of view. Spoth (1992) systematically explores the elegiac nature of the single *Heroides* for those who read German, while Rosati (1992), in Italian, and Fulkerson (2009), in English, are seminal and highly accessible regarding the crucial, Heroidean connection between the female voice and the genre of erotic elegy. The *Heroides*, *Amores* and the *Ars amatoria* are all at the centre of attention in Scivoletto's study (1976), in Italian, as are the same works, plus *Medicamina faciei feminea*, in Sabot's more extensive francophone monograph published the same year (1976), as well as in Thorsen (forthcoming), in English. Deremetz and Fabre-Serris (1999) offer, in French, a wide range of approaches to the *Heroides* together with the *Amores*. Boyd (1997) is a comprehensive study, which in its entirety is dedicated to Ovid's *Amores*. Luck (1969) on the *Amores* remains remarkably valuable, while Kennedy (1993) is brilliantly thought-provoking. Armstrong (2005) and Liveley (2005) give thorough presentations of Ovid's entire amatory output, which is explored in relation to Augustan politics by Davis (2006). Sharrock (1994) offers a sharp analysis of the second book, which includes plenty of sophisticated reflections on the genre of elegy. Conte's study (1989) is seminal for the understanding of the genre of Latin love elegy and for the *Remedia amoris*, and should be read together with Fulkerson (2004). For both the *Ars amatoria* and the *Remedia amoris*, see the rich volume edited by Gibson, Green and Sharrock (2006). Barchiesi (1993) on both the single and double *Heroides* is highly recommended, as are – for the latter – Kenney (1996), Barchiesi (1999) and Acosta-Hughes (2009). In general all three companions to Ovid, Boyd (2002), Hardie (2002a) and Knox (2009) remain highly useful for the scholar as well as the student of Ovid's love elegies.

PART III

The elegiac world

8

STEPHEN HARRISON

Time, place and political background

Time – chronology and politics

Chronology and historical context

Though proto-elegiac precursor texts such as Latin translations of Greek erotic epigrams are to be found in Roman literature from near the beginning of the first century BC,[1] Roman erotic elegy, in its 'classic' form which presents the male elegist addressing the *puella* or *puer* and leading the 'alternative' and angst-ridden life of love, seems to extend only over the second half of the first century BC. Gallus, probably born about 70 BC, is unlikely to have been writing elegy much before 50,[2] and Ovid's *Amores* were clearly completed by the end of the century,[3] by which point the poet had already turned to post-elegiac or even 'meta-elegiac' texts such as the *Ars Amatoria*.[4]

This two-generation literary life of love elegy can be integrally related to the tumultuous political, social and cultural changes of this period of Roman history. The fifty years following 50 BC saw the completion of several trends of the first century as a whole: the final breakdown of the traditional political system of the Roman Republic and the emergence of a monarchical regime, the unprecedented globalization of Roman culture in terms of conquest and military enterprise, and extended contact with and absorption of Greek and other non-Italian cultural influences.[5] The disastrous impact of Roman civil war in the first part of this period (between Caesar's crossing of the Rubicon

1 See Bessone (Chapter 2) in this volume.

2 On Gallus see Raymond (Chapter 3) in this volume.

3 See n. 28 below.

4 On Ovid's development and exhaustion of the genre cf. Gibson (Chapter 13) and Miller (Chapter 15) in this volume.

5 For these general tendencies see e.g. Raaflaub and Toher (1990), Edwards and Woolf (2006), Habinek and Schiesaro (1997).

in 49 and the future Augustus' victory at Actium in 31) is an especially notable feature.[6]

Most extant love elegy derives from the post-civil-war period. The disappearance of vicious internecine strife after Actium may well have stimulated a climate where 'peaceful' poetry such as love elegy could flourish, and where aspects of private life could receive literary emphasis now that public imperatives were less intense. The loosening of collectivist political and social traditions in the effective dismantling of the established Roman state which took place in the 40s may also have encouraged the relaxed approach to sexual morality which elegy projects in its presentation of leisured young men dominated by personal erotic concerns and (periodically) complaisant female and male lovers.[7]

In terms of detectable dates, the only love-elegies we know of which were certainly written before the battle of Actium are by Gallus. Gallus fr.2 Courtney (= fr. 4 Blänsdorf), celebrating the triumphant return of a Caesar to Rome, seems to refer to Julius Caesar in 45 BC,[8] especially given the undoubted citation of adjacent lines of Gallus in Virgil *Ecl.*10,[9] in a poetry-book most likely dated to *c.*38 BC.[10] The elegies of Propertius and Tibullus, though in some cases referring to earlier events from the civil-war period such as the sack of Perusia in 40 BC (see below), undoubtedly belong to a post-Actium Rome of peace and reconstruction; likely dates are *c.*30 for the first book of Propertius's elegies, *c.*26 for the first book of Tibullus, and *c.*26–24 for the poems known as Propertius 2.[11]

Elegy and war

Tibullus' first book begins and ends with poems which reject war. In 1.1–6 the life of wealth derived from fighting is famously rejected for the quiet, rural life, yet to be revealed as the life of love:

> diuitias alius fuluo sibi congerat auro
>   et teneat culti iugera multa soli,

6 For the impact of civil war on Roman culture from the first century BC see Jal (1963), Breed and Damon (2010).

7 For this background to elegy see especially Griffin (1985) 48–141.

8 For a detailed discussion see Nisbet in Anderson, Parsons and Nisbet (1979) 151–5 (= Nisbet (1995) 124–31).

9 See Hinds (1983).

10 I here follow Coleman (1979) 14–18 and Tarrant (1978) rather than Clausen (1994) xxii and Bowersock (1971).

11 See Lyne (1998a).

quem labor adsiduus uicino terreat hoste,
  Martia cui somnos classica pulsa fugent:
me mea paupertas uitae traducat inerti,
  dum meus adsiduo luceat igne focus.

Let another pile up riches for himself in tawny gold
And hold many acres of cultivated soil –
He who feels the fear of continuous labour with the enemy near,
Whose sleep is banished by the sound of war-trumpets;
For me, let my modest life move me to a life of inaction,
As long as my hearth gleams with an unquenched fire.

The linked topics of war and materialism, and their rejection for peace and modest self-sufficiency, look to the Roman foreign conquests of the post-Actium years; this way of life is clearly rejected for that of rustic peace. Here we have a clear ideological divergence from the rhetoric of Augustan conquest, voiced in the same period at the end of Virgil's *Georgics* (4.560–62) or the ninth epode of Horace and demonstrated publicly in the triple triumph of 29 BC. Tibullus wishes his patron Messalla well in his military career, but will himself remain at home engaged in the campaigns of love (1.1.51–6):

O quantum est auri pereat potiusque smaragdi,
  quam fleat ob nostras ulla puella uias.
te bellare decet terra, Messalla, marique,
  ut domus hostiles praeferat exuuias;
me retinent uinctum formosae uincla puellae,
  et sedeo duras ianitor ante fores.

May all the gold and emeralds there are perish
Rather than any girl should weep for my journeyings.
For you, Messalla, it is fitting to wage war by land and sea,
So that your house may display the enemy's spoils:
I am held prisoner by the chains of a beautiful girl,
And I sit as a doorkeeper at her pitiless gates.

The military language of *uinctum* and *sedeo* marks the key metaphor of the *militia amoris*, the military campaigning of love:[12] Tibullus is captured by Delia, not by the enemy, and he lays siege to her house, not to enemy cities. Messalla can decorate his house with military spoils, but for Tibullus the urban house is the place of the life of love (see pp. 144–8 below), and

[12] See Drinkwater (Chapter 12) in this volume.

material prosperity is replaced by the abject status of the prisoner/slave. For Tibullus himself this creates something of an inconsistency, since in this same book he clearly represents himself as joining Messalla on campaign (in 1.3 and 1.7); but it is clear that Tibullan elegy is cast as poetry of peace which rejects war.

In the final poem 1.10 this inconsistency remains: Tibullus presents himself as going to war, presumably again with Messalla (1.10.13), but his loyalty to his patron is subordinated to a passionate attack on fighting in general (1.10.1–6):

> quis fuit, horrendos primus qui protulit enses?
> quam ferus et uere ferreus ille fuit!
> tum caedes hominum generi, tum proelia nata,
> tum breuior dirae mortis aperta uia est.
> an nihil ille miser meruit, nos ad mala nostra
> uertimus, in saeuas quod dedit ille feras?

> Who was the first to produce terrible swords?
> How fierce and how truly made of iron he was!
> Then it was that slaughter and battles were born for the race of men,
> Then a shorter route to dire death was opened up.
> Or is it that he, poor man, deserves no blame, and that we
> Have turned to our own perdition what he gave us to use against wild beasts?

Here the emphasis on humans disastrously fighting each other (*ad mala nostra*, where *noster* as often might mean 'our Roman'[13]) reminds us that as Tibullus wrote Rome had not long emerged from a long period of civil war (see above). Elegy's constant argument that Roman males should serve as soldiers in the cause of love, not in actual war, needs to be understood in a post-civil-war context: in particular, the experience of war in Italy in the 40s BC was clearly important for the elegists.

Tibullus' attack on war at the end of his first book perhaps picks up something similar at the end of Propertius' first book.[14] That book closes with two interlinked short poems (1.21 and 1.22), closely related to types of sepulchral epigram, apparently marking the death, perhaps a decade before, of Gallus, a relative of Propertius, at the siege of Perugia in 40 BC.[15] The emphasis in context is certainly not on the victory of Caesar (the young Augustus), but rather on the tragedy of local loss for Propertius'

13 *OLD* s.v. 7: of civil war again at Horace *Odes* 2.1.36 *quae caret ora cruore nostro?*

14 This can be added to the dossier of Tibullan reaction to Propertius 1 in Lyne (1998a).

15 For full treatments see DuQuesnay (1992) and Cairns (2006b) 46–50; see also Keith (Chapter 6) in this volume.

homeland (see pp. 148–9). Such direct lamentation for the losses of civil war may underlie Tibullus' anti-war rhetoric in 1.10, and even his complaint about the deminution of inherited property at 1.1.41–2; Propertius also alludes to loss of ancestral land (4.1.128), and it seems possible that both poets suffered (as Virgil may have done) in the land-confiscations of 41–40 BC which provided pensions for the young Caesar's victorious army from Philippi.[16]

This tension between the world of love elegy and the world of war is a key element in the genre, and clearly affects its attitude to the conquering career of Augustus (see next section). Civil war continues to play a role: one of Propertius' first allusions to Actium is not encomiastic, but rather an ironic observation that if everyone led the life of love and luxury there would be no civil wars and consequent grief (2.15.41–6):

qualem si cuncti cuperent decurrere uitam
    et pressi multo membra iacere mero,
non ferrum crudele neque esset bellica nauis,
    nec nostra Actiacum uerteret ossa mare,
nec totiens propriis circum oppugnata triumphis
    lassa foret crinis soluere Roma suos.

If all desired to lead a life like this
And to lie back with limbs under the influence of much wine,
There would be no cruel weapon or warship,
And the sea of Actium would not toss our bones,
Nor would Rome, so often beset with triumphs against herself,
Be tired of loosing her hair in grief.

Here as at Tibullus 1.10.5, *nostra* means 'our Roman': the life of love is presented as a better alternative for all Romans than the life of war.

In the gradual movement of Propertian elegy towards a more Augustan stance outlined in the next section, this dichotomy is gradually deconstructed. The pair of poems Propertius 3.4 and 3.5 present first an encouragement for Augustus' upcoming eastern expedition (3.4.1–6):

arma deus Caesar dites meditatur ad Indos,
    et freta gemmiferi findere classe maris.
magna, Quiris, merces: parat ultima terra triumphos;
    Tigris et Euphrates sub tua iura fluent;
sera, sed Ausoniis ueniet prouincia uirgis;
    assuescent Latio Partha tropaea Ioui.

[16] For possible Propertian land-losses see Cairns (2006b) 54–8; for Tibullan, see Murgatroyd (1980) 7.

The god Caesar plans war against the rich Indians
And to cleave the straits of the jewel-bearing sea with his fleet.
Great is the gain, Roman: the earth's last land has triumphs ready,
The Tigris and Euphrates will flow subject to your laws;
Late, but yet a [new] province will come under Italian rods;
Parthian trophies will become used to Latium's Jupiter.

This thoroughly conventional nationalist position is tempered by the wish of Propertius (like Gallus before him) to see and praise the Princeps' triumphant return from his *puella*'s lap (3.4.15–18). Here the elegist goes as far as the traditional form of the genre allows in praising Caesar's war. But 3.4 is followed immediately by 3.5, in which the Tibullan pacifist position is at once adopted (3.5.1–4):

Pacis Amor deus est, pacem ueneramur amantes:
  sat mihi cum domina proelia dura mea.
nec mihi mille iugis Campania pinguis aratur,
  nec bibit e gemma diuite nostra sitis . . .

Cupid is the god of peace, it's peace that lovers worship:
I have enough hard battles with my mistress.
Rich Campania is not ploughed with a thousand yokes for my benefit,
Nor does my thirst drink from a luxurious jewelled vessel . . .

The poet then declares that all triumphs and wealth-getting are vain from the perspective of eternity, and that he will move on to consider philosophical issues as he gets older. The implicit disjunction between these peaceful pursuits and Caesar's campaign is then made brusquely explicit in the last couplet (47–8):

exitus hic uitae superet mihi: uos, quibus arma
  grata magis, Crassi signa referte domum.

Let this end of life remain for me: but you, to whom
War is more pleasing, bring Crassus' standards home.

Despite willingness to compromise, the poet cannot yet commit himself fully to the Augustan military project. The furthest he goes is in 4.6, where the battle of Actium, seen in 2.15 as the disastrous consequence of a wrong lifestyle choice, now becomes the triumphant origin of a great Roman cult-building. Here elegy and war can meet on the middle ground of Callimachean aetiology, and as stressed on pp. 140–4 below Propertius is responding to important positive treatments of the battle by Horace and Virgil.

A final aspect of this stand-off between love elegy and war is to be found in poems where love elegists address epic poets and discuss their two different sets of material. Here the dichotomy is between genres of literature rather than lifestyles, but the two are fundamentally related. In Propertius 1.7 the elegist addresses the epic poet Ponticus (1–6):

> Dum tibi Cadmeae dicuntur, Pontice, Thebae
> armaque fraternae tristia militiae,
> atque, ita sim felix, primo contendis Homero
> (sint modo fata tuis mollia carminibus),
> nos, ut consuemus, nostros agitamus amores,
> atque aliquid duram quaerimus in dominam...
>
> While Cadmus' Thebes is being narrated by you
> And the tragic war of the brothers' campaign,
> And (so may I prosper) you strive with supreme Homer
> (If only destiny is kind to your poetry),
> I, as is my wont, pursue that love of mine,
> And seek for something to use against my mistress's hard-heartedness...

For Propertius at least, the life of love and writing about it amount to the same thing, since poetry has a practical function in his love-affair in softening the *puella* (line 6). The second half of the poem argues that this will happen to Ponticus too (1.7.15–26): should he fall in love, he too will turn to writing elegy rather than epic, and life will influence literature.

The same scenario is set up in Ovid *Amores* 2.18, addressed to the epic poet Macer and clearly recalling Propertius' poem (1–4):[17]

> Carmen ad iratum dum tu perducis Achillem
> primaque iuratis induis arma uiris,
> nos, Macer, ignaua Veneris cessamus in umbra,
> et tener ausuros grandia frangit Amor.
>
> While you bring your poem to the anger of Achilles
> And put the first armour on the heroes who swore the oath,
> I, Macer, take it easy in the indolent shade of Venus,
> And soft Cupid breaks my force as I would attempt grand themes.

[17] It is possible that Tibullus 2.6 is addressed to the same Macer and makes the same intergeneric contrast symbolically (i.e. his apparently literal departure for the wars is a literary change from elegy to epic); for a sceptical discussion see Murgatroyd (1994) 239–40.

Here there is a play between literally putting on armour and putting on *arma*, i.e. epic poetry as represented by the first word of Virgil's *Aeneid* (*arma uiris* clearly puns on *arma uirum*).[18] The dichotomy between epic poet and elegist is set out, but again as in Propertius the poem suggests that the gap can be crossed: Ovid had ambitions to rise to epic (*ausuros grandia*), by the intervention of love, while Macer is expected to include the appropriate erotic stories in his account of the Trojan War before the *Iliad* (2.18.35–40):

> Nec tibi, qua tutum uati, Macer, arma canenti
> aureus in medio Marte tacetur Amor.
> et Paris est illic et adultera, nobile crimen,
> et comes extincto Laodamia uiro.
> si bene te noui, non bella libentius istis
> dicis, et a uestris in mea castra uenis.

> Nor is golden Love in the midst of war left in silence by you, Macer,
> At least where this is safe for a poet of battle:
> In that story there is Paris and his adulteress, a well-known crime,
> And Laodamia who went as companion to her dead husband.
> If I know you well, you narrate wars no more willingly
> Than this kind of material, and are coming over from your camp to mine.

The ideological stand-off between the poetry of love and the poetry of war can thus be defused, certainly in the realm of literature and perhaps in the realm of life.

Elegy and Augustus

In the years 30–24 BC, the young Caesar consolidates his hold on the state, takes the name 'Augustus' and spends a good deal of time away from Rome reinforcing Roman military dominion. But were the elegists our only source for the period, these crucial aspects would be hard to detect: Caesar/Augustus is decidedly low-profile in early elegy. Propertius mentions him only once in book 1, not very positively, as the sacker of Perugia (1.21.7), while Tibullus, patronized by the grand Messalla, does not mention him at all. Though the rise of elegy coincides with the self-establishment of Caesar's heir, in its initial phase it is distinctly uninterested in or antipathetic to the Augustan ideological cause.[19]

[18] See McKeown (1998) 388.

[19] Heyworth (2007a) argues that this remains Propertius' attitude throughout his career, but here I take the more evolutionary approach of La Penna (1977) or Cairns (2006b) 320–61.

This seems to change for Propertius in the mid 20s, in the course of books 2 and 3 (on the partial Augustan colour of 3.4 and 3.5 see pp. 134–40 above). One important factor is the intervention of Maecenas, trusted friend and adviser of Augustus and a man of high cultural and literary tastes, who had already early in the 30s 'recruited' Virgil and Horace for the new Caesarian cause.[20] It seems clear that Maecenas made approaches to Propertius: he is addressed in Propertius 2.1, where the campaigns of Caesar and Maecenas himself are discussed as potential topics, and Augustus (so named for the first time in Propertius) is feted in 2.10 (perhaps the final poem of the original Book 2); in both cases the poet suggests that his own more humble style of writing is not up to such grand subject matter in the typical *recusatio*, but its appearance on the poetic agenda even as a possibility marks something of a political shift since Propertius' first book.

Apart from the role of Maecenas, a further catalyst for Propertius' increased interest in public themes after his first book is the influential output of Virgil and Horace. Already in 2.34 Propertius shows knowledge of the forthcoming *Aeneid* (2.34.61–66),[21] though Virgil's epic was not to be published for some years, while book 3 is clearly in some sense a reaction to the publication of the first three books of Horace's *Odes* in about 23 BC and clearly postdates that year.[22] The evidently nationalist and Augustan engagement of these works, both of which contain (e.g.) encomiastic accounts of the battle of Actium (*Aeneid* 8.675–713, *Odes* 1.37), seems to have influenced Propertius towards more public themes, albeit very much on his own personal terms. The actual publication of the *Aeneid* c.19 BC had a clear impact on Propertius 4, emerging after 16 BC, which shows a much more nationalistic colour than the author's previous works and engages with many elements in Virgil's epic.[23] Poem 4.6 provides a full (if quirky) encomiastic statement of the Augustan position on Actium,[24] and it can be argued that the final three poems of the book, 4.9–11, provide a heavily Augustan closure to Propertius' extant oeuvre.[25]

Propertian elegy's increasing political engagement over the period 30–15 BC seems to have been at least partly the result of pressure from Maecenas

[20] For a useful characterization of Maecenas' *modus operandi* cf. White (1993) 133–8, and for the most recent substantial account of Propertius' relations with Maecenas see Cairns (2006b) 250–94.

[21] See e.g. Robinson (2006) 200–3, Heyworth (2007b) 275.

[22] See most conveniently Fedeli (1985) 32–3 and Keith (Chapter 6) in this volume.

[23] See the summaries of links at Hutchinson (2006) 6–7 and DeBrohun (2003) 263.

[24] See e.g. Cairns (1984), DeBrohun (2003) 210–35, and the suggestive brief treatment of Keith (2008) 164–5; for a more ambivalent view see e.g. Welch (2005) 79–111.

[25] Cf. Harrison (2005).

as well as a personal response to political events and cultural circumstances. Recent scholarship continues vigorously to debate the relation of Propertius to Augustan policy and ideology, but even those who see Propertius' poetry as fundamentally opposed to the 'Augustan project' have to admit that at least on the surface the reader of his four extant books finds a love elegist who begins with an element of defiance of Caesar's heir in Book 1 and ends with Book 4, whose Callimachean aetiological project presents the poet's own version of nationalism, largely leaves behind the traditional material of the life of love, and represents some form of accommodation (willing or unwilling, sincere or insincere) with the Augustan regime and its policies.[26]

Tibullus' second book, likely to have emerged incomplete after his death *c.*19 BC, shows little more engagement with Augustan themes than his first, though it seems to echo the *Aeneid* in 2.5.[27] Ovid's *Amores* (probably principally written *c.*25–12 BC, though the second edition we have was probably edited somewhat later),[28] resembles Tibullus in having little connection with the Augustan regime; it is interesting that the *Amores* never use the title 'Augustus'. It is possible that alternative sources of patronage and influence existed: we learn from Ovid's exile poetry that when young he had some encouragement from Tibullus' patron Messalla and links with his son Messalinus (*Ex Ponto* 1.7.27–8, 2.3.75–80), but the support of Messalla and his family is not at all apparent in the *Amores* themselves.

It might be argued that Ovidian elegy shadows Propertius to a degree by showing some movement over time towards more Augustan interests, in this case without the intervention of Maecenas, whose role with the poets clearly diminished after about 20 BC (he is not mentioned in the *Aeneid* or in Propertius' fourth book).[29] The first two books of the *Amores* mention the Princeps and Julian family only twice, both in ironic relation to Venus and Cupid, in a compliment urging Cupid to imitate the clemency of his great relative (*Amores* 1.2.51–2), and a suggestion that if Venus had followed Corinna's example and aborted Aeneas the world would have been (disastrously?) bereft of the Julian family (2.14.17–18). The third book, however, presents two complimentary references to Rome's leader and his

[26] For a recent survey and view see Heyworth (2007a).

[27] For the incompleteness see Reeve (1984), for the Virgilian engagement Murgatroyd (1994) 165–6.

[28] For the dating cf. McKeown (1987) 77–8.

[29] Scholars debate whether Maecenas fell from grace or simply took a back seat once Augustus himself was largely in Rome after 19 BC (having been absent for most of the 20s): cf. Williams (1990) and White (1991).

family which show a slightly more Augustan stance. At *Amores* 3.8.51–2 Julius Caesar is said to match Romulus/Quirinus, Bacchus/Liber and Hercules in achieving deification: here we find both an implicit compliment to Augustus as *diui filius* and an allusion to Horace's *Roman Odes* where the gods Quirinus, Liber and Hercules are presented as a model for Augustus' future apotheosis (*Odes* 3.3.9–16). At *Amores* 3.12.15–16 we finally find Augustus' achievements mentioned as a worthy potential poetic topic, though one which the poet unwisely rejects for Corinna:

> cum Thebae, cum Troia foret, cum Caesaris acta,
> ingenium mouit sola Corinna meum.

> Though Thebes, Troy, and the deeds of Caesar were available,
> Corinna alone stirred my talent to action.

This is one of several indications in the third book that the poet is moving out of love elegy into more obviously ambitious genres and topics.[30]

Legal considerations might be added to poetic ambition and nationalistic themes as a further explanation for the political evolution of love elegy. The introduction of the *leges Iuliae* strongly encouraging citizen marriage and heavily penalizing adultery in 19–18 BC[31] might be one reason why later elegy such as Propertius' fourth book turns away from its traditional narrative of the life of love (potentially adulterous) to more public themes. And yet post-*Amores* Ovid is far from playing safe: the series of erotodidactic works which engaged him in the last years of the first century BC (the *Ars Amatoria*, *Medicamina Faciei Femineae*, and *Remedia Amoris*) clearly gave instructions on non-marital relationships to citizen men and women, and despite the famous 'insurance' passage which warns off married women as readers (*Ars* 1.31–2), the *Ars Amatoria* could easily be interpreted as a handbook of adultery, as it seems to have been in the matter of Ovid's exile a decade later (*Tristia* 2.245–6).

The trajectory of love elegy over the period 45–15 BC is thus a double one. Love elegy focuses on but then moves away from its traditional content of the life of love and rejection of public life in various forms to a greater receptivity to political and nationalistic themes; in this it reflects larger social and historical trends as the Roman state moves towards a new construction of Augustan community and more conservative moral values. Concomitantly it also moves towards higher literary genres, through both

[30] See Harrison (2002) 81–2.

[31] For their provisions see Treggiari (1991) 277–98.

reaction to the loftier productions of Virgil and Horace and self-conscious internal development within the individual poet's literary career.[32]

Place – Rome and elsewhere

Rome: tales of the city

Latin love elegy is predominantly an urban genre; even Tibullus with his emphasis on the countryside sets only a small proportion of his poems in rural landscapes.[33] The default location is the city of Rome, and within it often a private residence of some kind: prominent examples are Propertius 1.3 or Ovid *Amores* 1.5, where key events in the life of love are enacted in a Roman house. The elegiac *puella* herself is essentially an urban creature, however we define her degree of fictionality or social status:[34] though Tibullus may fantasize about Delia helping with farming in the country, this is clearly a vain hope of escaping from the urban cycle of passionate erotic suffering.[35] The elegiac lover too is quintessentially a resident of Rome: though Tibullus may record himself as leaving Rome to campaign with Messalla (1.3.1–2, 1.7.9–12) and even set elegies abroad on his journeys (1.3), and though Propertius can present himself as being in a storm at sea (1.17) or in wild countryside (1.18) in attempts to escape slavery to Cynthia, the characteristic location of the elegist and the life of love is in Rome. The elegist thus primarily pursues an erotic career in the domestic enviroment of the city rather than the conventional Roman male elite career of foreign military service; such actual warfare is replaced in the elegiac world by the alternative of *militia amoris*, campaigning for love.[36] Even Gallus, later to command armies in the key new territory of Egypt, seems in the 40s BC to present himself as a stay-at-home spectator of Caesar's military glory (Gallus fr. 2 Courtney = fr. 4 Blänsdorf). The setting of many elegies in the personal, interior space of the Roman house emphasizes this overall rejection of the conventional world of public achievement.

Such urban and interior settings also relate to questions of readership and readerly environment. At 3.3.19–20 Apollo suggests to Propertius that his poetry is the literature of the boudoir:

32 For the self-construction of literary careers by Roman poets see Hardie and Moore (2010).

33 Though 1.1 is located in the country, 1.2 returns to the city, and only five of the sixteen extant Tibullan poems (1.1, 1.3, 1.10, 2.1, 2.3) are not set in an urban environment.

34 See P. A. Miller (Chapter 10) in this volume.

35 See Lyne (1980) 149–69.

36 See Drinkwater (Chapter 12) in this volume.

ut tuus in scamno iactetur saepe libellus,
    quem legat exspectans sola puella uirum.

so that your little book may often be tossed on a stool,
to be read by a girl alone waiting for her man.

To this explicit readership Ovid adds love-sick young men (*Amores* 1.15.38), and young people of both sexes who wish to learn about love (2.1.5–6). Though Propertius presents his poems on Cynthia (perhaps book 1) being read all over Rome and even in the forum (2.24.1–2), on the whole love elegy is a literature of the interior on both literal and metaphorical levels – a genre of brooding and introspection rather than poetry with a public function and location. This interior aspect is also evident in the close links between elegy's deployment of mythological scenes closely related to the kind of wall-painting characteristically found in the inner rooms of Roman town houses.[37] A good example is the opening of Propertius 1.3.1–8:

Qualis Thesea iacuit cedente carina
    languida desertis Cnosia litoribus;
qualis et accubuit primo Cepheia somno
    libera iam duris cotibus Andromede;
nec minus assiduis Edonis fessa choreis
    qualis in herboso concidit Apidano:
talis uisa mihi mollem spirare quietem
    Cynthia consertis nixa caput manibus . . .

Just as the Cretan girl, with Theseus' ship departing,
lay exhausted on deserted shores;
just as Andromeda, daughter of Cepheus, lay down
in her first sleep once freed from the hard cliffs;
and equally just as a Thracian woman, tired out from continuous dances
falls down on grassy Epidanus:
so Cynthia seemed to me to breathe soft rest,
supporting her head on her entwined hands . . .

Here the reader is invited to associate a catalogue of images of sleeping heroines with potential decorations of the domestic interior where the poem's action takes place.[38]

[37] For the distribution of mythological paintings in Campanian town houses see Wallace-Hadrill (1994) 149–60, and for the links of Propertius 1.3.1–8 with wall-painting (in which Ariadne abandoned by Theseus (cf. Elsner (2007) 91–109) and Andromeda freed from her rock (cf. *LIMC* Andromeda I.69–71) were standard topics) cf. Valladares (2005).

[38] For the relevance of the images to the poem's erotic scenario see Harrison (1994).

Outside the domestic interiors where much of love elegy is set, the landmarks of Rome play a significant part in the life of love. Propertius 2.31 opens with the elegist's apology for lateness at an appointment with the *puella* – he has been delayed by the opening of the porticoes of Augustus' temple of Palatine Apollo:

Quaeris, cur ueniam tibi tardior? aurea Phoebi
    porticus a magno Caesare aperta fuit.

You ask why I should come to you somewhat late?
The golden portico of Apollo has been opened by great Caesar.

The poem then goes on to spend the rest of its space on a full description of the Palatine temple which is one of the key sources for its reconstruction.[39] This constitutes a compliment to the young Caesar, part of the poet's movement towards Augustan interests noted above, but it also clearly integrates the Roman cityscape into the literary landscape of elegy. In the next poem (2.32), which is likely in fact to be a continuation of 2.31,[40] he goes on to suggest to Cynthia that she has no need to go outside Rome to flaunt her charms since the complex of Pompey's theatre provides ample opportunity (2.32.11–16):

scilicet umbrosis sordet Pompeia columnis
    porticus, aulaeis nobilis Attalicis,
et platanis creber pariter surgentibus ordo,
    flumina sopito quaeque Marone cadunt,
et leuiter nymphis tota crepitantibus urbe
    cum subito Triton ore refundit aquam.

Clearly then Pompey's portico with its shady columns disgusts you,
Though well-known for its Attalid hangings,
And its many rows of evenly-growing plane-trees,
And its streams which cascade down have put Maro to sleep,
And its nymphs who resound gently over the whole city
When Triton unexpectedly pours water from his mouth.

As with the description of the temple of Palatine Apollo, the lavish detail vividly evokes a particular locale of Augustan Rome. The theme of Roman public buildings and resorts as spots for the *puella*'s self-display for potential lovers is one repeated in love-elegy: Propertius 2.23.5–6 similarly suggests parks and porticoes as places where the *puella* can be found, while at Propertius 4.8.75–6 Pompey's complex, the Forum (when used for gladiatorial

[39] See now Miller (2009) 196–206. [40] See Heyworth (2007b) 246.

displays) and the theatre are seen as sites where the elegist might seek female company. Urban assignation spots are not a feature in Tibullus, but are common in Ovid: in Ovid *Amores* 2.2.3–4 the Palatine portico of the Danaids again occurs, this time as another place for assignations, while *Amores* 3.2 offers the elegist's commentary on the chariot-races at the Circus Maximus, delivered to the *puella* in a successful search for future erotic consummation (3.2.83–4). The *Ars Amatoria* codifies all this into formal advice. There the man in search of an available *puella* and the *puella* in search of a suitable man are given detailed instructions about where to find one in Rome (1.67–170, 3.381–96): Pompey's complex (once more), the porticoes of Octavia and Livia, the porticoes of Palatine Apollo (again), and the temples of Isis and Venus Genetrix, and (above all, and yet again) the theatres (of Pompey and Marcellus) and the Circus Maximus.

The urban setting of elegy also assigns a role to city-wide gossip in the life of love. Propertius' elegist is keen to report the views of the city on the progress or otherwise of his affair with Cynthia: in 2.26.2 he urges an admiring reaction in Rome (*tota . . . in urbe*) to the fact that the *puella* is now his slave, but more often the urban rumours are ugly, such as the unspecific scandal about Cynthia in 2.32.24 (again *tota . . . urbe*) or his own bad reputation *per totam urbem* at 2.24.7. The climax comes at the end of Book 3, where, in his apparent farewell to Cynthia, Propertius talks of his treatment by her becoming the humiliating subject of talk at parties (3.25.1–2):

> Risus eram positis inter conuiuia mensis
> et de me poterat quilibet esse loquax.

> I was a subject of laughter when tables were set out at feasts,
> And anyone could talk freely about me.

Propertius 4 presents a quite different attitude to the city of Rome in the context of love elegy, showing how far both author and genre have moved over time. The Callimachean aetiological programme of the book, to sing of the 'old names of places' (4.1.69), means that the city of Rome becomes a repository of past history and current political significance as well as a field of current erotic endeavour.[41] Though the story of Tarpeia in 4.4 combines aetiology and erotic narrative, and the two re-appearances of Cynthia in 4.7 and 4.8 are both set in an urban context (the latter explicitly in Propertius' own house on the Esquiline), the highlighting of the Palatine temple of Apollo in 4.6 and Jupiter Feretrius in 4.10 (and perhaps even of

[41] Well explored by Welch (2005).

the Bona Dea in 4.9) can be argued to have a largely encomiastic purpose and clearly have no erotic dimension.[42] Like the landscape of Rome itself, its representation in elegy has now become politicized in the Augustan interest.

Other locations – recreational, ancestral, imperial

One set of non-Roman locations in elegy mirrors the usual residential cycle of the urban Roman: Cynthia's excursion to the flesh-pots of Baiae in Propertius 1.11 reflects habitual Roman summer residence on the bay of Naples,[43] and journeys to Lanuvium, some 30 km SE of Rome (Propertius 4.8), or Falerii, some 50 km N (Ovid *Amores* 3.13), represent easy excursions from the capital; we find a full catalogue of such destinations for Cynthia at Propertius 2.32.3–6 (Praeneste, Tusculum, Tibur and Lanuvium). In the context of the urban life of love such journeys are usually represented as temporary desertions of the lover which provide rich opportunities for the *puella*'s infidelity; in *Amores* 3.6 Ovid presents himself as anxious to cross a river to reach the *puella* in Tibur – an anxiety perhaps driven by fears of infidelity.

Another set of non-Roman locations is provided by the elegists' deployment of their Italian home regions. For Tibullus we have no firm evidence of his place of origin,[44] but Propertius in book 4 is presented as coming from Assisi in Umbria (4.1.63–6, 121–26), consistent with his concern with the earlier civil war at nearby Perugia in 1.21 and 1.22, in which he seems to have lost relatives.[45] It is not until his second book, announcing his 'return' after book 1, that Ovid declares his ancestral link with the Sabine Paeligni (2.1.1), but we then find a poem wholly set in his birthplace of Sulmo (2.16) in which he (unusually) urges the *puella* to come and join him. Here as in allusions to recreational destinations near Rome, we can detect some indication of the real migratory patterns of elite Romans, who often visited property in their ancestral regions.

Further places outside the city occur in the mentions of Rome's overseas provinces. In the world of love elegy these locations, like Italian pleasure-resorts, are usually seen as destinations for separate travel by one of the erotic partners which seriously endangers the love-relationship. In 1.6 Propertius refuses service in the Greek East with his friend Tullus in order to stay with Cynthia in Rome, a gesture pointedly reversed in 3.22, when in an address

[42] Cf. Harrison (2005). [43] Cf. D'Arms (1970).

[44] Unless the location of Albius (surely Tibullus) *in regione Pedana* (near Praeneste) at Horace *Ep.*1.4.2 indicates his birthplace as well as a villa for relaxation; cf. Murgatroyd (1980).

[45] For literature see n. 15 above.

to the same friend some years later the elegist now wishes to leave Italy given the terminally poor state of his relationship with Cynthia.[46] In 1.8 (surely originally two poems)[47] Cynthia considers and is then dissuaded from going off to Illyria with a rival of the elegist; the theme of the *puella* departing for the provinces is found again at Ovid *Amores* 2.11, where Corinna seems to be about to sail away to foreign parts, abandoning Ovid and their love (2.11.7–8), a trip which clearly does not happen. In Tibullus 1.3 we find the elegist on Corfu, apparently fallen ill on the way with Messalla to the East, blaming himself for separation from Delia and looking forward to their reunion. This poem reminds us that travel to the provinces was often motivated by Rome's overseas wars and political expansion in this period, and the theme can illuminate political attitudes and their development. Propertius 3.12 blames an apparently real Roman Postumus, possibly a relative of the poet,[48] for abandoning his wife Galla in order to follow Augustus' Eastern campaigns, but 4.3, in a book of greater accommodation with Augustan ideology (see pp. 134–40 above), presents a *Heroides*-type letter of 'Arethusa' to her husband 'Lycotas' (clearly pseudonyms for real or imagined Roman elite members), again on Eastern campaign, which emphasizes more positive aspects and looks forward to the warrior's victorious return. Both the clear married status of the couple and the quasi-triumphalist tone of the poem suggest that we are now in a very different world from that of earlier elegy.[49]

Conclusion

Of all Latin literary genres, love elegy is the most specifically located in time (the last half-century BC) and place (essentially, Rome); that it did not survive more than two generations must be due to the unique circumstances of this location and period as well as to internal literary constraints. The social and political loosening which marked the end of the Roman Republic was an apt moment of genesis for an essentially countercultural genre, while moral legislation and an increasingly authoritarian monarchy clearly contributed to its passing.

Further reading

Pelling (1996) provides a good narrative of Roman history for the relevant period; for works of broader cultural and historical context on Augustan

[46] For this ring-compositional link between the two poems see Heyworth (2007b) 399.
[47] See Heyworth (2007b) 37–8. [48] See Cairns (2006b) 16–24.
[49] See Miller (Chapter 15) in this volume.

Rome see Galinsky (1996) and (2005). Griffin (1985) gives the most useful cultural framework for elegy at Rome. On political elements in Propertius, Heyworth (2007a) and Cairns (2006b) give interestingly different recent perspectives. The cityscape of Rome has been treated in connection with Propertius 4 by Welch (2005), but a substantial general treatment of Rome as the key scenario of elegy is lacking.

9

ALISON SHARROCK

The *poeta-amator*, *nequitia* and *recusatio*

Ovid proudly introduces his second book of elegies as the work of a poet (= creator/writer) of his own badness:

> HOC quoque composui Paelignis natus aquosis
> ille ego nequitiae Naso poeta meae;
> (Ov. *Am.* 2.1.1–2)

> This too I have composed, I myself, Naso, born among the watery Paeligni, the poet of my own badness.

All four canonical elegists wear this and other conventionally reprehensible characteristics as a badge of honour and a positive aesthetic choice. Even in the highly fragmentary work of Gallus, *nequitia* looks like a generic marker in its appearance, alongside the sadness which it inspires, in one of the lines published in 1979. Like love itself, this preferential option for badness can work either to undermine the holder's virility or to proclaim it: on the one hand, the lover is thus addicted to behaviour in direct opposition to central tenets of Roman manliness, but on the other hand the display of sexual (and poetic) power therein expressed can also celebrate the poet-lover's (*poeta-amator*) potency. This characteristic of *nequitia* is most easily seen when both Ovid (*Am.* 2.4 and 2.10) and Propertius (2.22a+b[1]) proclaim their insatiable and indefatigable desires for all things female. Ovid presents himself as wholly unable to resist this passion, despite his strong sense of its wickedness (*Am.* 2.4.1–10) – but we do not believe him for a moment. It is abundantly clear that the poet-lover is celebrating his erotic activity as an alternative – albeit outrageous – to conventional Roman manly pursuits. As Gale (1997: 80) says of Propertius: 'On the one hand, love

[1] Printed as separate but paired poems by Heyworth, who discusses the division at Heyworth 2007b: 200–2. Throughout this chapter, I use Heyworth's 2007 OCT edition of the poems of Propertius. Readers using other editions or translations may need to refer back to the OCT in order to follow the discussion.

is '*nequitia*', it involves the lover in suffering, loss of reputation, and all the other evils associated with erotic passion by moralists as different as Cicero and Lucretius. On the other, it is not only desirable – a death one would gladly die – but even, in some sense, as valid a "career" as the more conventional path pursued by Tullus.'

Ovid throws out a head-on challenge to conventional Roman masculinity when he takes the existing poetic conceit of *militia amoris*, the soldiering of love, and turns it into a proof (*Am.* 1.9) that elegiac lovers can match soldiers point for point on energy, hardiness, ruthlessness, skill, strength, strategy, tactics, drive and determination.[2] His climactic knockdown argument is his own experience: before he became a lover, he says, all those accusations of laziness, effeminacy, and weakness, generally directed at lovers, would have suited him exactly, but now that he has signed up in the army of love he is armed and ready for action:

> ipse ego segnis eram discinctaque in otia natus;
> mollierant animos lectus et umbra meos;
> impulit ignauum formosae cura puellae,
> iussit et in castris aera merere suis.
> inde uides agilem nocturnaque bella gerentem:
> qui nolet fieri desidiosus, amet.
> (Ov. *Am.* 1.9.41–6)

> I myself was sluggish (*segnis*) and born for unbuttoned leisure; bed and shade had softened (*mollierant*) my spirits; love for a beautiful girl gave a push to the lazy one (*ignauum*) and ordered me to earn my pay in her camp. Therefore you see me active (*agilem*, from *ago*) and waging nightly wars: whoever doesn't want to be lazy (*desidiosus*), let him love.

What Ovid does here is to reclaim for the lover the central tenets of Roman manliness, while transferring the effeminate characteristics conventionally assigned to the lover onto those who are not lovers.

If we look more closely at the conventions of Roman manliness with which Ovid is working here, however, we find something rather complex for the way Tibullus constructs his elegiac persona. The positive valuation of soldiering as true manliness comes from the same Roman ideological stable as the celebration of farming, both of them tough jobs for real men, both undermined by luxury and laziness – and love. A textbook expression of this attitude can be seen in the prologue to the Republican writer and politician Cato's treatise on agriculture: *at ex agricolis et uiri fortissimi et milites strenuissimi gignuntur* ('but from farmers are born both the

[2] See also Drinkwater (Chapter 12) in this volume.

very strongest/bravest men and also the most energetic soldiers', Cato, *On Agriculture* pr.4).

Tibullus, we discover gradually, is both a farmer (at least in imagination) and a soldier (if a sick one, 1.3). In his programmatic opening poem, Tibullus uses the positive Roman attributes of farming and its moral and social (if not actual) correlate, poverty, to introduce himself as lover and as poet.[3] He despises wealth (good traditional Roman), tends his farm (even better), honouring the *Lares* (Roman household gods, 1.1.20), displacing warfare onto those who, in opposition to traditional values, pursue wealth (1.1.1–4). All this seems remarkably close to one strand of Roman manliness. It is only gradually that the language of unconventional gender-positioning gains its elegiac programmatic force. First Tibullus' 'poverty' (which also has a poetological significance as a Callimachean preference for littleness) becomes associated with love:

> parua seges satis est; satis est, requiescere lecto
>   si licet et solito membra leuare toro.
> quam iuuat immites uentos audire cubantem
>   et dominam tenero continuisse sinu.
>
> (Tib. 1.1.43–6)

A small field is enough; it is enough to be allowed to rest in bed and to lighten your limbs on the accustomed couch. How pleasing it is to listen to the wild winds as you lie and to hold a mistress in tender embrace.

Then his laudatory (and dedicatory) address to his patron, Messalla, sets up a contrast between the Roman soldier (for glory, this time, instead of wealth?) and the poet in his most classic elegiac position:

> te bellare decet terra, Messalla, marique,
>   ut domus hostiles praeferat exuuias:
> me retinent uinctum formosae uincla puellae,
>   et sedeo duras ianitor ante fores.
> non ego laudari curo, mea Delia: tecum
>   dum modo sim, quaeso segnis inersque uocer.
>
> (Tib. 1.1.53–8)

It is right for you, Messalla, to make war on land and sea, to adorn your house with foreign spoils. The chains of a beautiful girl hold me bound and I sit as doorman before her hard doors. I don't care to be praised, my Delia; as long as I am with you let me be called sluggish and lazy.

[3] See also Lee-Stecum (Chapter 4) in this volume.

Now Tibullus has clearly ascribed to himself the accusations which conventional Roman manliness would level against the elegiac lover. He ends the poem with a farewell to warfare, again associated with the nefarious pursuit of wealth (1.1.75–6). Here, and throughout his poetry (see particularly poems 1.10 and 2.4), Tibullus makes wealth the enemy of both love and poetry, until in desperation he starts to reject elegy as hopeless, threatening to turn instead to slaughter and crime (2.4.19–22) in order not to be a locked-out (and therefore programmatically elegiac) lover. This 'slaughter and crime' stands for warfare and perhaps even elliptically for epic poetry. For Tibullus, paradoxically the only way to keep going as an elegist – to succeed – is to embrace the rhetoric of weakness and failure.

Those lines in 2.4 are a precursor to a stronger attempt to reject elegy in Tibullus' final poem (2.6). This poem offers Tibullus' nearest approximation to the explicit *recusatio*. He opens with that opposition between warfare and poetry which has run throughout the collection, exclaiming in dismay at the plans of his friend Macer to join the camp. This Macer was an epic poet to whom Ovid also addressed a poem about generic choice between epic and elegy (*Am.* 2.18). Tibullus, in his abject elegiac weakness, cannot even resist the call to the camp/epic, but as soon as he expresses his intention to apply himself to this manly pursuit, the closed door of elegy cuts off his escape:

> castra peto, ualeatque Venus ualeantque puellae:
>   et mihi sunt uires et mihi laeta tuba est.
> magna loquor, sed magnifice mihi magna locuto
>   excutiunt clausae fortia uerba fores.
> (Tib. 2.6.9–12)

> The camps I seek: farewell, Venus, farewell, girls. I've got the strength and now I love the war trumpet. Big talk – but while I am magnificently talking big, the closed doors shake out my strong words.

As he reflects in the next couplet (13–14), all his attempts to write something different end up in the same place. (There is probably a pun on metrical foot when he talks about his feet banging their own way back to his mistress's doorstep. As in English, the same Latin word is used for metrical and corporeal foot.) The poem and the collection end in classic elegiac form, with the lover blaming a *lena*, 'bawd', for his failure to achieve his desires.

As the comment from Gale quoted above suggests, Propertius presents his addiction to *nequitia* as a deliberate life choice – or rather, one which his love for Cynthia imposes on him. What Propertius has lost in giving himself over to love is that crucial upper-class male Roman ideal of autarky, being in control of oneself. Throughout the corpus, we hear again and again how Cynthia controls his life from beginning to end (1.12), how he cannot resist (2.3), how he has lost the freedom (*libertas*) to speak his mind (1.1.28), and how he himself is the subject of the passive form of *cogo* ('I force': 1.1.8, 1.7.8, 1.12.14, 1.18.8, 1.18.30[4]). One remarkable development of this persona of *nequitia* is an apparent association between the poet's presentation of himself and of Mark Antony (Griffin 1977), as a pair of dissolutes who let their lives be run by beautiful and fascinating women (see 3.11).

Poem 1.6 apologizes to the aristocratic dedicatee of the first book, Tullus, for the poet's inability to accompany his friend on the high seas of a military and socio-political tour of duty in the East, because Cynthia will not let him go. The poet's weakness and submission to love for a mere woman is contrasted with the fine upstanding youth of Tullus:

> nam tua non aetas umquam cessauit amori,
>   semper at armatae cura fuit patriae.
> et tibi non umquam nostros puer iste labores
>   afferat et lacrimis omnia nota meis.
> me sine, quem semper uoluit fortuna iacere,
>   hanc animam aeternae reddere nequitiae.
>   (Prop. 1.6.21–6)

> For your youth has never dawdled in love, but always your concern was for the defence of the fatherland. May that boy [Cupid] never bring you my labours and all things known by my tears. Allow me, whom fortune has wanted always to lie low, to give over this soul to eternal badness.

The choice of a life devoted to love and conventional laziness is closely paralleled in Propertius' programmatic self-presentation with a choice for elegy over epic in the doublet poems 1.7 and 1.9, addressed to the aspiring epic poet Ponticus. While the latter works away on a *Thebaid* of a nature to rival Homer (1.7.1–4), Propertius writes his love poetry, not, he initially claims, because this is the intellectual choice which he has made, but because his pain leaves him no option (1.7.7–8).

But then the position shifts: other lovers will read his account of his sufferings and will praise him for his life choice and his poetic choice (13–14), while even Ponticus might sometime himself be bitten by the love bug and then his *Thebaid* will be no use (17–18). Propertius, by contrast, will be the subject of posthumous praise, when the reader-lover draws together

[4] It will be noted that all these cases come from Book 1. There is an interesting example at 3.9.22, when *cogor* applies to Propertius' relationship with Maecenas, although not in a simple way. There, Propertius 'is forced' to follow the example of Maecenas by keeping his metaphorical sails closely trimmed.

the elegiac centrepieces of love and funerary commemoration in speaking a pentameter over the poet's grave (1.7.24). In poem 1.9, nemesis has reached Ponticus, and he is indeed in love. His words are no longer free (1.9.2), and his *graue . . . carmen* ('serious song', 1.9.9) is no use. His only option now being to learn elegiac love poetry, what better teacher than Propertius (1.9.5–8)? Weak elegy, then, has turned out to be better than strong epic.

One line of that poem introduces a point which underlies much of the Propertian programme, which is the poetic sleight of hand by which Propertius associates Hellenistic-style poetics[5] explicitly and particularly with love poetry:

> plus in amore ualet Mimnermi uersus Homero:
> (Prop. 1.9.11)
>
> The poetry of Mimnermus has more power in love than Homer.

While it is true that there is particular emphasis on emotions and plenty of erotic material in Hellenistic poetry, including from the master Callimachus, Propertius is hereby manipulating reality for his own purposes, enabling a choice of poetic style to appear naturally connected not only with a choice of poetic subject matter but also with the presentation of a particular kind of socio-political as well as poetic persona. We will see more of this below.

Whereas the opening poem of Book 1 presented a persona still struggling with the implications of a life of elegiac *nequitia* (1.1.25–8), the second book begins with more confidence, the poet wallowing in the luxury of his beloved's every feature as poetic inspiration (2.1.5–16). But then things turn serious. Propertius dedicates the book to his new patron, the politically powerful Maecenas, right-hand man of Augustus, with an explicit *recusatio*, which includes many of the features we associate with this topos: a claim of incapacity (2.1.17–18), rejection of epic subject matter, here epitomized by gigantomachy (19–20), and *praeteritio* – the practice of mentioning something by refusing to talk about it. There is a double refusal here: to paraphrase, *if* I had the strength, I would not write Homeric or Annalistic epic, but rather I would celebrate 'the wars and deeds of your Caesar' (25: i.e. Augustus), but I don't. The celebration of Augustus and of Maecenas which Propertius will not write goes on for twelve lines, until Callimachus puts a stop to it (39–40). Each man should sing of what he knows, so Propertius can only sing of love (43–6) – and he will only ever be able to do so, because his love and therefore his love poetry is until death (55–6). The politically

[5] See Hunter (Chapter 1, p. 25).

charged Roman language of praise for those who die in battle is appropriated in this poem for love-death (see Papanghelis 1987), then extended to praise for the life devoted to one love:

> laus in amore mori; laus altera si datur uno
> posse frui: fruar o semper amore meo.
> (Prop. 2.1.47–8)

> Praise for dying in love: another praise for the one to whom it is given to be able to enjoy one [love]: may I always enjoy my love.

Propertius plays here with the highly respectable Roman notion of the *uniuira*, the woman married to only one man, but with the outrageous gender inversion which claims the same praise for the man devoted to only one woman/love affair (Heyworth 2007b: 110). At the end of the poem, Maecenas himself is placed in the position held by the reader-lover in 1.7, speaking the poet's epitaph as an amalgamation of love and death (2.1.78), being thus forced to give his approval to the poet's disreputable choice.

The final poem of the second book also draws on this mixture of self-confidence and dissolution set in contrast to grander genres and more respectable poetry. A long and complicated poem, 2.34 keeps close to heart the essential link between being in love and writing love poetry, using a catalogue of other kinds of poetry to define the poet's position. The place of honour in the catalogue is given to Virgil, where it is introduced by a pointed contrast between the latter and Propertius:

> me iuuat hesternis positum languere corollis,
> quem tetigit iactu certus ad ossa deus;
> Actia Virgilio est custodis litora Phoebi
> Caesaris et fortes dicere posse rates,
> qui nunc Aeneae Troiani suscitat arma
> iactaque Lauinis moenia litoribus.
> cedite, Romani scriptores; cedite, Grai:
> nescioquid maius nascitur Iliade.
> (Prop. 2.34.59–66)

> It pleases me to loll about, placed amid yesterday's garlands, me whom the sure god has touched to the bone with his cast; it is for Virgil to be able to speak of the Actian coasts of guardian Phoebus and the brave ships of Caesar, [Virgil] who now arouses the arms of Trojan Aeneas and the walls cast down on Lavinian shores. Give way, Roman writers; give way, Greeks: something greater than the *Iliad* is being born.

The poem ends with Cynthia praised in the verse of Propertius (2.34.93–4). Elegiac values are thus reaffirmed.

The battle with epic has not, however, been so easily won as the first and last poems of the second book (as it stands) might imply. Poem 2.10, which may itself have originally been an ending poem (Heyworth 2007b: 153), presents the poet's intention 'now' to speak of 'the Roman camps of my leader' (2.10.4). He incites his mind to rise up to higher things (2.10.11–12), filling most of the extant poem with vicarious seriousness, including a direct address to Augustus (15). His powers are still – elegiacally – not up to the task (5), but the praise which poem 2.1 appropriated for love-death and devotion to one love is now glimpsed as a possibility for the daring poet of something more serious (Lyne 1998b). But there is a catch:

> bella canam, quando scripta puella mea est.
> (Prop. 2.10.8)

Scholars have argued about the exact meaning of this line, which would be simple to interpret if the last word were (the unmetrical) *erit*, or alternatively if *quando* here could easily have causal force ('since my girl has been written'). I am inclined (with Cairns (2006b) 327–8) to translate: 'wars I will sing, when my girl is [will have been] written'. (See Wyke (1987b) on the crucial phrase *scripta puella*.) Since we have been told that Propertius' devotion to Cynthia, and therefore his elegiac poetry, is for life (1.7.24, 1.12.20, 2.1.55–6), that means never.

Such a stalling game is at work also in 3.9. This poem presents itself as a response to a supposed request from Maecenas for an epic poem (by implication, in honour of Augustus), which is refuted by the argument that all artists should produce the kind of work for which they are suited, Propertius' skills being for love poetry in Hellenistic mode not for epic. It is likely that the literal request for encomiastic epic is a convenient fiction around which Propertius can develop his aesthetic position. This is not to say that both epic and political engagement were not major drives affecting the careers of Augustan poets, but rather that the choice to express those drives in a form such as that in 3.9 was an artistic one. The other strand to this poem, which is enabled by the introduction of Maecenas as someone expressing an interest in the content and style of Propertius' poetry, is the association between Propertius' poetic career and Maecenas' political choices. This second-in-command of the Augustan world was, notoriously, nominally a private citizen who rejected all the normal trappings of Roman political advancement. Propertius manages to offer an extended compliment to his powerful friend (23–34) in such a way as to present Maecenas as the model for the poet's career as a love elegist (21–2, placed after 34 by Heyworth). The culmination of the equation, Maecenas as private person/Propertius as lover, comes when Propertius makes another promise of future epic endeavour – under a blue moon:

te duce uel Iouis arma canam caeloque minantem
Coeum et Phlegraeis Oromedonta iugis;
(Prop. 3.9.47–8)

With you as leader I shall sing either the arms of Jupiter and Coeus threatening to heaven and Oromedon on the Phlegraean heights...

Propertius will undertake an epic, starting here with gigantomachy and moving on, via early Rome, to Augustus' military achievements, 'with Maecenas as leader', or 'when you are a general', i.e., never.

Although the refusal of 'serious' poetry is always at one level driven by the poet's disreputable life dominated by his love for a woman, it is, as we have seen, also an aesthetic choice, a choice for a poetics of littleness, skill, and beauty in the manner of Callimachus and other Hellenistic poets (Hunter 2006a). Or rather, a poetics which uses Callimachean discourse for its own aesthetic purposes. 'Callimachus' offers Propertius perhaps a more respectable alternative to Roman convention than does 'Cynthia', but nonetheless one which treads a narrow line between aesthetics and social construction. What I mean by this is to wonder whether the move from 'Cynthia' to 'Callimachus' (itself never a simple or one-way transition) might be not just a matter of increasing confidence and increasing respectability as the poet gets older, but a phenomenon whereby the Callimachean tradition itself is thus emasculated, or at least made to serve a new way of being a man and a Roman. The aesthetic values of the Hellenistic tradition at Rome are associated with the same side of the equation as the unconventional lifestyle choices summed up in the term *nequitia*.

The opening three (or even five) poems of Book 3 offer an intense and confident exploration of Propertian poetics in relation to Hellenistic aesthetics and Roman social politics. The book opens in mystical style, with the poet as priest seeking entry to the sacred grove of the Hellenistic poetic tradition (3.1.1–6), followed by a loyal statement of Callimachean allegiance constructed as an opposition to epic:

a ualeat, Phoebum quicumque moratur in armis.
exactus tenui pumice uersus eat.
(Prop. 3.1.7–8)

Farewell to anyone who would delay Phoebus in arms. May my verse go forth drawn out by slight pumice.

But then the muse of this poet who rejects war/epic becomes a triumphing general, accompanied in his chariot by Loves/love poems and followed by love poets (3.1.9–12). Is this a capitulation to Roman military values, or an appropriation of them for very different purposes? Next the triumphal chariot has become one for racing, with which some addressees (perhaps the other poets) are told not to compete, because the road is narrow (Callimachus, *Aetia* fr.1.28). It is others who will sing the praises of Rome (3.1.15), not Propertius, who seeks soft (elegiac, effeminate) garlands from the muses (3.1.19). If the envious (Callimachus, *Aetia* 1.17) crowd (Callimachus, *Epigrammata* 28.1) denies the poet honour during his lifetime, he will receive it with interest after his death (3.1.21–2). From this point on, the poem develops into a reflection on the immortalizing power of poetry, using the examples precisely of epic. Immortality through memory on the lips of men is as much a desideratum of the Roman statesman as of the writer. This poet who rejects epic will be praised by future generations of Romans just as the archetypal epic poet, Homer, is honoured by posterity (3.1.33–8). A complicated interweaving, then, of epic and elegy, epic and Callimachus, Roman power and poetic power.

The second poem meditates further on the power of poetry to bring immortality. Although the poet may not have achieved conventional success in the form of wealth (3.2.11–14), his power to immortalize the addressee is a greater gift. But this addressee is the beloved woman (3.2.17–18), and the poem opens with the suggestion that the previous poem might seem to have marked a move away from core Propertian values, to which the poet now returns:

> CARMINIS interea nostri redeamus in orbem
> gaudeat ut solito tacta puella sono.
> (Prop. 3.2.1–2)

Meanwhile let us return into the circuit of our own song so that a girl may rejoice, touched by the accustomed sound.

The third poem returns to the explicitly programmatic mode, with the poet dreaming of being Ennius and writing an epic of Roman history. This dream enters a complex intertextual web which takes in Ennius, Callimachus, Hesiod and Homer (for details see Keith (2008) 79–80 and n. 132), into which Callimachus forcibly intrudes in the form of a *reuocatio* scene: a god, paradigmatically Apollo, appears to the poet when he is actually or just about to sing an epic and tells him in no uncertain terms that he must turn to 'lighter' genres. The founding moment for this scene is the prologue to Callimachus' *Aetia*. Propertius has here again appropriated Callimachean aesthetics for his own purposes, making the designator which I have termed 'lighter' in my summary of the scene into an aesthetic which is explicitly erotic (3.3.20) and elegiac (3.3.23). Apollo's instruction is reinforced by another lesson, this time from the muse Calliope (= 'she of the beautiful face', 3.3.38), which makes the same point: not martial, Roman epic (3.3.41–6), but love elegy, in all its badness:

'... quippe coronatos alienum ad limen amantes
    nocturnaeque canes ebria signa morae,
ut per te clausas sciat excantare puellas
    qui uolet austeros arte ferire uiros.'
(Prop. 3.3.47–50)

'... Indeed you will sing of garlanded lovers on someone else's threshold and the drunken signs of nighttime loitering, so that through you whoever wants to strike down austere husbands by art may know how to charm out locked-up girls.'

That's telling it as it is. The poem ends with Calliope endorsing Propertius' association of Hellenistic aesthetics with elegiac *nequitia* when she sprinkles his lips with symbolic water of Philitas.

I suggested that poems four and five should also be included in the programmatic sequence of the opening of Book 3. The opening three poems have shown some anxiety over whether or not they are truly keeping faith with the Propertian programme. Such anxiety might very well be justified by the fourth poem, Propertius' most 'serious', Roman, Augustan poem to date, which opens with three very significant words, *arma deus Caesar*, 'god Caesar ... arms', the first of which is the opening word of Virgil's *Aeneid*. It is not surprising that Propertius feels it necessary to explain the subject position from which he speaks – as a spectator, in the embrace of his dear girl (3.4.15). And then poem five seems to offer another attempt to reclaim the erotic ground. 'We lovers honour peace', because, as the opening words say in answer to the opening words of the previous poem, *pacis Amor deus est*, 'Love is a god of peace'. The poem again tries to stress Propertius' addiction to poetry and love (3.5.19–24). But the peace which enables such behaviour is, or can be presented as, the gift of 'god Caesar's arms' (see Keith 2008). The closing couplet of 3.5 offers yet another *recusatio* of epic, but the reference to the returning standards of Crassus (a great Augustan propaganda coup) which is the subject of the refused epic may suggest that *nequitia* is no longer quite so edgy. Paradoxically, Propertian *nequitia*, which had based itself on an inversion of conventional Roman masculinity, actually loses potency when it begins to accommodate the dominant ideology.

Relatively rarely does Ovid follow the traditional pattern saying 'I would write in your praise, Caesar, if I were not so weak/unskilled/effeminate', which we could describe as being the Propertian pose, although it is the stance taken also by Virgil and Horace. His most conventional *recusatio* is in the complicated poem *Am.* 3.12, a poem which plays double bluff on the existence or otherwise of his mistress as a real person, claiming that poor reading (we think she is real) has prostituted her (because she is well-known through the poetry, others desire her). Here Ovid begins a motif which will flourish bitterly in exile, that his poems have harmed him (3.12.13–14) more than they have helped, then:

> cum Thebae, cum Troia foret, cum Caesaris acta,
> ingenium mouit sola Corinna meum.
> (Ov. *Am.* 3.12.15–16)

When there was Thebes or Troy or the deeds of Caesar to write about, Corinna alone stirred my genius.

Here, as is conventional, elegy and love are opposed to the poetry of epic and of political engagement. A further irony in this poem of hiding comes from the fact that Ovid makes his proclamation half-hiding behind the voice of Propertius, since line 16 reflects a number of classic Propertian lines, such as 2.1.4 and 1.11.23, 2.7.19. This is a poem in which Ovid is not really saying what he is saying – such is the idiom in which he toys with writing about the deeds of Caesar.

The deeds of Caesar apart, however, Ovid toys with the idea of writing epic throughout the *Amores* collection and indeed his whole corpus. Where Propertius used a probably invented request for politically engaged poetry as a vehicle through which to express his aesthetic choices, Ovid presents himself as a maker of aesthetic choices which also have political implications. Tibullus' friend Macer is again the fall-guy epic poet whose (pre)Iliadic daring is placed in opposition to the erotic susceptibility and weakness of the elegist:

> CARMEN ad iratum dum tu perducis Achillem
> primaque iuratis induis arma uiris,
> nos, Macer, ignaua Veneris cessamus in umbra,
> et tener ausuros grandia frangit Amor.
> (Ov. *Am.* 2.18.1–4)

While you draw out your song to angry Achilles and dress sworn men in their first arms, Macer, I am dawdling in the lazy shade of Venus, and tender Love breaks me as I am about to dare to speak in lofty mode.

Ovid claims that he keeps trying to get rid of his mistress and write epic, but her wheedling persuasions conquer him (11) and make him sing of 'things done at home' (*res . . . gestae* and *domi* are official Roman terms ironically appropriated for Ovid's discourse of love and leisure) and his own wars (12). And yet he did have a go at writing tragedy (13–14), until the love god laughed at his bombastic get-up and sent him right back to elegy. Most of the rest of the poem celebrates Ovid's own *Heroides*, until the last three couplets return to Macer and epic, to show that the *Iliad* and the poems of the epic cycle are, in fact, really all about sex, so Ovid wins and Macer has to end up in his erotic camp. This is the game which Ovid will play again, for much higher stakes, when in exile he writes to Augustus to teach the emperor how to read poetry (Barchiesi 2001) and to show, point by point, that all poetry, epic included, is love poetry (*Tristia* 2). Why would you need an excuse for not writing in serious genres if in fact all genres are versions of love elegy?

Nonetheless, Ovid keeps coming back to the possibility of taking on 'serious genres'. The programmatic opening poem of his third book sets up a contest between two personifications, Elegy and Tragedy, as females who contend for his attention just as Virtue and Vice contended for the soul of Hercules. It is clear that delightful, seductive Elegy, in whose metre and medium the contest takes place, is bound to win:

> exiguum uati concede, Tragoedia, tempus:
>   tu labor aeternus; quod petit illa, breue est.
>
> (Ov. *Am.* 3.1.67–8)

> Yield a little time to the poet, Tragedy: you are an eternal labour; what she seeks is brief.

What Tragedy offers may be greatness for posterity, while Elegy's reward is ephemeral – or perhaps Tragedy is long and boring (and sterile) while Elegy is aesthetically small and pleasing (and fertile). What Elegy really wants, it is implied, is sex.[6]

Ovid's most famous variation on the refusal of epic also presents the poet/lover as putty in the hands of Cupid, all his attempts at epic manliness (1.1.1–2) undermined by the love god's stealing of the final metrical foot of each second line.[7] Tricked by Cupid's action (the cutting down of the poet's feet may hint towards metaphorical emasculation), Ovid complains that he has no subject-matter suitable to the metre, whereupon the god shoots him with an erotic arrow to make him 'fall in love' and so write elegy (Kennedy 1993).

But for Ovid, less is more, failure is success, impotence is power (Sharrock 1995). His *pièce de résistance* on refusal to write epic and appropriation of

[6] The anonymous reader of the volume points out that, 'still, when Ovid says he will get back to Tragedy later, he will have her *a tergo* . . . ' = not only 'behind him', but also 'on [her] back'.

[7] See Thorsen (Chapter 23) in this volume.

the norms of Roman masculinity for the elegiac persona is the programmatic opening poem of the second book. The love god has ordered this poetry, from which the serious-minded are ritually excluded (2.1.3), whereas young lovers are invited to be amazed at just how right the poet has got it. (Interestingly, these appreciative readers are to include not only the standard young rakes, but also the innocent boy and even the virgin girl who is erotically alive to the prospect of marriage – a surprising confusion of the worlds of elegiac adultery/quasi-prostitution and realistic marriage, a confusion which usually only occurs displaced onto the world of myth.)

At this point, Ovid breaks off into a variation on the *recusatio*. He did not just think of writing epic, but actually did so, and the epic which he claims to have undertaken is nothing to do with the praise of Caesar and the glories of Rome but that epitome of epic greatness, the battle of gods and giants (Hinds 1987c). The poet takes to extremes the conceit whereby a poet 'does what he sings' and places himself alongside Jupiter casting his thunderbolts at the rebellious giants (2.1.11–16). Crucially, he rejects the topos of weakness with the claim *et satis oris erat* ('and my mouth/cheek was big enough', 2.1.12). But then, in three words, elegy asserted its greater poetic power with its programmatic closed door:

> clausit amica fores: ego cum Ioue fulmen omisi;
>   excidit ingenio Iuppiter ipse meo.
> Iuppiter, ignoscas: nil me tua tela iuuabant;
>   clausa tuo maius ianua fulmen habet.
> (Ov. *Am.* 2.1.17–20)

> My girlfriend closed the door: I dropped the bolt along with Jupiter; Jupiter himself fell out of my mind. Forgive me, Jupiter: your weapons were no help to me; the closed door has a bigger bolt than yours.

And so the poet returned to elegy in order to open the door. In this passage, soft, weak, effeminate elegy is more powerful than the most extreme epic. This power, moreover, is expressed in sexually suggestive terms: Jupiter wielding his thunderbolt is displaying his sexual power as well as military and political, as is shown by the story Ovid tells in the *Metamorphoses* when Semele is tricked into asking the king of the gods to make love to her as he does to his wife Juno – Jupiter tries to expend his potency by flashing thunderbolts all over the place in advance, although to no avail since his embrace is still too much for the poor mortal. Elegy's bolt, as wielded by Ovid, is more powerful than that. But its power, ironically, is to soften (i.e. weaken, emasculate) hard doors (2.1.22).

As Ovid in these lines has refused epic in the form of gigantomachy, so later in the poem he refuses the *Iliad* and the *Odyssey* (2.1.29–32) as models. I suggested above that this version of the recusatio was not directed towards the praise of Augustus, but this is only true at a superficial level. A poem working explicitly with the *Iliad* and *Odyssey* in order (in some sense) to praise Augustus has already, certainly by the date of the second edition of the *Amores*, become the ultimate epic poem, the *Aeneid*. And the association between Augustus and Jupiter, of which much play will be made in the exile poetry, is already gaining ground. With this in mind, the apology of line 19 takes on a new implication: 'forgive me, Jupiter, your weapons are no good' becomes a disrespectful variation on the topos of the *recusatio* of political poetry, while the comparison between size and strength of bolts does little to ameliorate the outrage. This is what it means for Ovid to be the poet of his own *nequitia* (2.1.2).

The elegists, then, celebrate their immoral and countercultural values as positive aesthetic choices – but only when it applies to themselves. Any display of *nequitia* on the part of the *puella*, by contrast, is wholly reprehensible. Where 'badness' for the elegist means a life of love and poetry rather than of political, military or commercial activity (and therefore, in elegiac newspeak, 'bad equals good – if you are a man'), 'badness' for the *puella* is rejection of the lover, the choice of a different lover (which could include someone with official status, potentially even a husband), desire for wealth and pleasure in luxuries, especially when these are provided by a rival. The attitudes which the elegists express towards their mistresses in this regard show barely any difference from the language of conventional morality. Gallus talks about his beloved's *nequitia* as behaviour which brings grief to himself.[8] For all that this grief might indeed be suitably elegiac, the beloved is by no means excused. Thus begins a long tradition: see for example Tib. 2.3.51, Prop. 1.2, 1.15.38, 2.5.2, 2.6.27, 3.10.24, 3.13, 3.19.10, Ov. Am. 3.4.10, 3.11b.37, 3.14.17. If you are an elegiac woman, bad equals bad.

Further reading

Kennedy 1993 is probably the best general discussion relating to the issues raised in this chapter, while an important voice in defence of the *puella* in this regard comes from James (2003). For Propertius, see Keith (2008); for Ovid, Armstrong (2005), Boyd (1997), Volk (2005). Little has been written specifically on Tibullus in this regard, but there is useful material in Lee-Stecum (1998).

[8] Hollis 2007: 244–5.

10

PAUL ALLEN MILLER

The *puella*

Accept no substitutions!

The story, as it was once told in undergraduate classrooms, goes something like this. The Romans were a dour lot, interested only in money, war, politics and low entertainments. After the Punic Wars and the conquest of Greece, wealth, purveyors of Greek culture and sophisticated courtesans flowed into the capital. To match the tastes of their newly sophisticated men, Roman women, with time and money on their hands, began to play the part of courtesans themselves. The record of this change and the corresponding corruption of Roman values can be found not only in the fulminations of Cicero and Sallust but also in the love elegists of the first century BC: Catullus, Gallus, Tibullus, Propertius, Ovid, as well as the lone woman, Sulpicia. In their texts, we read stories of sophisticated *puellae* (literally 'girls') and the poets who pursued them. And while certain allowances must be made for poetic exaggeration and convention, the record that these poems provide tells us stories of passion, pursuit, and poetic perfection worthy of *La Bohème*. Such is the story as it was once told and often still is.[1]

Nonetheless, by the 1980s, a reaction to this narrative had set in. While critics like Lyne still chose to speak of Catullus' and the elegists' desire for 'whole love' (1980), a new wave of criticism embodied in the work of scholars like Wyke (1989) and Veyne (1988) argued that the *puellae* were not real women in literary guise, but textual constructs. True, scholars had argued before against taking the poems as biographical evidence. However, the argument was largely aesthetic and formalist: appreciate the way a poem worked, not whether the poet was sincere or the beloved real. By contrast, Wyke and Veyne argued for the importance of the *puella*'s fundamental textuality. While Veyne argued that all the beloveds were ironic fictions (Catullus' Lesbia excepted), Wyke's more nuanced view allowed for the historical determination of the elegiac beloved by other images of women

[1] See inter alia, Luck (1960) 15; Hallett (1973) 105; Hallett (1974) 213; Boucher (1980) 447; Wyke (1987b) 165; White (1993) 90.

circulating within contemporary culture, while leaving the *puella* herself oddly underdetermined.

For us, however, it is not a question of which of these perspectives is correct. On the one hand, the *puellae* are beyond doubt textual. They are the pretexts around which are constructed elaborate poetic collections. These women, at least as we know them, do not exist outside this written world. They are the organizing elements around which the basic scenario of elegiac love is constructed – the genre does not exist without them. But the texts and languages out of which they are made are not mere abstract systems. They are deeply embedded tools that exist only in so far as they are intelligible, useful and/or enjoyable by the inhabitants of their world. While the first explanation of how Romans came to create this poetry may be overly simplistic, we know from Sallust and others that the Romans did in fact believe their mores had changed, and that these changes were associated with what could be seen as an increasing liberation of the behaviour of Roman women from the constraints of tradition. We also know that Augustus in his attempt at reform clearly believed that there had been a decline in the standards of moral behaviour, or at least that it was useful to portray himself as believing such. Moreover, he saw that the link between elegiac love poetry and moral decline as sufficiently credible that he could list the *Ars Amatoria* as one reason for Ovid's exile without appearing ridiculous. The *puellae* may be textual, but they have oddly real effects.

What we see, then, as we examine the issue is that the choice between fiction and reality, textuality and history, or language and referent in regard to the elegiac *puella* is false. These women only exist to the extent that they function within the textual system known as Latin erotic elegy, and that system only existed because it was intelligible to and usable by the inhabitants of Rome during this period. The question is not, who were the *puellae*, but how do they function and what do they stand for? That is to say, what sets of values do they substitute for in the textual economies constructed by the poetic collections in which they figure?

Catullus and Lesbia

In many ways, Lesbia is special. She is the first of the *puellae* and the first to be so named. In poem 2 line 1, we read *passer, deliciae meae puellae*, ('sparrow, plaything of my girl'). Lesbia, we learn, quiets her ardor by playing with a sparrow, the bird of Venus. Many see erotic undertones in this image, though there is no scholarly consensus. In poem 8, a disillusioned Catullus attempts to bid his beloved adieu (*uale, puella*, l.12). And in poem 11, the poet asks his erstwhile companions, Furius and Aurelius, to carry a few harsh words to Lesbia, (*pauca nuntiate meae puellae / non bona dicta*, ll. 14–15). Within the Catullan collection, *puella* functions as a generic term for the poet's beloved and, in that role, has no necessary connotation of age, social class, or marital status. It is arguably established within the poems themselves that Lesbia is married to another and of sufficiently high status that she could have been led to him in the type of elaborate procession that characterized elite marriage (68.143–46, cf. 61). Moreover, when this information is combined with external evidence from Apuleius and internal evidence from poem 79, the case becomes very strong that Lesbia is in fact Clodia Metelli, the wife – and, after 59 BC, the widow – of consul Quintus Caecilius Metellus Celer, sister of the tribune Clodius Pulcher, and the object of Cicero's scathing ridicule in the *Pro Caelio* (Skinner 2003: 81–3, 92–3, 107 and 2010: 121–45; Wiseman 1985: 166–7). This would, in fact, make Lesbia Catullus's superior in both age and social status. Thus, the Catullan *puella* may be referred to as a 'girl' in only the most extended sense.

This fact brings us to another way in which Lesbia is unique among the elegiac *puellae*. She alone, no matter how stylized the portrait, seems to be indubitably based on a real person.[2] Thus leading scholars of elegy as different as Veyne, who views the entire genre as an elaborate game (1988: 34–6, 174, 188), and James, who views it as a window onto the complex commerce that governed relations between upper class men and the women who erotically served them (2003: 250 n. 79, 272 n. 90), agree that Lesbia constitutes an exception. But if this is the case, does that mean that Lesbia also constitutes an exception to the methodological strictures laid down at the beginning of this chapter? Do we, therefore, not seek her meaning through the pattern of substitutions that characterizes her position within the textual economy of the Catullan corpus but rather predicate it on a pre-existing knowledge of her reality that allows us to read the poetry? The fact is, however, that the textual construct Catullus has produced only functions within the symbolic world that constitutes Roman life: the dividing line between poetic construct and prepoetic reality within that symbolic world is impossible to establish.

Poem 79 is not only one of the primary pieces of evidence for Lesbia's identity but also key to demonstrating the way that identity functions within this poetry.

> Lesbius est pulcer. quid ni? quem Lesbia malit
>   quam te cum tota gente, Catulle, tua.
> sed tamen hic pulcer uendat cum gente Catullum,
>   si tria notorum suauia reppererit.

[2] See Miller (2004) 61–73.

Lesbius is pretty. Why not? Lesbia prefers him
to you and your whole family, Catullus.
But nonetheless this pretty boy would sell both Catullus and his clan
if he could receive the kiss of just three friends.

The opening sentence is a pun that only works if we substitute Clodius for Lesbius. Lesbius is pretty (*pulcer*), and Clodius is Pulcher, the latter being the cognomen of P. Clodius Pulcher. This substitution in turn allows Clodia to be substituted for Lesbia, and brings with it an entire set of pre-existing perceptions. Cicero in the *Pro Caelio* famously accuses the brother and sister of promiscuity and incest. Catullus plays on his readers' knowledge of these rumoured perversities in his depiction of Lesbia's preference for Lesbius over Catullus. This information would not only have allowed readers to understand the final line, in which Clodius' friends will not give him the customary Roman greeting because they know where his mouth has been, but it also colours the sexual enormities of which Catullus accuses Lesbia in poems such as 11 and 58.

Clodia, nonetheless, was a woman of both beauty and sophistication. When addressed as Lesbia, a name derived from Sappho's island of Lesbos, she conjures not a geographical location but an atmosphere of refined erotic desire. Likewise when the poet in poem 35.16–17 refers to the *puella* of Caecilius as *Sapphica puella/ musa doctior* ('girl, more learned than the Sapphic muse'), he not only limns the qualification of the ideal *puella*, he also implicitly allows Lesbia, as an adjective derived from Lesbos, to be substituted for *Sapphica*,[3] a move that brings Clodia (and ultimately Clodius and Metellus Celer) in train.

In short, what poem 79 (see above) shows is that while the Catullan *puella* is exceptional, it is not because Lesbia is real and the others fictions. Lesbia is every bit a textual construct who only exists in a rarefied environment of puns, poetic allusion and an elaborate system of intertextual references. The Catullan *puella* is exceptional because the kind of substitutions Lesbia's identification with Clodia enables, in fact permits the economy of the Catullan text to function on a different level and in a different way from that of his successors. In Catullus, the prosopographical 'reality' of Roman life becomes an integral part of the poetic text, in which Clodia, Clodius, Cicero, Caesar, Pompey and others each have their roles.

Lesbia, however, is exceptional in her role as an elegiac *puella* not only because she is the first so named, and because she is the sole *puella* to have an established extrapoetic identity, she is also exceptional in so far as Catullus is not exclusively an elegist. Indeed many of the poems we have

[3] For this interpretation of a notoriously difficult line, see also Kutzko (2006).

cited are not written in the elegiac metre and, unlike his successors, Catullus' collection contains poems on a wide variety of topics of which love is only one. Nonetheless, as I have shown elsewhere, the elegists clearly regarded Catullus as their predecessor, and he established many of the thematic and formal precedents that founded the genre (Miller 2007). One of the key texts in this founding is poem 68, the longest elegy of the collection.[4]

Poem 68 falls into two parts. We will only be concerned with that portion traditionally labeled 68b: a poem thanking Allius for the loan of a house in which the poet and his beloved first made love. Lesbia enters, a shining goddess (*candida diua*, 68.70) and is compared to the mythic bride Laodamia crossing the threshold of her as yet incomplete home with Protesilaus. Their home is destined to remain unfinished, since, owing to a lack of proper sacrifice, Protesilaus is called away to the Trojan War where he is the first Greek to die. Through this comparison Lesbia is pictured as a bride entering her marriage chamber, but a chamber cursed with eternal unfulfilment due to lack of proper ritual observance. This initial substitution of Laodamia for Lesbia reveals both a desire for socially approved erotic fulfilment in marriage and its impossibility. The *puella*, here, stands for both.

In the following lines, the death of Protesilaus and the unappeasable grief of Laodamia are chronicled. The mention of Troy leads the poet to reflect on the death of his brother who is buried there. In this way, the poet's grief is implicitly equated with Laodamia's for Protesilaus. Therefore, when Laodamia is substituted for Lesbia, it also becomes possible to substitute the loss of Catullus' brother for the lack and grief associated by the poet with the nonfulfilment of his relationship with Lesbia. Thus each link in the complex chain of substitutions comes to function as the sign of an emotional wholeness that, if possessed, would unite the erotic, familial, and social into an impossible but ideal unity (Williams 1980: 59; Edwards 1991: 77; Janan 1994: 123–9).

In the course of this chain of substitutions something very subtle has occurred. Catullus has been substituted for Lesbia, for it is he that is grieved by the loss of Lesbia, and he that is grieved by the loss of his brother (Williams 1980: 55; Hubbard 1984: 34; Feeney 1992: 40; Skinner 2003: 57). Thus, on a profound level, the *puella* substitutes for the poet himself, for a fantasy of wholeness, in which all losses are made good. As we shall see, this pattern of loss and a fantasy of wholeness characterize the *puella* and her pattern of possible substitutions in the subsequent elegists too.

In sum, then, the *puella* as articulated in Catullus is the beloved as a dream of fulfilment: the sophisticated and beautiful *puella* (aligned in

4 See Miller (2004) chp. 2.

Catullan verse with the *Sapphica musa*) who exceeds the demands of social propriety. This is no traditional *matrona*, no mere vulgarian's girl of the moment (cf. 72.3). Nonetheless, she also functions as the image of that fulfilment's impossibility. She is a violation of social expectations. She cannot be integrated into a normative family structure. She is unfaithful, sexually omnivorous and associated with death. She is this contradictory pattern of substitutions.

Tibullus and Delia

In Tibullus' first book, half of the poems are dedicated to his love for Delia, with 1.4, 1.8, and 1.9 homoerotic poems. Catullus provides a precedent, for while the majority of his erotic poetry is dedicated to Lesbia, there is a 'cycle' of poems on Juventius. Neither Propertius nor Ovid include homoerotic poems, although they were common among the Hellenistic epigrams to which elegy owes a debt. Delia's social status is never made clear in the poems, nor are we given much description of her as a dramatic character. She does demand gifts from Tibullus, and this is often characteristic of *meretrices* or courtesans. She is also kept under lock and key by her *uir*, a term often translated 'husband' but possessing a wide semantic range and able to refer to any man with whom a woman has a long-term, exclusive relationship. It would not be uncommon for a *meretrix* to be in such a relationship, and her livelihood would depend on her ability to extract material benefits from her lovers (Veyne 1988: 1–2; Konstan 1995: 150–58; James 2003). Thus the conceit of the greedy *puella*, which we find throughout Tibullus, Propertius and Ovid, but not in Catullus, would point in the direction of someone without substantial means and a certain freedom on whom they bestow their favours. Normally, this would exclude aristocratic *matronae*, but the poets clearly play on the ambiguities of the beloved's status and are not always consistent in their characterizations (Fear 2000: 220 n. 7).

These ambiguities highlight what is at stake in these poems: not the 'reality' of the *puella*, but the pattern of substitutive relations she enacts. As with Lesbia, Delia represents both the fantasy of an idealized erotic and social fulfilment and its impossibility. But where for Catullus that fulfilment involved Lesbia substituting for a bride given in legitimate marriage, the brother torn away by death and an ideal of cultural sophistication through erotic possession, in the case of Tibullus, Delia stands for the impossible unity of a fantasy of rural ease and urban sophistication. Through Delia the poet constructs a world in which the opposites of loyalty to his patron, the wealthy general and politician Messalla, and a complete renunciation of military life are able to coincide. A fantasy world is constructed in which *otium*, 'leisure,' and the fruits of *negotium* or 'business,' coexist. Yet, while Delia stands for that unity, at the same time, the inability of the poet to possess her shows its impossibility. Delia, like Lesbia, stands at the centre of two contrary series of substitutions: private amorous plenitude and socially approved recognition.

We can illustrate this pattern by referring to poem 1.1. It begins with a lengthy fantasy of rural ease, which is contrasted with the life of the soldier (1.1.1–52). Near the end of this passage Tibullus dreams of possessing Delia in a world of simple pleasures and virtuous poverty (1.1.43–8). There is, then, a transition to Messalla's house lined with treasures captured on foreign campaign (1.1.53–4). This move brings us from the country to the city. The poet next has us imagine him as a slave chained to Delia's door (1.1.55–6). He then fantasizes about her weeping at his funeral envisioning an ideal of erotic reciprocity, but only at the precise moment it becomes impossible (1.1.59–64). The poem ends with a plea to the *puella* to make love while life permits and to the poet to enjoy the fruits of a moderate life (1.1.65–78).

In 1.2, the poet's rival is one who has rejected the life of rural ease and acquired the wealth needed to win Delia's favours. In 1.3, the poet accompanies Messalla on campaign and suffers from a fever as punishment for leaving Delia. In 1.5, at the moment when the poet dreams of having all he can imagine, a life of rural ease, the love of Delia, and the approval of Messalla, he reveals the whole construction to be a fantasy, a fiction created out of the opposed values for which Delia substitutes: *haec mihi fingebam* ('I made these things up for myself') (1.5.35).

Tibullus and Nemesis

In Tibullus' second book, he has a new mistress whose name reveals the change in her nature. The goddess Nemesis is the spirit of divine retribution, and Tibullus' *puella* in the second book represents the inverse of Delia. Where Delia represented the fantasized but impossible unity of two opposed series, private ease, and social recognition, Nemesis stands for their opposite: anxiety, labor and public humiliation. Whereas in book 1 Tibullus fantasizes a life reminiscent of the Golden Age in the company of Delia, in book 2 he envisions himself as a field hand with sunburned skin and blistered hands (2.3.9–10). Whereas in book 1 the poet pictures himself in a relation of ideal unity with Messalla, the exemplar of civic values and social approbation, in book 2 he fantasizes about a life of plunder to satisfy Nemesis' desire for luxury goods (2.3.35–58). In book 1 the impossible unity of competing goods is ultimately admitted to be a fiction; in book 2 its realization is a nightmare.[5]

Propertius and Cynthia

The case of Propertius and Cynthia is more complex than the two discrete movements that characterize the Tibullan corpus. In Propertius, the substitutions that characterize the poet's relation to the *puella* evolve over time as his aesthetic practice, patronage relations and political affiliations change. As I have argued at length (Miller 2004: ch. 3), in Propertius book 1, commonly known as the *Monobiblos*, Cynthia stands at the nexus of a particularly complex series of substitutive relations. On one level, she is the *Monobiblos*: ancient poetry books took their titles from their opening words: *Cynthia prima* ('Cynthia first'). This play on words, in which the words 'Cynthia first' serve as the opening of the collection, reveals a split between narrative content ('Cynthia was the first woman with whom I fell in love')[6] and metapoetic commentary ('Cynthia was the beginning of the book and hence its title'). From the first words of the first poem, then, we are involved in a substitutive series in which 'Cynthia' has two different values in two separate sequences of thought. This split is more explicit and more concentrated than anything seen in Catullus or Tibullus.

There is, however, another level of substitution present in these opening words: the first four lines of the poem translate an epigram by Meleager (*Anth. Pal.* 12.101). But where Meleager's poem is homoerotic, Propertius' is heteroerotic. Cynthia here substitutes not only for a self-conscious act of literary appropriation, indicating that the poetry to come will be literate, allusive, and modelled on the refined poetry of Propertius' Hellenistic predecessors, but also substitutes for a pederastic beloved, that is to say for a relation between males.

All of these themes find fuller expression throughout the *Monobiblos*. Cynthia stands not only for a fantasy of erotic fulfilment as in Catullus and Tibullus, but also for the genre of elegiac poetry per se and its intertextual relations with the competing genres of iambic (1.4) and epic (1.7), the latter being associated with narratives of political legitimacy and social recognition (1.6). In turn, the representatives of these genres are portrayed as potential or actual rivals for Cynthia. But there is also competition within elegy as Propertius' most intense rival is a certain Gallus, whom many identify with

[5] Furthermore, 'in 2.4.53–4 Tibullus trades in his ancestral love, his patrimony, for this tainted love of Nemesis' in the phrase of the volume's anonymous reader.

[6] See, however, Prop. 3.15.6, 43 on Lycinna.

Cornelius Gallus, often considered the first true elegist (1.5, 1.10, 1.13). Where Catullus provides the first example of sustained erotic elegy and also elaborates many of the themes that would become standard, Gallus was the first to write collections exclusively of elegiac verse devoted to a single beloved, Lycoris. Unfortunately, almost nothing of Gallus survives, though he is mentioned by Virgil in the *Eclogues* (6, 10) and clearly was a poet of influence.[7] In this light, Propertius presents a Gallus who is both a poet and a rival for the love of Cynthia; it is difficult not to interpret him as a rival for preeminence in the genre. Gallus moreover is directly addressed in the final full-length elegy in the *Monobiblos*, 1.20, a narrative poem on the love of Hercules for Hylas, a topic also treated by Gallus the poet. And Gallus himself was not only an accomplished poet but also a political figure, who was appointed prefect of Egypt by Octavian before falling into disgrace and committing suicide. In this context, it is particularly interesting that the collection ends with two short epigrams that feature another Gallus, this one a relative of Propertius who died as a result of Octavian's siege of Perugia. In this light, Cynthia as the object of desire and poetic rivalry comes to stand for Propertius' complex relations with a world of homosocial plenitude in which men are poets, politicians, friends and lovers: a world that political conflict and civil war had made impossible.[8]

In book 2 Gallus disappears and Propertius has entered the patronage of Maecenas, Augustus' astute political operative and informal minister of culture. In this new configuration, Cynthia comes to substitute less for the possibility of a lost homosocial unity than for poetry as the nexus between dreams of personal fulfilment and the growing power of the principate. Poem 2.1 opens with the poet saying that his *puella*, not Apollo or the muse, is the source of his poetry. If she comes dressed in Coan silks, then his entire book-roll will be made of this fabric. He will make poems out of her scattered locks, her playing of the lyre, her sleeping eyes. He will produce 'long *Iliads*' on the battles that ensue when he tears off her cloak (2.1.14). Thus, as in book one, Cynthia substitutes for the poems written about her. Those poems, in turn, are elegiac substitutions for epic. Indeed, immediately after this opening, the poet addresses Maecenas and claims that if he were gifted at leading men in battle he would produce epic verse, not on traditional mythological or historical subjects, but on the accomplishments of Augustus (2.1.17–36). There are, however, two caveats. Firstly, Propertius himself is not so gifted, and this passage is in fact an example of a poetic *recusatio* – the refusal to provide a requested poem, often, laudatory epic.[9] Secondly,

7 See Raymond (Chapter 3) in this volume.
8 See also Keith (Chapter 6) in this volume.
9 See also Sharrock (Chapter 9) in this volume.

and more subtly, it is far from clear that Maecenas and Augustus would have appreciated the topics Propertius wishes he could treat, many of which concern the recent civil wars and include one pointed allusion to the siege at Perugia. Thus, on the one hand, Cynthia, as poetry, represents the locus of interaction between Propertius, Maecenas and Augustus, and in that role she necessarily points to the possibility of his writing laudatory epic. On the other, Cynthia is erotic elegy and as such stands for a subject matter opposed to the martial exploits of epic. She represents a necessary resistance to the imperial power exemplified in the list of Augustus' exploits, a list that makes reference to the very losses the poet chronicles in 1.21 and 1.22.

This ambivalence continues throughout the book, with 2.7 for example chronicling the poet and his *puella*'s celebration of the repeal of a law that would have forced him to enter into a legitimate marriage. Here again amorous fulfilment and the new patronage relations he has entered into are shown to be in tension. Likewise, in poems 2.15 and 2.16, one marvellous night of lovemaking is juxtaposed with Cynthia's seduction by a praetor. While the first poem recalls the battle of Actium and asserts that if all men passed their lives like Propertius, the sea would not be churning Roman bones, the next blames Antony's amorous enslavement for the slaughter of his men at the battle. In each case, Cynthia stands as the nexus of an impossible sequence of substitutions in which, as both poetry and the object of erotic desire, she figures the poet's simultaneous rapprochement with and distance from Augustan power.

In Book Three this basic pattern continues till the final poem of the book when the poet claims to have now seen through the shallow beauty of a faithless mistress even as he had become the laughing stock of the town. He curses Cynthia and relishes imagining her coming age and the destruction of her looks. All of this signals the advent of a fundamentally new form of poetry in book 4. In Propertius' last essay in the genre, he turns to Callimachean aetiological poetry and recounts the origins of Roman monuments and customs (4.1.63–70). In this collection of poems on the origins of the statue of Vertumnus (4.2), the Tarpeian rock (4.4), the battle of Actium (4.6), the *ara maxima* (4.9) and the *spolia opima* (4.10), the voice of the *puella* would seem to have little place.[10] Yet oddly, the female speaker is heard more often in this book than any other. Nonetheless, that female speaker is not unitary and, in a real sense, not the *puella* at all but woman in general. In 4.3, rather than the voice of the beloved, we have that of Arethusa, a Roman *matrona* left behind by her husband, Lycotas, on campaign against the Parthians. She is by definition removed from the

[10] For a comprehensive treatment of this book, see Janan (2001).

chain of poetic substitutions that have defined Cynthia from the beginning of Book one. She looks forward to the writers of Ovid's *Heroides* rather than back to Catullus' Lesbia. In 4.4, the Vestal Virgin Tarpeia recounts her treasonous love for a Sabine prince. In 4.7 Cynthia returns as a ghost to chastise the faithless Propertius. In 4.8 we flashback to a period prior to her death when she had left town to participate in the snake cult of Lanuvium, before making a hasty return trip and surprising Propertius in the company of two women. The spectral quality of the Cynthia who appears in these poems highlights precisely the difference between the central role of the *puella* in the first books and her position now. The book ends with another ghostly voice, the dead Cornelia defending her life of upstanding virtue as a Roman *matrona* who spent her entire life married to a single man. She is everything the *puella* is not.

With book 4, the *puella* as a nexus of competing and often contradictory values has ceased to exist as coherent whole in relation to the elegiac speaking subject. Propertius in his final book anticipates the dispersal of both these figures, poet and *puella*, across a range of generic permutations in Ovid. That dispersal will signify both the final crystallization of the genre in the *Amores*, and its subsequent fracturing and self-parody in the *Heroides*, *Ars amatoria*, and *Medicamina faciei femineae*, where the *puella* becomes truly an interchangeable figure in a series of stock narrative frames.

Ovid and Corinna

Where Lesbia, Cynthia and Delia each in their own way stood at the nexus of competing chains of substitutive relations embodying amatory fulfilment and social recognition, with Nemesis standing as their negative image, Corinna stands in the first place for the formal tradition that creates her as fiction. Cynthia had certainly stood for both elegy in book 1 and poetry's constitutive role in the poet's relations to power and patronage in books 2 and 3, but Corinna substitutes for her own unreality, for the poet's ability to create her as another link in the chain of generic transmission that stands now for the resistance to epic, politics and normative civic life, while offering the fantasy of erotic fulfilment precisely as fantasy.

Amores 1.1 opens not with *Corinna prima*, but with the poet trying to write epic. Yet every other line Cupid steals a foot, turning the poet's dactylic hexameters into elegiac pentameters.[11] When the poet objects to the young god overstepping his bounds, the sprite responds by drawing his bow and shooting the poet in the heart. There is just one problem, while the poet may

[11] See Thorsen (Chapter 23) in this volume.

now be 'in love,' he is not yet 'in love' with anyone: '*me miserum! certas habuit puer ille sagittas:/ uror, et in uacuo pectore regnat Amor*' ('wretched me! That boy had unerring arrows!/ I burn and Love reigns in an empty heart'). The absurdity of the situation is only matched by the hilarity of its portrayal.

In 1.2 the poet is led in Love's triumph. The beloved not only does not yet have a name, it does not even have a sex (cf. 1.1.19–20). The poet's subjection to Love is purely abstract as he follows, hands bound, behind the triumphal chariot of his new *imperator*. His fellow captives Good Sense and Shame trail Love's companions, Flattery, Error and Madness (1.2.29–36). Where in 1.1 the formal object of desire stood for elegy's opposition to epic, in 1.2 that same object and the poetic genre it represents stand in stark and humorous contradiction to the moral virtues that Cupid's cousin, Augustus (1.2.51–2), was claiming to restore.

In 1.3 for the first time the word *puella* is used. Where in 1.2 the poet had been Cupid's prize (*praeda*, 1.2.19), in 1.3 he has become hers (*praedata puella est*, 1.3.1). With unusual clarity the pattern of substitutive relations is highlighted. The *puella* occupies the place of Amor, who stands in opposition both to epic and social recognition. The poet's deft revelation of the formal devices that lie at the heart of the elegiac fiction establish him as a recognized master of the genre before the fact. In the end, he prays that she will yield so that he can render both her and him immortal in verse (1.3.25–6).

In 1.4 the *puella* does not yet have a name, but like Lesbia and Delia, she has a *uir* (1.4.1). The status of this man is unclear. Other poems portray the *puella* as having a *lena* or 'madam' (1.8), which would indicate that she is a *meretrix* ('prostitute'). But within 1.4 the poet uses a variety of legal vocabulary to indicate that his own relationship should be seen as essentially adulterous (cf. 1.4.64; Davis 1993). In the context of the Augustan moral reform laws and the new legal ban on adultery in Rome, this can hardly have been accidental. The poet instructs his beloved on the use of hand signals and other forms of subterfuge to flirt and pet at a dinner party beneath the *uir*'s nose (1.4.15–44). The *puella* here occupies the position of both an object protected by the property rights of its possessor and of a moral agent whose actions are regulated by the state. At the same time, she stands as the possibility of the overturning of the law and normative morality in the name of a largely asocial image of sexual pleasure. The structure of the poem, and indeed the defining structure of the *puella* within these poems, depends upon the tension between these two opposed series of possible substitutions.

In poem 1.5 the *puella* finally receives a name: *ecce, Corinna uenit tunica uelata recincta/ candida diuidua colla tegente coma* ('Behold, Corinna comes wrapped in a high-belted tunic, radiant with her parted hair covering her neck.') The poem itself leads to a singular moment of erotic elan, as the poet unclothes his mistress before our eyes: *cetera quis nescit?* ('who does not know the rest?'). Yet the poem's real force is retroactive, in two senses. Firstly it looks back to the founding moments of the genre. In Catullus 68, when Lesbia first makes her entrance, she is referred to as the poet's *candida diua* ('shining goddess'). Ovid's *candida diuidua* both recalls and is divided from the founding *puella* of elegiac love, who did herself, as we have seen, occupy contradictory or divided positions within the chain of substitutions that defined her.[12] Secondly Corinna herself in poem 1.5 comes to crystallize and embody all the contradictory positions the poet has outlined for her in the first four poems of the collection. The moment the *puella* is named, what began as purely formal construct, and slowly became the nexus of competing and contradictory poetic, political, sexual, moral and legal values, acquires the unity of a single literary character, who in turn is defined by the chain of substitutions for which she stands.

Conclusion

The *puella*, then, is not a person. She is not even a fully formed literary character. Cynthia speaks rarely, Lesbia, Delia, Nemesis and Corinna never. Her physical features are described in passing and in the most general terms. Her social status is clear only in the case of Lesbia, who is a *matrona*, while the rest appear to be *meretrices*, though their portrayal is not always consistent. However, the *puella* is not simply a literary construct. While she may not refer, even in the case of Lesbia, to a single extra-textual reality (Clodia's lived experience was certainly not what Catullus or Cicero portrays), she is only intelligible to the poets' readers and able to function within their texts to the extent that she embodies certain sets of pre-existing erotic, social, moral, legal, political and poetic assumptions. What the *puella* does substitute for is the ability of these values to coincide: the impossible figure that reconciles amorous plenitude with social recognition, poetic perfection with political legitimacy, law with transgressive desire in first century Rome. Accept no substitutes!

Further reading

The standard realist view of the relation between poet and *puella* can be found in both conservative texts such as Luck (1960) and in those that take a critical, feminist perspective such as Hallett (1973). Lyne (1980) leaves these

[12] See Hinds (1987c = 2006) 20–1.

assumptions unchallenged in his exploration of the emotional world of the *Latin Love Poets*. In the later 1980s, the assumption that the elegiac *puella* represented a real person or persons with whom the poet was to be imagined as having a relationship was called into question by a series of articles by Wyke (1987a, 1989) and by the translation of Veyne's book (1988) into English. Both saw the *puella* as a semiotic construct functioning in a complex aesthetic and social game. Kennedy (1993) took this critique a step farther with his deconstruction of 'the rhetoric of reality' in elegiac criticism. Greene (1998) in turn portrayed the relationship between poet and *puella* as a power game that depended on a masculinist fantasy of sexual domination. With James' landmark (2003) the possibility of a woman reader, i.e. of an actual *puella* receiving the figure of the *puella*, is first envisioned and the semiotic fantasy is recontextualized in its materialist reality. My own book (2004), in turn, while indebted to the work of Janan (1994, 2001) was the first fully to develop the model of the *puella* as an object of substitution and exchange in a libidinal and semiotic economy.

11

LAUREL FULKERSON

Seruitium amoris

The interplay of dominance, gender and poetry

It may well be a universal phenomenon that those in love conceive of themselves as having lost control; different cultures find varying metaphors to describe this feeling. For the Roman elegists, loss of control is often theorized as a metaphorical slavery. The word *domina*, one of the primary names the elegiac lover has for his girlfriend, literally means 'mistress', i.e. the female version of 'master', but what is in English a dead metaphor was clearly very much alive in Latin. The word *domina* eventually comes to mean something not so different from *matrona*, i.e. 'female head of household', but this is not for some time; its original meaning is a woman who owns slaves.[1] So what does it mean that the lover in Roman elegy refers to his mistress as his mistress? Or (to ask the same question differently) that he conceives of his relationship with her as one of slavery?

The figure is in keeping with a trend of elegy as a whole, which consistently casts the powerful male lover in a position of submission of various kinds to his cruel and withholding girlfriend. Because the situation in elegy is a literary construct, it is difficult to speak authoritatively about the relative status of lover and *puella*, but the poets themselves were members of the highest property class, so assuredly members of the elite. For their girlfriends, the question remains very much open: wives of other upper-class Romans, unmarried or married freedwomen, and prostitutes (James 2003) have all been suggested, for the poetry itself is coy on the issue, deliberately conflating the vocabulary of different categories of women.[2] Many look to Catullus'

[1] See Lilja (1965) on nuances of *domina* in earlier literature and in the elegists, and on the relative frequency of terms for *seruitium* (81–86); as she notes, Ovid uses the word *domina* more frequently than other elegists, but with less detailed description (86).

[2] It has been suggested by many that this blurring of status is deliberate: whether as a reaction against Augustan attempts to unambiguously clarify the status of women, an attempt to leave narrative possibilities open or simply the result of the elegists' refusal to provide detailed information, is unclear.

Lesbia/Clodia, suggesting that her (elevated) status may apply also to the women of elegy.[3]

This is of course possible, but it is likelier that the elegiac lover, for all his pretence of virtuous poverty, will have been of a much higher social class than his beloved. So the pose of submission, however vividly portrayed, is best understood precisely as a pose, a chance for the elegiac *amator* to play at being less powerful than he really is (compare the elegist's figuration of himself as a 'soldier' of love, which enables him to appropriate some elements from the military life and to reject others). This 'trying-on' of different identities is a recurrent feature of the love poet's relationship to his mistress, and his poetry.

But unlike *militia amoris*, the metaphor of *seruitium amoris* adds more than narrative variation, for unless elegiac mistresses were prostitutes living at a subsistence level, they will inevitably have had some say in whom they spent their time with; only if they themselves were slaves, according to Roman thinking, would they have no choice at all about where to bestow their favours (see, for instance, Seneca *Controv.* 4 *praef.* 10 on sexual submission as *obsequium* (duty) for the freed but *necessitas* (requirement) for the enslaved). As it is, the paranoid persona of the elegiac lover magnifies the possibility of refusal, however limited or implausible, into a situation in which the *domina* has all of the power.

There is a further possibility that lurks behind the mask of enslavement to a mistress: Roman poets sometimes conceive of their artistic creation as play (cf. Catullus 50), sometimes as work. Because work was in the ancient world confined almost entirely to the servile classes (see below, pp. 188–90), any metaphor about work or expending effort will, to a Roman mind, implicitly suggest a kind of slavery, and any diminution in status will also suggest effeminacy. Scholars have shown the ways in which elegists' references to their relationship with their mistresses can also stand for the process of composing a book of poetry (which, as with Propertius' first book, derive their titles from their first word – in his case, Cynthia).[4] The 'fight' with a girlfriend may signify also a struggle for the right phrase; the beauty of the beloved can imply the quality of the composition; the compulsion to write may be figured as an all-consuming erotic relationship in which the difficult and intractable subject matter holds all the power, and this may itself be seen as a kind of enslavement.

Beyond metapoetic implications, however, lies a basic fact: elegiac poetry focuses on the ups and downs of a single erotic relationship (or at least, on

[3] Lesbia's status as a quasi-patron of Catullus is hinted at in Skinner (1997) 144.
[4] See, for a start, Wyke (1994), Sharrock (1991) 36 and *passim*.

only one at a time; Luck 1959: 166). The ups, as is well known to theorists of narrative, tend to be less interesting than the downs; when lovers 'live happily ever after', their story is over. A mistress who is alternately infuriating and enchanting offers the kind of unpredictable behaviour that makes a tale compelling (Connolly 2000: 75). The behaviour of actual slave-owners is likely to seem similarly opaque, even inscrutable, to those who serve them. So, on a narrative level, the capricious *domina* makes an ideal blocking character (Veyne 1988: 138).

Vocabulary and contexts of *seruitium amoris*

The word *domina* is first attested in elegy, at least for us, in Catullus 68.68 (*isque domum nobis isque dedit dominae,* 'he gave a house to me and my *domina*'),[5] the poem that many see as the origin of Augustan elegy. To be sure, in this line Lesbia is called a *domina* (if it is she) in order to connect her to the (illicit) *domus*, and only secondarily to describe Catullus' slavery to her,[6] but the use of *erae* (also literally 'mistress', here in the Latin genitive) at 68.136 suggests that the concept of being amorously enslaved was familiar to Catullus; perhaps indeed the casualness with which he uses the two words suggests that the metaphor was a regular feature of colloquial speech.[7] The word *domina* next appears in a fragment of the shadowy elegiac poet Gallus; this too may be where elegists derive the idea upon which they expand so fruitfully (2.6–7, with Courtney ad loc.).[8]

5 Translations, here and throughout, are my own, and make no claim to literary merit.

6 *Dominae* is an emendation of the ms. *dominam*; if accepted (as it is by few modern editors), *dominam* would suggest that Allius provided a woman to Catullus as well as a house. Wilkinson, who follows the manuscript reading, suggests that *domina* refers not to Lesbia but to the housekeeper who came with the house (1970: 290). So it may be that this passage does not imply *seruitium*. See too the use of *domina*, apparently for a girlfriend, at Lucilius 730M and Horace *Carm.* 1.33.14 and 2.12.13 (the latter of either Horace's mistress or Maecenas' wife; see Nisbet and Hubbard (1978) ad loc.). And, from a significantly later period, Martial 5.57 suggests that the masculine version of the word had lost any tone of deference, being used even for inferiors. Fantham notes that, whatever we are to make of the Catullan passage, the fact remains that Catullus' relationship to Lesbia posits her 'as a unique, dominant mistress to whom he was subordinated like a slave' (1996: 105). See too below, p. 185 for discussion of Catullus' positioning vis-à-vis Lesbia.

7 Courtney (1993) *ad* Gallus 2.7. The word *era* refers to a female head of household, but it is also used, by Ennius and Catullus, as a term of respect for goddesses (Enn. *inc.* 46, Catull. 64.395).

8 As Anderson, Parsons and Nisbet note, 'It would be intriguing if the masterful Gallus introduced the colloquialism to elegy with reference to a freedwoman' (1979: 144). Ross believes that Prop. 1.5 provides a hint that Gallus was the first to write explicitly about *seruitium amoris* (1975: 102–3).

...tandem fecerunt c[ar]mina Musae
quae possem domina deicere digna mea
(6–7)

At last the Muses have created songs which I can speak as being worthy of my mistress.

These poetic occurrences suggest that the word enjoyed some currency, and it has been suggested that the image of the lover as a slave was similarly colloquial, if not common (and not much attested in earlier literature).[9] As scholars note, it seems to be the case that when the lover is conceived of as a slave in literature prior to elegy, the focus is primarily on how powerful or miraculous love is, such that it makes him (occasionally her) behave in such uncharacteristic ways. This aspect is certainly present in erotic elegy, but it tends rather to emphasize the servility of the lover, the ways his behaviour is undignified and unseemly, rather than simply unusual.[10] In this vein, Ovid's *Amores* 2.17 is an extended discussion of whether it is or is not degrading to be enslaved to a woman and whether or not status matters in amorous relationships; it includes several non-canonical mythic exempla (see below, p. 185 for standard models).

It has often been noted that the imagery of slavery is most prevalent and most vivid in Propertius (Copley 1947: 297, Lyne 1979: 126), so the majority of my examples come from his poetry. The vocabulary used by the elegists is less varied than the uses to which they put it (*domina*, *seruus*, *seruitium*, *seruire* etc.); sometimes the elegists speak of themselves as slaves, sometimes of their girlfriends as mistresses, sometimes of slavery in general and sometimes of the humiliating tasks they must perform, the punishments they fear, suffer or deserve.[11] There are numerous 'casual' references, which seem simply to presume that the lover is enslaved but offer little comment.[12]

[9] Copley (1947) 285–90, Murgatroyd (1981) 590–4 and Lyne (1979) 118–22 outline the Greek and Latin precedents. These three articles, the most complete treatments of *seruitium amoris* as a whole, differ markedly from one another even in such details as their lists of passages that prefigure elegiac usage, but share a few similarities. Copley suggests that the metaphor is a way for elegists to bring themselves down to the level of their girlfriends, in order to minimize status differences (1947: 285), and that it derives ultimately from common speech (1947: 289). He notes that the imagery is most prevalent in Propertius (1947: 297). Lyne argues that the metaphor, while alluded to in earlier literature, is essentially an elegiac, indeed Propertian, invention (1979: 117), and that, although possibly familiar from colloquial speech, its prevalence and import in elegy are meant to be shocking (1979: 126). Murgatroyd believes that the metaphor was more prevalent in Hellenistic literature than our surviving evidence shows (1981: 594).

[10] See Copley (1947) 285, Lyne (1979) 117–21, Murgatroyd (1981) 604.

[11] See, for example, Tib. 1.6.37–8, 1.9.21–2, 2.4.1–12, Ov. *Am.* 1.7.1–4.

[12] See, for example, Prop. 1.4.1–4, 1.5.19–20, 1.7.7–8, 1.10.27, 1.18.25–6, which ironically claim that he has learned not to complain about his mistress's *iussa*, 'orders',

Somewhat more interesting are passages which imply the transference of *seruitium* from one mistress to another (e.g. Prop. 1.12.17–18), claim that the lover has become accustomed to servitude in general (Prop. 2.4.45–50) or conceive of a particular person as enslaving many (Tib. 4.5.3–4); these make it clear that it is difficult for the lover to envision a situation in which he would not be in thrall to someone or other.

Certain behaviours are denoted, either explicitly or implicitly, as slavish: standing outside the *puella*'s door all night long (often delivering a *paraklausithyron*, e.g. Prop. 2.17, Ov. *Ars* 2.523–8), kissing the *puella*'s feet (Ov. *Ars* 2.531–4) and taking a beating (Ov. *Ars* 2.531–4). Tibullus 1.4.39–52 outlines what a beloved boy might demand; his list includes deference in general, accompaniment on lengthy journeys, physical effort at the oars, work of various sorts (*duros . . . labores*), carrying hunting equipment, and letting him win in play-fights. There are similar, but even more servile, examples at Ovid, *Ars* 2.197–232, such as going where she says, laughing when she laughs, crying when she cries, letting her win at games, carrying an umbrella or a sunshade in case she needs one, warming her hands, holding her distaff, helping her in court cases, waiting patiently at appointed times and places, running to do her bidding, escorting her home late at night and accompanying her on journeys.[13] Although we might conceive of most of these examples as encompassing perfectly normal interactions between a couple, Romans would have seen most of these duties as suitable to the enslaved rather than the free.

The lover occasionally reflects on the origins of his slavery, and suggests that he has been captured either by Amor himself or by the *puella*. So, for instance, Prop. 1.1.1–4:[14]

> Cynthia prima suis miserum me cepit ocellis,
> contactum nullis ante cupidinibus.
> tum mihi constantis deiecit lumina fastus,
> et caput impositis pressit Amor pedibus,

2.20.19–20, of a *seruitium mite*, 'gentle servitude', 2.25.11–12, 3.11.1–8, 3.25.3; Tib. 1.1.46 and 55; Ov. *Am.* 1.3.5–6 (this list is by no means comprehensive).

13 Perhaps the most servile example of a slave of love is to be found in Ovid's version of the Homeric Briseis, who authors the letter we have as *Heroides* 3. The literal slave and war-captive of Achilles, she invokes the language of *seruitium amoris* in ways that some find poignant, others pathetic. Where it is for some elegists simply a metaphor, Briseis' expressions of willingness to be Achilles' maid/seamstress are deeply ironic (examples at Ov. *Her.* 3.5, 52, 69–82, 99–102; see Verducci (1985) 98–121 and Drinkwater (Chapter 12 in this volume)).

14 See too Prop. 2.3.9, also with the verb *cepit*. Other narratives of enslavement at Tib. 1.6.1–6 and 1.8.5–6, Ov. *Am.* 1.2.17–20; *Ars* 2.406 observes that Agamemnon was captured by (literally, 'made booty of', *praedae praeda*) Cassandra, his own slave-mistress.

> Cynthia first captured me with her eyes, poor me, who had been touched before by no desire. Then Amor cast down my eyes with their resolute pride, and with his feet on me, pressed upon my head...

To many, these lines are so well known that they engender little comment, but it is noteworthy that they initiate the collection with reference to enslavement. Warfare was one of the primary ways in which new slaves entered the Roman world, so here at least Propertius is realistic (and the image of stepping on a person is more suitable to prisoners than slaves).

Finally, the elegists sometimes trace a genealogy of *seruitium amoris*, attributing a mythological pedigree to it; the two most common *exempla* are Apollo, who was so in love with Admetus that he toiled in the fields for him (Tib. 2.3.11–28, discussed by Whitaker 1983: 79–83) and Hercules, so in love with Omphale that he willingly waited on her (Ov. *Ars* 2.221–2). But again, although these tales appear in literary works earlier than elegy, their previous incarnations tend to focus on incongruity rather than the debasing nature of slavery (Copley 1947: 285–8); indeed, previous versions of the Hercules/Omphale story have him literally enslaved to her, and include no erotic component at all.[15] And, of course, when elegists use mythological *exempla*, they tend to do so in order to make a point, usually a persuasive one (Whitaker 1983: 12–13). So, for instance, Tibullus uses Apollo as a divine justification for the degrading aspects of his own servitude (Whitaker 1983: 31, 82).

Gender and politics

We have already seen that the elegists' pretence of slavery is likely to be a rejection of their actual status in favour of a lower one. So too, positing a man as less powerful than a woman involves a reversal of the Roman norm. Women did, of course, own male slaves, but given the ideal of the free (wealthy) Roman man as the primary speaking subject, slavery itself can be seen as effeminizing, particularly to men. There is a clear connection in the Roman mind between slave, feminine and inferior (a point which must simply be stated, rather than argued).[16] Having to take orders, not

[15] E.g. Callim. *Hymn* 2.49 on Apollo as slave of Admetus. There is also an erotic precursor at Ter. *Eun.* 1026–7, where Thraso justifies his subservient behaviour by noting that Hercules was a slave to Omphale. See discussions of the mythological precedents at Copley (1947) 285–8.

[16] Others have argued this point at great length and with great persuasiveness. See, e.g. Wyke: 'In Roman moralising discourses, sexual relationships were constituted in terms of domination and subordination, of superiority and inferiority, of activity and passivity, of masculinity and femininity, and aligned with the relationships of master and

give them, is simultaneously servile and effeminate, and taking orders from a woman may be seen as particularly humiliating.[17]

Catullus had earlier assumed a traditionally feminine role in a series of sensitive poetic explorations of what love feels like to one who is not in control (e.g. 51, 63).[18] Rather than being the dominant partner in his relationship with Lesbia, he instead paints a portrait of himself as needing more than he gets from her, as more invested in the success and longevity of their liaison, as more vulnerable, and therefore more feminine. While it is perfectly possible that Catullus, or any Roman man, actually had feelings like this about a relationship with a particular woman, scholars have suggested that his pose is more about relative status in the public world than it is about gender roles in an intimate sphere. That is, Catullus uses his 'feminization' by Lesbia as a lens through which to focus anxieties about the decreasing role in public life for men of his class. This is a plausible suggestion, and need not preclude Catullus from also finding himself involved in an association with a particularly powerful woman, or merely from noticing that such women existed and imagining what a relationship with one would be like. Even if it is not correct that Catullus means to compare public and private morals to the detriment of both, his poetry provides an important precedent for the elegists' conflation of female and subservient in poetry (Skinner 1997: 145).[19]

Being in love does not automatically entail feeling powerless, and feeling powerless need not necessitate thinking of oneself as a woman or slave, but these connections seem to be at the forefront of how the elegists think of their amorous relationships.[20] Because she 'wears the trousers,' he must do as she says. Yet he is not silent about his sufferings; in fact, through his voluntary assumption of a position of slavery and complaints about that role, he paradoxically makes himself the hero of his own narrative (Greene

slave. The persistent Propertian strategy of casting the male lover in a submissive, servile role in relation to his beloved *puella* then realigns the gendered relations of domination and submission so intrinsic to Roman constructions of sexuality and social status. The male *ego* enacts the role of a faithful, submissive, subordinate woman' (1994: 116–17).

17 And apparently, not only the Roman mind: Barthes suggests that being in love always feminizes the lover (1978: 188–9).

18 Wiseman (1985: 143–6) discusses the ways in which Catullus shows us that Lesbia is in charge; see too the useful discussion in Skinner (1997).

19 See too Greene on the ways in which military and servile metaphors in the elegists show that they conceive of public and private discourses as implicated in one another (1998: 41).

20 As Greene notes, the inversion of 'normal' sex roles is extremely prevalent in all of elegy, and not only when the metaphor of love's slavery is being invoked: the elegist is regularly passive, devoted, feminine, enslaved, and his mistress is masterful, active and masculine, with interests other than her poet (1998: xiii; cf. Kennedy (1993) 31).

1998: 51, 66). He is at pains to suggest that his servitude is genuine, and to remind readers that it is freely chosen, and so only as real as he finds palatable at any given moment.[21] In fact, when the lover discourses on his metaphorical slavery, he is far more interested in his own role as subservient being than in the *puella*, or even in the relation of dominance itself. This too may reflect a political cast on the part of the elegists; about this there is much debate. Perhaps Roman poets fashion themselves as women/slaves because there is no place left from which to be a real man (Skinner 1997: 145, of Catullus; P.A. Miller 2004: 159, of Propertius).[22] Or perhaps they relish the escape from the demands of their own masculinity, in however tenuous and fictionalized fashion (Fitzgerald 2000: 41–3), in a way similar to that suggested for audiences of Roman comedy (Parker 1989, McCarthy 2000: ix–x, 20), and which we may find reminiscent of the Greek tragedies that centre on failed transitions to masculinity.

But either way, it is important to note that this is only one of a series of subject-positions adopted by the elegist; there are many other parts to the story and many other roles to play. So, for instance, it has been noted that the elegists also conceive of themselves as clients to their patron-*puella*[23] and worshippers of the *puella*-goddess; the metaphor of elegiac lovers as soldiers serving under the generalship of their mistresses or as captive booty of Amor is discussed by Drinkwater (Chapter 12) in this volume. These lenses also posit an unequal relationship, but as with *seruitium*, it is a metaphorical and temporary inequality. Perhaps most interestingly, when the elegist is not 'putting himself down', he is lording it over others, hoping or fantasizing

[21] E.g. Prop. 4.8.82, which speaks of *imperio . . . dato* (mastery which was given), Tib. 1.6.69–72, which asks for harsh treatment, and Ov. *Am.* 3.11a, which declares that his slavery is at an end. James too notes the fact that *seruitium amoris* is purely voluntary (2003: 147). See Benjamin on the pleasures of submission, particularly when it functions 'as a defensive strategy of the self', i.e. when it is, or can be conceived of, as a deliberate selection (1988: 81). She is concerned with voluntary submission to those who might subjugate or enslave anyway, which, if the political nuances suggested here are valid, may not be as irrelevant as it seems to the situation of Roman poets of the Augustan age.

[22] In this light, Fear's comments about the emperor Augustus' emasculating/seduction of the upper classes through providing *otium* and denying *negotium* are particularly interesting (2000: 237–8).

[23] On mistresses as patrons or quasi-patrons, see White (1993) 87–91. Oliensis persuasively shows the similarities between love and patronage, another difficult-to-understand but centrally Roman concept (1997) *passim*, e.g. 153; cf. Fitzgerald (2000) 72–3 on similarities between *seruitium amoris* and patronage. Gibson, by contrast, is at pains to differentiate between elegiac *seruitium* and *amicitia* (one way in which patronage is described); he suggests that Ovid and Propertius see themselves as behaving like *amici* but being treated like *serui* (1995: 74). McCarthy argues that such plays as Plautus' *Casina* substitute marriage for slavery, which is 'disorienting' (2000: 79–80). *Seruitium amoris* does essentially the opposite, and it is equally disorienting.

that his *puella* will become his slave (Prop. 2.26.22; cf. Veyne 1988: 139), abusing those who are lower than himself (see below, p. 189), reminding the *domina* of past gifts (Prop. 2.8.13–16), lauding his own power over the love-object or over love itself (e.g. Prop. 1.10.15–18, Tib. 1.4.15.16, Ov. *Am.* 3.7.11, where a sex partner calls him *dominum*, *Ars* 1.1–30, where the *praeceptor amoris* has mastery over love and 1.45–52, over the *puella*) or jeering at friends who have newly fallen under the spell of a dominating woman (e.g. Prop. 1.9). Indeed, the lover even occasionally threatens or resorts to violence against his *puella*, a move which makes clear in an extremely concrete way who holds the real power in the relationship.[24] So for the elegist, perhaps for the Roman man in general, relationships seem to centre on establishing who is on top, and slavery provides an extremely fertile metaphor for describing what it feels like to lose this contest, however temporarily.

Roman slavery, real and pretend

Because slavery was in Roman society not merely a metaphor, but a fact of daily life, it is worth exploring some aspects of slavery in the Roman world to see how they might affect our understanding of elegiac slavery. First, slavery and slaves were so prevalent in Roman society that they were almost invisible. For both Greeks and Romans, most kinds of work, particularly banausic labour, were seen as degrading, so the freeborn simply did not engage in them unless poverty required it. Romans of all but the very lowest classes owned slaves – anywhere from one to many hundreds – and these slaves performed a wide variety of tasks, including farm labour and factory work, personal service activities that range from administering medical care to grooming to entertaining, and even such tasks, odd to a modern audience, as reading out loud and remembering people's names. So for those reading and writing elegy, slaves are ubiquitous. In most of our ancient sources, slaves are like furniture: always presumed to be there, they are worthy of comment only when defective, exceptionally beautiful, or expensive.

This means that we know both a lot and very little about slavery in Rome. We know a great deal about the kinds of slaves there were, from such sources as their funerary epitaphs, lists of imperial slaves and incidental references to them in a wide variety of literature. The physical and sexual exploitation of slaves, both male and female, also seems to have been a regular feature

24 See, e.g. Prop. 2.8.25–8 (threatened), 2.15.17–20 (erotic), Ov. *Am.* 1.7, *Ars* 1.672–80 (erotic). The fact that the *puella* is sometimes envisioned as being violent (e.g. Prop. 3.8, 4.8.63–7) seems only to excite the lover.

of ancient life, as numerous scattered references show. What we do not and cannot know is the texture of ancient slavery, what it was actually like on a daily basis to own slaves or (even less accessible) to be one.[25]

Elegy itself regularly mentions those who are actual slaves, who work as maids, hairdressers, go-betweens, and guards (the *ianitor* is a key figure in elegy, as he polices the boundary between inside, where the girlfriend is, and outside, where the lover is).[26] These are all, as we should expect, domestic slaves, and primarily those who surround and/or control access to the *puella*. Generally, they are merely props for the elegist, but occasionally they take on personality, particularly in the elegies of Ovid. Yet where we might expect some reference to co-servitude to a single mistress as creating some bond, the elegists rarely suggest any fellow-feeling with other, less metaphorical slaves.[27]

In fact, when he is dealing with other slaves, the elegiac lover (particularly Ovid) tends to slip naturally into his normal role as master, ordering his subordinates around. In one lengthy and notable example, the diptych *Amores* 2.7 and 8, Ovid makes very clear his superiority to Cypassis, the hairdresser of Corinna, positioning himself as her angry *dominus* (2.8.23–4, with Davis 1989: 60–1). He threatens to tell her mistress he has had Cypassis as a way to make Cypassis have sex with him again. So too, in the *Ars Amatoria*, Ovid suggests seducing the maid (1.351–98; best after you have already had her mistress) and being friendly and generous to her so that she will speak well of you when you are absent (2.251–60).

The brief information I have provided about Roman slavery will, I hope, hint at yet another reason why the elegists find the pose of *seruitium amoris* so compelling. Because the slaves of elegy are in constant contact with the *puella*, and because slaves are the most likely (normally, the only) persons to attend upon the bodily wants and needs of the free, it is perhaps inevitable

[25] Fitzgerald (2000: 8), but see his chapter 1, esp. 24, for a reconstruction of living with slaves, which brings out the disturbing and comforting aspects of such intimacy.

[26] There are other mentions of domestic slaves at Prop. 2.23.23–4, 3.6, 4.7.35–48 and 73–6 (providing incidental evidence about household slaves), Ov. *Am.* 1.11 (addressed to Nape, the hairdresser and go-between of Corinna, entrusted with a tablet setting a rendezvous) and *Ars* 2.289–94, where it is suggested that the lover free a slave whom he was already planning to free at the *puella*'s request, in order to make her feel obligated to him. The *ianitor* features in a number of elegies, with pleas and curses addressed to him in Ov. *Am.* 1.6 and 2.2–3. Tibullus offers to take his place, and promises he will be a much more effective guardian (1.6.37–8), and Ovid claims that a *ianitor* should not be necessary for a truly virtuous woman (*Am* 3.4.33–6). There is, of course, a sense in which the lover, ever suspicious, would like literally to be able to watch his girlfriend when he is not around (Fitzgerald 2000: 75).

[27] Then again, there does not seem to have been much of this among actual slaves in ancient society as a whole.

that elegiac poets look to slavery as a way to express their desire for access and physical proximity to their *puellae*.[28] When they speak of the specific tasks they imagine performing (above, p. 184), they focus on those that are degrading, but also those that require being with their girlfriends. In this light, it is useful to note Fitzgerald's comments about the nature of relations between free and slave: although – perhaps because – the parties are of such unequal status, there is a frequent perception that a genuine bond of intimacy could exist between master and man (2000: 54–5). Given the exigencies of social relations between upper-class Romans, the metaphor of slavery may, ironically enough, be one of very few ways Romans had of envisioning a relationship that did not require worrying about who was the boss.[29]

Roman comedy and the *seruus callidus*

Elegy does not, as a whole, interest itself much in actual slaves, despite sometimes lengthy descriptions of the 'labour' the lover must undergo to keep his mistress happy (see above, p. 184). One of our most fruitful literary sources about Roman slavery is the comedies of Plautus and Terence, most of which feature multiple slaves of different statuses, roles, and personalities. As it happens, many scholars see Roman comedy as an important source for the genre of elegy (e.g. Day 1938: 85–101; James 1998: 3, 10–11), so it is worth devoting some attention to how slavery works in comedy, as it may provide us with further insights into its functions in elegy.

Actual *seruitium amoris* does not appear as such in Roman comedy. There are some references to young lovers as behaving slavishly because of their love or having no power to resist the wishes of their girlfriends,[30] but the elegists seem to have been the first to develop the metaphor. Two Plautine examples are worthy of further attention, if only to show how far the elegists have taken the concept from its origins. Phaedromus, the lover of the *Curculio*, obeys the orders of Venus and Cupid (*Venus Cupidoque imperat*) and

[28] Fitzgerald suggests that slavery also brings with it a kind of intimate knowledge: it provides a 'privileged position from which the master is observed' (2000: 19). See too McCarthy on slavery as linked to familiarity (1998: 179). Our word 'familiar' derives directly from the Latin *familia*, which denotes the Roman household, including (especially) slaves.

[29] See James on the equality, 'in fantasy and persuasive pretense, at least' of the *puella* and the *amator* (2003: 12).

[30] Slavish: Plaut. *Curc.* 1–11, *Poen.* 447–8. Powerless: Plaut. *Bacch. passim*, e.g. 55–6, 66–8, 102, 1123–8, *Truc.* 35–7, Ter. *Heaut.* 223–8, *Eun.* 46–80 and 186; these examples primarily use metaphors of hunting and military defeat, not enslavement per se.

so brings presents to his mistress; his servant notes that he is doing slave labor (*istuc quidem nec bellum est nec memorabile / tute tibi puer es*, 'this is neither pretty nor something to be discussed; that you yourself are your own slave', 8–9). The lover is a slave to Venus (or perhaps she is his commanding officer; the verb applies to both kinds of obeying), or to himself, but not to his girlfriend. Second, the lover of the *Poenulus* observes that Love has made him obey his own slave, although he is himself free (*quando Amor iubet / me oboedientem esse seruo liberum*, 447–8). Again we see the imagery nascent, but unrelated to the *puella*.

Although the specific similarities are few, the plot of many (though assuredly not all) comedies is similar to the basic structure of elegy: a resourceless young man falls helplessly in love with a woman he cannot have for one reason or another[31] (most often money is at issue, but sometimes his father forbids it, or both). In this situation, someone, usually the *seruus callidus*, 'clever slave', devises a brilliant plot to get the money and/or obtain the girl. Many of the ancillary characters in elegy clearly derive from comedy: the greedy *lena* who offers the girl mercenary advice which runs counter to the lover's interests, the wealthy but risible soldier who is his rival. It has even been suggested that the hapless *adulescens* makes his way into the persona of the elegiac lover, allowing poets to make fun of the characters they have created by showing them to be melodramatic and childish, even if likeable (James 1998: 10–11).[32]

Given that the affinities between the two genres are deep and pervasive, I would like to suggest that another character makes the transition from comedy into elegy, namely, the clever slave. He is a primary focus of interest in comedies, and his machinations to help his master get her girl provide much of the action of the plays. Although he does not behave ethically, he inevitably avoids punishment, at least for the duration of the play (Parker 1989: 233–5). McCarthy has persuasively argued that the figure of the clever slave would have touched a chord even in the freeborn and relatively powerful, and that they might have vicariously relished seeing the normally powerless triumph.[33] So too for elegy. The 'splitting' which Roman comedy

[31] Indeed, the fact that the status of the beloved in comedy is so variable may be one reason why it is difficult to pin down in elegy.

[32] There are also some key differences: Roman comedies, particularly those of Plautus, contain a great deal of farce, and the resolution of their plots is often a happy ending in the form of a love-marriage. Elegy, of course, does not want this kind of resolution, but it *is* concerned with the fulfilment of erotic desires.

[33] Her work is prefigured by Thalmann, who suggests that the *Captiui* naturalizes the ideology of domination and also of submission (1996: 112, 116). But she extends domination and submission to the same groups of people at different times, i.e. by suggesting that in some relations one is on top, and in others, on the bottom.

effects, by dividing the lover into an emotional youth and a scheming slave (Parker 1989: 242–3), is undone in the figure of the Roman elegist, who is alternately resourceless and Machiavellian, overcome by his feelings and plotting every move. The *adulescens*/lover himself is pathetic and innocent, but he only seems so because the scheming poet/slave has created the narrative and takes the blame.[34]

Conclusions

While *seruitium amoris* is normally read as an ironic reversal of status, designed to show that the lover refuses a relationship of equality,[35] I have suggested that it might also be the best way available to express a desire for equality. The paradigm of the clever slave in Roman comedy has provided us with a context suggesting that Romans viewed themselves in multiple subject positions at the same time, and so what looks to be contradiction may simply be juxtaposition: equality with, mastery of, and subordination to, the *puella* are simply different ways of expressing the varying aspects of how a relationship feels. *Seruitium amoris* well captures this multifold nuance. I close with a few lines of Sulpicia, a woman who is also an elegiac poet: when she invokes the metaphor of *seruitium amoris*, she does so in a way that explicitly seeks parity (4.5.13–16). I close with a few lines about Sulpicia:[36]

> nec tu sis iniusta, Venus: uel seruiat aeque
> uinctus uterque tibi, uel mea uincla leua.
> sed potius ualida teneamur uterque catena,
> nulla queat posthac nos soluisse dies.

> Venus, don't you be unjust: either let us each, enchained, be slaves equally, or lighten my chains. Instead, let us rather both be held by strong shackles, which no day coming later could loosen.

34 There are numerous references in Plautus to the 'clever slave' as author/plotmaker; they are most sustained in *Pseudolus* (e.g. 404–5).

35 See Lilja (1965: 203) for the notion that Ovid does not refer much to *seruitium* because he wants an equal relationship.

36 See too 4.6.7–10 for similar language also placed in the mouth of the *amicus Sulpiciae*. There is much scholarly debate about the authorship of these poems, some of which are written in the first person and some the third; further, some of those written in the first person are traditionally assumed not to have beeen written by Sulpicia, but instead by the *amicus*; see Skoie (Chapter 5) in this volume. The imagery is nearly identical in Prop. 2.15.25–6 (*atque utinam haerentis sic nos uincire catena/ uelles ut numquam solueret ulla dies*, 'would that you might be willing to bind us embracing with a chain such as no day could ever dissolve').

Further reading

There are three significant previous studies of *seruitium amoris*: Copley (1947), Lyne (1979) and Murgatroyd (1981); see note above for brief discussion of their points of contact. On relations of dominance in elegy, see Skinner (1997), Greene (1998) and P.A. Miller (2004), and for some of the possible political implications of elegy, see Fear (2000). Discussions of what we know, and cannot know, about the *puella*, are Wyke (1994), Sharrock (1991), James (2003) and P.A. Miller (Chapter 10) in this volume. Two excellent recent studies of literary conceptions of Roman slavery are Fitzgerald (2000) and McCarthy (2000).

12

MEGAN O. DRINKWATER

Militia amoris

Fighting in love's army

militiae species amor est: discedite, segnes;
non sunt haec timidis signa tuenda uiris.
nox et hiems longaeque uiae saeuique dolores
mollibus his castris et labor omnis inest.
(Ov. *Ars* 2.233–236)[1]

Love is a type of soldiery: depart, lazy ones;
these military standards are not to be observed by timid men.
Night and storm and long journeys and cruel pains
and all toil is within these tender camps.[2]

Roman masculine identity was oriented around warfare, as is perhaps most clearly shown in the Latin word for virtue (*uirtus*), which means specifically masculine virtue, courage and valour, with man (*uir*) at its very root. Any decision not to participate in Roman imperial expansion through military service was a failure to espouse cultural values, and could easily be construed as a renunciation of allegiance to the state. That military affairs were so integral to the cultural climate at the end of the republic is made clear by the protestations of the famed statesman and orator Cicero, one whose pen was ever mightier than his sword. His urging in the treatise *On Duties* that 'although most people believe that military affairs are more important than civil ones, this idea ought to be de-emphasized' (*cum plerique arbitrentur res bellicas maiores esse quam urbanas, minuenda est haec opinio*, *Off.* 1.74) well illustrates how overwhelmingly common opinion ran counter to his sentiment.[3] The pose thus adopted by the Roman elegists, that they were soldiers of Amor rather than of Roma, was a rejection of *Romanitas* itself, and more specifically the *Romanitas* promoted by the emerging *princeps*,

[1] All quotations from the *Ars Amatoria* and the *Amores* are from the text of Kenney (1995).
[2] All translations are my own.
[3] For assistance in clarifying the point, I thank Jim Abbot and Laurel Fulkerson. The text is that of Winterbottom (1994).

Augustus (Davis 1999: 438–42, Wyke 2002: 34–5).[4] The degree to which this renunciation should be taken seriously is a subject of disagreement among scholars of elegy: is it a playful game, meant only to be humorous for its ridiculousness (Murgatroyd, 1975)? Is it a serious attempt to undermine the Augustan program (Davis 1999)? Or somewhere in between (Gale 1997, Miller 2004 144–6)?

The interlacing of love and war has a long history in the literature of Greece and Rome. With seeds planted in Homer, initially nursed by Sappho[5] and cultivated in Greek drama, the Hellenistic poets and early Republican Roman literature, the trope comes to full flower with the Latin elegists of the first century BC (Murgatroyd 1975: 68–79; Lyne 1980: 71–2; Gale 1997: 78–9). With Tibullus, Propertius and Ovid, military imagery in love poetry developed into a sustained metaphor with several thematic variants. One such variant presents love itself as war and sex as a battle, with Love or the *puella* as a commanding officer and the lover as soldier. Another opposes love to warfare, sometimes as a career or lifestyle choice that is often linked to the poet's choice of *métier* or genre. The third variation I shall address conflates the first two through triumphal imagery, with the lover's defeat at the hands of love, or the lover's triumph over his girl. To complicate the issue, on occasion the *militia* and *seruitium amoris* tropes overlap, as in Prop. 1.1 with Cynthia's capture of the poet-speaker, with captivity and slavery as the inevitable result of war (see Fulkerson in this volume pp. 184–5). While the elegists all deploy military metaphors, each poet has his own particular preferences. As Propertius is the master of *seruitium* (see Fulkerson in this volume), so Ovid's favourite weapon is *militia*, and thus the bulk of my discussion centres on his work.

The quote that opens this chapter is from Ovid's manual of the lover's art, the *Ars Amatoria*, and is especially apt for introducing a discussion of *militia* as used by the three elegists whose work survives. I treat Tibullus, Propertius and Ovid in tandem, as the thematic focus of each loosely corresponds to the ideas the quote expresses. Because there is such extensive conflation and varied usage of the *militia amoris*, the boundaries between the sections and discussions of the poets are necessarily porous. I do not present a strict chronological development, or one that addresses each author in isolation from the others,[6] in hope that this approach will provide an overview of how

4 For a suggestive discussion of Propertius' self-identification with the notorious Mark Antony see Griffin (1986): 32–47.

5 Cf. especially Sappho's call to Aphrodite to be her comrade-in-arms, σύμμαχος, fr. 1.28, on which see Rissman (1983). The text cited is that of Lobel and Page (1955).

6 The chronology of the elegiac poems is difficult, especially in the case of Ovid, who on his own account reduced his *Amores* from five books to three. For the chronological

elegy and the *militia amoris* are a conscious choice each author makes in accordance with his own poetic interests. Each thematic section focuses on the author who best exemplifies that usage, with supplementary references to the other authors in order to show how the collective exploitation of *militia* makes up part of a dynamic and self-referential poetic system.

Discedite segnes: love vs. war

As Ovid's *Ars Amatoria* insists, elegiac love, like warfare, is not for the lazy. Tibullus, in his declaration that he would prefer to lie and loaf (*tecum/ dum modo sim, quaeso segnis inersque uocor*, Tib. 1.1.58 'as long as I may be with you, I pray that I am called sluggish and lazy'),[7] clearly opposes himself to what was to become Ovid's conception of the lover. It should be no surprise, then, that Tibullus' primary mode of addressing military values is one of opposition rather than assimilation. From the very start of his elegiac collection, Tibullus renounces warlike pursuits (Tib. 1.1.4–6) declaring that it is right for his patron Messalla to fight (*te bellare decet*, Tib. 1.1.53)[8] while instead he himself has been bound, *uinctum*, by a beautiful mistress (Tib. 1.1.55). At the close of this first poem, however, he shows the fluidity of *militia* under the elegists by engaging in the apparent assimilation of love and war:

> nunc leuis est tractanda Venus, dum frangere postes
>
>   non pudet et rixas inseruisse iuuat.
>
> hic ego dux milesque bonus. uos, signa tubaeque,
>
>   ite procul; cupidis uulnera ferte uiris,
>
> ferte et opes . . .   (Tib. 1.1.73–7)

> Now is the time for delightful sex, while it is not shameful to break the doorposts and it is pleasing to engage in quarrels. Here I am a general and a good soldier: you, martial insignia and war trumpets, go far away! Bring wounds to the men who desire them, and bring them riches!

In this merging of love and battle, Tibullus' version of war is clearly opposed to 'real' martial activity. His broken-in doors (Tib. 1.1.73) and brawls (Tib. 1.1.74) are those associated with sex (*Venus*, Tib. 1.1.73). It is under the goddess of love that the poet declares he will be a good general and soldier (Tib. 1.1.75), while the battle flags and military trumpets are urged to withdraw (Tib. 1.1.75) and bring their wounds and monetary rewards

order of the works of Propertius and Tibullus, see Lee-Stecum (Chapter 4), Keith (Chapter 6) and Thorsen (Introduction).

7 Or *in-ers*, Lat. art-less, 8 All quotations of Tibullus are from Maltby (2002).

to men who want them (Tib. 1.1.76). Yet it is a mark of Tibullan wit and sophistication that even this emphatic command contains its own conflation of love and war. Those who desire the wounds and riches they may bring are *cupidi*, 'desirous', the same word used in other elegiac contexts to describe lovers. Imagery that opposes love to war, and yet seems to assimilate lovers and fighters, appears in other poems of Tibullus (Tib. 1.2.67–76, 1.3.63–4 e.g.), but this presentation of *militia* is not unique to him. Just as in poem 1.10 Tibullus insists on *Pax* (Peace) as necessary for love, Propertius asserts that Love is the god of peace (*Pacis Amor deus est*, Prop. 3.5.1) and that battles (*proelia*, Prop. 3.5.2) with his mistress are enough for him (see also Prop. 4.7.20).[9] Similarly, Ovid asserts that war is for soldiers, while peace pleases lovers because it is during times of peace that love may be discovered (Ov. *Am.* 3.1.49–50).

An external figure, similarly named by both Tibullus (2.6) and Ovid (*Am.* 2.18), embodies a further possible connection for the elegists' use of the *militia* theme to point out the opposition between love and war. Tibullus notes that a certain Macer is off to war, and states that he will happily follow if it will free his mind of love (Tib. 2.6.1–10).[10] Unfortunately, his girlfriend shuts him out, and he is forced to remain in thrall, in hopes of overcoming her resistance (Tib. 2.6.11–20). Ovid's Macer, on the other hand, is a generic foil, one who writes military poetry (Ov. *Am.* 2.18.1–2) as opposed to actually engaging in military pursuits, while Ovid can only sing of his amorous-military exploits ('I sing of affairs conducted at home and of my own wars', *resque domi gestas et mea bella cano*, Ov. *Am.* 2.18.12).[11] This poem also engages in a complex generic game, as Ovid includes in it references to several of his literary heroines (on which see below), who themselves are a bridge between Macer's choice of epic and Ovid's of elegy. Ovid's elegiac imperialism depicts his Macer as heading inevitably to Ovid's own poetic camp (*in mea castra uenis*, Ov. *Am.* 2.18.40), despite the epic poet's best intentions. In this poem Ovid presents writing itself as a strenuous military undertaking, with the camps of elegy and epic in opposition to each other. Propertius will do much the same when he wishfully asserts that he is done with elegy and is ready for new poetic *castra* (Prop. 2.10.19), although for him the metaphor seems less sustained. Poetry that speaks of war, that is, is for serious poets, while love poetry is the right choice

9 All quotations of Propertius are from Heyworth (2007c).

10 On the identity of this figure, see most recently Maltby (2002) 466–7.

11 On Ovid's Macer, see McKeown (1998) 382–3 and 389. Although it is impossible to identify the characters satisfactorily, as McKeown (1998) 383 notes, 'Ovid is at least exploiting the fact that they have the same name'. See also Harrison (Chapter 8) and Sharrock (Chapter 9) in this volume.

for one of slender talents. This point is best not pressed too far in terms of *militia*, however; often the choice of genre is not simply between erotic elegy and martial epic, but between elegy and a variety of other more noble genres, such as astronomical poetry (Tib. 2.4.17–8), historical epic (Prop. 3.3) or tragedy (Ov. *Am.* 3.1). Another justification for the elegists' subject is that an inspirational power (Cupid: Ov. *Am.* 1.1.3–24, 2.1.3; Calliope: Prop. 3.3.39–50) or the capricious mistress (Tib. 2.6, Ov. *Am.* 2.1.17–20) imposes this *materia*, despite a poet's intent to treat lofty subjects.

Even given that love and war are opposites in Tibullus' usual practice, when in poem 1.10 he engages most fully with the idea of love as war the result is indeed full of Ovid's *saeui dolores* in a rather disturbing way. The poem begins with a discussion of real war and its inventor, with the root cause identified as money and men's desire for it. The poet now seems forced to engage in real *militia* (*nunc ad bella trahor*, 'now I am dragged to war' Tib. 1.10.13) while his preference is to let others have that honour (*sit alius fortis in armis*, Tib. 1.10.29). *Pax* is what the poet praises and desires (Tib. 1.10.45–50), as a necessary precedent to love, for only in times of peace can Venus heat up her own battles (Tib. 1.10.53). Yet these battles are not playful, but contain a violence that contrasts starkly with the poet's praise of peace in the preceding lines, exposing Love as a referee for sexual struggle rather than a sponsor of amorous activity:

> sed Veneris tunc bella calent, scissosque capillos
> femina perfractas conqueriturque fores.
> flet teneras subtusa genas, sed uictor et ipse
> flet sibi dementes tam ualuisse manus.
> at lasciuus Amor rixae mala uerba ministrat
> inter et iratum lentus utrumque sedet.
> (Tib. 1.10.53–8)

> But then the wars of Venus heat up, and the woman complains that her hair has been torn and her doorposts have been broken down. She weeps with her tender cheeks beaten, but the victor himself weeps that his frenzied hands have had such strength. But lascivious Love provides the wicked words of their conflict and sits unmoving between each of the angry parties.

Here in evidence is the darker side of elegy, which presents itself especially well in soldiers' garb, for the violence that underlies this use of the metaphor is quite menacing, more like a scene of rape than 'rough sex' with a girlfriend, complete with pulled hair, broken doors, bruises and tears (Lee-Stecum 1998: 280–5). That the repentant lover is described as the 'victor' is typical of elegiac violence, on which see more below. Even what follows, a repentant summation of appropriate force in the bedroom, is not much better, but rather softens the previous violence in a passage contrived to displace a rival who engages in real *militia*:

> sit satis e membris tenuem rescindere uestem,
> sit satis ornatus dissoluisse comae,
> sit lacrimas mouisse satis. quater ille beatus
> quo tenera irato flere puella potest.[12]
> sed manibus qui saeuus erit, scutumque sudemque
> is gerat et miti sit procul a Venere.
> (Tib. 1.10.61–66)

> Let it be enough to tear the delicate gown from her limbs; let it be enough to undo her elaborate hairstyle, let it be enough to have caused tears. He is four times blessed for whom his tender mistress can cry when he is angry. But the one who rages cruelly with his hands, let him wield his sword and his shield and be far away from soft Venus.

Even in this gentler description of sexual play there are dress-tearing and tears, tears which are in fact emphasized as a prize for the angered lover (cf. Ov. *Am* 1.7 and below). This limited attack is meant to be 'enough' (*satis*), which implies both that this is 'acceptable' violence, and that the lover would like to do more; the limit, significantly, is imposed by the male aggressor and not by his female counterpart. The next couplet seeks to reassert a separation between lovers and fighters, even following hard upon self-incriminating evidence that suggests the difference is sometimes both small and subjective.

Longae viae, saevi dolores: love as war

While the close of Tibullus 1.1 assimilates the experience of the lover and the fighter, poem 1.6 depicts Love as the general rather than the poet himself. It is Amor who has commanded him, and, as he asks, 'who carries weapons against gods?' (*iussit Amor; contra quis ferat arma deos?* Tib. 1.6.31). Similarly, Ovid posits himself as a loyal soldier of Cupid who does not deserve to be mistreated, asking 'why do you injure me, who as your soldier has never left your standards, and why am I myself wounded in my own camp?' (*quid me, qui miles numquam tua signa reliqui,/ laedis, et in castris uulneror ipse meis?* Ov. *Am.* 2.9.3–4). Propertius, too, assimilates love and war, asserting that he was not born for military glory, but that the fates had the *militia amoris* in mind for him instead (*hanc me militiam fata subire uolunt*, Prop. 1.6.30; Gale 1997: 80). Here, then, *militia amoris* is valorized as a type of martial activity, but one that is different from Rome's norm. Ovid,

[12] Cf. Ov. *Ars.* 2.447–8 about the psychological pain of jealousy.

too, refers to love as a type of *militia*, one in which those who help him assault his mistress's defences – such as her maid (Ov. Am. 1.11.11–2) – are comrades-in-arms, and one which figures the *puella*'s agreement to spend a night with him as a victory (Ov. *Am.* 1.11.25).

Just as the poets depict themselves as soldiers of love, engaged in an amorous war, on occasion they describe their erotic escapades as battles. While Tibullus resorts to blows less frequently than Propertius or Ovid, as the discussion of 1.10 shows, his conflicts can come disturbingly close to military encounters. Ovid, too describes sex as a battle, but with arguably less violence (although there are violent quarrels; cf. *Am.* 1.7 and below); after all, his *puella* is conquered by her own betrayal, namely her desire, in his view at least, to be conquered (*quae cum ita pugnaret, tamquam qua uincere nollet,/ uicta est non aegre proditione sua*, Ov. *Am.* 1.5.15–16; cf. Ov. *Ars* 2.743 and 3.1–6). It is in Propertius' writings that the theme of love as war takes more ample shape, and poem 2.15 embodies a transition in the poet's treatment of the *militia amoris*. While the poem professes to address the idea of love as an alternative to war, its threats of physical violence against the *puella* belie this stated impulse (James 2003: 184–97). The poem opens with the poet's delight at having finally spent the night with his girl, when they engaged in a great conflict (*rixa*, Prop. 2.15.8), and his girlfriend fought with him, amazon-like, with bared breasts (*nudatis mecumst luctata papillis*, Prop. 2.15.9). Even in this setting of fulfilment, however, the poet is not content, but threatens his *puella* with violence for coming to bed clothed. Should she persist in this provocation, she will feel his hands once he has torn her clothing (*scissa ueste meas experiere manus*, Prop. 2.15.18) and even have injured arms to show to her mother after their encounter (*ostendes matri bracchia laesa tuae*, Prop. 2.15.20). The poet's assertion later in the poem that if all men chose to live like him, there would be no war, and more pointedly no civil strife such as that which had plagued Rome in recent years (Prop. 2.15.41–6), may come as small consolation to his battered 'beloved'.

For Propertius and Ovid in particular, love also proves a source of inspiration for poetry that is either opposed to epic or equivalent to it. For Propertius, his amorous battles are transformed into *Iliads* (Prop. 2.1.13–4), and elsewhere he envisions himself, grown strong from the worship of Venus (Prop. 2.22a.21–4), as an Achilles or Hector of love (Prop. 2.22a.33–4). In the first poem of his own second book, Ovid also presents elegy as a generic choice dictated by material and refers to his flatteries and elegies as his weapons in the war of love (*blanditias elegosque leuis, mea tela*, Ov. *Am.* 2.1.21). Yet as these examples show, there is a conflation not only between the opposition and assimilation of love and war, but of action and word, living and writing. This authorial pose is emblematic of potential problems for readers of elegy; as scholars have long warned, it is dangerous to take the poets at face value and to impute to the individual authors the ideas their poetic speakers espouse.[13]

Even so, this conflation of life and poetry is apparent again in Propertius' professed joy that a law has been repealed that would require the poet to marry, and hence to terminate his affair with his mistress. He asserts that he will father no soldiers as the law seemed to require (*nullus de nostro sanguine miles erit*, Prop. 2.7.14), but follows up quickly with a reconsideration: but if he were following a real camp (*uera . . . castra* Prop. 2.7.15), that of his mistress (*meae . . . puellae*, Prop. 2.7.15), it would be an altogether different story. Propertius' relief that he need not marry runs counter to the Augustan program that encouraged marriage and childbearing in an attempt to repopulate Rome, officially depleted by years of civil conflict. That the *princeps* is specifically on his mind is made clear by his reference to Caesar in the assertion that even military accomplishments such as his are irrelevant in love (Prop. 2.7.5–6). And yet, Propertius' use of the *militia amoris* in claiming that service to his mistress is the only 'real' *militia* humorously deflates his own claim, thus prudently undercutting his objections to Augustan moral reforms (Gale 1997: 89). Thus even as words and the deeds they profess to report bleed together, the *militia amoris* trope can both provoke and demur even within the same poem.

Ovid's much-discussed *Amores* 1.9 is often viewed as the quintessential *militia amoris* poem, and links the presentation of love as war to the idea of love as conquest and success as triumph of (or for) Love. The poem's opening posits not only this poet/lover, but indeed all lovers, as recruits in Love's army (*militat omnis amans*, Ov. *Am.* 1.9.1), employing the immediacy of metaphor rather than the epic distancing of simile. The poem insists on parity in many categories: age (3), character (5), persistence (7–10; 19–20), tolerance of foul weather (11–16), and vigilance over one's foe (17–18) even in the darkest night (21–6). Indeed, love and war themselves are equally dubious affairs (Ov. *Am.* 1.9.29–30), he insists, and hence it is wrong to insist that love is 'idleness' (*desidiam*, Ov. *Am.* 1.9.31). The examples Ovid cites as proof at 33–40 are from the works most opposed to elegy, Homeric epic and Greek tragedy, as if this linkage of love and war in the 'respectable' genres is in itself proof of his claim that lovers and soldiers are on par. The lover/poet returns the focus to himself in the closing couplets, insisting that he himself had been 'lazy' (*segnis*, Ov. *Am.* 1.9.41) before love impelled him to descend into the field of battle (Ov. *Am.* 1.9.43–4). The insistence of

[13] Among many others, see Gale (1997) 90 on 'the distinction between poet and *persona*'.

Amores 1.9 on a sustained equivalence between lovers and soldiers is grist for the mill of those who see in Ovid a rejection of Roman ideology (Davis 1999: 442), while for others Ovid's emphatic exhaustiveness of the comparisons intentionally points up the ridiculousness of the claim (Murgatroyd 1999). As with Propertius 2.7, what begins to emerge from a sustained examination of *militia amoris* is precisely the question posed at the start of this chapter: how seriously should we take the elegiac conceit of love as war?

Labor omnis inest: the triumph of love

While the theme of success in love as a triumph appears in the poetry of Propertius (cf. Prop. 2.14.23–7 for Cynthia as military plunder, *praeda*, and 4.8.63–72 for Cynthia as triumphant general), it is Ovid who exploits this idea most fully. Early on, the poet presents Cupid as triumphing over him when he surrenders himself to the god and to elegiac poetry (Ov. *Am.* 1.2.19 ff.). The detailed account of this triumph is especially resonant for scholars who see subversion in Ovid's use of *militia* in that the correspondence to an actual military triumph – the highest and rarely achieved military honor a Roman could earn – may undercut a serious institution of great importance to Augustus (Davis 1999: 439). Indeed, referring at the poem's conclusion to the victorious Love as the kinsman of Caesar (*cognati*... *Caesaris*, Ov. *Am.* 1.2.51) may be especially tactless, given that under Augustus only members of the imperial family were allowed to celebrate a triumph. Such a conflation of Caesar's subjects and those of Love may both trivialize the princeps' authority and present an unpalatable picture of citizen subjection under his rule.

Amores 1.7, on the other hand, shows the range and flexibility of Ovid's presentation of love as triumph. This poem presents the lover not as conquered victim, but instead as a triumphant general who has achieved victory over his beaten mistress. Although the poet/lover triumphs over his mistress because he has hit her, he is, however, filled with remorse: the act was one of madness (*furor*, Ov. *Am.* 1.7.2–3), of a mindless barbarian (Ov. *Am.* 1.7.19). In the face of his literally dumb-struck mistress (Ov. *Am.* 1.7.20–2) he wishes his too-violent arms removed (Ov. *Am.* 1.7.23–4) or at least placed in shackles (Ov. *Am.* 1.7. 28). Indeed, the poet seemed on the verge of a proto-feminist protest: had he struck even the lowliest citizen, he asserts, he would have been made to pay; should his power over his mistress be greater? (*an, si pulsassem minimum de plebe Quiritem,/ plecterer – in dominam ius mihi maius erit?* Ov. *Am.* 1.7.29–30). The sarcastic paean to his victory (Ov. *Am.* 1.7.35–48) parallels the depiction of *Amores* 1.2, where the poet was instead the captive, and yet here the focus is not on the joyous celebration of the bystanders, but on the misery and unjust domination of the girl. Even so, this apparent invitation to readers to join in Ovid's empathy is soon undercut, deflating what seems to be a sustained critique of gender inequality at the poem's end (*contra* Cahoon 1988). The poem's close typifies the poet's vacillation between maintaining and undermining such a critique. At one moment he urges his injured mistress to scratch his face (Ov. *Am.* 1.7.64) and tear his hair in revenge (Ov. *Am.* 1.7.65). The next he asks that she at least make him feel less guilty by neatening herself up a bit: 'or so that such sad marks of my crime don't remain, redo your hair and put it back in order' (*neue mei sceleris tam tristia signa supersint,/ pone recompositas in statione coma*s Ov. *Am.* 1.7.1.67–8). Even here, though, when Ovid seems to return to the mundane in his request that his mistress neaten her hair, the military context remains in the word he chooses to describe this process: a *statio* is an armed post, a military garrison. The girl's just-beaten hair, then, must regroup for another battle.

The poet as conqueror is once again in evidence in *Amores* 2.12, this time with victory constituted not by battery, but by sex. Ovid compares his successful siege on Corinna with that against Troy (Ov. *Am.* 2.12.9–10), asserting that his is more impressive because achieved alone, entirely through his own effort (*cura*, Ov. *Am.* 2.12.16) with no help from soldiers (Ov. *Am.* 2.12.11–14) or luck (Ov. *Am.* 2.12. 15). Bombastic as this may sound, the poem lays an overt and curious emphasis on the victory as bloodless both at its opening and its close (Ov. *Am.* 2.12.6 and 27). One need only look to the following poems, *Amores* 2.13 and 2.14, for an explanation (McKeown 1998: 275). Corinna's abortion in *Amores* 2.12 has left her on the verge of death, and the poet is self-aware enough to recognize his responsibility (Ov. *Am.* 2.13. 5), although he does not tie her predicament specifically to the 'victory' of the preceding poem. The connection between abortion and warfare is made, however, in *Amores* 2.14, as Ovid muses over what good it is for women to be free of warfare if they nonetheless suffer wounds from their own hands through abortion (*quid iuuat inmunes belli cessare puellas . . . si sine Marte suis patiuntur uulnera telis*, Ov. *Am.* 2.14.1, 3; McKeown 1998: 294). Just as Ovid draws this parallel, though, he backs away from the responsibility he seemed to acknowledge in *Amores* 2.12, referring to the termination of a pregnancy, and a woman's death which may well be the result, as deserved punishment (Ov. *Am.* 2.14.37–40). The careful deflection of this view onto unnamed witnesses to such a woman's imagined funeral (Ov. *Am.* 2.14.39–40) only thinly conceals the lover/poet's view that abortion is a woman's own fault (*culpa*, Ov. *Am.* 2.14.44). This triptych of poems exposes not only the consequences of sexual intercourse, as has long been recognized, but also the casualties in the war of love (Gamel 1989). Ovid is unique among the elegists in engaging this 'real world' question in his poems, and his doing so under the aegis of the *militia amoris* theme shows at the same time both great inventiveness and unusual pathos.

This section's fitting conclusion is *Amores* 3.11, where the poet is not defeated by love, triumphant over his girl through physical dominance or persuasion, or musing on the consequences of the *militia amoris*. He has moved on, claiming victory over love: 'I have conquered and I tread upon Love, subdued, with my feet' (*uicimus et domitum pedibus calcamus Amorem*, Ov. *Am.* 3.11.5). Even so, as we have seen is so often the case in elegiac exploitation of military themes, the poet quickly undercuts his own assertions. The next poem sets the lover/poet and his readers straight, as he admits in *Amores* 3.11b that the victory the previous poem touted is not complete. Indeed, despite his best attempts, love appears to be winning: *puto, uincat amor* (Ov. *Am.* 3.11b.2). What this points to especially well is the impossibility of escaping military and poetic endeavours imposed by a god, and brings us full circle to the programmatic first poem of Ovid's first book, where Cupid dictates both his metre (Ov. *Am.* 1.1.4) and his material (Ov. *Am.* 1.1.24). Whether one chooses to see a parallel with Roman martial obligations and loss of citizen empowerment under an emerging imperial system is, of course, up to individual readers.

Coda: Ovid's *Heroides* and elegiac imperialism

Ovid's assertion that 'every lover is a fighter' is more inclusive than it might appear, even radically so in that Propertius 4.3 and Ovid's own *Heroides* collection show that his claim includes female lovers as well. Given the chronological uncertainties of Ovid's poetic output, it is difficult to know whether this collection of letters from abandoned heroines of myth and literature to their errant heroes pre- or postdates his *Amores*.[14] Further, scholars disagree as to whether Propertius' imagined letter from 'Arethusa' to her campaigning husband 'Lycotas' is the inspiration for Ovid's collection or was instead inspired by it. In either case these poems, in their use of the *militia amoris* from a female perspective, provide unique commentary on Roman masculine values, and do so from what might be termed a 'safe' distance. Propertius' 4.3 has been convincingly shown to disrupt the main line of Augustan propaganda (Janan 2001: 53–69, Wyke 2002: 87). Less

14 See Thorsen (Chapter 7) in this volume, and the discussion of Knox (1995) 3 and 5–6; consensus is in any case that the single letters are early works that predate the extant *Amores* collection.

attention of this sort has been paid to Ovid's *Heroides*, however, and they, too, may hint at an answer to the question posed at the start of this chapter.

As Thorsen has noted in this collection, *militia amoris* is among the weapons in Ovid's literary arsenal as deployed in the single letters (see Chapter 7 in this volume). In addition to the examples she notes, letter 3, from Briseis to Achilles, also conflates love and war in ways consistent with the more widely read elegies of Tibullus, Propertius and Ovid. These examples of 'female elegy', and especially their co-option of military imagery by female characters, may have particular resonance in a time of great change and uncertainty for Rome. In the nascent principate, after Rome had been so badly scarred by a generation or more of civil war, offloading covert military critiques onto women is both shockingly bold and deceptively safe. Shifting the first person narrator from an 'I' easily identified with the male poet to an 'I' that is clearly both fictional and female allows a poet critical of Augustus to speak from a safe distance. It is thus possible for Ovid's Briseis to allude (or not) to the years of Roman civil war by means of Homer's epic war, accusing her Achilles of not keeping his bargain. She asserts that she was 'an important part of her fatherland' (*patriae pars . . . magna*, Ov. *Her.* 3.46) as were Rome's citizens under the republican system, and that she had endured to be a war captive as part of a bargain for her safety, compensating for the loss of family and friends with the man responsible for their destruction: 'nevertheless, in you alone we sought compensation for so many lost' (*tot tamen amissis te compensauimus unum*, Ov. *Her.* 3.51). That this was an explicit, sustained promise and that it has not been upheld becomes clear in Briseis' reproachful reminder of this accord: 'you yourself used to tell me it was to my benefit to have been captured' (*utile dicebas ipse fuisse capi*, Ov. *Her.* 3.46). The resonances for Ovid's reader, although speculative, are clear: the bargain Rome struck with Octavian after Actium's defeat of Antony and Cleopatra in 31 BC, one that ensured Rome's safety in exchange for her citizens' traditional *libertas*, 'liberty', was one that may not have been to their unalloyed benefit.[15] Similarly, Briseis' reproach of Achilles' newfound pacifism may also point to contemporary concerns when she asks him pointedly 'did you only approve fierce wars while you were capturing me?' (*an tantum, dum me caperes, fera bella probabas . . .* ? Ov. *Her.* 3.123). In the context of the newly established *Pax Augusta*, and especially the dedication of the *Ara Pacis Augustae* in 9 BC, roughly contemporary with the publication of the single *Heroides*, such a critique may point to a perceived hypocrisy on the part of Rome's new leader.

15 On the rise of Octavian as a bargain between an exhausted and decimated Roman elite and the new *princeps*, see Osgood (2006) especially 397–403.

In the case of the *Heroides*, as with much of elegy, there is a literary dimension as well: when Ovid's heroines write, they are re-writing previous and definitive literary accounts, accounts that historically have been solely in the masculine domain.[16] Ovid's praxis in crafting his *Heroides* is a kind of generic imperialism related to Augustus' own political imperialism, and exposing the repercussions of both processes. As he rewrites Homeric epic, for example, Ovid shows that the translation of Homeric characters to a genre ostensibly more amenable to love is not to their benefit. The implication, tentative though it may be, is that the translation of the Roman people from the republic to the new regime, via generations of civil wars, may not be so beneficial either.

Further reading

Studies of *militia amoris* provide an excellent example of the varied scholarly approaches to elegy, depicting it as purely literary, violently misogynistic, gently renunciatory of social norms, politically subversive, and humorously self-undermining, to name a few. Murgatroyd (1975) traces in detail the origins and development of the love-as-war theme from Greek precedents to the unique Roman development in the hands of the elegists. Lyne (1980) remains essential reading; especially chapter 4, 'The Life of Love' with its particular emphasis on love's warfare at pages 71–8. Gale (1997) on Prop. 2.7 provides an excellent brief overview of *militia* as deployed by Tibullus and Propertius. Lyne (1998a) details the call and response between Propertius and Tibullus; in terms of *militia* see especially pp. 532–5. On Tibullus specifically, see Boyd (1984) and for Propertius, see Gale (1997). For Ovid, Cahoon (1988) traces the *militia* theme throughout Ovid's *Amores* in a study that shows the interpenetration of *militia* and *seruitium*, erotic war and captivity, with an emphasis on the violent underpinnings of Ovid's usage. For Ovid's quintessential *militia amoris* poem, *Amores* 1.9, McKeown (1995) urges a thorough literary appreciation while Murgatroyd (1999) responds to a series of readings of that poem, reminding readers of the humour in Ovid's manipulation of the theme. While there are numerous excellent studies of the *Heroides*, none attend much to the use of *militia* therein.

16 See Gold (1993) 84–6 for feminist readings of such disruptions in traditional 'master narratives', drawing on the work of Alice Jardine.

PART IV

The ends of Latin love elegy

13

ROY GIBSON

Loves and elegy

This chapter focuses on the relationship between the elegist's number of erotic partners and his concept of love.[1] The extant elegies of Gallus and Sulpicia are centred on one beloved person, but Tibullus directs his erotic attention to (at least) two women and one boy, while Propertius reveals the existence of numerous affairs with other women (three of whom are named), and Ovid, of course, develops into an omnivorous Don Giovanni who declares 'whatever girls anyone praises in all of Rome – my love is candidate [*ambitiosus amor*] for them all' (*Am.* 2.4.47–8). In the course of documenting the messy erotic careers of the elegists, questions will be raised about the extent to which a plurality of partners – and the continually shifting concept of love that it implies – tests the boundaries of elegy. Underneath these queries lies a much harder question: What is (elegiac) love?

One genre, one man, one woman?

In a notorious passage, the second-century writer Apuleius defends the use of pseudonyms in poetry by reference to earlier figures:

> ...they may as well accuse Caius Catullus for calling Clodia Lesbia, Ticida for substituting the name Perilla for that of Metella, Propertius for concealing the name Hostia beneath the pseudonym of Cynthia, and Tibullus for singing of Delia in his verse, when it was Plania who ruled his heart. (*Apol.* 10.3)

Apuleius is hardly seeking to provide a characterization of 'canonical' Roman love elegy: he makes no mention of either Gallus or Ovid. But his matching of each poet with just one lover reflects a common conception of the genre, whereby love elegy is a 'one man, one woman' type of poetry. Martial provides an essentially similar, if fuller list of poets and mistresses:

[1] Use of the following translations is gratefully acknowledged: H.E. Butler (Apuleius), G.P. Goold (Propertius), A.G. Lee (Tibullus), D.R. Shackleton Bailey (Martial), and G. Showerman (Ovid).

Cynthia made you a poet, sprightly Propertius;
fair Lycoris was Gallus' genius;
beauteous Nemesis is the fame of clear-voiced Tibullus;
Lesbia, elegant Catullus dictated your verse.
My poetry neither the Paelignians nor Mantua will spurn,
if I find a Corinna or an Alexis. (8.73.5–10)[2]

Lesbia and the Alexis of Virgil's *Eclogues* join Cynthia, Lycoris, Nemesis, and Corinna in the band of lovers whose names are joined to the poets who made them famous. If we concur with Martial and Apuleius in thinking of love elegy as essentially 'poet + [one] mistress', we cannot (pleasingly) blame ourselves too much. The same misconception is naughtily peddled by Ovid himself, in his first configuration (undoubtedly also at the same time a creation) of the Roman elegiac canon as we know it today:[3]

nos facimus placitae late praeconia formae:
nomen habet Nemesis, Cynthia nomen habet,
Vesper et Eoae nouere Lycorida terrae,
et multi, quae sit nostra Corinna, rogant.
(*Ars* 3.535–8)

It is we poets who herald the loved-one's beauty far and wide; renowned is Nemesis, Cynthia is renowned; evening and eastern lands know of Lycoris, and many inquire who my Corinna may be.

Ovid is trying to persuade his female pupils that poets (of course) make the best lovers, since they can make a girl famous: this much is proved by the renown of Nemesis and co.[4] In context, it is to Ovid's advantage that love elegy should be essentialized as a 'one man, one woman' genre. Fidelity to a single woman must be a prized asset from the viewpoint of Ovid's students in *Ars* 3, and the poet immediately adds confirmation of the quality of an elegiac poet's love: 'we know how to love with a loyalty excessively sure' (*Ars* 3.544). In fact, Ovid's choice of Nemesis – rather than the Delia highlighted by Apuleius – to illustrate the powers of Tibullus' poetry is deliberately designed to bolster the point about fidelity. For Nemesis appears

2 Cf. Mart. 5.10.10 (Ovid and Corinna), 12.44.5–6 (Catullus and Lesbia, Ovid and Corinna), 14.189 (Cynthia and Propertius), 14.193 (Nemesis and Tibullus).

3 For Ovid's other versions of the elegiac canon (none fully complete before this passage in *Ars* 3), cf. *Am.* 1.15.27–30 (Tibullus and Gallus), *Ars* 3.333–4, 343–4 (all four elegists, but not listed together as a 'canon'); *Tr.* 4.10.51–60, 5.1.17–20. On the politics of canon creation, see Hinds (1998) 52–83.

4 Ovid's underlining of uncertainty over the exact identity of Corinna, rather characteristically, undermines the attractiveness of immortalization by an elegist; see Kennedy (1993) 89–90, Gibson (2003) 312.

without rival for the poet's affections in Tibullus' second Book, whereas in Book 1 Delia is forced to share the stage with Marathus as her apparent competitor. In these circumstances, it is best for Ovid to stick with Nemesis and not to provoke memories of the complexities of book 1.

Ovid is not the only elegist to simplify his generic inheritance, since Propertius had already done so in the final poem of Book 2. Here he constructs a 'pre-elegiac' canon of love poets, where Cynthia and Propertius join such literary couples as Leucadia and Varro, Lesbia and Catullus, Quintilia and Calvus, and Lycoris and Gallus (2.34.85–94). As a celebration of the power of love poetry, it is memorable stuff; but layers of self-serving simplification are involved. For example, the poetry of Catullus contains several lovers alongside Lesbia (most notably Iuventius), while Calvus may have been notoriously unfaithful to Quintilia in his poetry and life.[5] And in Propertius Book 2, as will become clear later, the spotlight placed on Cynthia in the final poem is used, rather conveniently, to push episodes of infidelity narrated earlier in the Book to the margins.

One genre, many lovers

For all the obfuscation of the complexity of these poets' erotic careers, there are signs that, as the genre grew in confidence and stature, the elegists wanted us to think harder about what devotion to a single woman (or, for Sulpicia, single man) might mean: how it might be compromised or even abandoned altogether. That is to say, elegy shows increasing signs of self-consciousness about its own infidelities. In the poetry of Tibullus, we find several lovers paraded in the corpus of the poetry, but are offered no narrative about how these affairs fit together. Propertius, however, shows signs of creating a narrative of infidelity to Cynthia, to the extent that he begins to set problems for the reader in Books 3 and 4 about the course of his erotic career. But it is Ovid who is most open about his multiple appetites, and who in the *Amores* most seriously challenges the idea of 'poet + one mistress' that he himself would later promote in *Ars* 3.

Catullus, Tibullus, Lesbia, Iuventius, Delia, Marathus, Nemesis, plus some others

The messiness of the erotic careers of the elegists – and how they represent and deal with those careers – is best understood by going back to their predecessor, Catullus. Lesbia arguably dominates the first thirteen poems

[5] Cf. Ov. *Tr.* 2.431–2, Hollis (2007) 69–70.

or so of the polymetric collection[6] – whether so named or labelled 'my girl'[7] – but disappears thereafter until poem 36. In the poems which intervene between these points, we get a series of items on other lovers, including Ipsitilla – who is ordered to prepare 'nine fucks (*fututiones*) in a row' (32.8) – but most notably on a boy (15, 21), who is identified as 'flower of the Iuventii' (24).

Did the affair with Iuventius take place before or after the break up with Lesbia? In truth, the reader is given no hint on how this affair sits with the Lesbia sequence, since the polymetric poems display no overall chronology. So what concept of love is implied here? We ought not to assume an automatic cultural tolerance for a man conducting simultaneous affairs with a *puer* and a *puella*. After all, Catullus' own marriage hymn for Manlius playfully insists that the bridegroom must now give up his *puer* (61.119–48). However, there are even stiffer challenges for the 'one man, one woman' essentialization of Catullus found in later writers. In poem 48 Iuventius is awarded a version of the 'kiss' poems earlier addressed to Lesbia in 5 and 7. In the *Ars*, Ovid would later advise the lover intent on infidelity not to give to one lover a present that might be recognized by a second lover (*Ars* 2.391). Such advice arises naturally out of the world of the *Amores*, where (as we shall see later) Ovid creates narratives of simultaneous affairs. But no such narrative exists in Catullus. How, as readers, should we react on recognizing the same 'kiss' poem gifted to Iuventius that had already been given to Lesbia? Can we accommodate Iuventius within our conception of Catullan *amor*?

Nevertheless, if Catullus creates no narratives about the interaction of his affairs, he does find more formal ways of encouraging his readers to bring the poems for Lesbia, Iuventius (and Ipsitilla) together for simultaneous scrutiny. As Julia Dyson has pointed out,[8] we appear to be invited to compare and contrast the three sets of poems, since each employs closely similar but otherwise rare nouns (found elsewhere only in Martial): *basiatio* for Lesbia (7.1), *fututio* for Ipsitilla (32.8) and *osculatio* for Iuventius (48.6). This is clearly a strategy for forcing the reader to ponder the connections between these lovers.

6 It can be argued that the collection as we have it is a creation of the 3rd or 4th centuries AD. However, the shorter poems in a variety of metres perhaps formed a separate book not unlike our poems 1–53 (or 1–60, or 1–61 or all three in co-existence); see Butrica (2007) 19–24, with extensive reference to previous studies, also Skinner (2007).

7 See P.A. Miller (Chapter 10) in this volume.

8 Dyson (2007) 266. Cf. the similar problems set by the juxtaposition of poems 109 and 110.

Tibullus Book 1 also presents challenges to a reader expecting love poetry focused on a single lover. Here we find two named lovers, one a female (Delia) and one a boy (Marathus), but, as in Catullus, no 'narrative' explanation as to how these affairs and their poems fit together. However, the changed literary context between the 50s and 20s BC makes the case of Tibullus more problematic than that of Catullus. The polymetric and shorter elegiac productions of Catullus may have circulated as independent books, but it is not clear what involvement the poet himself had in their assembly. Book 1 of Tibullus, by contrast, clearly belongs to the world of the Augustan poetry book. If the reader of Catullus experiences only moderate pressure to make everything fit together, the pressure acting on the reader of Tibullus – following the high bar set by Virgil's *Eclogues* for expectations of interpenetration between poems – is rather greater.

The first three poems of Tibullus Book 1 present a consistent focus on Delia. The bulk of 1.4 is taken up with the pederastic lecture of the god Priapus, but no formal conflict with the Delia 'cycle' arises until the final verses, which – beginning with 'Alas, how Marathus in love's slow fire torments me!' (1.4.81) – reveal Tibullus' personal interest in Priapus' teachings. In the words of Lee-Stecum (1998: 153), ' the reader is forced to re-evaluate . . . has his *amor* for Marathus existed concurrently with his *amor* for Delia? Is the nature of each *amor* the same?'. Common critical solutions involve the construction of relative chronologies for the affairs;[9] but such solutions face the problem that '[none] explains the interweaving of the Delia and Marathus poems within the structure of the collection'.[10] That is to say, Delia returns as the main focus of 1.5 and 1.6, only for Marathus to reappear in 1.8 and 1.9,[11] prior to a more generalized poem on love at the close of the collection in 1.10. It would have been an easy matter for Tibullus to divide his Book up into separate sections devoted to Delia and Marathus respectively, merely by moving poem 1.4 to follow the current 1.6. Instead, Tibullus has taken the decision to intermingle the Marathus and Delia stories. Just as Catullus used rare nouns to connect the poems for his multiple lovers, so Tibullus has used the formal properties of the poetry book to set problems for the reader. In the first poem of the collection, the poet had envisaged a future with Delia of devotion to a single mistress and love till death (1.1.55–60). Where does Marathus fit into this scheme, and how does he affect the concept of love set out there? (No answers are given to these questions.)

[9] See Lee-Stecum (1998) 155. [10] Lee-Stecum (1998) 155; cf. ibid. 287–8.

[11] For the encouragement given to the reader to link 1.4, 1.8 and 1.9 into a narrative of a pederastic love affair between Tibullus and Marathus, see Murgatroyd (1980) 9, 235, 245; Lee-Stecum (1998) 227–31, 234, 239.

Intriguingly, the cross-currents of Book 1 are swept away in Book 2. Here a new beloved, Nemesis, appears without introduction and without a *puer* to distract the attention of either poet or reader. Apparently absent also is any correlation between the number of lovers and generic experimentation. Tibullus' reduction of his interests to a single mistress coincides with a notable expansion of the boundaries of the genre in terms of subject matter (e.g. 2.1, 2.2, 2.5). In Propertius, as we shall see, the pattern is reversed.

If neither Catullus nor Tibullus creates an actual narrative about their multiple affairs, Ovid does so on their behalf, despite his track record in *Ars* 3 of simplifying matters. For he grants recognition to the multiple loves of Catullus in his defence from exile of the *Ars*, at *Tr.* 2.429 *nec contentus ea* [sc. *Lesbia*], *multos uulgauit amores* ('and not content with Lesbia, he made public many other loves'). No need, here, to maintain the pretence of one lover per poet. Indeed, Catullus' philandering is to Ovid's advantage as he seeks to create a context for his great manual of infidelity. As for Tibullus, Ovid – in his lament for the poet at *Am.* 3.9 – asserts that Nemesis and Delia will both have their fame – Nemesis as the more 'recent love', and Delia as his 'first love' (3.9.31–2) – and later creates for the pair an altercation about the quality of their time spent with Tibullus (3.9.55–8). Nevertheless, even in Ovid there is no room for Marathus: his conception of elegiac love cannot accommodate the pederastic.[12]

Such willingness to recognize the multiple affairs of others is consonant with Ovid's own behaviour in the *Amores*. But first we must turn our attention to Propertius, who is the first to destabilize self-consciously the idea of the poet and his single mistress.

'*Prima Lycinna suis miserum me cepit ocellis*' (Prop. 1.1.(-)1)

Propertius' first elegy famously begins with the words *Cynthia prima* . . ., and Book 1 is littered with statements implying (exclusive) devotion to her.[13] At 1.18.11–12, Propertius swears that 'no other girl has ever set her dainty feet [*formosos . . . pedes*] on my threshold'. The mention here of dainty feet – where feet, as is common in elegy, are those of both mistress and metre – is a reminder that fidelity to a single mistress is bound up with faithfulness to a single genre. As will become clear below, Propertius' experiments with pushing the boundaries of elegy are matched by his increasing interest in other women or downplaying the figure of Cynthia.[14]

[12] Cf., however, *Am.* 1.1.19–20.

[13] 1.4.1–2, 1.6.27, 1.8.21–2, 45; 1.11.23–4, 1.12.19–20, 1.15.29–32, 1.19.5–6.

[14] Cf. Heyworth (2010).

Book 2 begins where Book 1 left off, with declarations of fidelity to a single woman (2.1.55 *una . . . femina*).[15] However, the reader's faith in Propertius' fidelity to Cynthia – and to the kind of elegy practised in Book 1 – is put to the test by the elegist's 'failure' to name her until 2.5.1, and by the content of 2.2–2.5, which play with the idea of abandoning love or the loved one. That faith is not seriously tested again until near the end of our Book 2,[16] where an 'infidelity' sequence begins at 2.22. Here we find the elegist in a mode more familiar from Ovid's *Am.* 2.4 and 2.10 (discussed below), openly declaring 'You know that of late many girls all charmed me equally' (2.22.1). Interest in other girls is not infidelity per se, but the elegist's statement of virility later in the poem is more explicit:

percontere licet: saepe est experta puella
    officium tota nocte ualere meum.
(2.22.23–4)

You may put the question: often a girl has discovered that I can do my duty all night through.

The obvious implication is that Propertius has demonstrated his sexual prowess with other women before now. The reader may ask 'when exactly?'; but will have to wait until Books 3 and 4 for some answers.

Some explanation for Propertius' behaviour emerges at the end of 2.22, where it appears to be implied that an extra girlfriend is needed to force Cynthia (unnamed) into greater compliance. But the poem seems almost tame by comparison with 2.23, where Propertius confesses an interest in common prostitutes:

cui fugienda fuit indocti semita uulgi,
    ipsa petita lacu nunc mihi dulcis aqua est . . .
[placet] cui saepe immundo Sacra conteritur Via socco,
    nec sinit esse moram, si quis adire uelit;
(2.23.1–2, 15–16)

I who was bent on fleeing the path of the ignorant mob now find tasteful even water taken from a public trough . . . [my fancy is taken by her] who oft treads the Sacred Way in dirty sandals, and brooks no delay if anyone wishes to come to her.

Given the references to paths and water sources and 'the crowd', this poem is inevitably also bound up with Callimachean poetics,[17] whereby Propertius

[15] On narrative progressions in the second Book, see also Keith (2008) 99–110.
[16] For poem 2.10 as probably the final member of the original second Book of Propertius, see Heyworth (2007b) 153.
[17] Cf. e.g. *AP* 12.43.1–4, *Aet.* fr. 1.25–8, *Ap.* 110–12.

is declaring the openness of his poetry to the lower genres, and not just to Callimachean elegiac style.[18] In other words, Propertius is using the idea of multiple lovers as a way of testing the stylistic boundaries of elegy.

A more explicit retrospective explanation for such infidelity to the ideal of one mistress is provided in the following poem, where the poet avers that 'if Cynthia were smiling indulgently upon me, I should not now be called the prince of debauchery . . . wonder not if I seek common women [*uilis*]' (2.24.5–6, 9). The stage is thus set for a return to 'normal', and renewed declarations of fidelity duly arrive later in 2.24 and then in 2.25, albeit with glances back to the women who crowd the streets of Rome in earlier poems (2.25.39–44). With that, a relatively tightly constructed *narrative* of infidelity comes to a close. Propertius may not have named his other lovers (unlike Tibullus); but he does create a story about how they relate to one another in time. However, Propertius' insistence at the end of Book 2 (2.34, quoted earlier) of his own devotion to Cynthia may now appear to be something of a whitewash of his own behaviour.

In Book 3, Propertius destabilizes the 'poet + Cynthia' ideal more radically. Not coincidentally, this Book also widens its generic remit – more aggressively than its predecessors – beyond a focus on love. The book contains its quota of declarations of fidelity to a single woman, alongside a good number of elegies which presuppose a longstanding affair with a single woman. There are also continuing signs of Propertius' interest in women more generally, including (apparently) prostitutes once more. But more disturbing than any of this is Propertius' decision not to name Cynthia until near the end of Book 3.

Such a 'failure' requires some context. In Book 1 her name occurs twenty-seven times, while in our book 2 her name is found twenty-one or twenty-two times (depending on the text of 2.25.1). In Book 3, Cynthia is named only at the moment when Propertius announces his intention to leave Cynthia (3.21.9–10), and only twice thereafter. The responsibility for determining the identity of the unnamed *puella* who features as the object of Propertius' interest in many poems in Book 3 is passed on to the reader. In fact, the readers' assumptions are put to the test, e.g. in poem 3.10, where the elegist instructs a *puella* to 'put on the dress in which you first ensnared the eyes of Propertius' (15–16). There are some disturbing discrepancies here with 1.1.1: there Cynthia catches Propertius with her eyes, and not with a dress. Indeed, Propertius spends the whole of poem 1.2 pretending to insist on the unattractiveness of an expensive eye-catching dress way beyond his means. Is the woman of 3.10 Cynthia? The reader could put a narrative together to

[18] For a discussion of this and other aspects of Prop. 2.23, see Gibson (2007) 24–34.

explain the discrepancies (obviously he really did find the dress of 1.2 attractive); but all the face-saving work is the job of the reader. Also troubling is poem 3.20, where Propertius looks forward to a first night of love with an unnamed woman (3.20.13), and emphasizes the drawing up of a contract in this 'new love' (3.20.15–16), before the celebration of the 'rites of marriage' (3.20.25–6). The problems for a Cynthia-based narrative are mounting.

In many ways, however, the biggest shock in Book 3 is found in an earlier poem, where Propertius seeks to reassure his lover of the irrelevance to him of a woman named Lycinna (3.15.3–6):

> ut mihi praetexti pudor est releuatus amictus
>   et data libertas noscere amoris iter,
> illa rudis animos per noctes conscia primas
>   imbuit, heu nullis capta Lycinna datis!

> When the restraint of boyhood's garb was lifted from me and I was given freedom to learn the ways of love, my accomplice on those first nights, who initiated my untried heart, was Lycinna, won, ah me, by never a gift of mine!

It is here that we learn that there was a lover prior to Cynthia, and that she has a name: a name that can easily be inserted into a rearranged Propertius 1.1.1 *Cynthia prima* . . . , to form a line which we may designate 1.1.(-)1:

> prima Lycinna suis miserum me cepit ocellis

> First Lycinna with her eyes ensnared me, poor wretch

In the blunt formulation of Heyworth (2007b) 366, 'this poem undermines the whole of the Propertian programme – Cynthia was not in fact the *prima*'. Furthermore, for a reader who now returns to Book 1 and starts again, the landscape of that Book will be altered. If the collection begins with a half-truth, suspicious readings may follow:

> hoc, moneo, uitate malum: sua quemque moretur
>   cura, neque assueto mutet amore locum.
> (1.1.35–6)

> Shun this plague, I counsel you: let everyone cling to his own sweetheart, nor switch his affections when love has grown familiar.

What are we now to make of this? Readers of 3.15 may have reason to understand Cynthia as the 'plague' and Lycinna as the 'love grown familiar'.

The boundaries of elegy – or rather the boundaries of our conception of Propertian elegy – are clearly being put to the test. Concomitant with this is the desire in Book 3 to test the generic boundaries of elegy in terms of subject matter, since Propertius includes here a series of poems which either have relatively little erotic content of the sort found in Books 1–2 or none.[19]

Further revisions of the ideal of fidelity to a single girl – and of the subject matter appropriate to love elegy – are to come in Book 4. Despite an opening prophecy that the elegiac poetry of Propertius will (continue to) focus on *una puella* (4.1.138–40), there is no trace of Cynthia in the series of the largely mythological and aetiological elegies which follow, and when a mistress appears as the pupil of a *lena* in poem 4.5, this woman is clearly not Cynthia.[20] In this sense, the absence of Cynthia from 4.1–5 is generically well matched to the more elevated subject matter of these poems. When a poem in Book 4 finally does include Cynthia, it is consistent enough in narrative terms with the end of Book 3, where Propertius had announced his split from his mistress. For in poem 4.7 Cynthia is dead, and returns in a vision to Propertius to complain of the lack of regard or expense devoted by him to her funeral (4.7.23–34). The poet's neglect of Cynthia in this regard is easily converted into a symbol of his poetic neglect of her in Book 4.

Nevertheless, a surprise awaits in 4.8: without explanation, Cynthia is alive and well, and erupts onto the scene to discover Propertius trying (and failing) to enjoy an evening with two prostitutes named Phyllis and Teia. How are we to make sense of this without further narrative explanation from the poet? In the words of one critic, 'Propertius does not have a life that makes sense'.[21] However, Propertius sets up the internal narrative of 4.8 with notable care: at lines 27–34 he explains that he decided to enjoy a night with these two prostitutes after Cynthia had insulted their bed so often that he needed to 'change bed and move camp'. Clearly, this is an episode which belongs – in narrative terms – to the 'five years of slavery' (3.24.23) covered by Books 1–3.

It can be argued that readers are being asked to go back to the beginning of the collection and start again, to read with this episode in mind. Of course, there are episodes of infidelity in Books 2–3; but what makes 4.8 different – and memorable – is that the 'infidelities' of 4.8 have a name: Phyllis and Teia. In effect, we now return to read Books 1–3 in the knowledge that – at some point – Propertius will start a night with this pair. The effect is to invite the reader to scrutinize elegies in which affairs with unnamed women are alluded to, and ask whether Phyllis and Teia belong here (or there). In effect, we must re-read the entire collection suspiciously, secure in the knowledge that Propertius will be defiantly unfaithful to Cynthia.

19 E.g. 3.4, 3.7, 3.12, 3.13, 3.18, 3.22.
20 Heyworth (2010) 101.
21 Heyworth (2010) 101.

In sum, Propertius gradually revises his conception of elegiac love, moving from an ideal of devotion to Cynthia in Book 1, through episodes of infidelity to her in Book 2, and on finally to Books 3 and 4, where it is the reader who must decide whether any given poem is addressed to Cynthia, and where Propertius reveals information which requires us to re-read earlier Books with suspicions that serve to destabilize our faith in his earlier devotion to Cynthia.

It is left to Ovid to develop a positive programme of sexual profligacy.

Ovid: 'The well-known singer of my own worthless ways' (*Am.* 2.1.2)

Amores Book 1 does not seriously disrupt the view that love for a single woman is the essence of elegiac poetry. That woman does not appear until 1.3, is not named as Corinna until 1.5, and will only be named once more in 1.11. But the tone of devotion is established by a deliberately cliché-ridden passage at *Am.* 1.3.11–20,[22] which aligns the author with his predecessors' dedication to their mistresses (however compromised that might turn out to be on a reading of the actual texts in question). Nevertheless, there are warning signs of what the future may hold, since Ovid goes on to compare his female addressee to women loved by Jupiter, all of them made famous by poetry (*Am.* 1.3.21–6). Jupiter, of course, was the philanderer par excellence.

In Book 2 Ovid does in fact display remarkably similar appetites to those found in his divine counterpart. Where *Am.* 1.3 had offered immortalization to a single *puella*, 2.1 issues a general invitation to all beautiful girls to flock to Ovid with the prospect of praise for their looks (2.1.37–8). *Am.* 2.4 then delivers on the promise of 2.1 and decisively wrecks any idea that we might be repeating Book 1's apparent narrative of fidelity to a single mistress.[23] For here Ovid, in a revision of the opening plea of *Am.* 1.3 ('let her either love me or give me reason ever to love'), reveals an openly libertine manifesto: 'There is no fixed beauty to call my love forth: there are one hundred reasons ever to love' (*Am.* 2.4.9–10). The poem continues for another twenty-eight lines with a catalogue of all the different kinds of women to whom Ovid is attracted, culminating in the brilliant assertion quoted in the opening paragraph of this chapter.

Ovid's self-conscious commitment to a libertine way of life in Book 2 extends to the supply of scenarios of infidelity to Corinna. In *Am.* 2.7 and 2.8, Ovid creates a small drama in which he is accused of infidelity by Corinna with her slave Cypassis – vehemently denied by the poet in 2.7 – only

[22] See McKeown (1989) 60–1, 69–73.

[23] For Corinna and her rivals in the *Amores*, see also Armstrong (2005) 53–66.

for the accusations to be shown in 2.8 to be well founded. Ovid, even more clearly than Propertius, and in direct contrast to Catullus and Tibullus, provides a narrative about his infidelities. Not only does he announce that he wants all of the girls in Rome, he takes us behind the scenes of his infidelities, where the sordid details are spelled out with the usual Ovidian clarity. It is perhaps no surprise that he alone should be alive to the multiple affairs of Catullus and make room for both Delia and Nemesis in his lament for Tibullus. Ovid's wicked purpose in continuing to promote Corinna as his 'one woman' in *Ars* 3 – before a whole new generation of Rome's available *puellae* – also stands out the more clearly.

Am. 2.10 brings the first half of the Book to a close with a further narrative of infidelity (to the idea of a single mistress), for here Ovid reveals he is managing to be 'in love with' two mistresses at once. After this point, any clear pattern of development in the *Amores* begins to break down, at least as regards Ovidian revisions of elegiac love.[24] Corinna makes a comeback in the second half of Book 2 with a series of poems dedicated to her (2.11–14, 17). But just as she appears to be building up a head of steam in the second half of the Book, after the more libertine first half, Corinna is gone again. For in *Am.* 2.19, Ovid urges an unnamed girl to act more the way he remembers Corinna behaving (2.19.9–20). She belongs now in his past. In the third Book, Elegy confirms the importance of Corinna to Ovid's elegiac poetry by naming her as part of the explanation why Ovid should persist with the genre (*Am.* 3.1.49ff.). However, the actions there described as typical also clearly belong to the past. The relegation of Corinna to the past tense, consonant with the implications of 2.19, could be said to continue right up till near the end of Book 3, where she is – without warning – suddenly reinstated as the poet's sole muse, at *Am.* 3.12.16 *ingenium mouit sola Corinna meum* ('Corinna alone has stirred my genius'). Shades here of Ovid's self-serving (and inaccurate) characterization of elegy in *Ars* 3. The shocks do not end there. In the very next poem we encounter Ovid accoutred – without explanation – with that most un-elegiac of appendages, a wife (*uxor*, *Am.* 3.13.1–2).

What is going on here? What, after all, is elegiac love? Can it accommodate Corinna (coming and going without explanation), a wife (of all things) and 'whatever girls anyone praises in all of Rome'? Clearly, it will have to. But (thankfully?), just as elegy and elegiac love threaten to burst at the seams, the *Amores* come to a close in 3.15 after a single intervening poem.

24 Nevertheless, for one attempt to follow the 'plot' of the *Amores*, see Holzberg (2002b) 46–66, also Booth (2009) 72–6.

But before pursuing the final dissolution of elegiac love in the *Ars Amatoria*, let us take a closer look at a single, all-too-interesting poem in *Amores* Book 3. In *Am.* 3.7 we encounter Ovid suffering from an embarrassing episode of impotence, on the pretext of which he catalogues his erotic successes from the past:

> at nuper bis flaua Chlide, ter candida Pitho,
> ter Libas officio continuata meo est;
> exigere a nobis angusta nocte Corinnam
> me memini numeros sustinuisse nouem.
> (*Am.* 3.7.23–6)

> Yet not long ago I satisfied blonde Chlide twice running with my performance, three times fair Pitho and three times Libas; I remember Corinna asking from me – and my supplying – nine measures on one short night.

Here we find three new names to add to Corinna (and Cypassis), much as Propertius had belatedly revealed the trio of Lycinna, Phyllis and Teia. More arresting, however, is the admission of impotence itself. Ovid, unlike Propertius, does not test the boundaries of elegy (in terms of subject matter) in tandem with an expansion of the number of admitted sexual partners. Rather the *Amores* display a fairly consistent reduction of the interests of love elegy to more exclusively amatory themes.[25] However, within these limits, we do find an expansion of elegy's range. For over the three books of the *Amores*, we move from declarations of fidelity in 1.3, to the Don Giovanni appetites of 2.4 and 2.10, to the impotence and deflation of 3.7. Evidently there are other ways in which to test the boundaries of love and elegy than by including non-amatory material.

The end of elegy: the *Ars amatoria*

The *Amores* ended on a note of dissolution, struggling to contain Corinna, multiple mistresses, and a wife. But Ovid, not content to rest there, brings before us the *Ars Amatoria*, which applies dissolving agents more liberally. Not only are the generic boundaries of elegy itself threatened by the heavy injection of elements from didactic epic in the *Ars*,[26] but – in keeping with the remit of didactic poetry addressed to a large audience – the women of the *Ars* bear little resemblance to the semi-divine beauties of Cynthia, Delia-Nemesis or Corinna, or even the nameless women who people the later Books of the *Amores*.[27] Rather, according to Ovid they are a 'crowd' (*turba*), composed of both 'beautiful and ugly girls' (*pulchrae turpesque puellae*), where 'the

[25] See McKeown (1987) 12–13. [26] Volk (2002). [27] Gibson (2003) 23–5.

worse are always more numerous than the good' (*pluraque sunt semper deteriora bonis*, *Ars* 3.255–6). Neither Ovid in his Don Giovanni guise in *Am.* 2.4, nor Propertius in his passing attraction to common prostitutes in 2.23, had actively contemplated pursuing the mass of *turpes puellae* who turn up in the *Ars*. But the elegiac woman is not alone in disappearing into the crowd. The unique male lover of elegy, who did not hesitate to identify himself as Tibullus (1.3.55, 1.9.83–4), Propertius (2.8.17, 2.14.27, 2.24.35, 2.34.93, 3.3.17, 3.10.15, 4.1.71, 4.7.49) or Naso (*Am. ep.* 1, 1.11.27, 2.1.2, 2.13.25), becomes the *si quis in hoc... populo* of *Ars* 1.1 ('If anyone among this people...').

More importantly, this pluralization and democratization of both *puella* and *amator* is accompanied by a threat to a classic formulation of the ideal of elegiac faithfulness to a single partner. In Book 2, assured that he and Cynthia would not have to part after the repeal of a threatening law, Propertius declares:

> tu mihi sola places: placeam tibi, Cynthia, solus:
> hic erit et patrio nomine pluris amor.
> (2.7.19–20)

> You alone are pleasing to me; may I alone be pleasing to you, Cynthia: this love means more to me than the name of 'father'.

Ovid, notoriously, hijacks the highlighted phrase at the very outset of the *Ars*:

> dum licet et loris passim potes ire solutes,
> elige cui dicas 'tu mihi sola places'.
> (*Ars* 1.41–2)

> While you may, and while you are able to proceed with loosened rein, choose one to whom you may say, 'You alone are pleasing to me'.

There is a palpable tension created by Ovid's importation of Propertius' impassioned declaration of utter devotion to Cynthia (cf. 2.7.3–4 'Not even Jupiter can part two lovers against their will') into a scenario where the lover surveys the women of Rome looking for a suitable candidate for this same declaration. The ideal of elegiac love has now become a chat-up line.

Further reading

The subject of the multiple lovers of the elegists (and Catullus) would benefit from further, more detailed research. Nevertheless for Catullus, see Dyson (2007); for Propertius, see Keith (2008) 86–114 and Heyworth (2010);

for Tibullus, see Lee-Stecum (1998) and for Marathus in Tibullus, see Drinkwater (2012 and forthcoming); and for Ovid's *Amores*, see Holzberg (2002b) 46–70 and Booth (2009). For the idea of 'narrative' in love elegy (broadly conceived), see the essays collected in Liveley and Mitchell (2008).

14

LISA PIAZZI

Latin love elegy and other genres

Self-sufficiency and inter-generic interference

If a literary genre can be said to construct a 'world model' sufficient to itself that tends to exclude all the rest, this is particularly true of Latin love elegy. For in its more serious programmatic declarations it feeds on *recusationes* and defines itself above all in the negative, in particular with respect to the 'high' genre par excellence, epic. And yet, despite this apparent closure, elegy is perhaps one of the genres most open to contamination, as though the elegiac poets meant to refer continually to the various types of poetry that they had chosen *not* to write. Alongside their clear inability to dedicate themselves to a more challenging poetry, there is always a desire to try their hand, if only in a few lines, at genres that are generally banished from the elegiac horizon.

From its origins Latin elegy was always an eclectic genre and, not surprisingly, the critical debate on its origins has brought to light the influence exercised by other genres, such as comedy (in particular with regard to specific figures like the young man in love and the temptress) and Hellenistic epigram.[1]

It is not only Ovid who constantly pushes back the boundaries of the genre and 'plays' with elegy (in the *Amores* and the *Ars*, but above all in the *Heroides*),[2] to the point of abandoning it and experimenting with other genres (tragedy in the lost *Medea*, hexameter poetry in the *Metamorphoses*). Propertius appears as a love poet in his first three books, while he becomes the 'Roman Callimachus' in the fourth, where he tackles aetiological poetry in a quest to find a 'third' space, that is, a mediation between the classical oppositions on which elegy feeds: public/private, war/peace, large/small, male/female, Roma/*amor*.[3]

Translated by Sophie Henderson.

1 See the well-known dispute of Leo and Jacoby over the origin of Latin elegy and Bessone (Chapter 2) in this volume.

2 See Thorsen (Chapter 7) in this volume.

3 On Propertius IV as the quest for a *tertium* (*tertium datur*!) see De Brohun (2003) 22–31.

Lucretius' fourth finale: *ante litteram* satire on elegiac love

The definition of what will become one of love elegy's pre-eminent topoi, the theme of the *exclusus amator*, derives from one of the texts that apparently has the least to do with elegy: the finale of Lucretius' fourth book, which ridicules the 'blindness' of the person who foolishly idealizes the object of their love. In *De rerum natura* 4.1177–84 there is a description of the lover outside a closed door, scattering flowers on the beloved's doorstep and covering it with kisses and perfume. It is likely that Lucretius means to make fun of Catullus' concept of an all-consuming love, although this cannot be demonstrated with certainty. The target might be all kinds of 'romantic' representations of love, as they appear for example in certain Platonic dialogues and in Greek epigram, but it is probable that Lucretius is also thinking of the young lovers of Latin comedy in their Greek setting.[4] Key expressions in love poetry that will become an integral part of elegy's linguistic terminology (*cura*, 'care'; *furor*, 'madness'; *flamma*, 'fire'; *ardor*, 'passion'; *Veneris tela*, 'the darts of Venus') occur in a discourse that is based on an absolutely anti-elegiac concept of love, founded on the demystification of woman and lovers' illusions. Not by chance the passage will serve as a model for the Ovid of *Remedia amoris*, who will take up in comic form the lines in Lucr. 4.1160–9 on the defects of women idealized by their lovers (cf. *infra*). Lucretius places typical Catullan diminutives, which clearly lose their emotional value, in alienating positions, such as in 4.1080 *dentes inlidunt saepe labellis* ('often fasten their teeth in the lips'),[5] where *labellis* is combined with the harsh *inlidunt*, to turn a kiss into a painful and violent collision.[6] Lucretius allows *libido* ('craving') to be positive and natural, being love understood as sexuality free of emotional involvement, but condemns *cupido* ('passion') outright as passionate love obsessively concentrated on one person, which is the very essence of elegiac love.[7] The description of the lover neglecting his duties and squandering his fortune on expensive clothes, shoes and pomades also anticipates the monomaniacal *nequitia* ('naughtiness') typical of the elegiac Augustans. The remedy suggested by Lucretius is the same proposed by other anti-elegiac poets such as Virgil and Horace:[8]

[4] On the literary background of the finale of the fourth book of *De rerum natura* cf. Brown (1987) 127–143.

[5] Trans. Bailey (1947). [6] Cf. Traina (1979).

[7] See however Gibson (Chapter 13) in this volume.

[8] In *Epode* XI, Horace vests the love poet with self-mockery and suggests the strategy of *clauus clauum eicit* ('when one door closes, another opens'): only a new passion (*alius ardor*, line 27) could turn his thoughts away from the last love to which he fell victim. Similarly, the bucolic Virgil consoles the shepherd Corydon, desperately in love with

uulgiuaga Venus ('freely-straying Venus'),[9] a non-exclusive love, causing no suffering, that is the exact opposite of elegiac love.

Elegy and epigram

The genre that presents the greatest affinity with elegy is probably epigram, to the extent that some experts declare it impossible to establish a clear distinction between the two. Both genres use the elegiac distich and both express, often in the form of a monologue, the poet's subjectivity with regard to the most varied themes (love, but also literature and choice of poetics, reflections on death, existence and so on). Latin elegy brings to completion the process of appropriation of themes, motifs and structures of Hellenistic epigram that began with the *poetae noui*, which in turn owe a great deal to authors such as Meleager and Philodemus.[10] The difference between elegy and epigram is often only quantitative – but there can be no firmly defined threshold in terms of the number of lines beyond which elegy kicks in.

It is therefore not surprising that genuine epigrams can be pinpointed within the text of some elegies by Tibullus, Propertius and Ovid, as well as more generic epigrammatic 'modulations' that are often found at the beginning or the end of the elegies themselves.[11] Among the epigrams that modern editors generally print in capitals in order to underline their nature as 'inscription' inserted within the body of the poem, several belong to the sepulchral genre. Tibullus 1.3.55–6 features an epitaph for the poet himself, who, having fallen ill in Corcyra during his patron Messalla's expedition to the Orient, imagines his own death and tombstone. The theme of the auto-epitaph is often integrated into the more general pathetic theme of longing for one's own death, which is frequent in elegy, where the first person poet-narrator, with the typical attitude of a victim wallowing in his pain, describes his own grave and funeral, imagining the reactions of the loved one, who is more or less directly saddled with responsibility for his death. The composition attributed to Lygdamus ([Tib.] 3.2.29–30) closes with an auto-epitaph by the poet ('Here Lygadmus is laid. Grief and love

Alexis (*Ecl.* 2.73): 'you will find another Alexis (*alium . . . Alexin*), if this one scorns you', where the association of *alius* with the name of the loved one represents the most anti-elegiac sentiment imaginable; the interchangeability of the object of love (would Propertius have contemplated the existence of an *alia Cynthia*? Any answer to this question must be approached through the lines of enquiry exposed by Gibson's preceding Chapter 13).

9 Trans. Brown (1984). 10 Cf. Giangrande (1986).

11 Identification of these epigrammatic characteristics, which often mark the conclusion of compositions, can also help to establish boundaries between elegies, that are often uncertain, in particular in the case of Propertius book 2: cf. Grondona (1977) 14–16.

for Neaera, the wife who was stolen from him, caused his death').[12] It is similar to that of a single line at the end of Prop. 2.1, 'an unrelenting girl was the death of this poor man',[13] where the poet imagines Cynthia standing beside his grave and recognizing that she is guilty of his death. Whereas in Propertius' elegy 4.7 Cynthia, appearing as a dead person before the poet, scolds him for his loss of interest and suggests that he compose an epitaph worthy of her: 'Here in Tibur's soil lies golden Cynthia:/ fresh glory, Anio, is added to thy banks' (85–6).

Funerary epigram in the first person returns in three Ovidian *Heroides*, those of Phyllis (2), Dido (7) and Hypermestra (14). These conclude with a brief epigram of one distich, in which the heroines prefigure their own death and lay blame at the door of cruel, ungrateful lovers. The funerary lament dedicated to Corinna's dead parrot at the end of *Amores* 2.6.61–2 is halfway between tragedy and parody. It can be linked to the vast Hellenistic and Roman literary tradition of the *epicedion* for the domestic animal. In this epitaph, again in the first person, the bird itself (by definition loquacious!) is imagined as talking and remembering the love that the young woman held for him.

Nor are examples of votive epigram lacking, as in Tibullus 1.9.83–4, where the poet imagines dedicating a golden palm to Venus when she takes her revenge on the unfaithful Marathus; Propertius 2.14.27–8, giving thanks to Venus for a joyous night of love with Cynthia; Ovid, *Am.* 1.11.27–8, dedicating tablets to Venus containing an invitation from Corinna to a lover's tryst. And finally, the genuine epitaph, Propertius' elegy 4.2, a monologue addressed by the statue of the god Vertumnus to a passer-by, where the four final distichs (57–64) imitate epigrams from the Hellenistic tradition in which a statue talks of himself in the first person and names the artist who sculpted him.

Elegy and epic

Epic is by definition *the* genre in opposition to love poetry. It is the genre that is rejected but remains the main point of comparison from which elegiac poets keep their distance. In their programmatic pieces, elegiac poets show a 'constitutional' inability to undertake epic that is expressed through the topos of *recusatio* ('I don't write epic poetry because I am unable to do so owing to the limitations of my genius and my inspiration').[14] In Propertius

[12] Trans. Lee (1990).
[13] Trans. Goold (1990): all translations of Propertius are from this edition.
[14] See Sharrock (Chapter 9) in this volume.

2.1 the impossibility of tackling traditional epic themes is explained in Callimachean terms: because Callimachus' *angustum pectus* ('narrow chest') is not appropriate for treating subjects such as the *Gigantomachy* or the *Thebaid*, Propertius can write of nothing but battles of love fought *angusto lecto* ('within the narrow confines of a bed': the use of the same adjective points to the connection between the choice of life and the choice of poetics). The only *Iliad* that Propertius composes will be a celebration of Cynthia's naked beauty (13–14 'if, her dress torn off, she struggles naked with me, then, be sure of it, I compose long *Iliads*'), given that the inspiration of his poetry comes not from the Muses or Apollo, but from the girl herself (3–4).[15] The intertextual relationship with Callimachus becomes explicit in Prop. 3.3: while he was asleep on Mount Helicon, the location of Hesiod's, Callimachus' and Ennius' poetic investiture, Propertius dreamed of celebrating the ancient story of Rome and Hannibal's battles in his verses. In short, he dreamed of writing Ennian poetry (5–6), but Apollo warned him to give up his epic ambitions, advising him not to 'burden the little bark of his genius' with themes that were unsuited to his inspiration.[16] Here there are clear references to the preface of the *Aetia* and *Hymn to Apollo* by Callimachus, which had already been used in a programmatic and metapoetical context by Virgil in *Eclogue* 6.3–5 ('When I was fain to sing of kings and battles, the Cynthian plucked my ear and warned me: "a shepherd, Tityrus, should feed sheep that are fat, but sing a lay fine-spun"').[17]

With a very different attitude to Propertius' serious proems, in *Amores* 1.1 Ovid ironically attributes his decision to dedicate himself to love poetry to mischievous Cupid's intervention. His vocation was to have been the epic, but, as he was on the point of composing hexameters, the spiteful god stole a foot, obliging the poet to use elegy's 'limping' metre. The first line (*arma graui numero uiolentaque bella parabam*: 'I was preparing to tell in heavy rhythm of arms and violent wars')[18] openly recalls the incipit of the *Aeneid*, leading one to expect content in keeping with the hexameter, while the pentameter disregards expectations and produces a disconnected effect, through the contradiction between what is being said and its metrical form (*materia conueniente modis*: 'with subject matching metre').[19]

[15] See Hunter (Chapter 1) in this volume.
[16] Cf. lines 22–4 'the little bark of your genius must not be burdened with a heavy load. With one oar skimming the waters, the other scraping the sand, you will be safe: out in mid-sea occur the roughest storms', where the image of two oars is probably a reference to the 'disparity' of the elegiac distich.
[17] Trans. Fairclough (1999). [18] Trans. Barsby (1973).
[19] See also Thorsen (Chapter 23) in this volume.

Another theme explicitly taken on by elegiac poets opposed to the choice of epic centres on its 'uselessness' in the courtship game: the only poem that the poet-lover will contemplate is the *werbende Dichtung*, the poetry of courtship aimed at celebrating and pleasing the beloved woman.[20] Epic poetry is no use in *amor* and cannot work towards conquering and keeping a *puella*. The concept is summarized in the famous line: *plus in amore ualet Mimnermi uersus Homero* ('in love Mimnermus' verse is worth more than Homer's' (Prop. 1.9.11), where the incommensurability of the two genres is emphasized by the fact that what is being placed in the balance are *one* line of the love poet Mimnermus and *all* of Homeric poetry. In the field of love, the latter turns out the loser.

However, the relationship between elegy and epic not only works through exclusion, but also by appropriation. Indeed, there is no lack of 'elegization' of epic themes and characters, i.e. the reduction and translation of situations originating in epic to an elegiac scale and key (in particular when epic characters become elegiac *exempla*, through the emphasizing of elements already present in the model).[21] This operation, systematically carried out by Ovid in some of the *Heroides*, where heroines from epic are transformed into elegiac lovers (Penelope, Briseis, Dido, Laodamia), also appears occasionally in certain Propertian elegies. At the end of elegy 2.8 for example, the entire story narrated by Achilles in the *Iliad* is re-read with an elegiac eye, reattributing all the Homeric hero's actions to a desire to get Briseis back: 'even great Achilles was forlorn when his wife was stolen from him and in the face of the Trojans stubbornly allowed his arms to lie idle' (Prop. 2.8.29–30) and '. . . enduring it all for the sake of lovely Briseis: such is the grief which sears a man when he is robbed of his sweetheart' (Prop. 2.8.35–6).

A further case of an epic character being subjected to elegiac reinterpretation is that of Calypso, who in at least three Propertian passages (and then in Ovid too)[22] is assimilated to the paradigm of the *relicta*, the unhappy, abandoned woman who, powerless and in tears, endures the departure of the man she loves. In this case, Propertius develops some of the Homeric text's 'elegiac potential', giving abundant space to what in Homer is only a detail. In the *Odyssey*, the nymph does not in fact cry at Odysseus' departure; on the contrary, she helps the hero to build the raft that will carry him far from Ogygia. Only when she receives Hermes' order to let Odysseus go does Calypso 'shudder', letting her fear at losing her guest come out (*Od.* 5.116). In elegy 1.15 Propertius rebukes Cynthia for her indifference and by way of contrast introduces examples of mythological heroines who suffered for their men, among whom the 'elegiac' Calypso stands out (9–14). 'Not

[20] Cf. Stroh (1971). [21] Cf. Benediktson (1985). [22] Cf. Ov. *Ars* 2.125–6.

thus was Calypso affected by the Ithacan's departure, when in ages past she wept to the lonely waves: for many days she sat disconsolately with unkempt tresses uttering many a complaint to the unjust sea, and although she was never to see him again, yet she still felt pain when she recalled their long happiness together'. A nod in the same direction can also be found in Prop. 2. 21.13–14 ('thus was Calypso cheated by the Dulichian hero: she saw her lover unfurl his sails') and in 3.12.31 'he [Odysseus] fled from the bed of Aeaea's weeping queen', within a bravura display in which the contents of the *Odyssey* are summarized in just a few lines. Rohde[23] suggested that, behind the transformation of episodes like that of Calypso into pathetic love stories, there lies a lost Hellenistic epyllion. In particular, he was thinking of Philitas' *Hermes*, which probably narrated the adventures of Odysseus with a new, modern and 'sentimental' sensibility.

The short epic's content is presented in the *Sufferings in Love* (Ἐρωτικὰ παθήματα) by Parthenius (an anthology of tales of disappointed love that provided material for poets and was dedicated to the canonical founder of Latin elegy, Cornelius Gallus); it told the tale of, amongst others, Polymela, daughter of Aeolus, and her unhappy love for their guest Odysseus, who seduced and then abandoned her.[24]

The elegiac text in which interference between love poetry and epic is most developed is certainly Ovid's *Heroides*, where the rewriting of myths already treated in epic (and in tragedy) in a female and monologue key allows for paradoxical outcomes with respect to the model text. For instance, the Heroidean letter of Laodamia (XIII) – by developing the theme already present in Propertius 4.3 (Arethusa's letter to her husband Lycotas, who had left for the war, which in many ways anticipates the *Heroides*) – overturns the traditional epic image of the perfect soldier and proposes an explicitly anti-heroic ideal. She counts on Protesilaus fighting with caution, and goes so far as to hope that he be the *last* to disembark from the Greek ships, so averting the destiny inscribed in his name (according to an oracle, the first Greek to touch Trojan soil would die). The lines in which Laodamia declares herself jealous of the Trojan women, who say goodbye to their husbands as they leave for battle and welcome them on their return, presuppose the 'archetypal' scene of the meeting between Hector and Andromache in *Iliad* 6. While Hector does not look back after saying goodbye to his wife (the act of turning back is a sign of unmanly weakness), the perfect soldier from Laodamia's elegiac point of view 'will fight with caution, and be mindful of his home' (*Her.* 13.146), i.e. will be prudent to the point of cowardice and will always have an eye for the wife awaiting

[23] Rohde (1914) 111. [24] Parth. *Amat. narr.* 2 in Lightfoot (1999) 310–12.

him.[25] Here Laodamia is in tune with the traditional elegiac ideology that condemns warlike activities and belittles martial ethos as the enemy of love.

Tragic love

In addition to the exempla taken from epic, Propertius often inserts references to tragic characters whose link with the elegiac context is represented by unhappy love: in 1.15, for example, tragic heroines such as Hypsipyle and Evadne are cited as paradigms of absolute love (Prop. 3.19.17–22, quite different from that of Cynthia!). While 3.19, on the theme of feminine passion, recalls Medea and Clytemnestra among mythical women who were driven by amorous desire to commit heinous crimes (Prop. 1.15.17–20).

Comparison between elegy and tragedy is at the centre of Ovid's *Amores* 3.1, which reviews the poet's initial career and announces his intention to dedicate himself henceforth to dramatic poetry. In this elegy the two genres are personified and meet each other for a contest that recalls the encounter between Vice and Virtue in the parable of Hercules at the crossroads narrated by Xenophon (*Mem.* 2.1.21–33, after the sophist Prodicus).[26] Elegy appears as a seductive woman with perfumed hair and transparent dress, who limps gracefully on ill-matched feet (another reference to the elegiac distich). Tragedy is grim, proceeds with violent gait, wearing a long cloak and buskins, offering the poet a chance to give up his dissipated life.

A reflection on the essential irreducibility of tragic characters in the 'lower' form of elegy underlies Medea's Heroidean letter (*Her.* 12), in which Ovid, elaborating the models provided by Euripides and Apollonius of Rhodes, attempts the impossible job of making the tragic heroine *par excellence* write an elegiac epistle. Naturally, the character reveals herself to be 'excessive' with respect to elegiac demands and the last line of the letter, besides prefiguring Medea's plans for revenge, also announces (metapoetically) an imminent return to the more suitable genre of tragedy. This announcement stands for Ovid's literary production too, since he was soon to write a *Medea* tragedy.[27]

Other Ovidian letters dedicated to tragic heroines are those of Deianira (a rewriting of the events of Sophocles' *Trachiniae*), Hypermestra (who draws on one of the most popular myths of tragic theatre, the Danaids) and Canace (protagonist of the tragedy *Aeolus* by Euripides, of which only fragments survive).

[25] Cf. Rosati (1991). [26] Cf. Hunter (2006a) 33–34.

[27] The metapoetic interpretation of Ov. *Her.*12.212 *nescio quid certe mens mea maius agit* ('something portentous, surely, is working in my soul') has been secured by Bessone (1997) 29.

The art of love

Mention has already been made of Lucretius' denunciation of the concept of the all-consuming love that would become standard in love elegy. But could the Lucretian model of the 'didactic epic' be incorporated into elegy? In 3.5.25–46, Propertius declares his desire to put off attempting scientific poetry for a time when age would cancel the pleasures of Venus: only as an old man would he occupy himself with Lucretian themes, such as the stars, the winds and the universe. In the lines immediately preceding, Propertius expresses his preference for love poetry by echoing Lucretius' programmatic declaration, playing on the phonetic similarity between *iuuat* (''tis my delight') and *iuuenta* ('youth', lines 19–22): ''tis my delight to have worshipped Helicon in my early youth and joined hands in the Muses' dance; 'tis my delight also to tie up my mind with deep draughts of wine and ever to have my head garlanded with the roses of spring'. The allusion, sealed by the repetition of the verb, is to Lucr. 1.927–30 ''tis my joy to approach those untasted springs and drink my fill, 'tis my joy to pluck new flowers and gather a glorious crown for my head...'.[28]

The dialogue with Lucretius turns out to be fundamental to both Ovid's didactic works on erotics, *Ars amatoria* and *Remedia amoris*; works that, with opposite and complementary precepts, respectively teach the art of seduction and strategies to cure oneself from painful love respectively. The famous passage in *De rerum natura* 4.1160–9, where Lucretius is ironic about the blindness of lovers who idealize women and euphemize their defects, is taken up again at *Ars* 2.657–662, where Ovid advises men to follow this procedure for the purposes of seduction ('With names you can soften shortcomings; let her be called swarthy, whose blood is blacker than Illyrian pitch; if cross-eyed, she is like Venus: yellow-haired, like Minerva; call her slender, whose thinness impairs her health...').

Whereas in *Remedia amoris* the precept is overturned to facilitate the 'curing' of amorous dependence: 'Where you can, turn to the worse your girl's attractions, and deceive your judgement with a narrow margin. Call her fat, if she is full-breasted, black, if dark-complexioned; in a slender woman leanness can be made a reproach...' (*Rem. am.* 325–30).[29]

[28] In establishing the text of the elegy, the identification of the Lucretian recollection leads one to choose, among other things, the indicative *iuuat... iuuat* instead of the subjunctive *iuuet... iuuet*, usually preferred by editors of Propertius: cf. Conte (2000).

[29] Translations of *Ars* and *Remedia amoris* are from Mozley (1962). On Ovid's didactic erotica cf. also Conte (1986a).

Erotic aetiologies

The fourth book of Propertius shows an attempt to enlarge the horizons of the elegiac genre towards greater civic commitment, without, however, completely abandoning the erotic theme and without renouncing the Callimachean poetic proclaimed in the preceding three books. The composite character of the book emerges in the first poem, which is clearly divided into two sections: in the first (Prop. 4.1.1–70), the poet accompanies an unspecified guest on an 'archaeological walk' through Rome, modelled on *Aeneid* VIII, where Evander shows his guest Aeneas his little kingdom on the Palatine hill. In the second half (Prop. 4.1.71–150), Horos the astrologer is introduced and chides Propertius for excessive ambition and prophesies his return to erotic poetry.[30] So book 4 signals a break from, but also continuity with, what Propertius had written before; the erotic component is definitely not absent, but is rather entangled with the aetiological discourse on the origins of certain traditions and cults of the Roman world. In 4.4 for example, the Vestal Virgin Tarpeia's betrayal of the city of Rome to Sabine invaders is traced to her passionate love for the King, Titus Tatius: Tarpeia's story is explicitly linked to those of other heroines who betrayed their people for love: Scylla, Ariadne and Medea.

Among the elegies of this book, one of the most complex and intertextually saturated is that of Hercules (4.9), which explains the origins of the cult of the *Ara Maxima*, retracing in Callimachean form, and not without irony, the myth that Virgil had narrated in epic-heroic style in *Aeneid* VIII. In particular, the scene where the demigod, parched with thirst, asks to enter the sacred wood of the Bona Dea, where her young female followers are playing (Prop. 4.9.23–6), reads as an elegiac *paraklausithyron*, pronounced by an anti-heroic Hercules, where he *iacit ante fores uerba minora deo* ('before the threshold utters words unworthy of a god', Prop. 4.9.32), where *minora* carries a metapoetic connotation, indicating the alienating belittlement and elegiac 'disguise' represented by a character translated from the 'higher' genres.[31] Turning to the priestesses, Hercules first puts forward his epic-heroic credentials, citing some of his famous labours. Then, fearing that his hyper-masculine and heroic identity would be unwelcome to the girls, he tells them that he had been in the service of Omphale too, carrying out women's tasks and even disguising himself as a woman (this episode of slavery to the oriental queen is compared in elegiac poetry to the *seruitium amoris* and,

[30] Prop. 4.1.135–138: 'Now you must compose Elegy, an alluring task (here lies your camp)... You will suffer active service in the tender warfare of Venus, and you will be a profitable adversary for Venus' boys.'

[31] Cf. Anderson (1964).

not by chance, finds plenty of space in the Ovidian letter by Deianira (*Her.* 9), based on the almost comic reduction of Hercules from a heroic character to an effeminate person obedient to the caprices of a woman.[32] Despite the hero's awkward *captatio beneuolentiae*, the priestess refuses to let Hercules enter and in the end he knocks the doors down, goes into the grove and drinks at the fountain anyway, deciding, out of pique, that women will be excluded from the cult of *Ara Maxima*.

Elegy and pastoral poetry

The text that most clearly demonstrates metapoetic reflection on the borders between bucolic-pastoral and elegy is Virgil's *Eclogue* 10. The protagonist of the work is the poet Cornelius Gallus, canonical founder of Latin elegy and victim of an incurable passion for the fickle Lycoris. Racked with pain at the departure of the beloved, the Virgilian Gallus seems to find momentary consolation and a cure for love in the world of bucolic poetry; indeed, in lines 50–51 he declares that from that moment on he will dedicate himself to pastoral poetry ('I will be gone, and the strains I composed in Chalcidian verse I will play on a Sicilian shepherd's pipe'). But the possibility of a poetic 'conversion' proves deceptive, because love is invincible and the suffering it brings is the essence of elegy.[33]

Virgil's *Eclogues* (and also *Georgics*) exercise a profound influence on Tibullus, for whom the yearning for an idealized rural world represents escape from amorous sufferings and the corruption of the age. Elegy 1.1 shows, through the typical structure of the priamel, the contrast between modest and serene country life and the ambitions of those who accumulate riches or dedicate themselves to military activities. Praise for the country people's happiness is clear, as in the close of *Georgics* 2: 'Wealth let others gather for themselves in yellow gold and occupy great acres of cultivated land – scared on active service, in contact with the enemy, their sleep put to flight by the blare of trumpet-calls. But let my general poverty transfer me to inaction, so long as fire glows always in my heart.'[34] In his bucolicized world it even becomes possible to imagine a happy and loving relationship that is not blighted by misfortune, as seen in the pastoral 'dream' of

32 Cf. Ov. *Her.* 9.47–118 and Casali (1995) 16–17 and 99. On the conflict of 'gender' vs. 'genre' incarnated by the Hercules of 4.9 cf. Janan (1998).

33 Cf. *Ecl.* 10.62–9: 'Once more Hamadryads and evensongs have lost their charms for me; once more farewell, even ye woods! No toils of ours can change that god . . . Love conquers all; let us, too, yield to Love!' For this interpretation cf. Conte (1984). On the countryside as a refuge from the agonies of failed love see also Ovid *Rem. am.* 169–98. Here he inserts a small sample of pastoral poetry into the book's didactic-elegiac fabric.

34 Trans. Lee (1990).

Tib. 1.5.21–30: 'I'll farm, I thought, and Delia will be there to guard the grain while the sun-baked floor threshes harvest in the heat . . . She will offer to the farmer God grapes for the vines, ears for the standing corn, a victim for the flock. She can rule us all, take charge of everything, but I'll enjoy being a nonentity at home.'

Tibullus' rural world represents partial recovery from the lacerations produced by civil war, the effects of which dominated the *Eclogues*. For example, in 1.1 Tibullus, now living modestly as a result of his family's decline, invokes the Lares, custodians of his estate in wealthy times. In this he echoes the words of the Virgilian Meliboeus, forced by exile to abandon his flock. But Tibullus' tone is more serene and less pathetic; even if the field is a poor one, he will nonetheless be the possessor of something and the Lares will still receive a sacrificial offering, albeit a humbler one.[35]

The importance of the *Eclogues* for elegiac poetry also emerges clearly in Propertius 2.34, a programmatic composition which affirms the rejection of epic poetry and proclaims adherence to Callimachean ideals.[36] At the end, Propertius retraces Virgil's poetic career, setting it alongside his own. If the peak of such a journey is represented by the monumental epic poem, whose imminent publication Propertius enthusiastically and movingly announces, it is also true that Virgil had commenced his career with the 'light' and Callimachean *Eclogues*, where the amorous theme was given plenty of space. Not surprisingly, in *his* 'retrospective', Propertius dedicates six lines to the *Aeneid* (2.34.61–66), four to the *Georgics* (2.34.77–80) but at least ten to the *Eclogues*, above all alluding to the eclogues in which the erotic theme takes the upper hand (I, II, III, V and VII): 'You sing beneath the pinewoods of shady Galaesus, of Thyrsis and Daphnis with his well-worn pipes, and how ten apples or the gift of a kid fresh from the udder of its dam may win the love of girls. Happy you, who can buy your love cheaply with apples! To her, unkind though she be, even Tityrus may sing . . .' (67–76).[37]

35 Tib. 1.1.19–20 'You, o Lares, also receive your gifts as guardians of a property once prosperous (*felicis quondam*), now poor'; Virg. *Ecl.* 1.74 'Away, my goats! Away, once happy flock (*felix quondam*)!' On this imitation of Virgil and more generally on the 'post-*Eclogue* setting' of Tibullus' elegies cf. Ziolkowski and Putnam (2008).

36 Within the vast bibliography on this complex elegy, I mention only Fedeli (2005) 948–1009 and Cairns (2006b) 295–319.

37 These considerations argue in favour of the textual structure proposed by Heyworth (2007c). He transposes lines 77–80 (on the *Georgics*) after line 66 ('something greater than the Iliad is coming to birth'): this moves the reference to the *Georgics* (the work that in this context is of less interest to Propertius) to a position halfway between the *Aeneid* and the *Eclogues*, while Prop. 2.34.81–2 would refer to these last, establishing a connection between Virgilian pastoral poetry (at least in part amorous in subject) and the neo-erotic-elegiac lineage of Varro Atacinus, Catullus, Calvus and Gallus on which Propertius wants a place. On this transposition cf. Heyworth (2007b) 276.

Elegy, comedy and mime

Together with epigram, comedy is the genre that has most often been considered 'parent' of the elegy. Both genres confront 'gender' conflict over amorous relations and call into question the axioms of traditional Roman morality. Both the youthful lover of comedy[38] and the elegiac poet assume reckless and scandalous behaviour as a result of amorous passion. They disregard the duties of the good Roman citizen, which include obeying their father, dedication to activities for the public good (war and politics) and control over women within the institution of marriage.[39] In comedy this subversion is usually temporary, since the young man on the loose will end up reintegrated into the family world of traditional values, whereas the *nequitia* of the elegiac poet-lover seems insuperable.[40]

Elegy's most 'comic' figure must be the procuress (*lena*) protagonist in Propertius 4.5 and Ovid, *Am.* 1.8. She represents perfectly all the anti-elegiac values in that she urges the young girl to scorn her poet-lover's verse and trade her body to rich admirers instead. The connection with comedy is explicit in Prop. 4.5.43–4, where old Acanthis advises the *puella* to follow the model of Menander's artful courtesan Thais. This *lena* recalls the figures of Cleareta in Plautus' *Asinaria* and Scapha in *Mostellaria*. In particular the scene where the boy in love listens unseen and at the end interrupts the 'lesson' given to the girl by the madame at *Most.* 157–312 is a chief model of *Amores* 1.8, in which the poet eavesdrops on Dipsas's discourse from behind a door and at the end, exasperated, can hardly hold himself back from coming to blows with the wicked old woman.[41] The characterisation of the go-between has also been traced back to the influence of the Greek mimographer Herodas, who in *Mime* 1, has old Gyllis try to convince young Metriche to betray her absent husband with a beau.

More difficult to determine is the role exercised by Roman mime, of which we know very little. A typical theme in this genre was the love triangle featuring adulterous wife, lover and cuckolded husband/fool. This can perhaps be detected in *Am.* 3.4, where Ovid demonstrates to a jealous husband how futile it is to check up on his wife, who will betray him in any case if she so wishes.[42] The same situation, with inverted roles, underlies Propertius 4.8, where a comic-'realistic' tone dominates, verging on farce. Cynthia surprises the poet in the company of two prostitutes and, like a new Odysseus taking his revenge on his wife's suitors, attacks and chases

[38] See also Fulkerson (Chapter 11) in this volume. [39] Cf. James (1998).
[40] See Sharrock (Chapter 9) in this volume. [41] Cf. Myers (1996) 3–4.
[42] On adultery-mime cf. Ov. *Tr.* 2.497–500, 505–506 and McKeown (1979) 72.

them off before she punishes Propertius himself and the slave who was accomplice to the crime.[43] It is therefore probable that elegiac poets drew inspiration from Roman mime as well, although the mediation of the higher genre of comedy cannot be excluded.[44]

Nostalgia for other genres

As has been shown in this brief survey, elegiac poets often exhibit the ambition (real or fictional) to go beyond the confines of the genre and ultimately to find the strength and the ability to dedicate themselves to a higher and more serious type of poetry (epic and didactic poetry in the case of Prop. 3.5, or tragedy in the case of Ovid). Furthermore, an original feature of elegy is that it is a composite and eclectic genre, interacting with and acknowledging upfront numerous other poetic forms such as epigram, comedy and pastoral.

Can we speak of elegy's 'nostalgia' for other genres? Just as, from the point of view of values, the elegiac lover goes against the rules by experimenting with amorous relationships but lives in intimate contradiction of this because he longs to anchor his own relationship in the traditional matrimonial ethos; so, with regard to literary choice, the elegiac poet often represents himself as though he were hanging in the balance, on the threshold of various different choices but unsure which to take. It is not by chance that Propertius closes his career with the ambiguous book 4, which is half patriotic elegy and only partly about love, and which represents a turning point in that it involves a greater thematic range and stylistic affiliation. Following his elegiac beginning, Ovid tries his hand at tragedy, didactic (still in distichs, but on a grander scale nonetheless) and (hexameter) epic, the ultimate metamorphosis of the elegiac poet himself.

Consideration of other genres provides coordinates for elegy. Although elegy represents itself as a self-sufficient world, there is always an aspiration to go beyond limits, and this often sparks fresh literary experiences. The competing genres represent a sort of 'escape route' to an alternative world longed for as consolation for the suffering of unhappy all-consuming love (and of a poem). These adventures across genres have a function analogous to that of myth in Propertius and the idealized countryside in Tibullus.

Further reading

On self-definition in Latin elegy cf. Fantham (2001). The exposition of elegiac intertextuality by O'Rourke (2012) covers the interaction between

[43] See also Gibson (Chapter 13) in this volume. [44] McKeown (1979) 72.

elegy and a number of non-elegiac genres. For the relationship between the genres of Roman erotic elegy and epigram Keith (2011) is a good starting point. Boyd (1997) remains a model study of the relationship between Latin love elegy and other genres in the case of Ovid's *Amores*, with particular attention paid to epic influences. In the vast bibliography on the influence of other genres on Ovid's *Heroides*, Jacobson (1974) is still valid and Jolivet (2001) (in French) is especially rich regarding influences from tragedy, while Lindheim (2003), Spentzou (2003) and Fulkerson (2005) contain plenty of useful material. Also useful are the commentaries (in Italian) on *Heroides* 1–3 by Barchiesi (1992), *Heroides* 9 by Casali (1995), *Heroides* 18–19 by Rosati (1996b), *Heroides* 12 by Bessone (1997), as well as *Heroides* 7 by Piazzi (2007), *Heroides* 8 by Pestelli (2007) and *Heroides* 13 by Reggia (2011). On Ovid's overcoming the contradictions of the elegiac genre, see Labate (1984), while Sommariva (1980) and Shulman (1981) trace Lucretian influences on Ovid's erotodidactic poetry. On various aetiological elegies of Propertius book 4 cf. Pinotti (2004); in particular, on a possible Homeric subtext in the scene of the meeting between Hercules and the young girls at Prop. 4.9 cf. Battistella (2006). For further aspects regarding Virgil and the elegy, see Kenney (1983) and Rosen-Farrell (1986). On elegy and comedy cf. Barsby (1996) and James (2003 and 2012); on elegy and mime, Fantham (1989); on the pantomime, Ingleheart (2008).

15

JOHN F. MILLER

Breaking the rules

Elegy, matrons and mime

The Augustan elegists' collections of first-person reflections on their erotic affairs at times gesture towards other modes (didactic, narrative, hymnic) and non-amatory themes (panegyric, aetiology, lament) found in the Hellenistic tradition from which Latin elegy descends.[1] Poems whose topics vary from the norm of what we call love elegy can seem to stand apart, such as Tibullus' birthday encomium of his patron Messalla (1.7) or Propertius' funeral elegy for Augustus' nephew Marcellus (3.18).[2] Other non-erotic elegies clearly reverberate within the larger amatory context – Propertius' evident panegyric of Augustus' military ambitions (3.4.1), for instance, is 'corrected' at the start of the succeeding poem (3.5.1). Still others are marked as the work of lover-poets by brief amatory tags at the start (Prop. 2.31 Temple of Apollo) or end (Prop. 3.7 Epicedium for Paetus) or by more extensive closural movements in ambitious 'public' presentations that seem to jolt the reader back to the world of erotic elegy (Tib. 2.1.67; 2.5.101). When the elegists' own erotic personae sharply recede or disappear altogether in Propertius' fourth book and Ovid's *Fasti*, two projects inspired by Callimachus' *Aetia* which announce their 'service' to the Roman state under Augustus, the poems' abiding elegiac sensibilities still include attention to *amor*. Indeed, erotic elements continue to be a defining characteristic of elegy in these compositions, albeit an *erōs* featuring different voices than the poet's, and often transmuted into more respectable conjugal situations or ribald mythological *Aitia* (Gr. 'origin-stories'). This chapter examines some striking cases of interplay with amatory themes in Propertius 4 and the *Fasti* and the generic and ideological dimensions of that interplay.

[1] See Bessone (Chapter 2) in this volume.

[2] The same seems true of Gallus' epigram on Caesar's expected triumph (fr. 2.2–5 Courtney). Ross (1975) argued that Gallus' *Amores* featured aetiology as well as *erōs*.

Propertius' Book 4

Propertius closes book 3 momentously with a bitter farewell to Cynthia, a goodbye both to the faithless girl and to love-elegy in the traditional sense of a lover-poet voicing his own erotic obsessions. His past verses celebrating such a sham beauty as Cynthia now bring him shame (3.24.3–8); to compensate, Propertius prophetically sings for her dire curses of future rejection and ugly old age (3.25.11–18). Though he will depart in tears, and the weeping Cynthia – again, deceitfully – tries to change his mind (3.25.5–6), 'her wrongs are greater than any tears' (3.25.7). The anguished lover has finally come to his senses, and Propertius indicates the finality of his gesture by echoing point by point the statement of his master passion for Cynthia at the start of book 1.[3]

After this strong closure, we find Propertius' next book striking out in a totally new direction, with the elegist guiding a visitor around Augustan Rome and musing on the city's earliest history. His experiments in the previous book with themes revolving around the emperor may in retrospect be seen as anticipating book 4's inaugural movement,[4] but nothing earlier really prepares us for the declaration that Cynthia's former slave will devote all of his 'limited' elegiac resources to serving the Roman state (4.1.59–60, 67). He proposes to turn now to antiquarian poetry, 'rites, festival days and the ancient names of places' (4.1.69 *sacra diesque canam et cognomina prisca locorum*), and thereby to Latinize Callimachus' *Aetia* and make his other *patria*, Umbria, swell with pride to have produced the Roman Callimachus (4.1.63–4). But no sooner has Propertius enunciated this bold new poetic direction than another, powerful voice emerges to take issue with the project. The astrologer Horos sternly warns him away from what Propertius proposes and justifies his objections by twice citing Apollo in the frame of his rambling horoscope for Propertius. The god of poetry and song is himself alleged to shun the poet's plan, his lyre unwilling (4.1.73–4). Likewise, back when Propertius was first coming of age, Horos reminds him by quoting the deity's words, Apollo urged the boy to write elegy instead of thundering in the forum and predicted his grim service to a single girl, Cynthia of course (4.1.131–46). The astrologer, whose name is the Egyptian equivalent of Apollo, thus implicitly enjoins Propertius to continue writing erotic instead of patriotic elegies. Since the scene cited from the elegist's youth clearly alludes to Apollo's injunction to the young Callimachus in the

[3] 1.1.1 *suis . . . ocellis* and 3.24.2 *oculis . . . meis*; 1.1.3 *constantis . . . fastus* and 3.25.15 *fastus . . . superbos*; 1.1.7 *toto . . . anno* and 3.25.3 *quinque . . . annos*; etc.

[4] 3.9.47–56 with Hubbard (1975) 111–15; 3.11 (Cleopatra), 3.18 (Marcellus' death).

prologue to the *Aitia*,[5] that foundation text for the *recusatio* and neoteric-elegiac poetics, the present alternatives for Propertius would seem to be contesting visions of 'Callimachean' poetry, namely love-elegy (for which he himself previously cited Callimachus as a model[6]) vs. Roman *aitia*, in which he would explicitly follow the great Alexandrian master.

That aetiology and *erōs* are hardly incompatible in the literary tradition that the elegists inherited from Hellenistic poetry may (among other things) point up the ridiculous character of Horos as poetic advisor.[7] In fact, all of the poles arising from the astrologer's evocation of the *recusatio* structure break down in the collection that is book 4 – national vs. personal, Augustus vs. Cynthia, aetiology vs. love, epicized vs. amatory elegy. This is not to say that Propertius' poetic identity in book 4 does not involve tensions with his previous stances – indeed, such tensions lie at the heart of the reader's experience of the book.[8] Yet in literary historical terms, book 4 puts on display a broadening of Propertius' range as a poet writing in the Hellenistic tradition. Aetiology and panegyric are the most conspicuous ingredients, both of them found in Callimachus. But no less striking is the array of female speakers, which makes the book, as much as anything else, a sustained meditation on the feminine voice.[9] I take up the first and last of these, the two married women, whose utterances at once illustrate the enlargement and interrogation of earlier Propertian poetry – whose alternative morality construes the decidedly unmarried lover and beloved in marital terms[10] – and enact Propertius' final valediction to amatory elegy.

First is Arethusa's sad letter from home to her Lycotas (4.3) who is campaigning against the Parthians (and other foes). Military (7–10, 35–6, 64–8) and urban details (55–62, 71) show clearly that the Greek names mask Roman characters, and we quickly learn (11) that the couple is married. Propertius himself earlier addressed a parallel situation by criticizing a friend who ignores his wife's pleas and heads off on a Parthian expedition with the Princeps (3.12.1–6):

5 Fr. 1.21–30; with the thunder compare also fr. 1.20.

6 2.34.30–2; 3.9.43–5. Cf. Ovid *Rem. am.* 759; *Tr.* 2.367–8.

7 E.g. the *Aitia* itself contains erotic elements. Propertius 2.34.32 names Callimachus as author of the *Aitia* among the proper models for love poetry. Sandbach (1962) 268 cites this passage in arguing that Horos in 4.1B does not oppose amatory and aetiological elegiacs. But see Prop. 2.1.11–12 (with Zetzel (1983) 92–3 and Miller (1986) 155–6), which suggests that Propertius could think of *amor* and *causae* as distinct poetic categories. So, while Horos is perverse, he is not utterly nonsensical, in attempting to fracture traditional Callimachean poetics.

8 Recently, Debrohun (2003).

9 Wyke (1987a) remains fundamental.

10 Cf. 2.6.41–2; 2.7; 2.13.36 and Lyne (1980) 79–80 and n. 20 on 'marriage thinking' in Propertius.

Postume, plorantem potuisti linquere Gallam,
 miles et Augusti fortia signa sequi?
tantine ulla fuit spoliati gloria Parthi,
 ne faceres Galla multa rogante tua?
si fas est, omnes pariter pereatis auari,
 et quisquis fido praetulit arma toro!

Postumus, could you leave Galla weeping and follow the brave standards of Augustus as a soldier? Was the glory of plundering the Parthians worth so much, when your Galla was begging you again and again not to do it? If I may say so, may all you greedy ones perish together, and whoever prefers arms to a faithful bed!

In these verses the names at line-ends and caesurae point up the questionable trade-off in Propertius' view – abandoning the distraught Galla to follow Augustus and seek glory in despoiling the Parthians. Propertius apologizes (*si fas est*) for characterizing the Augustan soldiery as motivated by gain (*auari*), and compensates somewhat by acknowledging their valour (*fortia*). At root here is the typical elegiac ethos that values love above military glory but the positive focus on married love in a contemporary context – for the first time in Propertius – complicates the cultural critique. For it was Augustus' concern to safeguard sexual morality in marriage (cf. 18) but the quest for imperial conquest distracts the Augustan warrior from appreciating his wife as a model of chaste devotion. One Augustan value is set against another, even if in the end the poem accents the wife who is more loyal than Penelope.

In 4.3 we hear the remarkable voice of a Roman wife deserted by her campaigning husband, by turns frustrated, angry, anxiously eager, and pensive. Book 4's promise of *sacra diesque* turns out here to be the *matrona*'s list of vain religious observances for her husband's return (17, 55–62; cf. 71). Augustan conquests are neither blamed nor praised outright. The contemporary reality of Parthian campaigning is kept in view throughout, but the world of war now serves as locus of suffering for the abandoned female lover more in human than in political terms. Especially noteworthy, in comparison with 3.12, is that the personal voice of Arethusa reveals, alongside the ample evidence of her constancy (tears, prayers, weaving his cloaks etc.), an erotic perspective akin to that of the male elegiac lover. When she questions the meaning of marital loyalty for the husband who abandons her, it is with memory of their embraces on their wedding night (11–12). The pentameter's *doubles entendres* with military terminology play on the familiar elegiac conceit of *militia amoris*[11] – now from the 'conquered' female's

[11] See Dee (1974) 83 and Hutchinson (2006) ad loc.

perspective – while the primary sense is the physical joining of their bodies, he pressing close (as well as pressuring), she surrendering. Likewise, in naively imagining Lycotas a raw recruit, Arethusa thinks about his body, worrying that the breastplate is chafing his 'delicate shoulders' and the spear blistering his 'arms not meant for war' (23–4). This conjures up for her the even more unpleasant thought of injury to him from another woman's love-bites, which she wishes away (25–6), before recounting to the husband her own lonely suffering at night in bed (29–32). The thrice recurring *mihi* in the same *sedes* (23 *dic mihi*, 26 *det mihi*, 29 *at mihi*) abets the continued focus on erotically charged physical details. Like the lovesick Propertius,[12] she endures bitter nights, complaining that she thrashes all over the bed (29–32). She kisses his weapons lying about the house (30), an eerie embodiment of the absent soldier. The gesture of fondness is ironically bestowed on the harsh source of her suffering; the alliterative *amaras*... *arma* may hint at the central elegiac opposition *amor/arma* (love/weapons) as well as recall the 'delicate shoulders' of Lycotas in her mind just a moment ago (23 *teneros*... *lacertos*, i.e. *armos*).[13]

The sexual undercurrent running through Arethusa's letter is absent from Propertius' address to the negligent husband Postumus. Apparently the poet felt it indecorous to broach such a topic in the case of another man's wife.[14] The only concrete picture of Galla's affection is her expected hanging on the husband's neck when he returns from abroad (3.12.21–2). Even so, the accent there falls on her chastity, as throughout the poem; the collocation at pentameter's end suggests that 'chaste' and 'yours' will be one and the same thing to the husband. When Propertius previously found himself in a position like that of Postumus, contemplating an invitation to join a military expedition abroad (1.6), he succumbed – not surprisingly – to Cynthia's pleas, as Postumus did not – and not only to her pleas, prayers and complaints, but also to her embraces (1.6.5). Propertius' girl friend dissuades him by proclaiming her passions in their all-night sessions (1.6.7). One may compare his curt dismissal here of the lover unresponsive to such appeals (1.6.12) with 3.12.5–6. In 4.3 Arethusa, too, underscores her loyalty to Lycotas – and insists upon his faithfulness to her (cf. 4.3.69). But Propertius also attributes to the speaking wife an erotic dimension that echoes his own prior persona, but that he all but withholds from his instructions to the negligent military husband. When, at the letter's end, Arethusa quotes the

[12] 1.1.33, 2.17.3–4; cf. Ov. *Her.* 12.169–70.

[13] Paul. Fest. 3 L. Cf. Serv. *Aen.* 4.495 and Maltby (1991) 52.

[14] Tib. 2.2 is likewise circumspect about his friend Cornutus' wife. A possible exception would be the sensual scenario at Hor. *Carm.* 2.12.25–8, if Licymnia is indeed a pseudonym for Maecenas' wife (but see Williams (1968) 301–3).

inscription that she plans to affix to the thankful offering for his return (72 *saluo grata puella uiro*, 'from a girl grateful for her man's safety'; cf. 3.12.21 above), her generalization has an amatory tinge. She calls herself *puella*, not *uxor* or *coniunx*;[15] the collocation *puella uiro* at verse's end alludes to an apposite moment in earlier Propertian elegy, a girl in precisely Arethusa's lonely situation, awaiting her man's arrival (3.3.20 *exspectans sola puella uirum*). The dedicatory inscription has the safely returned man enveloping his thankful girl, now enjoying what (hopefully) will have been denied to the rival *puella* (25) of Arethusa's fevered imagination.

Where in 4.3 the wife's letter to her absent husband offered Propertius the opportunity to combine elegiac *amor* with Roman *fides* – one approach to the polarities laid out in 4.1 – the final poem of the collection (4.11) stages a Roman *matrona*'s sustained proclamation of her virtue in which her spousal affection is only very obliquely expressed.[16] Here the speaker is the ghost of Cornelia, wife of Augustan associate Paullus Aemilius Lepidus (censor in 22), who instructs her surviving husband and children, while defending her chaste life before the judges of the Underworld. Though startling to the reader, the appearance of this noble woman brings book 4 to an effective, if contrastive, close. The book opened with the questionable prospect of patriotic Roman poetry and now ends with its most thoroughly Augustan poem.[17] A few elegies ago (4.7) Cynthia likewise spoke to Propertius from the dead, berating her lover for neglect both in life and death and loudly assuring him of her own fidelity – a transparent lie, to judge from Propertius' previous protestations; 4.11 counters with an imperial exemplar of female fidelity in traditional marital terms.[18] After Cynthia and the book's other disreputable women (treasonous Tarpeia in 4.4; the *lena* Acanthis in 4.5), with Cornelia we return to a figure like Arethusa, another steadfast Roman wife addressing her absent husband. But unlike her pseudonymous counterpart, the well-known aristocratic matron accentuates her public reputation; as the Augustanism of her matronly exemplarity moves to the foreground, the erotic elements of Arethusa's letter disappear.

In the same breath with which she first mentions her marriage to Lycotas, Arethusa recalls the couple's nuptial passion (4.3.11–12). But at the moment that Cornelia first directly identifies herself (to us) as Paullus' wife, she is

[15] *Puella* in elegy can apply to a married woman but the more common usage is for the elegiac mistress: Pichon (1902) 244–5. Applications to married females at Prop. 2.3.36 and 2.18.17 are in amatory contexts. See also P.A. Miller (Chapter 10) in this volume.

[16] Cf. Janan (2001) 146–7.

[17] Differently, the Augustan counterpart of 4.11 at the book's centre, 4.6 on the Battle of Actium, puts the imperial values that it expresses in dialogue with traditional elegiac poetics; Miller (2009) 232–3.

[18] Grimal (1953) on *fides* as the central theme of book 4.

pointing to the badges of her prominent status in Roman society: her well-connected marriage, her illustrious ancestors, and the children who guarantee her reputation (4.11.11–12). There are no offspring in 4.3's scenario of the wife gushing emotionally to her husband on campaign. Likewise, 4.11 picks up the linkage in 4.3 between the ideas of mournful solitary nights and another woman in her bed but subsumes both motifs under Cornelia's concern for her children. Where Arethusa thinks of a possible rival's love-bites vs. her own lonely agony (4.3.25–32), Cornelia bids her husband grieve for her alone at night instead of in their children's presence (4.11.79–84); when the possibility arises of a new bride occupying their/her marriage bed, she suddenly switches to address the children, urging them to accept Paullus' new arrangement (4.11.85–90). Both motifs have been all but emptied of the eroticism of 4.3 in what is fundamentally public discourse not unlike the book's central elegy on the Battle of Actium (4.6). Cornelia's pride in both her children and her chaste conjugal devotion makes her an embodiment of Augustan morality as it was recently enunciated in the *leges Iuliae*.[19] Yet in the larger context of elegy, such an ideal ironically comments on Propertius' provocative application of marital loyalty to his own extramarital love affair by restoring the value to its traditional context.[20] Where, for instance, the elegist's epitaph arrogates to his *seruitium amoris* the moral code of a wife married to only one man (2.13.36), Cornelia's gravestone reclaims the accolade (4.11.36). Like 4.3 featuring the married Arethusa, 4.11 is marked by the total absence of Propertius' first-person voice. In the final elegy, however, the elegiac values of Propertius are also absent.[21] Comparable is the last ode of Horace's fourth book, a celebration of the Augustan era that pointedly ends with the poet's surrender of his customary lyric ego to collective patriotic singing (4.15.29–32).

Ovid's *Fasti*

The final sequence of Ovid's *Amores* crystallizes the trajectory of the four books of Propertian elegy. The third from last poem (3.13) – the only non-erotic poem in the collection – concerns a festival in Falerii, thus echoing the *sacra diesque* of Propertius 4. In that connection it is probably no coincidence, given the prominence of marriage in book 4 of Propertius, that Ovid here shockingly – again, for the only time in the *Amores* – mentions his wife (3.13.1). The very last of the *Amores* (3.15) combines closural motifs of Propertius 3 and 4. Ovid follows Propertius' direct valediction

[19] Cf. Cairns (2006b) 358–61. [20] Holzberg (2001) 73–4; Wyke (1987a) 171–2.
[21] For a different view: Cairns (2006b) 358.

in 3.24–5, but predictably bids farewell to love elegy (*Am.* 3.15.19 *imbelles elegi*) and the deities of love (Venus and Cupid) rather than, like Propertius, to the exasperating girlfriend (3.25.7–9). Compared with the erotic experience driving Propertius, Ovid's imperative is literary and divinely ordained (cf. Cupid in *Amores* 1.1). He must leave elegy to accept Bacchus' summons to the *area maior* of tragedy (3.15.18), an expectation deferred at the start of *Amores* 3. At the same time, Ovid allusively evokes the enactment of Propertius' contested choice of a more elevated kind of poetry in 4.1. Ovid's final turn round the goalpost of love elegy (*Am.* 3.15.2 *raditur haec elegis ultima meta meis*), for instance, recalls Propertius' aim at the new poetic 'goal' of antiquarian patriotic elegy (4.1.70 *has meus ad metas sudet oportet equus*).

When with his *Fasti* Ovid himself takes up an extended Augustan aetiological elegy on the Roman calendar – like Propertius 4, based on Callimachus' *Aetia* – he embeds in it a running interaction with the tradition of love elegy. Alongside a solemn approach to religious festivals and a matter-of-fact antiquarianism are found narratives of rape, often burlesque in tone, and other erotic elements. It remains an open question among scholars to what extent these various features – not to mention, more generally, traditional elegiac perspectives and Augustan ideology – balance, harmonize, or clash with one another in the *Fasti*.[22] But there is indubitably an element of contrast in that love continues to be a marker of elegy – albeit a love relocated or transformed – even though Ovid claims to be engaged with a totally different kind of elegy.

Take the poet's embarrassed conversation with Venus at the start of April, her month, where he famously tries to explain that he never did actually desert her, even as we are constantly reminded of his leave-taking from Venus and love elegy at the close of the *Amores*.[23] The very opening of that valedictory (*Am.* 3.15.1) is audible in Ovid's opening supplication at *Fasti* 4.1. The 'grander course' of tragedy (*Am.* 3.15.18) for which he had to leave her then has now become the *area maior* (4.10) of ancient rites, their 'causes', and the constellations, which Ovid differentiates once again from amatory elegy, here called, after the passage of time, his youthful 'play' (4.9 *lusimus*: see *OLD* 4 and 8a). Now that he has reached the festivals of Venus' month, the elegist shamelessly asserts that he has never abandoned her standards (4.7), the very standards that he summarily bade her and Cupid remove from his field (*Am.* 3.15.16; cf. *Am.* 2.9.3). 'You have always been the object of my attention' (4.8). If, in Venus' teasing implication, Ovid has

22 The contrasting elements in equilibrium: Heinze (1919), Fantham (1998), Merli (2000); in tension with one another: Hinds (1992), Newlands (1995), Barchiesi (1997b).

23 Hinds (1987b) 118, Miller (1991) 29–34.

been breaking the rules of elegy, he convinces her that there is no damage after all. Unabashedly sophistical, Ovid's argument readily persuades the admittedly self-interested Venus, who responds to his request for favour (4.1 *faue*) by applying her sacred myrtle to his *tempora* (4.15–16), that is, both his temples and his poetry on 'the times' of the year (cf. 4.11, 1.1). It is telling that the only one of the many deities encountered by Ovid in the *Fasti* who thus formally consecrates him as a poet is Venus, the ancestor of the Julian family to be sure but at this point very conspicuously the divinity of Ovid's earlier amatory elegies. Accordingly, in the immediately ensuing movements Ovid figures the deity of April not only as Augustan progenitor, patroness of Rome, the deity of springtime, and universal procreative power, but also as the goddess of love in an elegiac context. His litany of her powers and accomplishments includes the striking allegation that the lover's *paraklausithyron* originated song (4.109–10), that stereotypical elegiac topos of the *exclusus amator* serenading on the girl's doorstep. Venus, too, in deserving the lovely springtime season in April, is said to be 'attached to her Mars, as usual' (4.130 *utque solet, Marti continuata suo est*). The adjective in particular naughtily points up that the familiar proximity of their months mirrors the divine couple's well-known adultery.[24]

Likewise, the proem to book 2 redirects Ovid's farewell address to his elegies that closes *Amores* 3.15 into an opening gambit which asserts 'Now, elegies, you are moving for the first time under greater sails.'[25] The 'grander' epicizing mode of the *Fasti* raises elegy above its former (and usual) status as 'slender' stuff (2.4 *exiguum . . . opus*)[26] and its previous erotic content in the youthful Ovid's hands (2.5–6). His new elegy on the calendar's *sacra* is akin to military service (9)[27] and honours Augustus in particular (2.15–18). For all that – the *amor* of previously slender elegy replaced by 'greater' subjects like Roman ceremonials and the Princeps – erotic passion stands out among the themes of *Fasti* 2. A tale of mythological or legendary rape occurs in each quarter of the book: the fast-paced catasterism of Callisto (155–92); Faunus' burlesque assault on Omphale as a 'foreign' *aition* for the Luperci's undress (303–58); Jupiter's stalled wooing of Juturna conjoined with Mercury's grim rape of the tattling nymph Lara, the Lares' mother (585–616); and the rape of Lucretia as book 2's climactic panel (721–852). These

[24] See further Barchiesi (1997b) 219–28 on the motifs of sexuality vs. morality in the ensuing entry for the feasts of Venus and Fortuna Virilis on April 1.

[25] The only two apostrophes to *elegi* before *Pont.* 4.5.1. The poet's 'memory' of his earlier elegy here (2.4 *memini*) glosses the allusion to *Am.* 3.15.19.

[26] Cf. Hor. *Ars P.* 77; Prop. 4.1.59; *Fasti* 6.22 and Bömer (1958) on 2.3.

[27] A claim that pointedly reconfigures the provocative elegiac idea of *militia amoris* even as it echoes Propertius' patriotic declaration at 4.1.60.

and similar stories throughout the *Fasti* may seem a world away from love elegy,[28] particularly in their tonal range anticipating that of the *Metamorphoses*, which swings from typically Ovidian lightheartedness to more sombre and even horrific scenes. But they do derive from Ovid's earlier elegiac experiments with mythological narrative, like the poet-lover's exempla of the river Anio wooing Ilia in *Amores* 3.6 and of Ceres and Iasius in 3.10 or the Rape of the Sabines in *Ars amatoria* 1 as a comic *aition* for finding available women in Roman theatres. The aetiological basis of such myths in the *Fasti* usually takes the place of an erotic referent in the body of the poem (the lover's experience, the erotic teacher's lessons), and more broadly comic and coarser mime-like sexual misadventures loom larger.[29] Love elegy nonetheless continues to resonate in the poetic calendar's amatory narratives.

The poem's very first 'sexual comedy' is also the most elaborately elegiac, an element adding texture and wit to Priapus' frustrated assault upon the nymph Lotis amidst the rustic merrymaking of satyrs and nymphs at a Greek festival of Bacchus (1.392–438). The atmosphere of the whole occasion is saturated with sexuality: those attending 'were not adverse to sexual play' (1.396 *quicumque iocis non alienus*),[30] particularly the males (397), whose lusts the pretty nymphs ignite (411, 413, 414). The catalogued variety of the women suggests that they themselves may be attempting to seduce the Pans and satyrs: they sport various hairstyles (405–6) as Ovid recommends in the *Ars amatoria*; this one reveals her legs (407), another her shoulder (409), that one her breast through a torn garment (408).[31] Most clearly reminiscent of love elegy is the behaviour of Priapus himself, the randy god of gardens who here ridiculously woos Lotis in the manner of an urban lover (cf. 425 *amans*). Unlike his fellow revellers, who are charmed by multiple beauties (411–13), Priapus is smitten (416 *captus*) by one nymph alone (417 *sola*). Like the elegiac lover, he sighs only for her (417), and subtly signals his affections with nods and expressive glances (418). Lotis, too, Ovid styles a typically arrogant elegiac beloved,[32] who mocks Priapus and scornfully looks down upon him (419–20). In spite of his goony wooing, therefore, this failed lover is not an entirely unsympathetic figure, even when in the end the raucous interruption of his assault upon the sleeping nymph leaves him a public laughing-stock (*omnibus . . . risus erat*) – 'all too erect' in the moonlight (437–8).

28 On the *Fasti*'s rape scenes and the tradition of love elegy see recently Murgatroyd (2005) 94–5.

29 On the background in mime see McKeown (1979), Fantham (1983) 200–1, Barchiesi (1997b) 238–51, Wiseman (2002).

30 See Green (2004) ad loc. for the meaning of *iocis* here (a secure emendation).

31 See Green (2004) ad locc. for parallels.

32 E.g. Prop. 3.24.2; Ov. *Am.* 1.17.9.

In book 6 Ovid retells this episode with a decisive change in the dramatis personae, Vesta in place of the nymph Lotis as the female victim – the story is an *aition* in the Vestalia panel. In the process, we are invited[33] to witness not only how the previous Priapic tale is abbreviated but also how its elegiac ethos evaporates when the chaste Roman goddess is introduced into the imaginary Greek divine festivities. In the course of the passage, Vesta is clearly shown to be incompatible with elegiac fun.

Throughout the *Fasti* Vesta is celebrated as an imperial icon by virtue of her cult's installation in Augustus' house when he became pontifex maximus in 12 BC. In Ovid's commemoration of that event on April 28, Vesta again emerges as a contrastive figure in relation to sexual licence, now that of the earthy festivity of the Floralia, which traditionally began on that day. Flora, goddess of blooming plants, arrives bedecked with richly multicoloured garlands; in her honour theatres stage the customary mimes featuring striptease and other lasciviousness (4.945–6). The feast will continue into May, and Ovid promises to resume at that point. But for the present 'a grander subject' is pressing (4.948 *grandius . . . opus*), so he cedes this day to Augustus' relative and new divine neighbour: 'Vesta, take away the day' (4.949). Ovid thus follows the priorities of the Augustan religious calendar, but pointedly casts the deferred feast of Flora in terms evocative of amatory elegy. Floral garlands (4.945) typify drinking parties. Here is the goddess honoured by satiric comedies like Ovid's lusty tales of Priapus and Faunus. The term for the risqué foolery on stage, *iocus* (4.946), is used elsewhere to characterize Ovid's own love elegy.[34] Most strikingly, the press of more serious business allusively echoes an earlier declaration that the poet is being pursued by a grander task than elegy (*Am.* 3.1.70 *grandius . . . opus*). There he was (temporarily) postponing the demands of his tragic muse in order to continue with *Amores* book 3; here he (temporarily) defers the celebration of a goddess redolent of amatory elegy in a sort of inverse *recusatio*.

If on 28 April Flora and Vesta seem to be ideological opposites, Flora does claim her own measure of respectability when she is afforded her time at the end of the Floralia on 2 May. In addressing her there (*Mater, ades, florum, ludis celebranda iocosis*, 5.183 'Mother of flowers, come hither, to be celebrated with playful games') Ovid once again (cf. 4.946) notes the deity's bawdy theatrical games but now balances this coarse feature with the dignified designation 'Mother of flowers,' an expression that evokes

33 From the start (6.319–20) Ovid clearly points back to his previous telling of the story. Comparisons of the two versions: Fantham (1983) 201–9, Newlands (1995) 124–45, Murgatroyd (2002) and (2005) 81–8, Frazel (2003).

34 *Ars* 2.600; *Rem. am.* 387; *Tr.* 2.354.

her honorific epithet in cult, *mater*.[35] The opening collocation *Mater, ades* recurs from an address to august Vesta at 4.828 (Romulus at Rome's foundation), an echo that in effect asserts their equality as well as reverses the preferential treatment given to Vesta at Flora's expense on 28 April. Flora herself, in answering Ovid's query about her identity, first of all tells the story of her rape (as her former self, the nymph Chloris) by the wind-god Zephyrus but instead of underlining her weakness like a typical Ovidian rape victim accents her future (and present) position as goddess and wife of Zephyrus. She omits any reference to her fear,[36] skips through the episode so quickly (one couplet: 5.201–2) that its spare counter-movements resemble a courtship ritual rather than a tumultuous event, and, most astonishing of all, excuses the violation, now that she has ended up a *matrona*. Zephyrus has compensated for his violence (5.205) by granting her the name of bride, a marriage bed free of complaints (5.206), a garden filled with flowers (5.209), and – the crowning glory – control of flowering as a goddess (5.212). Conjugal imagery runs throughout. Having in effect won divinity in exchange for her virginity (cf. Zephyr's charge at 5.212 'have divine control over flowers') – like Virgil's Juturna (*Aen.* 12.140–1) or Crane in *Fasti* 6 (127–8) – Flora downplays her suffering and highlights her present elevated status as wife of the mighty West Wind. The great divinity (or one who aspires to be great) goes on to boast of her variegated powers in nature, her extraordinary role in the birth of Mars, the festival awarded her by the Roman people, and the terrible punishment that she visited upon them when they slighted her.

As the poet and goddess discuss these matters for over 140 verses, there is no mention of the other side of her duality signalled in the opening address (5.183), Flora's infamous theatrical entertainments. It is only when, in line 331, Ovid gets up the nerve ('I was trying,' he says – *conabar*) to ask her why there is considerable salaciousness in her games (5.331–2), that the subject arises. It occurred to me, he continues, that she is not an austere divinity, that her floral gifts befit *deliciae* (5.333–4), that is, the convivial and erotic merrymaking that he goes on to detail (5.335–48). The negative expression *numen non esse seuerum* (5.333) as much as calls Flora *lasciua*.[37] Note

35 Cultic epithet at Cic. *Verr.* 2.5.36. Ovid recalls (and inverts) the verse-opening at Lucr. 5.739 *Flora quibus mater . . .*, Flora's first appearance in extant Latin poetry, where she likewise typifies springtime (cf. *Fasti* 5.194) and is in the company of Zephyrus (*Fasti* 5.201–12).

36 Victim's fear: e.g. *Met.* 1. 525, 4.228–9, 5.396, 5.605–6, 6.706; *Fasti* 2.799 etc.

37 *Lasciuus* vs. *seuerus*: Hor. *Ars P.* 107, Ov. *Am.* 2.10.16, 27, Mart. 3.20.6, Tac. *Ann.* 16.5.1.

that the talkative goddess is not allowed to answer this question herself, as if (somewhat paradoxically) to preserve decorum. Likewise, Ovid goes on to claim (5.349–40) that he needs no supernatural help in understanding why prostitutes throng her games. He can see for himself that 'she is not among the stern and grandiose' (5.351). When Flora does speak again, after thirty-two verses, the conversation seems to be back on safer ground as she fields the question about lights at her festival, for which she gives three alternative reasons (5.361–8). The final *causa* – the true one, she says – returns the topic to the feast's merriment: 'because nocturnal licence is appropriate to my *deliciae*' (5.367–8 *deliciis nocturna licentia nostris / conuenit*). This echoes Ovid's words above, uttered to us, about the appropriateness of Flora's gifts to *deliciae* (5.334). The goddess is thus made to follow the poet's lead in finally acknowledging the racier side of her festival. The whole conversation has been plotted to accent Flora's meretricious associations as a kind of punch line.

The word *deliciae* (these are the only two occurrences in the *Fasti*) and its referents here point unmistakably to love elegy. *Deliciae* in Ovid often signifies erotic pleasures[38] and at the programmatic close of the *Amores* the poet calls his elegies *deliciae*.[39] In itemizing the delights to which Flora's gifts are suitable, the calendrical poet suddenly ushers us into the world of amatory poetry: the rose-strewn table at a symposium, with its crowned symposiasts (5.335–7) – a scenario to which just below he compares the roses falling from Flora's garlands (5.359–60) – the drunken lover serenading at the harsh threshold of his girlfriend (5.339–40; cf. 4.109–10 in the list of Venus' *aretai*), and the wine-god Bacchus and his beloved Ariadne (5.345–6). Flora's attributed advice to enjoy life while in bloom (5.353) is in essence the love poet's injunction *carpe diem*. Ovid's exclusion of Flora from buskin-wearing goddesses styles her a kin to the personified Elegy of *Amores* 3.1, who faced off with Tragedy, the *dea cothurnata* par excellence.[40]

It is against this background of jocund games, courtesans and general revelry redolent of Ovid's earlier amatory poetry that the poet prays for his calendrical elegy's immortality to the floral deity whose fragrance lingered in the wake of her disappearance: *floreat ut toto carmen Nasonis in aeuo, / sparge, precor, donis pectora nostra tuis* (5.377–8, 'Scatter, I pray, my breast with your gifts so that the poem of Naso may flourish for all time'). The

[38] *Am.* 3.14.18, *Ars* 3.649, *Rem. am.* 154 and 374, *Tr.* 2.368. Cf. the juxtaposition elsewhere with *amor, amores, libidines*: *TLL* 5.448.81.

[39] *Am.* 3.15.4 *nec me deliciae dedecuere meae*, referring back to 2 *elegis . . . meis*; cf. *Tr.* 2.78, 349; 5.1.15.

[40] Newlands (1995) 108–9.

all-encompassing prayer and punning self-naming – both for the only time in the *Fasti* – mark this closural gesture as momentous. Its rich allusivity further charges the couplet with programmatic significance. Most conspicuous is the well-known reference to Callimachus' envoi to the Graces at the end of the first *aition* in the *Aetia*, the principal elegiac model of the *Fasti*: 'Come now and wipe your anointed hands upon my elegies so that they may live for many a year' (fr. 7.13–14). But Ovid's petition to Flora also recalls his assurance to his love elegies of their immortality at the end of the *Amores* (3.15.19–20) – that intertext again – a couplet itself looking to Callimachus' prayer. Another neglected allusion[41] is to the end (again) of Catullus 13:

> nam unguentum dabo, quod meae puellae
> donarunt Veneres Cupidinesque,
> quod tu cum olfacies, deos rogabis,
> totum ut te faciant, Fabulle, nasum.
> (13.11–14)

Catullus promises that the powerfully fragrant unguent which will make his friend pray to the gods to make him all nose – *totum nasum* – was a gift of Venuses and Cupids. Naso ('Nose') himself prays for the fragrant Flora's immortalizing gifts, which he just above situated firmly in sympotic and amatory contexts like that of Catullus' poem. Venus is otherwise evoked here at the close of the Floralia, as throughout the entry. Like Venus, Flora is goddess of gardens (5.209–12, 251–2, 315–18, 373), numbers the Horae and Charites as associates (5.217–20), and among all her flowers is emblematized by roses in particular (5.194; cf. 336, 344, 354, 360).[42] Much as Venus in *Aeneid* 1 departs from her son while exuding *diuinum odorem* (1.402–4 divine fragrance), Flora here ends her interview with Ovid by vanishing into thin air but leaving her divine fragrance behind (5.376). And perhaps most significantly, Ovid's closing request matches the programmatic moment at the start of *Fasti* 4, where he asks Venus, the patroness of his earlier elegy, for her favour upon his present work. In response she touched Ovid's temples with her sacred myrtle (4.15–16); Ovid would to similar effect have Flora scatter upon his breast her characteristic gifts. At two unique moments in his 'greater' national calendrical elegy Ovid asserts his poetic identity by strongly evoking the heritage of Latin love elegy even as he is broadening the elegiac genre.

41 Also relevant is a passage by Theocritus evidently imitating Callimachus' verses (*Id.* 17.36–7). Recall, too, Lucretius 5.739–40.

42 Venus and gardens: Varro, *Rust.* 1.1.6; roses: Paus. 6.24.7; cf. Eur. *Med.* 841; Bion 1.65–6.

Further reading

Here is a selection of the many contributions to the topic. The erotic and its transformation in Propertius 4 are explored in the path-breaking article by Wyke (1987b), and more recently with special attention to generic issues by DeBrohun (2003) and Hutchinson (2006); within a larger ideological problematic by Janan (2001) and P.A. Miller (2004). The studies of Hubbard (1975) and Rothstein's commentary (1924) remain fundamental to understanding book 4 within the Propertian oeuvre, as does the sorely neglected book by Ross (1975). On the generic identity of the *Fasti*, see Heinze (1919) and the responses by Hinds (1987b) and (1992) and Merli (2000); for ample attention to how the erotic code reverberates within the work's unique elegiac dynamic especially Newlands (1995) and Barchiesi (1997b); also J.F. Miller (1991a); see further Murgatroyd (2005) on erotic elements in the *Fasti*. On traces of mime in the poem see McKeown (1979), Fantham (1983), and Wiseman (2002).

PART V

Receptions

16

ROGER P.H. GREEN

Latin love elegy in Late Antiquity

Maximianus

In Late Antiquity (this period will here be taken as running from the early fourth century to the late sixth) there is plenty of love poetry, and there is plenty of poetry in the elegiac metre, but love elegy is notably scarce. It is almost as if *Elegia* (*amatoria*) had run into the bushes without taking care to be seen first,[1] but at least there is more of her in Late Antiquity than in the first and second centuries AD, when the love elegy of Tibullus, Propertius and Ovid, though better known, is not the object, as a genre, of close imitation. It is not the purpose of this chapter to examine or comment upon the earlier period, but it sheds interesting light (or darkness) on the state of affairs. In particular, it warns against overestimating the effects of Christian ideas and sensitivities on the genre, and simply attributing the apparent disappearance of the genre to Christian disapproval.

Love and elegies, not love elegy

For love poetry in general, Late Antiquity is outstanding, in terms of variety and innovation. Perhaps the best known work – for which a fourth century dating has now become more popular – is the incomparable *Peruigilium Veneris*, evidently written for a springtime festival of Venus, a poem which 'has caught the romantic imagination perhaps more than any other poem in ancient literature'.[2] The so-called *Latin Anthology* is graced by a wealth of amatory poems, such as Reposianus' *De Concubitu Martis et Veneris*,[3]

[1] Cf. Virgil, *Eclogues* 3.65. The important contributions of Virgil of the *Eclogues* and Horace of the *Odes* to love poetry lie outside the scope of this chapter – as does Catullus, though his work at times prefigured the form of love elegy. Gallus, however, will make a surprise appearance.

[2] Scourfield (2003) 1148. For the date see Cameron (1984) 209–34, and Shanzer (1990) 306–18. Cameron's paper includes a text; see also Shackleton Bailey (1982) 139–44 (it is no. 191).

[3] For Reposianus, see Shackleton Bailey (1982) 177–86 (no. 247) and Duff and Duff (1968) 524–38; and the short article of Scourfield (2003) 1309.

the anonymous *Cupido amans*, and Modestinus' *Cupido dormiens*.[4] This last conceit is developed by Ausonius in his poem *Cupido cruciatus* ('Cupid in Torment'), in which heroines of myth, in Virgil's Fields of Mourning, wreak their vengeance on the wicked boy . . . until he wakes from his dream.[5] Ausonius in fact offers a remarkable variety of amatory or erotic verse – but no love elegy. Best known for his *Cento nuptialis*, which sews together lines, half-lines, and little bits of Virgil to describe a wedding, and (more adventurously, as he claims with apologies to Virgil, and to any coy or censorious readers) the wedding night, he also composed, in assorted metres, the attractive but incomplete *Bissula*, which praises the beauties of a German slave. Ausonius also penned a touching elegy on his wife Sabina, looking back with undiminished grief at her death almost forty years before.[6] The purpose is memorialization, and the tone almost everywhere a sombre one, affectionate but never amatory. Ausonius' epigrams include ingenious and amusing pieces on love and sex. But perhaps his pupil Paulinus was not amused; at least his poetic corpus, which for the most part dates from his time as a monk at Nola, includes a virulently ascetic epithalamium.[7] A more conventional epithalamium was composed by Claudian, to greet the marriage of Honorius and Maria, and he also produced some rather more vibrant Fescennine verses,[8] and there are several epithalamia by Sidonius. There are erotic poems by Ennodius (who died in 521, then bishop of Pavia), while the work of Venantius Fortunatus has attracted interest for its spiritualizing renewal of aspects of Ovid's *Heroides*.[9]

Although most of these amatory poems were not in the elegiac metre, clearly it has not lost its connection with amatory themes. And it remained perfectly familiar, and writers use it with no less skill than before. It is the standard metre for the many prefaces which Claudian wrote for his major poems, and is used often by Sidonius and twice by Prudentius.[10] Rutilius Namatianus used it to narrate and describe his journey from Rome to Gaul, and in the same period Orientius of Auch wrote a lengthy homiletic poem in elegiacs.[11] Ausonius uses the metre for many purposes, in sequences such as the *Caesares* and *Fasti*, and for individual poems such as his 'farewell to his

4 For these see respectively Shackleton Bailey (1982) 170/1 (no. 233) and Duff and Duff (1968) 540–2; Shackleton Bailey (1982) 196 (no. 267) and Duff and Duff (1968) 538–40.
5 See Green (1999) 154–8, and (1991) 526–32.
6 See Green (1999) 35–6 and (1991) 31–2.
7 Poem 25 in Hartel and Kamptner (eds.) (1999).
8 See Hall (1985) 86–106, with Cameron (1970) 98–102.
9 W. Schmid (1959b). See also M. Roberts (2009) 246, 315, 318.
10 Prudentius, *Peristephanon* 8 and 11.
11 His so-called *Commonitorium* or 'admonition', see Ellis (1888) 193–243.

father', *Epicedion in patrem*. Dracontius chose the metre for his *Satisfactio ad Gunthamundum regem*, and it is a favourite metre of both Ennodius and Venantius Fortunatus.[12]

Classical love elegy in a post-classical age

The question naturally arises, how accessible to readers and potential imitators in Late Antiquity were the classical writers of love elegy? There are no extant manuscripts from this date, but that is no surprise. The writers are seldom mentioned in an educational context (for which the evidence is admittedly patchy, to say the least), and not part of the regular curriculum. It may be that 'the elegance of [Ovid's] style and his command of rhetorical technique' could have commended him as a school author, but perhaps the opportunity was not taken.[13] We know of no scholia or commentaries of any kind; none are mentioned in Jerome's list of commentaries, where (exaggerating, perhaps, to emphasize his point) he cites a large number of authors on whom commentaries of some sort were available: Virgil, Sallust, Cicero, Terence, Plautus, Lucretius, Horace, Persius, Lucan.[14] Then the grammarians of the period, although they quote frequently, refer hardly at all to the elegists; and in any case the material may well have been gathered long before. Writers on metrics use the occasional couplet from the elegists when analysing the metre.[15]

Sometimes a window is opened by a detail in the voluminous writings of the so-called 'Fathers of the Church', who may cite or mention classical writers, whether to argue or even agree with them.[16] Augustine appropriates Virgil and Sallust to develop his case against the integrity of early Rome in early books of *City of God*, and in *Confessions* actually quotes from mime and comedy.[17] But there is no mention of the elegists in Augustine's works; he shows little sign of knowing even the *Metamorphoses*.[18] The many writings of the learned Jerome are hardly more enlightening. He quotes but a single line from love elegy and seems unaware of its source: what is for us *Amores* 3.2.83 is for him *uersiculus ille uulgatus* ('that commonly used line') *risit et argutis quiddam promisit ocellis*.[19] The vagueness is surprising, for as a rule he is not afraid to show his knowledge where he can. Perhaps

12 For Dracontius see Vollmer (1984). 13 The quotation is from Tarrant (1983) 257.

14 Jerome, *Apologia aduersus Rufinum* 1.16 in P. Lardet (1982) 15.

15 For these writers see Keil (1857–80); there is an index in volume VII 579–668.

16 Notable here is the contribution of Hagendahl (1958). 17 Burton (2007) 37–52.

18 Hagendahl (1967). There is useful information on authors besides Virgil in the work of Mueller (2003).

19 'She laughed, and promised something with a twinkling eye.' This quotation is found in *Ep.* 123.4.2. See Hagendahl (1958) 253.

he shunned the mention of Ovid in the context of Christian marriage, or had simply forgotten. It has been noted that in his *Chronicle* Jerome added details about Ovid (born *in Paelignis*, died *in exilio*), but none for Propertius or Tibullus;[20] and it may be significant, too, that in a letter where he assures Paulinus that scripture's riches leave no need for classical poets (so David the Psalmist makes Catullus, Horace and Serenus redundant), he praises the Bible's Song of Songs yet says nothing of any classical writers that it might surpass.[21] Finally, if we turn to Ambrose, another 'Father' with a good classical education, there is again no sign of the love elegists, although he happily uses Virgil often enough. In sum, it looks as if the love elegists simply do not matter to Christian writers, and are not even worth condemning.

Detecting allusion to classical poets by the numerous poets of Late Antiquity has rightly been a popular pursuit, as one may see from the spoils of the perennial hunting expeditions conducted by editors and commentators. But the interpretation of such data is no easy task.[22] Propertius has been relatively well served in this connection, with Hosius, Enk and Shackleton Bailey making notable contributions.[23] Hosius thought that Ausonius, Claudian and Rutilius were the most likely to have made conscious use of Propertius, adding that it was uncertain if Propertius had 'touched the minds' of some ten Christian writers (the three just named being then considered 'pagan'). Perhaps he could not believe that they might be interested. Shackleton Bailey foregrounds Sidonius, and considers Orientius and Dracontius likely. The evidence now assembled by Kamptner increases the claims of Paulinus of Nola, likely in any case as the pupil of Ausonius, who has been shown to quote from all three elegists.[24] For Ovid, there is the dissertation of Eaton, who unearths many possible examples of the influence of Ovid on Claudian (far more than appear in Birt's massive edition) but after a rigid evaluation rejects most of them.[25] In a recent survey, conducted as it were from the opposite end (in methodological terms), Dewar confines himself to an example from the *Metamorphoses*, which was always better known.[26] Tibullus has perhaps received the least thorough treatment; certainly more should be done, if only by trawling through the editions of various Late Antique poets and yellowing theses of yesteryear, to confirm or refine the

[20] Kelly (1975) 75 n., citing Helm (1929) 92. One does not need good information to insert a floruit somewhere.

[21] *Ep.* 53.8.17, in Hilberg (1910) 461.

[22] There are some comments on this in Green (2010) 51–66.

[23] Hosius (1932) xxix–xxx; Enk (1946) 54–77 at 70–77; Shackleton Bailey (1952) 306–33 (at 320–30).

[24] For Paulinus see note 7; for Ausonius see Green (1991) *passim*.

[25] Eaton (1943); Birt (1892). [26] Dewar, in Boyd (2002) 383–412.

pessimistic diagnosis of K.F. Smith a century ago of a 'march to oblivion in the third and fourth centuries'.[27]

As well as seeking various small verbal echoes, or allusions, or imitations – these various words are all still useful – critics have looked for evidence of engagement with or appropriation of classical contexts or motifs, or (in metaphors that are rather strained) even 'dialogue' or 'correction'. It was suggested by Alfonsi,[28] that there is a reminiscence of a couplet of Tibullus (1.3.89–90) in a letter of Ausonius to Paulinus, at *Ep.* 23.43–52 and 24.16–124.[29] Tibullus dreams that he will suddenly (unannounced!) return and come to Delia; Ausonius imagines the receipt of a message that Paulinus is on his way home. There is no verbal similarity, even in the words that Alfonsi cites. (There may be a common source for Ausonius and for Jerome, who in *Ep.* 46.13 imagines the approach of a *uiator* with the news that Marcella, his correspondent, is arriving; but from what genre it might have come is anyone's guess.)[30] The influence of Tibullus has also been seen, in either Paulinus or Ausonius (not both: for the poem in question is more probably by Ausonius, as it forms an organic part of his *Ephemeris*, or 'Daily Round').[31] Ausonius' words *suprema diei cum uenerit hora* (line 72, 'when the final hour of life has come') represent with a slight change Tibullus' words at 1.1.59 *suprema mihi cum uenerit hora* ('when my final hour has come'). The theme is a common one, and not specifically amatory;[32] but it should be observed that the word *despiciam* in line 75 of Ausonius echoes the last line (78) of Tibullus' poem, where the word is repeated for emphasis. In rather mystical terms, Ausonius will one day despise everything, not just wealth as Tibullus says.

A most interesting echo of Ovid has been detected in the epithalamium of Paulinus of Nola, already mentioned, which makes a strong attack on the traditional discourse of marriage. In lines 9–10 of this long poem he writes *absit ab <his> thalamis uani lasciuia uulgi / Iuno Cupido Venus, nomina luxuriae* ('let the frivolity of the stupid populace be absent from this marriage, and Juno, Cupid and Venus, the names of self-indugence'); compare Ovid, in a poem urging his love to be less open about her nocturnal activities: *hinc simul exieris, lasciuia protinus omnis / absit et in lecto crimina pone tuo* (*Am.* 3.14.19–20, 'when you leave the place, let all frivolity be

[27] Smith (1913) 61. Smith mentions only Nemesianus, Ausonius and Paulinus of Nola.
[28] A. Alfonsi (1963) 117.
[29] References are to Green (1999) and Green (1991), where both the shorter and the longer versions of this missive are presented.
[30] It is certainly not from Ovid's development of the Tibullus passage at *Amores* 2.11.37–56.
[31] See Green (1991) 250.
[32] Weinreich (1927) 122–3.

absent forthwith, and leave your misdeeds in your bed'). Paulinus seems to be extracting Ovid's phrase *absit... lasciuia* and appropriating it to his ascetic purposes. He might have first read the poem in his youth and remembered it for prominent motifs such as *peccare* (Christian language for 'sin'), *crimina* ('misdeeds'), and *pudor* ('chastity') and related words. An even more striking case of what could be called *Kontrastimitation* – there are not many in this area, but the industry and ingenuity of scholars may in due course change this – was noted by Weyman and taken up by Schmid in the *Reallexikon für Antike und Christentum*.[33] In his account of creation (*De Laudibus Dei* 1.393) Dracontius presents the newly created Eve in the words *constitit ante oculos nullo uelamine tecta* ('she stood before his eyes, covered with no clothing'), fascinatingly close to a line in Ovid's description of Corinna *ut stetit ante oculos posito uelamine nostros* (*Am.* 1.5.17, 'as she stood before my eyes, her clothing removed'). Can one agree with Weyman that there is in Dracontius no trace of the Augustan poet's 'lewd sensuality'?[34]

No snakes in Iceland?

On 13 April 1778 Samuel Johnson was dining with a few friends, in taciturn mood. But an informant of Boswell recalled that he unwound to the point of boasting that his memory was able to retain the exact words of a whole book-chapter. This was chapter 72 of the *Natural History of Iceland from the Danish of Horrebow*, which ran: 'CHAP. LXXII Concerning Snakes. There are no snakes to be met with throughout the whole island'.[35] The present chapter has not taken this line, and does not need to. *Latet anguis in herba*. Perhaps, after all, the snake was not killed, either by Ovid – sometimes said to have killed elegy, with a surfeit of levity and playfulness – or by Augustus, who exiled him, creating a warning to any later poet and a justification for any subsequent ruler – but scotched? The work in question – to which the serpentine image will no longer be applied, for it deserves better – is traditionally known as the elegies of Maximianus, or Maximian, and usually dated to the mid-sixth century,[36] but there has been much rethinking over the last thirty years, which must now be briefly examined. At issue are

33 Weyman (1975) 147; Schmid (1959a).

34 '... ist doch von der lüsternen Sinnlichkeit... des augusteischen Poeten... bei Dracontius nichts zu verspüren'.

35 See Hill and Powell (1934) III 279. The anecdote is spoiled if one notes that the recollection is not totally accurate and that Horrebow was in fact systematically answering the statements of an earlier writer.

36 The traditional account is given in *OCD* 941 and in the older handbooks.

the author's name, the form and correct designation of the work, and its date and purpose.

The 686 lines which comprise the work have generally been seen as six elegies (or five if one treats its last twelve lines as an Epilogue). The many manuscripts seem to divide it into various poems or sections, but their testimony is far from unanimous. Critics must make the choice for themselves (as when editing manuscripts of Propertius), and since the edition of Pomponio Gaurico in 1501,[37] they have done so with little difficulty, presenting a long opening elegy (almost in fact half the total), and then four elegies averaging less than 100 lines, each dealing with a separate episode in the life of the disappointed old man through whose sad and frustrated eyes and mind the whole work is presented. Each of the four elegies centres on a particular woman: Lycoris, Aquilina, Candida, and an unnamed *Graea puella*. It has recently, however, been argued by Schneider that the work should be seen as an *opus continuum* ('continuous work'),[38] and that the notion of a series or cycle of elegies was unjustifiably imposed by Gaurico – who also attributed the poem to Gallus, because of the name Lycoris – in order to give the impression of classical love elegy. Certainly, the four episodes just mentioned are to be seen as exemplifications of the general lament over the troubles of old age in the long first section. The modes of introduction differ, some entering in *medias res*, others with a short introduction, but the variation is in line with the practice of the Roman elegists. There are, it is true, some verbal links between different parts of this work, though Schneider exaggerates their number and importance.[39] But these episodes also work well as individual elegies. If only one or two of them had survived, they would have been classed as self-sufficient poems without hesitation. What the poet has done is to marshal and exploit the episodic nature of classical elegy to give colour and vigour to the overall theme. In making such a linked set or series – it is perhaps unhelpful to speak of a 'cycle' (*Zyklus*) as scholars have done, and its unclarity makes Schneider's thesis harder to grasp[40] – he has gone further than Ovid and Tibullus, who only occasionally link two poems together,[41] and who do relatively little to outline the personality of the 'subjective love-poet'. Our work, moreover, looks back over a whole lifetime, and a series of women; it is a kind of *longue durée* collection, whereas the Augustans tend to present their adventures and reactions as if they happened only the other day. As we shall see, this new viewpoint has

[37] See Schneider (2003) 24–7. [38] Schneider (2003) 21–36. [39] Schneider (2003) 29.
[40] Szöverffy (1968) 351–67 speaks of 'a loosely connected series, a cycle', at 352.
[41] For example, Ovid, in *Amores* 2.7 and 8, and perhaps Tibullus in 1.8 and 9.

implications for his writing, which resorts to narrative and reported dialogue rather than Augustan soliloquy.

The name Maximianus comes from one line of the work, line 26 of Elegy 4, or 486 of the whole. There we are told that someone said, on hearing him sing the song he had heard from Candida the dancing girl, 'Maximianus loves a singer'.[42] Since the voice of the victim of old age and frustrated love is constant and ubiquitous in the work, one can call its owner Maximianus (or Maximian) without hesitation. But although many scribes and scholars have not done so, there are grounds for hesitating to call Maximianus author as well as narrator. The problem is not, of course, that a suitable author named Maximianus cannot be identified from the period in question, but simply that the narrator emerges throughout as something of a simpleton, a fool, a moaner, who (as he virtually says) deserves what he has got. (There may be a certain element of self-deprecation at times in the Augustan elegists, but never lamentation or even self-hatred on this scale.) It is easier to see the author as a distinct person, who has neither undergone such trauma nor is complaining of one, and who is to that extent not a 'subjective' love elegist' of the traditional kind. Our set of elegies has a skoptic, a satirical aim; whether the target is real or fictional need not be discussed here.[43]

The sixth-century date generally assigned to the work derives from the mention of Boethius in Elegy 3, and may be supported to some degree by the setting of the fifth elegy, an embassy to the other 'kingdom' of Constantinople.[44] Boethius is cast as a friend of Maximianus who advises him rather like the *praeceptor amoris* of love elegy. It is certainly surprising to find a real, (possibly) live, philosopher in a love elegy, and it is hard to reconcile his seemingly flippant and even amoral attitude after he fails with the gravity of the philosopher and martyr who wrote the *Consolation of Philosophy*, but it is unlikely that the name is a cipher, a 'speaking name' (so 'Helper'), or the result of textual corruption. It would not be the first example of a comic and mildly disrespectful story about a famous philosopher. Shanzer has given some reason to place this in his lifetime, that is before 524,[45] with evidence of a less serious side to Boethius, but a date in mid-century allows old Maximianus to have met Boethius when a young man, as well as matching various ambassadorial activity.

42 *Cantantem Maximianus amat.*

43 Öberg (1999) at 41–2 makes some suggestions as to his identity, but these are not authors.

44 In Late Antiquity the word *regnum* does not imply a *rex*, though in the West Gothic kings had replaced Roman emperors.

45 Shanzer (1983).

Arguments for a much later date have been advanced by Ratkowitsch,[46] who places the work in the ninth century, shortly before the date of a manuscript that contains a few lines from the work, wrongly attributed to Eugenius.[47] Her arguments from the intertextuality and metrical practice cannot be discussed here; suffice it to say that they have been either accepted en bloc and uncritically, or analysed and rejected. On one item of background detail – the *tristissima mater* guarding her daughter at 3.17, claimed by Ratkowitsch as certainly medieval – there has been spirited discussion by reviewers and reviewed.[48] Ratkowitsch has also suggested a novel explanation of the work's purpose: it was written with an apotreptic aim, to warn young monks of the dangers of sex. Maximianus' regrets carry an obvious lesson. But it is hard to think that a work which includes such matters as the classification of female physiognomies (1.75–100), a joke about their 'middle' (that is, genital) parts – a bawdy joke triggered by mention of the Aristotelian mean – at 1.81–4, the use of money to procure a girl's availability (3.63–74), and the importance, physically and emotionally, of the erect penis (5.49–80, 109–116), whose personal and indeed cosmic functions are extolled at some length, can seriously be meant as a deterrent. No amount of Ovid *ethicus* (as Ratkowitsch terms the letters from exile, which are often used) can neutralize the erotic elements; nor can allegory be invoked to cover them. It is totally misleading to dismiss, as Ratkowitsch did, the strong presence of love elegy – this will be exemplified below – and privilege the occasional verbal echoes of Christian Latin poets. *Enterotisierung* is just not possible. Rather than put anyone off a life of sexual activity, the work would surely have the opposite effect, arousing titters or mock-horror from the young, while their elders, whose attitude to sex is well attested, would, if they read it, be spluttering with rage. Schneider's interpretation of the work as *Widerrede* ('protest') is nearer the mark, though for him it covers a far greater range in ideological terms, traced by a remarkably subtle treatment of allusive possibility.[49]

The experience of elegiac love – with hindsight

In the survey that now follows we will assume an anonymous sixth-century author who wrote a series of love elegies contributing to the purpose of mocking an unhappy old man, named Maximianus, who may or may not

[46] Ratkowitsch (1986). [47] This is Paris Bibl. Nat. Lat. 2832.

[48] In a long article Ratkowitsch (1990) replies to various reviews, including that of Shanzer (1988).

[49] An example of its subtlety is given in the review of Butrica (2005).

have been a real person. The first poem, as already stated, develops the age-old theme of the troubles of old age, which in his misery he thinks infinitely protracted. Death would be rest, but life is pain.[50] Once, as a young man, he was respected and honoured as a speaker, a poet, and a successful pleader in court. As he talks in traditional terms of his achievements – swimming in the Tiber, managing with little food and drink (except in bibulous company: here too he could excel) and his eligibility, the impression of boastfulness and fantasizing increases. Fathers throughout a whole province (Italy, presumably) wanted him as a son-in-law, but he wished to live with his neck free of the chains of marriage (61–2); not for him the *coniugii uincula* reminiscent of Tib. 2.2.18. If we read the next line of Tibullus, with the happy words *tarda senectus* ('a late old age'), there is a notable reversal: for Maximianus old age and its *tarda quies* (line 2, 'sluggish rest') is too long. Girls blushed (*uisa puella*, 'the girl who has been seen', also of a bride in Ovid, *Am.* 2.5.36) and played hard to get; but none was worthy of him, and he remained a bachelor. Though at this point seemingly content, his words in line 76 resemble, ironically, the curse of [Ovid] *frigidus in uiduo destituere toro* (*Am.* 3.5.42 'you will be deserted on your empty bed'). Maximianus disliked the thin, the fat, the short and the tall; what he wanted was a woman slender but not skinny, with a pale complexion suffused by a rosy blush (*suffusa rubore* as in Ovid, *Amores* 3.3.5); someone with long hair and a milk-white neck, dark eyebrows, an open face, and dark eyes (*lumina nigra* are Propertian, 2.12.23; 4.3.14), someone with red lips, big enough to give a good kiss . . . but why mention everything? With the line *singula turpe seni quondam quaesita referre* (101, 'it is disgraceful for an old man to tell of his various ambitions') he recalls Ovid's *singula quid referam?* (*Am.* 1.5.23, 'why mention details?') that closes the detailed description of Corinna, combining it with an echo of another famous poem, 1.9.4 *turpe senex miles, turpe senilis amor* (*Am.* 1.9.4, 'a senile soldier is repulsive, a senile love repulsive').

In these last fifty lines the presence of love elegy is very clear. They could be seen as a kind of inversion of *Amores* 2.4, where Ovid unashamedly admits that all kinds of women attract him; Maximianus disdained almost all kinds, but then does feel shame for constructing his identikit lady-love. Indeed, these lines may be seen as an embedded or inset elegy, one which because of its position in his life story is more firmly rooted than the elegies that follow. The dotard then turns to the other woes of old age: physical decay,

50 This may echo the claim of Paul *uiuere mihi Christus, mors autem lucrum* (Phil. 1.21, Vulgate): 'for me to live is Christ, but death is gain'. Biblical echoes in this work may have been underestimated, but they are rare.

a deathly pallor, the inability to enjoy natural pleasures, the uselessness of being rich, the lack of people to talk to (*o sola fortes garrulitate senes!* 'Oh dear, old men brave only in their readiness to talk!'), illness, sleeplessness, the ridicule of the young. These are commonplaces, and not linked to any particular source. Elements of the language of love elegy are not absent from the remainder of this poem, but relatively inconspicuous among the gamut of authors from Virgil to Boethius collected by Öberg.

The first of the four shorter elegies is introduced by a sudden *en* ('look!'), as if Maximianus is racking his memory or looking back over a long space of time. He tells how he enjoyed a long and close relationship with Lycoris (longer at least than that of Gallus with his Lycoris, to judge from Virgil's *Eclogues* 10), until, seeking other loves (*alios . . . amores*) – these words recall the woman of Tib. 1.6.35 – she rejects him, as unmanly (*imbellis*) and decrepit. But, he contends, with a hint of Virg. *Eclogues* 2.25, he is not so unattractive even now. The proof of this seems to lie in the next line, *en facio uersus et mea facta cano* ('look, I make verses and sing of my own undertakings'): writing love poetry is a sign of a vigorous poet-lover.[51] There is another echo of Virgil's second eclogue in 2.14 *nonne fuit melius* 'was it not better?' (Virgil had *satius*, and a less drastic solution to the pain of rejection), but in the poem as a whole there are various Ovidian touches: the favourite collocation *turpe putet* at line 18, the arguments, whether amusing or not, from animal behaviour (43–52), and the point about ageing soldiers and animals (59–62: compare *Amores* 2.9.19–20), as well as material from the *Ars Amatoria* and the exile poems, with which we are not concerned.

Elegy 3 concerns Aquilina – the reasons for this choice of name are not clear – but the main element of interest is the role of Boethius, *praeceptor amoris*. Captivated by her (the words *captus amore tuo* are repeated, as in an 'anacyclic' couplet), Maximianus cannot attain her. They did not exchange signs of love (some resemblance to *Ars* 3.514), but later (27) they found they had to meet, walking noiselessly in the Tibullan manner (1.2.20). Her mother discovered this *furtiuus amor* ('furtive love', cf. Tib.1.5.75) and gave her a beating; but, as Ovid knew (*Amores* 1.2.11), fires are encouraged by such things, and they continued to rage. (The wording *saeuit amore dolor* (34) is exactly that of Prop. 2.8.36, of Achilles). When consulted, Boethius read the signs (line 58 *conscia signa*, *Am.* 2.1.8 and 2.8.8) and advised him to go for it (63 *fac . . . ut placitae potiaris munere formae*; cf. Ovid. *Ars* 1.385 *fac domina potiare prius*). Maximianus pleads the claims of *pietas* over love, but Boethius just laughs; when was love chaste? Loves are fed by fingernails

[51] *Facta* is read by a minority of manuscripts; most have *dicta*, which, like the emendation *fata*, is not easy to understand.

and bites (as so often in elegy). Boethius arranges a deal with Aquilina's parents, who happily succumb to greed. But then accessibility spoils desire, an Ovidian theme (*Am.* 2.19.3–4, 3.4.9–10, with the word *languidiora*, used twice in the relevant couplet, 77–8). Maximianus learns an important lesson, but is not impressed by Boethius' flippant congratulations; they both depart *ingrati* ('unwanted') and *tristes* ('sad'), with a possible echo of Propertius 1.6.10.[52]

Poem 4 begins with a short introduction saying that he will tell of disgraceful events, but also amuse his readers' hearts with a soft love-story (*molli pascere corda ioco*). There was a maiden by the name of Candida, a musician and a dancing girl, with whom Maximianus fell in love. He sang her tunes, and the secret was out. Worse, on one occasion he called out to her in his sleep that night was departing and the daylight, enemy of secrecy (*furtis inimica*), returning; as it happened, her father was lying beside him on the grass, and realized what was afoot. Maximianus' love was dashed, and with it his reputation as a person of principle and *grauitas*. Misery and shame followed, aggravating the woes of *serior aetas* ('advanced old age', an Ovidian phrase, from *Am.* 2.4.45, the poem used in the first elegy; but, more to the point, from Tibullus' picture at 1.4.33–4 of an old man regretting his wasted opportunities). This is a simple story of disappointment, again reflecting poorly on our would-be lover's lack of *savoir faire*. We can well imagine what Ovid might have made of this situation, perhaps expressing it in a soliloquy, briefly relating his gaffe with touches of humour. ('Did I really? Oh yes, I remember imagining something white, a singing bird perhaps . . . Or were you dreaming?'). But since our author has structured his work as an old man's fictive autobiography, he is always looking back, in predominantly narrative mode; he describes the various women, and his involvement with them, at some length and narrates the sequels leaving little to the imagination. At the dénouement, or, if the term is apt, climax, he generally resorts to dialogue, to vary his stance as a plain reporter.

In the last piece, he is on an embassy to Constantinople, but makes war (for himself) rather than peace for his political masters, when aroused and as he says tricked by a *Graia puella*. Here, in *altera Roma*, we have an inverted *paraklausithyron*: the woman is outside, the man in his room; the one seeking entry is not a reveller, but a professional; with no door or doorman to cause delay, she enters easily. If the echo in line 9 of Propertius' words *nocte fenestras* (3.20.29) is not mere coincidence, then it not only supports the atmosphere of a *paraklausithyron* but also underlines the man's ill luck,

52 Since Aquilina has left the scene in line 80, she is unlikely to be one of the two, though the match with Propertius would be better if she were.

for the Propertian context is a curse: may the mistress' windows never open, he says, and *semper amet, fructu semper amoris egens.*[53] There could hardly be a better description of Maximianus. The girl, who is never given a name, is described, first (lines 10–17) with some minor Ovidian echoes, (cf. *Am.* 2.4.25, 1.4.15, 2.6.62), but then in more detail, with line 26 recalling Ovid's 2.4.41 and line 27 recalling Ovid's 1.4.37), and the whole once more resembling the picturing of Corinna at *Am.* 1.5. The first night goes well enough, but not the second. She complains of the unsustainability of the missionary position,[54] with a vigour that brings on detumescence and panic, described with fine irony in the epicism *derigui* ('I went stiff', usually of fear). At line 50 ... *segnis ut ante fui* ('I was sluggish, as before') comes a notable echo of Ovid's poem on impotence, *nec uir, ut ante, fui* (*Am.* 3.7.60, 'and I was not a man, as before'). A dialogue, anxious and impassioned, begins, in which at line 51 she makes a reference to Paul, 1 Corinthians 7.3 *uxori uir debitum reddat* ('a man must give his wife what he owes her': Constantinopolitans knew their theology); she goes on to ask (like Tibullus' deputy date in 1.5.41–4) whose company has he been keeping. When nothing is achieved by digital solutions (81–4), she launches into a tirade against his *mentula*, including a ringing challenge from Lucan, *quo tibi feruor abit* (7.5: Cicero haranguing Pompey). But Maximianus confesses defeat, yielding up his useless *arma* ('[erotic] tools', 'weapons'). In her second grand speech, one of almost fifty lines, she laments not her own loss but that of the universal chaos that is threatened, and moves into a hymnic style. Two striking appropriations of Ovid contribute to a fitting climax. The first (line 130) takes line 20 of *Amores* 1.2 (on the triumph of Cupid) *porrigimus uictas ad tua iura manus* ('we stretch out our conquered hands to your laws'), mildly changing this to *porrigit inuictas ad tua iussa manus* ('she stretches out her unconquered hands to your commands') and applied to the *Sapientia* which rules the world,[55] the second (at line 144) echoes even more closely *excutere irato tela trisulca Ioui* (*Amores* 2.5.52 'shake the trident from furious Jove'), with *excutis irato tela trisulca Ioui* ('you shake the trident from furious Jove'), setting it in the aftermath of the war with the giants.[56] Here Ovid's tribute to Corinna's kisses is taken one step further in this serio-comic, bittersweet monologue – which leaves the Greek girl satisfied but makes Maximianus feel that he had witnessed his own funeral (compare *Amores* 3.7.16).

[53] 'May he be forever in love, forever deprived of the enjoyment of love'.
[54] There is here (line 34) a clear echo of Horace *Odes* 2.5.4 *tolerare pondus*.
[55] '... stretches its invincible (*inuictas*) hands to you, to do your commands'.
[56] 'You shake his three-forked thunderbolts from angry Jove'.

This is a remarkable poem, and its reception is marked by two remarkable developments. First, at some time in the early Middle Ages, it became one of the *octo auctores*, the standard collection of elementary Latin texts. The questions of how or why this happened deserve further investigation, but it was widely read, and even perhaps reached Chaucer in this way.[57] Secondly, as already mentioned, it was identified early in the age of printing with the lost work of the love-elegist Gallus, a notion which tralatitious editions disseminated for at least two hundred years.[58]

Further reading

There are attractive English translations of some of the love poems mentioned at the beginning of this article in H. Isbell (1971), but no translation into modern English of 'Maximianus'' work. There is a fine study of the age of 'Maximianus' in A.D. Momigliano, (1960: 191–229 = 1955: 207–45), and several of Boethius, most recently *The Cambridge Companion to Boethius* (ed. J. Marenbon 2009). The supposed anniversary of the great man's birth produced Chadwick (1981) and M. Gibson (ed.) (1981). There is a conjectural reconstruction of the milieu of 'Maximianus' by Barnish (1990) 16–32.

57 Schneider (2003) 151–5. 58 Szöverffy, (1968) 353 and n. 13.

17

MAREK THUE KRETSCHMER

The love elegy in medieval Latin literature (pseudo-Ovidiana and Ovidian imitations)

. . . [sint] in Turonica emissiones paradisi cum pomorum fructibus, ut ueniens Auster perflaret hortos Ligeri fluminis et fluant aromata illius . . .

. . . may branches of paradise shoot forth and yield fruit in Tours, so that the arriving south wind may blow through the gardens of the Loire and spread its spices . . . [1]

Aetas Ouidiana

When it comes to love poetry in Medieval Latin literature, we have neither a canon nor a clear-cut definition of the genre that corresponds to Roman love elegy. Firstly, Medieval love poetry was not necessarily composed in the elegiac metre.[2] Secondly, up to about the year 1000, elegy was first and foremost associated with its original tradition as a song of lament.[3] Isidore of Seville († 636) gives the following etymologically founded definition: 'the elegiac metre is thus called because the beat of this particular poem goes well with miserable subjects'.[4] It is significant that modern scholars place medieval love poetry under the general term of lyric poetry.[5]

A century ago, Ludwig Traube, who held the first chair of Medieval Latin in Germany, invented the terms *Aetas Virgiliana* (eighth and ninth centuries), *Aetas Horatiana* (tenth and eleventh centuries) and *Aetas Ouidiana* (twelfth and thirteenth centuries), to describe thus the different periods of medieval poetry inspired by the Roman *auctores*.[6] The works of Ovid were continuously and zealously copied, studied and imitated during that era,

[1] Alcuin, letter 43 to Charlemagne; *PL* 100, col. 208. All translations are mine.

[2] Brinkmann (1979) *passim*.

[3] Beissner (1965) 24–45.

[4] *Etymologiae* 1.39.14: *Elegiacus autem dictus eo, quod modulatio eiusdem carminis conueniat miseris* Lindsay (1911) 78.

[5] Cf. Dronke (1968) 229–31; Mantello and Rigg (1996) 589–96; and Szövérffy (1992–5) II 385–90.

[6] Traube (1911) 113.

whereas the poems of Propertius and Tibullus were, with very few exceptions, unknown to the medieval men – and occasional women – of letters. However, this Ovidian literary activity was a local phenomenon limited to northern and central France and especially to the Loire Valley.[7] The cathedral school of Orléans[8] was the most important centre for the revival of Ovid and other Roman classics. In the heyday of the so-called Twelfth-Century Renaissance,[9] one of the Orléans teachers, Matthew of Vendôme, redefined elegy as the literary genre of love poetry. In his *Ars uersificatoria* (*ca.*1170), a guide to poetics, he opens the second book with a personification of the different forms of poetry. Inspired by Ovid, Boethius and Martianus Capella, he describes his nightly vision of a vernal appearance of Lady Philosophy accompanied by the four maidens Tragedy, Satire, Comedy and

Quarta pharetratos Elegia cantat amores (cf. *Rem. am.* 379)

> fauorali supercilio, oculo quasi uocatiuo, fronte expositiva petulantiae, cuius labella prodiga saporis ad oscula uidentur suspirare; quae ultima procedens non ex indignitate, sed potius ex inaequalitate pedum: tamen in effectu iocunditatis staturae claudicantis uindicat detrimentum, iuxta illud Ouidii:
>
> In pedibus uitium causa decoris erit[10] (cf. *Am.* 3.1.10).
>
> A fourth, Elegy, 'sings of quiver-bearing cupids'. She has dainty brows, seductive eyes and a wanton look. Her succulent lips seem to sigh for kisses. She comes forth last, not because of unworthiness, but rather because of her uneven feet. Yet, the effect of her enchanting stature compensates for the defect of limping, according to the following line from Ovid: 'A defect in the gait is what causes the grace'.

Thus the Medieval Latin love elegy is a literary phenomenon pertaining to the Ovidian Age, that is, to north-central France of the twelfth and thirteenth centuries. Now, the term *Aetas Ouidiana* may be well known, but the student who wants to explore its contents, the Ovidian literature, faces a confusing puzzle of desperately scattered bits and pieces. The aim of this chapter is therefore to present an overview of the chief Medieval Latin poets and poems inspired by Ovid, though such an overview must necessarily be a simplification. We have chosen to concentrate here on Ovidian imitations and the so-called pseudo-Ovidiana.[11] By Ovidian imitation we mean a poem

7 Moser (2004) 17–65. 8 Cf. Moser (2004) 157 and Rouse (1979).

9 Cf. Haskins (1927) and Melve (2006). 10 Faral (1924a) 153.

11 Lehmann (1927a). Lenz published a series of articles in the 50s and 60s on single pseudo-Ovidian titles. One article is a general comment: Lenz (1959a). A new pseudo-Ovidian project was recently announced in *Mittellateinisches Jahrbuch*: Klein (2006).

where the author consciously and more or less consistently imitates Ovidian lines, themes or topics, while the term pseudo-Ovidiana denotes poems ascribed to Ovid in at least one manuscript. Both categories include poems in hexameters, and when relevant we will include such poems in the following discussion, but our focus will be on elegiac poetry.

Pseudo-Ovidiana

Elegiac comedy

Many pseudo-Ovidian poems are short satirical tales or fables containing moral or political criticism. Invectives against clerics, monks, rulers, teachers and so forth hide behind titles such as *De lupo*,[12] *De pediculo*,[13] *De uentre*[14] and so forth, where the Ovidian mask and thematical concealment protect the author against open conflicts.[15] This was hardly the case for the pseudo-Ovidian love poems. With the name of elegiac comedy[16] we designate some twenty dramatic tales written in elegiac distichs, many of them composed by men of letters from the Loire Valley in the twelfth century.[17] The dramatic or narrative element varies greatly from piece to piece – though some are pure narrative and others are pure drama, most mix narrative lines with dialogues and monologues – and scholars[18] have long debated whether the comedies are to be considered as actual plays or not. The controversies regarding the problematic nature of the genre need not concern us here. Of interest, however, is that the plot often involves an amorous intrigue and that the themes, language, style and metrical techniques are clearly Ovidian.[19] What is more, some of the anonymous comedies are attributed to Ovid in the manuscripts and belong thus to the group of pseudo-Ovidiana: *Ouidius*

[12] Lenz (1963). [13] Lenz (1955). [14] Lenz (1959b).

[15] Thus Lenz objected to Lehmann's interpretation (Lehmann 1927a), according to which many pseudo-Ovidiana are simply innocent pieces of humour. Cf. Lenz (1959a) 179.

[16] Bertini (1993) 217–30; Manitius (1931) 1015–40; and Raby (1934) II 54–69.

[17] *Geta* and *Aulularia* by Vitalis of Blois, *Alda* by William of Blois, *Milo* by Matthew of Vendôme, *Lydia* and *Miles gloriosus* by Arnulf of Orléans, *De clericis et rustico* by Hugo Cancellarius, *De tribus sociis* by Geoffrey of Vinsauf, *De uxore cerdonis* by Jacob of Benevento, *De Paulino et Polla* by Richard of Venosa and the anonymous *Babio*, *Baucis et Traso*, *Pamphilus Gliscerium et Birria*, *De nuncio sagaci*, *Pamphilus*, *De tribus puellis*, *De mercatore*, *De Lombardo et lumaca*, *Asinarius*, *Rapularius*, and *De more medicorum*. Cf. Bertini et al. (1976–98), and Cohen et al. (1931). Cohen's edition does not contain the following: *De lombardo et lumaca*, *Asinarius*, *Rapularius*, *De more medicorum*, *De uxore cerdonis* and *De Paulino et Polla*. Some comedies are also edited separately: Becker (1972) and Lieberz (1980).

[18] Cf. among others Bate (1979), Dronke (1973), Faral (1924b), Hagendahl (1939), Roy (1974) and Vinay (1952).

[19] For an excellent overview, see Goullet (1998).

puellarum or *De nuncio sagaci*, *Pamphilus de amore*, *De tribus puellis*, and *De Lombardo et lumaca*.[20]

The comedies of seduction *De nuncio sagaci* and *Pamphilus* both relate how a young man, afflicted by the darts of Love, begs the gods for help, and by the sly stratagem of a go-between manages to seduce a girl. The similarities of plot are striking, with one example being the act of seduction. In both cases the go-between facilitates the seduction by suddenly disappearing after having brought the unwitting girl together with the young man to a spot suitable for defloration. After the involuntary liaison, the go-between reappears and plays innocent: 'Why do you cry? What has happened?' etc. Compare how the two go-betweens interrogate the girl upon reappearing:

> Cur oculos tergis? dic que sit causa doloris.
> Lesit te quisquam? mox accipiet sibi penam!
> (206–7)

> Why do you wipe away tears? Tell me what caused the affliction. Has someone hurt you? He will soon be punished!

> Cur, Galathea, tuo corrumpis lumina fletu,
> Quem michi demonstras, hic dolor unde uenit?
> Absens donec eram, quid tecum Pamphilus egit?
> (725–7)

> Why, Galathea, do you spoil your eyes with weeping? What causes this sorrow that you reveal to me? While I was absent, what did Pamphilus do to you?

In fact, thorough analyses[21] indicate that *Pamphilus* was modelled on *De nuncio sagaci*.

Even if the internal evidence and the incompleteness of *De nuncio sagaci* – it breaks off after 375 lines, compared with the 780 lines of the full-length *Pamphilus* – do not allow a definitive answer, *Pamphilus* reads as a later, expanded variation. However, the two comedies differ when it comes to form. As the few lines above show, *De nuncio sagaci* is composed in hexameters with monosyllabic leonine rhyme or assonance (between the penthemimeral caesura and the line-end) instead of the conventional elegiac distichs. The entire piece is told by a narrator in the first person, and the

[20] *De Lombardo et lumaca* has thematically more in common with the above-mentioned satirical fables and has been interpreted as a political satire on Emperor Frederick Barbarossa's warfare in Lombardy (Lenz) or more generally as a satire on Lombard cowardice (Novati). Cf. Lenz (1957) and Novati (1905). The latest editor, Magda Bonacina, follows Novati's explication. Cf. Bertini et al. (1976–98), IV 95–135.

[21] Blumenthal (1976), Creizenach (1911–16), Jahnke (1891), Lehmann (1927b), Morawski (1917) and Pittaluga (1979).

plot develops with alternating sections of narrative lines and lines of dialogue and monologue, whereas the 390 distichs of *Pamphilus* consist solely of dialogue and monologue, except for one single narrative hemistich.[22]

De nuncio sagaci (*ca.*1080) and *Pamphilus* (*ca.*1100) are the earliest extant elegiac comedies, and both the Loire Valley and south-west Germany (Tegernsee) have been suggested as their geographical origin.[23] It is worth mentioning that *Pamphilus* is extant in some sixty manuscripts, and just as many florilegia and incunabula, together with several vernacular translations and paraphrases.[24] That the title survives today in the word pamphlet is also a sign of its former popularity.

De tribus puellis is a somewhat later pseudo-Ovidian comedy of 150 distichs. It is a most charming pastiche on the story of the judgement of Paris, in which Paris is replaced by the poet-narrator, who meets three maidens. These dispute about who is the best singer. A song contest is arranged, and the poet chooses the winner, who remunerates him with an unforgettable night.

Of the elegiac comedies, *De tribus puellis* is clearly the most Ovidian. Nearly every other line contains an echo, reminiscence or citation from Ovid.[25] The final love scene may serve as a good example. The young lady, clearly resembling the naked Corinna of Amores 1.5, undresses before the delighted poet:

> Se facit hec nudam, uoluit quoque nuda uideri,
> At non in tenera carne fuit macula.
> . . .
> Hach! quales humeros et qualia brachia uidi;
> Candida crura nimis non ualuere minus.
> Parua papilla fuit, fuit apta, fuit speciosa,
> Si paulo rigida, non minus apta fuit.
> Pectus erat planum, planus sub pectore uenter,
> Formabat medium corpus utrumque latus.
> Non referam, quamuis poteram meliora referre
> Illam cum uidi, sed tibi non referam.
> (249–50, 255–62)

She stripped herself naked, and naked she wanted to be seen. There was not a flaw on her tender body. (. . .). Ah! What shoulders and what arms I saw.

22 Line 71: *Tunc Venus hec inquit . . .* 23 Dronke (1979).

24 Thirteenth-century translations in old Venetian and old Norse: editions by Tobler (1885–6), and Holm Olsen (1940). Fourteenth-century paraphrases in old French and Spanish by Jean Bras-de-Fer and Juan Ruiz: editions by Morawski (1917) and Gybbon-Monypenny (1988). See also Becker (1972) 132–3; and Manitius (1931) 1034.

25 Pittaluga (1976–7).

> The dazzling legs were no less impressive. The breasts were small, shapely and beautiful, and even if quite firm, no less shapely. The bosom was smooth, and smooth was the belly beneath. The sides formed perfect curves. I will not reveal the best part, although I could. For I saw it, but reveal it to you I will not.

Didactic love poetry (and prose) and *Streitgedichte*

Among the many Ovidian themes that appear in the pseudo-Ovidiana, we will here focus on a key topic, namely the influence of didactic love poetry. When for example Pamphilus applies to Venus for help, she assists him with a series of *praecepta amoris*, and her reply (lines 71–142)[26] takes the shape of an *Ars amatoria* in miniature. Moreover, the eroto-didactic element had an impact not only on the elegiac comedies, but also on love poetry in general. In a series of articles[27] Erich Joseph Thiel published what he believed to be the first critical edition of two elegiac poems ascribed to Ovid in many of the twenty-five extant manuscripts, of which twenty-four belong to the fifteenth and sixteenth centuries. The first poem is a *pseudo-Ars amatoria* in ninety-five distichs of free paraphrase on Ovid's *praecepta* (how to find the right girl, how to conquer her etc.), while the second is a *pseudo-Remedia amoris* in 32 distichs. The latter is thematically even more remote from the Ovidian model: the short treatise, beginning *qui fuerit cupiens ab amica soluere colla* ('he who wishes to escape the embrace of his lady') teaches the lover to find flaws and faults in every woman. The female is described according to which temperament she belongs to – the choleric, melancholic, phlegmatic or sanguine – and the poem is thus little more than a misogynistic, quasi-medical catalogue. In fact, these two pseudo-Ovidian didactic love poems are parts of the so-called *Facetus*,[28] composed by a certain Aurigena. Peter Dronke dates it to the 1130s or 1140s, and envisages south-west Germany as a likely provenance.[29] This poem gives advice on conduct to the clergy and the laity, with sections on lovers (131–384),[30] friends (385–438), physicians (455–66), soldiers (467–88), and old age (489–510).

In a satirical mode the topic of clerical versus knightly love was reflected in the well-known *Concilium Romarici Montis* (*ca.*1150),[31] the 'Love

[26] Blumenthal has pointed out how closely this part follows Ovid both in structure and contents. Cf. Blumenthal (1976) 236–44.

[27] Thiel (1968), (1970) and (1973).

[28] Edition by Morel-Fatio (1886).

[29] Dronke (1979). Interestingly, in the same article Dronke points out certain verbal parallels between *Facetus* and *Pamphilus*, and on this basis assumes that they are directly related. See also Dronke (1976).

[30] Lines 131–320 = Pseudo-*Ars amatoria*; lines 321–384 = Pseudo-*Remedia amoris*.

[31] First edited by Waitz (1849). Later editions by Lee (1981) and Meyer (1915); and text with commentary in Pascal (1993). See also Dronke (1968) 229–31; Faral (1913),

Council of Remiremont', a parody on a church council. The nuns of Remiremont in the diocese of Toul (Lorraine) are united to discuss matters of love, and the 'gospel of Ovid', that is the *Ars amatoria*, is being read:

In eo concilio de solo negocio
amoris tractatum est, quod in nullo factum est;
sed de euangelio nulla fuit mencio. (7–9)
...
Intromissis omnibus uirginum agminibus
lecta sunt in medium quasi euangelium
praecepta Ouidii, doctoris egregii. (25–7)

The only issue discussed in this council was love, an unprecedented matter. There was, however, no mention of the gospel... But after the rows of maidens were let in, the precepts of Ovid, the distinguished instructor, were read as a gospel in their midst.

The proceedings here are led by a *cardinalis domina*, and the god of love himself has ordered her to inquire into the love life of the nuns. In short, the majority fancy clerical love, a final decree demands the excommunication of those who favour knightly love, and the poems thus ends with an *excommunicatio rebellarum* (lines 215–40).

A far less known example is the pseudo-Ovidian poem entitled by its first editor *De distributione mulierum*.[32] The twenty-two distichs contain a satirical story not very different from the *Concilium:* by turns, clergymen, laymen (merchants and soldiers) and finally monks enter a pagan temple in Rome. Each member hopes to obtain a *pulchra puella* from Venus, the goddess of the temple, but only the clergymen have their wish granted.

It is against this literary background that we must view the famous Ovid-inspired prose treatise *De amore* (*ca.*1180),[33] which Andreas Capellanus wrote to a certain Walter, a helpless victim of love, in order to teach him how love is conquered, maintained and resisted (books 1–3, respectively). A central theme in *De amore* is a long series of model wooing-dialogues which instruct Walter in how to engage in amorous conversation with members of the same or different social classes.

210–17; Lehmann (1963); Raby (1934) II 294–6; Szövérffy (1992–5), II 385–90; Walther (1920) 145–7; and Warren (1907).

32 Lehmann (1927a) 88–9. Later editions and commentaries by Hinz (2006) and Lenz (1959c). In the only extant manuscript, the fourteenth-century Vatican lat. 1602, the poem, on f. 49rv, refers to *puellae*; hence, *De distributione puellarum* would perhaps be a better title.

33 Edition by Trojel (1892). Dronke suggests that *De amore* is a product of the Parisian university milieu of the 1230s rather than of the Parisian court of the 1180s. Cf. Dronke (1994).

Andreas probably drew on both elegiac comedy and didactic love poetry for his guidelines to amorous conversation. With numerous dialogues illustrating the amorous procedures, the elegiac comedies were literary repertories for approaching and seducing a woman. Also the *Facetus* included advice on amorous conversation (205–54), and Peter Dronke has convincingly argued that the *Facetus* served as a source for Andreas.[34] In both *Facetus* and *De amore*, the narrative goes directly from *ars* (*Facetus* 131–320/*De amore* 1–2) to *remedia* (*Facetus* 321–84/*De amore* 3), and both poems warn against seeking love among nuns or prostitutes (*Facetus* 133–40/*De amore* 1.8 and 1.12).

What is more, Andreas may have combined these readings with another source of inspiration: a sort of *Streitgedicht* where knightly and clerical love is contested, such as the above-mentioned *Concilium Romarici Montis*.[35] In his last dialogue for wooers, for instance, Andreas gives voice to members of the higher nobility:

> . . . ineuitabili uobis necessitate probabo, quod magis in amore clericus quam laicus est eligendus. Clericus enim in cunctis cautior et prudentior quam laicus inuenitur et maiori moderamine se suaque disponit et competentiori mensura solitus est omnia moderari, et quia clericus omnium rerum scientiae habet scriptura referente peritiam. Unde potior ipsius quam laici amor est iudicandus, quia nil in mundo tam necessarium inuenitur, quam omnium industria rerum amorosum esse peritum.

> With infallible reasoning I will prove to you that the cleric should be preferred in love to the layman. In everything the cleric is found to be more cautious and experienced than the layman. He organizes his life with greater control and he is used to manage everything with finer judgement. Since he is a cleric he attains knowledge of everything from scripture. Hence, his love should be judged to be better than the layman's, because nothing in the world is found to be more fundamental than that the lover must be experienced in all things.

Autobiography

During the Ovidian centuries, Richard de Fournival (1210–60), bibliophile and chancellor of the cathedral of Amiens, was supposedly one of many

34 Dronke (1976).

35 Other *Streitgedichte* from the same period are poems such as the *Altercatio Phillidis et Florae*. The date of *De distributione mulierum* is uncertain, and the poem may well be later than *De amore*. Cf. Raby (1934) II 290–7. See also Lee (1981) 137–40; and Vinay (1951).

who wrote a poem under the false name of Ovid. *De uetula*,[36] possibly to be counted among Richard's works, consists of 2,400 hexameters divided into three books. In some manuscripts a preface in prose explains that the poem was discovered in Ovid's tomb in the kingdom of Colchis and sent to the Byzantine Emperor who had Ovid's alleged swan song published by a certain Leo, an imperial secretary skilled in Latin. The poem opens in book one with a long description of Ovid's superficial life as a happy playboy addicted to love and pleasure. Book two includes the unhappy tale of how Ovid falls in love with a girl and seeks out her old nurse, hoping thus that this go-between will lead him to his object of desire. When the promised night comes, Ovid, deceived, finds himself in bed with the old woman instead of the girl, who shortly afterwards marries another man. Twenty years later, he meets the now widowed old flame again and finally wins her love, but depressed by age, eventually decides to renounce erotic adventures and embrace a life of philosophical and religious contemplation. Book three is a display of both ancient and medieval lore[37] and ends with the poet-philosopher Ovid relating various prophecies on Christ and offering a prayer to the Virgin, mother of God. In other words, this is Ovid's own *metamorphosis*, a sort of memoir narrating the moral journey from *ars amatoria* to *remedia amoris*, and the transformation of *Ouidius praeceptor amoris* into *Ouidius ethicus* and *Ouidius christianus*. The poem, extant in some forty manuscripts, was apparently a fair success and was translated into old French in the fourteenth century by Jean Le Fèvre.[38]

The forgery is by no means typical. *De uetula* by far exceeds the length of the other pseudo-Ovidian poems, and with respect to contents and genre the reader may easily feel himself to be in a literary no-man's land. Formally an epic, the poem, written in a satirical tenor, offers an autobiographical narrative, where the characters involved are the typical dramatis personae of comedy: the young man (Ovid), the aristocratic love interest and the go-between (the hag). Towards the end, however, the satirical/comical autobiography becomes a didactic epic, and the poem thus reveals its true nature. Paul Klopsch[39] has fittingly placed *De uetula* among the allegorical poems in vogue in the second half of the twelfth century, namely Bernard Silvester's *prosimetrum Cosmographia*[40] (*ca.*1150) and the epics of Alan of Lille and

[36] Klopsch (1967) and Robathan (1968). See Klopsch (1967) 15–159 for an excellent analysis of the poem.

[37] See the notes to book 3 in Robathan (1968) 155–63.

[38] Cochéris (1861).

[39] Klopsch (1967) 152–9.

[40] Dronke (1978).

John of Hauteville, respectively the Anticlaudianus[41] and Architrenius (both *ca.*1185).[42]

Ovidian imitations

Deidamia Achilli *('Medieval* Heroides' *1)*

Perhaps the finest product of the Ovidian age is the poetical epistle or epistolary poem, developed by the Loire poets[43] around the turn of the eleventh to the twelfth century. The anonymous eleventh-century *Deidamia Achilli*,[44] an early (*ca.*1070) example of a medieval *Heroides*, is a poem of sixty-five distichs (with monosyllabic leonine rhyme) representing Deidamia's letter lamenting the absence and infidelity of Achilles. The story of how Thetis, in order to prevent her son Achilles' participation in the Trojan war, disguised him as a girl and concealed him among the daughters of King Lycomedes, was well-known in the Middle Ages through the highly respected Statius and his Achilleid. Statius' epic contains the account of Achilles' union with Deidamia, the fair daughter of Lycomedes, and of their inevitable parting once Achilles was tracked down by Odysseus and Diomedes. *Deidamia Achilli* is both a continuation of the *Achilleid* and a pendant to *Heroides* 3 (*Briseis Achilli*).[45] The *Achilleid* remains incomplete[46] shortly after Deidamia's last words to her beloved (1.931–955), with her final plea (1.952–955) being that Achilles remember their son and remain faithful, to which Achilles swears to comply and also promises to bring presents on his return (1.957–60). This becomes, then, the object of reproach in *Deidamia Achilli*: unmindful of both her and their son, he never came back. The main points may be presented as follows:

41 Bossuat (1955). 42 Schmidt (1974).

43 Baudri of Bourgueil (1046–1130), Marbod of Rennes (1035–1123) and Hildebert of Lavardin (1055–1133) often appear under the now contested term 'the Loire School' or 'the Loire Circle'; see for instance Tilliette (1998–2002), I xxxiv, and Szövérffy (1992–5) II 106 ff. Godfrey of Reims († 1095) is also associated with the Loire poets, although he, geographically speaking, belonged in the province of Champagne. We are thus speaking of a poetical relationship. All four wrote love poems towards the end of the eleventh century. My presentation of this poetry is thematic rather than strictly chronological.

44 Edited with excellent commentary by Stohlmann (1973).

45 Stohlmann's admirable apparatus of Ovidian echoes is an indispensable tool for spotting the constant allusions. For Briseis' letter to Achilles (Ov. *Her.* 3), see Drinkwater (Chapter 12) in this volume.

46 Book 2 of the *Achilleid* contains little more than Achilles' departure from Scyros with Odysseus and Diomedes.

Dixisti . . .
Tempus erit, cum me spectabis laeta redire,
    Troica cum niueos praeda sequetur equos
Cumque peregrinae uenient tibi munera gazae . . .
(19–21)[47]

You said . . . there will be a time when you will rejoice at the sight of my return, when snowy horses will drag booty from Troy, and when foreign treasures will be your presents.

Uxor abesse meum quotiens queror aegra maritum,
    Condolet absentem natus abesse patrem . . .
(41–2)

In endless suffering I, your wife, weep over my absent husband, and the child laments the absence of a missing father.

Rumor sollicitam Licomedis uenit in aulam
    Te dominum seruae succubuisse tuae . . .
(65–6)[48]

A rumour stirs the palace of Lycomedes: that you, the master, have fallen for your slave girl.

Non ita iurabas, dum me uiolenter amabas –
    Et satis ex aequo tunc redamabar ego –:
'Per tibi te iuro, soli michi iungere, quaeso;
    Iungar ego soli, Deidamia, tibi!'?
(73–6)

Was this your oath when you loved me with passion, a time when you responded to my feelings with equal affection: 'By you to you I swear that I will be the only one for you, and I beg you, Deidamia, please be the only one for me!'?

Next, Deidamia prays to Venus for revenge, recapitulates her accusations and eventually begs Achilles to come back.

[47] The allusion to Achilles' oath at *Achilleid* 1.957–60 is evident:

talia dicentem non ipse immotus Achilles
solatur iuratque fidem iurataque fletu
spondet et ingentes famulas captumque reuersus
Ilion et Phrygiae promittit munera gazae.

As she utters these words, Achilles, himself not unmoved, consoles her, and he swears fidelity and binds himself to his vow with tears, promising to return from conquered Troy with stout handmaidens and gifts of Phrygian treasure.

[48] These lines allude to *Heroides* 9.2–3 (*Deianira Herculi*). Cf. Stohlmann (1973) 227.

Heroides 3 functions as an antithetical reference, and one of the main themes of the intertextual relation consists of the antagonism between *uxor/nupta* (wife/bride, Deidamia) and *amica* (girlfriend, Briseis). A single example will have to suffice. In the opening of her letter, Briseis flirts with Achilles by addressing him in a way that challenges the non-marital status of their relationship:

> Si mihi pauca queri de te dominoque uiroque
> fas est, de domino pauca uiroque querar.
> (*Her.* 3.5–6)

If I am allowed to utter a few words of complaint against you, my lord and man, a few words of complaint against my lord and man I will utter.

Deidamia opens her letter reversing the game and ironically questions if a legitimate wife also can be a lover to her husband:

> Legitimam nuptam si dici fas sit amicam,
> haec tibi casta suo mittit amica uiro.
> (1–2)

If a legitimate spouse rightly can be called a lover, your chaste lover sends these words to her man.

In addition, the opposition between *dominus/uictor* (master/victor, Achilles) and *serua/captiua* (slave/captive, Briseis) also implies an underlying irony. The attributions agree with the reality on the battlefield, but in the field of love[49] Achilles and Briseis change roles: he becomes the *captiuus* and she the *domina*.[50] The continuation of the rumour from lines 65–66 above illustrates this:

> ... et post barbaricos raptos ex hoste triumphos
> victus ab ancilla diceris esse tua.
> Seruula Briseis titulos incrustat Achillis
> Victoremque Frigum uincit amica uirum;
> (67–70)
> ...
> Tu nunc captiua frueris plus captus amica. (81)

... and that you, after having vanquished in triumph the barbarian enemy, are said to be conquered by your slave girl. Briseis, the little slave, defiles the glory of Achilles, and a concubine gains victory over the man who gained victory over the Phrygians; ... You now enjoy your captive girl, more captured than her.

49 See Drinkwater (Chapter 12) for further reflections on the erotic-elegiac trope *militia amoris*.

50 See Fulkerson (Chapter 11) for the erotic-elegiac trope *seruitium amoris*.

Baudri of Bourgueil ('Medieval Heroides' *2)*

Even if we cannot identify the author of *Deidamia Achilli*, there is no reason to doubt that he was a precursor of the Ovidian revival associated with the Loire Valley at the turn of the twelfth century.[51] Baudri of Bourgueil, perhaps inspired by poems such as Deidamia's letter,[52] brought the sprout of Ovidian epistles to full flower. At some point during the 1080s, Baudri became abbot of the Benedictine monastery Saint-Pierre of Bourgueil, midway between Angers and Tours (where he remained until 1107, when he was nominated archbishop of Dol-de-Bretagne). Baudri's poetry dates from his abbacy. His 256 poems, for the most part epitaphs and epistolary poems in hexameters or elegiac distichs, are preserved in only one manuscript, the Vatican reg. lat. 1351, Baudri's authorized copy,[53] and the *editio princeps* came as late as in 1926.[54] Among the epistles we find poems 7–8,[55] which are Baudri's imitation of Heroides 16–17 (the billets-doux of Paris and Helen), and poems 200–1,[56] a sort of contemporary double *Heroides*, that is, the correspondence between Baudri and his domina, a nun named Constance. (Baudri also invented a third pair of epistolary poems, 97–8,[57] modelled on the *Ex Ponto*, in which he imagined an exchange of letters between a fictitious Florus and Ovid in exile.)

The message from Baudri's Paris does not differ from that of his Ovidian counterpart – 'Leave Mycenae and Menelaus and be my queen in Troy!' – but if Ovid's letter is all about Paris' burning passion, Baudri, instead, develops a play of antagonism between Troy and Greece. On the surface, the condemnation of Greece and praise of Troy (7.95–227)[58] are meant to encourage Helen, but at the same time, Baudri elaborates a playfully allusive association of ancient Troy with present-day Loire that blurs the borders between persona and poet and between the poem and the real world. For instance, when describing the Trojan *locus amoenus*, Paris compares the vines of Troy with those of Orléans (with the witty remark that they refreshed the belligerent King Henry I), and the Trojan rivers Simois and Xanthus with the Loire and the local stream Cambio, which sprinkles the

[51] Stohlmann (1973) 216–17.
[52] Stohlmann (1973) 216–17, note 63. [53] Tilliette (1983).
[54] The mediocre edition of Abrahams (1926) has been replaced by Hilbert (1979) and Tilliette (1998–2002), from which I quote in the following.
[55] Cf. Albrecht (1982), Bond (1987 and 1995), Kretschmer (2011), Ratkowitsch (1991), and Tilliette (1994).
[56] Cf. Bond (1987); Dronke (1984) 84–91; Offermanns (1970) 106–11; and Tilliette (1992).
[57] Cf. Offermanns (1970) 94–7; Ratkowitsch (1987); and Schülper (1979).
[58] For considerations of space the Baudrian and Ovidian lines are not quoted. The poems are discussed more extensively in Kretschmer (2011).

gardens of Bourgueil (7.188–209). What is more, Baudri, always in the mood for another joke, concludes his poem with an allusion to *Amores* 2.15 (7.279–300), namely by expressing his wish to become his own letter, the parchment which Helen will keep under her breast.

Helen's reply, poem 8, is a long series of moral and religious arguments (8.1–319), but in the end (8.320–370) she yields and gives Paris precise instructions on how to conquer her: 'Come to Greece with three ships, disguised as a merchant. When I enter your ship to inspect your merchandise, pull the oars!'

Baudri wrote his version of *Heroides* 16–17 in hexameters, probably to give them an epic touch, but for his modernization of the double *Heroides* he chose the traditional elegiac metre; in fact, poems 200 and 201 are of identical length, each consisting of 89 elegiac distichs.

Poem 200 is a sort of *Kontrastimitation*[59] of the Ovidian genre of *Heroides*. Like Paris, Baudri writes to his *domina*, and Baudri too, condemns the Greek, but not in order to seduce his *domina*. In Baudri's letter the criticism of the Greek becomes explicitly ideological. The love of Paris for Helen was carnal, so the entire Greek world was permeated by carnal and literal myths. Baudri's love for Constance, on the other hand, is spiritual, and he will teach her to unfold the (spiritual) truth hidden behind the gentiles' false and fictitious *fabulae*. Baudri teaches Constance how to see the reality behind the veil of mist, with the clue being to interpret the myths allegorically (200.89–134).[60] This brings us to the higher meaning, and, as Baudri tells Constance: *Omnia, si nosti, talia mistica sunt* ('Everything of this sort is allegorical, if you have the right knowledge').

Constance replies with a most affectionate letter, poem 201, in which she exposes her tender reflections on their spiritual love. She has spent the day reading Baudri's letter, the night passionately absorbing its contents, and now, the next morning, she confides her thoughts to the tablets.

Marbod of Rennes ('Medieval Amores' *1)*

The letters of Baudri and Constance were written a few years before the famous correspondence between Abelard and Heloise,[61] and the question naturally arises whether Constance was a historical person or Baudri's

59 Thraede (1962).

60 Cf. the medieval theory of *integumentum*: Brinkmann (1971); Chenu (1955); Dronke (1985) *passim*; and Jeauneau (1957).

61 Muckle (1953) and Könsgen (1974). For the highly debated question of the authenticity of the epistles, see Marenbon (2000) and Ziolkowski (2004).

invention. In fact, scholarly opinion is divided between those[62] who claim that Baudri wrote poem 201 himself and those[63] who identify the author with a nun at the convent of Le Ronceray near Angers. Apparently, Baudri wrote poems to a few other penfriends at Le Ronceray, and in so doing he was perhaps following the example of his senior fellow-poet Marbod of Rennes.[64] Before becoming bishop of Rennes in 1096, Marbod led the cathedral school of Angers from 1069, and it is quite possible that Baudri studied under him at some point during the 1070s. From this period there are nine poems of Marbod *ad amicam* or *ad puellam* (poems 24, 36–42, and 50) and the poem of reply by a *puella ad amicum* (poem 27); *puellae amicae* may possibly be identified with girls at Le Ronceray, trained in Latin and engaged in a veritable poetical correspondence with the learned scholar at Angers.[65] These poems are short (from twelve to twenty-six lines) occasional love poems written in the spirit of the *Amores*. Marbod's Ovidian vein is perceptible in various intertextual references, plays and allusions. Poem 36 for instance describes the happy situation of the man who has received a letter that announces the love of his sweetheart:

> A te missa michi gaudens, carissima, legi
> namque tenetur ibi me placuisse tibi.
> (36.1–2)

Rejoicing I read, dearest, the letter you have sent me. For it maintains that you have taken a fancy to me.

[62] Notably Tilliette (1992).

[63] Notably Dronke (1984). See also Dronke (1968) 213–20 and Schaller (1966).

[64] Cf. poems 137 (to Muriel), 138 (to Agnes), 139 and 153 (to Emma). The identification of Agnes is uncertain, that of Muriel contested. Although Dronke (1984) 85 and Dronke (1968) 217 claims that Muriel was at Le Ronceray, it seems more likely that she was a nun at Wilton Abbey in England. Interestingly, both Hildebert of Lavardin and Serlo of Bayeux wrote poems to her. Cf. Scott (2001), pp. xxvii–xxviii and 17–18. See also Baudri's poem 86 (to Marbod). It is worth mentioning that Hilarius of Orléans, before becoming a pupil of Abelard, had been a canon at Le Ronceray, where he too, around the year 1110, charmed the girls with his poems. Cf. Bulst and Bulst-Thiele (1989) 1–4.

[65] These poems were practically unknown until 1950, when Bulst (1950) had them re-edited after more than 400 years of oblivion. Our knowledge of Marbod's poems largely depends on the *editio princeps* of 1524, a text preserved in one exemplar only, the Rés. p. Yc. 1533 of the Bibliothèque Nationale. Dom A. Beaugendre was in charge of an edition of the works of Hildebert and Marbod in 1708. For Marbod he took the *editio princeps* as his basis, but the priggish monk evidently chose to pass over the spicy poems. J. J. Bourassé, who edited the works of Hildebert and Marbod for volume 171 of *PL* in 1854, made few changes to Beaugendre's text. Although he added a few poems (*PL* 171, 1684–1685), the love poems lay undisturbed for another century. Seven years after Bulst's edition, Raby failed to include this important addition in his second edition (1934/1957).

The silent countertheme that comes to the reader's mind is the opening of *Amores* 1.12:

> Flete meos casus – tristes rediere tabellae
> infelix hodie littera posse negat.
> (*Am.* 1.12.1–2)

> Weep for my bad luck – sad tablets have come back: The unhappy letter announces that today she can't.

And when Marbod in the middle of the poem gives his blessing to the tablets (36.9–10) . . .

> Felices tabulae, felix grafiusque manusque
> Et felix dextra littera facta tua.
> (36.9–10)

> Happy tablets, happy pen and hand, and happy letter written by your right hand.

. . . he tacitly juxtaposes his exultation with the curse (*Am.* 1.12.7–30) from the rejected Ovid:

> Ite hinc, difficiles, funebria ligna, tabellae,
> tuque, negaturis cera referta notis!
> (*Am.* 1.12.7–8)

> Go away, annoying tablets, fatal pieces of wood, and you, wax crammed with words of denial.

Poem 39 presents the apology of the lover who has been unjustly reproached. This is Marbod's variation on *Amores* 2.7, and we will quote the outburst contained in the last couplet, the final line of which expresses the essence of the Ovidian model:

> Quod quia non nescis, crucias crudelis amantem,
> Criminibus falsis insimulando reum.
> (39.13–14)

> Since you are not unaware of this, cruel one, you torment your lover by charging him with false crimes.

Godfrey of Reims (An example of Descriptio puellae*)*

Though the Ovidian epistolary love poem culminates with Baudri and Marbod, poems on female beauty existed as a sort of subgenre alongside the medieval *Heroides* and *Amores*. In fact, with these poems the physiological merits of the poet's girl become the main topic, and the Ovidian link tends to be more stylistic than thematic. Baudri himself was greatly influenced by an author of one such *descriptio puellae*,[66] namely Godfrey († 1095), chancellor of the cathedral of Reims, whom Baudri declares to be *secundum Nasoni*[67] in a poem dedicated to him. We possess four epistolary poems[68] (the so-called *Epistolarum Liber*) from Godfrey's hand, but only one of them was dedicated to a girl, the *Parce, precor, uirgo*. In the first twenty-five elegiac distichs, Godfrey urges the unnamed *uirgo* to give up all cosmetics and ornaments. She must confide in her natural beauty, and Godfrey assures her that nothing in this world can compete with her grace and elegance. In the second half of the poem, Godfrey compares his girl to Helen. If she had been abducted by Paris, it would not have taken the Greeks more than a month to finish off the Phrygians; and, like Baudri, Godfrey associates himself with Paris by affirming that if he himself were judge, she would be more worthy than Helen of being the cause that made the flames burn the city of Troy. And, of course, had she presented herself as a fourth contestant in the famous beauty contest, the apple would have been hers.[69]

The Ovidian love poem remained a French phenomenon, but with so many students coming to France from across the Channel, it was perhaps only a question of time before the new soil would raise new Godfreys and Marbods. We will conclude our survey by mentioning one such outstanding intellectual.

Serlo of Wilton ('Medieval Amores' *2)*

Serlo of Wilton (*ca.*1105–81) moved to Paris and taught grammar there until a vision made him enter the Cluniac order in the mid twelfth century. Subsequently he joined the Cistercians and became abbot at L'Aumône in 1171.[70] Serlo's literary production counts eighty-four poems,[71] and his verses range from the grammatical to the satirical. Among such delightful poetical variety we find some ten graceful love poems, certainly written

[66] For this literary topos, see Brinkmann (1979) 88–93; Bruyne (1946) 173–94; Cizek (1991); Faral (1913) 99–109; and Offermanns (1970) 129–56. A later author of such a *descriptio* is the Welshman Gerald de Barri (1146–1223). Cf. Brewer (1861) 349–52.

[67] Poem 39, lines 3–4. Poems 35–8, 99 and 100 are also dedicated to Godfrey.

[68] Edited by Bröcker (2002). Worthwhile introductions to Godfrey are Boutemy (1947) and Williams (1947).

[69] The theme of natural beauty and the comparison with Helen would suggest a Propertian inspiration (1.2.1–8 and 2.3.32) rather than Ovidian, and, in fact, Propertius was available/known in Northern France at the time. Cf. Butrica (1984) 29. For a discussion of Godfrey's use of the Latin classics, see Williams (1947).

[70] Cf. Rigg (1996). [71] Edition by Öberg (1965).

before his conversion. Serlo's love poems, like Marbod's, are modelled on the *Amores*. In poem 7 (*In biuio ponor*), for instance, Serlo declares his love for two girls, evidently inspired by *Amores* 2.10. But Serlo pushes the imitation a step further, and like Baudri appropriates Ovid by means of emulation. If Baudri's emulation consists of the poetical development of cultural superiority,[72] Serlo's aim is, as Peter Dronke has observed,[73] to be more Ovidian than Ovid himself! Serlo's seduction of his girl in poem 29 (*Quadam nocte*) leaves less to the reader's imagination than Ovid's seduction of Corinna in *Amores* 1.5 (*singula quid referam?... cetera quis nescit?*). Ovid, and Gallus[74] too, may have known the ways of love, but Serlo knew better:

Pronus erat Veneri Naso, sed ego mage pronus,
    Pronus erat Gallus, sed mage pronus ego.
Nasoni, Gallo placuere Corinna, Liquoris –
    Queque mihi...   (20.1–4)

Ovid was obsessed with love, but I am more obsessed; Gallus was obsessed with love, but I am even more obsessed. Corinna charmed Ovid, and Lycoris charmed Gallus – every lady charms me...[75]

A final comment on the 'Post-Ovidian Age'

Commentators[76] and translations

At about the same time, towards the end of the twelfth century, Arnulf of Orléans wrote his comments on Ovid's poetry.[77] During the next two centuries, he was followed by scholars such as John of Garland[78] (*ca.*1195–1272), Giovanni del Virgilio (*fl.* early 14th century)[79] and Pierre Bursuire[80] (1290–1362). Vernacular translations and reworkings[81] appeared in succession from Chrétien de Troyes' lost translations of *Ars amatoria* and *Remedia amoris* (*ca.*1170) to the paraphrase of *Remedia amoris* embedded into the anonymous *Échecs amoureux*[82] (*ca.*1380), but, as it seems, elegy in Latin did not come back into fashion until the humanists rediscovered the classics and gave them new life throughout the fifteenth and sixteenth centuries. That will be the topic for the next chapter.

72 Cf. Kretschmer (2011). 73 Cf. Dronke (1968) 241.
74 The knowledge of Gallus and Lycoris may stem from *Am.* 1.15.29–30. The mention of Gallus in medieval literature is extremely rare. Another example is to be found in the *Roman de la Rose*.
75 See Gibson (Chapter 13) in this volume. 76 Cf. Hexter (1986).
77 Cf. Ghisalberti (1932). See also Roy and Schooner (1996). 78 Cf. Ghisalberti (1933a).
79 Cf. Ghisalberti (1931). 80 Cf. Ghisalberti (1933b).
81 Cf. Segre (1968). 82 Cf. Körting (1871).

Further reading

An all-embracing monograph on medieval Ovidian literature still remains to be written, but see now Clark, Coulson and McKinley (2011).[83] Useful are also the relevant chapters in Anderson (1995), Binns (1973), Martindale (1988) and Rand (1925). Brill, Cambridge University Press and Blackwell have all recently published companions to Ovid with useful chapters on the Medieval Ovid: Dimmick (2002), Fyler (2009) and Hexter (2002). An excellent bibliographical guide for medieval Ovidian literature is Coulson and Roy (2000). Introductions to the pseudo-Ovidian literature are Lehmann (1927a) Lenz (1959a) and Hexter (2011). The following histories of Medieval Latin (love) poetry are highly recommended: Brinkmann (1979), Dronke (1968), Moser (2004), Raby (1934) and Szövérffy (1992–5). There exists no systematic study of the Ovidian imitations, but Offermanns (1970) contains many highly relevant observations.

[83] Published after the completion of this chapter.

18

LUKE B.T. HOUGHTON

Renaissance Latin love elegy

If the triumph of Callimachus, as Wendell Clausen asserted, took place not in Hellenistic Alexandria but in Rome under Catullus and the following generation,[1] it can be argued that the triumph of Latin love elegy is to be seen not in its brief initial flowering at Rome from Cornelius Gallus to Ovid, but in the vast elegiac output of fifteenth- and sixteenth-century Europe, the full extent of which remains even now difficult to gauge. In addition to the productions of individual poets, whose elegiac endeavours enjoyed differing degrees of celebrity and circulation, a range of compilations – such as the *Poetae tres elegantissimi*, various collections of *Delitiae*, and two separate volumes entitled *Carmina quinque illustrium poetarum* – were issued, comprising the works of more than one author or offering a selection of items representative of a particular genre or nationality.[2] A comprehensive overview of this mass of material is beyond the scope of this chapter, and a bald catalogue of the principal Renaissance elegists and their poetic collections would give little impression of the literary character of these works. The following pages will therefore concentrate on three recurring themes that play a significant role throughout the surviving corpus of Renaissance Latin love elegy: the appropriation and revival of classical models; the combination and enhancement of this poetic inheritance from Catullus, Propertius, Tibullus and Ovid with other literary material, both antique and more recent; and the poets' attempts to situate their work within the literary tradition of ancient erotic elegy by presenting their poetry as part of a generic succession, a strategy of self-definition familiar from the works of the Roman elegists themselves.

[1] Clausen (1964) 181; for doubts over elegiac engagement with Callimachus, see e.g. DeBrohun (2003) 3–8, Lyne (1980) 136, 147–8, 297 n. 20 – but see now Hunter (2006a).

[2] See Perosa and Sparrow (1979) xxiii–xxv; also Sparrow (1976).

Recreation

An important part of the *raison d'être* of almost all Renaissance Latin poetry is the recreation of ancient literary models; and yet it is precisely the imitative character of this body of verse that was responsible for the low estimate of its literary value until well into the twentieth century. Even as the Latin literature of antiquity began to achieve emancipation from charges of parasitic servility to the masterpieces of ancient Greece, something of the same stigma still clung to the Renaissance revivers of Virgil, Horace and the elegists, their efforts dismissed as derivative, artificial and almost by definition emotionally deficient in comparison to contemporary developments in the vernacular – despite the fact that many of the most distinguished proponents of neo-Latin poetry were also prolific and accomplished authors in their own tongues. But not only does the denigration of Renaissance Latin verse, much of it erotic in content, on the grounds of excessive dependence on ancient models do less than justice to the theory of imitation within which these poets were operating, as John Sparrow pointed out;[3] in an age which can appreciate both the pleasure of recognition and the serious point about the palimpsestic nature of amatory expression in the 'Elephant Love Medley' of Baz Luhrmann's *Moulin Rouge* (2001), the time is surely ripe for a reappraisal.

Far from seeking to conceal what has been perceived as their lack of originality, Latin love elegists of the Renaissance are quite open about their relationship with ancient elegy – indeed this feature of their work constitutes their principal claim to literary attention. At the very beginning of one of the earliest collections of Renaissance love elegy, the *Cinthia* of Enea Silvio Piccolomini (1405–64, later Pope Pius II),[4] we find explicit acknowledgement of the poet's Propertian aspirations, encapsulated – as he points out himself – in the opening word of the book (Piccolomini, *Cinthia* 1):

> Cinthia, si qua meo debetur fama labori,
> abs te suscipiam quicquid honoris erit.
> Tu mihi das ipsas scribenda in carmina uires,
> tu facis ingenium, tu facis eloquium.
> Te duce concedunt diuae in mea uota sorores,
> te duce Castalio somnia fonte bibo.

[3] Sparrow (1960) 363–7; on Renaissance theories of literary imitation more generally, see McLaughlin (1995).

[4] For the text of Piccolomini's *Cinthia*, see Van Heck (1994); studies include Paparelli (1964) and (1987); Baca (1971–2); Galand-Hallyn (1993); Pieper (2008) 83–90. Another fifteenth-century *Cynthia* is the elegiac collection of Marcantonio Aldegati, who also wrote a (now fragmentary) *Gigantomachia*: see Bottari (1980).

Summa tibi, fateor, debentur praemia: summo
    te quoque, si liceat, carmine ad astra feram.
Et nostri prima uenies in parte libelli:
    tu mihi principium, tu mihi finis eris.

Cinthia, if any renown is due to my toil, it's from you I shall receive whatever honour there'll be. It is you who give me strength for writing poetry, you who supply my talent, you who supply my eloquence. Under your guidance the heavenly sisters grant my prayers, under your guidance I drink dreams from the Castalian spring. The loftiest prizes, I declare, are owed to you: and you too I shall bear, if I may, with loftiest song to the stars. You shall turn up at the opening of my little book as well: you shall be my beginning, and you my end.

In this opening poem there are at least two clear echoes of well-known passages in Propertius (the declaration that Cynthia alone supplies Propertius' *ingenium*, 2.1.4; and the assertion that Cynthia will be both the speaker's beginning and his end – *Cynthia prima fuit, Cynthia finis erit*, 1.12.20); but what is perhaps more striking is the highly self-conscious way in which Piccolomini advertises his adoption of Propertian precedent here. In an evident comment on the position of the name of the beloved at the start of his predecessor's elegiac collection, Piccolomini not only gives the name Cinthia pride of place in his *libellus* (a programmatic term for Latin love poetry: cf. Catull. 1; Prop. 2.13.25; Ovid, *Am.* 2.17.33), but draws attention both to the fact that he is doing so and to the fact that he is not the first person to do this – *et nostri prima . . . in parte libelli* ('in the first part of my little book too', 1.9), *te quoque . . . feram* ('you too I shall bear', 1.8). The epigonal status of Piccolomini's neo-Propertian brand of elegy is thus established from the outset of the collection, much as Petrarch (Francesco Petrarca, 1304–74) had announced his entry into the pre-existing tradition of Ennian epic by beginning his *Africa* with the words *Et mihi . . . Musa, uirum referes* ('to me too, Muse, will you recall the man . . .', 1.1–2).[5]

What the Renaissance elegists considered to be the defining features of Latin love elegy can be partly deduced from what they chose to imitate. Particularly revealing in this respect is a passage in the second book of the *Xandra*, the influential three-book collection of love elegies by the Florentine poet, literary critic and philosopher Cristoforo Landino (1424–98).[6] Here Landino lays out his conception of what Latin love elegy entails, in terms immediately recognizable from the works of his ancient predecessors in the genre (*Xandra* 2.23.31–42):

[5] See e.g. Hardie (1993) 296–7.

[6] For a text and English translation (to be used with caution) see Chatfield (2008); for discussion of the *Xandra* see especially Wenzel (2010), Pieper (2008) and Tonelli (2002).

Sed nimis heu gracili tam grandia proelia uersu
ludo: meos humeros non onus omne decet.
Est furor, est cymba uasto me credere ponto
exigua; fluuios nostra phaselus amet.
Sitque satis dominam miseris urgere querelis,
mulcere et gracili pectora dura lyra,
imparibusque modis teneros disponere amores:
haec tibi materies, parue libelle, datur.
Nec tamen exiguum talem dixisse puellam
duxeris: haec laudis gloria magna mea est.
Gloria magna quidem talem dixisse puellam,
cui similis quondam nulla puella fuit.

But alas – I'm playing at such mighty battles in too slender verse: not every burden suits my shoulders. It's madness to entrust myself to the vast ocean in a miniature vessel: let my skiff cherish the rivers. Let it be enough to importune my mistress with sorry complaints, and to caress her hard heart with the slender lyre, and to set my tender loves / love poems in order in an uneven metre: it's this subject matter that's given to you, little booklet. And yet you shouldn't think it a slight thing to have told of such a girl: this is my great vaunt of praise. It's a great glory, indeed, to have told of such a girl, to whom no girl has ever been comparable.

One after another, the programmatic themes and vocabulary of erotic elegy as defined by its ancient practitioners pass before us in rapid succession: the opposition between the heroic struggles of martial epic and the 'slender verse' (*gracili . . . uersu*, 31) of refined elegy; the rejection of the vast sea of elevated poetry for the restricted stream of elegiac composition (see e.g. Propertius 3.9.3–4, 35–6), characterized by the quintessential epithet of elegy, *exiguus* ('miniature', 'tiny': see e.g. Horace, *Ars poetica* 77; Ovid, *Ars amatoria* 2.286; id., *Fasti* 2.4, 6.22); the lover's devotion to a hard-hearted mistress, *domina*, whom he assails with *querelae*, complaints – another distinctive designation of the elegiac genre;[7] the small-scale nature of elegy (*parue libelle* (38): the diminutive *libellus* – on which see above – already indicates smallness, reinforced further by the adjective); and the paradoxical 'glory' that celebration of the *puella* brings to her poet, a glory superior to more conventional forms of military distinction (see especially Propertius 1.6.29–30). Characteristic also is Landino's description of the process of elegiac composition as *imparibus . . . modis teneros disponere amores* ('to set my tender *amores* in order in an uneven metre', 37) – not only is *tener* an epithet used repeatedly of elegiac love poetry (see e.g. Ovid, *Amores* 2.1.4,

[7] Saylor (1967).

Remedia amoris 757), but *amores* can denote either love affairs or the poetry that enshrines them, or both.[8] Finally, the claim that the lover-poet's girl is beyond compare is a typical sentiment of the besotted protagonist of elegy – the irony here, of course, (as elsewhere) is that the supposedly nonpareil Xandra, as Landino portrays her, is obviously comparable (*similis*, 42) to any number of previous elegiac mistresses, precisely because she and her lover's reaction to her are directly modelled on elements in earlier elegy!

Like Piccolomini, Landino can give self-conscious expression to his awareness of the imitative quality of his interactions with previous Latin love poetry, although he does so in a more implicit fashion. This is evident above all in the following lines from the first book of *Xandra*, where the relentless insistence on memory and recollection combines with unmistakable reminiscences from classical and post-classical Latin love elegy to point towards the operation of poetic memory in Landino's construction of his mistress (*Xandra* 1.28.13–24):

Et nunc qui uultus, quae sit tibi gratia formae
    nunc memini, qualis rideat ore nitor,
sideribusque oculos similes et cygnea colla
    et niueum pectus, pectora nostra domans.
Et memini cantum quo se pulcherrima uictam
    non, modo sit uerax, Calliopea neget;
et memini in numerum soleant ut mollia crura
    ludere et in girum molliter ire pedes.
Omnia quae memori monitus dum mente retracto
    materiam, infelix, ignibus addo meis.
Sic infelices nostros nutrimus amores,
    gaudia praeteriti dum meminisse iuuat...

And now I remember your features, now what grace your figure has, what kind of gleam smiles on your face, and your eyes like stars and your swan-like neck and your snow-white breast, taming the heart in my breast. And I remember your singing, by which most beautiful Calliope would not deny herself beaten – if she were being truthful, that is. And I remember how your soft limbs tend to play in rhythm and your feet go softly round in a circle. While I go over and over all these things in my remembering mind, reminded of them, I add – poor wretch – fuel to my fire. Like this I unhappily nourish my love / love poetry, while I take pleasure in remembering the joys of the past...

Here the pleasure of 'remembering the joys of the past' (*gaudia praeteriti... meminisse*, 24) seems to be as much about the savouring of

[8] See e.g. Kennedy (1993) 24–6, 50–1, 69.

literary recollection as it is about nostalgia for the presence of the beloved – and again, as the memory of Xandra's many attractions nourishes his love (*amores*, 23), so the memory of earlier elegiac texts gives sustenance (and literary subject matter: *materia*, 22) to Landino's love poetry. Indeed, Landino's use of *in numerum* ('in rhythm' or 'in metre', 19) in describing the motion of Xandra's limbs, together with the stylistic adjective *mollia* (see e.g. Prop. 2.1.2), repeated in *molliter* in the following line, seems to point towards a recognition of the textual nature of the female body in Roman love elegy, arguably in line with the observations of Maria Wyke on Propertius.[9]

Contamination

From its earliest phase in the works of Giovanni Marrasio (1400/4–52),[10] who begins and ends the *Angelinetum* with addresses to Leonardo Bruni, and Piccolomini, whose *Cinthia* includes two *encomia* on Virgil and a number of satirical and epitaphic pieces, Renaissance elegy demonstrates a recognition that the subject matter of elegy is not exclusively erotic. This is in keeping with the variegated character of classical elegy, and over the course of their tripartite elegiac collections both Cristoforo Landino and his follower Naldo Naldi (1436–*c*.1513) stage a progressive dilution of amatory material with poetry on other, particularly contemporary Medicean, topics, in the manner of Propertius in his first three books.[11] Likewise, among the *Elegiae* of the Dutchman Johannes (or Janus) Secundus (1511–36), the first book is devoted to love elegies addressed to one Julia, the second book addresses a variety of mistresses, and the final book largely abandons the subject of love, although one elegy here (3.3) is given over entirely to celebration of Catullus, Tibullus and Propertius.[12] This diversification reaches its apogee in the elegies of Iacopo Sannazaro (1458–1530) and the leading German elegist Petrus Lotichius Secundus (1528–60),[13] in which erotic pieces are very definitely in a minority. But even within the sections of their work devoted to amatory themes, the Renaissance elegists intersperse and fuse

9 Collected in Wyke (2002).

10 For Marrasio and the *Angelinetum*, see Resta (1976); Pieper (2008) 78–83, 122–31.

11 On Naldi see Grant (1962) and Martelli (1985); for the text of his *Elegiae*, see Juhász (1934).

12 Text and translation in Murgatroyd (2000); see also Endres (1981), and for discussion Godman (1988). Secundus was also responsible for the influential *Basia*, a collection of nineteen poems on kisses in imitation of Catullus.

13 On the *Elegiae* of Sannazaro, best known for his *De partu Virginis* and *Piscatory Eclogues*, see Putnam (2009) and Tateo (1987) 58–60; for Lotichius, Ludwig (1976) 177–90 and essays in Auhagen and Schäfer (2001).

their imitation of Roman erotic elegy with elements from other literature, both ancient and modern. In the final poem of the *Angelinetum*, Marrasio tells his patron Bruni *O utinam de te possem componere uersus, | quales Virgilius Callimachusque tulit!* ('would that I might be capable of composing verses about you like those Virgil and Callimachus produced!', *Angelinetum* 9.11–12); and an extreme example of this generic expansion with regard to classical poetry is the opening erotic elegy in the *Amores* of the French humanist Joachim Du Bellay (*c.*1525–60),[14] who playfully takes advantage of the traditional elegiac refusal of grander forms of poetry to echo the opening lines of all the Roman epics (Lucan's *Civil War*, Statius' *Thebaid*, Virgil's *Aeneid*, Ovid's *Metamorphoses*, Claudian's *De raptu Proserpinae*) he will not be producing – rather as Ovid teasingly begins his *Amores* with the epic keyword *arma* – before misleadingly alluding to the incipit of Lucretius' *De rerum natura* to announce the erotic programme of the poems to follow (Du Bellay, *Amores* 2.1–6).

It is in their incorporation of motifs from more recent vernacular poetry, however, that the Renaissance Latin elegists principally supplement and transform the classical genre of love elegy; in Italy, in particular, as Charles Fantazzi has demonstrated with reference to the *Elegiae* of Angelo Poliziano (1454–94), 'there was a living, active exchange between the two languages, a cross-fertilization, an interplay of vocabulary and imagery, so that, to resurrect a verb of John Donne's, the two may be said to have "inter-inanimated" one another'.[15] Although Petrarch, despite owning a manuscript of Propertius and intermittently drawing on the corpus of Latin love elegy in his Italian lyrics,[16] did not attempt to revive the genre of amatory elegy in Latin, his contribution – via the medium of his vernacular erotic poetry – to the development of the Latin elegy of the later Renaissance is nonetheless profound.[17] So in *Xandra* 1.14 Landino inserts a Virgilian reminiscence (*pergite Pierides*, 2; cf. Virgil, *Eclogues* 6.13), elegiac *querela* (8, 10) and the quintessential elegiac epithet *miser* ('wretched', 10: cf. Propertius 1.1.1 etc.) into what is at times a fairly close Latin translation of a popular Petrarchan sonnet (*Canzon.* 132), featuring the latter's characteristic antithesis of sweet and bitter,[18] and his recurring image of the lover's ship in troubled waters (see especially *Canzon.* 80, 189, 235):

[14] See Hawkins (2004); Ginsberg (1985). [15] Fantazzi (1996) 128.

[16] On Petrarch and Propertius see Caputo (1998); Dolla (1987); Petrie (1983) index s.v. 'Propertius', esp. 1–2, 139–44; La Penna (1977) 254–61; Ullman (1973); De Nolhac (1907) I 157, 170–2, 175.

[17] See Coppini (2006); Fantazzi (1996), esp. 129–30, 135, 137–8; McFarlane (1980) 66; Ludwig (1976) 173.

[18] Houghton (2009) 171 with n. 45; Petrie (1983) 174–6.

Si non uexat amor, quidnam mea pectora uexat?
    Pergite Pierides, dicite quaeso, deae!
Vel mihi, quid sit amor qualisue, referte Camenae,
    si mala tot nobis congerit asper Amor;
si dulcis, dulci cur tot permiscet amara,
    dulcia uel qui dat, si sit amarus Amor,
aut mihi si flammae consumunt corda uolenti,
    unde igitur nobis tanta querela uenit?
Inuito uel si comburunt ossa calores
    quid misero tantum proderit usque queri?
Talibus, heu, fragili in lembo me fluctibus aequor
    iactat et in scopulos iam ruit ipsa ratis.

If it's not love that's harassing my heart, what is harassing it, then? Come on, then, goddesses of Pieria, tell me – I beg you! Or, Camenae, relate to me what love is or what it's like, if harsh Love heaps up so many sufferings for us; if it is sweet, why does it mingle so much bitterness with the sweet, or who gives sweetness, if Love be bitter? Or, if flames devour my heart in accordance with my will, where's all this complaining of ours coming from, then? But if the heat is burning up my bones against my will, what good will it do me to spend my time complaining, wretch that I am? On waves like these, alas, does the ocean toss me in my fragile boat, and now the raft itself is rushing onto the rocks.

Secundus adds the equally familiar Petrarchan opposition of fire and ice,[19] here conjoined with a diminutive (*flammeolis*) and an endearment (*mea lux*) of the kind beloved by exponents of the Catullan tradition: *Flammeolis, mea lux, oculis cum cuncta peruras, | frigidius Scythica cur niue pectus habes?* ('My light, since you burn up everything with your little flaming eyes, why do you have a heart colder than Scythian snow?', *Elegiae* 2.3.1–2). The same paradox, which in Petrarch's most distilled formulation appears as '*et ardo, et son un ghiaccio*' ('I both burn and am made of ice', *Canzon.* 134.2), is expressed also in the *Flametta* of Landino's imitator Ugolino Verino (1438–1516), where the very name of the eponymous mistress suggests her fiery effect on the lover (*Flametta* 1.6.9–10, 19–22):

Me solum flammae rapiunt, me feruidus ignis
    urit, et in tanto frigore feruet amor.
. . .
Hei mihi, riualem nunc hunc, nunc aspicis illum,
    frigidius glacie tunc mihi pectus erat.
Et tamen in gelido caluerunt pectore flammae,
    tempore sic uno frigus et ardor erat.

[19] See Forster (1969) index s.v. 'ice–fire'.

Me alone the flames seize, me the blazing fire burns, and in such great cold my love blazes . . . Woe is me, you catch sight of now this rival, now that – then my heart was colder than ice. And yet in my chill heart flames grew warm: thus at one and the same time there was both cold and burning.

In the following century Marcantonio Flaminio (1497/9–1550) was to praise Francesco Maria Molza (1489–1544), whose Latin poetry includes an elegy *Ad Beatricem Hispanam* in imitation of Ovid, *Amores* 1.14, another *Ad Venerem* on his girl's illness, and an elegiac epistle from Catherine of Aragon to Henry VIII in the manner of Ovid's *Heroides*,[20] for his successful emulation of both Tibullus and Petrarch – though this probably refers to Molza's proficiency in both Latin and vernacular poetry, rather than to his amalgamation of the two traditions (Flaminio, *Carmina* 2.19):[21]

Postera dum numeros dulces mirabitur aetas
    siue, Tibulle, tuos, siue, Petrarca, tuos;
tu quoque, Molsa, pari semper celebrabere fama,
    uel potius titulo duplice maior eris:
quidquid enim laudis dedit inclita Musa duobus
    uatibus, hoc uni donat habere tibi.

While a later age will marvel at sweet measures, whether yours, Tibullus, or yours, Petrarch, you too, Molza, will be fêted with equal renown – or rather, you shall be greater through a double title: for whatever praise the glorious Muse has given to those two poets, she bestows that on you alone.

Despite their acknowledged debt, then, to their ancient predecessors, the authors of Renaissance Latin elegy had at their disposal a more varied palette than the (admittedly luminous) colours available from the art of Propertius, Tibullus and Ovid. Of these the principal novelty, at least in the earlier stages of elegiac revival in Renaissance Italy, was the infusion of the spirit and imagery of Petrarch's *Rerum uulgarium fragmenta*, but once the Latin genre was re-established, subsequent poets in centres such as Florence, Naples and Ferrara could also draw on the works of their *concittadini* and others to enrich their own syntheses of elegiac ingredients. From this repertoire the most talented of the humanists succeeded in creating a new poetic compound – as Fantazzi characterizes the Latin love poetry of Poliziano, 'a

[20] For further examples of the Renaissance vogue for the *Heroides*, see also the *Liber Isottaeus* of Basinio Basini (on whom see below), three books of elegiac epistles between Sigismondo Malatesta of Rimini and his mistress Isotta degli Atti; and the *Heroides Christianae* of the prolific German Helius Eobanus Hessus (1488–1540), featuring letters from Christian heroines from the Virgin Mary onwards – for text and translation see Vredeveld (2008).

[21] Text from Cuccoli (1897) 231.

variegated work of intarsia with all the pieces cut to precision, fitted into place and carefully polished'.[22]

Succession

In the opening poem of Piccolomini's *Cinthia* (above), we saw the poet explicitly positioning himself as a successor to a previous author, in his declaration that the mistress's name would appear at the start of his book too. But like Propertius himself, who claims in the introductory elegy to his fourth book the title *Callimachus Romanus* ('the Roman Callimachus', 4.1.64), the Renaissance elegists can be even more direct in their advertisement of a relationship to a prestigious predecessor. As Propertius begins his third book of elegies by invoking *Callimachi Manes* ('the shades of Callimachus', 3.1.1), so in turn Johannes Secundus opens his second book by conjuring up the shade of Propertius himself, a quite literal reanimation of the spirit of ancient elegy (*O tantum faueas, Umbri leuis umbra poetae, | Cynthia si nostro semper in ore sonat*: 'Just grant me your favour, insubstantial shade of the Umbrian poet, if Cynthia always sounds on my lips', *Elegiae* 2.1.19–20). One of the most influential and productive of neo-Latin poets, Giovanni Gioviano Pontano (1429–1503),[23] author of two books of erotic elegies, *Parthenopaeus siue Amores*, and of the three-book *De amore coniugali*, in which the genre of love elegy is thoroughly domesticated, with poems celebrating the blessings of peace and the birth of a son, and a long series of *Naeniae* – lullabies – at the end of the second book, prays that his love poetry may achieve an immortality comparable to that of his fellow-countryman Propertius (Pontano was born near Spoleto; *Parthenopaeus* 1.18.21–6).[24]

Once the revitalised elegiac tradition had taken root in Renaissance Italy, this impulse to locate oneself within a sequence, to set oneself consciously in the tracks of a pioneer, could be applied equally to more recent practitioners of the genre. So Ugolino Verino, with a nod to Ovid (cf. *Her.* 15.28, *Am.*

[22] Fantazzi (1996) 145–6; for a different (but no less apposite) metaphor see Sparrow (1960) 367 – 'the hybrid blossoms that emerge from the crossing of so many strains – ancient and modern, pagan and Christian, classical and vernacular . . . '

[23] On Pontano's love poetry, see essays in Baier (2003); also Tateo (1987) 53–8; La Penna (1977) 267–9. For the texts, see Oeschger (1948).

[24] Strikingly, we find here the same phrases – *et nostri . . . libelli* ('my little books too', 21), *me quoque* ('me too', 23) – used by Piccolomini to emphasize the secondary character of his work. On this passage see La Penna (1977) 268–9; note also Secundus, *Elegiae* 1.2.65–6, where Cupid advises the poet (via his nurse) to take lessons from his own instructor Ovid, maintaining *tu quoque cum Belgis non inhonorus eris* ('you too will not be without honour, along with the Belgae').

1.15.7–8, *Ars* 2.740, *Rem. am.* 363, *Tr.* 2.118), situates himself in the wake of Landino (*Flametta* 1.20.29–38; the speaker is Apollo):

At nunc Landini, Medicum Petrique fauore,
    cantatur toto nomen in orbe tui,
qui cecinit Xandram miro inflammatus amore
    et mox magna Petri dicere gesta parat.
At tu, qui tanti sequeris uestigia uatis,
    haec illi nostro nomine dicta refer.
Nec tua Lethaeas mergetur uirgo sub undas,
    Flametta ardoris maxima flamma tui,
inter et Etruscas cantabitur ipsa puellas,
    et sua post cineres fama superstes erit.

But now, through the favour of Pietro and the Medici, the name of your Landino is sung throughout the world: he who, fired by wondrous love, sang of Xandra and is preparing to tell soon of the mighty exploits of Pietro. But you, who follow the tracks of so great a poet, report these words to him in my name. Neither will your maid sink beneath the waves of Lethe – Flametta, the greatest flame of your passion – and she herself will be sung of among the girls of Tuscany, and after she is ash her renown will survive.

Verino's fiery heroine will take her place *inter . . . Etruscas . . . puellas* (37), 'among the elegiac women of Tuscany', confirming her author's entry into the restored elegiac succession.

The strategy of literary self-definition through enumeration of predecessors in the genre is one that occurs prominently in the works of the Roman elegists, most notably in the final poem of what has come down to us as the second book of Propertius, where the poet runs through the sequence of Virgil (here tendentiously presented as a love poet), Varro of Atax, Catullus, C. Licinius Calvus and Cornelius Gallus, before adding, in final position (2.34.93–4):

Cynthia quin etiam uersu laudata Properti,
    hos inter si me ponere Fama uolet.

Cynthia too, moreover, praised in the verse of Propertius, if Fame is willing to set me among these people.

Ovid, too, in the epilogue to his first book of *Amores*, prophesies the continued life of a more eclectic range of poetic antecedents (including Tibullus and Gallus), and concludes with an anticipation of his own survival, in terms we have already seen echoed by Verino: *ergo etiam cum me supremus adederit ignis | uiuam, parsque mei multa superstes erit* ('therefore also, when the final fire has eaten away at me, I shall live, and a great part of me will survive', *Amores* 1.15.41–2). At a number of points in his exile poetry, moreover, Ovid constructs an elegiac succession, in which the canonical sequence of Gallus, Propertius and Tibullus is presented as culminating in Ovid himself, the latest instalment in an unbroken line of elegiac enterprise (see *Tristia* 2.445–70, 4.10.51–4).[25]

Time and again we find the elegists' would-be successors among the neo-Latin poets of the Renaissance drawing on one or more of these elegiac catalogues to locate themselves within this established literary ancestry.[26] Membership of such a company can also be conferred upon an elegist by a fellow-poet, as a means of commendation: so Maffeo Vegio, best-known for his Supplement to Virgil's *Aeneid*, locates Marrasio within the elegiac succession in a poetic epistle composed in the voice of the latter's beloved Angelina (*Carmen ad Marrasium Siculum pro Angelina* 89–94).[27]

> Ut quondam Gallo placuit sua blanda Licoris
> Lesbiaque, ut fertur, grata, Catulle, tibi;
> ut fuit Ouidii cantata Corinna, Properti
> Cinthia et ut Nemesis pulchra, Tibulle, tua;
> sic ego Marrasii ferar Angelina Sicani,
> aeternumque tuo carmine nomen erit.

> As once his seductive Lycoris found favour with Gallus, and as Lesbia is said to have been pleasing to you, Catullus; as Ovid's Corinna was celebrated in song, and Propertius' Cynthia, and your beautiful Nemesis, Tibullus; so I shall be called Sicilian Marrasio's Angelina, and I shall have an everlasting name through your poetry.

A comparable accolade can be seen in a letter from Leonardo Bruni to Marrasio in response to the latter's dedication of the *Angelinetum* to the Florentine chancellor, setting the poet *inter Nasones et Propertios et Tibullos* (among the Ovids and Propertiuses and Tibulluses).[28]

Conversely, the capacity to withhold the honour of enrolling a mistress among the ranks of celebrated elegiac *puellae* if the girl is less than compliant with the lover-poet's wishes can be employed as a weapon in the elegists' techniques of amatory persuasion. In the *Cyris*, a collection of twelve elegies by Basinio Basini (Basinio da Parma, 1425–57), the mistress' decision to

[25] For discussion see Ingleheart (2010a).

[26] On such catalogues in Renaissance elegy see Charlet (2005) 283 with 293 nn. 4–6.

[27] For the complete poem see Resta (1976) 135–9; yet more generously Landino, in the earlier redaction of the first book of *Xandra*, declares that his friend Francesco da Castiglione's Theoplasma will become even more celebrated than Lesbia, Nemesis and Cynthia, making her poet 'equal to Callimachus everywhere' (*Xandra*, earlier redaction 1.26).

[28] See Resta (1976) 147.

marry an elderly rival prompts the following jealous assertion of the power of elegiac poetry (*Cyris*, 6.17–22):

> Cynthia lasciui uiuit formosa Properti
> carmine, carminibus digna puella suis;
> Galli carminibus uiuit formosa Lycoris,
> Delia carminibus, clare Tibulle, tuis.
> Forsitan et nostris fueras cantanda tabellis,
> si non acciperes, bella puella, senem.

> Beauteous Cynthia lives on through the poetry of naughty Propertius, a girl worthy of the poems dedicated to her; beauteous Lycoris lives on through the poems of Gallus, and Delia through your poems, famous Tibullus. Perhaps you would have been worthy of being sung by my tablets as well, if you, a pretty girl, weren't accepting an old man.

Secundus (*Elegiae* 1.7.35–6) sounds a similar note, while Tito Vespasiano Strozzi (1424–1505), from Ferrara, even goes so far as to misrepresent the painfully recalcitrant *puellae* of Propertius and Tibullus in order to hold them up to his mistress as a model of the rewards contingent upon properly acquiescent conduct, claiming *Cynthia clara minus Nemesisque obscurior esset, | sed facilis Nemesis, Cynthia mitis erat* ('Cynthia would have been less famous, and Nemesis more obscure, but Nemesis was yielding and Cynthia gentle', *Erotica* 1.2.77–8)![29]

Less modest exponents of the genre can even claim that their work will set them above the canon of classical elegists: Giovannantonio Campano (1429–77), author of eight books of elegies and epigrams,[30] proudly declares *Paeligni cedant lusus et blanda Tibulli | Delia; Galle, meis uinceris a numeris* ('let the games of the Paelignian [Ovid] give way, and Tibullus' seductive Delia; Gallus, you're beaten by my measures', *Elegiae et epigrammata* 1.14.5–6), while Landino devotes an entire poem of the *Xandra* (2.27) to a review of the varied charms of past elegiac mistresses, whose manifest attractions are nonetheless surpassed, in the verdict of Rome herself, by those of his own incomparable Xandra.

One of the most memorable formulations of the concept of elegiac succession is to be found at the end of Ovid's elegy for Tibullus (*Amores* 3.9), where the younger elegist imagines his predecessor arriving in the Elysian fields, to be greeted by a welcome party of like-minded love poets: Catullus,

[29] See also Strozzi, *Erotica* 1.8.281–6. For the text of Strozzi's *Erotica* (or *Eroticon*), see Della Guardia (1916); in addition to the analysis in Tateo (1987) 41–9, there are a number of studies on Strozzi's elegiac poetry by Béatrice Charlet-Mesdjian, e.g. Mesdjian (1997).

[30] See Tateo (1998).

Calvus and Gallus (3.9.59–66). This scenario too is appropriated by the Renaissance elegists, envisaging the posthumous reception of themselves or of a colleague in the genre, which like the acclamation accorded to Tibullus will reflect the nature of their literary achievement. Pontano, for instance, imagines the *Musa Catulli* waiting to receive him in his Elysian destination, a mark of his indebtedness to the Catullan style (*Parthenopaeus siue Amores* 1.19.29–34)

Perhaps even more alluring is the welcome foreseen by Pontano in his *Tumuli*, a collection of elegiac epitaphs, for his fellow epigrammatist Michele Marullo (*c.*1453–1500), who will be met by the musical mistresses of classical love elegy, disporting themselves in a suitably literary fashion (*Tumuli* 1.14.9–14):

> Nil praeter nomen tumulo: per opaca uagaris
> culta, per Elysium, docte Marulle, nemus;
> hinc tibi se ad cantum adiungit formosa Corinna,
> cantat et ad calamos Delia culta tuos;
> illinc compositos exercet Cynthia saltus,
> exercet raros Lesbia blanda choros.

The tomb holds nothing but your name: through the shady fields, through the Elysian grove you wander, learned Marullus; on this side beauteous Corinna attaches herself to you for singing, and cultivated Delia sings along to your pipes; on that side Cynthia practises her artistic leaps, and seductive Lesbia practises exquisite dances.

Such company would no doubt be congenial, as Pontano saw it, for the 'learned' Marullus, a just reward for his elegiac *doctrina* (cf. Ovid's apostrophe to *docte Catulle* at *Amores* 3.9.62) – and every aspect of this Elysian beauty pageant is carefully calibrated to reflect the poetic interests of its beneficiary.

Finally, the first volume of Serassi's edition of the poetry of Francesco Maria Molza concludes with a long elegy attributed to Paolo Pansa (who appears along with Molza in the catalogue of poets in Ariosto, *Orlando furioso* 46.13) which is clearly modelled on Ovid's elegy for Tibullus; here Molza is received into the Elysian fields by a full-blown genealogy of poetic predecessors ancient and modern (including Petrarch and Boccaccio), Latin and vernacular (*Paulli Pansae de Molsae obitu elegia* 161–72).[31]

What the Latin love elegists of the Renaissance may be getting up to in Elysium, and what company they are keeping there, are obviously matters of

[31] Serassi (1747) 261–6 at 265–6. For a similar poetic genealogy (though not in an Elysian setting) including Callimachus, Propertius and Petrarch, see Landino, *Xandra* 2.4.1–12 with Tateo (1987) 51–2.

speculation; but that their aspirations for the afterlife achieved some measure of fulfilment, at least, in the terrestrial sphere is indicated by the existence of manuscripts containing the texts of both the Roman elegists and their later imitators (including the notorious *Hermaphroditus* of Antonio Beccadelli (Panormita, 1394–1471)).[32]

By using the resonant names of their predecessors in the elegiac genre, as those predecessors had themselves peppered their work with the names of Callimachus and Philitas (see Propertius 2.34.31–2, 3.1.1, 3.9.43–4), the Renaissance elegists attempt to harness for their own productions the cultural cachet attaching to the literature of antiquity. How far the results live up to the comparisons they invite is for the individual reader to decide. Not even the most ardent supporter of Renaissance Latin love elegy would maintain that every neo-Latin collection of erotic elegies displays the same degree of inventiveness or achieves equal success in its imitation of classical and post-classical models; but given the relative attention each has received from scholars of Latin poetry, it is perhaps even truer of Renaissance elegy than it is of its ancient counterpart to say that with closer scrutiny (to resort to a conceit of the kind enjoyed by the elegists themselves)[33] you will undoubtedly find more in *amores*.

Further reading

Complete texts of Renaissance elegiac collections are not always easily available, and indeed some still exist only in manuscript, or in early printed editions; there are generous selections in Arnaldi et al. (1964), Perosa and Sparrow (1979) and Laurens and Balavoine (1975), and the Anglophone reader may profit from a smaller selection with translations in McFarlane (1980) 39–65. Thanks to the I Tatti Renaissance Library (published by Harvard University Press), and to recent editions such as Murgatroyd (2000), many more neo-Latin texts of the period are now accessible in English translation than was previously the case. For the study of Renaissance Latin elegy, as for any aspect of neo-Latin literature, Ijsewijn and Sacré (1990–8) remains indispensable. Useful introductory surveys in English can be found in Parken (2012), Fantazzi (1996), Ludwig (1976) and Sparrow (1960) – the last on Renaissance Latin verse more generally, but an excellent point of departure for further study. Pieper (2008) ranges more widely than its subtitle (the Latin title is derived from a line of Marrasio) would suggest,

32 See Tateo (1987) 53. For Beccadelli see Parker (2010); O'Connor (2001); Coppini (1990).

33 Cf. Propertius 2.1.47 with Papanghelis (1987) 41–5, 64; Tibullus 1.1.69–70; Ovid, *Amores* 2.7.10, *Ars amatoria* 1.372.

and includes discussions of Beccadelli, Marrasio and Piccolomini, as well as Landino; an important new collection is Cardini and Coppini (2009). On the fortunes of Propertius in particular, see La Penna (1977) 263–74, Coppini (1981), Tateo (1987) and Gavinelli (2006); and on the Catullan tradition (which encompasses lyric and hendecasyllabic pieces as well as erotic elegy), Gaisser (1993) can be warmly recommended, along with the work of Walther Ludwig – see e.g. Ludwig (1990). But reliable texts of individual authors are still urgently required, even for some of the most celebrated neo-Latin poets, and the field as a whole is clearly open for further research.

19

VICTORIA MOUL

English elegies of the sixteenth and seventeenth century

There are plenty of poems titled or described as 'elegies' in early modern England, and a considerably larger volume of occasional Latin verse composed in elegiac couplets. But for the classicist interested in the reception of Latin love elegy even a cursory survey of this material presents an obvious problem: most of the best known English Renaissance 'elegies' are not concerned with love. These are poems of death and mourning (the modern English 'elegiac'), or of praise, usually of one man for another; and while many of them are beautiful, they have relatively little to say to the reader fresh from Propertius, Tibullus and Ovid who wants to know what happened to that material, how it was read and what it meant, to authors in the sixteenth and seventeenth century.[1]

If we set about to look specifically for British love elegy in this period, we find two things. Firstly, a small set of English poems which do follow closely in the tradition of the Augustan elegists, including Marlowe's fine translations of Ovid, and a group of English elegies which have been of particular interest to literary historians for their uncertain allocation between Ben Jonson and John Donne.[2] Secondly, if we venture from English into the substantial but understudied terrain of early modern Latin poetry, we find a very considerable body of verse in detailed and often imaginative dialogue with Roman elegy. These two closely related sub-traditions are the focus of this essay.

Before looking closely at a selection of authors, collections and poems, we should consider the bibliographical background. By 1500, all three Latin elegists had appeared in several editions, and new editions continued to be produced throughout the sixteenth century, chiefly on the continent. Major textual work and commentary on these poets was still however fairly

[1] For an introduction to elegy as lament, see Bloomfield (1986) and Clymer (2010).
[2] *The Underwood*, 38–41 in Herford and Simpson (1925–52).

recent, and dominated by Julius Caesar Scaliger (1484–1558) and Marc Antoine Muret (1526–85). Muretus was a friend of Ronsard, whose *Amours* (1552) and *Amours diverses* (1578) show the influence of the Latin elegists: although they are not the focus of this essay, French and Italian vernacular and neo-Latin literature stand alongside sixteenth century classical scholarship as influences upon British Latin elegiac poets. Luke Houghton's chapter in this volume offers an excellent survey of the most significant fifteenth and sixteenth century continental elegists.

English translations of the Roman elegists are, however, harder to come by: Golding's translation of the *Metamorphoses* was published in 1565, and Turbeville's version of the *Heroides* in 1567, but Marlowe's *Amores* was in 1599 the first published translation of the love elegies into English, and no English translations of Propertius or Tibullus were printed until the eighteenth century. This is not of course to say that none were being made – manuscript commonplace books and miscellanies often include passages of translation from these authors, though not always marked as such, and translation into and out of Latin verse was a standard school exercise.

Finally, while modern classicists are used to talking about 'love elegy' as a genre of its own, early modern scholarship, like the ancient critics, spoke simply of 'elegiac verse'. Ovid's Renaissance popularity – and presence in the curriculum – extended, for instance, to the *Tristia* and *Fasti*, works read much less often than the erotic verse today. 'Latin elegy' probably looked to an early modern imitator, on average, somewhat broader and less necessarily a genre of love and subjection than it does to a typical modern student.

This background, of good – but quite recent – Latin editions, few or no English translations, and a hint of continental glamour lies behind the vogue for Latin elegy within a certain circle of well-educated young men in the 1590s. In this decade we find Marlowe's accomplished translations of Ovid's *Amores* book I as well as Campion's *Liber Elegiarum* (published in the *Poemata* of 1595). Given a very large amount of material, both English and (especially) Latin, such a brief discussion as this must be necessarily selective; but the influence of Marlowe in English and of Campion in Latin is felt upon each of the British elegists discussed in this chapter (Ben Jonson, John Donne, John Milton and Abraham Cowley). In my discussion of these authors, I will focus in particular upon three main aspects of their appropriation of the classical genre: the combination of conventional elegiac features with generic innovation and extension; the adoption of and variation upon the motif of *recusatio*; and the ways in which elegy is used to mark poetic ambition and identity.

Recasting the familiar

Several of Marlowe's translations are of the very highest order – it is hard to think of a better translation of *Amores* 1.5 than his, beginning 'In summer's heat, and midtime of the day'. The love elegies of Ben Jonson and of John Donne stand at several removes from such close translation, but nevertheless derive many key features from Latin love elegy, especially Ovid – and, within Ovid, from the first book of the *Amores* in particular. Donne's first elegy, for instance, imitates Ovid *Amores* 1.4: both poems describe the conduct of two covert lovers at a dinner at which the woman's husband is also present. Ovid's poem is prospective – he looks forward to the dinner (though lamenting the husband's very existence), and describes to his mistress the various ways in which they can contrive to communicate with one another without him realizing. Compare Donne's version of the scenario:

> O give him many thanks, he's courteous,
> That in suspecting kindly warneth us.
> Wee must not, as wee us'd, flout openly,
> In scoffing ridles, his deformitie;
> Nor at his boord together being satt,
> With words, nor touch, scarce lookes adulterate.
> Nor when he swolne, and pamper'd with great fare,
> Sits downe, and snorts, cag'd in his basket chaire,
> Must wee usurpe his owne bed any more,
> Nor kisse and play in his house, as before.
> Now I see many dangers; for it is
> His realme, his castle, and his diocesse. (15–26)

Dramatically, Donne's poem appears to follow Ovid's. The lovers have clearly practised their Ovidian tricks at previous dinners at the husband's house ('at his boord [table] together being satt', 19), and he has become suspicious ('in suspecting kindly warneth us', 16). Donne's elegist suggests a solution: they should simply go elsewhere:

> But if, as envious men, which would revile
> Their Prince, or coyne his gold, themselves exile
> Into another countrie, 'doe it there,
> Wee play'in another house, what should we feare?
> There we will scorne his houshold policies,
> His seely plots, and pensionary spies,
> As the inhabitants of Thames right side
> Do Londons Major, or Germans, the Popes pride.
> (27–34, end)

In this way, Donne begins his collection of elegies with a homage to Ovid that is also a sequel: an imitation that acknowledges – and makes humorous play of – its own secondary status.

We find a similar combination of allusion and comment, once again probably upon *Amores* 1.4, and certainly upon the elegiac scenario of a married lover, in Jonson, *Underwoods* 19 ('An Elegie'). In this apparently straightforward love poem, which begins by enumerating the charms of his beloved's eyes, brow, hair, cheeks and lips, the beloved's husband makes an unexpected appearance in the final sentence:

> To use the present, then, is not abuse,
> You have a husband is the just excuse
> Of all that can be done him (21–3)

We recognize the sentiment here – a pithy version of the same *carpe diem* motif in Marvell's 'To His Coy Mistress', alongside many others – but the concise cynicism goes beyond anything we find even in Ovid.

In these two examples, Jonson and Donne depend upon familiarity with elegiac text and convention in order to create poetic energy from their comment and extension upon it. Jonson (perhaps with an eye upon the critique of elegiac lament in Horace) titles his poem an 'elegie', but develops the theme in the direction of satire. Donne 'updates' the scenario both in dramatic relation to Ovid's poem and in the links he makes between the domestic politics of the unfaithful lovers and the political and religious affiliations of contemporary England and Germany.

Campion too makes a point of juxtaposing the classical conventions of the genre with contemporary references. The fourth poem in his 1595 collection of Latin elegies, 'De Mellea Lusus', begins:

> Pulchra roseta inter mea Mellea pulchrior illis
> Dum legit umbroso mollia fraga solo:
> uenit Amor, qui iam pharetra positisque sagittis . . .
> (1–3)[3]

> While in a fair rose-garden my Mellea, fairer still, was picking tender strawberries from the shady ground. Love came and now, his quiver and arrows set aside . . .

If we pause at the end of line 3, at which point Cupid has arrived (*Venit Amor*), and laid aside his quiver and arrows (*qui iam pharetra positisque sagittis*), we might expect a motif of 'Cupid-in-love', or the love-god disarmed – a fairly conventional twist. But our expectations are

[3] Campion's Latin is cited from Vivian (1909). Translations are my own.

confounded – as we read on from lines 3 to 4 we discover that Cupid has set down his arrows only to replace them with a more modern weapon: *gestitat igniuomo ferra forata cauo* ('... was wielding bored-out irons with fire-belching muzzles', 4). Campion's Cupid sports a musket.

Poetic originality

Campion's joke, like Jonson's unexpected husband, relies upon the reader's knowledge of the conventions of the genre to appreciate the departure from them. With varying degrees of sophistication, all the British elegists demonstrate their ability to recast the tropes of Latin love elegy in this way. But an explicit declaration of originality is itself an elegiac trope. At the opening of his third book, Propertius announces his own originality in terms (ironically) familiar from Callimachus, Theocritus, Horace, Virgil and Lucretius before him: *primus ego ingredior puro de fonte sacerdos / Itala per Graios orgia ferre choros*, 'I am the first to enter, a priest from a pure spring and bear the mystic emblems of Italy in Greek dances' (3. 1. 3–4).

Accordingly, Campion too imitates both this motif and its self-conscious appropriation from earlier authors. Consider the opening lines of the first elegy in his 1595 collection:

Ite procul tetrici, moneo, procul ite seueri,
    Ludit censuras pagina nostra graues.
Ite senes nisi forte aliquis torpente medulla
    Carminibus flammas credit inesse meis.
Aptior ad teneros lusus florentior aetas,
    Vel iuuenis, uel me docta puella legat.
Et uatem celebrent Bruti de nomine primum
    Qui molles elegos et sua furta canat.
(1–8)

Get away you gloomy men: I warn you – depart, those who are austere. My page makes light of stern censures. Begone old men, unless by chance some one of you with his sluggish marrow believes that there is fire in my poems. The age of flowering is more suitable for tender games – may either a young man or a learned young girl read me, and may they celebrate me as the first British bard to sing gentle elegies and to tell of his tricks.

Perhaps most striking is Campion's claim that he will be celebrated as the first British poet (*uates*, a strong term, with a religious force that overlaps with Propertius' *sacerdos*) to sing of elegiac love. But in fact the passage is an artful combination of multiple classical passages, drawn from Ovid as well as Propertius.[4] At *Amores* 2.1.3–4 Ovid introduces his second volume of elegies: *hoc quoque iussit Amor – procul hinc, procul este, seueri! / non estis teneris apta theatra modis* (Amor commands this too – get far away, far away, you solemn types! / You are not a fit audience for my tender lines) (*Am.* 2.1.3–4). Ovid goes on to designate those for whom his verse is suitable: the *non frigida uirgo* (5) and the *puer* in love for the first time (6). Campion has imitated both the gesture of rejection – *ite procul tetrici, moneo, procul ite seueri*' (1) – and the description of his intended audience: *uel iuuenis, uel me docta puella legat* (6). The *docta puella* is of course herself a well-known feature of Latin love elegy, found for instance at Ovid's *Ars amatoria* (2. 281). Other elements can also be traced to classical poetry: Campion's *sua furta*, for instance, perhaps looks towards Leander's expression, in his letter to Hero at *Heroides* 18.64: *flecte, precor, uultus ad mea furta tuos* ('turn your gracious attention, I beseech you, upon my stolen pleasures'). Finally, the *teneros lusus* (5) for which Campion claims his age fits him may derive from Ovid, *Amores* 3.1: *quod tenerae cantent, lusit tua Musa, puellae, / primaque per numeros acta iuuenta suos*, 'Your Muse has been playing at the songs soft girls sing, the mere juvenilia of her poetry' (27–8).

This combination of models is plainly programmatic: Campion is marking out his poem as an elegy in the tradition of the first century BC; he lays claim, too, to the traditional (and paradoxical) mode of originality – to be the first, as a British Latin poet, to emulate Propertius' self-declared act of combined imitation and innovation. There is nothing careless about the appropriation here: notice how the list of echoes includes *Amores* 2.1 and 3.1 and Propertius 3.1 – all the opening poems of their books.

John Milton, who certainly knew Campion's Latin poetry well, revisits this claim of innovation in the fourth of his remarkable collection of elegies. Published in the 1645 *Poems*, the seven poems of Milton's *Liber Elegiarum* include two to Milton's friend Charles Diodati (*E.* 1 and 6), two marking deaths (of the beadle of Cambridge University, *E.* 2, and of the Bishop of Winchester, *E.* 3), one to Milton's previous tutor, Thomas Young (*E.* 4), and two more conventional pieces: on the coming of spring (*E.* 5) and on love (*E.* 7).

E. 4 dates from early in Milton's career. He was eighteen in 1627 at the time of its composition, and it is addressed to his old tutor Thomas Young – not a university tutor, but a home tutor, probably dating from the years immediately before he started at St. Paul's, perhaps between the ages of around nine and twelve.

[4] There are hints here too of Martial (*Epigrams* 11.2) and Catullus (5).

Primus ego Aonios illo praeeunte recessus
  Lustrabam, et bifidi sacra uireta iugi;
Pieriosque hausi latices, Clioque fauente,
  Castalio sparsi laeta ter ora mero.
(29–32)[5]

With him as my guide I first wandered the Aonian retreats and the sacred glades of the twin-peaked mountain. There I drank of the Pierian waters and, favoured by Clio, three times I wet my joyful lips with pure Castalian wine.

Milton uses here the same passage of Propertius 3.1 alluded to by Campion, but he blends it with the opening of Virgil's *Georgics* 3 (of which Propertius' own lines are themselves an imitation): *primus ego in patriam mecum, modo uita supersit, / Aonio rediens deducam uertice Musas*, 'I will be first, if only I live long enough, to return from the peak of Helicon and bring the Muses with me into my native land' (*G.* 3.10–11).[6] The *primus* which denotes in Virgil the originality of laureate achievement, and the innovation of Greek forms in Latin verse, becomes Milton's literal and biographical 'first': Thomas Jones, the addressee, is the man with whom Milton quite literally first read these authors. The reversal of first writing to first reading is rather moving, but it does not detract from the statement of confidence and authority that the allusion encodes. In the *Georgics*, Virgil goes on to speak of bringing Greek palms to Mantua, and of how he will build a temple for Caesar on the banks of the Mincius – a temple usually supposed to refer to the *Aeneid* itself. Whereas Propertius 3.1 (like Ovid's *Amores* 1.1) is a *recusatio*,[7] in which the poet banishes epic poetry in preference for the elegy of national peace, Milton's poem pushes elegy explicitly towards epic, describing Thomas Young as a Puritan exile from England, reimagined as the hero of a Biblical epic.

Elegy in an English landscape

Milton's first elegy exerts similar pressure upon the elegiac genre. Addressed from London to his friend Charles Diodati, holidaying in Chester during their Christmas vacation from Cambridge, Milton poses in this poem as a cheerful exile:

Me tenet urbs reflua quam Thamesis alluit unda,
  Meque nec inuitum patria dulcis habet.

5 Milton's Latin is cited from Carey and Fowler (1968). Translations are my own.

6 This well-known passage is imitated repeatedly in classical literature, and is itself an imitation (of Lucretius and Ennius); see Hinds (1998), 52–5.

7 See Sharrock (Chapter 9) in this volume.

Iam nec arundiferum mihi cura reuisere Camum,
    Nec dudum uetiti me laris angit amor.
Nuda nec arua placent, umbrasque negantia molles,
    Quam male Phoebicolis conuenit ille locus!
. . .
Si sit hoc exilium patrios adiisse penates,
    Et uacuum curis otia grata sequi,
Non ego uel profugi nomen, sortemue recuso,
    Laetus et exilii conditione fruor.
O utinam uates nunquam grauiora tulisset
    Ille Tomitano flebilis exul agro;
Non tunc Ionio quicquam cessisset Homero
    Neue foret uicto laus tibi prima Maro.
(9–12 and 17–24)

That city upon which the Thames tide laps holds me fast. This sweet homeland detains me – not unwillingly. I've no longing to revisit the reedy Cam, nor do I suffer from a love for a home long denied me. Bare fields that offer no gentle shade give no pleasure. How badly that place suits followers of Phoebus! . . . If exile means to return to my father's house, and, carefree, pass the time in pleasant pursuits, then I do not reject either the name or the fate of a fugitive, and I enjoy the exile's state with pleasure. Would that the poet had suffered no worse in the fields of Tomis, sorrowing exile as he was – then he would have ceded nothing to Ionian Homer; and the highest praise would no longer be yours, defeated Maro.

In the fifteenth and final poem of *Amores* I, Ovid compares his work – and resultant fame – to a string of Greek and Latin poets, from Homer to Gallus. In the same way, Milton here compares himself boldly to Ovid, but with their situations reversed. The bare and shadeless fields of Cambridge – from which he declares himself a happy exile – echo those of Ovid's exile by the Black Sea (*Pont.* 1.3.55–6: *quocumque aspicies, campi cultore carentes / uastaque, quae nemo uindicat, arua iacent*, 'wherever you look, you see a spread of uncultivated plains, and enormous fields which no-one tends'). By contrast, Milton's London offers all the delights of Rome – especially the particularly Ovidian pleasures of beautiful women of many kinds (*Gloria uirginibus debetur prima Britannis*, 'The chief glory is owed to British girls', 71).

By claiming that, had Ovid avoided exile, he might have outdone Homer and Virgil, Milton at once alludes to, and dismisses *Amores* 1.15, while implying that his own work – untrammelled by such misfortune – may succeed where Ovid failed. Whereas Donne's first elegy is set dramatically after the Ovidian poem to which it alludes (*Amores* 1.4), here Milton compares his own first elegy to Ovid's very latest work. At only 17, Milton recasts not – as we might expect – the start of Ovid's career, but its end.

Such pronounced poetic ambition marks, too, the second poem to Diodati (*E.* 6), in which Milton revisits the question of genre, and distinguishes between his friend's naturally elegiac temperament and his own more austere poetic vocation. 'Light Elegy' (*E.* 6.49) plays host to Bacchus, Erato, Ceres, Venus and *cum purpurea matre tenellus Amor* ('Tender little Cupid with his purple mother', 51); whereas Milton's own sober Muse is destined to reach beyond elegy towards epic and religious themes: *At qui bella refert, et adulto sub Ioue caelum, / Heroasque pios, semideosque duces*..., 'But as for [the poet] who tells of wars, and heaven beneath the command of a full-grown Jove, / of pious heroes, and semi-divine commanders' (*E.* 6. 55–6). Those 'pious' heroes and 'semi-divine' warriors are designed to remind us of the *Aeneid* and the *Iliad* respectively: once again, Milton's elegiacs begin with Ovid, but extend beyond him towards all that the conventional *recusatio* appears to reject.

Milton's less solemn fourth elegy praises London, and claims that British women outdo those of the *Heroides*, of Greece, Rome and of the Bible. Campion's first elegy moves similarly from love to national feeling, characterized by the beauty of the country's river nymphs and its literary heritage.

> Quid sacras memorem nymphis habitantibus undas,
> Siue tuas Thamesis, siue, Sabrina, tuas?
> Mille etiam Charites siluis, totidemque Napaeae,
> Tot Veneres, tot eunt Indigenaeque deae.
> Ut taceam musas, toto quas orbe silentes
> Chaucerus mira fecerat arte loqui.
>
> (*Elegy* 1, in 1595 *Poemata*)

What should I recount about the nymphs in your holy waters, Thames, or in yours, Severn? A thousand nymphs pass through our forests, and a thousand valley sprites, Venuses, and native English goddesses. To say nothing of the Muses, once silent, whom by his wonderful art Chaucer taught to speak throughout the world!

Despite the programmatically Latin and elegiac cues with which Campion's first elegy begins, it ends by redefining elegy in forcefully sixteenth-century terms: the love, leisure and strictly erotic battles of elegy are a product, he claims, of Elizabethan military victory and religious independence from Rome: *Iuris sola sui gentes procul Anglia ridet / Tendentes Latio libera colla iugo* ('Only far-off England, living by its own law, laughs at the nations stretching their free necks into the yoke of Latium', 33–4). Key tropes of love elegy – the servitude of love, and love as a kind of military service[8] – are recast by Campion with political force: because they are free of the real slavery and unrest on the continent, the English are free to sing of the *arma* ('weapons', 40) and *fera bella* ('wild battles', 39) of love.

Elegiac women and the female voice

This link between elegy and national feeling is related to the pressure that propels Milton's elegy away from the *recusatio* of his classical models towards an epic register. But one aspect of modern interest in Latin love elegy that we have not seen much reflected in the early modern genre is an imaginative engagement with the depiction of gender, both male and female, or any instance of the female perspective we find in the *Heroides*. In the final section of this essay, I would like to turn to a remarkable series of Latin elegies dating from the middle of the seventeenth century – the first two books of Abraham Cowley's *Plantarum Libri Sex* ('Six Books of Plants'). The elegies were published alone in 1662, and then again as the first two of six books in 1668 (the others being in lyric metres and hexameter).

Cowley's elegies share certain features with Milton and Campion: a version of elegy that is politically serious and strongly positive about the British future, both politically and poetically. Moreoever, this version of elegy is strongly gendered. With the exception of the opening lines, each of the herbs in the first two books, all of whom are female, speak *in propria persona*; and while the first book is a kind of medley, the second has a dramatic structure – a meeting of herbs useful for women in pregnancy and childbirth, held at night in the botanic garden at Oxford. In addition, Cowley's work is didactically serious: each poem is accompanied by a substantial body of Latin notes pointing us to the relevant authorities both scientific and literary.

This surprising combination amounts to a substantial redeployment of elegiac convention. The maiden-hair fern (*Capillus Veneris*), for instance, describes the origin of her own name in the following lines:

> Funditur augurio noster meliore Capillus,
>   Et non de nihilo nomen Amoris habet.
> Ipsa mihi multum scit se debere Venustas,
>   Ipse meis telis retia nectit Amor.
> A me formosi lasciua uolumina Crinis,
>   Plaudentisque humeros umbra decora comae,

[8] See Fulkerson (Chapter 11) and Drinkwater (Chapter 12) in this volume.

> Me cole quisquis amas; laetam nutrire memento
> Caesariem, et toto uertice tende plagas.
> (Maiden-Hair fern, *Capillus Veneris* 11–18)[9]

> My hair was born of far better origins [than other ferns], it is not for nothing that it has the name of Love. Beauty herself knows that she owes me much, and Love ties his nets from my threads. Wanton curls of beautiful hair come from me, and shoulders finely shaded by sweeping locks. Whoever you are, worship me if you are in love; remember to nourish your fine hair and spread your nets around your whole head.

There are several points to be made here. As elegy, these lines have a conventional feel, marked by the personification of beauty (*Venustas*) and love (*Amor*), the erotic connotations of long hair (the curls are *lasciua*, 15), and a tone of mildly ironic instruction in the techniques of grooming and courtship. These conventional features have however been harnessed to didactic effect: the maiden-hair fern who speaks the poem is so called because her fronds resemble hair; but also, according to these lines (and a substantial note) because the plant itself is good for hair – basically, an effective conditioner. The tone of humorous instruction in these lines owes much to the *Ars amatoria*, which mentions the importance of careful hair-styling for a woman (*Ars* 3.132) and lists a variety of options, including long hair worn down (*Ars* 3.141–2).[10] Cowley has marked the Ovidian register with a specific allusion: the *tende plagas* of line 18 echoes *Ars* 1.269–70: *Prima tuae menti fiducia, cunctas / posse capi; capies, tu modo tende plagas*, 'First be assured: all women can be caught; only spread your nets, and you will catch them'. Cowley's speaking fern makes beautiful tresses stand in for Ovid's more general array of seductive ploys.

The joke is that in each Ovidian poem the voice is strongly male, whether advising women on their hairstyles or other men on their courtship; whereas in Cowley the roles are reversed: a female plant is telling *men* (not women) how to look good. In fact, Cowley goes rather further than this. We associate women speaking in elegy either with the *puella* or with a tragic heroine, generally destined for rape and abandonment. Cowley's version of this motif develops that tradition in a peculiarly positive direction – a positivity that is related, I think, to the national pride and epic certainty we found in Milton and Campion, but combined in Cowley with a peculiarly mid-seventeenth century optimism about emergent scientific knowledge.

9 There is no modern edition of the *Plantarum*. Quotations are taken from Cowley (1668), images of which can be found on Early English Books Online (http://eebo.chadwyck.com/home).

10 Note too Ovid, *Amores* 1.14, addressed to a woman who has ruined her hair with harsh dyes.

Later in book 1, for instance, we find the poem on Nymphea, the water-lily who, it turns out, has an elegiac story of her own: a beautiful nymph, she was seduced and then abandoned by Hercules:

Nympha fui, *Dea* postremae non infima classis;
    Venit *Amor*: quid tum profuit esse *Deam*?
Flammipotens iubet Ille: accendor in *Hercule* uiso,
    Totque *Triumphorum* pars *Dea* parua fui.
[...]
Ille meos (quid multa?) ferus decerpsit honores
    Ille meae *Florem Virginitatis* habet.
(5–8, 17–18)

I was a nymph, a goddess of no small rank; but then Love came: what good was my godhead then? In his flaming power he ordered me: I took fire at the sight of Hercules, and I a goddess was but a small part of his total triumphs. [...] For he (what more is there to say?) fiercely plucked my honour and took the flower of my virginity.

In her shame and misery, she wishes to die; but, as a goddess, cannot. At this point, we are still in plainly elegiac territory, and Cowley signals as much. The pool created by her ceaseless weeping is described, at line 42, with a phrase that echoes the abandoned Ariadne of Catullus 64, the bereft Cornelia of Propertius 4.11 and finally Gallus, addressed by Propertius in a poem that compares Gallus' beloved to Hylas, whom Hercules loved.[11]

Interea lacrymas fundo noctemque diemque,
    Hac mihi Clepsydra tempora longa fluunt.
Fit Lacus e denso tandem mirabilis imbre,
    Et collecta meos alluit unda pedes.
(39–42)

Meanwhile I pour forth tears both day and night, and by that – my water-clock – long ages flow past. At length a remarkable pool is created from the ceaseless shower, and the collected waters lap at my feet.

At this point, however, the poem takes a surprising turn. Jupiter, taking pity on Nymphea, turns her into a plant that grows in wet conditions with a

[11] Catullus 64.67: *omnia quae toto delapsa e corpore passim / ipsius ante pedes fluctus salis adludebant* ('the waves of the very sea were lapping against all the clothes shed from her entire body'); Propertius 4.11.16: *et quaecumque meos implicat unda pedes* ('whatever wave enfolds my feet'); Propertius 1.20.8: *siue Aniena tuos tinxerit unda pedes* (7–8, 'whether the wave of the Anio moistens your feet'). Interestingly, Propertius 1.20 is also the source of an extended allusion in Milton's seventh elegy.

sturdy root, the so-called 'club of Hercules'. In her new form, Nymphea is no longer sorrowful, but, on the contrary, considers herself cheerful, lucky and, above all, useful – because her suffering has seen her transformed into a plant with the power to ease exactly that painful experience by which she was defeated.

Certe hominum miseret, quos mille incommoda uitae
    Et ferus exercet, Maxima pestis, Amor.
Non ignara mali, ueterumue oblita dolorum,
    Extinguo flammas, saeue Cupido, tuas,
Victoremqe meum tandem uicisse triumpho.
    Iniusta has iustum est Regna subire uices.
Ne te mireris uictae cessisse, Cupido,
    Me meus Alcides uincere Monstra docet.
(61–8)

I pity men, whom a thousand cares harass, and, the greatest plague of all, ferocious love. While not unaware of my suffering, or forgetful of my ancient griefs, I extinguish your flames, fierce Cupid, and I am triumphant in my victory over my conqueror. It is right for unjust rule to suffer such reversals. Don't be surprised, Cupid, that you have lost to her whom you conquered before; my Hercules taught me to conquer monsters.

As Cowley's note makes clear, preparations made from the water-lily plant are believed to assuage lust and fevers of various kinds. This metamorphosed woman-cum-herb not only has the power to speak, and retains it after her transformation (unlike in Ovid), she is able to be positively constructive – her typically elegiac suffering functions as a source of (and aide-memoire for) her scientific usefulness.

Cowley's female herbs are far removed from Donne's knowing version of *Amores* 1.4, or Campion's armed Cupid. But each of these pieces relies for its effect upon a knowledge of the tropes and conventions of classical Latin elegy, and a pleasure in their extension and variation. Cowley's six books of plants will move on from elegy to higher genres and subjects – lyric and hexameter, the conquest of America, the English civil war and the Restoration. But just as Milton uses elegy to look towards epic, so too does Cowley extend the range of subject and diction which his elegiac verse – and the female characters who speak it – can be made to sustain. The second and last book of his elegies concludes with a remarkable example of this kind of expansion. The book ends when Robert, the gardener, interrupts Myrrh in a long and technical account, marked by Lucretian vocabulary, of the origin and conception not only of children, but of life and indeed of the elements themselves.

Conclusion

This brief survey is necessarily selective, and a great deal has gone unmentioned – in particular, I have not discussed any of the examples of elegiac verse, whether English or Latin, found in the rich manuscript sources of this period; nor have I considered any of the examples of love elegies addressed to historical women – such as Jonson's interesting *Eupheme* sequence (*UW* 84, in memory of Lady Venetia Digby). Much work remains to be done on the reception of the Roman elegists in these works. We find in English and Latin elegies of the sixteenth and seventeenth century, as we might expect, charming appropriations of the tone and tropes of Roman love elegy; but also a great deal more – a body of work which is marked by flexibility and innovation, and which uses a given familiarity with the Latin genre to think in unexpected ways about poetic and political identity, gender and even emergent science.

Further reading

Relatively little critical work discusses early modern elegies, whether English or Latin, in relation to the classical genre. Braden (2010) includes a brief discussion of Donne in the context of continental neo-Latin poetry, but does not discuss British Latin elegiacs. Ijsewijn in Ijsewijn and Sacré (1990–8) has a very concise but stimulating overview of neo-Latin elegy, with a useful bibliography – but again, no treatment of British authors. Binns (1974 and 1990) and Bradner (1940) provide some information on the Latin poetry of Campion, Milton and Cowley, but with no particular focus upon elegy. A few articles do consider British authors specifically as elegists, though these can be hard to find – among the most useful are Peacock (1975 and 1979) and Skulsky (1973). Of the British neo-Latin poets, Milton is by far the best served: Carey and Fowler's (1968) annotated edition of Milton's verse includes good notes on classical parallels and Revard (2009) includes a reliable parallel text translation of the Latin verse. Readers new to neo-Latin literature as a whole may consult Helander (2001) for a recent overview.

20

STEPHANIE LOUBÈRE

Translation and imitation of classical elegy in the French eighteenth century

The history of ancient elegiac poetry in eighteenth-century France is particularly unusual on account of that century's complex relationship with both poetry and antiquity.

The French poetry of the Enlightenment was passing through a crisis. Alongside poetic turmoil manifested by the prevailing 'metromania' and the proliferation of collections of poetry, a debate arose concerning the value of the genre, seen from two points of view. The question was not only whether the poetry of the Moderns could match the models inherited from the past, but also how its merits compared with other genres, all of which were affected by mutations that were upsetting the literary landscape during this century. Poetry needed to find a dignity that constantly eluded it: what was its position, faced as it was with the flowering of the novel, an explosion in the taste for drama and the expansion of the literature of ideas? The question of modernity as posed by the great Quarrel between the Ancients and the Moderns that arose in France in the second half of the seventeenth century and continued far into the eighteenth likewise influenced and often complicated poetry's relationship to its models. Before it was possible to speak of 'a return to antiquity' during the second half of the eighteenth century, an ongoing debate had repeatedly compared the authors of the century of Louis XIV to those of the century of Augustus and the French language to Latin and Greek, in an attempt to assess the relative value and define the limits of a modernity that was unable to find its identity without constantly measuring up to the ancient model.

The place of ancient elegy within the field of French literature was affected by this context pervaded by tensions and a debate that both looked beyond it and yet included it. Moreover, it is impossible to dissociate the history of the fortunes of ancient elegy from the progressive emancipation that now characterized the production of national poetry: French elegy became

Translated by Janet Lloyd

involved in a redistribution of poetic inspiration when it discovered a new lyricism that prefigured the explosion of Romanticism and played its part in liberating poetry from the dead-end in which it had seemed to be trapped.

The presence of ancient elegy in French literature up to the eighteenth century

In France, the elegiac legacy had a somewhat complicated history. The ancient genre was undeniably much appreciated but also met with a degree of distrust which accounts for the mixed reputation attached to this poetic genre.

Up until the seventeenth century, with the exception of Ovid, who constitutes a special case, the authors of the elegiac corpus (Catullus, Tibullus and Propertius), among whom Maximian,[1] wrongly believed to be the proto-elegiac Gallus,[2] is sometimes included, were published as a group, often in expurgated versions, and translations into French were rare. However, the philological efforts that developed in the classical age made it possible to access texts established by increasingly strict methods. The publication of these reached a high point in the edition produced by the *ad usum Delphini* collection. Between 1670 and 1698, among the sixty or so volumes that constituted this collection, the elegiac poets received rather unusual treatment that was ruled by two contradictory principles. In order to produce a complete edition but one that also respected the conventions of the day, the edition of the elegies of Catullus, Tibullus and Propertius, which appeared in two volumes in 1685, included passages that had been suppressed (indicated in the text by blank spaces and rows of dots), and these were repositioned at the end of the volume. This *ad usum Delphini* edition did not contain a translation but was accompanied by notes which, positioned at the bottom of the pages, occasionally suggested a prose transposition of the verse text or an *interpretatio* that clarified the meaning. However, at the end of the seventeenth century, when the use of Latin was diminishing, that type of edition came increasingly into competition with translations. These eighteenth-century translations repeated a practice that has been noted above: Ovid was treated quite differently from the elegiac trio composed of Catullus, Tibullus and Propertius. The admiration that the elegiac works of Ovid attracted was sometimes ambiguous. Reservations were regularly expressed, bringing his qualities as an elegiac poet into question. It was Ovid's *Heroides* that finally established his fame as an elegiac poet, – not his *Amores* or his *Tristia*. In the second half of the eighteenth century, the *Heroides* became positively

[1] See Green (Chapter 16) in this volume. [2] See Raymond (Chapter 3) in this volume.

fashionable, restoring Ovid to the stature of an elegiac model and conferring upon elegy a status that it had lost. The *Heroides* became part of the debate about elegy, concentrating attention on its protean nature, with the epistolary mode being recognized as one possible form for it to take, and at the same time identifying elegy with a particular elegiac tonality that was now reduced to its plaintive dimension, whereas in the past it had been associated with a wide range of different feelings.

The fortunes of the other elegiac poets differed from that of Ovid, their most notable aspect being the fact that they were treated as a group. Catullus, Tibullus and Propertius were known as 'the elegiac triumvirate',[3] and their works seldom appeared in individual editions. In 1653 the Abbé de Marolles had produced a translation of the three elegiac poets (*Les Poésies de Catulle, Tibulle et Properce en latin et en français*) in which their poems were grouped together; and in the following century most translators combined at least two of the ancient models. La Chapelle produced his version of the *Amours de Catulle* (1680), followed by that of the *Amours de Tibulle* (1712), then combined the two in a single edition (*Les Amours de Catulle et de Tibulle*, 1716). Later, the marquis de Pezay collected the poems of the two authors together with those of Gallus in his *Traduction en prose de Catulle, Tibulle et Gallus* (1771). Gillet de Moyvre applied a style of novelettish imitation similar to that adopted by La Chapelle for the works of both Propertius and Tibullus. He published his *La Vie et les amours de Tibulle, chevalier romain* in 1743, following it up with *La vie de Properce, chevalier romain* in 1746. Not many translators, having tackled one of the elegiac poets, failed to follow up that first volume by translating the works of at least one of his fellows. *Les élégies de Properce* (1772), translated by Longchamps, were thus followed by *Les élégies de Tibulle* (1776). Later on, a Latinist such as Charles-Louis Mollevaut felt in duty bound to publish in succession his verse translations of the elegies of Tibullus (1806), Catullus and Propertius (1816) and Ovid's *Amores* (1822) and to accompany his work as a translator by the publication of a volume of *Elégies* of his own (1816) that testified to the strength of the poetic inspiration generated by imitation of the ancient elegiacs.[4]

The influence of Latin elegiacs in eighteenth-century France

The insistent presence of ancient elegiac poets in the French literary scene of the eighteenth century is manifested by the respectable number of Latin

[3] Nicéron (1731) 158.

[4] Both before and towards the end of the eighteenth century there were women writing elegies, but during the Age of the Enlightenment they are curiously absent.

editions or re-editions and, above all, by a flowering of translations and imitations. Their presence exerted a by no means negligible influence on the development of the aesthetics and poetics of the Enlightenment. The transmission of elegiac models was a feature of the debate about the 'return to antiquity' that continued throughout the century and, more specifically, the thought about genres that gradually developed around the subject of elegy and the definition of elegiac poetry contributed to the emergence of a poetics well aware of its aims and practices.

The debate on the 'return to antiquity'

The eighteenth century's relations with antiquity were somewhat paradoxical. On the one hand, the study of ancient languages was declining, but at the same time interest in that legacy was returning, as was evident in every domain of artistic creation (literature to be sure, but also painting, sculpture, architecture and so on). This was not so much a return to antiquity, rather a re-evaluation and re-interpretation of it, which made it possible for artists to relate their modern preoccupations to re-visited ancient ideals. Translating and imitating Latin elegies, models that were recognized thanks to their sometimes abrasive reputation, enabled poets to propagate, yet tone down the hedonistic streak that ran through the thought of the Enlightenment. Their works, vouched for by these ancient or pseudo-erudite references, conveyed a commonplace sensuality and constituted a centre for trying out an Epicureanism that was now rendered innocuous.

Understandably, then, the essential character of the transmission of ancient models lay in a desire to acclimatize those works to the spirit of the age and the French nation. In his famous *Art poétique* (1674), Boileau had already taken over Ovid's definition of elegy as poetry of a plaintive and erotic nature.[5] In the debate that crystallized around this genre, whose protean nature made it hard to categorize, a number of voices were raised in defence of its intrinsic ability to absorb the particular characteristics of the various nations and periods that used it.[6]

The process of acculturation seemed complete when, in a piquant reversal of perspectives, Latin elegiacs were judged by the yardstick provided by French poets: in an essay devoted to Tibullus, P.A. Guys (1779) wrote as follows: 'Tibullus is a courtier; his style is pure and limpid. He is a tender and sensual lover who writes poetry with the facility of La Fare, Chaulieu and de Gresset.'[7]

The affinities of ancient elegies with the spirit of the age and with French poetry were deliberately cultivated and account for the spate of translations

[5] See *Canto* II, lines 39–42. [6] See Michault (1743) 119–20. [7] Guys (1779) 11.

and imitations that smoothly adapted the themes bequeathed by the ancient tradition. The way in which, in ancient elegy, the feelings of love were explored in depth thus initially suited the exploration of *galanterie* and *libertinage* within the devious workings of the heart and mind. The presentation of a poet as a *praeceptor amoris* ('an instructor in love'), which we find in Ovid and the other elegiac poets, chimed particularly with a period obsessed with a desire to establish control and tempted by the idea of a system. An entire section of the poetic production of the Enlightenment was devoted to this attempt to found an art of loving, which was prompted by the desire to understand, the better to control, the sphere of feelings and amorous sensations. It thus seems perfectly natural that Ovid's *Ars amatoria* was so popular in the eighteenth century. It can be explained by a deep complicity between the Age of Augustus and the Age of Enlightenment: in Augustan society as among the nobility of the Enlightenment, love occupied a central place. The *Art of Love* expresses erotic and literary preoccupations to which a man of the Enlightenment was bound to be sensitive, attracted by its acute psychological understanding, its obsessive preoccupation with the senses and pleasure, its praise of freedom and its taste for formal sophistication and witty remarks. This affinity was a matter of content as much as form. The quest for pleasure generated a playful concept of love and, at the same time, favoured a hedonistic approach to feeling and the act of love: it was an affinity that in itself was enough to account for the fact that the oeuvre of this ancient poet was so easily integrated into the literary heritage of the France of the Age of Enlightenment.

But this complicity spread well beyond Ovid and his *Art of Love*. It was connected with the major aesthetic trends of the century. From the second half of the eighteenth century onward, the emergence of an aesthetic of sensibility recaptured the field of knowledge of love, while personal poetry in quest of a new lyricism discovered a regenerated model in the poetic novels that the collections of ancient elegies constituted. Furthermore, the theme of lamentation, which progressively became a distinctive characteristic of elegy, also echoed the mood of the time, particularly after the French Revolution.

The destiny of the elegiac poets was thus inseparable from the aesthetic debates that animated the eighteenth-century republic of letters. That destiny went hand in hand with an evolution in taste, which it is possible to trace through the history of the eighteenth-century reception of the ancient elegiac poets.

The influence of ancient elegiac poetry in France was mostly purveyed through the Latin heritage. However, the debt that Latin poets owed to their Greek models was regularly recalled, in particular in order to suggest a kind of historical continuity of elegiac inspiration, which would make it possible to strengthen the sense of affiliation and hence legitimacy that Enlightenment poetry expressed. This is what the duc de Nivernais was suggesting when he asked: 'Should we not, following the Latins, be doing what they did following the Greeks?'[8] In a century in which the question of progress was at times the subject of ferocious polemic, the revelation of an elegiac heritage was inevitably accompanied by thought about the possible decadence of this genre. Jaucourt, in the *Réflexions* that he devoted to elegy for the *Encyclopédie*, formulated this idea rather vaguely when he expressed his regret at the degradation of the genre introduced by Latin elegy, in comparison to its Greek models ('The Latins, taking over various forms of verse from the Greeks, reduced them to a type of correctness that borders on sterility and monotony').[9] Jaucourt was equally hard on the poets of his own time: 'A number of modern poets have also devoted themselves to elegy. Unfortunately they have, for the most part, substituted falsity for truth, pompousness for simplicity and the language of wit for that of nature!'[10]

Theorists of the elegiac genre, taking as their models sometimes Latin authors (e.g. Batteux and Marmontel in the early eighteenth century), sometimes Greek ones (e.g. Millevoye and Treneuil at the beginning of the nineteenth century), testify to this evolution in taste. Among the elegiac poets of the late eighteenth century, preference for the Greek rather than the Latin model came to reflect a desire to return to sources, to the 'purity' or 'naivety' of the genre (to borrow the terms that were later to be used by Chénier). It so happens that the greater part of the Greek elegiac corpus has been lost. But far from discouraging a return to the Greek model, that disappearance contributed to the aura that surrounded it and that has been increasingly affirmed as the centuries have passed. In his *Réflexions sur l'élégie*, Jaucourt reviews these paradoxical models that were both hallowed yet little known. Most of the works have come down to us only in the form of fragments (Sappho, Philitas, Mimnermus, Hermesianax . . .). The fascination that they exerted was partly due to the disappearance of the bulk of their work, a fact that chimed with the development of a taste for ruins and incompleteness in the last years of the eighteenth century. The Latin model, with its narrative thread that ruled the composition of elegiac collections, was now superseded by the Greek model, which accommodated disorder and encouraged the cultivation of a new taste for flashes of brilliance and discontinuity in the expression of human feelings.

The question of the internal hierarchy of the various Latin elegiac poets is also worth mentioning, for this too reflects a number of interesting

[8] Nivernais (1743) 276. [9] Jaucourt (1755) 488. [10] Jaucourt (1755) 491.

mutations. The early eighteenth-century tendency to prefer Ovid to the other poets was reversed as the taste for literature of feeling increased. A further debate which, moving on from the ancient elegiac corpus as a whole, concentrated on aesthetic choices of a more general nature, concerned the respective merits of the three authors considered to be the trumpeters of elegy: Ovid, Tibullus and Propertius. Catullus, who, as we have seen, used to be regularly associated with Tibullus and Propertius, was left out of this debate. In a chapter devoted to elegy in his *Traité de la poésie française* (1724), M. Mourgues takes Ovid as a model and adds Tibullus and Propertius, but expresses reservations with regard to Catullus and Gallus: 'The elegant Tibullus, the gallant Propertius and the brilliant Ovid were foremost in devoting all the charms of their diverse minds [to elegy]. Ovid, more natural, more moving and more passionate than the other two, seems to me to have had a better understanding of the nature of elegy. Those are the masters to consult, and so too would be Catullus and Cornelius Gallus [i.e. Maximian, see above] were it not for the liberty of some of their writings, which makes them more dangerous than useful.'[11]

But the marked preference for Ovid over the other elegiac poets, expressed so crisply by Mourgues, was progressively called into question. Another theorist of elegy, J.-B. Michault, devotes part of his *Réflexions critiques sur l'élégie* (1734) to a description of this debate on the hierarchy of the three poets. He recalls the verdict of Father Rapin in the preceding century, who regarded Ovid as the most natural, the most moving and the most passionate of the three elegiac poets, but Michault, for his part, criticizes him for his excessive liberty and lasciviousness. Propertius' elegies were, in his opinion, 'too flowery and sometimes also too obscure', so he pronounced Tibullus to be the model for French writers of elegies, since 'he is clearer and his elegies are much more graceful'.[12] In the mid-eighteenth century, Marmontel expressed a rather different view of this debate, in his article for the *Encyclopédie*. In it, he tries to describe the style of each of the poets and to draw attention to their respective merits, aiming to characterize them rather than evaluate them in a hierarchical order. The elegiac Ovid stands out for 'his gracious manner', Propertius is described as 'passionate' and 'learned', while the main characteristic of Tibullus' elegies is that they are 'tender'. Unlike the qualities associated with the elegies of Ovid and Propertius, which could sometimes be regarded as faults, the essential 'tenderness' of the elegies of Tibullus placed him beyond unfavourable criticism, and did so all the more as the general taste for sensitive and personal poetry spread. So it comes as no surprise to find that, by the end of the century, Tibullus wore the crown

[11] Mourgues (1724) 271–2. [12] Michault (1743) 97–8.

as prince of the elegiac poets. The poet Le Brun praised him in a speech in which he reaffirmed Tibullus' superiority over Ovid (who manifested 'more wit than feeling' and likewise over Propertius ('he sighs so learnedly and his passion is so erudite').[13] In this period, the praise lavished on Tibullus and the criticisms levelled at Ovid and Propertius became commonplaces that surface repeatedly: for example in the works of La Harpe, who reiterates a verdict that reflects the way that aesthetics and poetic criteria were evolving: 'Tibullus has less fire than Propertius, but he is more tender and more delicate. This is the poet of feeling . . . He has a charm of expression that no translation can capture, and he can be appreciated only by one's heart.'[14]

The fortunes of the Latin elegiac poets were thus closely linked with the evolution of aesthetics in the course of the century. The varied judgements passed on Ovid, the admiration mixed with disdain aroused by his 'slickness' and 'wit', correspond to the ambiguous relationship that the century had with poetic creation, a relationship that combined formality and familiarity, literary ambition and social panache. By supplanting the wit of Ovid by his own delicacy and elegance, Tibullus set elegy on the path of sensibility, thereby adjusting it to the taste of the day.

Reflections on literary genres and metapoetics

It was not only the models of elegy that fluctuated during the eighteenth century: the genre itself was the subject of much critical examination and stimulated debates with a theoretical significance that was reflected in scholarly publications, the prefaces of translators and the productions of contemporary poets.

Elegy pinpoints a number of questions that refer back more or less directly to the 'poetry crisis' that affected the eighteenth century. Applying the terms used in the analysis by May (1963) of the status of the novel, one might even speak of 'the dilemma of elegy'. On the one hand, this poetic genre became the subject of a veritable craze, which found expression in an increasing production and publication of elegies, on the other hand it is the target of philosophic-moral disapproval that condemned it on the grounds of, in particular, its 'softness' and its lack of form.[15] Elegy was a disparaged genre, yet one that was rapidly expanding. Its bad reputation resulted, paradoxically, from its success, which, according to commentators, elicited both 'boredom' and 'disgust'.[16] Rémond de Saint-Mard identified the use of the

[13] Le Brun (1763) 394–5. [14] La Harpe (1834) 169. [15] See Loubier (2006).

[16] Leblanc starts his *Discours sur l'élégie* (1731) with a description of the public's distaste for elegy ('The fact is that, despite the great number of elegies that are produced, there

elegiac couplet as the cause of the 'unbearable monotony' produced by reading ancient elegies. According to him, the pentameter was guilty of impeding the free expression of feeling: 'It is impossible for meaning not to lose its force or its gentleness if it is always entrapped in such a confined space. It is bound to suffer sometimes from being constrained in this way.'[17] According to Saint-Mard, the imitation of such imperfect models explained the mediocrity of contemporary elegy, which he considered to be 'the most insipid genre of our poetry'.[18]

Other critics developed the less categorical but more common idea of a decadence in this genre and thereby involved the debate about elegy in the major quarrel between Ancients and Moderns. This idea of decadence underlies the articles that Marmontel and Jaucourt wrote for *Encyclopédie*: these define elegy and discuss it as a genre made famous by the Ancients; and if they do cite any modern poets, they do so somewhat reservedly. As we have seen, Jaucourt criticizes them for the excessive artifice and wit in their elegies. Le Brun, who himself composed elegies and encouraged Chénier to do so likewise, wrote a *Discours sur Tibulle* (1763) that affirms the absolute superiority of the ancient elegiac poets over the moderns who, in his view, do not bear comparison to their illustrious models: 'One should not hope to find even a shadow of them in Hamilton, La Fare or Chaulieu, nor in the modern crowd of gentlemen-authors, writers in pastel shades and poets with a superficial glitter'.[19]

André Chénier expressed a similar view when, in an attempt to discover 'the causes and effects of perfection and decadence in literature and the arts', he drew a contrast between, on the one hand, 'the ancient elegies, which were simple, natural and passionate and in which nudity was always kept decent' and, on the other, 'these insipid and enigmatic subtleties known as *galanteries*, which make these erotic writers of ours seem so fastidious to any readers who combine straightforward and just minds with real sensibility and souls that are receptive to all aspects of the passions, whether they be gentle or stormy'.[20]

The fortunes of ancient elegiac poetry in French eighteenth-century literature should therefore be examined within a context of wide-ranging aesthetic thought that contributed to the theoretical elaboration of Enlightenment poetics. The debate prompted by the 'minor genre' of elegy provides us with

are few of them that can be read without boredom', 3), and he later returns to the 'fashion' for elegy ('Elegies used to be very fashionable, and many people only became disgusted by them because they became increasingly common but without becoming better', 29–30).

17 Rémond de Saint-Mard (1734) 179.

18 Rémond de Saint-Mard (1734) 149–50.

19 Le Brun (1763) 396.

20 Chénier (1958) 661.

an insight into the perceptive critical awareness not only of scholars but of poets too, for 'an eighteenth-century poet does not separate the practice of his art from thought about that art'.[21] The rehabilitation of this minor genre, which took off definitively at the turn of the century, is inseparable from the theoretical thought of the principal actors already mentioned. Now we must be more specific as to its various aspects and what was at stake.

The recovery of interest in this poetic genre bequeathed by antiquity prompted attempts to define it, and these concentrated in particular upon the main characteristics of the elegiac genre. In 1680, La Mesnadière was pondering upon 'the character of elegy', while Leblanc and Saint-Mard declared it to be 'a poetic genre' and commentators frequently referred to the 'tone' of elegy. The hesitant critical terminology reflects the difficulties presented by a genre that was sometimes defined by its form (a particular type of verse), sometimes by its content (lamentations, a lyrical expression of the feelings of happy or unhappy love or sentiments of loss or exile . . .). In an effort to resolve this ambiguity, Jaucourt even invented a new term: he set up an opposition between 'elegiac poets' (who practised elegy, that is to say a type of poetry that 'lamented . . . some misfortune or . . . depicted the sadness [or] joy of lovers') and 'elegiographs' (who composed 'written pieces in pentameter and hexameter verse', the content of which was not necessarily elegiac).[22]

Elegy eluded strict definition, for formal and thematic criteria did not always coincide. The quest for a purely formal criterion (through the use of the elegiac couplet in Latin or a particular type of versification or stanza in French) generally provided no solution. The problem was above all how to define the thematic field of elegy; and two conflicting approaches to this developed. Some writers favoured restricting elegy to the treatment of doleful subjects and limited it to its plaintive dimension (in some cases adding a further restriction according to which only the laments of lovers were suited to elegy). Others, on the contrary, extended the domain of elegy to include a wide range of subjects, whether plaintive or not, personal or collective. Gradually, a solution to the dilemma emerged: another criterion for defining it, which was of neither a formal nor a thematic nature, but was instead linked to the effect that the poem produced. Now elegy could be defined as a poetic genre that was particularly suited for moving the reader and touching his or her heart. This redefinition of elegy according to the criterion of its effect may explain both the phenomenon of the re-evaluation of the Latin authors mentioned above, which set the 'tender Tibullus' above

[21] The expression is borrowed from Guitton (1974) 12.
[22] See Leblanc (1731) and Rémond de Saint-Mard (1734).

the witty Ovid, and also the rise of the elegiac genre in French poetry, at the end of the century, thanks to a widespread taste for 'sensitive' literature. Michaut, in his *Réflexions* on elegy, had already tackled the reversal in critical taste, venturing to suggest that 'an elegiac poem must awaken our sensibility... Elegy should gently move us'.[23] Later, in the opening and the final lines of his *Encyclopédie* article on the desired effect produced by elegy, Jaucourt confirmed this change of view. He began by reminding the reader that the lamentations of the ancient elegies 'moved one's soul' and ended by associating the 'thousand attractions' of the elegiac genre with the fact that 'it stirs our passions..., imitates things that interest us..., allows us to understand men who are deeply moved and who make us sensitive both to their sorrows and to their pleasures'. For – as he takes care to remind us – 'we really do love to feel emotion'. Then, significantly enough, he refers the reader to the *Encyclopédie* article on 'Emotion'.

All these attempts to define elegy indicate how difficult it is to get a grasp on a genre that is characterized by its openness and its formal and thematic flexibility. The reflections of these authors help us to understand the importance of the role that the Latin models played in the elaboration, at the turn of the eighteenth century, of a new type of aesthetics that was more in tune with the times.

The fascination exerted by the elegiac genre, which accounts for the rediscovery of the ancient poets and the increasing production of similar contemporary works, can be better understood if one bears in mind that the modern authors were prompted by their ancient models to develop their own investigations into the status of poets and the role of poetry. Even the history of elegy revolves around the conjunction of, on the one hand, a lyrical expression of feelings and, on the other, critical reflection on the practice of writing poetry: all the elegiac poets were also theorists of their art. The fleeting poets of the eighteenth century, conscious of being practitioners of a 'minor genre' but nevertheless anxious to defend its paradoxical value, inevitably found themselves involved in a *recusatio* designed to justify their honour as minor poets. They also detected in the ancient models an echo of the tension that pervades elegiac poetry, which reflects a conscious hedonism at the same time as a tragic perception of existence. La Harpe put his finger on all that the ancient authors contributed to justify the claims of this poetry that was seeking recognition. He describes the tragic depth of ancient elegiac hedonism as follows: 'We should note in passing that the most sensual of the ancient authors, Anacreon, Horace,

[23] Michault (1743) 17 and 19.

Tibullus and Catullus were perfectly prepared to intermingle images of death with images of pleasure. They invited death to their festivities and, so to speak, offered her a seat at their table, as if she was a guest who, far from saddening them, encouraged them to go ahead and enjoy themselves.'[24] That statement could apply equally well to the underlying gravity that was inseparable from most of the fleeting poetry of the age of the Enlightenment.

The poetry of the ancient elegists thus mirrors the questioning and experiments of the modern poets. The attempts to define elegy that accompanied the production of elegiac poetry testify to the establishment of an aesthetics shot through by contradictions: on the one hand, it recognized the unifying principle of imitation (as described by Abbé Batteux in his essay entitled *Les Beaux-Arts réduits à un même principe* ('The Fine-arts reduced to a single principle', 1740); on the other hand, it called for a new definition of inventiveness, one which set a high value on the emerging aesthetic category of originality. The diverse qualities of elegiac poetry, described on the basis of its ancient legacy, crystallize those aesthetic tensions and account for the permanence of the elegiac model in modern creativity: a desire for things natural, a quest for truth and a cult of feeling and sweetness became the criteria for this poetry that was on the point of developing its lyrical bent. The establishment of the poet in person within his work, even accompanied by a distancing of himself that was tinged with the cynicism introduced by a metapoetic stance, made it possible for the eighteenth century to move on from the etiolated poetry of polite society and commit entirely to what would turn into lyrical Romanticism.

Modern realizations of this poetic aesthetics

Among the poets who were involved in this mutation of modern elegy, yet without ever dissociating it from its ancient origins, we should first mention the 'discreet' elegists of the early years of the eighteenth century, men such as Chaulieu and Dorat, who discovered their particular talent above all thanks to the example of erotic inspiration and nonchalance set by the Latin authors. A number of 'recognized' elegiac poets promoted the transition by writing elegy as it would be practised in the following century. One was Le Brun, known as Le Brun-Pindar, the author of a *Discours sur Tibulle* and a series of elegies composed in the style of Ovid's *Amores*, in which he celebrated the pleasures and pains of his life with Fanni, his wife and muse. He compares himself, in passing, to Tibullus, Catullus and Ovid:

[24] La Harpe (1834) 145.

Là, chantant les attraits dont tu fus embellie
Mes vers rendront jaloux et Tibulle et Délie.
Gallus, Catulle, Ovide et La Fare et Chaulieu
A ma flamme, à mes chants reconnaîtront leur Dieu.[25]

Here, singing of the charms that made you so lovely, my verses will prompt the jealousy of Tibullus and Delia. Gallus, Catullus, Ovid, La Fare and Chaulieu will hail their God in my passion and my songs.

His four books of elegies intertwine a chronicle of his own loves with translations of Tibullus, Propertius and Ovid and a few poems in which he refers to Gallus and Moschus. In his case, elegiac inspiration was certainly inseparable from the impact of the ancient models.

With the half-caste poets Parny and Bertin, French elegy enjoyed a palpable success and progressively acceded to an autonomy of its own without, however, ever failing to honour its origins. Parny, the 'French Tibullus', and Bertin, the 'new Propertius', chose to stress the link that united them with their predecessors and constructed their works and their careers as poets around the gratitude that they owed them. This constitution of an 'elegiac fraternity' that linked them to their models and strove to establish itself as a poetic movement testified to their desire to perpetuate their affiliation with the Ancients and to become part of elegiac 'history'. Evariste Parny published his *Poésies érotiques* in 1778 and immediately enjoyed considerable success. This collection of elegies, organized around the figure of Eléonore, constituted another novel about love in the manner of Ovid, but it reflected a new stream of inspiration and an updating of elegiac language. Seeking simplicity, Parny's poems did without rhetorical ornamentation and mythological comparisons, the better to concentrate on expressing feelings and emotion. The first poem in this collection thus sings of 'the day after' and expresses the poet's desire to reconcile elegy with erotic verse in a combination of lamentation and tranquil enjoyment:

Enfin, ma chère Eléonore,
Tu l'as connu ce péché si charmant
Que tu craignais, même en le désirant;
En le goûtant tu le craignais encore.
Eh bien! Dis-moi: qu'a-t-il donc d'effrayant?[26]

At last, dear Eleonore, you have experienced this delightful sin that you feared even as you desired it and even savouring it, feared it still. Well now, tell me: what is there to fear about it?

[25] Le Brun (1811) *Elégies*, I, 5, 2; 14. [26] Parny (1862) I.

However, the rest of the collection introduces notes of a profound melancholy, in which the creation of past joys gives way to expressions of the poet's distress.[27] The Romantics were happy to hail Parny as a precursor. Chateaubriand, for instance, knew his poems by heart and regarded him as 'the only elegiac poet that France has, as yet, produced'.[28]

Antoine de Bertin, a friend of Parny's, published three books of *Amours* between 1780 and 1784. In them he sings of Eucharis and Catilie and, in the *recusatio* with which the first book of his elegies opens, he immediately signals his allegiance to Ovid and the 'minor genre' of elegy:

> Je chantais les combats; le Dieu de l'harmonie
> Des feux de Calliope échauffait mon génie:
> Côte à côte rangés, mes vers présomptueux
> Déployaient en deux temps, six pieds majestueux.
> De ces vers nombreux et sublimes
> L'Amour se riant à l'écart,
> Sur mon papier mit la main au hasard,
> Retrancha quelques pieds, brouilla toutes les rimes;
> De ce désordre heureux naquit un nouvel art.[29]

> I used to sing of battles; the God of harmony kindled my talent with the fires of Calliope, one by one my lines full of pretention set out two groups of six majestic feet. Love, laughing up his sleeve at all my sublime lines, set his hand at random on those pages of mine, knocked out a few feet, mixed up all the rhymes; and from this happy disorder a new art was born.

Paradoxically enough, we still have to wait for the appearance of the poet most fully sustained by all the above references, the one who constructed his oeuvre according to the principle of an 'inventiveness' inseparable from imitation and thereby achieved a very real lyrical emancipation for elegy at the very end of the eighteenth century. André Chénier's watchword was 'Let us make ancient poetry about new ideas' (*Sur des pensers nouveaux faisons des vers antiques*), and his poetic creativity was nurtured by his readings of the Ancients. He experimented with forms that broke away from the legacy of antiquity and adapted elegiac writing to suit his own personal aims. He continued to swear by his affiliation to the Ancients and to the models that haunt his poems,[30] but he also insisted upon a Modernity that took the form of increasingly open borrowings from other poetic genres (odes, bucolic verse etc.) and, although he acknowledged his models, he was constantly changing them, dreaming now of Gallus, now of Propertius or

[27] Parny (1862) 116. [28] Chateaubriand (1978) 105.
[29] Bertin (1780). See Ovid, *Amores*, 1.1.1–4. [30] Chénier (2005) II 13, 243.

Tibullus. He allowed Ovid's *Amores* and *The Art of Love* to leave their mark upon his poetry but never let the voices of his prestigious predecessors override his own. Heartfelt lyricism was highly praised by Boileau; 'In elegy, the heart alone must speak' (Book II, line 57), and it found intense expression in Chénier's work. The more or less completed fragments that constituted his elegiac oeuvre drew on ancient models only the better to nurture the authenticity of a voice that sought to use creative inspiration to discover the most faithful means of expressing the personal feelings of a 'heart' that never lied:

> L'art des transports de l'âme est un faible interprète,
> L'art ne fait que des vers; le coeur seul est poète.[31]

> Art is a feeble translator of the surges of the soul that merely puts words together in verse; only the heart is a Poet.

He does return to the vision of a personified elegy that first Ovid, and later Boileau (Book II, lines 39–42), had invoked:

> Mais la tendre élégie et sa grâce touchante
> M'ont séduit: l'élégie à la voix gémissante,
> Au ris mêlé de pleurs, aux longs cheveux épars,
> Belle, levant au ciel ses humides regards.[32]

> But tender elegy, with her touching grace, has won me over: elegy, with her sorrowful voice and her laughter mixed with tears and her long, flowing hair, so lovely as she lifts her brimming eyes heavenward.

However, he does so in order to appropriate the beguiling power of this eminently lyrical form, capable of conveying emotion, which attains a universal meaning in its expression of the most personal of sentiments. The cry that Chénier attributes to a poet reading his work,

> 'Ce poète amoureux, qui me connaît si bien
> Quand il a peint son coeur, avait lu dans le mien'.[33]

'This love-lorn poet who knows me so well in depicting his heart has seen into mine', suggests that the historical model behind the elegiac voice has dropped away. This elegiac voice was one now destined to enjoy a fine lyrical future in the hands of the Romantics. With the emergence of Romanticism, elegiac poetry abandoned the *boudoirs* and scribbles of the perfumed nobility and at the same time liberated itself from its ancient models, thereby acquiring its own credentials and acceding to a new modernity.

[31] Chénier (2005) *Elégies*, IV 33, 317.
[32] Chénier (2005) *Elégies*, II 13, 242.
[33] Chénier (2005) *Elégies*, II 13, 244.

Further reading

For thought about the genre of elegy based on the historical texts, see the informative article by Denis (2008) and also the study by Loubier (2006). Loubère (2002) offers a number of insights on the fortunes of Ovid's erotic elegies. On the creation of French elegy at the end of the eighteenth century, see Potez (1898), which is somewhat dated but does present a suggestive panorama, which may be expanded by consulting the special number (no. 25, 2006) of the *Cahiers Roucher-André Chénier* that is devoted to *L'Elégie et la poésie élégiaque autour d'André Chénier*; see also Seth (1998).

21

ANDREW KAHN

Russian elegists and Latin lovers in the long eighteenth century

From the 1750s Russian poets have excelled in writing about intimate feelings, and produced a tradition rich in miniature stories of rapture and heartbreak. Until the 1820s, the period when a secular literary culture conclusively eclipsed ecclesiastical domination, Roman love poetry proved to be a formative influence. It should be no surprise that interest in the Latin model surged with the establishment of classicism encouraged by Catherine the Great from 1762 (Segel 1973, Kahn 1993). But the Russian assimilation of Western literary models tended to telescope several trends simultaneously before moving quickly on. Imitation of Horace, Tibullus and Propertius on a significant scale was concentrated in this period, proceeding in parallel with other literary influences, especially from France. After the 1820s the influence of the Roman model eventually became attenuated. The legacy of classicism was manifest less in overt imitation and more as a stylistic legacy in the language of elegy. From the 1820s, love poetry calqued on a generalized sense of the Roman model merged with the broader emphasis that the genre of elegy acquired on self-regret and poems of place. For these reasons this chapter will focus on the seventy years 1760–1830 that form an important episode in the history of Russian lyric poetry and its representation of the language of feeling and the passions.

The first generation

The first generation of Russian writers committed to the creation of a secular literature were the classicists of the eighteenth century. Their double task was to define a new literary practice, establishing the rules of genre and expression, and to put those rules into practice by assimilating European models to a newly stable modern literary language. Lyric poets proved to be the most successful, and most experimental, in the transition, formally from an outdated system of versification and topically from civic poetry, to more personal themes. The invention of love as a literary theme in Russia began in 1730 with the adaptation by Vassily Trediakovsky of Tallemant's *roman précieux Voyage a l'isle d'amour*. For the first time Russian characters in prose and verse spoke in the vernacular of certain emotions – despair, longing, erotic desire – rather than in the standard ecclesiastical language. In this work, and in the elegies he composed at the same time, Trediakovsky, a fine Latinist, transferred the emotional language of funerary elegy to the description of erotic feeling, and coined new idioms in which characters not only 'weep out their eyes' (*plakat' ochi*) in 'bitter tears' (*gorkie slezy*) for the first time at the death or departure of a beloved and a cruel fate (*sud'ba zhestoka*), but also treat love as a 'most cruel illness' (*prezhestokaia bolezn*), a fever (*zhar*), a cancer (*iazva*), and an implacable fever (*liutyi zhar*). Although he failed to cement new trends,Trediakovsky's elegiac language and idiom of grief and rapture eventually informed the expressions that poets crafted in the 1770s when love elegy became a staple of the new Russian literature (Lotman 1992).

The look of love

Enthusiasm for self-expression and poetry of feeling derived from two sources. To begin with, the first generation of Russian poets, drawn from the educated elite, wished to import to Russia the emotional postures they discovered in classical Latin poetry and modes of 'ephemeral' poetry (*poésie fugitive*) and 'tearful' poetry (*poésie larmoyante*) as practised by French erotic elegists. Secondly, from the 1760s a burgeoning interest in theatre informed the practices of lyric. The establishment in 1783 of the Imperial Theatre in St Petersburg provided a home stage on which the great French neoclassical dramas by Corneille and Racine were performed, inspiring Russian imitators who quickly mastered the idiom of soliloquies in which heroes and heroines weighed duty and patriotism and agonized over transgressions in love (Karlinsky 1985). The most important proponent of the rules of the new classicism was Alexander Sumarokov, poet, theorist and director of the Imperial Theatre from the reign of Peter the Great's daughter, Elizabeth I (1741–61). Often dubbed the Russian Boileau, Sumarokov authored a large number of mournful (*plachevnyi* or *skorbnyi*) and erotic elegies (*liubovnye*).[1] Cognate with the soliloquies he created for the characters of his many tragedies, and composed in Alexandrines, the tragic metre of

[1] For the eighteenth-century Russian writers quoted in this essay, see Frizman (1991) esp. 56–126.

choice, his love elegies create a highly stable, and repetitive idiom, in which characters mainly lament the end of love. As a rule Sumarokov's poems are cast in the present tense, which fits their emotional profile as statements about current feelings of loss rather more than retrospective accounts of a relationship. In speeches of about 80 lines, a considerable length for Russian lyric at the time, his protagonists plumb the depths of erotic anguish, and muster stoic consolation. Written at a time when Russians first began to read the Roman Stoics such as Seneca and Cicero, Sumarokov's heroes are prone to blame fate and the laws of the universe. Both terms denoting 'fate' (*sud'ba*) and 'destiny' (*rok*) are blamed for causing passion that cannot be requited (*neutolima strast'*) (Kahn 2003).

Typically poems begin with a statement of explicit loss – the Russian verb *lishat'sia* meaning 'to forfeit' recurs throughout his corpus of texts – but a specific reason, either death or rejection, is rarely given because Sumarokov prefers to castigate a malign fate as the cause. One of the more individual features of his poems is their focus on the looks and glances that lovers once shared, and the recollection of the gaze of the lover. Love is intensely visual in these elegies, and speakers repeatedly reignite their passion and sorrow just as they begin to calm down by recalling the moment when they first set eyes on the beloved. To love, and to elegize, is to represent visually (*izobrazit'*) in the mind how the lover's gaze (*tvoi vzor*) penetrated his soul (*vozmog ego pronzit'*) and ignited extreme feelings of passion. The vocabulary of such a sequence reflects Sumarokov's credentials as a follower of John Locke, a rare instance of Locke's reception in Russia (Levitt 2009). The sense-impressions associated with love do not originate within the individual's soul but originally must stem from an external source. In Locke's thought perception records the images that the eyes of others generate, and once these impressions are stored in the mind they can be replayed to the subject. Sumarokov's speakers are caught in a vicious circle: the more they seek to escape love by complaining, the more they remind themselves of their original feelings. Such memories repeatedly and ineluctably stimulate new statements of feeling (*chuvstvovat'*) because his philosophical model of love object, perception, mind and memory makes this process of feeling anguish all over again an inevitable sequence. If love is fated to act this way, and the speaker doomed to repeat the feelings in elegy after elegy, it is because Sumarokov construes emotions according to psychological laws. Resolution of the impasse will come only through the Stoic resolve to achieve equanimity and is never guaranteed. Tranquillity rarely comes to the elegist, and more poems in which the speaker enjoins his soul 'to suffer, to tolerate' these torments result.

Numerous minor poets emulated his example as an elegist, turning out Alexandrine couplets[2] at enormous length. The lyrics of writers and followers like S.V. Naryshkin (1732–85), the actor I.A. Dmitrevskii (1734–1821) and V.D. Sankovskii (b.1741), among others, approach love in similar terms of deprivation, loss of freedom, torment and suffering, although few lay on the grief quite so thickly and relentlessly. Alexander Rzhevskii (1737–1804), a more significant acolyte of Sumarokov, faithfully perpetuates the same tropes of anguished exclamation and topoi of seeing, feeling and remembering.[3] Yet his speakers also depart from the model because they are less self-centred and pay more attention to the beloved and why she elicited such feelings. Caresses as well as glances, charm as well as pain, sparks of wit as well as feverish longing vary the picture. These poets exceed Sumarokov in the psychological complexity they confer on love as a dilemma: their speakers are trapped between acts of realistic renunciation and desperate self-delusion. The harder the post-Sumarokov lover tries to avoid the beloved, the more inclined he is to seek her once again:

> I hide from you
> But in hiding feel sad
> And cannot contain my thoughts,
> I look for you again
> I will see you again
> I shall grieve again when I see you
> And hate you again.

Fedor Kozel'skii (b.1734), another accomplished elegist, expresses the same problem as an even greater paradox. His poetic monodramas recapitulate the standard predicament and self-pitying postures that dominate in this period. But, like Rzhevskii, his speakers are reluctant to break completely with the beloved. Through an exquisitely tortured logic, they persuade themselves that while, on the one hand, forgetting the beloved would set them free, the process of attempting to forget would in itself be so painful, on the other hand, that the lover would never achieve the detachment he seeks. Love remains for all of these male speakers a state of 'eternal unfreedom',[4] a complaint that becomes habitual among male elegists writing until the 1780s.

2 For the 'elegiac' character of the Alexandrine couplet, see Ziolkowski (Chapter 22) in this volume.

3 For these texts, see *Russkaia elegiia*.

4 See also Fulkerson (Chapter 11) in this volume on the erotic-elegiac trope of *seruitium amoris*, 'slavery of love'.

Of the small handful of female poets who make a mark on Russian classicism, the Princess Ekaterina Urusova (b.1747) has been largely overlooked despite her striking gifts and legacy as a playwright. In Russia she has the distinction of being the first major imitator of Ovid, and her skilful adaptation of the *Heroides* creates the first feminine perspective on love before the Romantic elegists (Carocci 1988). Urusova understood perfectly that her decision to imitate Ovid and to speak of female love and loss represented a break with current practice. In her introduction to her volume of *Heroides* she makes two important assertions, connecting poetry to politics; and to autobiography and female sensibility. She declares that the sign of the new age is the flourishing of its poetry (Urusova (1777) 1, ll. 15–16). In her view, Catherine's wisdom has brought Russia enlightenment – an argument that is unremarkable and conventional for the period. But the proem then makes more precise claims that go beyond the standard topoi of praise. For Urusova defines Enlightenment as the specific phenomenon of having female poets whose talent has been fostered by a female ruler. Because voice and writing have been identified with patriarchal authority in the culture, the authority of the female ruler newly confers authority on female rhetorical culture (Proskurina (2006) 1–30). She then makes a second feminist claim. Urusova argues that personal experience and an intensity of feeling equal to that of her subjects authenticates the true poet of the passions. The source of such insight into the passions is the unique privilege of the female poet, whose sex as much as her poetic gift makes her uniquely able to render the passions. If female eloquence is psychologically privileged and more adept than male eloquence, as Urusova claims, then her choice of the female epistle as a genre achieves a good match between form and ideology. The epistolary poem, a largely neglected form in Russia, allowed her (as it arguably allowed Ovid) to create a new female perspective on amatory discourse and human relationships that goes beyond the proven, and somewhat fossilized, norms of the theatre. The choice of genre is itself proof of a literary dynamism driven by self-conscious awareness of the writer's womanhood.

In these poems, her chief aim is to show emotion in action, rather than to create activity out of emotion. The epistolary monologue is that activity. Passion emerges as a complex manifestation of impulses. It is the inability of the single female subject to contain extremes of jealousy and love, vengefulness and relinquishment, prudence and daring, reason and unreason that buffets the speaker. Throughout the collection the depiction of mortal viragos serves to illustrate the volatility of women by comparison with men, whose descriptions are one-dimensional. There is also another dimension to sexual typology. While the male speakers of elegy are paralyzed by love, women in this collection rise above their moments of hysteria to titanic acts of bravery (this word in Russian, *muzhestvo*, also means 'masculinity'). Urusova's males rarely display such 'masculinity'. There are six female narrators of the Russian *Heroides*. Letters 2 and 3 are an exchange beginning with the letter of the guilty male. Letter 5, from one male to his best friend, narrates how the aptly name Promest fell in love with a woman, and has therefore promised her the love he always bore for the male addressee. The sixth and seven of Urusova's poems represent the only dialogues with a successful outcome, departing from the relentless grief of Ovid's epistles. The five other letters all replay standard tragic plots. Circumstances are unimportant in the plotting of the poems. These female characters tell their own story with such conviction and authentic emotion that their emotions require no scene-setting. And for once, male narrators are the creations of a female author. All the monologues ring changes on the key theme of passion and its consequences. Certain heroines seem to step out of the pages of Corneille: their drama arises from the unbearable dilemma that forces a choice between duty and love. Other heroines, victims of sexual infidelity or misguided male ambition, employ Racinian language about inescapable fate; some are resigned, others are determined to use the letter to win back their love, which is what happens a number of times.

The Ovidian soliloquy, however, differs rhetorically in an important way from dramatic monologue. It is conventional in neoclassical theatre for the heroes and heroines to be caught in isolated meditation, and to be heard speaking aloud by the audience: development of the plot will emerge out of the resolve or despair that is phrased in such soliloquies. In most of the *Heroides* the reader is aware of an ironic playfulness that Ovid has in creating heroines who are abandoned and on their own, whose pleas fall on deaf ears, yet who also write letters that the reader must be willing to hear or read in order to experience their plight and eloquence. For the modern writer of *Heroides*, who liberates the heroines' speeches from master texts, their supposedly unfiltered performance is the drama, their minds and passions and not their status as rewritings, provide theatre. Like the Ovidian heroines, Urusova's women lament eloquently and aggressively. Their plight is psychologically devastating as they confront betrayal and repeatedly try to apply their eloquence to winning back their lovers. But feminist readings of the *Heroides* have rightly identified how strongly the generic model of the female controls the model of gender in Ovid's text, undermining his representation of female psychology (Spentzou 2003: 24). The rhetorical difference between Ovid and Urusova lies in a more fundamental subversion of certain cultural norms – or at the very least their adjustment to a culture where a woman, famed for her eloquence as well as for her indiscrete passions, reigns as lawgiver. The context of Catherine's reign to which

Urusova pays so much attention in her preface, is not merely part of a ritual tribute. It also gives Urusova confidence to signal a shift in the rhetoric and emotional posture of her heroines. Catherine's own writings sought to promote an ethical system based on law consistent with feeling or an intuitive knowledge of the good. Like Ovid's heroines, Urusova's speakers conceive of the epistle as an erotic agent of persuasive power. But unlike his heroines, who are restricted to negative eloquence and locked in their own woe, several of Urusova's speakers demonstrate their command of the masculine language of virtue and reason. For example, in the final section of her lament, Zaida (*Epistle* I) achieves what Ovid's heroines usually find impossible. She reconciles both heart and reason. She finds it possible to regulate passion according to an ideal of love, and in the final lines to assert self-control. Above all, she articulates loyalty to the self and to the emotional capacity of the female. The poem does not argue that passion must be subordinated to reason, but that reason must serve passion – an argument that goes against the current of much Enlightenment philosophy. And, insofar as passion has been seen throughout as part of the gender identity of the female, the poem espouses rather than condemns a new model of female identity strong in feeling and in mind. If the gendered self, as Judith Butler says, is 'produced by the regulation of attributes along culturally established lines of coherence', then in aligning civic codes and emotional truths Urusova's heroine begins the blurring of gender boundaries that we associate with sentimentalism a decade later, and more prominently with the feminization of the male (Butler 1990: 33). For these reasons, Urusova's first heroine leaps out of the world of Catherine's Russia rather than belonging to the pages of Ovid.

Erotic-elegiac themes, multifarious forms

Among Russian writers between the Age of Enlightenment and early Romanticism a lull in elegy writing sets in from the 1780s until the 1810s. Rationalism is one cause of its decline. As early as 1770 the greatest lyricist of the period, Gavriil Derzhavin, mocked pining lovers in his 'To Nina', in which he says that he'd prefer his beloved to kiss him only once rather than hundreds of times; that the flame of love expires rather quickly; and for that reason it is better to embrace, enjoy but not 'die' of anguish. To the unreason of the love elegy, in which people often lost control, Derzhavin preferred the metaphysical argument of the elegy of mourning which created opportunities to ponder the nature of the soul (material or spiritual), to celebrate dead soldiers and to pose questions of natural philosophy. A second reason for the decline of the love elegy is the rise of sentimentalism and sensibility. On the surface this looks paradoxical in a literature that places a premium on extrovert demonstrations of feeling, especially weeping. However, the feminization of the male that has been associated with the movement in Russia also led to the de-eroticizing of relationships represented in literature (Hammarberg 1994: 103–20). The sublimation of passions into the courtesies shared between the sexes as friends more than lovers dislodges traditional displays of ardour and despair. For example, the opening of Nikolai Karamzin's poem 'Melancholy' ('Melankholia', 1800), an imitation of the French poet Jacques Delille, initially sounds like a love elegy, but the passion that he apostrophizes is melancholy itself rather than love. Among the few remaining practitioners of the art is Vassily Kapnist (1758–1823), a fine translator and imitator of Horace. His versions of Horace *Odes* II.viii and *Epode* XV shift the emphasis from regret to anger. Such extrovert and manifestly dramatic outbursts must have appealed to a love of extreme and lurid expression fostered by the gothic strain in early Romanticism.

By 1814, however, Kapnist was contributing to the revival of the love elegy, much modified from the neoclassical style of expression. Numerous lyrics like 'Woe' ('Gorest''), 'On the death of Julia' ('Na smert'' Iulii') and 'Yearning for the beloved' ('Toska po milom') reprise the traditional postures of the abandoned male speaker while repositioning the genre. Formally, poets drop the Alexandrine favoured by Sumarokov and his followers, now favouring mixed iambs (though rarely employing the elegiac distich as such). The newer prosody accompanies a more fluid syntax and prosodic effects like enjambment that suit the more labile state of emotions conveyed in poems. Whereas earlier poems achieved closure, the love elegy of the 1810s and 1820s focuses on the devastating emotional legacy of love interrupted by rejection or death, and the ongoing impact on the sensibility of the speaker whose affection transcends both rejection and death. Poets are increasingly inventive in devising seemingly artless and spontaneous language to express emotion, but the conventions of the elegy standardize certain topoi and tropes: the image of the beloved is 'sweet' (*milyi*) and 'unforgettable (*nezabvennyi*), the memory of her voice is unfailingly sweet (*golos milyi*), yet bitterness rarely obtrudes.

Frequently, the language of friendship replaces erotic longing, nowhere more strikingly than in the work of Konstantin Batiushkov, the most accomplished elegist of the period, famed for his adaptations of Roman and Italian poets, especially Propertius and Tibullus; thanks to its fluent emotional expressivity and musicality his free translation of Tibullus I.10 set a new standard for elegiac expression in 1809. 'The shade of a friend' ('Ten' Druga', 1810), composed in elegiac distichs, takes its theme from Propertius who supplies an epigraph: '*Sunt aliquid manes: letum non omnia finit: /luridaque euictos effugit umbra rogos*' ('The souls of the dead are something: in death everything does not cease:/the pale shade escapes the pyre') (Batiushkov 1977: 222–24). Batiushkov locates his speaker on a ship leaving the misty banks of Albion. The liminal space, misty weather, lapping of the waves on the oars, provide the perfect setting for a series of 'fancies' that conjure the ghost of a beloved friend to whom he reaches out. The centrepiece is a soliloquy in which the poet, as he interrogates his own thoughts, sees the shade of his friend. Initially the live image of the beloved – and he is male – prompts the speaker to recall and rehearse the elegy he delivered graveside at the burial of his friend. But gradually joy at the encounter dispels his incredulity and he beseeches the friend to answer him and to allow him to embrace and kiss him. At its conclusion, the speaker awakes from his reverie, regretting how the ghost disappeared 'like smoke, like a meteor', but finds that part of his own soul has departed with his friend. Other elegies associate the fleeting pleasures of love, gratefully recalled, with the passing of youth. 'Elysium' ('Elizii', 1810, cf. Tib. I.3), an example of the exquisite musicality for which Batiushkov was famed, imagines an underworld in which the speaker enjoys perpetual love surrounded by the dancing Graces and Nymphs who link arms around him and include Horace with Tibullus' Delia (poetic licence on Batiushkov's part who rhymes the Russianized name 'Goratsii' with 'gratsii' for Graces).

Poets of Alexander Pushkin's generation tend to assimilate the celebration of love to other Epicurean pleasures, and to mix commemoration of past love affairs with eulogy of the dead. In the first line of 'To Evgenii' (1819), Anton Del'vig, Pushkin's school friend best known for his imitations of Theocritean idylls, declares that when he writes as the 'priest of love' he 'is Horace', dedicated to celebrating calm and pleasure as well as the 'fiery ecstasy of love', and to imitating Horace whose instruction in 'the marvellous science, in pleasure' is invaluable to a poet. This is the message of a number of other poems, including his 'First Horatian ode' in which Del'vig recalls past loves (Themira, Daphne, Lileth) who exist for the poet only at the back of his mind until his current love unleashes pleasures that mingle in his sleep with the memory of past raptures. Another poem, entitled 'On the death of ***', in mixed iambs, strives for Horatian wistfulness by eulogizing the virtues of the lover (intelligence, passion, charm, fidelity) and noting how uncannily the deceased foresaw her own early death, proof of her superior spirituality. The idyll 'Friends' ('Druz'ia', 1826) attests to the strength of the classical impulse among this final generation of faithful practitioners. Written in heroic hexameter as a formal indication of its classical tone, it transports the reader to Arcadia and celebrates the friendship in terms of a homosocial bond, and ponders the pain of parting with a beloved friend, wondering aloud whether friends who part can ever again love 'as they loved before in olden days'. But by 1826 Del'vig was beginning to look like an anachronism. Poets of a younger generation like Mikhail Lermontov turned to Byron for lessons in how to love and regret.

The greatest elegist of that generation is Evgenii Baratynskii (1800–44). References to classical antiquity recur throughout his poetry, and poems about Rome and Greece powerfully allegorize disenchantment with the industrial world and longing for a lost Golden Age. Yet the love poetry for which he is most famous shows no clear affiliation with any one elegiac tradition. Occasional references to Delia or Aphrodite are nothing more than ornamental, vestigial clichés that signal tone and mood. These poems represent the synthesis and culmination of a well-established tradition of writing about love that has seamlessly blended the idioms of several overlapping strands. Over the past half century even as poets enriched the range of expression by experimenting with the genre, and by blending Latin, French and English styles of voicing emotion, the tendency was to subsume their personal voice in the idiom of the genre. The achievement of a recognizable personal voice – in Baratynsky's case one that is caustic, embittered, forever full of regret and even in love with regret – shows a mastery of the elegiac idiom developed over the course of the past fifty years.

It is necessary to distinguish between neoclassical stylization and genuine imitation in the poetry of Alexander Pushkin (1799–1837), one of the greatest Russian elegists and love poets. Where classical reference occurs in his love lyrics the effect is generally more of stylization than imitation. This is by contrast with his philosophical and political poetry, which more genuinely emulates Horace and Juvenal, and in his poems of exile Ovid is a towering presence (Sandler 1989: ch. 1). His love poetry sports abundant references to Venus, Delia, Leda and Cupid, but their primary function is to suggest urbanity and an affinity with French *poésie légère* as a tradition of erotic verse rather than signal a substantive connection to Latin lyric. In poems like the 'Triumph of Bacchus' ('Torzhestvo Bakkha', 1819), which celebrates erotic and sympotic pleasures, Pushkin draws easily and simultaneously on several reinforcing traditions by alluding to Catullus 64, a popular ballet on a mythological subject, and an elegy from the third book of the collection *Les Amours* of Antoine de Bertin (Pushkin (2004) II 506).[5] Pushkin is overt about his technique of overlaying traditions in a short poem of 1826 that pays tribute not to the deity of religion but the god of beauty, listing the poets Évariste Parny, Tibullus[6] and Thomas Moore as masters. Yet a more meditative strain of elegy employs the elegiac distich in order to suggest a

[5] For Bertin 'the new Propertius', see Loubère (Chapter 20) in this volume.
[6] For Parny 'the new Tibullus', see Loubère (Chapter 20) in this volume.

deeper sense of regret over lost love. Among the more celebrated poems of this type 'On the hills of Georgia' ('Na kholmakh Gruzii', 1829) commemorates in stark images and halting expression an affair and the speaker's own capacity to love. 'Under azure skies' ('Pod nebom golubym', 1826) is also composed in this classical line and draws strongly on the language of Stoicism in preserving the memory of a beautiful woman who died too young, as does the poem 'To ***' ('K***', 1832) which stages a contest between the 'turmoil of love' and 'tranquillity' by using philosophical vocabulary (Kahn 2007).

The legacy

Although in the next generation a great elegist like Fedor Tiutchev (1803–73) occasionally produced overt imitations of Horace and Tibullus, his lyric heroes speak the language of *Sturm und Drang*, and conceive of love philosophically as defined by Schopenhauer. Another great lyricist, Afanasii Fet (1820–92), renowned for the exquisite musicality of his own verse, produced rather laboured versions of selections from Ovid's *Epistulae ex Ponto*, Tibullus' elegies as well as Horace's *Ars poetica*; these efforts appear to have left little trace on his own lyric persona. From the 1850s when poetry of a more civic cast dominates, love elegy yielded ground to public statement. And from the 1880s, when the development of a more personal voice recurred in the history of Russian poetry, writers like the Symbolists were more inspired by the widespread historical and anthropological interest in Greek culture than Roman models, and in equal measure turned to Baudelaire and the Parnassians to learn about decadence, and to Ruskin to learn about aesthetics (Polonsky 1998). In the next generation the most renowned classicizing poet was Osip Mandelstam (1891–1938), who pays tribute to both Ovid and Tibullus as elegists in '*Tristia*' (1918), a famous poem about separation caused by war. Its title directly echoes Ovid, but the female figure who crosses the elegiac speaker's mind is Tibullus' Delia. The overlay of Roman poets is a typical example of Modernist allusion. During the Soviet period it would not be until the 1970s that world-class poets like the Nobel laureate Joseph Brodsky (1940–96) and Aleksei Tsvetkov (b.1947) once again revived interest in Propertius, Catullus and Horace. The classical turn has been intermittent and highly individual rather than a sustained fashion. The story of the Russian reception of the Latin love elegy, when considered as a concentrated phenomenon, largely comprises a single chapter – yet one of great importance to the history of Russian poetry and of intrinsic merit for the quality of poems and poets.

Further reading

There is relatively little on this topic in English (more in Russian and French), but these titles appropriately complement the bibliography in the chapter and are thus useful for further reading: Sobol (2009), the only study to date that is dedicated to the topic of literary lovesickness in Russian literature. Wes (1992) provides an overview of classics in eighteenth-century Russia. For the use of neoclassical topoi in the aesthetic of the period, see Baehr (1992). Segel (1967) and Brown (1980) cover the period more broadly in terms of literary history, for which see also Garrard (1973). For the literary achievements of women in this field, see Kelly (1994a and 1994b (ed.)).

22

THEODORE ZIOLKOWSKI

German elegies

From Baroque beginnings and classical culminations to twentieth-century Hollywood

In German literature the term 'elegy' is ambiguous to a degree unusual even in a discipline whose terminology is as notoriously inconsistent as literary criticism and poetics. Since Roman antiquity it was believed that the elegiac distich constituted the proper form for that genre, and Horace's formulation in his *Ars poetica* was traditionally cited as the proper model for the expression of lamentation (*querimonia*) and feeling of a wish come true (*uoti sententia compos*) that was later to be linked to erotic elegy.[1]

> Versibus impariter junctis querimonia primum,
> Post etiam inclusa est uoti sententia compos.
> (*Ars P.* 75–76)

> Verses yoked unequally first embraced lamentation, later also the sentiment of granted prayer.[2]

Horace's formula was repeated by the Middle High German poet Eberhard der Deutsche in his thirteenth-century *Laborintus*, which specified that the appropriate form for narratives is the hexameter and for lamentation the elegiac pentameter, while songs of praise use strophic forms:

> Historias habet hexametrum, seruitque querelae
> Pentametrum, laudes cetera metra canunt.[3]

> (The hexameter tells of tales and the pentameter serves the lament, all the other metres sing of praise.)

But during the *aetas Ouidiana* of the twelfth and thirteenth centuries the elegiac distich became so popular that it was increasingly used for almost

[1] Thanks to an ancient scholium *Ars poetica* 75 'persuaded older commentators (wrongly as it happens) that the love elegy was involved': Brink (1971), 166–7. See also C. Gottsched below.

[2] Translation, R. Fairclough (1970) 457.

[3] Beissner (1941) 13–34.

any subject matter.[4] Eberhard's own work exemplifies the fact that the distinctions were becoming blurred because he used the distich for didactic purposes, just as other authors began to use the distich for epic narrative. By the end of the Middle Ages in Germany as elsewhere any precise sense of elegy as a genre had been effaced because distich form had expanded to embrace virtually any and every subject.

This tendency continued in the poetry of Neo-Latin humanism. To be sure, a certain refocusing took place: in contrast to the medieval poets, who still regarded lamentation as the central matter of the elegy, German poets writing in Latin followed the practice of the Roman poets rather than Horace's prescriptions, putting erotic love into the centre of the genre: e.g. the *Amores* (1502) of Konrad Celtis, the *Basia* (1539) of the Dutch Humanist Johannes Secundus and the four books of *carmina* by Petrus Lotichius Secundus, which included elegies on war along with those on love.[5]

With the emergence of vernacular poetry during the Renaissance the situation changed. Poets in Germany, France and England sought in their respective languages to recreate the elegiac distich. In general, as formal criteria vanished, content became the single means of identifying elegy in France and England.[6]

The Baroque elegy: a matter of form

In Germany, in contrast, the characteristic feature of Baroque elegy was not so much subject matter as form. In Martin Opitz's *Buch von der deutschen Poeterey* (1624), to be sure, the genre is still defined wholly in terms of subject matter: 'In elegies were written, originally, only sad matters and then, subsequently, also love affairs, lovers' laments, desire for death, letters, longing for absent ones, accounts of one's own life and similar things.'[7] But this fact stems from the circumstance that Germany was more than a century later than most other countries in adapting classical forms and genres to the vernacular. As a result, when Opitz wrote the first German poetics, he had at his disposal not only the theoretical works of such Renaissance critics as Scaliger but also the practical examples of French and Italian poetry, where the genre was identified by its subject matter. It was Opitz's practice rather than his theory that influenced the development of the genre in Germany. For his own 'elegies' he devised a form whose rhythms more closely approximate the classical distich than the rhyming of the French. Opitz's elegiac alexandrines – with alternating feminine and masculine rhymes – retain two

[4] For the *aetas Ouidiana*, see Kretschmer (Chapter 17) in this volume.
[5] See Houghton (Chapter 18) in this volume.
[6] See Moul (Chapter 19) and Loubère (Chapter 20) in this volume.
[7] Opitz (1954) 21.

characteristics of the distich: the six-beat line in both elements and the alternating acatalectic and catalectic endings. These effects are evident in the opening lines of his 'Beschluss-Elegie' ('Conclusion Elegy'):

Das blinde Liebeswerk, die süße Gift der Sinnen
    Und rechte Zauberei, hat letzlich hier ein End':
Es wird das lose Kind, so mich verführen könne,
    Gott lob, letzt ganz und gar von mir hinweggewendt.[8]

The blind work of love, the sweet poison of the senses,
    And actual magic has finally here its end:
The wanton child that could seduce me,
    Thank God, has now at last been turned away from me.

By mid-century Opitz's practice had obscured his theory. When Enoch Hanmann reedited Opitz's poetics (1658) he wrote simply that 'Elegies are alexandrine verses in which a feminine and masculine are alternated.'[9] The practice of many poets – Johannes Rist, Caspar Ziegler, Christian Hofmann von Hofmannswaldau and others – substantiated the general observation that the elegy of this period is identifiable by its formal characteristics alone.

Towards popularity

For a variety of reasons elegy failed to attract the major poets of the Baroque. But during the eighteenth century it became once again one of the most popular literary forms in Europe. In Germany, in particular, its appeal is evidenced by such anthologies as Klamer Schmidt's *Elegien der Deutschen* (1776) and Hans Heinrich Füssli's *Oden und Elegien der Deutschen* (1785). Many volumes by representative poets contain clearly specified examples of the genre, and no issue of a journal was deemed to be complete without an elegy. Yet paradoxically and for several reasons the very popularity of the genre caused it to lose definition as to both form and subject matter.

First, Baroque elegy in Horace's sense continued to exist as a viable form until the end of the century, largely because of the authority of Johann Christoph Gottsched, whose *Versuch einer Critischen Dichtkunst* (1730) is prefaced by a translation of the *Ars poetica* and reinterprets Horace's lines to include erotic elegy in rhyming alexandrines:

Die Elegie war sonst ein Werk der Traurigkeit,
Allein sie ward hernach zugleich der Lust geweiht.[10]

The elegy was once a work of sadness,
But it was later also dedicated to pleasure.

[8] Opitz (1869) 69. [9] Cited in Beissner (1941) 63. [10] Gottsched (1962) 17.

In his extended commentary on this passage Gottsched states that the subject matter 'should be composed in a natural and flowing manner, should have a sad content and consist almost wholly of laments'[11] and opposed the tendency of the late Baroque to restrict elegy to erotic poetry. In his consideration of the form Gottsched first criticizes the French and English for writing poems that are elegies in name and content alone but not in form. He is especially contemptuous of the rhyming couplets employed by Marot, Ronsard, Desportes, and Rochester. Opitz did much better for the Germans, he asserts, by creating elegies that, while not identical in form with the Latin distichs, at least bear a close resemblance to them.

Second, around the middle of the century many poets of the Rococo, turning back directly to the model of Catullus, resurrected the animal epicedium as a variety of elegy. The lament over the death of a favourite bird, like Lesbia's sparrow (Catull. 3) and Corinna's parrot (Ovid *Am.* 2.6), becomes virtually a subgenre in German Anacreontic poetry. We find elegies to sparrows (J.W.L. Gleim), canaries (Anna Luise Karschin), quails (Karl Wilhelm Ramler), doves (Johann Martin Miller), starlings (Friedrich Matthisson) and a flock of other fowl – not to mention pet lapdogs, cats and sundry other beasts. This trivialization of subject matter was accompanied by a relaxing of the strict Baroque form of cross-rhyming alexandrines. Virtually any couplet comprising lines of unequal length was felt to be elegiac. The first strophe of Hölty's elegy 'Auf den Tod einer Nachtigal' ('On the Death of a Nightingale', 1771) is representative:

> Sie ist dahin, die Maienlieder tönte,
> Die Sängerin,
> Die durch ihr Lied den ganzen Hain verschönte,
> Sie ist dahin![12]
>
> She's gone, who sounded May songs,
> The songstress,
> Who through her song brightened the whole grove,
> She's gone!

Third, Friedrich Wilhelm Gotter's translation of Gray's 'Elegy written in a country churchyard' into alexandrine rhymed couplets introduced yet another topic into the eighteenth-century German elegy: the melancholy meditation composed in some such isolated spot as a cemetery, castle ruin or battlefield. In 1771, the year that Gotter's translation appeared, Hölty produced elegies inspired both by country and city cemeteries. The first strophe of the former leaves little doubt about the source of inspiration:

[11] Gottsched (1962) 657–68, here 657. [12] Hölty (1966) 36.

Mit dem letzten Schall der Abendglocke,
  Die den jungen Maitag
Weinend jetzt zu Grabe läutet, wandle
  ich in diese Schatten.[13]

With the last peal of the evening bell
  which sounds the young May day
tearfully to its grave, I stroll
  into these shadows.

Matthisson used an elegiac stanza similar to Gray's for his 'Elegie auf einem Gottesacker geschrieben,' ('Elegy written in a graveyard') but he created a different strophe for his 'Elegie in den Ruinen eines alten Bergschlosses geschrieben' ('Elegy written in the ruins of an old mountain castle'):

Schweigend in der Abenddämmrung Schleier,
  Ruht die Flur, das Lied der Haine stirbt,
Nur daß hier, im alternden Gemäuer,
  Melancholisch noch ein Heimchen zirpt.[14]

Silently in the veil of evening's dusk
  The meadow rests, the song of the groves dies,
Only here, in the ageing ruins,
  A cricket chirps mournfully.

C.A. Tiedge selected for his popular elegiac meditations a legend-veiled precipice in the Harz Mountains, 'Elegie am Roßtrapp', and the battlefield where Frederick the Great suffered his worst defeat in the Seven Years' War, 'Elegie auf dem Schlachtfelde bei Kunersdorf', ('Elegy on the battlefield near Kunersdorf').

Finally, the elegiac distich was gradually adapted for use in German poetry, a circumstance that emphatically distinguishes German literature from other European literatures. As early as the sixteenth and seventeenth centuries there had been occasional experiments with the distich, but these were in general too sporadic to have any authority. Then in 1748 the enormous success of Friedrich Klopstock's *Der Messias*, with its swelling hexameters, undermined the hegemony of alexandrine verse in German literature, which was soon replaced in drama by blank verse and in epic poetry by hexameters patterned after classical models. In the wake of this success classically oriented poets began experimenting with other Greek and Latin forms – the Alcaic, the Asclepiadean and Sapphic odes as well as the distich. Among the various forms at which Klopstock tried his hand during the

[13] 'Elegie auf einen Dorfkirchhof', ibid. 37. [14] Matthisson (1787) 5.

fifties and sixties we find occasional poems in distichs. His first of this sort, 'Die künftige Geliebte' ('The future beloved', 1748), in fact, was originally called simply 'Elegie'. But despite the allusion to melancholy in the first couplet –

> Dir nur, liebendes Herz, euch, meine vertraulichsten Thränen,
> Sing' ich traurig allein dies wehmütige Lied.[15]

> To you alone, loving heart, to you, my most intimate tears,
> I sadly sing this mournful song.

– the poem is an elegy only in the formal sense of the word because it contains no real lament. Instead, as the title suggests, it is a speculation about the nature of the girl, presently growing up somewhere, who will become his future beloved. Klopstock's poems in distichs stimulated wide imitation after they appeared in 1771 in his volume of odes. During that decade Johann Heinrich Voss, whose widely acclaimed translation of *The Odyssey* (1781) fully naturalized the hexameter for German versification, succeeded in such poems as 'Die Trennung' ('The Separation', 1776) and 'An Selma' (1776) in writing metrically correct pentameters in German. His example was imitated by various poets, such as Ludwig Theobul Kosegarten, who wrote erotic elegies to a chorus-line of girls with names like Agnes, Alma, Ida, Jinny, Minona and Rosa. In 1783, following various prose versions, K.F. Reinhard published the first translation of a Roman elegist into German distichs. And that same decade witnessed the appearance of other poems in distichs. Johann Gaudenz von Salis-Seewis' 'Elegie an mein Vaterland' ('Elegy to my fatherland', 1785) is written in distichs inspired by Voss. In 1791, as though there were something about mountains that inspired distichs, Friederike Brun wrote 'Der Tempel der Freundschaft' ('The temple of friendship'), an elegy celebrating the Jura mountains, and Friedrich Matthisson composed his 'Elegie an Sophie von Seckendorf und Eleonore von Kalb', in which the poet sits at sunset beside a mountain spring and thinks of his distant friends. However, there was still no firm association of the form with a fixed subject matter. Most of the poems in distichs are elegies only in the formal sense of the word.

This, then, was the situation in 1795, when three works appeared in the journal *Die Horen* that canonized elegy in German literature. Goethe's cycle of 'Römische Elegien' authoritatively established the elegiac distich as a viable form in German literature and especially for the love elegy. Schiller's essay *Über naive und sentimentalische Dichtung* provided the theoretical

[15] Klopstock (1981) I 21–4, here 21.

basis for the genre that may rightly be called 'the classical German elegy' in distinction from other more traditional forms of the genre. And Schiller's poem 'Der Spaziergang' ('The walk') exemplified that form.

Goethe's 'Roman elegies'

In June 1788, when the thirty-eight-year-old Goethe arrived back in Weimar after almost two years in Italy, the psychic wrench he felt at leaving the eternal city, he reports in the last paragraph of *Die Italienische Reise* (*The Italian Journey*), was so 'heroic-elegiac' that he wanted to write an elegy to commemorate the occasion. But several factors precluded any immediate composition. First, the vivid recollection of Ovid's elegy to Rome (*Tristia* I.3) intruded into his meditations and prevented him from composing a poem of his own. Then his liaison with the twenty-three-year-old commoner Christiane Vulpius, whom he met shortly after his return and took into his house and life, alienated the prim ladies of Weimar. Though eager to give poetic expression to his new domestic bliss, he had to find a mode that would not be flagrantly indiscreet. Finally, his friend Ludwig von Knebel, translator of various classical works, sent him a fine Latin edition of what he termed the 'cloverleaf of poets' ('das Kleeblatt der Dichter')[16] – Tibullus, Catullus and Propertius – and Goethe plunged immediately into their perusal. This re-acquaintance with the Latin erotic elegists under totally new auspices was the catalyst that precipitated the poetic treatment of Goethe's Italian years and his new-found love at home. The transposition of his Weimar experience to a Roman setting and the translation of his autobiography into a classical form enabled him to achieve a twofold distance, spatial and temporal, from his experience and to render it with poetic objectivity. By the end of October 1788 he began writing occasional poems in distichs that celebrated his love for Christiane as transposed to a Roman setting. In his letters from the period Goethe referred to these poems simply as his 'Erotica', and he gathered them in an album that he kept under a cast of Raphael's skull.

By April 1790, when he decided to conclude the collection, he had written at least twenty-four poems in elegiac distichs, which he shared with a few close friends. Several of them strongly urged him to keep the poems as a private memento, a diary in verse, fearing that a prudish public might be offended by such passages as the one in which the poet recounts how he lay in bed with his beloved, gently scanning his verses with his fingers on her bare back:

[16] Goethe, letter of 25 October 1788 to Knebel. All relevant passages from letters and reviews concerning the 'Römische Elegien' are conveniently reprinted in Leitzmann (1912) 24.

Oftmals hab ich auch schon in ihren Armen gedichtet
    Und des Hexameters Maß leise mit fingernder Hand
Ihr auf den Rücken gezählt. (V, 15–17)

Often I composed in her arms
    And counted the hexameter's measure with fingering hand
On her back.[17]

Goethe followed this well-meant advice for several years. But when Schiller asked him in 1794 for a contribution to *Die Horen*, he made up his mind to release the poems under the title 'Elegien. Rom 1788', omitting two 'priapic' poems and ultimately deciding to leave out two more that contained 'objectionable passages'. Even Schiller, who felt that the elegies belong among Goethe's finest works, privately found them 'lascivious' ('schlüpfrig') and 'not entirely respectable' ('nicht sehr decent').[18]

Although the reception of the elegies was enthusiastic among liberal spirits, the opinion of the minor poet Johann Baptist von Alxinger is more typical of the general public reaction. 'It was all right for Propertius to boast that he had spent a happy night with his girl. But who can approve when Herr von Goethe practices con-cubitus with his Italian mistress before the eyes of all Germany in *Die Horen*?'[19] One contemporary letter reports that 'all the respectable ladies are incensed at the bordello-like nakedness exposed in the elegies'.[20]

It is difficult for modern readers to appreciate the furore of indignation that greeted Goethe's poems – especially in Weimar, where people soon realized that the girl of the poems, even though she was called by an Italian name, looked exactly like Christiane. On one level, to be sure, the elegies contain the record of a love affair – a story told with great restraint, with an unusual degree of understanding for the woman's point of view and with a disarming degree of humour. However, the poems do not amount to a tightly or systematically organized novel in verse form. What we find, rather, are incidents and episodes from a Roman love affair arranged in a roughly chronological sequence. In the course of the twenty poems we are provided with many isolated details, which reveal a suggestively complete picture of the affair with Faustine, a young widow with an infant son. Yet despite the vividness of detail, the poems do not constitute an autobiography in verse of Goethe's sex life. In the first place, it turns out repeatedly that the most charming details are literary in origin, borrowed from the poems

[17] Writing on a body is a concept also employed by Ovid in his *Ars amatoria*, cf. 3.625–6.
[18] Schiller's letter of 20 Sept. 1794, to his wife; Leitzmann (1912) 50.
[19] Letter of 25 March 1795, to Böttiger; Leitzmann (1912) 55.
[20] Letter of 27 July 1795, from Böttiger to Schulz; Leitzmann (1912) 52.

of the Roman elegists. In the second place, love is only one of three large themes in the cycle. The designation 'Erotica' may have been appropriate for the earliest poems, but Goethe knew full well what he was doing when he changed the title to 'Elegien. Rom 1788' and then, for publication in his collected poems, to the now familiar title 'Römische Elegien'. The city of Rome is as meaningful to the poet-narrator as is his mistress, the Rome of classical antiquity and not contemporary or even Renaissance Rome. When he is not with Faustine, the poet is studying the architectural monuments of antiquity, reading its authors and recapitulating its history. The poet uses his lover's body in the very act of love-making to educate himself about ancient sculpture, as in the famous passage:

Und belehr ich mich nicht, indem ich des lieblichen Busens
    Formen spähe, die Hand leite die Hüften hinab?
Dann versteh ich den Marmor erst recht: ich denk und vergleiche,
    Sehe mit fühlendem Aug, fühle mit sehender Hand. (V,7–10)

And do I not instruct myself when I spy the lovely bosom's
    Forms, guide my hand down her hips?
Then I finally understand marble: I think and compare,
    See with feeling eyes, feel with seeing hand.

The connection between the city and the love affair, between Roma-Amor in the ancient palindrome, introduces the third major theme of the cycle: mythology and its representative, Amor himself, along with various mythological loving couples.

August Wilhelm Schlegel, reviewing the 'Elegien' in 1796, shrewdly foresaw that 'the objection will be raised against these poems, with great pomposity, that they are not elegies'.[21] For two centuries scholars have been debating precisely that question. Yet surely only the most provincial pedantry would deny the poems their proper designation. Goethe's elegies are not lamentations, but to the extent that the erotic distichs of Tibullus, Propertius and Ovid are elegies, Goethe's poems deserve the label as well. His poems resemble nothing in Western literature so much as the elegy books of his beloved Roman triumvirate. The most accurate description of the relationship between Goethe's elegies and the Latin elegies was stated by Schlegel in his review: 'the truest poetical re-creations of the Ancients . . . original works in the genuine antique style'.[22] It was Goethe's contribution to conquer the elegiac distich for German literature: a supple form in which it was possible to write a long poem and to express virtually everything. Yet for the very reasons that Schlegel cites, Goethe's elegies cannot properly be called

[21] Leitzmann (1912) 36. [22] Leitzmann (1912) 33.

'classical German elegies': it would be more accurate to describe them as 'Roman elegies in German'. He created in his own language an ideal form for all shadings of experience, from the most personal to the most universal. But he did not reshape the genre of the European elegy in doing so. Before classical German elegy could be created, it was necessary to have a suitable elegiac mode to match the new elegiac form. This was Schiller's accomplishment.

Schiller's elegiac 'Walk' and Goethe's 'Euphrosyne'

While such authorities as Zedler's *Universal Lexicon* (1734) followed Gottsched's wholly normative definition of elegy according to Horace's form and subject matter, the standard dictionary at century's end provided a more generous understanding: 'In a wider sense elegy, even among the ancients, was a poem dedicated to the gentle sensations of sorrow or joy, especially the amorous sensations of an affection either happy or sad.'[23] This shift in definition should be seen as a specific case within the more general movement from the normative poetics of the early eighteenth century to an increasingly psychological understanding of genre – from a conception of genre as form and content to one of genre as mood, from genre as a literary kind to genre as a mode of sensation. This shift, in turn, resulted from the new sensationist theory of aesthetics represented by Edmund Burke's *Philosophical Enquiry into . . . the Sublime and Beautiful* (1757), which introduced the notion of a 'mixed sense of pleasure' to explain such passions as love and fear. As Moses Mendelssohn explained in his *Briefe über die Empfindung* (1755), our sensations are rarely pure and unmixed. Rather, they are mixtures involving varying degrees of pleasure and pain. This theory of mixed sensations was immediately productive for such thinkers as G.E. Lessing in the analysis of drama and its emotions. At the same time, Thomas Abbt incorporated the new ideas into his essay on the elegy, which appeared in 1762 as the review of a volume of Anacreontic love elegies. He begins and ends his comments by attacking that insipid genre. 'It is not always possible, without a certain effrontery, to expect the public to listen to an author whining his laments – especially when we are talking about the laments of a lover!'[24] This misconception stems from the fact that most poets have too narrowly limited the range of elegy, which might more generally be described as 'the sensually perfect description of our mixed sensations'. J.G. Herder in his various passages on elegy was even more explicit than Abbt in distinguishing between elegy as a literary form and the elegiac as a mode: 'poetic lamentation,

[23] Adelung (1793) cols 1787–8. [24] Abbt (1762) 69–83, here 69.

Horace's *uersus querimoniae*, no matter where they are found – in epic or ode, in tragedy or idyll'.[25]

It is against this background of familiar aesthetic theory that Schiller's discussion of elegy in his essay 'Über naive und sentimentalische Dichtung' must be read. Schiller betrays himself as an heir of his age in his tendency to characterize the mode rather than the genre and to define the mode by its degree of mixed sensations. The modern poet – and here Schiller also includes the Romans in distinction from the Greeks – is no longer at one with nature, for consciousness has interposed itself between him and the world. Unable to accept experience naturally and without mediation, the modern poet 'reflects on the impression that the objects make upon him'.[26] As a result, he is constantly aware of the discrepancy between reality as he experiences it and the ideal as he imagines it. It is this state of mixed sensations that accounts for the three principal modes of expression open to the sentimental poet: satire elegy and the idyll, depending on the relative view of reality and the ideal. 'In elegy, grief may flow only from an enthusiasm aroused by the ideal':[27] e.g. laments over lost happiness, the vanished Golden Age or the bliss of youth. Subject matter becomes suitable for elegiac lament only if it can be enhanced to a condition at which it represents 'moral harmony'.

It is this view that informs the poems in elegiac distichs that Schiller wrote from 1795 to 1799, but nowhere more paradigmatically than in 'Der Spaziergang', which provided for the next century the model of what may be called 'the classical German elegy' – a model, indeed, that even Goethe followed in his greatest 'classical German' elegy 'Euphrosyne' (1799). In both cases we find an extended poem in elegiac distichs, organized as a first-person framework embracing a central meditative core and moving from thematic tension toward resolution. In Schiller's poem the poet's thoughts on cultural history as he walks up the small mountain outside Jena are triggered by the landscapes he sees: from the heroic age still subject to necessity suggested by the rural countryside, to a diversified civilization already moving toward unbridled freedom as represented by the city seen below. In this dialectically balanced work of mixed sensations the historical moment of cultural equilibrium slips past unnoticed. It is only through the poetic structure achieved when the poet returns to his room and writes his poem that the balance of nature and reason, which never existed in reality, can be achieved.

Similarly, Goethe's 'Euphrosyne' is a sustained composition based thematically on the antithesis between the eternal order of nature and the arbitrary lot of mankind. The central meditative core is embraced by a framework

[25] Herder (1877–1913) III 23. [26] Schiller (1967) V 720. [27] Schiller (1967) V, 728.

locating the poetic persona in a mountain landscape, where he has the vision of a young actress recently deceased, who implores him not to let her descend unsung into the underworld, for only in poetry can the dead live on.

> Laß nicht ungerühmt mich zu den Schatten hinabgehn!
> Nur die Muse gewährt einiges Leben dem Tod.

> Let me not go unpraised down to the shades!
> Only the Muse grants death a certain life.

We realize on putting the text aside that the poem itself exemplifies the fulfilment of Euphrosyne's wish that she might be immortalized through means of art. What is viewed as an impossible obstacle within the poem is resolved by means of the poem.

It should be stressed again that we are talking here not about 'the elegy', 'the elegiac', 'the modern elegy' or any other such general category, but only about the genre that we have specifically delimited as 'the classical German elegy'. However, this model was enormously influential on German poetry of the nineteenth century and beyond. Thus we find essentially the same pattern not only in Knebel's slavish imitation, 'Die Wälder' (1799) but, more significantly, in Hölderlin's two greatest efforts in the genre, 'Menons Klagen um Diotima' ('Menon's lament for Diotima') and 'Brot und Wein' ('Bread and wine'). 'Menons Klagen' (1799), which in its original form bore the simple normative title 'Elegie', leads Menon from his present despair over the loss of his beloved to his culminating realization of Diotima's eternal presence and his insight into the poet's mission – a development that reflects with great precision the 'tonal modulations' that Hölderlin theorized as necessary in the reconciliation of the poem's 'basic tone' ('Grundton') and its more conspicuous artistic effect ('Kunstcharakter').[28] If 'Menons Klagen' can be viewed as Hölderlin's attempt to compete with Goethe's 'Euphrosyne', then 'Brot und Wein' constitutes his effort to rewrite 'Der Spaziergang' in its movement from naive harmony through erotic alienation to ideal unity.

Many poets of the nineteenth century followed Schiller's model: Karl Ludwig von Knebel's 'Die Wälder' ('The Forests', 1799), in which the poet recuperates from the humiliation of defeat by the French through communion with nature; Wilhelm von Humboldt's meditative poem 'Rom' (1806), which surveys the history of the empire; Karl Immermann's 'Der Dom zu Köln' ('The Cologne Cathedral', 1823), which contrasts past glory and present decline in Germany; August von Platen's 'Im Theater von Taormina' ('In the theater at Taormina', 1835), a meditation on the great poetry of

[28] See Ziolkowski (1980) 119–22.

the past and present mediocrity; Adolf Friedrich von Schack's 'Im Theater des Dionysos' (1839) with its vision of murder and mercy in Aeschylus' *Eumenides*; Heinrich Leuthold's 'Elegie aus dem Süden' ('Elegy from the South' *c.*1870), with its recognition of the beauty of a vanished antiquity in a procession of contemporary Italian youth; the concluding elegy in Emanuel Geibel's 'Spätherbstblätter' ('Late autumn leaves', 1877), which contemplates the literary past in the light of present society; or Ferdinand von Saar's 'Wiener Elegien' ('Viennese elegies', 1893), which with its resolution of past and present through cyclical regeneration of man and nature is perhaps the finest embodiment of the classical elegy since Goethe and Schiller.

The powerful examples of Schiller and Goethe did not immediately replace the older literary kinds known traditionally as elegies. Goethe himself in his 'Marienbader Elegie' (1823) reverted to sestinas in iambic pentameter to recount the poignant love of his old age in a version of the ancient erotic elegy. At the same time, the elegiac distich was so widely used in the first decades of the nineteenth century that the situation resembled that in the late Middle Ages. Because so many varieties of poetry were being composed in that metre, the genre threatened to lose its distinctive outline. We can distinguish several other categories sometimes labelled as 'elegies' for their use of the elegiac distich. The distich continued to occur in traditional poems of 'mixed sensations' by such poets as Christian Ludwig Neuffer, Siegfried Schmid, C.U. Boehlendorff or Adelbert Chamisso; in didactic verse, as in Goethe's own 'Die Metamorphose der Pflanzen' (1799), August Wilhelm Schlegel's 'Die Kunst der Griechen' (1799) or Friedrich Schlegel's 'Herkules Musagetes' (1801), which amounts to a survey of modern German literature followed by a theory of criticism; and even in Achim von Arnim's 'Elegie aus einem Reisetagebuche im Schottland' ('Elegy from a travel journal in Scotland', 1808). The influence of the Goethe-Schiller 'Xenien' popularized the use of distichs for satirical epigrams. None of these genres can properly be called elegiac. But in addition to Schiller's 'Der Spaziergang' two other models continued to exert a powerful influence: Goethe's 'Römische Elegien' and Hölderlin's elegies.

Almost immediately there were imitations of Goethe's cycle. In 1797 the Swiss poet Heinrich Keller published four poems in which the poet reenacts with his Italian mistress many of Goethe's adventures with his Faustine. In Ludwig Robert's 'Elegien' (1804) the scene has shifted from Rome to Vienna, but the model is still clearly Goethe's cycle when the poet has an affair with a Viennese *Mäderl* ('girl') who could have stepped out of a bitter-sweet tale by the Austrian erotic novelist and dramatist Arthur Schnitzler. Similarly Ernst Schulze used the pattern in the thirty-three 'Elegien' that he wrote in 1812 to commemorate his brief romance with a girl who had died earlier that year. Even the twelve elegies that Ludwig I, the king of Bavaria, wrote during his travels in Italy in 1805, 'Erinnerung aus Italien im Jahr 1805' (Memory of Italy in the year 1805'), sublimating his erotic lust into lofty thoughts, followed Goethe's model. And Goethe's cycle continued to provide the pattern for poets down to Rudolf Alexander Schröder and the seven erotic poems of his 'Römische Elegien' (1913–1940).

The greatest German elegies of the twentieth century, Rilke's *Duineser Elegien* ('Duino elegies', 1923), seem at first glance to have little in common with the elegies we have considered up to this point. Two of the ten poems are written in blank verse, and the others feature a loosely dactylic *parlando* that is so flexible as to defy precise categorization. The opening lines of the First Elegy are typical:

> Wer, wenn ich schrie, hörte mich denn aus der Engel
> Ordnungen? und gesetzt selbst, es nähme
> einer mich plötzlich ans Herz: ich verginge von seinem
> stärkeren Dasein. Denn das Schöne ist nichts
> als des Schrecklichen Anfang, den wir noch grade ertragen,
> und wir bewundern es so, weil es gelassen verschmäht,
> uns zu zerstören. Ein jeder Engel ist schrecklich.
>
> Who, if I cried out, would hear me from the angels'
> Orders? And even if one should take me
> Suddenly to his heart: I would perish from his
> More powerful being. For the Beautiful is nothing
> But the start of the Terrifying which we scarcely bear,
> And we admire it so because it serenely declines
> To destroy us. Every angel is terrifying.

What we hear is a clearly dactylic line with a generally five-beat rhythm. But out of this rhythm there emerges in lines 5 and 6, so inconspicuously as to be almost imperceptible, a perfect elegiac distich. As we examine the cycle more closely, we find that these distichs appear rather insistently in all the dactylic elegies but the Fifth. Moreover, the work as a whole reveals a long meditative core revolving around the tension between consciousness and innocence, embraced by a personal framework consisting of the first and last elegies. In the Tenth Elegy the poet has transcended the elegiac conflict between the real and the ideal with a new sense of fulfilment in the present: 'Hiersein ist herrlich.' ('Being here is splendid'). In further confirmation, we know that Rilke's work on his elegies was directly triggered by his encounter with Goethe's 'Euphrosyne' and Hölderlin's elegies.

The other major poet of the twentieth century with an elegiac temperament was the Austrian Georg Trakl, who, lacking any classical education, was generally indebted to Hölderlin for his acquaintance with poetic elegies. His 'Abendländisches Lied' ('Occidental Song', 1913) begins with a basically dactylic rhythm:

> O der Seele nächtlicher Flügelschlag:
> Hirten gingen wir einst an dämmernden Wäldern hin . . .
>
> O the nightly wing-beat of the soul:
> As shepherds we once walked beside dusking woods . . .

In the following lines the poet re-experiences in a vision four stages in the history of humankind: from innocence through consciousness and guilt to an awakening to harmony and unity. So we find the traditional elegiac pattern familiar since Goethe and Schiller: a meditative poem written in a generally dactylic rhythm consisting of the familiar framework and core and culminating in a moment of anagnorisis.

Brecht brings elegy to Hollywood

German poets of the twentieth century continued to write 'elegies' even after the dissolution of the classical German elegy, just as they had done before its creation by Schiller, Goethe, and Hölderlin. But few of their elegies belong to the category which characterizes the finest poems. Poets who attempted to extend the tradition were unable to go beyond the vanishing point to which Trakl had brought the genre. As a result, they tended to turn back to Rilke or earlier models, either in imitation or in parody.

In the 'Elegien und Hymnen' (1936) of the Austrian poet Josef Weinheber we find examples that amount virtually to a reworking in a Rilkean dactylic *parlando* of the principal themes of the Duineser Elegien, as the poet sought desperately to offset the chaos of his world through aesthetic organization. In the 'Hollywood Elegien' of Bertolt Brecht, who felt nothing but contempt for Rilke, we hear parodic allusion to Rilke's elegies. Brecht makes much of the circumstance, for instance, that Hollywood – actually Los Angeles – is named for the angels, but these angels are utterly un-Rilkean, reeking as they do of perfume, carrying gold pessaries and shading their eyes as they feed the writers in the swimming pools.

Weinheber's imitations and Brecht's parodies exemplify the problem of any genre that has been pushed to the limits of its potentialities. At the beginning of its history the classical German elegy emerged in response to the specific modal need for a reflective poem that could deal with problems presented by the new German notion of *Bildung* ('education'). By the end of the First World War the values and mode of thought that produced the meditative elegy had vanished, leaving intact only the form, in the idiosyncratic extreme to which it was carried by Rilke. It is this form to which Weinheber and Brecht were responding, not to any meditative impulse of their own or to any perception of the tradition of the genre as a whole. In general, post-Rilkean poets who were moved by a genuinely 'elegiac' emotion tended not to adapt the form of the classical German elegy, which had become so stylized that it obscured its own content. Only the resistance poetry of the period 1933 to 1945 returned to traditional forms: notably the sonnet and, in the case of F.G. Jünger's 'Der Mohn' ('Poppy') or Hans Carossa's 'Abendländische Elegie' ('Occidental Elegy'), to elegy. In general, the classical German elegy has thrived during periods when poets were obsessed with the notion of *Bildung* and including specifically the elegiac sense of its loss: poetry, in sum, that requires grand historical or philosophical themes for its meditations. Beyond the closed genre of the classical German elegy, which dominated German poetry for over a century, other 'elegies' have continued to be written, but they are so loosely defined that the generic label often has no specific meaning.

Further reading

On preclassical elegy see Beissner (1941); on elegy from 1795 to 1950 see Ziolkowski (1980); on theory and elegy, Schuster (2002); on elegy and epigram, Frey (1995); and on free-verse elegies, Weissenberg (1969).

PART VI

Metre

23

THEA S. THORSEN

The Latin elegiac couplet

Perhaps surprisingly, Latin love elegy is easily defined, both by its content, which is (mainly) erotic-persuasive-pathetic, and by its form, the elegiac couplet. Perhaps even more surprising is the poetic significance of the metrical form of the genre, a significance that will be explored in this chapter.

Metre matters

The significance of the elegiac couplet is most acutely expressed in the first poem of Ovid's *Amores*:

Arma graui numero uiolentaque bella parabam
    edere, materia conueniente modis.
par erat inferior uersus; risisse Cupido
    dicitur atque unum surripuisse pedem.
'...
cum bene surrexit uersu noua pagina primo,
    attenuat neruos proximus ille meos.
nec mihi materia est numeris leuioribus apta,
    aut puer aut longas compta puella comas.'
questus eram, pharetra cum protinus ille soluta
    legit in exitium spicula facta meum
lunauitque genu sinuosum fortiter arcum
    'quod'que 'canas, uates, accipe' dixit 'opus!'
me miserum! certas habuit puer ille sagittas:
    uror et in uacuo pectore regnat Amor.
sex mihi surgat opus numeris, in quinque residat;
    ferrea cum uestris bella ualete modis.

Stephen Harrison and the anonymous reader of Cambridge University Press have kindly improved this chapter.

cingere litorea flauentia tempora myrto,
    Musa[1] per undenos emodulanda pedes.
(*Am.* 1.1)

Arms and violent wars I prepared to pour forth in a heavy rhythm, a theme matching my metre. The second verse was equal [to the first]; then, it is said, Cupid laughed and stole a foot. '... Although the new page rose well in its first verse, the next [verse] weakened my strength. And I do not even have a theme that is apt for lighter rhythms, neither a boy nor a well-coiffed girl with long locks.' Thus I complained [to Cupid], when he suddenly chose a dart that was made for my undoing from his loosened quiver. Bending the flexible bow over his knee like a crescent, he said, 'Take, bard, the task you are to sing.' Poor me! That boy had unfailing arrows, I am burning and Amor reigns in my heart that used to be free. Let the work rise in six rhythmical units and sink back in five; farewell, you ironclad wars with your metre. Crown your blond temples with the beach-loving myrtle, you Muse, to be measured in poems of eleven feet.[2]

In technical terms, the elegiac couplet is a unit consisting of two lines (Gr. δίστιχος, distich) consisting of a six-foot dactylic hexameter and a five-foot dactylic pentameter that together amount to a total number of eleven feet (cf. *Am.* 1.1.30). In the hexameter each trisyllablic dactyl (–⏑⏑) can be substituted by a disyllabic spondee (– –), normally with the exception of the last two feet: the fifth foot is regularly a trisyllabic dactyl, while the sixth foot is disyllabic, closing with an *anceps* (two-fold, double); the *anceps* can be long or short, so the sixth foot can be a spondee or a trochee (–⏑). In the dactylic pentameter, which the ancients thought of as two and a half feet plus two and a half feet (= five feet), only the first two dactyls can regularly be substituted by spondees. The entire elegiac couplet thus appears as follows:

–⏕ | –⏕ | –⏕ | –⏕ | –⏑⏑ | –⏓
–⏕ | –⏕ | – || –⏑⏑ | –⏑⏑ | –

The process of identifying the different feet of a metre is called 'scansion'. The scansion of e.g. *Am.* 1.1.17–18 is as follows:

–   ⏑ ⏑| – – |– – | – ⏑ ⏑|– ⏑ ⏑| – –
cum bene surrexit uersu noua pagina primo,

– ⏑ ⏑|– – | – || – ⏑ ⏑|– ⏑ ⏑| –
attenuat neruos proximus ille meos.

[1] 'In the hexameter, the Muse is clearly personified; in the pentameter, the sense is rather "poetic composition".' McKeown (1989: 30). For 'hexameter' and 'pentameter', see below.

[2] All translations are my own.

As seen from this example, the metrical feet need not coincide with the division of words in the couplet; that regularly occurs only after the first two and a half feet of the pentameter. When the metrical foot is divided between two words, this is called a *caesura* ('cutting'), which gives a sense of pause to the line. The most important caesura of the elegiac hexameter is regularly found in the third foot, most frequently after the first syllable, and is called 'strong': – || – if the foot is a spondee or – || ⏑⏑ if it is a dactyl.[3] Alternatively, the caesura of the third foot may occur after the second syllable of a dactyl and is called 'weak': –⏑||⏑. In the elegiac pentameter there is a mid-line caesura, which occurs without exception after the first five half-feet (Gr. *penthemimeres*). When the end of a metrical foot and the end of a word do coincide, this is called a *diaeresis* (Gr. 'division').[4] Finally, an elegiac poem consists of a certain number of elegiac couplets, normally more than four (= eight lines), since a poem in this metre shorter than that (and often of one or two couplets) would customarily be regarded as an epigram (see Introduction).

Ovid's *Amores* 1.1 dramatizes the one-foot difference between the stichic (continuous) dactylic hexameter of epic and the dactylic hexameter alternating with the dactylic pentameter of elegy. In his *Musa Pedestris: Metre and Meaning in Roman Verse* (2010), Morgan repeatedly points out how the epic hexameter is the metre par excellence against which almost all other Roman verse forms are identified. In the case of the elegiac couplet, the constant comparison with the epic metre becomes all the more acute inasmuch as the first verse line *is* precisely a dactylic hexameter, a point that is at the very heart of Ovid's *Amores* 1.1, as we saw above. The hallmark of the epic genre is its stichic character founded in the unbroken continuity of dactylic hexameters, which accommodates the genre's strong association with narrative. Actually, as many as three hexameters arguably start within the span of an elegiac couplet. Obviously, however, only the first of these three hexametrical starts is brought to its hexametrical finish, while the subsequent hemistichs (Gr. 'half-lines') of the pentameter refuse to roll onto their closure. In an elegiac couplet the epic expectation of flowing verse lines is thus frustrated three times over, creating a sense of abruptness and incompletion, hesitation and circumspection. These undercutting effects are in line with the aesthetics associated with the tradition after Callimachus, where the small and brilliant is valued more highly than the grand and conventional.

[3] For a technical and thorough analysis of 'strong' and 'weak', common, rare, possible and impossible caesurae, see Platnauer (1951) 4–16.

[4] The term *diaeresis* is also used when the two vowels in a diphthong are pronounced separately, so as to add an extra syllable to the word for the sake of the metre.

Suitably, it is the god of love, Cupid/Amor, who aggressively forces Ovid, apparently bent on epic projects, to change his metre and turn to love in *Amores* 1.1. However, compared with the erotic theme, the technical aspect of the genre seems to be of primary importance. Thus, Ovid admits that his intended heroic verse (cf. *arma... uiolentaque bella*) feebly diminishes into a pentameter in the next verse (*Am.* 1.1.17–8), *before* he complains that he lacks a suitable love interest for such light verses (*Am.* 1.1.19–20). Likewise, when the god of love finally shoots his dart into Ovid's heart, the poet refers to the immediate erotic-emotional consequences in passing (notably still without any mention of a proper love interest, cf. *Am.* 1.1.25–6), while the metrical consequences seem paramount (*Am.* 1.1.27–30). In other words, the *elegiac couplet* is the most conspicuous sign of a poet in love!

The elegiac couplet at Rome: a story of polishing brilliance

The complex affinity between the metres of epic and elegy, which is fundamental to the metrical joke employed in Ovid's *Amores* 1.1, is already embedded in the Greek tradition of the genre (see Garner 2011 and Hunter (Chapter 1) in this volume). While in terms of subject matter Latin love elegy was to become distinctly different from its Greek counterpart, the Latin genre arguably came to converge with Greek elegy in terms of metre. McKeown shows that while the frequency of dactyls in the first four feet in Greek elegists like Theognis and Meleager is around 550 per 300 lines, the corresponding frequencies for Catullus, Tibullus, Propertius and Ovid are roughly 330, 440, 440 and 500 per 300 lines (1987: 114). The difference between Catullus and the two Greek examples 'reflects a fundamental difference between the Greek and Latin languages: in Greek, short syllables are approximately twice as common as long; in Latin the proportions are reversed'.[5] The further development, from Catullus onward, attests to the elegists' successful efforts in fitting the Latin language to the Greek metre. These efforts were thus to result in a smooth regularity, which is first and foremost marked by the absence of elisions, especially in the crucial position of the third foot (where the most important caesura occurs), and by a disyllabic word at the end of each pentameter.

By comparison with hexameter verse, the elegiac couplet found its shape rather late in the history of Latin literature,[6] and because its development took place in a relatively short period, it is fairly easy to trace. In Catullus' epigrammatic elegiac couplets we find the greatest metrical licence, which even includes elision over the point of the mid-caesura of the pentameter

[5] McKeown (1987) 114. [6] Raven (1965) 104.

(||): *quam modo qui me unum atque* || *unicum amicum habuit* (Catull. 73.6, 'than him who just now had in me his one and only friend') and *ei misero eripuisti* || *omnia nostra bona* (Catull. 77.4,[7] 'you stole from wretched me all my blessings'). Such 'harsh' elisions never occur in the elegists. Compared with Tibullus, whose metrical perfection is closer to that of Ovid, Propertius nevertheless has a few more features in common with Catullus, such as more elisions and polysyllabic words at the end of the pentameter.[8] Regarding the Hellenization of the Latin elegiac couplet, Tibullus should be mentioned for his relatively extensive use of a weak caesura after the second syllable of a third-foot dactyl: 'This is normally combined with "strong" caesuras in the second and fourth feet as in 1.3.5: *abstineas,* || *Mors atra,* || *precor:* || *non hic mihi mater* "I beg of you, dark Death, stay away: My mother is not here". This weak caesura is much more common in Greek than Latin hexameters, (again) as Greek has many more words ending and beginning with short vowels than Latin'.[9]

Considering the approximately twenty years between the floruit of Catullus (late 60s– early 50s BC) and the publication of Propertius' *Monobiblos* and Tibullus' first book,[10] which are both already considerably smoother with regard to metre, it is tempting to ponder on what efforts the 'lost generation' of neoteric poets and others who used the elegiac couplet may have made in order to Latinize the Greek verse form. Unfortunately, of these poets only scarce fragments remain, and very few in elegiac metre. We know that Helvius Cinna (*c.*90–44 BC) wrote epigrams in the elegiac couplet (frr. 14, 15, 16 Hollis) and *carmina amatoria* (cf. Ov. *Tr.* 2.435 and Hollis 2007: 17–20, 46). Of Licinius Calvus (*c.*82–54/53 BC, cf. Hollis 2007: 57–8), Hollis observes that the 'close relationship in metre (as in subject matter) between Calvus and Catullus is very striking: they share hexameters, *elegiacs*, hendecasyllables and choliambs' (2007: 6, my italics). Furthermore, Ticida, who probably was executed in 46 BC (cf. Hollis 2007: 159), did write love poetry (cf. Ov. *Tr.* 2.433–4) in praise of Perilla, a pseudonym for Metella (Apul. *Apol.* 10), perhaps in elegiacs (cf. fr. 103 Hollis). Finally, Varro Atacinus (*c.*82–53 BC) wrote love poetry to a Leucadia, perhaps in elegiacs, although his other works are supposed to have been in hexameters (Prop. 2.34.85–6, cf. Ov. *Tr.* 2.439–40, Hollis 2007: 5, 177). Obviously, very little can be known about the metrical habits of these almost entirely lost poets.

[7] For both examples, see Raven (1965) 105.

[8] 'Many of the features of elegiac verse which later become associated with Ovid in fact originate with [Tibullus].' Maltby (2002) 68.

[9] Maltby (2002) 69.

[10] For the disputed chronological order between the first publications of Propertius and Tibullus, see the Introduction.

However, the elegiac couplets of Virgil's friend Gallus, famously recovered in the Qaṣr Ibrîm papyrus published in 1979,[11] offer some indications as to what must have been going on in the interval between Catullus and Propertius:[12]

Tristia nequit[ia . . . .]a, Lycori, tua
Fata mihi, Caesar, tum erunt mea dulcia, quom tu
maxima Romanae pars eri<s> historiae
postque tuum reditum multorum templa deorum
fixa legam spolieis deiuitiora tueis.

. . . . .] . . . tandem fecerunt c[ar]mina Musae
quae possem domina deicere digna mea.
. . . .]atur idem tibi, non ego, Visce
. . . .] . . . . . .] Kato, iudice te uereor.
. . . [ ].
] . . . . [ ].Tyria.[13]
].

A feature that Gallus' hexameters have in common with those of Catullus is the use of words occupying a *molossus* (a metrical foot consisting in three long syllables – ; i.e. *multorum* 4, *fecerunt* 6), which recurs for example in Catullus 64. Furthermore there is no elision between the final nasal of *tum* and the subsequent initial short vowel of *erunt* in the second line. This has been called a '"prosodic hiatus" of a type hitherto unparalleled in elegy'.[14] It has however also been argued that this may in fact not be 'a hiatus, but the survival of an old license' and 'might be considered . . . a sign of Gallus' less than perfect technique'. Hollis, who makes this observation (2007: 245), concludes that 'Propertius would never have written *tum erunt*'.[15] But if Propertius 'would never have' resorted to such metrical solutions, he did however employ words of both three and four syllables at the end of a pentameter more frequently than any other extant elegist, a phenomenon of which we find several examples in these very few Gallan lines (cf. vv. 3, 9 and 11).[16]

11 Anderson, Parsons and Nisbet (1979).

12 For the approximate date of the fragment of Gallus, see Anderson, Parsons and Nisbet (1979) 128.

13 For critical apparatus and translation, see Raymond (Chapter 3) in this volume.

14 Anderson, Parsons and Nisbet (1979) 148.

15 Hollis (2007) 251.

16 Platnauer (1951) 17 gives a survey of polysyllabic endings in pentameters, in which we find the following figures for quadrisyllabic words: Tibullus, 18 + 4 (Lygd.) + 1 (*App. Tib.*); Propertius, 166; and Ovid, 31 (of which two are in the *Fasti*, three in the double *Heroides* and twenty-six in the exile poems).

The efforts made by Roman elegists to adapt the Latin language to the Greek form did eventually consolidate a metrical system, which in terms of regularity provides a striking parallel to the equally consistent range of themes in Latin love elegy. While Catullus' elegiac couplets can seem rudimentary, the hallmark of Ovidian verse remains a steady, decorously hesitant progression that appears entirely natural; there is no doubt that elegiacs from Catullus to Ovid attest a development towards metrical refinement and regularity. Ovid has more dactyls, fewer elisions and more disyllabic pentameter-endings than the other Augustan elegists. The opening verse of Ovid's *Amores*, quoted above, is a good example: although the choice of words solemnly heralds epic intentions (cf. *arma . . . uiolentaque bella*), the line betrays metrically that the turn from epic to elegy has already taken place (and in fact, the encounter with Cupid is referred to in the past tense), as it is one of only seventeen hexameters in all three books of Ovid's *Amores* that contain the maximum number of dactyls, an obtrusive pattern that rarely occurs in epic, whose hexameters regularly sport at least one spondaic foot.[17] Similarly, when the (overall) dactylic rhythm is the rule, the distribution of spondees arguably becomes all the more meaningful; McKeown has pointed out many striking examples of this phenomenon.[18]

Likewise, among Ovid's relatively few examples of elision[19] we find one that is unparalleled in Augustan elegy, namely *fluminum amores*. The elision occurs in the following passage, where the poet, hampered by a river swelling with spring-waters, has been distracted into narrating a whole catalogue of noble rivers:

> huic ego uae demens narrabam fluminum amores?
>   iactasse indigne nomina tanta pudet.
> nescioquem hunc spectans Acheloon et Inachon amnem
>   et potui nomen, Nile, referre tuum?
>
> (*Am.* 3.6.101–3)

> Did I – oh, insane – tell of the rivers' loves to this one? It is shameful to have thrown about such great names in an unworthy manner. Could I [really], looking at that good for nothing stream, mention both Achelous and Inachus and your name, Nile?

Regarding this elision, McKeown must be right that 'combined with the harsh elision in *nescioquem hunc*, [it] may emphasise Ovid's irate disgust'.[20]

17 McKeown (1987) 117.   18 McKeown (1987) 115–6.

19 See McKeown's survey of different kinds of elision in Catullus and the elegists (1987) 114.

20 McKeown (1987) 120.

Similarly, in yet another example from McKeown's rich analysis, it becomes clear that deviation from Ovid's regular use of caesurae may also facilitate more profound interpretation of the lines in question: 'Caesurae and sense-pauses within the couplet are also exploited effectively. 3.11.33 *luctantur pectusque leue in contraria tendunt* ("[love and hate] fight about my light chest and pull it in opposite directions") is the only hexameter in the *Amores* which neither has a strong third-foot caesura nor compensates for its absence by having strong caesurae in both the second and fourth foot. The rhythm conveys an impression of tortured conflict, an impression which is quickly dispelled by the light and swift pentameter: *hac amor, hac odium, sed, puto, uincit amor.*[21] (*Am.* 3.11.34, "love on this side, hate on that, but love, I think, is winning").'[22] Thus form and subject matter in the lines match each other's meaning perfectly.

Correctly understood, these examples of pointed contravention reinforce the fact that Ovid's output represents the *culmen* of the gradually more polished brilliance of the elegiac couplet at Rome. Against an entirely linear, close-to-teleological understanding of the development of the Latin elegiac couplet during the late Roman Republic and subsequent Augustan age, it might be useful to recall that for example the distinct feature of metrical regularity – the disyllabic pentameter ending – is not strictly observed by the 'perfectionist' Ovid in his later output, from the *Fasti* onwards (see note above). In fact, towards the end of his poetic career, the poet arguably reverses a development found in Propertius, whose quadrisyllabic pentameter endings were distributed among his oeuvre (books 1–4) as follows: 36%, 10.5%, 3.2% and 1%.[23] Ovid's recovery of an 'earlier' feature of the Latin elegiac couplet could serve to underscore the same point as the occasional deviations observed by McKeown in Ovid's *Amores*, namely that the rigid observation of self-imposed rules in the field of metrics is a matter of choice and not necessarily maturity – or at least not maturity alone.[24]

The meaning of metre, or: further examples of Ovid's wit

Subversion of conventional values and self-sufficiency are two fundamental qualities of Latin love elegy. The elegiac couplet strikingly embodies and dramatizes these qualities in a way that demonstrates not only the meaning of Latin love elegy, but also the meaning of its metre.

[21] McKeown (1987) 120. [22] McKeown (1987) 120. [23] Platnauer (1951) 17.

[24] Commenting on the occurrence of quadrisyllabic words as in the survey presented above, Butler and Barber remark: 'Clearly [Propertius'] maturer judgement preferred the sound of a disyllabic ending' (1933: xvi).

The elegiac couplet is on unequal footing with itself, as it were, by including the epic, long and heavy hexameter as well as the anti-epic, shorter and lighter pentameter. The power play of elegy is consequently captured in its very couplet. This power play may be activated by referring to established literary conventions, according to which epic is the heroic, lofty genre, while elegy is the small and humble genre. A second way of rendering the elegiac couplet semantically significant is by the transposition of elegiac subject matter to the epic hexameter of the elegiac couplet, thus associating the conventional importance of the epic genre with elegy, and, conversely, by relegating epic subject matter to the elegiac pentameter. Finally, the metrical power play in question is particularly conspicuous in the metrical device known as *uersus echoici* (pl. 'echoing verses') that discloses the ultimate dominance of the pentameter over the hexameter in an elegiac couplet in the genre of Latin love elegy.

Conventionally, then, epic is a 'high' genre of valour, while elegy is the weaker and lowlier art form. The epic hexameter is accordingly described as *bene surrexit*, 'it rose well' at *Am.* 1.1.17, while the elegiac pentameter, the next verse line, *proximus ille*, weakens the poet's vigour (*Am.* 1.1.18, *attenuat*... *neruos meos*). Figuratively, Ovid may consequently compare Corinna to the lofty hexameter and himself to the humble pentameter in the following attempt to seduce her:

> non...
> ...
> collatum idcirco tibi me contemnere debes:
>   aptari magnis inferiora licet.
> ...
> carminis hoc ipsum genus impar, sed tamen apte
>   iungitur herous cum breuiore modo.
> (*Am.* 2.17.11–22)

> You should therefore not disdain pairing yourself with me: it is allowed to let that which is inferior to be adapted to that which is great.... the genre of this poetry is uneven, but it is fitting to join the epic metre with the shorter measure.

So Ovid readily pays lip service to the conventionally superior status of epic compared to the lowlier standing of elegy through their proper metrical forms in the literary context of *Amores* 1.1.17–18 as well as in the figurative speech of *Amores* 2.17.11–22.

In Latin love elegy, however, what is conventionally powerless is frequently empowered, a process that may take place in the case of the pentameter, as in the case of the poet-lover under the sway of his own *nequitia* (see Sharrock (Chapter 9) in this volume) or enslaved by his love for his mistress in his *seruitium amoris* (see Fulkerson (Chapter 11) in this volume). One example of such arch-elegiac subversion involves the elevation of elegy to the superior verse line of epic, thus associating the strength, grandeur and importance of epic with its generic adversary elegy. This subversive act in favour of elegy is often followed by the transferring of epic to the inferior line of the pentameter, which vouches for the association between epic and the lowlier status of elegy. Thus at *Amores* 1.1.28–9, the description of the entire elegiac metre (*sex mihi surgat opus numeris, in quinque residat*) is reserved for the (epic) hexameter, while the metrical form as well as the subject matter of epic is squeezed into the (elegiac) pentameter (*ferrea cum uestris bella ualete modis*). In these lines, elegy has, in metrical fact, taken the elevated place of epic. Furthermore, the same metrical strategy arguably elevates elegy to the detriment of epic when Ovid 'rewrites' literary history, Greek as well as Roman. Thus, in the passage of *Remedia amoris*, which amounts to an *ars poetica Ouidiana*, Ovid lectures his readership, telling us that *Callimachi numeris non est dicendus Achilles,/ Cydippe non est oris, Homere, tui* (Ov. *Rem. am.* 381–2, 'Achilles is not to be described in the metre of Callimachus, Cydippe [in Callimachus' *Aet.* frr. 67–75] is not meant for your mouth, Homer'). Here, the Hellenistic elegist Callimachus occupies the superior hexameter line, while the father of epic, Homer, is relegated to the lowlier pentameter. Notably, the same inversion of elegist versus epic poet is found in the couplet that closes Ovid's excursus on poetic genres and their subject matter: *tantum se nobis elegi debere fatentur,/ quantum Vergilio nobile debet epos* (*Rem. am.* 395–6, 'Elegies admit they owe me as much as noble epic owes Virgil.') Literary history, Greek as well as Roman, is thus summed up in the genres of epic and elegy, and the way in which the various verse lines are married with their respective subject matters places the elegy above epic in a way that suggests that elegy – contrary to the conventional hierarchy of literary genres in antiquity – is the superior genre.

It should come as no surprise, then, that even the lowlier pentameter can gain the upper hand in the universe of Latin love elegy. One example of how the pentameter may in fact emerge 'stronger' than the hexameter is the aforementioned *uersus echoici*, a favourite device of Ovid (McKeown 1989: 260–1). One example of this kind of device is found in *Amores* 3.6, the poem where the unusual elision (*fluminum amores*) pointed out above occurs. Here the poet recalls a number of stories in which river gods fall in love. One of these river gods is Anien, who tries to seduce the unresponsive girl Ilia with the following words: *Ilia pone metus: tibi regia nostra patebit,/ teque colent amnes: Ilia pone metus* (*Am.* 3.6.61–2, 'Ilia, do not be afraid: my palace will be open for you, rivers will adore and attend to you: Ilia, do not be afraid'). In these lines the first five half-feet of the hexameter and the last five half-feet of the pentameter are entirely interchangeable. Thus, in the words of the anonymous reader of this volume for Cambridge University Press, the *uersus echoicus* is a most acute example of 'how the second half of the pentameter's invariance infects the hexameter with its "levity" ... it creates the couplet'. Though the hexameter comes first in the couplet, it is in fact the non-spondaic second half of the elegiac pentameter that preconditions the start of the hexameter that precedes it, which as a consequence also must be non-spondaic. Elegy, again, has the upper hand!

A further way in which the elegiac couplet underpins the meaning of Latin love elegy concerns the concept of unity and self-sufficiency, which, in various ways, marks the genre in question. To the list of one time, one place, one theme, one form and one canon, 'one syntactical unit' may be added (for the other items in this list, see the Introduction). The unit of the elegiac couplet corresponds with a striking regularity with the unit of a sentence, which thus contributes to the impression of unity and self-containment that is so distinct in the genre of Latin love elegy. In Ovid's *Amores* there are several scenes where the poet-lover is on the brink of losing control. One such scene takes place when the poet-lover regrets that he has beaten his girl (*Am.* 1.7), another when he fears for her life after she has had an abortion (*Am.* 2.14) and a third when the poet shamefully recounts the one occasion when he proved to be impotent in bed (*Am.* 3.7). Yet, none of these situations results in the disruption of the obvious control with which the syntactical units are brought to their closures within the span of each couplet. Almost without exception, each hexameter sports a proper syntactical start, between the end of each hexameter and beginning of each pentameter there is regularly a conjunction, and each pentameter ends with a syntactical closure. This is contravened in only a few instances,[25] as for example when the poet-lover is suddenly discovered, after having listened to the bawd Dipsas' attempt at seducing his beloved girl to take many lovers in order to secure an (increasing) income:

uox erat in cursu, cum me mea prodidit umbra;
  at nostrae uix se continuere manus
quin albam raram<u>que</u> comam lacrimosa<u>que</u> uino
  lumina rugosas distraherent<u>que</u> genas.
(*Am.* 1.8.109–12)

She was still talking, when my shadow betrayed me; but my hands could hardly contain themselves from disfiguring the white, thin hair, the eyes flowing with tears from wine and the wrinkled cheeks.

[25] See *Am.* 1.1.21–5, 1.4.35–45 and McKeown (1987) 111–2.

These lines describe how close the poet-lover was to losing control, an effect aptly conveyed by the way in which the sentence is extended over two couplets, as the adversative particle *at* ('but') disrupts the regular rhythm of the pentameter, which normally brings the sentence begun in the hexameter to a close, and the triple *-que* enhances the impression of a breathless pace. This exception aside, the elegiac couplet in general and the Ovidian elegiac couplet in particular[26] appear self-sufficient, in the sense that syntactical units are regularly contained within units of the couplets.

In sum, then, the meaning of metre in Latin love elegy is rich indeed. The elegiac couplet captures the inherent and paradoxical urge of Latin love elegy to defy and be defined by the poetic genre of epos. Furthermore, the subversive dynamics of power play essential to the elegiac genre are crucial to the couplet as well, where the seemingly and conventionally weak (elegy/pentameter) appears just as strong as the conventionally mighty (epic/hexameter). The couplet also corroborates the self-sufficiency and unity of elegy not only by being one metrical form, but also by encapsulating syntactical units that tend to coincide with the unit of the couplets.

Further reading

Anyone interested in the significance and sophistication of metre in Roman poetry can do no better than consult Morgan's stimulating and delightful works on Latin verse, elegy included (2010, 345–59; 2012). However, in the wise words of Robert Maltby (2002, 72): 'more comparative work needs to be done on the metre of the elegists . . . the statistics provided by Platnauer need to be reviewed in the light of more recent scholarly work on these texts.' Platnauer's study (1951) remains the one book-length study dedicated to the Latin elegiac couplet. Although it covers all imaginable and unimaginable aspects of the metrical form from a technical point of view, it remains hard to access, since Platnauer hardly considers the significance of metrical features in relation to the subject matter expressed in the verses in question. Very brief but comprehensible is Raven (1965) 103–9 on the elegists in general; highly commendable is Maltby (2002) 68–72 on the characteristics of Tibullus; and absolutely splendid is McKeown's (1987: 108–23) analysis of the carefully calibrated connection between form and content in the elegiac couplets of Ovid's *Amores*.

[26] In Propertius the sentence may sometimes be brought to a close within the pentameter, e.g. 3.11.49 and 4.7.53.

DATELINE

Some of these dates are necessarily approximate or speculative.

BC

754 date of the founding of Rome according to Varro (21 April)
648 total eclipse of the sun, recorded by Archilochus (6 April), iambic poet who also composed elegiac couplets. Tyrtaeus, a composer of elegiac couplets is active in the second half of the seventh century
*c.*550 the active years of the elegist Mimnermus commence; Solon, a composer also of elegiac couplets, is active, as is Echembrotus, who composes laments in elegiac couplets
522 Anacreon, of great importance to Roman love elegists, comes to Athens
*c.*400 Antimachus *floruit*
426 approximate date of Euripides' tragedy *Andromache*, where a lament in elegiac metre occurs
320 in these or the following years Callimachus, composer also of elegiac couplets, is born, Philitas, an important predecessor for the Roman elegists, is active, as is Hermesianax
246 Callimachus composes the *Lock of Berenice* in elegiac couplets in celebration of king Ptolemy Euergetes' wedding to the queen. The composition is added to his masterpiece in elegiac couplets, the *Aetia*, which might have been published in the preceding years
*c.*240 Callimachus dies
106 Cicero is born
100 Julius Caesar is born; epigrammatist Meleager of Gadara *floruit*
*c.*95 Clodia, widely admitted to be the model for Catullus' Lesbia, is born
90 Helvius Cinna, composer of epigrams in elegiac couplets, is probably born
*c.*85 Catullus is born in Verona
82 Varro Atacinus and Licinus Calvus are born

73 Parthenius of Niceae, later friend of Gallus, is brought to Rome as a slave
70 Virgil is born 15 October
69 approximate date of Gallus' birth
65 Horace is born at Venusia 8 December; Didymus of Alexandria is born
63 Octavian, later Augustus, is born; Cicero is consul
55 sometime between this year and 48 Tibullus is born
54 Catullus dies, in this or the following year Licinus Calvus dies, sometime between this year and 47 Propertius is born
49 Caesar crosses Rubicon; Civil War begins
46 Caesar is dictator; Ticida, probably the same Ticida who wrote love poetry in praise of Perilla, is executed
44 Caesar is assassinated 15 March; Helvius Cinna dies
43 Ovid is born 20 March; Cicero is assassinated 7 December; Sulpicia's father dies, the year is thus the *terminus ante quem* of her birth; the erotic-elegiac poet Lygdamus claims to be born, alternatively he is born after 11 or in the Flavian period
42 Horace participates in the battle of Philippi on the side of Caesar's murderers
39 Asinius Pollio opens the first public library in Rome; this or the following year Virgil publishes his *Bucolics*
31 Octavian emerges victorious from the naval battle of Actium against Cleopatra and Mark Antony; Mark Antony commits suicide
30 Cleopatra commits suicide
29 Virgil reads from the *Georgics* to Octavian
28 the most commonly accepted publication date for Propertius' first book of elegies about Cynthia, the *Monobiblos*
27 Octavian takes the name Augustus; this or the following year, Gallus commits suicide, which is thus the *terminus ante quem* for the publication of his four-book collection of elegies about Lycoris, entitled *Amores*; this or the following year Ovid begins publicly reciting poems about Corinna, later to appear in his *Amores*
26 the most commonly accepted publication date for Tibullus' first book of elegies about Delia and Marathus
25 Propertius' second volume of elegies
23 Horace publishes *Odes* 1–3
22 Propertius' third volume of elegies
*c.*20 Ovid abandons a public career for poetry; the first five-book edition of his *Amores* appears
19 Tibullus dies, marking the *terminus ante quem* for his second book of elegies about Nemesis; Virgil dies, leaving behind his unfinished *Aeneid* to be published posthumously. Virgil's Dido (*Aen.* 4) evidently precedes

Ovid's Dido (*Her.* 7), which marks the *terminus post quem* for Ovid's single *Heroides* 1–15

16 Propertius' fourth book of elegies appears; this is thus the *terminus post quem* for the death of Propertius

*c.*13 Horace's fourth book of *Odes*; his *Ars poetica* is probably later than this year

12 Valgius Rufus, a poet of homoerotic elegies, is consul

8 Horace dies 27 November

AD

4 before this year, Ovid's second three-book edition of his *Amores*, his *Medicamina faciei femineae*, his *Ars amatoria* 1–3 and his *Remedia amoris* appear, probably in a collective volume

8 Ovid and Julia minor are banished from Rome; before this date Ovid composes most of the extant *Metamorphoses* and the six books of his *Fasti*

10 Didymus of Alexandria dies

14 Augustus dies, Tiberius succeeds him

17/18 Ovid dies in exile; during the last nine years he has composed the four books of *Tristia*, the three books of *Epistulae ex Ponto*, the curse poem *Ibis* and, probably, the double *Heroides* 16–21

310–93 Ausonius; during this century the *Peruigilium Veneris* is composed

*c.*550 the most probable date for Maximianus' floruit

*c.*1070 Marbod of Rennes and Baudri of Bourgueil are active

1105–1181 Serlo of Wilton

1304–1374 Francesco Petrarcha

1405–1464 Enea Silvio Piccolomini, later Pope Pius II

1424–1498 Cristoforo Landino

1424–1505 Tito Vespasiano Strozzi

1501 Pomponio Gaurico edits Maximianus's elegies presenting them as those of Cornelius Gallus

1502 Konrad Celtis publishes his *Amores*

1511–36 Johannes Secundus

1525–60 Joachim Du Bellay

1484–1558 Julius Caesar Scaliger

1526–85 Marc Antoine Muret (= Muretus)

1552 publication of Ronsard's *Amours*

1572–1631 John Donne

1572–1637 Ben Jonson

1578 publication of Ronsard's *Amours diverses*

1567 publication of Turbeville's translation of Ovid's *Heroides*
1595 publication of Campion's *Liber elegiarum*
1599 publication of Marlowe's translation of Ovid's *Amores*
1608–74 John Milton
1618–67 Abraham Cowley
1653 translation by Abbé de Marolles of Catullus, Tibullus and Propertius
1680 translation by La Chapelle of Catullus' *Amours* (sic!)
1712 translation by La Chapelle of Tibullus' *Amours* (sic!)
1716 joint edition of the two above-mentioned translations by La Chapelle
1743 publication of Gillet de Moyvre's *La vie et les amours de Tibulle, chevalier roman*
1746 publication of Gillet de Moyvre's *La vie et les amours de Properce, chevalier roman*
1747 Princess Ekatarina Urusova is born
1749–1832 Johann Wolfgang von Goethe
1753–1814 Évariste de Parny
1759–1805 Friedrich Schiller
1762–94 André Chénier
1763 publication of Le Brun's *Discours sur Tibulle*
1768–48 René Chateaubriand
1770–1843 Friedrich Hölderlin
1771 Marquis de Pezay's *Traduction en prose de Catulle, Tibulle et Properce en latin et en français*
1772 Longchamps' translation of *Les élégies de Properce*
1776 Longchamps' translation of *Les élégies de Tibulle*
1799–1837 Alexander Pushkin
1806–22 Charles-Louis Mollevaut's translation of Tibullus, Propertius, Catullus and Ovid's *Amores*
1816 publication of Charles-Louis Mollevaut's own *Élégies*
1875–1926 Rainer M. Rilke
1885–1972 Ezra Pound
1887–1914 Georg Trakl
1891–1938 Osip Mandelstam
1898–1956 Bertold Brecht
1919 publication of Ezra Pound's *Homage to Sextus Propertius*
1930 Nobel Laureate Derek Walcott is born
1940–96 Nobel Laureate Joseph Brodsky
1987 Publication of Derek Walcott's *Arkansas testament*, which includes 'A Propertius Quartet'

WORKS CITED

Abbt, T. (1762) *Briefe die neueste Litteratur betreffend*. Berlin

Abrahams, P. (1926) *Les Oeuvres poétiques de Baudri de Bourgueil*. Paris

Acosta-Hughes, B. (2009) 'Ovid and Callimachus: Rewriting the Master', in Knox (2009): 236–52

Adelung, J.C. (1793) *Grammatisch-kritisches Wörterbuch der Hochdeutschen Mundart*, 2nd edn. Leipzig

Adkins, A.W.H. (1985) *Poetic Craft in the Early Greek Elegists*. Chicago

Albrecht, M. von (1982) 'La correspondance de Pâris et d'Hélène: Ovide et Baudri de Bourgueil' in R. Chevallier (ed.), *Colloque Présence d'Ovide* (Paris): 189–93

Alfonsi, A. (1963) 'Ausoniana', *Aevum* 37: 117

Alfonsi, L. (1965) 'Il problema dell'origine dell'elegia latina', *Studi Urbinati* 39: 354–65

Allen, A.W. (1950) 'Elegy and the Classical Attitude towards Love: Propertius I.1', *Yale Classical Studies* 11: 255–77

Aloni, A. (2009) 'Elegy', in Budelmann (2009): 168–88

Aloni, A. and Iannucci, A. (2007) *L'elegia greca e l'epigramma dalle origini al V secolo. Con un'appendice sulla 'nuova' elegia di Archiloco*. Florence

Ancona, R. and Greene, E. (2005) (eds.) *Gendered Dynamics in Latin Love Poetry*. Baltimore

Ancona, R., Maltby, R., et al. (2004) (eds.) *Writing Passion: a Catullus Reader*. Mundelein, Ill.

Anderson, R.D., Parsons, P.J. and Nisbet, R.G.M. (1979) 'Elegiacs by Gallus from Quaṣr Ibrim', *Journal of Roman Studies* 69: 125–55

Anderson, W.S. (1964) 'Hercules Exclusus: Propertius, IV, 9', *American Journal of Philology* 85: 1–12

(1973) 'The *Heroides*', in Binns (1973): 49–83

(1995) (ed.) *Ovid. The Classical Heritage*. New York

Antolín, F.N. (1996) *Lygdamus. Corpus Tibullianum III.1–6: Lygdami Elegiarum Liber*, trans. J.J. Zoltowski. Leiden

Argentieri, L. (1998) 'Epigramma e libro: Morfologia delle raccolte epigrammatiche premeleagree', *Zeitschrift für Papyrologie und Epigraphik* 121: 1–20

Armstrong, R. (2005) *Ovid and his Love Poetry*. London

Arnaldi, F., Gualdo Rosa, L. and Monti Sabia, L. (1964) (eds.) *Poeti latini del Quattrocento*. Milan

Asquith, H. (2005) 'From Genealogy to *Catalogue*: the Hellenistic Adaptation of the Hesiodic Catalogue Form', in Hunter, R. (ed.), *The Hesiodic Catalogue of Women* (Cambridge) 266–86

Auhagen, U. and Schäfer, E. (2001) (eds.) *Lotichius und die römische Elegie*. Tübingen

Baar, M. (2006) *Dolor und Ingenium: Untersuchungen zur römischen Liebeselegie*. Stuttgart

Baca, A.R. (1971–2) 'Propertian Elements in the *Cinthia* of Aeneas Silvius Piccolomini', *The Classical Journal* 67: 221–6

Baehr, S. (1992) *The Paradise Myth in Eighteenth-Century Russia*. Stanford

Baier, T. (2003) (ed.) *Pontano und Catull*. Tübingen

Bailey, C. (1947) *Titi Lucreti Cari*: De rerum natura *libri sex*, 3 vols. Oxford

Baker, R.J. (1990) *Propertius I*. Warminster

Ball, R.J. (1983) *Tibullus the Elegist: A Critical Survey*. Göttingen

Barbantani, S. (2001) Φάτις νικηφόρος. *Frammenti di elegia encomiastica nell'età delle Guerre Galatiche: Supplementum Hellenisticum 958 e 989*. Milan

Barchiesi, A. (1981) 'Notizie sul "nuovo Gallo"', *Atene e Roma* 26: 153–66

(1992) *P. Ovidii Nasonis Heroidum Epistula 1–3*. Florence

(1993) 'Future Reflexive: Two Modes of Allusion and Ovid's *Heroides*', *Harvard Studies in Classical Philology* 95: 333–65

(1997a) 'Elegia', in *Enciclopedia oraziana*, II (Rome) 42–4

(1997b) *The Poet and the Prince. Ovid and Augustan Discourse*. Berkeley

(1999) 'Vers un'histoire à rebourse de l'élégie latine: Les *Héroïdes* "Double" (16–21)', in A. Deremetz and J. Fabre-Serris (eds.), *Élégie et épopée: Mélanges offerts à S. Viarre* (Lille) 53–67

(2001) 'Teaching Augustus through Allusion', in M. Fox and S. Marchesi (eds. and trans.), *Speaking Volumes: Narrative and Intertext in Ovid and Other Latin Poets* (London) 79–104

(2005) 'The Search for the Perfect Book: A PS to the New Posidippus', in Gutzwiller (ed.), *The New Posidippus. A Hellenistic Poetry Book* (Oxford) 320–42

(2006) 'Women on Top', in R. Gibson, S. Green and A Sharrock (eds.), *The Art of Love: Bimillennial Essays on Ovid's* Ars Amatoria *and* Remedia Amoris (Oxford) 96–120

Barchiesi, A. and Hardie, P. (2010) 'The Ovidian Career Model: Ovid, Gallus, Apuleius, Boccaccio' in P. Hardie and H. Moore (eds.) *Classical Literary Careers and Their Reception* (Cambridge) 59–88

Bardon, H. (1956) *La littérature latine inconnue*: II *L'époque impériale*. Paris

Barnes, H.R. (1995) 'The Structure of the Elegiac Hexameter: A Comparison of the Structure of Elegiac and Stichic Hexameter Verse', in M. Fantuzzi and R. Pretagostini (eds.), *Struttura e storia dell'esametro Greco*, I (Rome) 135–61

Barnish, S.J.B. (1990) 'Maximian, Cassiodorus, Boethius, Theodahad: Literature, Philosophy and Politics in Ostrogothic Italy', *Nottingham Mediaeval Studies* 34: 16–32

Barsby, J.A. (1973) (ed.) *Ovid, Amores Book 1*, with translation and commentary. Oxford

(1996) 'Ovid's *Amores* and Roman Comedy', in F. Cairns and M. Heath (eds.), *Papers of the Leeds International Latin Seminar* 9: 135–57

Barthes, R. (1968) 'L'effet de réel', *Communication* 11: 84–9
(1978) *A Lover's Discourse: Fragments*, trans. R. Howard. New York
Bate, A.K. (1979) 'Twelfth-Century Latin Comedies and the Theatre', in F. Cairns (ed.), *Papers of the Liverpool Latin Seminar* 2: 249–62
Batiushkov, K.N. (1977) *Opyty v stikhakh i proze*, ed. I.M. Semenko. Moscow
Batstone, W.W. (2000) 'Sulpicia and the Speech of Men', www.wbatstone.com/Sulpicia.htm
Battistella, C. (2006) 'L'"errore" elegiaco di Ercole', *Studi Italiani di Filologia Classica* 4: 229–40
(2010) *P. Ovidii Nasonis* Heroidum Epistula 10: Ariadne Theseo: *Introduzione, testo e commento*. Berlin
Beard, M. (2007) *The Roman Triumph*. Cambridge, Mass
Becker, F.G. (1972) 'Pamphilus – Prolegomena zum Pamphilus (*de amore*) und kritische Textausgabe' (Beihefte zum Mittellateinischen Jahrbuch) 9. Düsseldorf
Beissner, F. (1941) *Geschichte der deutschen Elegie*. Berlin
(1965) 'Geschichte der deutschen Elegie', *Grundriss der germanischen Philologie* 14, 3rd edn. Berlin
Bellandi, F. (2003) '*Ad inferias*: Il c. 101 di Catullo fra Meleagro e Foscolo', *Materiali e Discussioni* 51, 65–134
(2007) *Lepos e pathos: Studi su Catullo* (Bologna) 271–341
Benediktson, D.T. (1985) 'Propertius' "Elegiacization" of Homer', *Maia* 37: 17–26
(1989) *Propertius: Modernist Poet of Antiquity*. Carbondale, Ill.
Benjamin, J. (1988) *The Bonds of Love: Psychoanalysis, Feminism, and the Problem of Domination*. New York
Bernays, J. (2004) 'Zur Elegie Tib. 3.9 und zur Problematik der Sulpicia-Gedichte', *Mnemosyne* 70: 209–15
Bernsdorff, H. (2007) '*P. Oxy*. 4711 and the Poetry of Parthenius', *Journal of Hellenic Studies* 127: 1–18
Bertin, A. de (1780) *Les Amours, élégies en trois livres*. London
Bertini, F. (1993) 'La commedia elegiaca', in G. Cavallo, C. Leonardi and E. Menestò (eds.), *Lo Spazio Letterario del medioevo. 1: Il medioevo latino. 1: La produzione del testo* (Rome) 217–30
Bertini, F., et al. (1976–98) (eds.) *Commedie latine del XII e XIII secolo*, 6 vols., Genoa
Bessone, F. (1997) *P. Ovidii Nasonis* Heroidum Epistula XII. Medea Iasoni. Florence
(2003) 'Saffo, la lirica, l'elegia: Su Ovidio, Heroides 15', *Materiali e discussioni* 51: 209–43
Bielohlawek, K. (1940) 'Gastmahls- und Symposionlehren bei griechischen Dichtern', *Wiener Studien* 58: 11–30
Binder, G. and Hamm, U. (1998) 'Die "Locke der Berenike" und die Ursprünge der römischen Liebeselegie', in A.E. Radke (ed.), *Candide iudex: Beiträge zur augusteischen Dichtung. Festschrift für W. Wimmel zum 75. Geburtstag* (Stuttgart) 13–34
Binns, J.W. (1973) (ed.) *Ovid*. London
(1974) (ed.) *The Latin Poetry of English Poets*. London and Boston
(1990) *Intellectual Culture in Elizabethan and Jacobean England. The Latin Writings of the Age*. Leeds
Biondi, G.G. (1976) 'Il carme 101 di Catullo', *Lingua e stile* 11: 409–25

Birt, T. (1892) (ed.), *Claudi Claudiani Carmina* (Monumenta Germaniae Historica Auctores Antiquissimi X). Berlin

Bishop, J.D. (1972) 'Catullus 76: Elegy or Epigram?', *Classical Philology* 67: 293–4

Block, E. (1984) 'Carmen 65 and the Arrangement of Catullus' Poetry', *Ramus* 13: 48–59

Bloomfield, M.W. (1986) 'The Elegy and the Elegiac Mode: Praise and Alienation', in B.K. Lewalski (ed.), *Renaissance Genres: Essays on Theory, History and Interpretation* (Cambridge, Mass.) 147–57

Blumenthal, W. (1976) 'Untersuchungen zur Komödie Pamphilus', *Mittellateinisches Jahrbuch* 11: 224–311

Boedeker, D. and Sider, D. (2001) (eds.) *The New Simonides: Contexts of Praise and Desire*. New York

Bömer, F. (1958) *P. Ovidius Naso: Die* Fasten, II: *Kommentar*. Heidelberg

Bonamente, G. (2004) 'Properzio, un esponente dell'aristocrazia municipale di Asisium nella Roma di Augusto' in C. Santini and F. Santucci (eds.) *Properzio tra storia, arte, mito* (Atti del convegno internazionale, Assisi, 24–26 maggio 2002). Assisi, 17–74

Bond, G.A. (1987) 'Composing Yourself: Ovid's *Heroides*, Baudri of Bourgueil and the Problem of the Persona', *Mediaevalia* 13: 83–117

(1995) *Loving Subject: Desire, Eloquence, and Power in Romanesque France*. Philadelphia

Bonvicini, M. (2000) *Le forme del pianto. Catullo nei* Tristia *di Ovidio*. Bologna

Booth, J. (1991) *Publius Ovidius Naso: The Second Book of* Amores. Warminster

(2009) 'The *Amores*: Ovid Making Love', in Knox (2009): 61–77

(forthcoming) *Commentary on Propertius I*. Cambridge

Bossuat, R. (1955) *Anticlaudianus*. Paris

Bottari, G. (1980) *Marcantonio Aldegati: Poeta latino del Quattrocento*. Palermo

Boucher, J-P. (1965) *Études sur Properce: Problèmes d'inspiration et d'art*. Paris

(1966) *Caius Cornelius Gallus*. Paris

(1980) *Études sur Properce: Problèmes d'inspiration et d'art*, 2nd edn. Paris

Boutemy, A. (1947) 'Autour de Godefroid de Reims', *Latomus* 6: 231–55

Bowersock, G.W. (1971) 'A Date in the *Eighth Eclogue*', *Harvard Studies in Classical Philology* 75: 73–80

Bowie, E. (1986) 'Early Greek Elegy, Symposium and Public Festival', *Journal of Hellenic Studies* 106: 13–35

(1997) 'The *Theognidea*: A Step Towards a Collection of Fragments?', in G.W. Most (ed.), *Collecting Fragments. Fragmente sammeln* (Göttingen) 53–66

(2001) 'Ancestors of Historiography in early Greek Elegiac and Iambic Poetry?', in N. Luraghi (ed.), *The Historian's Craft in the Age of Herodotus* (Oxford) 45–66

(2007) 'From Archaic Elegy to Hellenistic Sympotic Epigram?', in P. Bing and J.S. Bruss (eds.), *Brill's Companion to Hellenistic Epigram* (Leiden and Boston) 95–112

Boyd, B.W. (1984) '*Parva seges satis est*: The Landscape of Tibullan Elegy in 1.1 and 1.10', *Transactions of American Philological Association* 114: 273–80

(1997) *Ovid's Literary Loves: Influence and Innovation in the* Amores. Ann Arbor

(2002) (ed.), *Brill's Companion to Ovid*. Leiden and Boston

Boyle, A.J. (1986) *The Chaonian Dove: Studies in the* Eclogues, Georgics, *and* Aeneid *of Virgil*. Leiden
Braden, G. (2010) 'Classical Love Elegy in the Renaissance (and After)', in K. Weisman (ed.), *The Oxford Handbook of the Elegy* (Oxford) 153–69
Bradner, L. (1940) *Musae Anglicanae: A History of Anglo-Latin Poetry 1500–1925*. New York and London
Breed, B. and Damon, C. (2010) (eds.) *Citizens of Discord: Rome and its Civil Wars*. Oxford
Breguet, E. (1946) *Le Roman de Sulpicia*. Geneva
Bremer, J.M. and Parsons, P.J. (1987) *The Oxyrhynchus Papyri*, LIV (London) no. 3723, 58–64
Brewer, J.S. (1861) *Giraldi Cambrensis Opera, I*. London
Bright, D.F. (1978) Haec mihi fingebam: *Tibullus and His World*. Leiden
Brink, C.O. (1971) *Horace on Poetry. The* Ars Poetica. Cambridge
Brinkmann, H. (1971) 'Verhüllung ("*integumentum*") als literarische Darstellungsform im Mittelalter', *Miscellanea Mediaevalia* 8: 314–39
(1979) *Geschichte der lateinischen Liebesdichtung im Mittelalter*, 2nd edn. Darmstadt
Bröcker, E. (2002) *Gottfried von Reims: Kritische Gesamtausgabe: Mit einer Untersuchung zur Verfasserfrage und Edition der ihm zugeschriebenen* Carmina. Frankfurt am Mainz
Brown, P.M. (1984) *Lucretius:* De rerum natura *I*. Bristol
Brown, R.D. (1987) *Lucretius on Love and Sex: A Commentary on* De rerum Natura *IV.1030–1287, with Prolegomena, Text and Translation*. Leiden
Brown, W.E. (1980) *A History of 18th Century Russian Literature*. Ann Arbor
Brugnoli, G. (1968) *Studi Suetoniani*. Lecce
Brunt, P.A. (1988) *The Fall of the Roman Republic*. Oxford
Bruyne, E. de (1946) *Études d'esthétique médiévale*, 3 vols. Bruges
Budelmann, F. (2009) *The Cambridge Companion to Greek Lyric*. Cambridge
Bulloch, A.W. (1973) 'Tibullus and the Alexandrians', *Proceedings of Cambridge Philological Society* n.s.19: 71–89
Bulst, W. (1950) 'Liebesbriefgedichte Marbods', in B. Bischoff and S. Brechter (eds.), *Liber Floridus: Mittellateinische Studien Paul Lehmann zum 65. Geburtstag gewidmet* (St. Ottilien) 287–301
Bulst, W. and Bulst-Thiele, M.L. (1989) *Hilarii Aurelianensis Versus et ludi, Epistolae, Ludus Danielis Belouacensis* (Mittellateinische Studien und Texte 16). Leiden
Burton, P.H. (2007) *Language in the Confessions of Augustine*. Oxford
Butler, H.E. and Barber, E.A. (1933) *The Elegies of Propertius*. Oxford
Butler, J. (1990) *Gender Trouble: Feminism and the Subversion of Identity*. New York
Butrica, J.L. (1984) *The Manuscript Tradition of Propertius*. Toronto
(1996a) 'Hellenistic Erotic Elegy: the Evidence of the Papyri', *Papers of the Leeds international Latin Seminar* 9: 297–322
(1996b) 'The Amores of Propertius: Unity and Structure in Books 2–4', *Illinois Classical Studies* 21: 87–158
(2005) 'Review: Maximian W.C. Schneider: *Die elegischen Verse von Maximian: Eine letzte Widerrede gegen die neue christliche Zeit. Mit den Gedichten der*

Appendix Maximiana *und der* Imitatio Maximiani: *Interpretation, Text und Übersetzung*', *Classical Review* 55: 562–3
(2007) 'History and transmission of the text', in M. Skinner (ed.), *A Companion to Catullus* (Malden, Mass., Oxford and Carlton) 13–34
Cahoon, L. (1988) 'The Bed as Battlefield: Erotic Conquest and Military Metaphor in Ovid's *Amores*', *Transactions of the American Philological Association* 118: 293–307
Cairns, F. (1969) 'Propertius i. 18 and Callimachus, Acontius and Cydippe', *Classical Review* 19: 131–4
(1972) *Generic Composition in Greek and Roman Poetry*. Edinburgh
(1979a) *Tibullus. A Hellenistic Poet at Rome*. Cambridge
(1979b) 'Propertius on Augustus' Marriage Law (II,7)', *Grazer Beiträge* 8: 185–204
(1984) 'Propertius and the Battle of Actium', in T. Woodman and D. West (eds.), *Poetry and Politics in the Age of Augustus* (Cambridge) 129–68
(2006a) 'Propertius and the Origins of Latin Love-Elegy', in Günther (2006a): 69–95
(2006b) *Sextus Propertius: The Augustan Elegist*. Cambridge
(2007) *Papers on Roman Elegy: 1969–2003*. Bologna
(2011) 'Cornelius Gallus and the River Hypanis', *Rivista di filologia e di istruzione classica* 139: 326–38
Calame, C. (1999) *The Poetics of Eros in Ancient Greece*. Princeton
Cameron, A. (1970) *Claudian: Poetry and Propaganda at the Court of Honorius*. Oxford
(1984) 'The *Pervigilium Veneris*', in S. Costanza (ed.), *La Poesia Tardoantica: tra retorica, teologia e politica* (Messina) 209–34
(1993) *The Greek Anthology: From Meleager to Planudes*. Oxford
(1995) *Callimachus and his Critics*. Princeton
Camps, W.A. (1961) *Propertius, Elegies Book I*. Cambridge
(1965) *Propertius, Elegies Book IV*. Cambridge
(1966) *Propertius, Elegies Book III*. Cambridge
(1967) *Propertius, Elegies Book II*. Cambridge
Cancelli, F. (1986) 'Spunti ideologico-politici in Tibullo', in *Atti del Convegno Internazionale di Studi su Albio Tibullo (Roma – Palestrina, 10–13 maggio 1984)* (Rome) 233–50
Capasso, M. (2003) *Il ritorno di Cornelio Gallo*. Lecce
Caputo, R. (1998) 'Petrarca e Properzio: "Che d'amor cantaro fervidamente"', in G. Catanzaro and F. Santucci (eds.), *A confronto con Properzio (da Petrarca a Pound)* (Assisi) 113–23
Cardini, R. and Coppini, D. (2009) (eds.) *Il rinnovamento umanistico della poesia: L'epigramma e l'elegia*. Florence
Carey, J. and Fowler, A. (1968) (eds.) *The Poems of John Milton*. London
Carocci, R. (1988) *Les* Héroides *dans la seconde moitié du XVIII*[e] *siècle (1758–1788)*. Paris
Casali, S. (1995) *P. Ovidii Nasonis* Heroidum Epistula IX. Deianira Herculi. Florence
Caston, R.R. (2012) *The Elegiac Passion: Jealousy in Roman Love Elegy*. Oxford
Chadwick, H. (1981) *Boethius: The Consolations of Music, Logic, Theology, and Philosophy*. Oxford

Charlet, J.-L. (2005) 'La marque de Catulle sur la renaissance de l'élégie latine au Quattrocento (Beccadelli, Enea Silvio Piccolomini, Landino)', in R. Poignault (ed.) *Présence de Catulle et des élégiaques latins* (Clermont-Ferrand) 283–94
Chateaubriand, F.-R. de (1978) *Essai historique, politique et moral sur les revolutions*, in *Essai sur les révolutions. Génie du christianisme* (orig. 1797). Paris
Chatfield, M.P. (2008) (trans.) *Cristoforo Landino: Poems*. Cambridge, Mass.
Chénier, A. (1958) *Essai sur les causes et les effets de la perfection et de la décadence des lettres et des arts*, in *Œuvres complètes*. Paris
(2005) *Œuvres poétiques*, ed. G. Buisson and É. Guitton. Orléans
Chenu, M.-D. (1955) 'Involucrum – le mythe selon les théologiens médiévaux', *Archives d'Histoire Doctrinale et Littéraire du Moyen Âge* 22: 75–9
Citroni, M. (1995) *Poesia e lettori in Roma antica*. Rome
Cizek, A. (1991) 'Das Bild von der idealen Schönheit in der lateinischen Dichtung des Frühmittelalters', *Mittellateinisches Jahrbuch* 26: 5–35
Clark, J.G., Coulson, F.T. and McKinley, K.L. (eds.) (2011) *Ovid in the Middle Ages*. Cambridge
Clausen, W.V. (1964) 'Callimachus and Latin Poetry', *Greek, Roman and Byzantine Studies* 5: 181–96
(1970) "Catullus and Callimachus", *Harvard Studies in Classical Philology* 74: 85–94
(1994) *A Commentary on Virgil:* Eclogues. Oxford
Clymer, L. (2010) 'The Funeral Elegy in Early Modern Britain: A Brief History', in K. Weisman (2010) 170–86
Coarelli, F. (2004) *Gli scavi di Roma 1878–1921* (Lexicon topographicum urbis Romae, Suppl. II.1). Rome
Cochéris, H. (1861) La Vieille *ou les dernières amours d'Ovide*. Paris
Cohen, G., et al. (1931) *La "comédie" latine en France au XIIe siècle*, 2 vols., Paris
Coleman, R.G. (1979) *Vergil:* Eclogues. Cambridge
Comber, M. (1998) 'A Book Made New: Reading Propertius, Reading Pound. A study in Reception', *Journal of Roman Studies* 88: 37–55
Commager, S. (1974) *A Prolegomenon to Propertius*. Norman, Okla
Connolly, J. (2000) 'Asymptotes of Pleasure: Thoughts on the Nature of Roman Erotic Elegy', *Arethusa* 33: 71–90
Conte, G.B. (1984) 'Il genere e i suoi confini: Interpretazione della *decima Egloga*', in *Virgilio. Il genere e i suoi confini* (Milan) 13–42
(1986a) 'L'amore senza elegia: *I Rimedi contro l'amore* e la logica di un genere', in C. Lazzarini (ed.), *Ovidio*, Rimedi contro l'amore (Venice) 9–53
(1986b) *The Rhetoric of Imitation: Genre and Poetic Memory in Virgil and other Latin Poets*. Ithaca, NY
(1987) *Letteratura latina: Manuale storico dalle origini alla fine dell'impero romano*. Florence
(1989) 'Love without Elegy: The *Remedia amoris* and the Logic of a Genre', trans. G. Most, *Poetics Today* 10: 441–69
(1991) *Generi e lettori*. Milan
(1992) 'Proems in the Middle', *Yale Classical Studies*, 29: 147–159
(1994a) *Genres and Readers*, trans. G. Most. Baltimore
(1994b) 'Love without Elegy: The *Remedia Amoris* and the Logic of a Genre', in *Genres and Readers*, trans. G. Most (Baltimore) 35–65

(2000) 'A Humorous *Recusatio*: on Propertius 3.5', *Classical Quarterly* 50: 307–310
(2002) 'Aristeo, Orfeo e le *Georgiche*: Una seconda volta', in *Virgilio. L'epica del sentimento* (Turin) 65–89
(2006) 'Risposta a Luigi Galasso', in C. Ampolo (ed.) *Aspetti dell'opera di Felix Jacoby* (Pisa) 145–8
(2007) 'Aristaeus, Orpheus and the *Georgics*: Once again', in S. Harrison (ed.) *The Poetry of Pathos: Studies in Virgilian Epic* (Oxford) 123–49
Copley, F.O. (1947) '*Servitium Amoris* in the Roman elegists', *Transactions of the American Philological Association* 78: 285–300
Coppel, B. (1973) *Das Alliusgedicht*. Heidelberg
Coppini, D. (1981) 'Properzio nella poesia d'amore degli umanisti', in F. Santucci and S. Vivona (eds.), *Colloquium Propertianum (secundum)* (Assisi) 169–201
(1990) (ed.) *Antonii Panhormitae Hermaphroditus*. Rome
(2006) 'I "canzonieri" latini del Quattrocento: Petrarca e l'epigramma nella strutturazione del libro elegiaco', in F. Lomonaco, L.C. Rossi and M. Scaffai (eds.), *Liber, fragmenta, libellus. Prima e dopo Petrarca* (Florence) 209–38
Coulson, F.T. and Roy, B. (2000) Incipitarium Ovidianum: *A Finding Guide for Texts in Latin Related to the Study of Ovid in the Middle Ages and Renaissance* (Publications of the Journal of Medieval Latin 3). Turnhout
Courtney, E. (1965) 'Ovidian and Non-Ovidian *Heroides*', *Bulletin of the Institute of Classical Studies* 12: 63–66
(1968) 'The Structure of Propertius Book I and Some Textual Consequences', *Phoenix* 22: 250–8
(1969) 'Three Poems of Propertius', *Bulletin of the Institute of Classical Studies* 16: 70–87
(1970) 'The Structure of Propertius Book 3', *Phoenix* 24: 48–53
(1993) *The Fragmentary Latin Poets*. Oxford
(1998) 'Echtheitskritik: Ovidian and Non-Ovidian *Heroides* Again', *Bulletin of the Institute of Classical Studies* 12: 63–6
Cowley, A. (1668) *Poemata Latina*. London
Creekmore, H. (1966) *The Erotic Elegies of Albius Tibullus with the Poems of Sulpicia Arranged as a Sequence Called 'No Harm to Lovers'*. New York
Creizenach, W. (1911–16) *Geschichte des neueren Dramas*, 4 vols. Leipzig
Crowther, N.B. (1983) 'C. Cornelius Gallus: His Importance in the Development of Roman Poetry', *Aufstieg und Niedergang der römischen Welt* II.30.3: 1622–48
Crusius, O. (1905) 'Elegie', *RE* V 2, 2260–307
Cuccoli, E. (1897) (ed.) *M. Antonio Flaminio*. Bologna
D'Alessio, G.B. (2009) 'Defining Local Identities in Greek Lyric Poetry', in R. Hunter and I. Rutherford (eds.), *Wandering Poets in Ancient Greek Culture* (Cambridge) 137–67
D'Arms, J.H. (1970) *Romans on the Bay of Naples*. Cambridge, Mass
Dalzell, A. (1956) 'Maecenas and the Poets', *Phoenix* 10: 151–62
Davies, C. (1973) 'Poetry in the "Circle" of Messalla', *Greece and Rome* 20: 25–35
Davis, J.T. (1977) *Dramatic Pairings in the Elegies of Propertius and Ovid*. Bern
(1989) Fictus Adulter: *Poet as Actor in the* Amores. Amsterdam
(1993) 'Thou Shalt Not Cuddle: *Amores* 1.4 and the Law', *Syllecta Classica* 4: 64–9

Davis, P.J. (1999) 'Ovid's *Amores*: A Political Reading', *Classical Philology* 94: 431–49
(2006) *Ovid and Augustus*. London
Day, A.A. (1938) *The Origins of Latin Love-Elegy*. Oxford
DeBrohun, J.B. (2003) *Roman Propertius and the Reinvention of Elegy*. Ann Arbor
De Nolhac, P. (1907) *Pétrarque et l'humanisme*, 2 vols., 2nd edn. Paris
Dee, J.H. (1974) 'Arethusa to Lycotas: Propertius 4.3', *Transactions of the American Philological Association* 104: 81–96
Della Guardia, A. (1916) (ed.) *Tito Vespasiano Strozzi: Poesie latine tratte dall'Aldina e confrontate coi codici*. Modena
Denis, D. (2008) 'De l'élégie à l'élégiaque: Un débat théorique à l'âge classique', in L. Gaudin-Bordes and G. Salvan (eds.) *Les Registres: Enjeux statistiques et visées pragmatiques* (Leuven) 65–78
Dennis, R.G. and Putnam, M. (2012) *The Complete Poems of Tibullus, Lygdamus and Sulpicia* (trans. with Parallel Latin Text and Introduction by J.H. Gaisser). Berkeley
Deremetz, A. and Fabre-Serris, J. (1999) (eds.) *Élégie et épopée: Mélanges offerts à S. Viarre*. Lille
Dettmer, H. (1980) 'The Arrangement of Tibullus Books 1 and 2', *Philologus* 124: 68–82
Dewar, M. (2002) '*Si quid habent veri vatum praesagia*: Ovid in the 1st–5th Centuries A.D.', in Boyd 2002: 383–412
Dimmick, J. (2002) 'Ovid in the Middle Ages: Authority and Poetry', in P. Hardie (ed.), *The Cambridge Companion to Ovid* (Cambridge) 264–87
Dimundo, R. (2002) 'Properzio e gli Augustei', in G. Catanzaro and F. Santucci (eds.), *Properzio alle soglie del 2000: Un bilancio di fine secolo, Atti del convegno internazionale, Assisi Maggio 2000* (Assisi) 295–318
Dissen, L. (1835) *Albii Tibulli* Carmina *ex recensione Lachmanni*. Göttingen
Dixon, S.M. (2001) *Reading Roman Women: Sources, Genres and Real Life*. London
Dolla, V. (1987) 'Echi properziani nella cultura e nella poesia dei secoli XIII e XIV', in S. Pasquazi (ed.), *Properzio nella letteratura italiana. Atti del Convegno Nazionale (Assisi, 15–17 novembre 1985)* (Assisi) 21–40
Dörrie, H. (1971) *P. Ouidii Nasonis* Epistulae Heroidum. Berlin
(1975) *P. Ouidius Naso. Der Brief der Sappho an Phaon* (Zetemata 58). Munich
Drinkwater, M.O. (2012) 'His Turn to Cry', *The Classical Journal* 107: 423–50
(2013) 'The Woman's Part: The Speaking Beloved in Roman Elegy', *Classical Quarterly* 63: 329–38
Dronke, P. (1968) *Medieval Latin and the Rise of European Love-Lyric*, 2 vols. Oxford
(1973) 'The Rise of the Medieval Fabliau: Latin and Vernacular Evidence', *Romanische Forschungen* 85: 275–97
(1976) 'Pseudo-Ovid, Facetus, and the Arts of Love', *Mittellateinisches Jahrbuch* 11: 126–31
(1978) *Bernardus Silvestris – Cosmographia*. Leiden
(1979) 'A Note on Pamphilus', *Journal of the Warburg and Courtauld Institutes* 42: 225–30
(1984) *Women Writers of the Middle Ages: A Critical Study of Texts from Perpetua († 203) to Marguerite Porete († 1310)*. Cambridge

(1985) *Fabula – Explorations into the Uses of Myth in Medieval Platonism* (Mittellateinische Texte und Studien 9). Leiden
(1994) 'Andreas Capellanus', *The Journal of Medieval Latin* 4: 51–63
Duff, J.W. and Duff, A.M. (1968) (eds.), *Minor Latin Poets*. Cambridge, Mass
DuQuesnay, I.M. Le M. (1992) '*In Memoriam Galli:* Propertius 1.21', in A.J. Woodman and J.G.F. Powell (eds.), *Author and Audience in Latin Literature* (Cambridge) 52–85
Dyson, J.T. (2007) 'The Lesbia Poems' in M.B. Skinner (ed.), *A Companion to Catullus* (Malden, Mass.) 254–75
Eaton, A.H. (1943) 'The Influence of Ovid on Claudian', diss., Catholic University, Washington, D.C.
Edwards, C. and Woolf, G. (2006) (eds.) *Rome: The Cosmopolis*. Cambridge
Edwards, M.J. (1991) 'The Theology of Catullus 68b', *Antike und Abendland* 37: 68–81
Elder, J.P. (1962) 'Tibullus: *Tersus atque elegans*', in J.P. Sullivan (ed.), *Critical Essays on Roman Literature: Elegy and Lyric* (London) 65–105
Ellis, R. (1888) (ed.) *Poetae Christiani Minores*, 1 (Corpus Scriptorum Ecclesiasticorum Latinorum XVI). Vienna
Elsner, J.R. (2007) *Roman Eyes*. Princeton
Endres, C. (1981) *Johannes Secundus: The Latin Love Elegy in the Renaissance*. Hamden, Conn.
Enk, P.J. (1946) (ed.), *Sex. Propertii* Liber 1*: Pars prior*. Leiden
Fain, G.L. (2008) *Writing Epigrams: The Art of Composition in Catullus, Callimachus and Martial*. Brussels
Fairclough, H.R. (1970) *Horace,* Satires, Epistles *and* Ars Poetica, 11th edn. Cambridge, Mass.
(1999) *Virgil,* Eclogues, Georgics, Aeneid *I–VI*, with an English translation by H.R.F., revised by G.P. Goold, Cambridge, Mass.
Fairweather, J. (1984) 'The "Gallus Papyrus": A New Interpretation', *Classical Quarterly*, n.s., 34: 167–74
Fantazzi, C. (1996) 'The Style of Quattrocento Latin Love Poetry', *International Journal of the Classical Tradition* 3: 127–46
Fantham, R.E. (1983) 'Sexual Comedy in Ovid's *Fasti*: Sources and Motivation', *Harvard Studies in Classical Philology* 87: 185–216
(1989) 'Mime: The Missing Link in Roman Literary History', *The Classical World* 82: 153–63
(1996) *Roman Literary Culture from Cicero to Apuleius*. Baltimore
(1998) *Ovid* Fasti *Book 4*. Cambridge
(2001) 'Roman Elegy: Problems of Self-Definition and Redirection', in E.A. Schmidt (ed.) *L'histoire littéraire immanente dans la poésie latine* (Entretiens sur l'Antiquité classique 47) (Vandœuvres) 183–211
(2006) 'The Image of Women in Propertius' Poetry' in Günther (2006a): 183–98
Fantuzzi, M. and Hunter, R. (2002) *Muse e modelli. La poesia ellenistica da Alessandro Magno ad Augusto*. Rome and Bari
(2004) *Tradition and Innovation in Hellenistic Poetry*. Cambridge
Faral, E. (1913) *Recherches sur les sources latines des contes et romans courtois du Moyen Age*. Paris

(1924a) *Les arts poétiques du XIIe et du XIIIe siècles*. Paris
(1924b) 'Le fabliau latin au moyen âge', *Romania* 50: 321–85
Faraone, C.A. (2008) *The Stanzaic Architecture of Early Greek Elegy*. Oxford
Farrell, J. (2003) 'Classical Genre in Theory and Practice', *New Literary History* 34: 383–408
(2012) 'Calling out the Greeks: Dynamics of the Elegiac Canon', in Gold (2012) 11–24
Fear, T. (2000) 'The Poet as Pimp: Elegiac Seduction in the Time of Augustus', *Arethusa* 33: 217–39
(2005) 'Propertian Closure: the Elegiac Inscription of the Liminal Male and Ideological Contestation in Augustan Rome', in Ancona and Greene (2005): 13–40
Fedeli, P. (1965) *Properzio*, Elegie: Libro *IV*. Bari
(1974) 'Properzio 1, 3: Interpretazione e proposte sull'origine dell'elegia latina', *Museum Helveticum* 31: 23–41
(1980) *Sesto Properzio: Il libro primo delle* Elegie, *Introduzione, testo critico e commento*. Florence
(1983) 'Propertii *Monobiblos*: struttura e motivi', *Aufstieg und Niedergang der römischen Welt* 30.3: 1858–1922
(1984) *Properti* elegiarum libri *IV*. Stuttgart
(1985) *Properzio: il* Libro Terzo *delle Elegie*. Bari
(1994) *Il libro di Cinzia*: Elegia *I*, Marsilio
(2005) *Properzio*, Elegie, Libro *II*, *Introduzione, testo e commento*. Cambridge
Feeney, D. (1992) '"Shall I compare thee . . . ?" Catullus 68B and the Limits of Analogy', in A.J. Woodman and J.G.F. Powell (eds.) *Author and Audience in Latin Literature* (Cambridge) 33–44
(2009) 'Catullus and the Roman Paradox Epigram', *Materiali e Discussioni* 61: 29–39
Feldherr, A. (2000) '*Non inter nota sepulchra*: Catullus 101 and Roman Funerary Ritual', *Classical Antiquity* 19: 209–31
Fernandelli, M. (2004–2005) 'Catullo 65 e le immagini', *Incontri triestini di filologia classica* 4: 99–150
Fisher, J.M. (1981) 'The Life and Work of Tibullus', *Aufstieg und Niedergang der Römischen Welt* II.30.3: 1924–61
Fitzgerald, W. (2000) *Slavery and the Roman Literary Imagination*. Cambridge
Flach, D. (1967) 'Das literarische Verhältnis von Horaz und Properz', diss. Gießen. Marburg
Flaschenriem, B.L. (1999) 'Sulpicia and the Rhetoric of Disclosure', *Classical Philology* 94: 36–54
Flower, H. (2006) *The Art of Forgetting. Disgrace and Oblivion in Roman Political Culture*. Chapel Hill
Fordyce, C.J. (1961) *Catullus: A Commentary*. Oxford
Formicola, C. (2003) 'Il pomo della concordia (Catull. 65, Callimaco e l'elegia latina)', *Vichiana* 4 serie, 5: 183–205
Forster, L. (1969) *The Icy Fire: Five Studies in European Petrarchism*. Cambridge
Forsyth, P.Y. (1977) 'Comments on Catullus 116', *Classical Quarterly* 27: 352–3
Francke, V. (1816) *Callinus Siue Quaestionis de Origine Carminis Elegiaci Tractatio Critica*. Hamburg
Frazel, T.D. (2003) 'Priapus's Two Rapes in Ovid's *Fasti*', *Arethusa* 36: 61–97

Frey, D. (1995) *Bissige Tränen. Eine Untersuchung über Elegie und Epigramm seit den Anfängen bis Bertolt Brecht und Peter Huchel*. Würzburg
Frizman, L.G. (1991) *Russkaia elegiia XVIII-nachala XX veka*. Leningrad
Fuhrer, T. (1992) *Die Auseinandersetzung mit den Chorlyrikern in den Epinikien des Kallimachos*. Basel
Fulkerson, L. (2004) '*Omnia vincit amor*: Why the *Remedia* fail', *Classical Quarterly* 54: 211–23
(2005) *The Ovidian Heroine as Author: Reading, Writing and Community in the* Heroides. Cambridge
(2009) 'The *Heroides*: Female Elegy?' in Knox (2009): 78–90
Fyler, J.M. (2009) 'The Medieval Ovid', in Knox (2009): 411–22
Gagné, R. (2006) 'What is the Pride of Halicarnassus?', *Classical Antiquity* 25: 1–33
Gaisser, J.H. (1983) '*Amor, Rura* and *Militia* in Three Elegies of Tibullus: 1.1, 1.5 and 1.10', *Latomus* 92: 58–72
(1993) *Catullus and his Renaissance Readers*. Oxford
(2007) *Catullus*. Oxford
Galand-Hallyn, P. (1993) 'La poétique de jeunesse de Pie II: La *Cinthia*', *Latomus* 52: 875–96
Galasso, L. (2006) 'Jacoby e l'elegia latina', in C. Ampolo (ed.), *Aspetti dell'opera di Felix Jacoby* (Pisa) 133–44
Gale, M.R. (1994) *Myth and Poetry in Lucretius*. Cambridge
(1997) 'Propertius 2.7: *Militia Amoris* and the Ironies of Elegy', *Journal of Roman Studies* 87: 77–91
Galinsky, K. (1996) *Augustan Culture*. Princeton
(2005) (ed.) *The Cambridge Companion to the Age of Augustus*. Cambridge
Gamel, M.-K. (1989) '*Non sine caede*: Abortion Politics and Poetics in Ovid's *Amores*', *Helios* 16.2: 183–206
Gardner, H.H. (2013) *Gendering Time in Augustan Love Elegy*. Oxford
Garner, R.S. (2011) *Traditional Elegy: The Interplay of Meter, Tradition, and Context in Early Greek Poetry*. Oxford
Garrard, J.G. (1973) (ed.) *The Eighteenth Century in Russia*. Oxford
Gärtner, Th. (2006) 'Überlegungen zur Genese der römischen Liebeselegie aus der Hellenistischen Dichtung', *Acta antiqua academiae scientiarum Hungaricae* 46: 213–37
Gavinelli, S. (2006) 'The Reception of Propertius in Late Antiquity and Neolatin and Renaissance Literature', in Günther (2006a): 399–415
Gentili, B. (1968) 'Epigramma ed elegia', in A.E. Raubitschek et al. *L'Épigramme grecque* (Entretiens sur l'antiquité classique, 14), (Vandoeuvres): 39–81
Gerber, D.E. (1991) 'Early Greek Elegy and Iambus 1921–1989', *Lustrum* 33: 7–225
(1997) 'Elegy', in D.E. Gerber (ed.), *A Companion to the Greek Lyric Poets* (Leiden) 91–132
(1999) *Greek Elegiac Poetry*. Cambridge, Mass.
Ghisalberti, F. (1931) 'Giovanni del Virgilio, espositore delle "Metamorfosi"', *Giornale dantesco* 34: 1–110
(1932) 'Arnolfo d'Orléans: Un cultore di Ovidio nel secolo XII', *Memorie del Reale Istituto Lombardo di Scienze e Lettere* 24: 157–234
(1933a) *Giovanni di Garlandia. Integumenta Ovidii, poemetto inedito del secolo XIII*. Messina and Milan

(1933b) 'L'Ovidius moralizatus di Pierre Bersuire', *Studj romanzi* 23: 5–136
Giangrande, G. (1968) 'Sympotic Literature and Epigram', in A.E. Raubitschek et al., *L'Épigramme grecque* (Entretiens Hardt 14) (Vandoeuvres) 93–172
(1986) 'La componente epigrammatica nella struttura delle elegie di Properzio', in *Bimillenario della morte di Properzio. Atti del convegno internazionale di Studi properziani, Roma-Assisi 21–26 maggio 1985* (Assisi) 223–64
Gibson, R. (1995) 'How to Win Girlfriends and Influence Them: *Amicitia* in Roman Love Elegy', *Proceedings of Cambridge Philological Society* 41: 62–82
(2003) *Ovid:* Ars Amatoria *Book 3*. Cambridge
(2005) 'Love Elegy', in S. Harrison (ed.), *A Companion to Latin Literature* (Malden, Mass., Oxford and Carlton) 159–73
(2007) *Excess and restraint: Propertius, Horace and Ovid's* Ars Amatoria. London
Gibson, R., Green, S. and Sharrock, A. (2006) *The Art of Love. Bimillennial Essays on Ovid's* Ars Amatoria *and* Remedia Amoris. Oxford
Gibson, M.T. (1981) *Boethius, his Life, Thought, and Influence*. Oxford
Ginsberg, E.S. (1985) 'The *Amores* of Joachim du Bellay: a Neo-Latin Cycle of Love Poems', in R. J. Schoeck (ed.), *Acta Conventus Neo-Latini Bononiensis. Proceedings of the Fourth International Congress of Neo-Latin Studies* (Binghamton) 483–90
Girard, R. (1976) *Deceit, Desire, and the Novel*, trans. Yvonne Freccero. Baltimore
Godman, P. (1988) 'Johannes Secundus and Renaissance Latin Poetry', *Review of English Studies* n.s. 39: 258–72
Godwin, J. (1995) *Catullus: Poems 61–68*. Warminster
(1999) *Catullus: The Shorter Poems*. Warminster
Gold, B.K. (1993) '"But Ariadne Was Never There In the First Place": Finding the Female in Roman Poetry', in N.S. Rabinowitz and A. Richlin (eds.), *Feminist Theory and the Classics* (London) 75–101
(2012) (ed.) *A Companion to Roman Love Elegy*. Chichester
Goold, G.P. (1983) (ed.) *Catullus*. London
(1990) (ed.) *Propertius,* Elegies. Cambridge, Mass., and London
Goold, G.P., Cornish, F.W., Postgate, J.P. (1988) *Catullus, Tibullus*. Cambridge, Mass.
Gottsched, J.C. (1962) *Versuch einer Critischen Dichtkunst*, 4th edn (orig. 1751). Darmstadt
Goullet, M. (1998) 'Métamorphose d'Ovide: La représentation du sentiment amoureux dans la "comédie élégiaque" du XIIe siècle', *Revue des études latines* 76: 241–69
Granarolo, J. (1980) 'Catulle à l'origine de l'élegie latine?', in *L'élégie romaine. Enracinement, thèmes, diffusion. Actes du colloque international organisé par la Faculté de Lettres et sciences humaines de Mulhouse en mars 1979 sous la direction d'André Thill* (Bull. de la Fac. de Lettres de Mulhouse 10) (Paris) 27–36
Grant, W.L. (1962) 'The Major Poems of Naldo Naldi', *Manuscripta* 6: 131–54
Graverini, L. (1997) 'Un secolo di studi su Mecenate', *Rivista storica dell'anticità* 27: 231–89
Green, R.P.H. (1991) (ed.) *The Works of Ausonius*. Oxford
(1999) (ed.) *Ausonii* Opera. Oxford

(2010) 'Victorius' Vergil: Some Comments on a Passage of the *Alithia*', *Millennium. Jahrbuch zur Kultur und Geschichte des ersten Jahrtausends n. Chr.* 7: 51–66
Green, S. (2004) *Ovid*, Fasti *Book 1. A Commentary*. Leiden
Greene, E. (1998) *The Erotics of Domination: Male Desire and the Mistress in Latin Love Poetry*. Baltimore
Griffin, J. (1977) 'Propertius and Antony', *Journal of Roman Studies* 67: 17–26
(1985) *Latin Poets and Roman Life*. London
(1986) *Latin Poets and Roman Life*. Chapel Hill
Grimal, P. (1953) *Les intentions de Properce et la composition du livre IV des 'Elegies'*. Brussels
Grondona, M. (1977) 'Gli epigrammi di Tibullo e il congedo delle elegie (su Properzio e Virgilio)', *Latomus* 36: 5–29
Gruen, E.S. (2005) 'Augustus and the Making of the Principate', in K. Galinsky (ed.), *The Cambridge Companion to the Age of Augustus* (Cambridge) 33–51
Grüner, A. (1993) 'Zur Topographie des Esquilin in der frühen Kaiserzeit: Das Haus des Properz: Versuch einer Lokalisierung', *Boreas* 16: 39–55
Gruppe, O.F. (1838) *Die römische Elegie*. Berlin
Guitton, E. (1974) *Jacques Delille et le poème de la nature en France de 1750 à 1820*. Paris
Günther, H.-C. (2006a) (ed.) *Brill's Companion to Propertius*. Leiden
(2006b) 'The Fourth Book', in Günther (2006a) 353–95
Gutzwiller, K.J. (1997) 'The Poetics of Editing in Meleager's Garland', *Transactions of the American Philological Association* 127: 169–200
(1998) *Poetic Garlands. Hellenistic Epigrams in Context*. Berkeley
(2005) (ed.) *The New Posidippus: A Hellenistic Poetry Book*. Oxford
(2007) 'The Paradox of Amatory Epigram', in P. Bing and J.S. Bruss (eds.), *Brill's Companion to Hellenistic Epigram* (Leiden) 313–32
Guitton, E. (1974) *Jacques Delille, 1738–1813, et le poème de la nature en France de 1750–1820*. Paris
Guys, P.A. (1779) *Essai sur les élégies de Tibulle, auquel on a joint quelques poésies légères*. Paris
Gybbon-Monypenny, G.B. (1988) *Libro de buen amor*. Madrid
Haarhoff, T.J. (1960) 'Vergil and Cornelius Gallus', *Classical Philology* 55: 101–8
Habinek, T. and Schiesaro, A. (1997) (eds.) *The Roman Cultural Revolution*. Cambridge
Hagendahl, H. (1939) 'La comédie latine au XIIe siècle', *Dragma: Martino P. Nilsson anno 1939 dedicatum* (Leipzig) 222–55
(1958) *Latin Fathers and the Classics: a Study on the Apologists, Jerome and Other Christian Writers* (Acta Universitatis Gothoburgensis 64). Gothenburg
(1967) *Augustine and the Latin Classics*, 2 vols. (Studia Gothoburgensia 20.1–2) Gothenburg
Haight, E.H. (1932) *Romance in the Latin Elegiac Poets*. London
Hall, J.B. (1985) (ed.) *Claudiani* Carmina. Leipzig
Hallett, J. (1973) 'The Role of Women in Roman Elegy: Counter-Cultural Feminism', *Arethusa* 6: 103–23
(1974) 'Women in Roman Elegy: A Reply', *Arethusa* 7: 211–17

(2002a) 'Sulpicia and the Valerii: Family Ties and Poetic Unity', in B. Amden et al. (eds.) *Noctes Atticae. 34 Articles on Greco-Roman Antiquity and its Nachleben. Studies Presented to Jørgen Mejer on his Sixtieth Birthday March 18, 2002* (Copenhagen) 141–9

(2002b) 'The Eleven Elegies of Sulpicia', in L.J. Churchill and E. Jeffrey (eds.), *Women Writing Latin in Antiquity, Late Antiquity and the Early Christian Era* (London) 45–65

(2006) 'Sulpicia and Her *Fama*: An Intertextual Approach to Recovering her Latin Literary Image', *Classical World* 100: 37–42

(2009a) 'Sulpicia and her Resistant Intertextuality', in D. van Mal-Maeder, A. Burnier and L. Núñez (eds.), *Jeux de voix: Enonciation, intertextualité et intentionnalité dans la littérature antique* (Bern) 141–53

(2009b) 'Absent Roman Fathers in the Writings of their Daughters: Cornelia and Sulpicia', in S. Huebner and D.M. Ratzan (eds.), *Growing up Fatherless in Antiquity* (Cambridge) 175–91

Hammarberg, G. (1994) 'The Feminine Chronotope and Sentimentalist Canon Formation', in A.G. Cross and G.S. Smith (eds.) *Literature, Lives, and Legality in Catherine's* Russia (Nottingham) 103–20

Hansen, P.A. (1983) *Carmina Epigraphica Graeca Saeculorum VIII–V a. Chr. n.* Berlin and New York

Harder, A. (2012) (ed.) *Callimachus' Aetia*. Oxford

Hardie, P.R. (1993) 'After Rome: Renaissance Epic', in A. J. Boyle (ed.), *Roman Epic* (London and New York) 294–313

(2002a) (ed.) *The Cambridge Companion to Ovid*. Cambridge

(2002b) *Ovid's Poetics of Illusion*. Cambridge

Hardie, P. and Moore, H. (2010) (eds.) *Classical Literary Careers and their Reception*. Cambridge

Harrauer, H. (1981) 'Epigrammincipit auf einem Papyrus aus dem 3. Jh. v.Chr.', in Bagnall, R.S., Browne, G.M., Hanson, A.E. and Koenen, L. (eds.), *Proceedings of the Sixteenth International Congress of Papyrology. New York, 24–31 July* (Chico) 49–53

Harrison, S. (1994) 'Drink, Suspicion and Comedy in Propertius 1.3', *Proceedings of the Cambridge Philological Society* n.s. 40: 18–26

(2002) 'Ovid and Genre: Evolutions of an Elegist', in Hardie (2002a): 79–94

(2005) 'Hercules and Augustus in Propertius 4.9', *Papers of the Langford Latin Seminar* 12: 117–32

Hartel, W. and Kamptner, M. (1999) (eds.) *Paulinus Nolanus* Carmina (Corpus Scriptorum Ecclesiasticorum Latinorum 30). Vienna

Hartz, C. (2007) *Catulls* Epigramme *im Kontext Hellenistischer Dichtung*. Berlin and New York

Harvey, A.E. (1955) 'The Classification of Greek Lyric Poetry', *Classical Quarterly* n.s. 5: 157–75

Haskins, C.H. (1927) *The Renaissance of the Twelfth Century*. New York

Hawkins, H.W. (2004) (trans.) *The Amores of Faustina, Latin Epigrams and Elegies of Joachim du Bellay*. Manquin

Heinze, R. (1919) *Ovids elegische Erzählung*, in *Sitzungsberichte Akademie Leipzig*, phil.-hist. Klasse, 71

Helander, H. (2001) 'Neo-Latin Studies: Significance and Prospects', *Symbolae Osloenses* 76: 5–102
Helm, R. (1929) *Hieronymus' Zusätze in Eusebius'* Chronik *und ihr Wert für die Literaturgeschichte* (Philologus Supplementum 21). Göttingen
(1956) (ed.) *Die Chronik des Hieronymus*, 2nd edn. Berlin
Hemelrijk, E.A. (1999) Matrona docta*: Educated Women in the Roman Élite from Cornelia to Julia Domna*. London and New York
Herder, J.G. (1877–1913) *Sämmtliche Werke*, ed. B. Suphan, 33 vols. Berlin
Herford, C.H., Simpson, P. and Simpson, E. (1925–52) (eds.) *Ben Jonson*, 11 vols. Oxford
Hexter, R.J. (1986) *Ovid and Medieval Schooling: Studies in Medieval School Commentaries on Ovid's* Ars Amatoria, Epistulae ex Ponto, *and* Epistulae Heroidum. Munich
(2002) 'Ovid in the Middle Ages: Exile, Mythographer, Lover', in Boyd (2002): 413–42
(2011) 'Shades of Ovid: Pseudo- (and Para-) Ovidiana in the Middle Ages' in J.G. Clark, F.T. Coulson, and K.L. McKinley (eds.) (Cambridge) 284–309
Heyne, Chr. F. (1755) (ed.) *Albii Tibulli Carminum libri tres cum libro quarto Sulpiciae et aliorum*. Leipzig
Heyworth, S.J. (1986) 'Notes on Propertius, Books III and IV', *Classical Quarterly* 36: 199–211
(1995) 'Propertius: Division, Transmission, and the Editor's Task', *Papers of the Leeds International Latin Seminar* 8: 165–85
(2007a) 'Propertius, Patronage and Politics', *Bulletin of the Institute of Classical Studies* 50: 93–128
(2007b) *Cynthia: A Companion to the Text of Propertius*. Oxford
(2007c) *Sexti Properti* Elegi. Oxford
(2010) 'An Elegist's Career: from Cynthia to Cornelia', in P. Hardie and H. Moore (eds.), *Classical Literary Careers and their Reception* (Cambridge) 89–104
Hilberg, I. (1910) (ed.), *Eusebii Hieronymi* Epistulae, *Pars 1*. Vienna
Hilbert, K. (1979) *Baldricus Burgulianus:* Carmina. Heidelberg
Hill, G.B. and F.L. Powell (1934) (eds.) *Boswell's Life of Johnson*. Oxford
Hillard, T.W. (1981) '*In Triclinio Coam, in Cubiculo Nolam*: Lesbia and the Other Clodia', *Liverpool Classical Monthly* 6: 149–54
(1989) 'Republican Politics, Women, and Evidence', *Helios* 16.2: 165–82
Hinds, S.E. (1983) '*Carmina Digna*. Gallus *P. Qaṣr Ibrîm* 6–7 Metamorphosed', *Papers of Langford Latin Seminar* 4: 43–54
(1987a) 'The Poetess and the Reader: Further Steps towards Sulpicia', *Hermathena* 143: 29–46
(1987b) *The Metamorphosis of Persephone: Ovid and the Self-Conscious Muse*. Cambridge
(1987c) 'Generalizing about Ovid', *Ramus* 16: 4–31, reprinted in P.E. Knox (2006) (ed.) *Oxford Readings in Ovid*. Oxford
(1992) '*Arma* in Ovid's *Fasti*', *Arethusa* 25: 81–153
(1998) *Allusion and Intertext: Dynamics of Appropriation in Roman Poetry*. Cambridge
Hinz, V. (2006) 'Kann denn Liebe Sünde sein? Kleriker im Gefolge der Venus beim mittelalterlichen Ovid', *Mittellateinisches Jahrbuch* 41: 35–52

Hoffmann, F., Minas-Nerpel, M., Pfeiffer, S. (2009) *Die dreisprachige Stele des C. Cornelius Gallus*. Berlin

Hollis, A. (1977) *Ovid:* Ars Amatoria *Book 1*. Oxford

(2007) *Fragments of Roman Poetry c.60 BC–A.D. 20*, ed. with an intr., transl., and comm. Oxford

Holm Olsen, L. (1940) 'Den gammelnorske oversettelsen av Pamphilus med en undersøkelse av paleografi og lydverk', *Avhandlinger, Det Norske videnskaps-akademi II: Historisk-filosofisk klasse*. Oslo

Hölty, L.C.H. (1966) *Werke und Briefe*, ed. U. Berger. Berlin

Holzberg, N. (1990) *Die römische Liebeselegie. Eine Einführung*. Darmstadt

(1999) 'Four Poets and a Poetess or a Portrait of the Poet as a Young Man? Thoughts on Book 3 of the *Corpus Tibullianum*', *Classical Journal* 94: 169–91

(2001) *Die römische Liebeselegie. Eine Einführung*, 2nd edn. Darmstadt

(2002a) *Catull. Der Dichter und sein erotisches Werk*. Munich

(2002b) *Ovid: The Poet and his Work*. Ithaca

Höschele, R. (2009) 'Catullus' Callimachean Hair-itage and the Erotics of Translation', *Rivista di Filologia ed Istruzione Classica* 137: 118–52

Hose, M. (1994) 'Die römische Liebeselegie und die griechische Literatur. Überlegungen zu POxy 3723', *Philologus* 138: 67–82

Hosius, C. (1932) (ed.) *Sexti Propertii* Elegiarum Libri IV, 3rd edn. Leipzig

Houghton, L.B.T. (2009) 'Two letters to Horace: Petrarch and Andrew Lang', in L.B.T. Houghton and M. Wyke (eds.), *Perceptions of Horace. A Roman Poet and his Readers* (Cambridge) 161–81

Hubbard, M. (1974) *Propertius*. London

(1975) *Propertius*. New York

Hubbard, T.K. (1984) 'Catullus 68: The Text as Self-Demystification', *Arethusa* 17: 29–49

(2004/5) 'The Invention of Sulpicia', *Classical Journal* 100.2: 177–94

(2005) 'The Catullan "Libelli" Revisited', *Philologus* 149: 253–77

Hunter, R. (1983) *Eubulus. The Fragments*. Cambridge

(1993) 'Callimachean Echoes in Catullus 65', *Zeitschrift für Papyrologie und Epigraphik* 96: 179–82

(2005) 'The Hesiodic Catalogue and Hellenistic poetry', in R. Hunter (ed.), *The Hesiodic Catalogue of Women* (Cambridge) 239–65

(2006a) *The Shadow of Callimachus: Studies in the Reception of Hellenistic Poetry at Rome*. Cambridge

(2006b) 'Sweet Nothings – Callimachus fr. 1, 9–12 Revisited', in G. Bastianini and A. Casanova (eds.), *Callimaco. Cent'anni di papiri. Atti del Convegno internazionale di studi Firenze, 9–10 giugno 2005* (Florence) 119–31

(2008) *On Coming After: Studies in Post-Classical Greek Literature and its Reception*. Berlin

(2010) 'The Reputation of Callimachus', in D. Obbink and R. Rutherford (eds.), *Culture in Pieces* (Oxford) 220–38

(2012) 'Callimachus and Roman Elegy', in B. Gold (eds.) 155–71

(2013) 'One Verse of Mimnermus? Latin Elegy and Archaic Greek Elegy', in T. Paphangelis, S. Harrison and S. Frangoulidis (eds.) *Generic Interfaces in Latin Literature* (Berlin) 337–49

Huskey, S.J. (2005) 'In memory of Tibullus: Ovid's Rememberance of Tibullus 1.3 in *Amores* 3.9 and *Tristia* 3.3', *Arethusa* 38: 367–86
Hutchinson, G.O. (1981) 'Notes on the New Gallus', *Zeitschrift für Papyrologie und Epigraphik* 41: 37–42
(2003) 'The Catullan Corpus, Greek Epigram and the Poetry of Objects', *Classical Quarterly* n.s. 53: 206–21
(2006) *Propertius:* Elegies *Book IV*. Cambridge
Huys, M. (1991) *Le poème élégiaque hellénistique P.Brux.Inv. E8934 et P.Sorb.Inv. 2254*. Brussels
Ijsewijn, J. and Sacré, D. (1990–98) *Companion to Neo-Latin Studies*, 2 vols. Leuven
Ingleheart, J. (2008) 'Ovid on Pantomime', in E. Hall and R. Wyles (eds.), *New Directions in Ancient Pantomime*. Oxford
(2010a) 'The Literary "Successor": Ovidian Metapoetry and Metaphor', *Classical Quarterly* n.s. 60: 167–72
(2010b) *A Commentary on Ovid,* Tristia 2. Oxford
Ingleheart, J. and Radice, K. (2011) *Ovid:* Amores *III. A Selection: 2, 4, 5, 14*. London
Irigaray, L. (1985) *This Sex which Is Not One*. New York
Irwin, E. (2005) *Solon and Early Greek Elegy*. Cambridge
Isbell, H. (1971) (ed.) *The Last Poets of Imperial Rome*. Harmondsworth
(1990) (trans.) *Ovid:* Heroides. London
Jacobson, H. (1974) *Ovid's* Heroides. Princeton
Jacoby, F. (1905) 'Zur Entstehung der römischen Elegie', *Rheinisches Museum für Philologie* 60: 38–105
(1909–10) 'Tibulls erste Elegie. Ein Beitrag zum Verständnis der tibullischen Kunst', *Rheinisches Museum für Philologie* 44: 601–22; 45, 22–87
(1961) *Kleine philologische Schriften*, ed. H.J. Mette, 2. Berlin
Jahnke, R. (1891) *Comoediae Horatianae Tres*. Leipzig
Jal, P. (1963) *La guerre civile à Rome*. Paris
James, S.L. (1998) 'Introduction: Constructions of Gender and Genre in Roman Comedy and Elegy', *Helios* 25: 3–16
(2003) *Learned Girls and Male Persuasion: Gender and Reading in Roman Love Elegy*. Berkeley
(2006) 'A Courtesan's Choreography: Female Liberty and Male Anxiety at the Roman Dinner Party' in C. Faraone and L. McClure (eds.), *Prostitutes and Courtesans of the Ancient World* (Madison) 224–62
(2012) 'Elegy and New Comedy' in Gold (2012): 253–68
Janan, M. (1994) '*When the Lamp is Shattered': Desire and Narrative in Catullus*. Carbondale
(1998) 'Refashioning Hercules: Propertius 4.9', *Helios* 25: 65–77
(2001) *The Poetics of Desire: Propertius IV*. Berkeley and Los Angeles
Janka, M. (1997) *Ovid* Ars Amatoria *Buch 2. Kommentar*. Heidelberg
Jaucourt, L. (1755) 'Réflexions sur l'élégie', in *Encyclopédie ou Dictionnaire raisonné des sciences, des arts et des métiers*, vol. 5. Paris
Jeauneau, E. (1957) 'L'usage de la notion d'*integumentum* à travers les gloses de Guillaume de Conches', *Archives d'Histoire Doctrinale et Littéraire du Moyen Âge* 24: 35–100

Jolivet, J.-C. (2001) *Allusion et fiction épistolaire dans les* Héroïdes*: Recherches sur l'intertextualité ovidienne* (Collection de l'École Française de Rome 289). Rome

Juhász, L. (1934) (ed.) *Naldus de Naldis:* Elegiarum libri *III ad Laurentium Medicen.* Leipzig

Juster, A.M. (2012) *Tibullus'* Elegies (Trans. with Parallel Latin Text and Introduction and Notes by R. Maltby). Oxford

Kahn, A. (1993) 'Readings of Imperial Rome', *Slavic Review* 52: 745–68

(2003) '"Blazhenstvo ne v luchakh porfira": Histoire et fonction de la tranquillité (spokojstvie) dans la pensée et la poésie russes du XVIIIe siècle: De Kantemir au sentimentalisme', *Révue des Études Slaves* 4: 669–88

(2007) 'Pushkin's Lyric Identities', in A. Kahn (ed.), *The Cambridge Companion to Pushkin* (Cambridge) 26–40

Kapnist, V.V. (1973) *Izbrannye proizvedeniia*. Leningrad

Karlinsky, S. (1985) *Russian Drama from its Beginnings to the Age of Pushkin.* Berkeley

Katz, V. (2004) (trans.) *The Complete Elegies of Sextus Propertius*. Berkeley

Keil, H. (1857–80) (ed.) *Grammatici Latini*, 8 vols. Leipzig

Keith, A.M. (1994) '*Corpus eroticum*: Elegiac Poetics and Elegiac *puellae* in Ovid's *Amores*', *Classical World* 88: 27–40

(1997) '*Tandem venit amor*: A Roman Woman Speaks of Love', in J.P. Hallett and M. Skinner (eds.), *Roman Sexualities* (Princeton) 295–310

(2000) *Engendering Rome: Women in Latin Epic*. Cambridge

(2006) 'Critical Trends in Interpreting Sulpicia', *Classical World* 100: 3–10

(2008) *Propertius: Poet of Love and Leisure*. London

(2011) (ed.) *Latin Elegy and Hellenistic Epigram: A Tale of Two Genres at Rome.* Newcastle upon Tyne

Kelly, C. (1994a) *A History of Russian Women's Writing, 1820–1992*. Oxford

(1994b) (ed.) *An Anthology of Russian Women's Writing: 1777–1992*. New York

Kelly, J.N.D. (1975) *Jerome: His Life, Writings, and Controversies*. London

Kennedy, D.F. (1993) *The Arts of Love: Five Studies in the Discourse of Roman Love Elegy*. Cambridge

Kenney, E.J. (1983) 'Virgil and the Elegiac Sensibility', *Illinois Classical Studies* 8: 44–59

(1995) *P. Ovidi Nasonis* Amores, Medicamina Faciei Femineae, Ars Amatoria, Remedia Amoris, 2nd edn. Oxford

(1996) *Ovid:* Heroides *XVI–XXI*. Cambridge

Keyser, P.T. (1992) 'Propertius' Horoscope: A Suggested Birthdate', *Classical Philology* 87: 328–34

King, J. (1975–6) 'Propertius' Programmatic Poetry and the Unity of the *Monobiblos*', *Classical Journal* 71: 108–24

(1988) 'Catullus' Callimachean *Carmina*, cc. 65–116', *Classical World* 81: 383–92

Klein, T. (2006) 'Hallenser Studien zum christlichen Ovid des Mittelalters', *Mittellateinisches Jahrbuch* 41: 33–4

Klopsch, P. (1967) *Pseudo-Ovidius* De Vetula*: Untersuchungen und Text* (Mittellateinische Texte und Studien 2). Leiden

Klopstock, F. (1981) *Ausgewählte Werke*, 2 vols. Munich

Knox, P.E. (1993) 'Philetas and Roman Poetry', *Papers of the Leeds International Latin Seminar* 7: 61–83
(1995) *Ovid:* Heroides: *Select Epistles*. Cambridge
(2005) 'Milestones in the Career of Tibullus', *Classical Quarterly* 55: 204–16
(2006) 'Propertius and the Neoterics', in Günther (2006a): *Brill's Companion to Propertius* (Leiden) 127–44
(2007) 'Catullus and Callimachus', in M.B. Skinner (ed.), *A Companion to Catullus* (Malden, Mass.) 151–71
(2009) (ed.) *A Companion to Ovid*. Chichester
Könsgen, E. (1974) Epistolae duorum amantium: *Briefe Abaelards und Heloises?* (Mittellateinische Texte und Studien 8). Leiden
Konstan, D. (1986) 'Love in Terence's *Eunuch*: the Origins of Erotic Subjectivity', *American Journal of Philology* 107: 369–93
(1995) *Sexual Symmetry: Love in the Ancient Novel and Related Genres*. Princeton
Körte, A. (1912) (ed.) *Menandrea*, 2nd edn. Leipzig
Körting, G. (1871) *Altfranzösische Übersetzung der* Remedia Amoris *des Ovid (ein Theil des allegorisch- didaktischen Epos les Échecs amoureux) nach der Dresdener Handschrift*. Leipzig
Kowerski, L.M. (2005) *Simonides on the Persian Wars: A Study of the Elegiac Verses of the "New Simonides"*. New York and London
Kretschmer, M.T. (2011) 'Bourgueil, la nouvelle Athènes (ou Troie), et Reims, la nouvelle Rome: La notion de *translatio studii* chez Baudri de Bourgueil', *Latomus* 70: 1102–16
Krevans, N. (1993) 'Fighting against Antimachus: The *Lyde* and the *Aetia* Reconsidered', in M.A. Harder, R.F. Regtuit, G.C. Wakker (eds.), *Callimachus* (Hellenistica Groningana I) (Groningen) 149–60
(2007) 'The Arrangement of Epigrams in Collections', in P. Bing and J.S. Bruss (eds.), *Brill's Companion to Hellenistic Epigram* (Leiden) 131–46
Kutzko, D. (2006) 'Lesbia in Catullus 35', *Classical Philology* 101: 405–10
La Harpe, J.-F. de (1834) *Lycée ou Cours de littérature ancienne et moderne* (orig. 1798), 1. Paris
La Penna, A. (1977) *L'integrazione difficile: Un profilo di Properzio*. Turin
(1982) 'I generi letterari ellenistici nella tarda repubblica romana: Epillio, elegia, epigramma, lirica', *Maia* 34: 111–30
Labate, M. (1984) *L'arte di farsi amare: Modelli culturali e progetto didascalico nell'elegia ovidiana*. Pisa
(1987) 'Elegia triste ed elegia lieta: Un caso di riconversione letteraria', *Materiali e Discussioni* 19: 91–129
(1990) 'Forme della letteratura, immagini del mondo', in A. Schiavone (ed.), *Storia di Roma*, 2.1 (Turin) 923–65
(1994) 'La forma dell'amore: Appunti sulla poesia erotica oraziana', in *Bimillenario della morte di Q. Orazio Flacco. Atti dei Convegni*, 3: *Atti dei Convegni di Venosa Napoli Roma (novembre 1993)* (Venosa) 69–87
Lachmann, K. (1816) (ed.), *Sextii Aurelii Propertii* Carmina. Hildesheim
Laigneau, S. (1999) *La femme et l'amour chez Catulle et les Élégiaques augustéens* (Collection Latomus 249). Brussels
Lardet, P. (1982) (ed.) *S. Hieronymi Presbyteri opera*, B.1. Turnhout

Laurens, P. (1989) *L'abeille dans l'ambre: célébration de l'épigramme de l'époque alexandrine à la fin de la Renaissance*. Paris
Laurens, P. and Balavoine, C. (1975) (eds.) *Musae Reduces. Anthologie de la poésie latine dans l'Europe de la Renaissance*, 2 vols. Leiden
Le Brun, P.-D.E. (1811) 'Discours sur Tibulle' (orig. 1763), in *Œuvres*, 4 vols. (Paris) at IV 392–403
Leach, E.W. (1980) 'Poetics and Poetic Design in Tibullus' First Elegiac Book', *Arethusa* 13: 79–96
Leblanc, J.-B. (1731) *Discours sur l'élégie*, in *Élégies de Mr L. B. C. avec un discours sur ce genre de poésie, et quelques autres pièces du même auteur* (Paris) 1–16
Lee, A.G. (1958–9) 'The Date of Lygdamus and his Relationship to Ovid', *Proceedings of the Cambridge Philological Society* 185: 15–23
(1968) (trans.) *Ovid's Amores*. London
(1990) *Tibullus:* Elegies. *Introduction, Text, Translation and Notes*. Leeds
(1994) *Propertius*. Oxford
(1998) *Catullus: The Complete Poems*. Oxford
Lee, R.R. (1981) 'A New Edition of "The Council of Remiremont"', diss. University of Connecticut
Lee-Stecum, P. (1998) *Powerplay in Tibullus*. Cambridge
(2000) 'Poet/Reader, Authority Deferred: Re-Reading Tibullan Elegy', *Arethusa* 33: 177–215
Lefèvre, E. (1991) 'Propertius Pindaricus. Der Sinn der Elegie 3,17 und ihr Verhältnis zu 3,18', in *Studi di filologia classica in onore di G. Monaco*, II (Palermo) 1001–5
Lehmann, P. (1927a) *Pseudo-Antike Literatur des Mittelalter*. Berlin (repr. Darmstadt 1964)
(1927b) 'Der schlaue Liebesbote', *Zeitschrift für romanische Philologie* 46: 699–705
(1963) *Die Parodie im Mittelalter* 2nd edn. (Stuttgart) 110–12
Leitzmann, A. (1912) (ed.) *Goethes römische Elegien nach der ältesten Reinschrift*. Bonn
Lenz, F.W. (1955) '[P. Ovidii Nasonis] *De pediculo libellus*', *Eranos* 53: 61–74
(1957) 'Das pseudo-ovidische Gedicht *De Lombardo et lumaca*', *Maia* 9: 204–22
(1959a) 'Einführende Bermerkungen zu den mittelalterlichen Pseudo-Ovid', *Das Altertum* 5: 171–82
(1959b) 'Das pseudo-ovidische Gedicht *De ventre*', *Maia* 11: 169–211
(1959c) 'Die Verteilung der Frauen', *Rivista di cultura classica e medioevale* 1: 97–105
(1963) 'Bemerkungen zu dem pseudo-ovidischen Gedicht *De lupo*', *Orpheus* 10: 21–32
Leo, F. (1895) *Plautinische Forschungen*. Berlin
(1900) 'Elegie und Komödie', *Rheinisches Museum für Philologie* 55: 604–11
Levine, P. (1985) 'Catullus c. 67: The Dark Side of Love and Marriage', *Classical Antiquity* 4: 62–71
Levitt, M. (2009) *Early Modern Russian Letters: Texts and Contexts*. Boston
Lieberz, G. (1980) '*Ovidius puellarum* ("*De nuncio sagaci*")' (Lateinische Sprache und Literatur des Mittelalters 8). Frankfurt
Lightfoot, J.L. (1999) (ed.) *Parthenius of Nicaea. Extant Works*, edited with Introduction and Commentary. Oxford

(2009) (ed.) *A Hellenistic Collection*. Cambridge, Mass.
Lilja, S. (1965) *The Roman Elegists' Attitude to Women*. (Annales Academiae Scientiarum Fennicae 135.1). Helsinki
Lindheim, S.H. (2003) *Mail and Female: Epistolary Narrative and Desire in Ovid's Heroides*. Madison
Lindsay, W.M. (1911) *Isidori Hispalensis Episcopi* Etymologiarum sive originum libri XX. 2 vols. Oxford
Little, D. (1982) 'Politics in Augustan Poetry', *Aufstieg und Niedergang der römischen Welt* 2.30.1: 254–370
Liveley, G. (2005) *Ovid: Love Songs*. London
Liveley, G. and Salzman-Mitchell, P. (2008) (eds.) *Latin Elegy and Narratology: Fragments of Story*. Columbus
Lobel, E. and Page, D. (1955) (eds.) *Poetarum Lesbiorum fragmenta*. Oxford
Lotman, Y. (1992) '"Ezda v. ostrov liubvi" Trediakovskogo i funktsiia perevodnoj literatury v russkoi kul'ture pervoi poloviny XVIII veka', in his *Izbrannye stat'i v trekh tomakh*, 1, (Tallinn) 22–8
Loubère, S. (2002) *L'Art d'aimer au siècle des Lumières*. Oxford
Loubier, P. (2006) 'Mollesse de l'élégie, 1778–1829', *Orages* 5: 23–37
Lowe, N.J. (1988) 'Sulpicia's Syntax', *Classical Quarterly* 38: 193–205
Lucarini, C.M. (2008) 'Una fonte di Properzio 3.14 e le origini greche dell'elegia d'amore romana', *Philologus* 152: 246–69
Luck, G. (1959) *The Latin Love Elegy*. London
(1960) *The Latin Love Elegy*. New York
(1969) *The Latin Love Elegy*, 2nd edn. London
(1998) (ed.) *Albii Tibulli aliorumque carmina*. Stuttgart
Ludwig, W. (1976) 'Petrus Lotichius Secundus and the Roman Elegists: Prolegomena to a Study of Neo-Latin Elegy', in R.R. Bolgar (ed.), *Classical Influences on European Culture* AD *1500–1700* (Cambridge) 171–90
(1990) 'The Origin and Development of the Catullan Style in Neo-Latin Poetry', in P. Godman and O. Murray (eds.), *Latin Poetry and the Classical Tradition. Essays in Medieval and Renaissance Literature* (Oxford) 183–97
Lulli, L. (2009) 'Appunti per una storia grafico-editoriale del genere letterario dell'elegia in età ellenistico-romana', *Scripta* 2: 135–57
(2011) *Narrare in distici. L'elegia greca arcaica e classica di argomento storico-mitico*. Rome
Lyne, R.O.A.M. (1979) '*Servitium Amoris*', *Classical Quarterly* 29: 117–30
(1980) *The Latin Love Poets: From Catullus to Horace*. Oxford
(1996) *The Latin Love Poets: From Catullus to Horace*, 2nd edn. Oxford
(1998a) 'Propertius and Tibullus: Early Exchanges', *Classical Quarterly* 48: 519–44
(1998b) 'Propertius 2.10 and 11 and the Structure of Books "2A" and "2B"', *Journal of Roman Studies* 88: 21–36
(2007) *Collected Papers on Latin Poetry*. Oxford
MacLeod, C. (1983) *Collected Essays*. Oxford
Maggiali, G. (2008) (ed.) *Il carme 68 di Catullo: Edizione critica e commento*. Cesena
Magnelli, E. (1999) *Alexandri Aetoli testimonia et fragmenta*. Florence
Maltby, R. (1991) *A Lexicon of Ancient Latin Etymologies*. Leeds
(2002) (ed.) *Tibullus:* Elegies*: Text, Introduction and Commentary*. Cambridge

Manitius, M. (1931) *Geschichte der lateinischen Literatur des Mittelalters 3: Vom Ausbruch des Kirchenstreites bis zum Ende des zwölften Jahrhunderts*. Munich

Mantello, F.A.C. and Rigg, A.G. (1996) (eds.) *Medieval Latin: An Introduction and Bibliographical Guide*. Washington, D.C.

Manuwald, G. (2006) 'The First Book', in Günther (2006a): 219–43

Manzoni, G.E. (1995) *Foroiuliensis poeta. Vita e poesia di Cornelio Gallo*. Milan

Marenbon, J. (2000) 'Authenticity Revisited', in B. Wheeler (ed.) *Listening to Heloise: The Voice of a Twelfth-Century Woman* (New York) 19–33

(2009) (ed.) *The Cambridge Companion to Boethius*. Cambridge

Marinone, N. (1997) *Berenice da Callimaco a Catullo*. Bologna

Martelli, M. (1985) 'Le elegie di Naldo Naldi', in R. Cardini, E. Garin, L. Cesarini Martinelli and G. Pascucci (eds.), *Tradizione classica e letteratura umanistica. Per A. Perosa*, 2 vols. (Rome) 1. 307–32

Martindale, C. (1988) (ed.) *Ovid Renewed: Ovidian Influences on Literature and Art from the Middle Ages to the Twentieth Century*. Cambridge

Matthews, V.J. (1996) *Antimachus of Colophon: Text and Commentary*. Leiden

Matthisson, F. (1787) *Gedichte*. Mannheim

Maxwell, M. (2002) 'H.D.: Pound's Sulpicia', *Arion* 10: 15–48

May, G. (1963) *Le Dilemme du roman au XVIIIe siècle*. New Haven

McCarthy, K. (1998) '*Servitium amoris: amor servitii*', in S.R. Joshel and S. Murnaghan (eds.), *Women and Slaves in Greco-Roman Culture: Differential Equations* (London) 174–92

(2000) *Slaves, Masters, and the Art of Authority in Plautine Comedy*. Princeton

McFarlane, I.D. (1980) *Renaissance Latin Poetry*. Manchester

McKeown, J.C. (1979) 'Augustan Elegy and Mime', *Proceedings of Cambridge Philological Society* 25: 71–84

(1987) *Ovid:* Amores. *I: Text and Prolegomena*. Liverpool

(1989) *Ovid:* Amores. *II: A Commentary on Book One*. Leeds

(1995) '*Militat omnis amans*', *Classical Journal* 90: 295–304

(1998) *Ovid:* Amores. *III: A Commentary on Book Two*. Leeds

McLaughlin, M.L. (1995) *Literary Imitation in the Italian Renaissance: The Theory and Practice of Literary Imitation in Italy from Dante to Bembo*. Oxford

McNamee, K. (1993) 'Propertius, Poetry, and Love', in M. DeForest (ed.) *Woman's Power, Man's Game: Essays in Honor of Joy K. King*. Wauconda, Ill

Melve, L. (2006) 'The Revolt of the Medievalists: Directions in Recent Research on the Twelfth-Century Renaissance', *Journal of Medieval History* 32: 231–252

Melville, A.D. (1998) (trans.) *Ovid: The Love Poems*, with notes by E.J. Kenney. Oxford

Menés, E. (1983) 'The External Evidence for the Division of Propertius, Book 2', *Classical Philology* 78: 137–43

Merli, E. (2000) *Arma canant alii: Materia epica e narrazione elegiaca nei Fasti di Ovidio*. Florence

Merriam, C.U. (1990) 'The New Gallus Revisited', *Latomus* 49: 443–52

(2006) 'Sulpicia: Just Another Roman Poet', *Classical World* 100: 11–16

Mesdjian, B. (1997) 'Éros dans l'*Eroticon* de T.V. Strozzi', in P. Ford and I. De Smet (eds.), *Éros et Priapus. Erotisme et obscénité dans la littérature néo-latine* (Geneva) 25–42

Meyer, W. (1915) 'Das Liebesconcil in Remiremont, neu herausgegeben', in *Nachrichten von der Königlichen Gesellschaft der Wissenschaftten zu Göttingen, Philologisch-historische Klasse* (Berlin) 1–19
Michault, J.-B. (1743) *Réflexions critiques sur l'élégie*. Dijon
Miller, J.F. (1982) 'Callimachus and the Augustan Aetiological Elegy', *Aufstieg und Niedergang der Römischen Welt* II 30.1: 371–417
(1983) 'Propertius 3.2 and Horace', *Transactions of the American Philological Association* 113: 289–99
(1986) 'Disclaiming Divine Inspiration: A Programmatic Pattern', *Wiener Studien* n.F. 99: 151–64
(1991a) *Ovid's Elegiac Festivals: Studies in the* Fasti. Frankfurt
(1991b) 'Propertius' Hymn to Bacchus and Contemporary Poetry', *American Journal of Philology* 11: 77–86
(2009) *Apollo, Augustus and the Poets*. Cambridge
Miller, P.A. (1999) 'The Tibullan Dream Text', *Transactions of the American Philological Association* 129: 181–224
(2004) *Subjecting Verses: Latin Love Elegy and the Emergence of the Real*. Princeton
(2007) 'Catullus and Roman Love Elegy', in M.B. Skinner (ed.), *A Companion to Catullus* (Malden, Mass.) 399–417
(2010) '"What's Love Got to Do With It?": The Peculiar Story of Elegy in Rome', in Weisman (2010): 46–66
Momigliano, A. (1960) *Secundo contributo alla storia degli studi classici*. Rome
Monella, P. (2002) 'Tra dolore e poesia: Catullo, il fratello e l'usignolo della Daulide', *Pan* 20: 95–103
(2005) *Procne e Filomela: dal mito al simbolo letterario*. Bologna
Morawski, J. de (1917) *Pamphile et Galatée par Jehan Bras-de-Fer-de-Dammartin-en-Goele – Poème inédit du XIVe siècle*. Paris
Morel-Fatio, A. (1886) 'Facetus', *Romania* 15: 224–35
Morelli, A.M. (1984) Review of L. Nicastri, *Cornelio Gallo e l'elegia ellenistico-romana*. Naples 1983, *Quaderni dell'AICC di Foggia* 4: 151–7
(1985) 'Rassegna sul nuovo Gallo', in V. Tandoi (ed.), *Disiecti membra poetae: Studi di poesia latina in frammenti*, 2 (Foggia) 140–83
(1994) 'Sul papiro di Ossirinco LIV 3723: Considerazioni sui caratteri dell'elegia erotica ellenistica alla luce dei nuovi ritrovamenti papiracei', *Rivista di Filologia ed Istruzione Classica* 122: 385–421
(2000) *L'epigramma latino prima di Catullo*. Cassino
(2007) 'Hellenistic Epigram in the Roman World from the Beginnings to the End of the Republican Age', in P. Bing and J.S. Bruss (eds.), *Brill's Companion to Hellenistic Epigram* (Leiden and Boston) 521–41
(2008a) '*Epigramma longum*: In cerca di una *básanos* per il genere epigrammatico', in A.M. Morelli (ed.), *Epigramma longum: Da Marziale alla tarda antichità*, 2 vols. (Cassino) 17–51
(2008b) 'Gli epigrammi erotici "lunghi" in distici di Catullo e Marziale. Morfologia e statuto di genere', in A.M. Morelli (ed.), *Epigramma longum. Da Marziale alla tarda antichità*, 1 (Cassino) 81–130
Morgan, K. (1977) *Ovid's Art of Imitation: Propertius in the* Amores. Leiden
Morgan, L. (2010) *Musa Pedestris: Metre and Meaning in Roman Verse*. Oxford

(2012) 'Elegiac Meter: Opposites Attract' in Gold (2012): 214–18
Moser, T.C. (2004) *A Cosmos of Desire: The Medieval Latin Erotic Lyric in English Manuscripts*. Ann Arbor
Mourgues, M. (1724) *Traité de la poésie française*. Paris
Mozley, J.H. (1962) *Ovid:* Art of Love. Cosmetics. Remedies for Love. Ibis. Walnut-tree. Sea Fishing. Consolation. Cambridge, Mass.
Mueller, G.A. (2003) *Formen und Funktionen der Vergilzitate und Anspielungen bei Augustin von Hippo*. Paderborn
Murgatroyd, P. (1975) '*Militia amoris* and the Roman Elegists', *Latomus* 34: 59–79
(1980) (ed.) *Tibullus 1*. Pietermaritzburg (repr. Bristol, 1991)
(1981) '*Servitium amoris* and the Roman Elegists', *Latomus* 40: 589–606
(1989) 'Some Neglected Aspects of Catullus 67', *Hermes* 117: 471–8
(1994) (ed.) *Tibullus:* Elegies *II*. Oxford
(1999) 'The Argumentation in Ovid, *Amores* 1.9', *Mnemosyne* 52: 569–72
(2000) (ed. and trans.) *The Amatory Elegies of Johannes Secundus*. Leiden
(2002) 'The Rape Attempts on Lotis and Vesta,' *Classical Quarterly* 52: 622–4
(2005) *Mythical and Legendary Narrative in Ovid's* Fasti. Leiden
Murgia (1986a) 'The Date of Ovid's *Ars Amatoria* 3', *American Journal of Philology* 107: 74–94
(1986b) 'Influence of Ovid's *Remedia Amoris* on *Ars* 3 and *Amores* 3', *Classical Philology* 81: 203–20
Murray, J. (2010) 'Hellenistic Elegy: Out from Under the Shadow of Callimachus', in J.J. Clauss and M. Cuypers (eds.), *A Companion to Hellenistic Literature* (Malden, Mass.) 106–16
Murray, O. (1985) 'Symposium and Genre in the Poetry of Horace', *Journal of Roman Studies* 75: 39–50
Mutschler, F.-H. (1985) *Die poetische Kunst Tibulls*. Frankfurt
Myerowitz, M. (1985) *Ovid's Games of Love*. Detroit
Myers, S.K. (1996) 'The Poet and the Procuress: The *lena* in Latin Love Elegy', *The Journal of Roman Studies* 88: 1–21
Mynors, R.A.B. (1958) (ed.) *C. Valerii Catulli* Carmina. Oxford
Nagle, B.R. (1980) *The Poetics of Exile: Program and Polemic in the Tristia and Epistulae ex Ponto of Ovid*. Brussels
Nagy, G. (2010) 'Ancient Greek Elegy', in Weisman (2010): 13–45
Nethercut, W.R. (1970) 'The Ironic Priest', *The American Journal of Philology*, 91: 385–407
Neumeister, K. (1983) *Die Überwindung der elegischen Liebe bei Properz (Buch I–III)*. Frankfurt am Main
Newlands, C.E. (1995) *Playing with Time. Ovid and the* Fasti. Ithaca
Newman, J.K. (1997) *Augustan Propertius: The Recapitulation of a Genre*. Hildesheim
(2006) 'The Third Book: Defining a Poetic Self', in Günther (2006a): 319–352
Nicastri, L. (1984) *Cornelio Gallo e l'elegia ellenistico-romana*. Naples
Nicéron, J.-P. (1731) *Mémoires pour servir à l'histoire des hommes illustres dans la République des Lettres*, 16. Paris
Nilsson, I. (2009) (ed.) *Plotting with Eros: Essays on the Poetics of Love and the Erotics of Reading*. Copenhagen
Nisbet, R.G.M. (1995) *Collected Papers on Latin Literature*. Oxford

Nisbet, R.G.M. and Hubbard, M. (1978) *A Commentary on Horace:* Odes *Book II*. Oxford
Nivernais, L.J. duc de (1743) *Dissertation sur l'élégie*, in *Œuvres* (1796), 4 (Paris), 259–90
Nobili, C. (2011) 'Threnodic Elegy in Sparta', *Greek, Roman and Byzantine Studies* 51: 26–48
Norden, E. (1954) *Die römische Literatur*, 5th edn. Leipzig
Novati, F. (1905) *Attraverso il medio evo*. Bari
O'Connor, E. (2001) (trans.) *Antonio Panormita: Hermaphroditus*. Lanham
O'Rourke, D. (2012) 'Intertextuality in Roman Elegy', in Gold (2012): 390–409
Obbink, D. (1999) 'Anoubion, Elegiacs', in N. Gonis, J. Chapa, W.E.H. Cockle, D. Obbink, P.J. Parsons, J.D. Thomas (eds.), *The Oxyrhynchus Papyri* 66: 67–109
(2006) 'A New Archilochus Poem', *Zeitschrift für Papyrologie und Epigraphik* 156: 1–9
Öberg, C.S. (1999) (ed.) *Versus Maximiani* (Studia Latina Stockholmensia 43). Stockholm
Öberg, J. (1965) *Serlon de Wilton – Poèmes latins* (Studia Latina Stockholmiensia 14). Stockholm
Oeschger, J. (1948) (ed.) *Ioannis Ioviani Pontani carmina: Egloghe, elegie, liriche*. Bari
Offermanns, W. (1970) *Die Wirkung Ovids auf die literarische Sprache der latinischen Liebesdichtung des 11. und 12. Jahrhunderts* (Beihefte zum Mittellateinischen Jahrbuch 4). Stockholm
Oliensis, E. (1997) 'The Erotics of *amicitia*: Readings in Tibullus, Propertius, and Horace', in J.P. Hallett and M.B. Skinner (eds.), *Roman Sexualities* (Princeton) 151–71
O'Neill, K. (2005) 'The Lover's Gaze and Cynthia's Glance', in R. Ancona and E. Greene (eds.), *Gendered Dynamics in Latin Love Poetry* (Baltimore) 243–68
Opitz, M. (1869) *Ausgewählte Dichtungen*, ed. J. Tittmann. Leipzig
(1954) *Buch von der deutschen Poeterei*, ed. W. Braune, 6th edn. Tübingen
Osgood, J. (2006) *Caesar's Legacy: Civil War and the Emergence of the Roman Empire*. Cambridge
Otis, B. (1965) 'Propertius' Single Book', *Harvard Studies in Classical Philology* 70: 1–44
Page, D. (1936) 'The Elegiacs in Euripides' *Andromache*' in C. Bailey, C.M. Bowra, A.E. Barber, J.D. Denniston and D.L. Page (eds.), *Greek Poetry and Life: Essays Presented to Gilbert Murray on his Seventieth Birthday* (Oxford) 206–30
(1964) 'Archilochus and the Oral Tradition', in J. Poilloux et al., *Archiloque* (Entretiens sur l'antiquité classique 10) (Vandoeuvres): 117–63
Palmer, A.P. and L.C. Purser (1898) *P. Ouidii Nasonis* Heroides *with the Greek Translation of Planudes*. Oxford
(2005) *P. Ouidii Nasonis* Heroides *with the Greek Translation of Planudes with New, Additional Introduction by D.F. Kennedy*. Bristol
Papanghelis, T.D. (1987) *Propertius: A Hellenistic Poet on Love and Death*. Cambridge
Paparelli, G. (1964) 'Enea Silvio Piccolomini, poeta d'amore', *Helikon* 4: 253–60

(1987) 'Properzio nella poesia giovanile di Enea Silvio Piccolomini', in S. Pasquazi (ed.), *Properzio nella letteratura italiana. Atti del convegno nazionale (Assisi, 15–17 novembre 1985)* (Assisi) 65–70
Parker, H.N. (1989) 'Crucially Funny or Tranio on the Couch: The *servus callidus* and Jokes about Torture', *Transactions of the American Philological Association* 119: 233–46
(1994) 'Sulpicia, the *Auctor de Sulpicia* and the Authorship of 3.9 and 3.11 of the *Corpus Tibullianum*', *Helios* 21.1: 39–62
(2006) 'Catullus and the *amicus Catulli*: The Text of Learned Talk', *Classical World* 100: 17–30
(2010) (ed. and trans.) *Antonio Beccadelli: The Hermaphrodite*. Cambridge, Mass.
Parny, E.D. (1862) *Œuvres de Parny: Élégies et poésies diverses*. Paris
Parsons, P.J. (1988) 'Eine neugefundene griechische Liebeselegie', *Museum Helveticum* 45: 65–74
Parsons, P.J. and Kassel, R. (1977) 'Callimachus: *Victoria Berenices*', *Zeitschrift für Papyrologie und Epigraphik*, 25: 1–51
Pascal, P. (1993) *Concilium Romarici Montis* (Bryn Mawr Latin Commentaries). Bryn Mawr
Pasoli, E. (1980) 'Appunti sul ruolo del c. 68 nell'origine dell'elegia latina', in *L'élégie romaine. Enracinement, thèmes, diffusion. Actes du colloque international organisé par la Faculté de Lettres et sciences humaines de Mulhouse en mars 1979 sous la direction d'André Thill* (Bull. de la Fac. de Lettres de Mulhouse 10) (Paris) 17–26
Peacock, A. (1975) 'Donne's Elegies and Roman Love Elegy', *Hermathena* 119: 20–9
(1979) 'Ben Jonson's "Elegies" and Roman Love Elegy', *Études anglaises* 32: 20–27
Pearcy, L.T. (2006) 'Erasing Cerinthus: Sulpicia and her Audience', *Classical World* 100: 31–6
Pelling, C. (1996) 'The Triumviral Period', in A.K. Bowman, E. Champlin and A. Lintott (eds.), *The Cambridge Ancient History*, X: *The Augustan Empire, 43 BC – AD 69* (Cambridge) 1–69
Perkell, C.G. (1996) 'The "Dying Gallus" and the Design of *Eclogue* 10', *Classical Philology* 91: 128–40
Perkins, C.A. (2011) 'The Figure of Elegy in *Amores* 3.1: Elegy as *puella*, Elegy as *poeta*, *puella* as *poeta*', *Classical World* 104: 313–31
Perosa, A. and Sparrow, J. (1979) (eds.) *Renaissance Latin Verse: An Anthology*. London
Perutelli, A. (1979) *La narrazione commentata: studi sull'epillio latino*. Pisa
(1990) 'Lutazio Catulo poeta', *Rivista di filologia e di istruzione classica* 118: 257–81
(2002) 'Lutazio Catulo poeta', in *Frustula poetarum. Contributi a poeti latini in frammenti* (Bologna) 31–58
Pestelli, A. (2007) *P. Ovidii Nasonis* Heroidum Epistula VII, ed. H. Oresti. Florence
Petersmann, G. (1980) *Themenführung und Motiventfaltung in der* Monobiblios *des Properz*. Graz
(1983) 'Cornelius Gallus und der Papyrus von Qaṣr Ibrîm', *Aufstieg und Niedergang der römishcen Welt* II 30.3: 1649–55

Petrie, J. (1983) *Petrarch: The Augustan Poets, the Italian Tradition and the Canzoniere*. Dublin
Petrovic, A. (2007) *Kommentar zu den simonideischen Versinschriften*. Leiden
Pfeiffer, R. (1949–53) (ed.) *Callimachus*, 2 vols. Oxford
Piazzi, L. (2007) *P. Ovidii Nasonis* Heroidum Epistula VII. Dido Aeneae. Florence
Pichon, R. (1902) *De sermone amatorio apud Latinos elegiarum scriptores*. Paris
Pieper, C. (2008) Elegos redolere Vergiliosque sapere. *Cristoforo Landinos 'Xandra' zwischen Liebe und Gesellschaft*. Hildesheim
Pinotti, P. (2002) *L'elegia Latina: Storia di una forma poetica*. Rome
(2004) Primus ingredior*: Studi su Properzio*. Bologna
Pittaluga, S. (1976–7) 'Le *De tribus puellis*, Comedie Ovidenne', *Vita Latina* 61: 2–13 and 62: 2–14
(1979) '*De nuncio sagaci* e *Pamphilus*: Studio parallelo', in S. Pittaluga, *La scena interdetta: Teatro e letteratura fra Medioevo e Umanesimo* (Nuovo Medioevo 61) (Naples): 13–22
Platnauer, M. (1951) *Latin Elegiac Verse*. Oxford
Plessis, F. (1884) *Études critiques sur Properce et ses élégies*. Paris
Polonsky, R. (1998) *English Literature and the Russian Aesthetic Renaissance*. Cambridge
Pomeroy, S. (1975) *Goddesses, Whores, Wives and Slaves*. New York
Potez, H. (1898) *L'Elégie en France avant le Romantisme, de Parny à Lamartine, 1778–1820*. Paris
Proskurina, V. (2006) *Mify imperii: Literatura I vlast' v epokhu Ekateriny II*. Moscow
Puelma, M. (1982) 'Die *Aitien* des Kallimachos als Vorbild der römischen Amores-Elegie', *Museum Helveticum* 39: 221–46, 285–304
(1996) '*Epigramma*: Aspekte einer Wortgeschichte', *Museum Helveticum* 53: 123–39
Pushkin, A.S. (2004) *Stikhotvoreniia: Kniga Pervaia (Petersburg, 1817–20)*. Petersburg
Putnam, M.C.J. (1970) *Virgil's Pastoral Art: Studies in the Eclogues*. Princeton
(1980) 'Propertius and the New Gallus Fragment', *Zeitschrift für Papyrologie und Epigraphik* 39: 49–56
(2005) 'Virgil and Tibullus 1.1', *Classical Philology* 100: 123–41
(2009) (trans.) *Jacopo Sannazaro: Latin Poetry*. Cambridge, Mass
Quinn, K. (1970) (ed.) *Catullus: The Poems*. London
(1972) *Catullus: An Interpretation*. London
Raaflaub, K. and Toher, M. (1990) (eds.) *Between Republic and Empire: Interpretations of Augustus and His Principate*. Berkeley
Raalte, M. van (1988) 'Greek Elegiac Verse Rhythm', *Glotta* 66: 145–78
Raby, F.J.E. (1934) *A History of Secular Latin Poetry in the Middle Ages*, 2nd edn 1957, 2 vols Oxford
Radford, R.S. (1923) 'Tibullus and Ovid', *American Journal of Philology* 44: 1–26, 230–59, 293–318
Ramírez de Verger, A. (2003) *Publius Ovidius Naso:* Carmina Amatoria. Munich
Ramsby, T.R. (2007) *Textual Permanence: Roman Elegists and the Epigraphic Tradition*. London
Rand, E.K. (1925) *Ovid and His Influence*. New York

Randall, J.G. (1979) 'Mistresses' Pseudonyms in Latin Elegy', *Liverpool Classical Monthly* 4: 27–35

Ratkowitsch, C. (1986) *Maximianus amat: zu Datierung und Interpretation des Elegikers Maximian*. Vienna

(1987) 'Baudri von Bourgueil, ein Dichter der inneren Emigration', *Mittellateinisches Jahrbuch* 22: 142–65

(1990) 'Weitere Argumente zur Datierung und Interpretation Maximians', *Wiener Studien* 103: 207–39

(1991) 'Die keusche Helena: Ovids *Heroides* 16/17 in der mittelalterlichen Neudichtung des Baudri von Bourgueil', *Wiener Studien* 104: 209–36

Raven, D.S. (1965) *Latin Metre: An Introduction*. London

Rayor, D.J. (1993) 'Korinna: Gender and the Narrative Tradition', *Arethusa* 26: 219–31

Reeve, M.D. (1984) 'Tibullus 2.6', *Phoenix* 38: 235–9

Reeve, M.D. and Rouse, R.H. (1983) 'Tibullus', in L.D. Reynolds (ed.), *Texts and Transmission. A Survey of Latin Classics* (Oxford) 420–5

Rei, A. (1998) 'Villains, Wives, and Slaves in the Comedies of Plautus', in S.R. Joshel and S. Murnaghan (eds.), *Women and Slaves in Greco-Roman Culture: Differential Equations* (London) 92–108

Reitzenstein, R. (1907) 'Epigramm', *RE* VI 1: 71–111

Rémond de Saint-Mard, T. (1734) *Réflexions sur la poésie en général, sur l'églogue, sur la fable, sur l'élégie [. . .] suivies de trois lettres sur la décadence du goût en France*. La Haye

Resta, G. (1976) (ed.) *Johannis Marrasii* Angelinetum *et Carmina Varia*. Palermo

Revard, S.P. (2009) (ed.) *John Milton: Complete Shorter Poems*. Malden, MA and Oxford

Richardson, L. (1992) *A New Topographical Dictionary of Ancient Rome*. Baltimore

Rigg, A.R. (1996) 'Serlo of Wilton: Biographical Notes', *Medium Aevum* 65: 96–101

Rissman, L. (1983) *Love as War: Homeric Allusion in the Poetry of Sappho* (Beiträge zur klassischen Philologie 157). Königstein

Robathan, D.M. (1968) *The Pseudo-Ovidian* De Vetula. Amsterdam

Roberts, M. (2009) *The Humblest Sparrow: The Poetry of Venantius Fortunatus*. Ann Arbor

Robinson, M. (2006) 'Augustan Responses to Virgil', in B. Currie, M. Clarke, R.O.A.M. Lyne (eds.), *Epic Interactions* (Oxford) 185–216

Roessel, D. (1990a) 'The Significance of the Name Cerinthus in the Poems of Sulpicia', *Transactions of the American Philological Association* 120: 243–50

(1990b) 'Or perhaps Sulpicia: Pound and a Roman Poetess', *Paideuma* 19: 125–35

Roggia, A. (2011) *P. Ovidii Nasonis* Heroidum Epistula XIII, ed. L. Protesilao. Florence

Rohde, E. (1914) *Der griechische Roman und seine Vorläufer*, 3rd edn. Leipzig

Rohr Vio, F. (2009) 'Gaio Cornelio Gallo nella poesia augustea tra storia e propaganda', in B. Delignon and Y. Roman (eds.), *Le poète irrévérencieux: Modèles hellénistiques et réalités romaines* (Paris) 65–78

Romano, A.J. (2009) 'The Invention of Marriage: Hermaphroditus and Salmacis at Halicarnassus and in Ovid', *Classical Quarterly* 59: 543–61

Rosati, G. (1991) 'Protesilao, Paride e l'amante elegiaco: Un modello omerico in Ovidio', *Maia* 43: 103–14

(1992) 'L'elegia al femminile: Le Heroides di Ovidio (e altre heroides)', *Materiali e Discussioni* 29: 71–94
(1996a) 'Sabinus, the *Heroides* and the Poet-Nightingale: Some Observations on the Authenticity of the *Epistula Sapphus*', *Classical Quarterly* n.s. 46: 207–16
(1996b) *P. Ovidii Nasonis* Heroidum Epistulae XVIII–XIX. *Leander Heroni, Hero Leandro*. Florence
(2005) 'Elegy after the Elegists: From Opposition to Assent', *Papers of the Langford Latin Seminar* 12: 133–50
Rosen, R.M., and Farrell, J. (1986) 'Acontius, Milanion, and Gallus: Vergil, *Ecl.* 10.52–61', *Transactions of the American Philological Association* 116: 241–54
Rosokoki, A. (1995) *Die* Erigone *des Eratosthenes*. Heidelberg
Ross, D.O. (1969) *Style and Tradition in Catullus*. Cambridge, Mass.
(1975) *Backgrounds to Augustan Poetry: Gallus, Elegy and Rome*. Cambridge
Rostagni, A. (1944) *Suetonio* De Poetis. Turin
(1956) 'L'influenza greca sulle origini dell'elegia erotica latina', in *L'Influence grècque sur la poésie latine de Catulle à Ovide* (Entretiens sur l'antiquité classique 2) (Vandoeuvres), 40–63
(1979) *Suetonio* De poetis *e biografi minori*. New York
Rothstein, M. (1924) (ed. and comm.) *Die Elegien des Sextus Propertius. Drittes und viertes Buch*. Berlin
Rougemont, D. de (1958) *L'Amour et L'Occident*, 2nd edn. Paris
(1983) *Love in the Western World*, trans. M. Belgion. Princeton
Rouse, R.H. (1979) 'Florilegia and Latin Classical Authors in Twelfth- and Thirteenth-Century Orléans', *Viator* 10: 131–60
Roy, B. (1974) 'Arnulf of Orléans and the Latin "Comedy"', *Speculum* 49: 258–66
Roy, B. and Schooner, H.V. (1996) 'Arnulfi Aurelianensis Glosule de *Remediis amoris*', *The Journal of Medieval Latin* 6: 135–96
Rychlewska, L. (1971) (ed.) *Turpilius Sextus* Fragmenta. Leipzig
Sabot, A.-F. (1974) *Ovide: Poète de l'amour dans ses œuvres de jeunesse:* Amores, Héroïdes, Ars Amatoria, Remedia Amoris, De Medicamine Faciei Femineae. Paris
Sandbach, F.H. (1962) 'Some Problems in Propertius', *Classical Quarterly* 56: 262–76
Sandler, S. (1989) *Distant Pleasures: Alexander Pushkin and the Writing of Exile*. Stanford
Santirocco, M.S. (1979) 'Sulpicia Reconsidered', *Classical Journal* 74: 229–39
Sarkissian, J. (1983) *Catullus 68: An Interpretation* (Mnemosyne Supplementum 76). Leiden
Saylor, C.F. (1967) '*Querelae*: Propertius' Distinctive, Technical Name for his Elegy', *Agon* 1: 142–9
Scaliger, J. (1577) *Catulli, Tibulli, Properti nova editio. Iosephus Scaliger Iul. Caesaris f. recensuit. Eiusdem in eosdem Castigationum liber*. Paris
Schaller, D. (1966) 'Probleme der Überlieferung und Verfasserschaft lateinischer Liebesbriefe des hohen Mittelalters', *Mittellateinisches Jahrbuch* 3: 25–36
Schiller, F. (1967) *Sämtliche Werke*, ed. G. Fricke and H. Göpfert, 5 vols. Munich
Schmid, W. (1959a) 'Elegie', in T. Klauser (ed.), *Reallexikon für Antike und Christentum*, 4 (Stuttgart) 1060

(1959b), 'Ein christlicher Heroidenbrief des sechsten Jahrhunderts', in H. Dahlmann and R. Merkelbach (eds.), *Studien zur Textgeschichte und Textkritik* (Cologne and Opladen) 253–63
Schmidt, P.G. (1974) *Johannes de Hauvilla: Architrenius*. Munich
Schneider, W.C. (2003) *Die elegischen Verse von Maximian* (Palingenesia 79) Wiesbaden
Schülper, S. (1979) 'Ovid aus der Sicht des Balderich von Bourgueil dargestellt anhand des Briefwechsels Florus-Ovid', *Mittellateinisches Jahrbuch* 14: 93–118
Schuster, J. (2002) *Poetologie der Distanz: Die klassische deutsche Elegie 1750–1800*. Freiburg im Breisgau
Scivoletto, N. (1976) Musa iocosa*: Studio sulla poesia giovanile di Ovidio*. Rome
Scott, A.B. (2001) *Hildebertus Cenomannensis episcopus:* Carmina Minora, 2nd edn. Leipzig
Scourfield, J.H.D. (2003) '*Pervigilium Veneris*' and 'Reposianus', in S. Hornblower and A. Spawforth (eds.), *The Oxford Classical Dictionary*, 3rd rev. edn. (Oxford) 1148 and 1309
Sedgwick, E.K. (1992) *Between Men: English Literature and Male Homosocial Desire*. New York
Segel, H. (1967) *The Literature of Eighteenth-Century Russia*. New York
(1973) 'Classicism and Classical Antiquity in Eighteenth and Early Nineteenth-century Russian Literature', in J.G. Garrard (ed.), *The Eighteenth Century in Russia* (Oxford) 48–74
Segre, C. (1968) '*Ars amandi* classica e medievale', in H.R. Jauss and E. Köhler (eds.), *Grundriss der romanischen Literaturen des Mittelalters*, VI.1: *La litterature didactique, allegorique et satirique* (Heidelberg) 109–116
Selle, H. (2008) *Theognis und die Theognidea*. Berlin
Serassi, P. (1747) (ed.) *Delle poesie volgari e latine di Francesco Maria Molza*, 1. Bergamo
Seth, C. (1998) *Les poètes creoles du XVIIIe siècle*. Paris and Rome
Shackleton Bailey, D.R. (1952) 'Echoes of Propertius', *Mnemosyne* series 4, 5: 306–33
(1982) (ed.), *Anthologia Latina*. Stuttgart
Shanzer, D. (1983) 'Ennodius, Boethius, and the Date and Interpretation of Maximianus' *Elegia* III', *Rivista di filologia e di istruzione classica* 111: 183–95
(1988) Review of Ch. Ratkowitsch *Maximianus amat. Zu Datierung und Interpretation des Elegikers Maximian*, *Gnomon* 60: 258–61
(1990) 'Once again Tiberianus and the *Pervigilium Veneris*', *Rivista di filologia e di istruzione classica* 118: 306–18
Sharrock, A. (1991) 'Womanufacture', *Journal of Roman Studies* 81: 36–49
(1994) *Seduction and Repetition in Ovid's* Ars Amatoria *II*. Oxford
(1995) 'The Drooping Rose: Elegiac Failure in *Amores* 3.7', *Ramus* 24: 152–80
(2000) 'Constructing Characters in Propertius', *Arethusa* 33: 263–84
(2012) 'Ovid' in Gold (2012): 70–85
Showerman, G. (1977) *Ovid.* Heroides, Amores, *With an English Translation*, 2nd edn. rev. by G. Goold. Cambridge, Mass
Shulman, J. (1981) '*Te quoque falle tamen*: Ovid's Anti-Lucretian Didactics', *Classical Journal* 76: 242–53

Skinner, M.B. (1997) '*Ego mulier*: The Construction of Male Sexuality in Catullus', in J.P. Hallett and M.B. Skinner (eds.), *Roman Sexualities* (Princeton) 129–50
(2003) *Catullus in Verona: A Reading of the Elegiac* Libellus, *Poems 65–116*. Columbus
(2007) 'Authorial Arrangement of the Collection: Debate Past and Present', in M.B. Skinner (ed.), *A Companion to Catullus* (Malden, Mass.) 35–53
(2010) *Clodia Metelli: The Tribune's Sister*. Oxford
Skoie, M. (2002) *Reading Sulpicia: Commentaries 1470–1990*. Oxford
(2008) 'Telling Sulpicia's Joys: Narrative at the Receiving End', in G. Lively and P. Salzman-Mitchell (2008) 239–54
Skulsky, H. (1973) 'Milton's Enrichment of Latin Love Elegy', in J. Ijsewijn, E. Kessler and L.V. Ryan (eds.), *Acta Conventus Neo-Latini Lovaniensis: Proceedings of the First International Congress of Neo-Latin Studies* (Munich) 603–11
Skutsch, F. (1906) *Gallus und Vergil: Aus Vergils Frühzeit*, II. Leipzig and Berlin
Skutsch, O. (1963) 'The Structure of the Propertian *Monobiblos*', *Classical Philology* 58: 238–9
(1975) 'The Second Book of Propertius', *Harvard Studies in Classical Philology* 79: 229–33
Slavitt, D.R. (2011) *Love Poems, Letters and Remedies of Ovid*. Cambridge, Mass.
Smith, K.F. (1913) (ed.) *The Elegies of Albius Tibullus, The Corpus Tibullianum. Edited with Introduction and Notes on Books I, II, and IV.2–14*. Darmstadt
Snyder, J.M. (1989) *The Woman and the Lyre: Women Writers in Classical Greece and Rome*. Carbondale, Ill.
Sobol, V. (2009) *Febris erotica: Lovesickness in the Russian Literary Imagination*. Seattle
Solmsen, F. (1948) 'Propertius and Horace', *Classical Philology* 43: 105–9
(1962) 'Tibullus as an Augustan Poet', *Hermes* 90: 295–325
Sommariva, G. (1980) 'La parodia di Lucrezio nell'*Ars* e nei *Remedia* Ovidiani' *Atene e Roma* 25: 123–48
Sparrow, J. (1960) 'Latin Verse of the High Renaissance', in E.F. Jacob (ed.), *Italian Renaissance Studies. A Tribute to the Late Cecilia M. Ady* (London) 354–409
(1976) 'Renaissance Latin Poetry: Some Sixteenth-Century Italian Anthologies', in C.H. Clough (ed.), *Cultural Aspects of the Renaissance: Essays in Honour of Paul Oskar Kristeller* (Manchester) 386–405
Spentzou, E. (2003) *Readers and Writers in Ovid's* Heroides. *Transgressions of Genre and Gender*. Oxford
Spoth, F. (1992) *Ovids* Heroides *als Elegien*. Munich
Stahl, H.-P. (1985) *Propertius: 'Love' and 'War'. Individual and State under Augustus*. Berkeley
Stevenson, J. (2005) 'Classical Latin Women Poets', in *Women Latin Poets. Language, Gender, and Authority: From Antiquity to the Eighteenth Century* (Oxford) 31–48
Stickler, T. (2002) '*Gallus amore peribat?' Cornelius Gallus und die Anfänge der augusteischen Herrschaft in Ägypten*, II. Rahden
Stohlmann, J. (1973) 'Deidamia Achilli. Eine Ovid-Imitation aus dem 11. Jahrhundert', in A. Önnerfors, J. Rathofer, F. Wagner (eds.), *Literatur und Sprache im europäischen Mittelalter. Festschrift für Karl Langosch* (Darmstadt) 195–231

Stroh, W. (1971) *Die römische Liebeselegie als werbende Dichtung*. Amsterdam
(1983) 'Die Ursprünge der römischen Liebeselegie: Ein altes Problem im Licht eines neuen Fundes', *Poetica* 15: 205–46
Sturz, F.W. (1820) *Orionis Thebani Etymologicon*. Leipzig
Suits, T.A. (1976) 'The Iambic Character of Propertius 1.4', *Philologus* 120: 86–91
Sullivan, J.P. (1976) *Propertius: A Critical Introduction*. Cambridge
(1984) 'Propertius Book IV: Themes and Structures', *Illinois Classical Studies* 9: 30–4
Sweet, D.R. (2006) 'Catullus 65: Grief and Poetry', in C. Deroux (ed.), *Studies in Latin Literature and Roman History* 13 (Brussels) 87–96
Syme, R. (1939) *The Roman Revolution*. Oxford
(1978) *History in Ovid*. Oxford
(1986) *The Augustan Aristocracy*. Oxford
Syndikus, H.P. (1990) *Catull: Eine Interpretation*, II: *Die großen Gedichte (61–68)*. Darmstadt
(1998) 'Horaz und die elegischen Dichter', in A.E. Radke (ed.), *Candide iudex. Beiträge zur augusteischen Dichtung. Festschrift für W. Wimmel zum 75. Geburtstag* (Stuttgart) 375–98
(2006) 'The Second Book', in Günther (2006a): 245–318
Szöverffy, J. (1968) 'Maximianus a Satirist', *Harvard Studies in Classical Philology* 72: 351–67
(1992) *Secular Latin Lyrics and Minor Poetic Forms of the Middle Ages: A Historical Survey and Literary Repertory from the Tenth to the Late Fifteenth Century*, 4 vols. Concord, N.H.
Tandoi, V. (1992) *Scritti di filologia e di storia della cultura classica*, ed. F.E. Consolino, G. Lotito, M.P. Pieri, G. Sommariva, S. Timpanaro, M.A. Vinchesi, 2 vols. Pisa
Tarrant, R.J. (1978) 'The Addressee of Virgil's Eighth Eclogue', *Harvard Studies in Classical Philology* 82: 187–99
(1983) 'Ovid' in L.D. Reynolds (ed.), *Texts and Transmission: a Survey of the Latin Classics* (Oxford) 257–84
(2006) 'Propertian Textual Criticism and Editing', in Günther (2006): 45–65
Tateo, F. (1987) 'Properzio nella poesia latina del Quattrocento', in S. Pasquazi (ed.), *Properzio nella letteratura italiana. Atti del convegno nazionale (Assisi, 15–17 novembre 1985)* (Assisi) 41–64
(1998) 'Le elegie "Properziane" di Giovannantonio Campano', in G. Catanzaro and F. Santucci (eds.), *A confronto con Properzio (da Petrarca a Pound)* (Assisi) 125–40
Tatum, W.J. (1997) 'Friendship, Politics, and Literature in Catullus: Poems 1, 65 and 66, 116', *Classical Quarterly* 47: 482–500
Thalmann, W.G. (1996) 'Versions of Slavery in the *Captivi* of Plautus', *Ramus* 25: 112–45
Theodorakopoulos, E. (2007) 'C. 68: Love and Death, and the Gifts of Venus and the Muses', in M.B. Skinner (ed.), *A Companion to Catullus*. (Malden, Mass.) 527–52
Thiel, E.J. (1968) 'Mittellateinische Nachdichtungen von Ovids *Ars amatoria* und *Remedia amoris*', *Mittellateinisches Jahrbuch* 5: 115–80

(1970) 'Beiträge zu den Ovid-Nachdichtungen *Pseudo-Ars amatoria* und *Pseudo-Remedia amoris*', *Mittellateinisches Jahrbuch* 6: 132–48

(1973) 'Neue Handschriften der mittellateinischen Nachdichtungen von Ovids *Ars Amatoria* und *Remedia Amoris* und Nachträge', *Mittellateinisches Jahrbuch* 9: 248–68

Thilo, G. and Hagen, H. (1961) *Servii grammatici qui feruntur in Vergilii* Bucolica *et* Georgica *commentarii*. Hildesheim

Thomas, R. (1983) 'Callimachus, the *Victoria Berenices* and Roman poetry', *Classical Quarterly* 33: 92–113

Thorsen, T.S. (2012) 'Sappho, Corinna and Colleagues in Ancient Rome: Tatian's Catalogue of Statues (*Oratio ad Graecos* 33–4) Reconsidered', *Mnemosyne*, 65: 696–715

forthcoming *Ovid's Early Poetry. From his* Heroides *to his* Remedia amoris. Cambridge

Thraede, K. (1962) 'Epos', *Reallexikon für Antike und Christentum* 5: 983–1042

Tilliette, J.-Y. (1983) 'Note sur le manuscrit des poèmes de Baudri de Bourgueil (Vatican, Reg. Lat. 1351)', *Scriptorium* 37: 241–45

(1992) 'Hermès amoureux ou les métamorphoses de la Chimère: Réflexions sur les carmina 200 et 201 de Baudri de Bourgueil', *Mélanges de l'École française de Rome. Moyen Âge* 104: 121–61

(1994) 'Savants et poètes du moyen âge face à Ovide: Les débuts de l'*aetas Ovidiana* (v. 1050 – v. 1200)', in M. Picone and B. Zimmermann (eds.), *Ovidius Redivivus: Von Ovid zu Dante* (Stuttgart) 63–104

(1998–2002) *Baudri de Bourgueil. Poèmes*, 2 vols. Paris

Tobler, A. (1885–6) 'Il Panfilo in antico veneziano col latino a fronte', *Archivio glottologico italiano* 9–10: 177–255

Tonelli, N. (2002) 'Landino: la "Xandra" e il codice elegiaco', *Giornale storico della letteratura italiana* 179: 193–211

Torlone, Z. (1999) *Gallus in Arcadia: Eclogues and Elegy*. New York

Traina, A. (1954) 'Catullo e gli dei: Il carme LXXVI nella critica più recente', *Convivium* n.s.1: 358–68

(1979) 'Dira libido (sul linguaggio lucreziano dell'eros)', in *Studi di poesia latina in onore di A. Traglia* (Rome) 259–76

(1998) 'Introduzione a Catullo: la poesia degli affetti', in A. Traina, *Poeti latini (e neolatini). Note e saggi filologici*, V (Bologna) 19–50

Tränkle, H. (1990) (ed., comm.) *Appendix Tibulliana*. Berlin

Traube, L. (1911) *Vorlesungen und Abhandlungen*, II: *Einleitung in die lateinische Philologie des Mittelalters*. Munich

Treggiari, S. (1991) *Roman Marriage*. Oxford

Trojel, E. (1892) *Andreae Capellani Regii Francorum* De amore *libri tres*. Copenhagen

Tuplin, C.J. (1981) 'Catullus 68', *Classical Quarterly* 31: 113–39

Tzounakas, S. (2006) '*Rusticitas* versus *Urbanitas* in the Literary Programmes of Tibullus and Persius', *Mnemosyne* 59: 111–28

Ullman, B.L. (1973) 'Petrarch's Acquaintance with Catullus, Tibullus, Propertius', in *Studies in the Italian Renaissance*, 2nd edn. (Rome) 177–96

Urusova, E. (1777) *Iroidy muzam posviashchennye*. St. Petersburg

Valladares, H. (2005) 'The Lover as a Model Viewer: Gendered Dynamics in Propertius 1.3', in R. Ancona and E. Greene (eds.), *Gendered Dynamics in Latin Love Poetry* (Baltimore) 206–42
Van Heck, A. (1994) (ed.) *Enee Silvii Piccolominei postea Pii pp. II* Carmina. Vatican City
Van Sickle, J.B. (1968) 'About Form and Feeling in Catullus 65', *Transactions of the American Philological Association* 99: 487–508
(1977) '*Et Gallus cantavit*: A Review Article', review of Ross (1975) *Classical Journal* 72: 327–33
(1981) 'Style and Imitation in the New Gallus', *Quaderni Urbinati di Cultura Classica* n.s. 9: 115–24
Verducci, F. (1984) 'On the Sequence of Gallus' Epigrams: *molles elegi, vasta triumphi pondera*', *Quaderni Urbinati di Cultura Classica* 45: 119–36
(1985) *Ovid's Toyshop of the Heart:* Epistulae Heroidum. Princeton
Veyne, P. (1983) *L'élégie érotique romaine: L'amour, la poésie et l'occident*. Paris
(1988) *Roman Erotic Elegy: Love, Poetry, and the West*, trans. D. Pellauer. Chicago
Vinay, G. (1951) 'Il *De amore* di Andrea Capellano nel quadro della letteratura amorosa e della rinascita del secolo XII', *Studi medievali* 17: 203–76
(1952) 'La commedia latina del secolo XII', *Studi medievali* 18: 209–71
Vivian, P. (1909) (ed.) *Campion's Works*. Oxford
Volk, K. (2002) *The Poetics of Latin Didactic: Lucretius, Vergil, Ovid, Manilius*. Oxford
(2010) *Ovid*. Chichester
Vollmer, F. (1984) (ed.) *Fl. Merobaudis Reliquiae, Blossii Aemilii Dracontii Carmina* (Monumenta Germaniae Historica, Auctores Antiquissimi 14). Munich
Vredeveld, H. (2008) (ed. and trans.) *The Poetic Works of Helius Eobanus Hessus*, 2. Tempe
Waitz, G. (1849) 'Das Liebesconcil', *Zeitschrift für deutsches Altertum und deutsche Litteratur* 7: 160–7
Walcott, D. (1987) *The Arkansas Testament*. London
Wallace-Hadrill, A. (1994) *Houses and Society in Pompeii and Herculaneum*. Princeton
Walther, H. (1920) *Das Streitgedicht in der lateinischen Literatur des Mittelalters*. Munich (repr. Hildesheim 1984)
Warden, J. (1980) *Fallax opus: Poet and Reader in the Elegies of Propertius*. Toronto
(2006) 'Catullus in the Grove of Callimachus', in C. Deroux (ed.), *Studies in Latin Literature and Roman History*, 13 (Brussels) 97–153
Warren, F.M. (1907) 'The Council of Remiremont', *Modern Language Notes* 22: 137–40
Watson, L.C. (2003) *A Commentary on Horace's Epodes*. Oxford
Weinreich, O. (1927) 'Die Christianisierung einer Tibullstelle', *Hermes* 62: 122–3
Weisman, K. (2010) *The Oxford Handbook of the Elegy*. Oxford
Weissenberger, K. (1969) *Formen der Elegie von Goethe bis Celan*. Bern
Welch, T. (2005) *The Elegiac Cityscape: Propertius and the Meaning of Roman Monuments*. Columbus
Wenzel, A. (2010) *Die Xandra-Gedichte des Cristoforo Landino*. Heidelberg

Wes, M. (1992) *Classics in Russia, 1700–1855: Between Two Bronze Horsemen*. Leiden
West, M.L. (1971/1992) *Iambi et Elegi Graeci ante Alexandrum cantati*. Oxford
(1974) *Studies in Greek Elegy and Iambus*. Berlin and New York
(1982) *Greek Metre*. Oxford
Weyman, C. (1975) *Beiträge zur Geschichte der Christlich-lateinischen Poesie*. Hildesheim
Whitaker, R. (1983) *Myth and Personal Experience in Roman Love-Elegy: a Study in Poetic Technique*. Göttingen
White, P. (1991) 'Maecenas' Retirement', *Classical Philology* 86: 130–8
(1993) *Promised Verse: Poets in the Society of Augustan Rome*. Cambridge, Mass
(2005) 'Poets in the New Milieu: Realigning', in K.Galinsky (ed.), *The Cambridge Companion to the Age of Augustus* (Cambridge) 321–39
Wickert, L. (1974) 'Neue Forschungen zum römischen Principat', *Aufstieg und Niedergang der römischen Welt* II.1: 3–76
Wilamowitz, U. von (1924) *Hellenistische Dichtung in der Zeit des Kallimachos*, 2 vols. Berlin
Wilkinson, L.P. (1970) '*Domina* in Catullus 68', *Classical Review* 20: 290
Williams, G.D. (1994) *Banished Voices. Readings in Ovid's Exile Poetry*. Cambridge
Williams, G.W. (1968) *Tradition and Originality in Roman Poetry*. Oxford
(1980) *Figures of Thought in Roman Poetry*. New Haven
(1990) 'Did Maecenas Fall from Favor? Augustan Literary Patronage' in K.A. Raaflaub and M. Toher (1990): 258–75
(1995) '*Libertino patre natus*: True or False?' in S. Harrison (ed.), *Homage to Horace: A Bimillenary Celebration* (Oxford) 296–313
Williams, J.R. (1947) 'Godfrey of Reims: a Humanist of the Eleventh Century', *Speculum* 22: 29–45
Wimmel, W. (1960) *Kallimachos in Rom: Die Nachfolge seines apologetischen Dichtens in der Augusteerzeit*. Wiesbaden
(1976) *Tibull und Delia*, I: *Tibulls* Elegie *1,1*. Wiesbaden
(1983) *Tibull und Delia*, II: *Tibulls* Elegie *1,2*. Wiesbaden
Winterbottom, M. (1994) (ed.) *M. Tulli Ciceronis De officiis*. Oxford
Wiseman, T.P. (1969) *Catullan Questions*. Leicester
(1979) *Clio's Cosmetics. Three Studies in Graeco-Roman Literature*. Leicester
(1985) *Catullus and his World: A Reappraisal*. Cambridge
(2002) 'Ovid and the Stage', in G. Herbert-Brown (ed.), *Ovid's* Fasti. *Historical Readings at its Bimillennium* (Oxford) 275–99
Woodman, A.J. (1997) 'The position of Gallus in *Eclogue 6*', *Classical Quarterly* 47, 593–7
Wray, D. (2003) 'What Poets Do: Tibullus on "Easy" Hands', *Classical Philology* 98: 217–50
(2012) 'Catullus, the Roman Love Elegist?' in Gold (2012): 25–38
Wyke, M. (1987a) 'The Elegiac Woman at Rome', *Proceedings of the Cambridge Philological Society* 33: 78–114
(1987b) 'Written Women: Propertius' *scripta puella*', *Journal of Roman Studies* 77: 153–78
(1989) 'Mistress and Metaphor in Augustan Elegy', *Helios* 16: 25–47

(1994) 'Taking the Woman's Part: Engendering Roman Love Elegy', *Ramus* 23: 110–28
(2002) *The Roman Mistress: Ancient and Modern Representations*. Oxford
Yardley, J.C. (1990) 'Cerinthus' *pia cura* ([Tibullus] 3.17.1–2)', *Classical Quarterly* 40: 568–70
Ypsilanti, M. (2005) 'Literary Loves as Cycles: From Meleager to Ovid', *L'Antiquité classique* 74: 83–110
Zetzel, J.E.G. (1983) 'Recreating the Canon: Augustan Poetry and the Alexandrian Past', *Critical Inquiry* 10: 83–105
Ziolkowski, J.M. (2004) 'Lost and Not Yet Found: Heloise, Abelard, and the *Epistolae duorum amantium*', *Journal of Medieval Latin* 14: 171–201
Ziolkowski, J.M. and Putnam, M.C. (2008) (eds.), *The Virgilian Tradition: The First Fifteen Hundred Years*. New Haven
Ziolkowski, T. (1980) *The Classical German Elegy, 1795–1950*. Princeton

INDEX

Cambridge Companions to . . .

AUTHORS

Edward Albee edited by Stephen J. Bottoms
Margaret Atwood edited by Coral Ann Howells
W. H. Auden edited by Stan Smith
Jane Austen edited by Edward Copeland and Juliet McMaster
Beckett edited by John Pilling
Aphra Behn edited by Derek Hughes and Janet Todd
Walter Benjamin edited by David S. Ferris
William Blake edited by Morris Eaves
Brecht edited by Peter Thomson and Glendyr Sacks (second edition)
The Brontës edited by Heather Glen
Frances Burney edited by Peter Sabor
Byron edited by Drummond Bone
Albert Camus edited by Edward J. Hughes
Willa Cather edited by Marilee Lindemann
Cervantes edited by Anthony J. Cascardi
Chaucer, second edition edited by Piero Boitani and Jill Mann
Chekhov edited by Vera Gottlieb and Paul Allain
Kate Chopin edited by Janet Beer
Coleridge edited by Lucy Newlyn
Wilkie Collins edited by Jenny Bourne Taylor
Joseph Conrad edited by J. H. Stape
Dante edited by Rachel Jacoff (second edition)
Daniel Defoe edited by John Richetti
Don DeLillo edited by John N. Duvall
Charles Dickens edited by John O. Jordan
Emily Dickinson edited by Wendy Martin
John Donne edited by Achsah Guibbory
Dostoevskii edited by W. J. Leatherbarrow
Theodore Dreiser edited by Leonard Cassuto and Claire Virginia Eby
John Dryden edited by Steven N. Zwicker
W. E. B. Du Bois edited by Shamoon Zamir
George Eliot edited by George Levine
T. S. Eliot edited by A. David Moody
Ralph Ellison edited by Ross Posnock
Ralph Waldo Emerson edited by Joel Porte and Saundra Morris
William Faulkner edited by Philip M. Weinstein
Henry Fielding edited by Claude Rawson
F. Scott Fitzgerald edited by Ruth Prigozy
Flaubert edited by Timothy Unwin
E. M. Forster edited by David Bradshaw
Benjamin Franklin edited by Carla Mulford
Brian Friel edited by Anthony Roche
Robert Frost edited by Robert Faggen
Elizabeth Gaskell edited by Jill L. Matus
Goethe edited by Lesley Sharpe
Günter Grass edited by Stuart Taberner
Thomas Hardy edited by Dale Kramer
David Hare edited by Richard Boon
Nathaniel Hawthorne edited by Richard Millington
Seamus Heaney edited by Bernard O'Donoghue
Ernest Hemingway edited by Scott Donaldson
Homer edited by Robert Fowler
Horace edited by Stephen Harrison
Ibsen edited by James McFarlane
Henry James edited by Jonathan Freedman
Samuel Johnson edited by Greg Clingham
Ben Jonson edited by Richard Harp and Stanley Stewart
James Joyce edited by Derek Attridge (second edition)
Kafka edited by Julian Preece
Keats edited by Susan J. Wolfson
Lacan edited by Jean-Michel Rabaté
D. H. Lawrence edited by Anne Fernihough
Primo Levi edited by Robert Gordon
Lucretius edited by Stuart Gillespie and Philip Hardie
David Mamet edited by Christopher Bigsby
Thomas Mann edited by Ritchie Robertson
Christopher Marlowe edited by Patrick Cheney
Herman Melville edited by Robert S. Levine
Arthur Miller edited by Christopher Bigsby
Milton edited by Dennis Danielson (second edition)
Molière edited by David Bradby and Andrew Calder
Toni Morrison edited by Justine Tally
Nabokov edited by Julian W. Connolly

Eugene O'Neill edited by Michael Manheim
George Orwell edited by John Rodden
Ovid edited by Philip Hardie
Harold Pinter edited by Peter Raby (second edition)
Sylvia Plath edited by Jo Gill
Edgar Allan Poe edited by Kevin J. Hayes
Alexander Pope edited by Pat Rogers
Ezra Pound edited by Ira B. Nadel
Proust edited by Richard Bales
Pushkin edited by Andrew Kahn
Rilke edited by Karen Leeder and Robert Vilain
Philip Roth edited by Timothy Parrish
Salman Rushdie edited by Abdulrazak Gurnah
Shakespeare edited by Margareta de Grazia and Stanley Wells
Shakespearean Comedy edited by Alexander Leggatt
Shakespeare on Film edited by Russell Jackson (second edition)
Shakespeare's History Plays edited by Michael Hattaway
Shakespeare's Last Plays edited by Catherine M. S. Alexander
Shakespeare's Poetry edited by Patrick Cheney
Shakespeare and Popular Culture edited by Robert Shaughnessy
Shakespeare on Stage edited by Stanley Wells and Sarah Stanton
Shakespearean Tragedy edited by Claire McEachern
George Bernard Shaw edited by Christopher Innes
Shelley edited by Timothy Morton
Mary Shelley edited by Esther Schor
Sam Shepard edited by Matthew C. Roudané
Spenser edited by Andrew Hadfield
Laurence Sterne edited by Thomas Keymer
Wallace Stevens edited by John N. Serio
Tom Stoppard edited by Katherine E. Kelly
Harriet Beecher Stowe edited by Cindy Weinstein
August Strindberg edited by Michael Robinson
Jonathan Swift edited by Christopher Fox
J. M. Synge edited by P. J. Mathews
Tacitus edited by A. J. Woodman
Henry David Thoreau edited by Joel Myerson
Tolstoy edited by Donna Tussing Orwin
Mark Twain edited by Forrest G. Robinson
Virgil edited by Charles Martindale
Voltaire edited by Nicholas Cronk
Edith Wharton edited by Millicent Bell
Walt Whitman edited by Ezra Greenspan
Oscar Wilde edited by Peter Raby
Tennessee Williams edited by Matthew C. Roudané
August Wilson edited by Christopher Bigsby
Mary Wollstonecraft edited by Claudia L. Johnson
Virginia Woolf edited by Sue Roe and Susan Sellers
Wordsworth edited by Stephen Gill
W. B. Yeats edited by Marjorie Howes and John Kelly
Zola edited by Brian Nelson

TOPICS

The Actress edited by Maggie B. Gale and John Stokes
The African American Novel edited by Maryemma Graham
The African American Slave Narrative edited by Audrey A. Fisch
Allegory edited by Rita Copeland and Peter Struck
American Modernism edited by Walter Kalaidjian
American Realism and Naturalism edited by Donald Pizer
American Travel Writing edited by Alfred Bendixen and Judith Hamera
American Women Playwrights edited by Brenda Murphy
Arthurian Legend edited by Elizabeth Archibald and Ad Putter
Australian Literature edited by Elizabeth Webby
British Romanticism edited by Stuart Curran
British Romantic Poetry edited by James Chandler and Maureen N. McLane
British Theatre, 1730–1830, edited by Jane Moody and Daniel O'Quinn
Canadian Literature edited by Eva-Marie Kröller

Children's Literature edited by M. O. Grenby and Andrea Immel

The Classic Russian Novel edited by Malcolm V. Jones and Robin Feuer Miller

Contemporary Irish Poetry edited by Matthew Campbell

Crime Fiction edited by Martin Priestman

Early Modern Women's Writing edited by Laura Lunger Knoppers

The Eighteenth-Century Novel edited by John Richetti

Eighteenth-Century Poetry edited by John Sitter

English Literature, 1500–1600 edited by Arthur F. Kinney

English Literature, 1650–1740 edited by Steven N. Zwicker

English Literature, 1740–1830 edited by Thomas Keymer and Jon Mee

English Novelists edited by Adrian Poole

English Poets edited by Claude Rawson

English Poetry, Donne to Marvell edited by Thomas N. Corns

English Renaissance Drama, second edition edited by A. R. Braunmuller and Michael Hattaway

English Restoration Theatre edited by Deborah C. Payne Fisk

Feminist Literary Theory edited by Ellen Rooney

Fiction in the Romantic Period edited by Richard Maxwell and Katie Trumpener

The Fin de Siècle edited by Gail Marshall

The French Novel: from 1800 to the Present edited by Timothy Unwin

German Romanticism edited by Nicholas Saul

Gothic Fiction edited by Jerrold E. Hogle

The Greek and Roman Novel edited by Tim Whitmarsh

Greek and Roman Theatre edited by Marianne McDonald and J. Michael Walton

Greek Mythology edited by Roger D. Woodard

Greek Tragedy edited by P. E. Easterling

The Harlem Renaissance edited by George Hutchinson

The Irish Novel edited by John Wilson Foster

The Italian Novel edited by Peter Bondanella and Andrea Ciccarelli

Jewish American Literature edited by Hana Wirth-Nesher and Michael P. Kramer

The Latin American Novel edited by Efraín Kristal

The Literature of the First World War edited by Vincent Sherry

The Literature of World War II edited by Marina MacKay

Literature on Screen edited by Deborah Cartmell and Imelda Whelehan

Medieval English Literature edited by Larry Scanlon

Medieval English Theatre edited by Richard Beadle and Alan J. Fletcher (second edition)

Medieval French Literature edited by Simon Gaunt and Sarah Kay

Medieval Romance edited by Roberta L. Krueger

Medieval Women's Writing edited by Carolyn Dinshaw and David Wallace

Modern American Culture edited by Christopher Bigsby

Modern British Women Playwrights edited by Elaine Aston and Janelle Reinelt

Modern French Culture edited by Nicholas Hewitt

Modern German Culture edited by Eva Kolinsky and Wilfried van der Will

The Modern German Novel edited by Graham Bartram

Modern Irish Culture edited by Joe Cleary and Claire Connolly

Modernism edited by Michael Levenson

The Modernist Novel edited by Morag Shiach

Modernist Poetry edited by Alex Davis and Lee M. Jenkins

Modern Italian Culture edited by Zygmunt G. Baranski and Rebecca J. West

Modern Latin American Culture edited by John King

Modern Russian Culture edited by Nicholas Rzhevsky

Modern Spanish Culture edited by David T. Gies

Narrative edited by David Herman

Native American Literature edited by Joy Porter and Kenneth M. Roemer

Nineteenth-Century American Women's Writing edited by Dale M. Bauer and Philip Gould

Old English Literature edited by Malcolm Godden and Michael Lapidge

Performance Studies edited by Tracy C. Davis

Postcolonial Literary Studies edited by Neil Lazarus

Postmodernism edited by Steven Connor

Renaissance Humanism edited by Jill Kraye

Roman Satire edited by Kirk Freudenburg

The Roman Historians edited by Andrew Feldherr

The Spanish Novel: from 1600 to the Present edited by Harriet Turner and Adelaida López de Martínez

Travel Writing edited by Peter Hulme and Tim Youngs

Twentieth-Century Irish Drama edited by Shaun Richards

The Twentieth-Century English Novel edited by Robert L. Caserio

Twentieth-Century English Poetry edited by Neil Corcoran

Victorian and Edwardian Theatre edited by Kerry Powell

The Victorian Novel edited by Deirdre David

Victorian Poetry edited by Joseph Bristow

War Writing edited by Kate McLoughlin

Writing of the English Revolution edited by N. H. Keeble